Policy and Practice in European Human Resource Management

This volume presents the findings of the Price Waterhouse Cranfield survey of international strategic human resource management. It provides a wealth of data and analysis drawn from a major three year survey of employing organisations, in all sectors of the economy in fourteen major European states.

The volume lays out and considers the evidence of trends in HRM in a variety of areas: overall strategy, the role and education of HR professionals, recruitment, training and development, pay, industrial relations, communication, flexibility, equal opportunities and EC social policy. A unique feature of the research is its comprehensive coverage, not only geographically within Europe, but also in terms of sector, including data from manufacturing, services and the public sector. Because the research examined data at the organisational level, the book is able to provide a unique analysis of what is happening in HRM in the very different cultures of the European states, both EC and EFTA.

With contributions by experts from across Europe, this volume is an indispensable source for all teachers and students of European HRM practices and policies. Including a unique tabular database that supports detailed analysis of the major themes within HRM, this book is also a key reference source for practitioners wishing to understand HRM in the various European countries and to 'benchmark' their organisation against current practice.

Chris Brewster is Director of the Centre for European HRM at Cranfield School of Management. **Ariane Hegewisch** is also at the Centre, where she is a Senior Researcher.

Policy and Practice in European Human Resource Management

The Price Waterhouse Cranfield Survey

Edited by Chris Brewster and Ariane Hegewisch

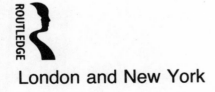

London and New York

First published 1994
by Routledge
11 New Fetter Lane, London EC4P 4EE

Simultaneously published in the USA and Canada
by Routledge
29 West 35th Street, New York, NY 10001

Typeset in Times by J&L Composition Ltd, Filey, North Yorkshire
Printed and bound in Great Britain by
Clays Ltd., St Ives PLC

British Library Cataloguing in Publication Data
A catalogue record for this book is available from the British Library

Library of Congress Cataloging in Publication Data
Policy and practice in European human resource management / edited by Chris Brewster and
  Ariane Hegewisch.
      p.   cm.
    Results of the Price Waterhouse Cranfield Survey of European human resource management.
    Includes bibliographical references and index.
    ISBN 0–415–06529–1 – ISBN 0–415–06530–5 (pbk.)
    1. Personnel management – Europe. I. Brewster, Chris. II. Hegewisch, Ariane,
1958– . III. Price, Waterhouse & Co. IV. Cranfield School of Management.
HF5549.2.E9P65   1994
658.3′0094 – dc20   93–43235
                                                                          CIP

ISBN 0–415–06529–1 (hbk)
ISBN 0–415–06530–5 (pbk)

Contents

Figures

Tables

Notes: 1 Unless otherwise indicated all tables and data are original and are drawn from the Price Waterhouse Cranfield Survey data.

2 Tables use the following country abbreviations:

CH	– Switzerland	IRL	– Ireland
D	– West Germany	N	– Norway
DK	– Denmark	NL	– Netherlands
E	– Spain	P	– Portugal
F	– France	S	– Sweden
FIN	– Finland	T	– Turkey
I	– Italy	UK	– United Kingdom

Contributors

Frank Bournois: Université Jean Moulin, Lyon 3, France.
Chris Brewster: Cranfield School of Management, United Kingdom.
Jean-Hugues Chauchat: Groupe ESC Lyon, France.
Françoise Dany: Groupe ESC Lyon, France.
Jaime Filella: ESADE, Barcelona, Spain.
Patrick Gunnigle: University of Limerick, Ireland.
Ariane Hegewisch: Cranfield School of Management, United Kingdom.
Henrik Holt Larsen: Handelshøjskolen I København, Denmark.
Lesley Mayne: Cranfield School of Management, United Kingdom.
Mike Morley: University of Limerick, Ireland.
Sylvie Roussillon: Groupe ESC Lyon, France.
Magnus Söderström: IPF, Uppsala, Sweden.
Paul Teague: University of Ulster, Northern Ireland.
Véronique Torchy: formerly Groupe ESC Lyon, France.
Olga Tregaskis: Cranfield School of Management, United Kingdom.
Shaun Tyson: Cranfield School of Management, United Kingdom.
Lennart Wikander: Uppsala University, Sweden.

Acknowledgements

There are a considerable number of people who have made this book possible, in addition to those who appear as contributors. We would like to place on record our thanks to them all.

The European network would not have existed in its present form, the research would not have been undertaken without the substantial support of Price Waterhouse. So many people there have helped to make this research possible that it is not possible to name them all, but we must take this opportunity to register formally our gratitude to Gavin Adam, who initiated the Price Waterhouse Cranfield Project and whose support and enthusiasm continued throughout. It has been an instructive and a pleasurable experience working with him. Within the other, Cranfield, half of the title, our champions have been Professors Leo Murray and Shaun Tyson. Without the positive enthusiasm of these three people the project would not have existed and prospered as it has done. Lastly we would like to acknowledge the important role of Michel Syrett as one of the initiating directors of the project.

The team at the Centre for European HRM at Cranfield School of Management currently consists of ourselves, Trixy Alberga, Lesley Mayne and Olga Tregaskis. Previous members of the team have been Terry Lockhart, Len Holden and Emma Godfrey and, on six-month secondments from Price Waterhouse, Chris Smith, Pat Metcalf, Jonathan Skan and Sally Smith. We have also been assisted on shorter placements from their universities by Maria Figueras, Joaquim Candel and Christian Sirnes. All of these have made important contributions to the research process.

We would like to record our appreciation to our colleagues throughout Europe who have been a vital part of our network but do not appear as contributors to this book. Their contribution to our research has, none the less, been vital and is visible in various articles and reports. It has been a pleasurable learning experience to work with them all and we thank them.

There have been a considerable number of people throughout Europe and the world who have assisted us to understand HRM, its role in Europe and the import of our data. These include the practitioners who have acted as panel members in each of the countries surveyed and a very wide academic community who have acted in the true sense of those words, critiquing, discussing, arguing and commenting on our results, encouraging us to carry our work forward and providing platforms for us to disseminate our work. They are too numerous to mention them by name, but they know who they are and they have our thanks.

This book, as the main output of our research, is the result of an initiative by and continuing indulgent but firm pressure from Rosemary Nixon of Routledge. We hope that it is worthy of her efforts.

Finally and, as always, we thank Sarah Atterbury. Her organisational skills brought the text to fruition. She is the best.

Chapter 1

Human resource management in Europe
Issues and opportunities

Chris Brewster and Ariane Hegewisch

Human resource management (HRM) has achieved significant importance in the last few years: in practice and in the literature. In both arenas the focus is increasingly international. Management of all kinds is ever more often conducted across national borders. This is the case not only for the giant private sector multinationals but also for organisations in the public sector and amongst smaller employers. The growth of major international trading 'blocs' – in South East Asia, North America and, in its most advanced form, in Europe – has accelerated these trends.

There is therefore a need to explore international differences in the way people are managed. With more organisations operating across international boundaries and more managers being transferred internationally (Dowling and Schuler 1990; Brewster 1991; Black, Gregerson and Mendenhall 1993) and with the increasing influence of international trading blocs such as the European Community the importance of comparative knowledge about such areas as labour markets, skills, legislation and trade unions is apparent (see, for example, Brewster *et al.* 1992).

It has been argued that there is a direct correlation between strategic HRM and economic success. Porter (1985) believed that HRM can help a firm obtain competitive advantage. Schuler and Macmillan (1984: 242) make a similar point, that 'effectively managing human resources' gives benefits which 'include greater profitability'. Other authors make the point explicitly that 'firms that engage in a strategy formulation process that systematically and reciprocally considers human resources and competitive strategy will perform better . . . over the long term' (Lengnick-Hall and Lengnick-Hall 1988: 468); HRM has even been propounded as 'the only truly important determinant of success' (Beyer 1991: 1). Salaman (1991) comments 'this is an obvious but important point'. Later texts by Porter (1985, 1991) and, in Europe, Pieper built on this to argue that 'since HRM is seen as a strategic factor strongly influencing the economic success of a single company one can argue that it is also a strategic factor for the success of an entire nation' (1990: 4). Such arguments have to be set in the context of the lack of empirical data to support them. Indeed on the autonomous, non-union, unregulated model that casual commentators often imply within the term HRM the evidence points in the opposite direction. Thus, those nations who are furthest from that model, those with most legal regulation and trade union influence, tend to have been most successful in recent years. This requires further empirical investigation.

These pragmatic rationales for comparative studies of HRM are linked to social science studies. Comparative international research for several decades now has examined production systems and management strategies in different cultural and national circumstances. Indeed, globalisation has been argued to be the most significant trend in modern business, with extensive implications for strategic management (Bartlett and Ghoshal 1989; Levitt 1983; Prahalad and Doz 1987). The implications of these and earlier international studies (Haire, Ghiselli and Porter 1966; England 1978; Ronen and Shenkar 1985) for HRM were manifest, but have only more recently been the focus of international comparative research. There is already, in addition to this strong tradition of research into international management practices, a stream of research into international cultural values (Hofstede 1980, 1991; Laurent 1983; Tayeb 1988). This provides a broad basis on which to study HRM internationally (Brewster and Tyson 1991).

Such studies have a value beyond the intrinsic interest of examination of different ways of doing things. They challenge our assumptions of the manner in which business is most effectively conducted and people are managed. Authors such as Hofstede (1980) have pointed out that assumptions about what objectives should be achieved in people management, how people should be trained and valued, what motivates them and how they should relate to colleagues and supervisors, vary from culture to culture.

There is a strong argument to be made, then, for the value of comparative studies. This book reports the results of such a study, focused on organisational policies and practices in human resource management in Europe. This first chapter has two objectives. The first is to outline the conceptual rationale for studying HRM in Europe, and to outline the form of study that we have been involved in. The second is to explain how the results of the study are presented in the rest of the book and to outline key findings.

CONCEPTUAL CONCERNS

Comparative studies are not unproblematic. In addition to methodological problems (examined in relation to our project in Appendix I) there are conceptual issues. An initial question concerns the universality of management practice. There are arguments both for universality and particularity (see Brewster and Tyson 1991: introduction). A fascinating recent study (Craig et al. 1992) has shown that on some very 'hard' measures – such as infant mortality, cost of living, cars, electricity use and telephones amongst others – countries in Europe, the United States and Japan are tending to diverge rather than converge. In general terms researchers who focus on the content of management tend to find similarities across national borders; those who focus on process tend to identify differences (Tayeb 1988). There is the associated question of the geopolitical focus that is taken. Clearly there are universal features of management; regional blocs (for example, North America, Pacific, European); and national state differences. Within the regional blocs there may be further regional variations as well as sector, size, ownership and other groupings that will provide sufficient similarities within them, and differences from other groupings, to be taken as units of analysis.

There is also a national comparative perspective. Many of the following chapters focus on HRM at this level. Internationally comparative data, particularly from the organisational level, is not common and we believe that a major contribution of this book is to add to that stock. Because international comparisons are much less frequent than within-country comparisons it is perhaps worth emphasising the point that over and over again in our data it is the differences between countries that prove to be more significant variables in HRM than, for example, the differences between organisational size or industrial sector. Given the importance of national cultures, governments, legislation, economics, ownership patterns, labour markets, trade unions, this should be no surprise – except that the within-country perspective often leads to this fact being ignored.

Pulling wider there is a regional perspective. It has been pointed out elsewhere, using our data (Filella 1991), that regional patterns (Nordic, Northern European, Latin) can be discerned. The direct correlation with some of the research by authorities on national cultures (Hofstede 1980, 1983, 1991; Laurent 1983; Adler 1986) is instructive.

Finally, it is also clear that from a global perspective Europe has a coherence of its own, and a distinctiveness from other major blocs. Such a perspective involves a considerable degree of generalisation: conflating differences elsewhere and, particularly, within Europe. However, the point has been made by another commentator on 'the conditions and circumstances within Western Europe' that although there are differences in HRM in each country, taken as a whole 'they stand out as being distinct from other economic areas like the USA, USSR or Japan'. (Remer 1986: 363).

We have explored these distinctive features of European HRM elsewhere (Brewster 1993) and they are touched upon in other places throughout this text. Suffice it to say here that in many areas beyond the scope of this text – in culture, government, legislation and ownership patterns again, and in labour markets and trading relationships – Europe has both internal differences but also commonalities. Furthermore, within the HRM areas covered in this book will be found further evidence of similarities in issues and in trends: and further distinctions from other regions of the world. It can be found in, for example, decentralisation and devolvement, pay flexibility, the attention paid to training and development, in industrial relations and employee communications and the growth of flexible working patterns and perhaps most of all in the development of a social policy by Europe's unique supranational level of government, the European Community.

HRM as a concept has come to Europe from the United States. It has been subject to significant criticism in Europe. Poole (1990) and Hendry and Pettigrew (1990) start from the Beer *et al.* (1985) model and wish to amplify it to include environmental factors. Hendry and Pettigrew add three headings: under 'economic' they include ownership and control, organisational size and structure, the growth part of an organisation, industry structure and markets; under 'technical' they refer to skill, work organisation and labour force require-ments of technologies; 'socio-political' encompasses the institutional framework, particularly the national education and training system.

The environmental factors have been central to discussions of this issue in other European countries (see, for example, Bournois 1990 in France). A more explicit instance can be taken from Remer (1986), discussing personnel management in the more administrative German context: he does so in terms of 'external characteristics' (economy, technology, society, employers, politics, law, science, culture).

Pieper categorised the environmental factors affecting HRM similarly to Beer *et al.*, or to Hendry and Pettigrew. However, he felt that this approach does not overcome the problem of presenting 'lists' of things and, in the last instance, is atheoretical and forced to rely once again on the black box of culture to explain international differences (1990: 22).

Whether these lists of environmental issues are external or are an intrinsic aspect of the HRM concept may be more than a matter of semantics. It is noteworthy that it is in general the American authors who have seen it as external. Focusing on these environmental issues as external to the concept has led to the often very detailed, case-study based, and sophisticated attempts to create a 'contingency' approach to HRM. Thus Schuler (1989), a leading figure in this movement, has attempted to link HRM strategies to lifecycle models (as did Fombrun and Tichy 1983 and Kochan and Barocci 1985) and to Porter's models for achieving competitive advantage in different industry conditions (Schuler and Jackson 1987; Schuler 1989). Other authors have argued that HRM should be contingent upon markets (Baird, Meshoulam and Degive 1983; Dertouzos, Lester and Solow 1989) and upon groupings within organisational levels (Lorange and Murphy 1984). The examples could be multiplied (see also Macmillan and Schuler 1985, where the reciprocity of HR and strategy is clearly stated; Lengnick-Hall and Lengnick-Hall 1988; Schuler and Macmillan 1984; Schuler 1992).

This contingent determinism has been adopted by some authors in Europe (Staffelbach 1986; Ackermann 1986; Besseyre des Horts 1987, 1988). However contingency theory has come under attack in the corporate strategy literature (originated by Child 1976 and followed through by such authorities as Porter 1985 – see the recent debate on organisational economics led by Donaldson in the *Academy of Management Review* 1990). A major critique is that it allows little role for managerial action other than that of identifying the current position and matching strategy to it. Many of the 'contingency' school of HRM writers fall into a form of strategic determinism in which management's task is essentially no more than to establish the 'fit' of HRM to a given – usually corporate-strategy driven – scenario. Such attempts have been sharply criticised by Conrad and Pieper (1990); by Staehle (1987), who criticises the American literature accessible in Germany for its derivative approach to personnel management which is seen as dependent upon corporate strategy, rather than contributory to it; and by Poole (1990: 5): 'strategic choices imply discretion over decision-making (i.e. no situational or environmental determinism)'.

THE EUROPEANISATION OF THEORY

There is a general trend in theorising on the eastern side of the North Atlantic towards arguing that an over-ready acceptance of American models has gone beyond its provable value: and that the time is now ripe for distinguishing specifically European approaches.

It is surely no coincidence that this coincides with the revitalisation of the European Community and Europe's economic success compared to the USA.

Thurley and Wirdenius, for example, were concerned with the development of a functional model of management, particularly in the context of international business activities, rather than with HRM in particular or the comparative analysis of different national models of HRM. But they are relevant here because they try to distil what is particular to 'Europe' rather than the US or Japan. They focus on the cultural context of management, and, in the face of the predominance of American and Japanese conceptions of management, the need 'now to distinguish "European Management" as a possible alternative approach' (1991: 128). They see this as necessary to reflect the different cultural values and legal-institutional practices that are dominant in Europe. Such a European approach is said to be:

emerging, and cannot be said to exist except in limited circumstances;

broadly linked to the idea of European integration, which is continuously expanding further into different countries (i.e. the twelve);

a reflector of key values such as pluralism, tolerance, etc., but is not consciously developed from these values;

associated with a balanced stakeholder philosophy and the concept of Social Partners.
(Thurley and Wirdenius 1991: 128)

There has been criticism of the importation of American theory elsewhere too (Cox and Cooper 1985). In the context of HRM specifically, European authors have argued that 'we are in culturally different contexts' and, 'Rather than copy solutions which result from other cultural traditions, we should consider the state of mind that presided in the search for responses adapted to the culture' (Albert 1989: 75, translations in Brewster and Bournois 1991).

A 'EUROPEAN MODEL' OF HRM?

Despite the clear national or regional distinctions, there is an identifiable difference between the way in which HRM is conducted in Europe and the situation in the United States of America; a difference which allows us to speak of a European form of HRM and to question the appropriateness of the American concept of HRM in this other continent. (We would add that intuitively we believe that there may also be questions about the relevance of the US form of the concept in other continents.)

A model of HRM is required that re-emphasises the influence of such factors as culture, ownership structures, the role of the state and trade union organisation. Clearly the European evidence suggests that managements can see the unions, for example, as social partners with a positive role to play in human resource management: and the manifest success of many European firms which adopt that approach shows the, explicit or implicit, anti-unionism of many American views to be culture bound (Brewster 1994). Guest discerns signs that even in the United Kingdom 'the American model is losing its appeal as attention focuses to a greater extent on developments in Europe' (Guest 1990: 377).

The inapplicability of American models in Europe has also been noted in Germany. Gaugler concludes that because of different legal, institutional and economic contexts there is no uniform model of personnel management: 'An international comparison of HR practices clearly indicates that the basic functions of HR management are given different weights in different countries and that they are carried out differently' (Gaugler 1988: 26). Another German, Pieper, surveying European personnel management similarly concluded that 'a single universal model of HRM does not exist' (1990: 11). Critiques of any simplistic attempts to 'universalise' the American models have also come from France (see, e.g., Bournois 1991a, 1991b).

It is our contention that HRM theory needs to adopt the wider perspective of the model proposed by Kochan *et al.* (1986), and a more comprehensive view of the actors in the system, if it is to become a theory that stands the test of international application.

We have therefore proposed a model of HRM (outlined in Figure 1.1) which places HR strategies firmly within, though not entirely absorbed by, the business strategy. The two-dimensional presentation doesn't show, but must be taken to include, an interaction between the two rather than one following from the other. The model also

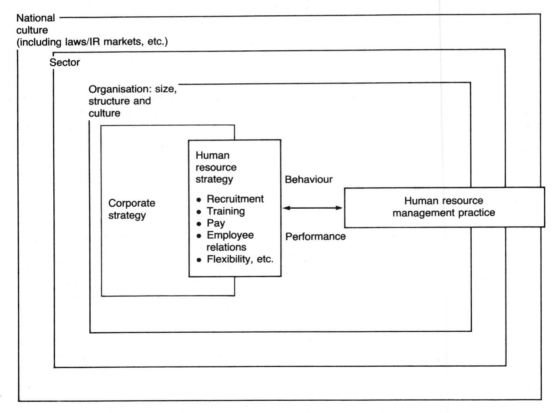

Figure 1.1 A model for investigating human resource strategies: the European environment
Source: Adapted from Brewster and Bournois 1991

shows, in a simplistic form, that the business strategy, HR strategy and HR practice are located within an external environment of national culture, power systems, legislation, education, employee representation and all the other issues discussed above. The organisation and its human resource strategies and practices in turn interact with and are part of that environment. The model places HR strategies in close interaction with the relevant organisational strategy and external environment in a way that is not unforeshadowed in much of the literature but is indicated simply and clearly here.

This presentation of the HRM concept points towards a model which places HRM within the national context: thus allowing fuller understanding of situations which differ from that existing in the United States. The advantages of this approach include a better fit of the model to the European scene and experience. This changes the debates in Europe from two angles. From the normative side, where commentators and consultants have criticised employing organisations for not adopting the 'American' model, this approach allows a change. Rather than searching for, and not finding, traditional HRM, and then criticising employing organisations and their personnel specialists for not adopting these 'modern' approaches, the model enables the consultants to be more modest and employers to be less defensive. From the analytical side, where academics have found little evidence of HRM in practice and significant shortcomings in the concept as it has come across to us from the USA, the model enables analysts to move beyond discussions of whether HRM should be 'accepted' or 'rejected' to a more positive debate about the forms and styles of change in people management.

By allowing for a greater input into HRM from the environment in which the organisation is located this approach also enables the analysts to link HRM more clearly with international contextual variations. It can be argued that Europe has some of the advantages in international competition which leading strategic theorists claim will accrue where organisations take greater account of personnel requirements, are more tolerant of ambiguity and challenge, are in a position to take greater risks and are more accepting of variability (Bartlett and Ghoshal 1989; Hedlund and Rolander 1990). Perhaps based partly on this reasoning the model provides a closer fit between HRM and national success. The fact that personnel aspects are brought into corporate strategy by culture, legislation, union involvement can be encompassed here: thus going a considerable way towards explaining why some countries, even including those with limited natural resources, that do not meet the traditional criteria of HRM are none the less amongst the most successful in the world (Porter 1991).

Developing the concept to take account of the more limited autonomy (or greater support) of organisational managers which is evidenced in Europe, and including the external factors within the concept of HRM, has a value beyond the presentation of simple diagrams. Without some adaptation to take account of the European (and perhaps other?) non-American situations, the HRM concept will continue to attract fundamental critiques, even in its most sophisticated form, for its failure to accept different degrees of managerial independence, different approaches to working with employee representatives and governmental involvement and, most damagingly, its inability to link HRM to economic performance. This model, by attempting to clarify some of these fundamental bases of the concept, suggests one way forward (Brewster 1994).

One oversimplification in the model, and one where it clearly needs development, is in its relation to MNCs. The international model emphasises the need for international organisations, and particularly international managers (Brewster 1991) to be aware of, and to adapt to, local environments – as in practice they frequently do (Brewster 1994). However a more complicated, perhaps three-dimensional, model would be required to provide a full picture of the world environment within which many international organisations operate.

Of course, our focus here on the Europeanisation of HRM should not be taken to imply that, from a closer focus, we are not aware of the differences between countries within Europe nor, from a closer one still, of the differences within countries in terms of such factors as size, sector or ownership. Indeed, the rest of the book addresses these issues specifically.

THE SURVEY

Studying HRM comparatively at the organisational level invariably leads researchers to notice the gap between national level labour market data and the detailed and instructive – but partial and non-comparable – case studies. The decision to do something about this gap originated at Price Waterhouse. A journalist, Michel Syrett, introduced them to researchers at Cranfield School of Management. With Gavin Adam of Price Waterhouse and Chris Brewster of Cranfield they established the Price Waterhouse Cranfield Project on International Strategic Human Resource Management. This snappily titled body was a collaborative venture between the two partners. It was agreed at a very early stage that this was to be a joint programme, not a piece of commissioned research. There were inevitably some tensions in this relationship, but they were few and were more than compensated for by the sharing of costs and administration, the mutual learning, the recruitment of Cranfield MBAs to Price Waterhouse via six-month assignments on the project and the shared information gathered and public exposure received as an outcome of the research. Once the project was underway (recruiting first Len Holden and Ariane Hegewisch and then a succession of other researchers) a further major benefit for both partners became apparent – the forging of a powerful and effective network of contacts across Europe.

The first issue in establishing the network was the selection of countries. In the first year it was decided to concentrate on a small group of countries. The amount of work involved in creating these links, establishing a research framework and instrument, and managing the resulting data was already clear. We decided to start with West Germany, France and the United Kingdom. These were three of the four big economies in the European Community and it was felt that any research which did not include them would lack credibility. Italy was left out because our contacts told us that postal survey research was difficult there (we subsequently confirmed this) and we felt that establishing the project would involve enough work without such additional problems. We also wanted a 'southern' European country, to establish whether HRM was different there and a non-EC European country to see whether HRM was different between EC and non-EC states. In the event we chose the two biggest, Spain and Sweden. Our decision here was aided by Price Waterhouse's extensive consultancy operation in Spain and Cranfield School of Management's close relationship with colleagues in Sweden.

In the first year the network was chosen, in the main, from the United Kingdom. Numerous visits were made to these countries, talking to business schools and universities, the local Price Waterhouse consultants and managerial contacts, to identify the appropriate academic partners. The criteria for selection were clear but difficult to fulfil. We were looking for institutions with considerable academic prestige and a significant profile amongst the managerial community in their country; they had to have a powerful HRM or personnel department with a respected specialist who was interested in international comparisons and prepared to work with us through the inevitable difficulties, compromise and pressure that comparative research entails; the specialists had to be able to invest time and money in the enterprise: and we had to feel comfortable working together. In the end our selection proved to have been successful; positive and continuing relationships developed.

The partners in the first year were:

Cranfield School of Management

Prof. Dr Dr h.c. E. Gaugler
Universität Mannheim

Professor Jaime Filella
ESADE

Dr Frank Bournois
Groupe ESC Lyon

Dr Magnus Söderström
IPF Uppsala

We wanted to extend the number of countries in the subsequent years. This was done rather differently. First, we had the benefit of having the original five country partners involved in the selection both of other countries and of appropriate academic partners. Second, the subsequently joining countries had less opportunity to vary the instruments we used – they had, to a considerable degree, to accept what we had developed. Third, they had less financial support from the centre – this became increasingly difficult as the number of countries expanded. Partners in different countries responded differently, some being prepared to cover the costs themselves, others attracting sponsors. Fourth, the project now had a product (data and networks) to offer, the benefits were more tangible and we found partners much readier, indeed even eager and in some countries competing, to join. Finally, following the experience of the first year we had identified more clearly the benefits of involving local personnel management associations and this was a feature of the network as it developed.

We added Italy and the Netherlands as the two missing major EC economies. The first year had shown Sweden to be distinct from the other countries and we wanted to explore that further, so we added Norway, to establish whether Sweden was unique or one of a Nordic bloc with Denmark. The Danes share much of the Scandinavian culture but are a European mainland and European Community country. We also added Switzerland as one of the most international countries in the world as a non-Scandinavian, non-EC European country.

The partners that were added in the second year were:

Professor Martin Hilb Ph.D.
University of St Gallen

Professor Henrik Holt Larsen
Copenhagen Business School

Mr Jonathan Cooper
SAIS, Bologna

Knut Lange
Handelshoyskolen BI, Oslo

Drs J Hoogendoorn
Rotterdam School of Management

In the third year Italy dropped out – mainly for reasons of financial constraints – and so did Switzerland. The Swiss felt that repeating the survey on an annual basis would not be acceptable to practitioners there and response rates would be very low. To the remaining countries we added Finland, Portugal, Ireland and our first country from outside Western Europe, Turkey. Our partners in these countries were:

Merja Mattila
University of Tampere

Rita Cantos e Cunha
Universidade Nova de Lisboa

Patrick Gunnigle
University of Limerick

Doç Dr Ayse Can Baysal
I.U. Isletma Fakültesi

As we write the survey is also being conducted in Greece; (Dr Nancy Papalexandris, Athens University of Economics and Business); in Austria (Dr Wolfgang Mayrhofer, Abteilung für Personalwirtschaft Wirtschaftsuniversität Wien); and in the Czech republic (Dr Josef Koubek, Prague School of Economics). A separate, but linked, project is being conducted in the Eastern Länder of Germany (what was the GDR), funded by the Anglo-German Foundation and run jointly with the Technical University of Dresden. A full report on the Eastern German project will be available in 1994.

FORMAT OF THE BOOK

It is within this view of a specifically European model, based on the specific history and developments within Europe (see Hegewisch and Brewster 1993, introduction) that our research programme was created and conducted. Full details of the methodology of the project are given in Appendix I. Here it suffices to point out that our objective was to collect, as far as possible, hard data on organisational level HRM practices from the most senior personnel specialists across all sectors of the economy of a variety of European countries. In the research, and in this text except where otherwise indicated, we define HRM (see Chapter 2) as a broad subject area rather than as either a set of particular approaches to the management of labour or as a specifically strategic approach. We therefore include within our remit all major areas covered in the planning, resourcing, development and motivation of employees and employee relations. In this sense the survey was aimed at establishing a basic infrastructure of organisational level data on human resource management practices, in response to the absence of European comparative data sources in the area. We wanted to go beyond the collection (and even presentation) of data however. The network of researchers that was established to conduct the research, therefore, included key authorities and significant business schools or universities in each country: and the research programme and the findings utilised, in each country, a panel of practitioners from leading organisations. Thus we were in a position to use the data – the evidence that had been collected – to address some of the major debates within human resource management (see for example Guest 1993 for a British overview of debates) and the broad assumptions that lie behind them; and to see these within the differing national contexts (see Brewster *et al.* 1992).

This is a lengthy book. What has been attempted here makes the length almost inevitable. The book is intended to be a report upon, and summation of, one of the largest independent research projects on human resource management practices in Europe. It is our belief that the rigour and representativeness of our data, and its trans-national collection of directly comparable data across all sectors of these economies, makes it a particularly powerful and useful database (see Appendix I on methodology for a more detailed discussion). The book therefore has two aims: to present the data in a meaningful way so that it informs serious commentaries on the areas under discussion; and to present sufficient of the data that other researchers can use it to extend, or even challenge, those commentaries or to take the discussions into new areas not covered here.

All of the chapters in this book focus on the 1992 data (the third year of our research), though they occasionally refer to the evidence gathered in previous years. These chapters have been written specifically for this book. They do however draw on earlier analyses of the data from previous years which have been presented in a variety of articles, working papers and reports.

This book brings together authors from seven different countries most of whom have been directly involved in the development of the survey as part of our network of European business schools or universities. This national diversity is reflected in their choice of issues within each area, in theoretical approaches and in the selection of relevant debates. We feel that this variety in approach is not only an inevitable but also a desirable outcome of European collaboration at this level.

In broad terms the book, and the presentation of tables at the end of the book, follow the outline of the questionnaire on which our research is based (Appendix II). As explained in the methodological appendix this changed marginally over the three years of data collection but the main headings remained the same. In this section of the introductory chapter we outline the topic area covered in each of the following chapters and, in a form of 'executive summary', outline the main findings.

CHAPTER 2
THE INTEGRATION OF HUMAN RESOURCE MANAGEMENT AND CORPORATE STRATEGY
BREWSTER

The debates about the role and function of HRM are continued in the next chapter, which takes a careful look at the concepts and the evidence. The data shows considerable stability over time – and considerable variation between countries. Spain and France for example consistently report a majority of organisations having an HR Director on the Board (or equivalent). Italy and Germany have a small proportion of organisations in the same position. Most of the others show a little less than half of the organisations with HR departments directly represented at the top decision making level. Some of the reasons for the variations are made clear: they relate to culture and task. Germany tends to have more 'administrative' personnel departments, but with personnel issues being brought into corporate thinking through employee representation at the top level. Italy has personnel departments that are focused on industrial relations issues. On perhaps the key question, of HR influence on corporate strategy, there is more uniformity: in most countries the personnel specialists claim to be involved 'from the outset' in strategy formulation in around half the organisations.

CHAPTER 3
THE EDUCATION AND TRAINING OF HUMAN RESOURCE MANAGERS IN EUROPE
TYSON AND WIKANDER

The role and function of the personnel department varies across Europe. The training that personnel specialists receive is closely related to their educational background and their progress through the personnel department.

Germany, Ireland, France, the Netherlands and the United Kingdom stand out in that more top level personnel specialists have had more than five years' experience in personnel. An interesting career pointer for personnel specialists is that Portugal is the only EC country in our sample to appoint as many as 3 in 10 of their top personnel specialists from within the company's own personnel department. Elsewhere it seems that in order to reach the top, managers have to be prepared to change organisation or function.

CHAPTER 4
HUMAN RESOURCES AND LINE MANAGEMENT
BREWSTER AND SODERSTRÖM

The decentralisation of personnel management and the devolvement of personnel tasks to line management have been claimed as distinctive features of HRM as opposed to 'personnel management'. In practice they vary widely across Europe. Most organisations with more than 200 employees have policies on various aspects of HR determined mainly at the level of the national HQ (more so for pay and industrial relations; less so for recruitment and selection, and health and safety). In terms of devolvement to the line, most organisations share responsibility between the HR department and the line for most issues. Where there has been a change in the last three years (a minority of cases) it tends to be in the direction of giving more responsibility to line management.

Denmark and the United Kingdom tend to be at the more decentralised end of the personnel management spectrum. Devolution, the sharing of responsibility for personnel issues with line management, is currently a live issue in the HRM debates. On a range of personnel issues it is the Italians who are most likely to hold responsibility within the personnel department. The British come next. This stands in sharp contrast to the Danes, for example, who on all issues tend to give much greater responsibility to line managers. Furthermore the trend in most European countries is to give increasing amounts of responsibility for HR issues to line managers.

CHAPTER 5
RECRUITMENT AND SELECTION IN EUROPE: POLICIES, PRACTICES AND METHODS
DANY AND TORCHY

Getting the right people into the organisation is a vital component of HRM. Analysis of the data identifies four distinct groupings of countries in terms of recruitment and selection. Germany stands alone, with recruitment organised within the codetermination framework and extensive use of flexible working as a means of encouraging recruitment. The Nordic countries form a bloc with few recruitment problems; despite the generally lower levels of unemployment potential recruits are better skilled. They also have more line management involvement in the process and longer-term planning horizons. The central European group (France, Ireland, United Kingdom, Netherlands) tend to use a wide range of recruitment methods and to give responsibility for recruitment to the local establishment. Finally the southern countries (Spain, Portugal, Turkey) are more likely to use informal recruitment techniques, tend not to use flexible working to aid recruitment, have short planning horizons and experience difficulty in hiring technically qualified people.

CHAPTER 6
EUROPEAN EXPERIMENTS WITH PAY AND BENEFITS POLICIES
FILELLA AND HEGEWISCH

Most countries in Europe have seen a decentralisation in bargaining structures away from the national or industry-wide level to more company or even individual bargaining. Nevertheless the picture remains very diverse and, across Europe, centralised pay determination is still common. Spain, France and Britain have the smallest number of organisations who bargain over basic pay for manual workers at national or industrywide level. Indeed, in the United Kingdom private sector negotiations at company level are now more frequent than at industry level for all staff groups, including manual workers. This is a very different picture from countries such as Germany, Ireland or the Netherlands where there is a national and industrywide framework for negotiations; though of course this does not preclude top-up negotiations at plant level, especially in times of tight labour markets.

The 1980s saw the beginning of a more rigorous focus on pay, not just as a means of attracting, retaining and motivating employees, but as a strategic weapon in ensuring the cost-effectiveness of human resources. The more rigorous focus on pay has also included the development of a new 'received wisdom': that the way forward lies in variable, particularly performance related, pay. Again, there continue to be differences across Europe. Merit or performance related pay is a practice much emphasised in Britain and Italy (where it is provided for in national agreements for managers), but used by less than a quarter of Dutch organisations even for the managerial staff. In any case it seems that the rise of performance related pay in Britain has been halted by the recession: compared to 1990–1 the latest survey has seen a falling off in the numbers of organisations offering performance related pay in all staff categories.

CHAPTER 7
KEY ISSUES IN TRAINING AND DEVELOPMENT
HOLT LARSEN

Training and staff development is the leading issue for most personnel departments across Europe. It is consistently ranked as the number one strategic objective for the next three years in our survey, irrespective of the differing education and training systems and Government found in the different countries. The amount spent on training per employee has increased or stayed the same in all staff categories, but it has increased most for management and professional/technical staff. Portugal, Spain and France all show a high degree of increase. The United Kingdom is not far behind, especially within management. There is little evidence of cutbacks during the recession of the early 1990s. We should add a note of caution here: across Europe between 30 and 40 per cent of organisations do not know how much they spend on training; the decentralisation of training budgets to line managers and general difficulties in costing on the job training for example are given as explanations. Nevertheless, this raises doubts about the seriousness with which organisations view investment in training: other decentralised areas of spending are still monitored centrally. A more positive response lies in the careful analysis of training needs and monitoring of the effectiveness of training. In most countries a clear majority of organisations do both – though the monitoring of effectiveness is often done largely through the mechanism of informal feedback from participants and line managers, and immediate course-end evaluation. In terms of training subjects there is a clear and consistent identification of the three main areas for the immediate future as business administration and strategy; people management; and computers and new technology.

CHAPTER 8
TRAINING AND MANAGEMENT DEVELOPMENT IN EUROPE
BOURNOIS, CHAUCHAT AND ROUSSILLON

Management development is both important and complicated. It varies significantly by country across Europe, and although the countries can be grouped, they do not clearly fall into any previously noted patterns. There are differences in the kind of management training undertaken in the various countries, with, for example, emphasis on languages in Spain and Finland; on communicaiton in Ireland and Norway; on delegation in Sweden and Norway; team building and performance appraisal in the United Kingdom and motivation in Germany. There are also differences in the use of particular approaches such as performance appraisal as a training analysis, assessment centres and career planning. Overall management development is a complex issue, related to the educational background and managerial roles.

CHAPTER 9
EUROPEAN INDUSTRIAL RELATIONS: CHANGE AND CONTINUITY
GUNNIGLE, BREWSTER AND MORLEY

Trade unions are not 'going away'. Despite the view (fears or hopes?) of some commentators, relationships with trade unions are still a key issue for personnel departments in most European organisations. Of course, union membership varies considerably – it is high in Scandinavia and low in France. However, individual membership is not a good indicator of trade union influence within organisations: recognition levels are higher – our survey shows that amongst organisations with more than 200 employees a clear majority recognise trade unions for collective bargaining. Even this underestimates the collective influence given the mandatory consultation arrangements in many European countries. Union influence is stable in most countries; reduced in a large proportion of organisations in some countries (the United Kingdom, France, Italy) and in some countries such as Germany and Spain more organisations report that union influence has increased than report it as decreased. Overall, trade unions continue to play an important part in European HRM. The reasons for this are complex: they include the trade union role in communication and consultation which is legally determined in many European countries; the attempts by some European governments and the European Community to emphasise the position of the 'social partners' as the EC calls them; and the related fact that in most countries the unions are not seen, and do not see themselves, as 'adversaries' of management. Rather, they are seen as partners. They work with the organisation for the success of the enterprise and those who work in it. This raises again the question of the applicability of the 'anti-union' bias underlying many concepts of HRM.

CHAPTER 10
EMPLOYEE COMMUNICATION AND PARTICIPATION
BREWSTER, HEGEWISCH, MAYNE AND TREGASKIS

HRM texts tend to give a central place to employee communication. In many European countries this is controlled by detailed legislation – legislation with fundamental national differences. The data shows considerable national differences in communication within organisations; but no obvious correlation with national legislative systems. Across Europe there are general increases in the extent of communication, with between a third and two-thirds of organisations (depending on country) increasing verbal and written communication direct to employees, and hardly any reducing it. Increases in communication through collective channels also outweigh decreases although there are more of the latter than there are in individual communication. There is also evidence of the existence of a 'glass floor': information on economic performance and strategy does not get down to the lower levels of the organisation in most cases.

CHAPTER 11
FLEXIBLE WORKING PRACTICES: THE CONTROVERSY AND THE EVIDENCE
BREWSTER, HEGEWISCH AND MAYNE

Flexible working practices are spreading fast. There is a widespread increase in nearly all forms of flexible working; and their adoption across all sectors of the economy in all European countries. Some forms of flexibility, like the use of overtime or weekend working, are increasing or decreasing in different countries – depending largely on the current state of the economy. Amongst other types of flexibility, however, three general trends are apparent. First, the most substantial growth has been in areas of non-permanent employment: temporary contracts, fixed-term contracts and subcontracting. Second, the use of shiftworking and part-time work continues to grow – but the growth of part-time work tends to be concentrated in the middle of Europe. It is less used in the southern countries and may even be reducing in its stronghold in the Nordic states. Third, the ideas which have perhaps attracted most attention amongst practitioners – annual hours and home working or teleworking – remain very much minority concerns. The take-up in practice has been low. The findings on home working in particular confound many predictions: it seems that the importance of the social aspect of work was underestimated. The growth of flexibility raises important policy questions. At the European Community level, two arguments could be addressed to the EC's latest Directives on flexible working, which aim to protect employees from exploitation and to prevent unfair competition. Either such protection is overdue and will be only just in time; or it is flying in the face of an overwhelming Europe-wide trend to achieve greater contract flexibility. At the company level, our data shows that the growth of flexibility has little correlation with strategic HR policies: it appears to be, in general, an ad hoc response to external pressures. Flexible working practices clearly are seen by many organisations across Europe as a more efficient way of working, but to be successful they need careful management, investment and training.

CHAPTER 12
EQUAL OPPORTUNITIES POLICIES IN EUROPE
HEGEWISCH AND MAYNE

The common EC framework for the prevention of discrimination on the grounds of gender is not matched by common policies on racial discrimination or discrimination against the disabled. However there is little correlation between legislative provision and the extent to which organisations monitor recruitment, training or promotion in these three areas. Nor is there any evidence of a follow through into practice, through targeted recruitment or the development of what have been called 'family friendly' practices. In overall terms organisations are paying more attention to gender issues than to race or disablement. Although there is evidence here that public sector organisations are more likely to apply gender monitoring, USMNCs tend to reflect national practice in the country they are operating in, rather than import US practices. 'Family friendly' or flexible work practices which enable women to continue to take responsibility for 'caring' duties whilst working are more common in the northern European countries and are correlated with the public provision of childcare facilities.

CHAPTER 13
EC SOCIAL POLICY AND EUROPEAN HUMAN RESOURCE MANAGEMENT
TEAGUE

The uneven development of EC social policy has made it difficult to evaluate its relationship to the practicalities of organisational human resource management. Overall, this untidiness has probably made the practical impact of the policy minimal – and indeed human resource management specialists claim to be untroubled by it. Arguably the role of EC social policy is in practice to reflect and consolidate changes rather than to direct them.

THE APPENDICES

 I Methodology of the Price Waterhouse Cranfield Project
 II Questionnaire (1992)
III Tables

The appendices form a valuable, and substantial, part of this text. The methodological appendix presents details of the form and nature of our research programme and the tests that have been conducted to assess the representativeness of the responses. We are grateful for the work of Olga Tregaskis of the Centre for European HRM at Cranfield on this appendix. The second appendix consists of the English language questionnaire used in the third year (1992) of the study. The third appendix presents the results collected in that year; by country, by size (above and below 1000 employees) and by public or private sector. This book, and our publications elsewhere, are the attempts by those involved in the research to draw analytical and theoretical conclusions from what remains one of the largest and most comprehensive of organisational level research projects into HRM. The data collected so far is presented here so that other researchers, policy makers and practitioners can draw upon it to check, extend, or challenge, our interpretations.

    Of course the data is susceptible to extensive further detailed analyses and these are being progressed within the Centre for European HRM.

RESEARCH INTO EUROPEAN HRM

European HRM is a continuing area of research within the Cranfield School of Management's Centre for European HRM. Plans are in hand to collect similar data in the United States of America. The survey will be repeated in the winter of 1994; we have the ambition from then onwards to resurvey across Europe on a triennial basis.

This chapter has only touched on some of the issues involved in conducting internationally comparative research. We have been struggling with them for four years now. It seems valuable to conclude this section with three general points.

First, this form of organisational level survey provides limited information. It has neither the generality of national (usually governmentally sponsored) surveys of the labour force, nor the explanatory power of case studies. However, it does fill a major gap in our understanding, enabling researchers, policy makers and practitioners to evaluate policy and practice implications at organisational level and to generalise from the inevitably limited and partial number of case studies.

Second, such research requires the cooperation of partners based in each country. One conclusion that we have come to is that it must be almost impossible to undertake genuine explanatory, internationally comparative, work without spending considerable time in a country, working with the national cultural background, statistics, legislation and practitioners. Since for any researcher (or research group) this limits them to perhaps the two or three countries that they can physically spend time in, broader surveys can only be undertaken by internationally cooperating teams. We believe that such teams also have considerable value: they challenge our assumptions; they are a valuable learning opportunity; and they are a lot of fun.

Third, the importance of cross-national studies is, we believe, manifest. As the world, and particularly Europe, becomes ever more international, the implicit value of studies of management which challenge our assumptions is increasingly matched by the value of comparative information for organisations and their managers. There are obvious additional difficulties in conducting research internationally – but enormous value in taking up the challenge.

REFERENCES

Ackermann, K. F. (1986) 'A contingency model of HRM strategy – empirical research findings reconsidered', *Management Forum*, 6: 65–83.

Adler, N. (1986) *International Dimensions of Organisational Behaviour*, Boston: PWS-Kent.

Albert, F. J. (1989) *Les ressources humaines, atout stratégique*, Paris: Editions L'harmattan, p. 75.

Baird, L., Meshoulam, I., Degive, G. (1983) 'Meshing human resources planning with strategic business planning, a model approach', *Personnel*, 60(5): 14–25.

Bartlett, C. A. and Ghoshal, S. (1989) *Managing Across Borders*, Boston: Harvard Business School Press.

Beer, M., Lawrence, P. R., Mills, Q. N. and Walton, R. E. (1985) *Human Resource Management*, New York: Free Press.

Besseyre des Horts, C. H. (1987) 'Typologies des pratiques de gestion des ressources humaines', *Revue française de Gestion*, Sept.–Oct.: 149–55.

Besseyre des Horts, C. H. (1988) *Vers une Gestion Stratégique des Ressources Humaines*, Paris: Editions d'Organisation, pp. 69–84.

Beyer, H. T. (1991) 'Personalarbeit als integrierter Bestandteil der Unternehmensstrategie' paper to the 1991 DGFP Annual Congress, Wiesbaden.

Black, S., Gregerson, H. and Mendenhall, M. (1993) *Global Assignments*, San Francisco: Jossey-Bass.

Bournois, F. (1990) 'La place de la fonction Ressources Humaines en Europe: similitudes et différences', *Actes du 1er Congrès de l'Association française de Gestion des Ressources Humaines*, Bordeaux, November: 107–22.

Bournois, F. (1991a) 'Gestion des RH en Europe: données comparées' *Revue française de Gestion*, March–May: 68–83.

Bournois, F. (1991b) *La Gestion des Cadres en Europe*, Paris: Editions Eyrolles.

Brewster, C. (1991) *The Management of Expatriates*, London, Kogan Page.

Brewster, C. (1993) 'The paradox of adjustment: UK and Swedish expatriates in Sweden and the UK', *Human Resource Management Journal* 4(1): 1–14.

Brewster, C. (1994) 'Human Resource Management in Europe: Reflection of, or Challenge to, the American Concept?' in Kirkbride, P. (ed.) (1994) *Human Resource Management in the New Europe: Perspectives on the 1990s*, London: Routledge.

Brewster, C. and Bournois, F. (1991) 'A European perspective on human resource management', *Personnel Review* 20(6): 4–13.

Brewster, C., Hegewisch, A., Holden, L. and Lockhart, T. (eds) (1992) *The European Human Resource Management Guide*, London: Academic Press.

Brewster, C. and Tyson, S. (eds) (1991) *International Comparisons in Human Resource Management*, London: Pitman.

Child, J. (1976) 'Organisational structure, environment and performance: the role of strategic choice', *Sociology* 6: 1–22.

Conrad, P. and Pieper, R. (1990) 'HRM in the Federal Republic of Germany' in R. Pieper (ed.) *Human Resource Management: an International Comparison*, Berlin: Walter de Gruyter.

Cox, J. and Cooper, L. (1985), 'The irrelevance of American organisational sciences to the UK and Europe', *Journal of General Management* 11(2): 27–34.

Craig, C. S., Douglas, S. P. and Grein, A. (1992) 'Patterns of convergence and divergence among industrialised nations: 1960–1988', *Journal of International Business Studies* 4: 773–87.

Dertouzos, M. L., Lester, R. K. and Solow, R. M. (1989) *Made in America: Regaining the Productive Edge*, Cambridge, Mass.: MIT Press.

Dowling, P. and Schuler, R. (1990) *International Dimensions of Human Resource Management*, San Francisco: PWS-Kent.

England, G. W. (1978) *The Manager and His Values: an International Perspective from the United States, Japan, Korea, India and Australia*, Cambridge: Ballinger.

Filella, J. (1991) 'Is there a Latin model in the management of human resources', *Personnel Review* 20(6): 15–24.

Fombrun, C. and Tichy, N. M. (1983) 'Strategic planning and human resources management: at rainbow's end', in R. Lamb (ed.) (1983) *Recent Advances in Strategic Planning*, New York: McGraw-Hill.

Fox, S. and McLeay, S. (1992) 'An approach to researching managerial labour markets: HRM, corporate strategy and financial performance in UK manufacturing', *International Journal of Human Resource Management* 3(3): 523–54.

Gaugler, E. (1988) 'HR management: an international comparison', *Personnel* 65(8); 24–30.

Guest, D. (1990) 'Human resource management and the American dream', *Journal of Management Studies*, 27(4): 377–97.

Guest, D. (1993) 'Current perspectives on human resource management in the United Kingdom', in C. Brewster and A. Hegewisch (eds) (1993) *European Developments in Human Resource Management*, Cranfield Research series, London: Kogan Page.

Haire, M., Ghiselli, E. E. and Porter, L. W. (1966) *Managerial Thinking: an International Study*, New York: Free Press.

Hedlund, G. and Rolander, D. (1990) 'Action in heterarchies – new approaches to managing the MNC', in C. A. Bartlett, Y. Doz and G. Hedlund, (eds) (1990) *Managing the Global Firm*, London: Routledge, pp. 15–46.

Hegewisch, A. and Brewster, C. (eds) (1993) *European Developments in Human Resource Management*, Cranfield Research series, London: Kogan Page.

Hendry, C. and Pettigrew, A. (1990) 'HRM: an agenda for the 1990s', *International Journal of Human Resource Management* 1(1): 17–25.

Hofstede, G. (1980) *Cultures Consequences: International Differences in Work-related Values*, Beverly Hills: Sage.

Hofstede, G. (1983) 'The cultural relativity of organisational practices and theories', *Journal of International Business Studies* 13(3): 75–90.

Hofstede, G. (1991) *Cultures and Organisations*, London: McGraw-Hill.

Kochan, T. A. and Barocci, T. A. (1985) *Human Resource Management and Industrial Relations*, Boston: Little Brown.

Kochan, T. A., Katz, H. C. and McKersie, R. B. (1986) *The Transformation of American Industrial Relations*, New York: Basic Books.

Laurent, A. (1983) 'The cultural diversity of western conceptions of management', *International Studies of Management and Organisation* 13(1–2): 75–96.

Lengnick-Hall, C. A. and Lengnick-Hall, M. L. (1988), 'Strategic human resources management: a review of the literature and a proposed typology', *Academy of Management Review* 13(3): 454–70.

Levitt, T. (1983) 'The globalisation of markets' *Harvard Business Review* May–June: 92–102.

Lorange, P. and Murphy, D. (1984) 'Bringing human resources into strategic planning: systems design considerations', in C. J. Fombrun, N. M. Tichy and M. A. Devanna (eds) *Strategic Human Resource Management*, New York: John Wiley.

Macmillan, I. C. and Schuler, R. S. (1985) 'Gaining a competitive edge through human resources', *Personnel* 62(4): 24–9.

Pieper, R. (ed.) (1990) *Human Resource Management: an International Comparison*, Berlin: Walter de Gruyter.

Poole, M. (1990), 'Human resource management in an international perspective', *International Journal of Human Resource Management* 1(1): 1–15.

Porter, M. (1985) *Competitive Advantage*, New York: Free Press.

Porter, M. (1991) *The Competitive Advantage of Nations*, New York: Free Press.

Prahalad, C. K. and Doz, Y. (1987) *The Multinational Mission* New York: Free Press.

Remer, A. (1986) 'Personnel management in Western Europe – development, situation and concepts', in K. Macharzina and W. H. Staehle, (eds) (1986) *European Approaches to International Management*, Berlin: Walter de Gruyter.

Ronen, S. and Shenkar, O. (1985) 'Clustering countries on attitudinal divisions: a review and synthesis', *Academy of Management Review* 10(3): 435–54.

Salaman, G. (ed.) (1991) *Human Resource Management Strategies*, Milton Keynes: Open University Press.

Schuler, R. A. (1989) 'Strategic human resource management and industrial relations', *Human Relations* 42(2): 157–84.

Schuler, R. S. (1992) 'Strategic human resource management: linking the people with the strategic needs of the business', *Organisational Dynamics* summer: 18–31.

Schuler, R. S. and Jackson, S. E. (1987) 'Linking competitive strategies with human resource management practices', *Academy of Management Executive* 1(3): 209–13.

Schuler, R. and Macmillan, S. (1984) 'Gaining competitive advantage through human resource management practices', *Human Resource Management* 23(3): 241–55.

Staehle, W. H. (1987) 'Human resource management', *Zeitschrift für Betriebswirtschaft* 5(6): 26–37.

Staehle, W. H. (1990) 'Human resource management and corporate strategy', in R. Pieper (ed.) (1990) *Human Resource Management: an International Comparison*, Berlin: Walter de Gruyter.

Staffelbach, B. (1986) *Strategisches Personalmanagement*, Bern-Stuttgart.

Tayeb, M. (1988) *Organisations and National Culture: a Comparative Analysis*, London: Sage.

Thurley, K. and Wirdenius, H. (1991) 'Will management become "European"? Strategic choices for organisations', *European Management Journal*, 9(2): 127–34.

Chapter 2

The integration of human resource management and corporate strategy

Chris Brewster

Increasingly, in the literature and within employing organisations, the concept of human resource management (HRM), and the associated concept of strategic human resource management, is achieving greater prominence.

This chapter reviews, briefly, the concept of HRM and the associated concepts of strategic HRM and international HRM. It identifies the integration of senior specialists within the top management team as a key issue and presents data concerning the extent of such integration in Europe. This is not a straightforward task: there are both conceptual and methodological difficulties. On the conceptual side, the definition of HRM is far from clearly established in the literature: different authorities imply or state different definitions and draw on different evidence. On the methodological side, there are inherent problems in assessing the concept and in identifying relevant data. These issues are addressed first.

DEFINITIONS OF HUMAN RESOURCE MANAGEMENT

Conceptually, a range of definitions of human resource management is possible: from an almost etymological analysis at one end to a clearly normative perspective at the other. Within this range three broad categories can be discerned.

HRM as a broad subject area

From the words 'human resource management' alone the subject can be defined as the processes by which an organisation deals with the labour it needs to perform its functions.

Such a broad definition would therefore encompass, but go beyond, traditional definitions of personnel management, manpower planning, resourcing, development, industrial relations etc. It would also, because it does not refer to personnel or employees, include subcontracting, outsourcing and similar approaches.

This approach to HRM can be seen in attempts to provide all-encompassing classifications of the various areas which HRM covers: seeing, in one of the classic texts, a four-fold typology – employee influence, human resource flow (into, through, and out of the organisation), reward systems and work systems (Beer *et al*. 1985); or four rather different areas – the acquisition, maintenance, motivation and development of human resources (e.g. DeCenzo and Robbins, 1988); or a five-step HRM cycle – selection, performance, appraisal, rewards and development (Storey 1989). At one point Hendry and Pettigrew (1990: 24) seem to adopt this view defining HRM as 'a range of things affecting the employment and contribution of people, against the criteria of coherence and appropriateness'.

HRM as a 'model' approach

Many authorities have tried to narrow the concept to distinguish HRM from these related topics, particularly from personnel management. Legge (1989), in her review of British and American writing on HRM, sees HRM as distinctive in the following three areas: it gives greater emphasis to the development of the management team than personnel management; it differs from personnel management as an activity for line managers because it is more firmly integrated in the general coordinating activity of line managers, including a greater 'bottom-line' emphasis; it emphasises the management of corporate culture as a senior management activity (Legge 1989: 27, 28).

Guest (who emphasises the more 'human' resources aspects of the American theories and their roots in occupational psychology) conceives of HRM not as an alternative to personnel management but as a particular form of personnel management, which stresses 'the goal of integration, the goal of employee commitment, the goal of flexibility/adaptability, the goal of quality' (Guest 1987). A later paper by the same author discusses a range of 'innovative techniques of the sort typically associated with HRM' including such issues as flexible working practices, quality circles, training in participative skills and job enrichment (Guest 1990: 385).

Storey (1992) identifies fifteen differences between personnel management and HRM under the four headings of beliefs and assumptions; strategic aspects; line management; and key levers. Mahoney and Deckop (1986) also examined the differences between 'personnel' and 'HRM'. They argue that, overall, HRM involves a wider and broader view in six specific areas:

1 *Employment planning*: from a narrow technical focus to closer links with business strategy.
2 *Communication with employees*: from a collective, negotiating focus to a more general approach to more direct communication with employees.
3 *Employee feelings*: from job satisfaction to concern with the total organisational culture.

4 *Employment terms*: from selection, training, compensation policies focused on individuals to a concern with group working and group effectiveness.

5 *Employment cost-benefits*: from a concern with cost-reduction through such strategies as reducing turnover, controlling absenteeism to a focus on organisational effectiveness and the 'bottom line'.

6 *Employee development*: from individual skills to longer-term employment capabilities.

(Mahoney and Deckop 1986)

In a similar, but slightly different way, Beaumont identifies five 'major items typically mentioned' in the US literature as part of HRM:

1 Relatively well-developed internal labour market arrangements; in such areas, for example, as promotion, training, individual career planning.

2 Flexible work organisation systems.

3 Contingent compensation practices and/or skills or knowledge-based pay structure.

4 High levels of individual participation in task-related decisions.

5 Extensive internal communications arrangements.

(Beaumont 1991)

Together, these attempts to synthesise the elements of HRM show some areas of consistency (wider communication for example); some areas of greater or less detail (presumably, for example, flexible work organisation is intended to be a contribution to the bottom line; training for the longer term is an aspect of developing an internal labour market); and some areas of uncertainty (not only are the elements of compensation which are seen to be evidence of HRM different but even within Beaumont's synopsis he finds two different elements).

HRM has been characterised as having specific objectives which include high commitment, trust or involvement (Walton 1985; Guest 1987; Kochan and Dyer 1992). Alternatively HRM has been seen as encompassing specific practices in relation to employees including, for example, team working, flexible working practices, direct communication, non-unionism and 'quality' programmes (Purcell 1991; Storey 1992).

A specific problem with this level of definition is that different authors emphasise different approaches or practices, and/or are unclear about the relationship between them. Often the lists of potential practices include some that are incompatible (performance measurement and quality programmes, for example: see Brewster 1992). Sometimes they raise incompatibilities within the topic (as when Beaumont includes contingent compensation practices and/or skills or knowledge-based pay).

'Strategic' HRM

There is also a group of authorities who distinguish HRM from other approaches in that it is closely integrated with organisational strategies and objectives (Schuler and Jackson 1987; Lengnick-Hall and Lengnick-Hall 1988; Hendry and Pettigrew 1990; Miller 1991; Schuler 1992; Wright and McMahon 1992). Hendry and Pettigrew (1986) have summarised this clearly. They focus on HRM as strategic integration, defined by:

1 the use of planning;
2 a coherent approach to the design and management of personnel systems based on an employment policy and manpower strategy, and often underpinned by a 'philosophy';
3 matching HRM activities and policies to some explicit business strategy; and
4 seeing the people of the organisation as a 'strategic resource' for achieving 'competitive advantage'.

(Hendry and Pettigrew 1986)

Later they say explicitly, 'We see HRM as a perspective on employment systems, characterised by their closer alignment with business strategy' (Hendry and Pettigrew 1990: 36). This approach to HRM is the one that informs this chapter.

Of course these three definitions can be, and often are, overlapping. Arguably, the moves by IBM at the end of the 1980s and Hewlett Packard at the beginning of the 1990s show this. They were often held up as exemplars of the HRM 'model' approach with a range of practices including lifetime employment. However the response to their worsening market position at that time was extensive redundancies – showing perhaps that in the event where model HRM and strategic HRM no longer coincide one has to be chosen at the expense of the other. One of the problems in the literature is that individual texts either do not specify which of these broad definitional levels they are addressing, or assume mutual interlinking, or drift between them. Theoretically it is quite possible that a closely integrated, strategic approach to HRM will involve nearly all the specific HRM objectives and practices and hence drive all aspects of the way labour is managed. Equally however, it is possible that the close integration of HRM with corporate strategy could, in some sectors for example, lead to a heavy emphasis on cost-reduction, eliminating all 'people frills' such as training or employee benefits and making extensive use of outsourcing.

Throughout the book we utilise the concept of HRM as a broad study area, except where specifically noted otherwise. This chapter, though, concentrates upon strategic HRM, addressing first the debate in the literature, and secondly using proxy data to outline the extent of integration in a number of European countries. Underlying the concept of strategic HRM is the idea that human resources are not only the major operating cost for most organisations but are also a crucial factor in utilising all the organisation's other resources in the most effective way. HRM becomes strategic when, in private sector terms, 'human resources are elevated to a position where the firm sees and treats these (human resource) issues as a source of competitive advantage' (Kochan and Dyer 1992: 3). A defining feature of strategic HRM therefore is its close linkage to business strategy which will be called here 'integration'. By *integration* is meant the degree to which the HRM issues are considered as part of the formulation of business strategies (see, for European examples, Schreyögg 1987; Butler 1988; Wohlgemuth 1988; Guest 1989). There is – in research as well as in the business community – an increasing awareness of the relationship between business strategy and HRM (Storey 1989; Freedman 1991). Indeed, in Germany particularly, the debates about HRM have tended to focus on the issue of 'strategy' (see Conrad and Pieper 1990, for a full review of the German debate on HRM).

The argument that there is a direct correlation between strategic HRM and economic success has been made many times. Porter (1985) believes that HRM can help a firm obtain competitive advantage. Schuler and Macmillan (1984: 242) make a similar point, that 'effectively managing human resources' gives benefits which 'include greater profitability'.

Indeed, Schuler has gone on to argue that effectively managing human resources has a positive impact on the firm's overall success through improving productivity, advantage and assuring workforce flexibility (Schuler and Huber 1993). Other authors, as we pointed out in the first chapter, argue that organisations which engage in a strategy formulation process systematically and reciprocally consider human resources and competitive strategy will perform better over the long term' (Lengnick-Hall and Lengnick-Hall 1988: 468). Pieper builds on the view that HRM is the key to organisational success to argue that 'since HRM is seen as a strategic factor strongly influencing the economic success of a single company one can argue that it is also a strategic factor for the success of an entire nation' (1990: 4). Porter (1991) makes similar arguments.

The problem is that there is a marked dearth of evidence to support those points. Indeed at the most visible level, the national level, there is some evidence that on the most generalised assumptions taken here the evidence points in the opposite direction: countries with less evidence of autonomous company international 'model' HRM, (countries where HR departments are most administrative, with most legal regulation and trade union influence), tend to have been most successful in recent years. National differences in human resource management and in 'model' practices have no correlation with national differences in economic performance.

Part of the answer to this problem is undoubtedly methodological, based around the impossibility of finding nations (or organisations) which are equal in all substantial areas except HRM strategies. It seems unlikely however that better methodology would resolve the issue. This raises two possibilities: the first is that the link with economic success, despite its apparent logic, is a fallacy. The second, more promisingly, is that current conceptions of HRM are inadequate. If this is so, it would help to explain the lack of correlation of a narrowly conceived view of organisational HRM strategies with economic success – by failing to include the external constraints, the autonomous 'model' HRM concept ignores important factors.

According to Lengnick-Hall and Lengnick-Hall (1988: 459–60), the integration of business strategy and HRM has four advantages: it provides a broader range of solutions for solving complex organisational problems; it ensures that human, financial, and technological resources are given consideration in setting goals and assessing implementation capabilities; and that organisations explicitly consider the individuals who comprise them and who implement policies; and finally it ensures that human resource considerations contribute to, rather than are subordinate to, strategic decisions.

This stands in opposition to the widespread belief that HRM is the dependent variable and the business strategy the independent variable in this relationship: the view that HRM should in some sense 'follow' business strategy (see, e.g., Tichy et al. 1982; Ackermann 1986; Miller 1989). 'The critical managerial task is to align the formal structure and the HR systems so that they drive the strategic objectives of the organisation' (Fombrun, Tichy and Devanna 1984: 37). The assumption is that human resource management is in some sense 'strategic' when it follows closely the corporate strategy of the organisation. This conception is widespread in the United States.

This is a view popular with those who identify the strategic HRM definition directly with model HRM policies or practices: they tend towards the normative 'one best way' approach. It is argued that the Taylorist or in its later forms Braverman-style labour process approach (Braverman 1974) has been outdated by technological developments and the resultant increases in flexibly specialised production (Piore and Sabel 1984); in the requirement for highly skilled, well educated and well trained workers (Daniel 1987) and in the consequent need for either more normative, indirect controls (Ramsey 1977; Friedman 1977; Collins 1979; Edwards 1979) or for a move away from control towards commitment. Thus it would be argued that strategic HRM has to include a focus on employee commitment (Walton 1985; Kochan and Dyer 1992); or must of necessity be non-union (Purcell 1991); or involve a unitary framework (Guest 1987).

A different strand of the strategic HRM literature eschews the one-best-way approach but, (like Fombrun, Tichy and Devanna 1984; Ackermann 1986; Staffelbach 1986; Besseyre des Horts 1987, 1988; and Miller 1989), gets locked into a form of contingent determinism. The elements of the corporate strategy that dominate the HR strategy vary. Thus Purcell (1987) indicates that certain organisational forms will find it virtually impossible to adopt strategic HRM, whilst Marginson et al. (1988) state that foreign companies are more likely to adopt it. Other authors have linked HR strategies to different factors: Schuler has indicated that they should be based on the type of market as defined by Porter (Schuler and Jackson 1987) or on a particular position in a company's lifecycle (Schuler 1989). The market approach has also been propounded by others (Baird, Meshoulam and Degive 1983; Dertouzos, Lester and Solow 1989) and the lifecycle approach has been adopted by others too (Fombrun and Tichy 1983; Kochan and Barocci 1985). Cohen and Pfeiffer (1986) argue that sector and type of organisation can be determining factors, with public sector and large, high visibility organisations more likely to adopt strategic HR practices.

METHODOLOGICAL ISSUES

Our survey illuminates this issue on a broad, internationally comparative, basis. Inevitably with such a research approach the rigour and explanatory value of detailed, multimethod or longitudinal case studies is lost. However, what is gained is the ability to draw clearly comparative analyses of the degree of integration typical in the different countries. To do this, questions were asked, not directly about integration, but about a series of surrogate measures that allowed more objective comparison. The surrogate measures that were chosen were drawn from the literature (see, for example, Schuler 1989, 1991; Schuler and Jackson 1987).

They build on the assumption that HRM will be integrated with corporate strategy when the function is represented at the top decision making level of the organisation and involved in decisions there at an early stage, and when the function's role is operationalised through the development of an HR policy. Therefore the following were taken as surrogate measures of integration: HR specialist involvement in the main policy making forum of the organisation (Board of Directors or equivalent); HR specialist involvement in the development of corporate strategy; and whether or not such strategies are linked with HR policies.

In European countries personnel or HR specialists rarely reach the very highest positions in employing organisations (Coulson-Thomas 1990; Coulson-Thomas and Wakeham 1991). Of course, the degree of HR access to CEO and similar positions varies by country and would appear to be more common in Scandinavia. It is also true that there are numerous CEOs who may not have come from the personnel function but exhibit a particular interest in HRM. However, these are still exceptions. The assumption taken in the research followed the literature in assuming that an informed HR input to top-level debates is most likely only where there is an organisational structure which provides for the head of the HR functions to be present at the key policy making forum.

FINDINGS

Tables 2.1 and 2.2 indicate the proportion of companies with an HR presence at the level of the Board (or equivalent); and the role that such Board-level HR specialists play in the development of corporate strategy. These show significant differences across Europe. In six countries a clear majority of organisations have an HR presence at the top strategic level: as many as seven out of ten organisations in Sweden, France, Spain and Norway. However in some countries, notably West Germany and Italy, the HR function is only rarely represented at Board level.

When we examine personnel department involvement in the development of corporate strategy the picture changes somewhat. In Germany and Italy our respondents tell us that human resource issues are taken into account from the outset in the development of corporate strategy by more organisations than the number who have Board-level responsibility for the HR function: a point explored below. In the Netherlands and the United Kingdom HR influence from the outset approximately mirrors Board-level involvement. In the other six countries there are considerable numbers of HR specialists with a place on the Board who, nevertheless, are not involved in the development of corporate strategy until a later stage.

Generally, between a third and a half of all organisations in all the other countries have an early HR involvement at this critical level: slightly more than that in Norway, Sweden, France, Spain and the United Kingdom.

The next stage in this analysis of integration is to examine those organisations who have

Table 2.1 Head of personnel or human resources function on the main Board of directors or equivalent (%)

Country	CH[a]	D(W)	DK	E	F	FIN	I[a]	IRL	N	NL	P	S	T	UK
	58	30	49	73	84	61	18	44	71	42	46	84	37	49

Note: [a] 1991 data

Table 2.2 HR involvement in development of corporate strategy (%)

Country	CH[a]	D(W)	DK	E	F	FIN	I[a]	IRL	N	NL	P	S	T	UK
From the outset	48	55	47	54	54	48	32	50	65	50	42	56	45	53
Consultative	20	25	31	25	27	23	23	31	24	36	30	31	9	32
Implementation	6	10	15	18	16	10	17	10	9	10	18	8	33	9
Not consulted	14	10	7	4	3	7	3	9	3	3	10	6	13	7

Note: [a] 1991 data

Table 2.3 Personnel/HR management strategy (%)

Country	CH[a]	D(W)	DK	E	F	FIN	I[a]	IRL	N	NL	P	S	T	UK
Written	58	18	72	37	34	52	33	41	71	44	34	73	29	50
Unwritten	32	42	20	41	52	29	40	34	16	33	41	24	41	24
No strategy	9	32	4	16	10	14	11	15	9	13	14	3	18	19
Don't know/Missing	1	2	1	0	0	1	16	9	0	1	3	0	1	1

Note: [a] 1991 data

formal HR strategies which the organisation takes seriously enough to translate into work programmes and deadlines and to monitor. The figures for HR strategies are given in Table 2.3. Again they show considerable variation. In Germany only 18 per cent of organisations have a written personnel or HR strategy, with 42 per cent claiming to have an 'unwritten strategy'. Arguably, this may be a response to the possibility of close scrutiny of any written document by the powerful Works Councils. In Norway, at the other extreme, 71 per cent of organisations have a written strategy and a further 16 per cent have an 'unwritten strategy'. There is a broad correlation between having the head of the HR group on the Board, or equivalent, and having a written HR strategy. Perhaps Board membership encourages HR specialists to feel that formalised strategies are as important for their function as for other areas of the business. The noticeable exceptions to this broad correlation are in the Latin countries of Spain, France and Italy. In Spain and France Board-level representation is high, but formal policies exist in only half as many organisations: and in Italy formal strategies exist in twice as many organisations as have Board-level representation for the HR function. The high rating on Board membership and early involvement in the creation of corporate strategy compared to its much lower rating on HR policy in France and Spain fits in with stereotypes (supported by some evidence, see Laurent 1983 and Hofstede 1980) of these as rigidly hierarchical countries: the influential senior HR specialists do not want their autonomy restricted by written policies (see also Filella 1991). In Italy, by contrast, the predominant role for the HR specialist concerns trade union relationships and employment legislation (Cooper and Giacomello 1992). In consequence, many HR activities are formalised into clearly visible policies.

Comparing the general ordering of the countries on these criteria some other anomalies stand out. Spain appears to be one of the least consistent countries, being near the top of the scale on Board membership, much further down in terms of written HR strategies and their translation into work programmes and otherwise in central positions. This volatility is understandable given the dramatic and comparatively recent change from fascism to democracy in Spain, rapid economic growth following accession to the EC, and the subsequent attempts of the personnel function to clarify its new role.

AN INTEGRATION RANKING

The different measures indicate difference degrees of integration but also show some consistency. Thus, the data shows that Sweden, Norway and France always rank amongst the top four countries; Italy always at the bottom. On this basis, these European countries

Table 2.4 Integration ranking for fourteen European countries

Group I (most integrated)	Sweden
	Norway
	France
Group II	Switzerland
	Spain
	Finland
	Netherlands
Group III	United Kingdom
	Denmark
	Ireland
	Portugal
	Turkey
Group IV (least integrated)	Germany
	Italy

can be ranked according to the likelihood of their organisations integrating HRM and business strategy (see Table 2.4).

Discussion

This ranking raises three immediate issues, concerning: the conceptual limitations of the process; methodological issues; and the value of this analysis.

Conceptually, this paper has addressed the issue of the formulation of strategy and the link to HRM as if they were essentially unproblematic. However, although space limitations preclude any detailed discussion here it would be inappropriate to ignore these difficulties. The two key problems concern the meaning of 'strategy' and the measures of integration.

Many of the discussions of strategy and HRM are based on a misunderstanding of the process of strategy formulation. Mintzberg (1978: 935) indeed argues that 'formulation' of strategy does not take place – it is much less explicit, conscious or planned than that implies. He suggests using the term 'formation' instead. The development of strategy is in fact a complex, interactive and incremental process, so that it is difficult to define a point at which the corporate strategy can be 'finalised' sufficiently to allow the 'HRM strategy' to be created. (For a brief, clear view of this issue see Hendry and Pettigrew 1990: 34.)

There is considerable evidence from the United States (Springer and Springer 1990; Devanna *et al.* 1982; Quinn Mills and Balkaby 1985; Burack 1986) that the integration of HRM with business strategy is in practice rare there even amongst large corporations (see Guest 1990). British authors have gone so far as to suggest that, like previous theories of management, American texts on HRM 'need to be read, therefore, as indictments of what American industry largely was not' (Hendry and Pettigrew 1990: 19). The data indicates that in Europe HRM may, for some organisations in some countries at least, be integrated into the strategic level.

The process described in the United States is built on different assumptions than those which operate in much of Europe. The American 'rational/logical' approach leads to a view that HRM strategies should be determined by experts closely following the business strategy. It is a direct importation of this approach that informs the research reported above. The attempt to measure national differences by Board membership, involvement in corporate strategy and HR policies reflects this conception of the strategic role of HRM. The ranking is therefore limited by this conception of the manner in which HRM can be integrated with corporate strategy and by the implied autonomy of organisations (Brewster 1994). In particular, by measuring the integration of the HR function at the top decision making level, this measure allows very little role for the inclusion of HRM in strategic decision making through the process of having many senior executives who have been promoted 'spirally', including spending time in the HR department, as happens in Japan.

Nor, more relevantly for Europe, does this discussion of strategy allow for the inclusion of HRM at the strategic level through the role of government and legislation or through consultative or trade union requirements. Thus, discussing how what he calls 'modern personnel management' could be more closely integrated with the organisation's strategy a German author draws the immediate conclusion that 'this could perhaps mean that staff participation in the organisational process . . . might be more feasible now than was the case in the past' (Remer 1986: 361). American texts tend not to make the assumption that employees will be involved in the process of strategy formation. In Europe employees may quite possibly be so involved. In Germany, for example, the Codetermination Act of 1976 required the Executive Boards of large companies to have a labour director with responsibility for staff and welfare matters. Furthermore, the Executive Board is overseen by a Supervisory Board on which, depending on size and sector, legislation provides for a third or a half of the seats to be reserved for employee representatives (Gaugler and Wiltz 1992). These state-determined requirements are in addition to, or perhaps supplement, having the head of the function on the main Board. Inevitably they mean that human resource issues are an integral part of corporate decision making. The Netherlands and Denmark also have two-tier Boards with union representation on the Supervisory Board. Other requirements for consultation and disclosure (Brewster *et al*. 1992) may also have the effect of raising awareness of HR issues at the top level.

This emphasises the European position and provides some explanation of the position of Germany and Italy in the integration ranking. The ranking measures the link between the HR function and corporate strategy. HR functions in Germany are essentially administrative and mechanistic (see e.g. Ackermann 1986; Pieper 1990; Lawrence 1991; Gaugler and Wiltz 1992). However, the strong adherence to a detailed legal or quasi-legal basis for the employment relationship in the context of powerful works councils, employee representatives on the Board and an open cooperative approach to trade unions mean that HR issues are raised in all key managerial decisions – but through a different route. The legislative position and powerful trade unions in Italy may possibly, though less obviously, perform a similar function (Sirianni 1992). Thus, in Germany at least, a focus on the integration of HRM and corporate strategy through the HR department may miss crucial factors.

Methodological limitations are outlined in detail in Appendix I. Three issues are relevant here. First, our data is limited to organisations with more than 200 employees. It is likely that small organisations have quite different approaches to integration. Their HR issues are rarely handled by a separate HR department and HR issues therefore are intrinsically 'integrated' by the few people who, whatever their level of competence in this field, take all key decisions.

Second, and linked to one of the conceptual concerns, our objective of comparing organisational HR policies and practices across national boundaries has led us to collect data through a broad, representative, and large-scale survey. We have, therefore, had to use a limited number of general, surrogate measures to identify levels of integration and involvement. More qualitative measures within organisations may find, on a consistent, nationally determined basis, that the senior personnel specialists responding to our survey have provided information which is in some way biased by their position. It would be interesting to know, for example, whether senior line managers or even personnel specialists outside headquarters share our respondents' perceptions of the integration of the HR function.

Third, the rankings are relative, not absolute. It may well be, for example, that typical organisations in Sweden and Norway have a far from integrated HRM. What we can say is that they are closer to it than the other countries for which we have data.

As far as the value of this analysis is concerned it is noticeable that with the exception of the two countries in the least integrated group there is a broad correlation between rank order and national wealth. (Once the conceptual issues concerning the position of Germany and Italy are included, it can be argued that the correlation is very close.) To this extent the data provides at least some empirical evidence for the suggestion (see, for example Porter, 1985, 1991) that there is a link between the seriousness with which a country addresses human resources and national success. Furthermore, there is a broad correlation between these groupings and some of the analyses of national culture, in particular Hofstede's (1980) dimensions of power distance and individualism.

Finally, this chapter shows the value of national-level comparisons. Obviously, there will be (as the tables show) a range of organisations within each country. It is arguable that HRM is determined to a considerable degree by state boundaries. There will be clear similarities within states, and differences between states, in their culture, government, legislation, demography, labour markets, patterns of ownership and trade union position. This is not to deny that there are differences between industrial sectors or different sized organisations, for example. However, because most studies are nationally bound and focus on these differences it is worth making the point that here, as in other analyses of our data (Brewster and Bournois 1991; Hegewisch 1991; Hoogendoorn and Brewster 1992; Brewster and Holt Larsen 1992; Gunnigle et al. 1993) the national variable is the more significant. This has obvious theoretic implications, but practical ones too for MNCs locating in different countries and for expatriate managers.

REFERENCES

Ackermann, K. F. (1986) 'A contingency model of HRM strategy – empirical research findings reconsidered' *Management Forum* 6: 65–83.

Baird, L., Meshoulam, I., Degive, G. (1983) 'Meshing human resources planning with strategic business planning, a model approach', *Personnel*, 60(5): 14–25.

Beaumont, P. B. (1991) 'The US human resource management literature: a review' in G. Salaman (ed.) (1991) *Human Resource Strategies*, Milton Keynes: Open University Press.

Beaumont, P. (1992) 'Trade unions and HRM', *Industrial Relations Journal* 22(4): 300–8.

Beer, M., Lawrence, P. R., Mills, Q. N. and Walton, R. E. (1985) *Human Resource Management*, New York: Free Press.

Besseyre des Horts, C. H. (1987) 'Typologies des pratiques de gestion des ressources humaines', *Revue française de Gestion*: 149–55.

Besseyre des Horts, C. H. (1988) *Vers une Gestion Stratégique des Ressources Humaines*, Editions d'Organisation, pp. 69–84.

Beyer, H. T. (1991) 'Personalarbeit als integrierter Bestandteil der Unternehmensstrategie', paper to the 1991 DGFP Annual Congress, Wiesbaden.

Braverman, H. (1974) *Labour and Monopoly Capitalism*, New York: Monthly Review Press.

Brewster, C. (1992) 'Managing industrial relations' in B. Towers (ed.) (1992) *Handbook of Industrial Relations Practice*, London: Kogan Page (2nd edition).

Brewster, C. (1994) 'Human resource management in Europe: reflection of, or challenge to, the American concept?', in P. Kirkbride (ed.) (1994) *Human Resource Management in Europe: Perspectives for the 1990s*, London: Routledge.

Brewster, C. and Bournois, F. (1991) 'A European perspective on human resource management', *Personnel Review* 20(6): 4–13.

Brewster, C. and Holt Larsen, H. (1992) 'Human resource management in Europe: evidence from ten countries', *International Journal of Human Resource Management* 3(3): 409–34.

Brewster, C., Hegewisch, A., Holden, L. and Lockhart, T. (eds) (1992), *The European Human Resource Management Guide*, London: Academic Press.

Burack, E. H. (1986) 'Corporate business and human resource planning practices, strategic issues and concerns', *Organisational Dynamics* 15: 73–87.

Butler, J. E. (1988) 'Human resource management as a driving force in business strategy', *Journal of General Management* 13(4): 88–102.

Collins, R. (1979) *The Credential Society*, New York: Academic Press. Commerce Clearing House (1989) *The 1989 ASPA/CCH Survey: Corporate Restructuring*, Chicago: CCH, Inc.

Conrad, P. and Pieper, R. (1990) 'HRM in the Federal Republic of Germany', in R. Pieper (ed.) (1990) *Human Resource Management: an International Comparison*, Berlin: Walter de Gruyter.

Cooper, J. and Giacomello, G. (1992) 'Italy', in C. Brewster, A. Hegewisch, L. Holden and T. Lockhart (eds) *The European Human Resource Management Guide*, London: Academic Press.

Coulson-Thomas, C. (1990) *Professional Development of and for the Board*, London: Institute of Directors.

Coulson-Thomas, C. and Wakeham, A. (1991) *The Effective Board: Current Practice Myths and Realities*, London: Institute of Directors.

Daniel, W. W. (1987) *Workplace Industrial Relations and Technical Change*, London: Frances Pinter.

DeCenzo, D. A. and Robbins, S. P. (1988) *Personnel/Human Resource Management*, Englewood Cliffs, NJ: Prentice Hall (3rd edn).

Dertouzos, M. L., Lester, R. K. and Solow, R. M. (1989) *Made in America: Regaining the Productive Edge*, Cambridge, Mass.: MIT Press.

Devanna, M. A., Fombrun, C. J., Tichy, N. M. and Warren, L. (1982) 'Strategic planning and human resource management', *Human Resource Management* 21: 1–17.

Edwards, R. (1979) *The Contested Terrain*, New York: Basic Books.

Filella, J. (1991) 'Is there a Latin model in the management of human resources?', *Personnel Review* 20(6): 14–23.

Fombrun, C. and Tichy, N. M. (1983) 'Strategic planning and human resources management: at rainbow's end', in R. Lamb (ed.) (1983) *Recent Advances in Strategic Planning*, New York: McGraw-Hill.

Fombrun, C., Tichy, N. and Devanna, M. (eds) (1984) *Strategic Human Resource Management*, New York: John Wiley.

Freedman, A. (1991) *The Changing Human Resources Function*, New York: The Conference Board.

Friedman, A. (1977) *Industry and Labour*, London: Macmillan.

Galbraith, J. R. and Nathanson, D. A. (1978a) *Strategy Implementation: the Role of Structure and Process*, St Paul, Minn.: West Publishing.

Galbraith, J. R. and Nathanson, D. A. (1978b) *The Value Adding Corporation*, University of Southern California: CEO Publications.

Gaugler, E. and Wiltz, S. (1992) 'Germany', in C. Brewster, A. Hegewisch, L. Holden and T. Lockhart (eds) *European Guide to Human Resource Management*, London: Academic Press.

Guest, D. (1987) 'Human resource management and industrial relations', *Journal of Management Studies*, 24(5): 503–22.

Guest, D. (1989) 'HRM: implications for industrial relations', in Storey, J. (ed.) (1989) *New Perspectives on Human Resource Management*, London: Routledge.

Guest, D. (1990) 'Human resource management and the American dream', *Journal of Management Studies* 27(4): 377–97.

Gunnigle, P., Brewster, C. and Morley, M. (1993) 'Developments in European human resource management', *European Foundation for the Improvement of Working and Living Conditions*, Working Paper no. WP/93/42/EN.

Hegewisch, A. (1991) 'The decentralisation of pay bargaining: European comparisons', *Personnel Review* 20(6): 28–35.

Hendry, C. and Pettigrew, A. (1986) 'The practice of strategic human resource management', *Personnel Review* 15(5): 3–8.

Hendry, C. and Pettigrew, A. (1990) 'HRM: an agenda for the 1990s', *International Journal of Human Resource Management* 1(1): 17–25.

Hofstede, G. (1980) *Cultures Consequences: international differences in work-related values*, Beverly Hills: Sage.

Hoogendoorn, J. and Brewster, C. (1992) 'Human Resource Aspects of Decentralisation and Devolution', *Personnel Review* 21(1): 24–38.

Kochan, T. A. and Barocci, T. A. (1985) *Human Resource Management and Industrial Relations*, Boston: Little Brown.

Kochan, T. A. and Dyer. L. (1992) 'Managing transformational change: the role of human resource professionals', Sloan Working Paper 3420–92–BPS, Mass.: MIT.

Laurent, A. (1983) 'The cultural diversity of western conceptions of management', *International Studies of Management and Organisation*, 13(1–2): 75–96.

Lawrence, P. (1991) 'The personnel function: an Anglo-German comparison', in C. Brewster and S. Tyson (eds) *International Comparisons in Human Resource Management*, London: Pitman.

Legge, K. (1989) 'Human resource management: a critical analysis', in J. Storey (ed.) (1989) *New Perspectives on Human Resource Management*, London: Routledge.

Lengnick-Hall, C. A. and Lengnick-Hall, M. L. (1988) 'Strategic human resources management: a review of the literature and a proposed typology', *Academy of Management Review* 13(3): 454–70.

Macmillan, I. C. and Schuler, R. S. (1985) 'Gaining a competitive edge through human resources', *Personnel* 62(4): 24–9.

Mahoney, T. and Deckop, J. R. (1986) 'Evolution of concept and practice in personnel administration/ human resource management' *Journal of Management*, 12(2): 223–41.

Marginson, P., Edwards, P. K., Martin, R., Purcell, J. and Sisson, K. (1988) *Beyond the Workplace. Managing Industrial Relations in the Multi-establishment Enterprise*, Oxford: Blackwell.

Miller, P. (1989) 'Strategic HRM: what it is and what it isn't', *Personnel Management* February: 46–51.

Miller, P. (1991) 'Strategic human resource management: an assessment of progress', *Human Resource Management Journal* 1: 23–39.

Mintzberg, H. (1978) 'Patterns in strategy formation', *Management Science* 24(9): 934–48.

Pieper, R. (ed.) (1990) *Human Resource Management: an International Comparison*, Berlin: Walter de Gruyter.

Piore, M. J. and Sabel, C. F. (1984) *The Second Industrial Divide: Possibilities for Prosperity*, New York: Basic Books.

Popper, K. R. (1945) *The Open Society and Its Enemies*, London: Routledge & Kegan Paul.

Porter, M. (1985) *Competitive Advantage*, New York: Free Press.

Porter, M. (1991) *The Competitive Advantage of Nations*, New York: Free Press.

Purcell (1987) 'Mapping management styles in industrial relations', *Journal of Management Studies* 24(5): 535–48.

Purcell (1991) 'The rediscovery of the management prerogative: the management of labour relations in the 1980s', *Oxford Review of Economic Policy* 7(1): 33–43.

Quinn Mills, D. and Balkaby, M. (1985) 'Planning for morale and culture', in R. Walton and P. Lawrence (eds) (1985) *Human Resource Management – Trends and Challenges*, Boston, Mass.: Harvard Business School Press.

Ramsey, H. (1977) 'Cycles of control: work participation in sociological and historical perspective', *Sociology* 11(3): 481–506.

Remer, A. (1986) 'Personnel management in western Europe – development, situation and concepts', in K. Macharzina and W. H. Staehle (eds) (1986) *European Approaches to International Management*, Berlin: Walter de Gruyter.

Schreyögg, G. (1987) 'Verschlüsselte Botschaften: Neue Perspektiven einer Strategischen Personalführung', *Zeitschrift Führung und Organisation* 56(3): 151–8.

Schuler, R. S. (1989) 'Human resources strategy: focusing on issues and actions', *Organisational Dynamics* 19(1): 4–20.

Schuler, R. S. (1992) 'Strategic human resource management: linking the people with the strategic needs of the business', *Organisational Dynamics*, summer: 18–31.

Schuler, R. S. and Huber, V. L. (1993) *Personnel and Human Resource Management*, St Paul, MN: West.

Schuler, R. S. and Jackson, S. E. (1987) 'Linking competitive strategies with human resource management practices', *Academy of Management Executive* 1(3): 209–13.

Schuler, R. S. and Macmillan, I. (1984) 'Creating competitive advantage through human resource managment practices', *Human Resource Management* 23: 241–55.

Sirianni, C. A. (1992) 'Human resource management in Italy', *Employee Relations* 14(5): 23–38.

Springer, B. and Springer, S. (1990) 'Human resource management in the UK – celebration of its centenary', in R. Pieper (ed.) *Human Resource Management: an International Comparison*, Berlin: Walter de Gruyter.

Staffelbach, B. (1986) *Strategisches Personalmanagement*, Bern-Stuttgart.

Storey, J. (1992) 'HRM in action: the truth is out at last' *Personnel Management* April: 28–31.

Storey, J. (ed.) (1989) *New Perspectives on Human Resource Management*, London: Routledge.

Tichy, N. M., Fombrun, C. J. and Devanna, M. A. (1982) 'Strategic human resource management', in *Sloan Management Review* 24: 47–61.

Walton, R. E. (1985) 'From control to commitment in the workplace', *Harvard Business Review* 64(2): 77–84.

Wohlgemuth, A. C. (1988) 'Human resources management und die wirkungsvolle Vermaschung mit der Unternehmungspolitik', *Management-Zeitschrift Industrielle Organisation* 56(2): 115–18.

Wright, P. and McMahon, A. (1992) 'Theoretical perspectives for strategic human resource management', *Journal of Management* 18(2): 295–320.

Chapter 3

The education and training of human resource managers in Europe

Shaun Tyson and Lennart Wikander

The growing economic and political ties of the European Community and the extension of collaborative business ventures across Europe raise important questions for the human resource function. Adjusting educational institutions and training systems to the new political and economic situations emerging will be a priority as the twentieth century draws to a close.

Human resource managers are especially concerned with some of the 'softer' aspects of management through which values are expressed, including management style, inter-departmental relationships, bargaining processes, employee development, employee involvement and organisation culture (Guest 1987). Practitioners are often at the nexus of different values, and are expected to manage cultural and value differences over national boundaries (Tyson 1983, 1987). How managers are educated and trained to fulfil a European role is significant on this reading of their work. With a diversity of educational systems across Europe, this chapter offers an insight into how these differences impact on an occupation which is at the heart of the management ideologies and value systems adopted by companies in Europe.

From what is known of the formal development systems we are aware that there are many different approaches to the training of human resource specialists. In the United Kingdom the Institute of Personnel Management (IPM) and, to a lesser extent, in Sweden the Sverges Personaladministrativa Föreng (SPF) offer a 'professional' form of training, through national associations which have tried to take on the role of a professional body by establishing qualification schemes, and have attempted to sustain human resource practitioners as a separate managerial profession (Watson 1977; Tyson 1983). In other parts of Europe there are different perceptions of professional associations. The French Association Nationale des Directeurs et Chefs de Personnel (ANDCP) like the IPM and

SPF has helped to create personnel management programmes in the technical universities, but has not sought to offer qualifications itself in the way of the British IPM. In Germany the Deutsche Gesellschaft für Personalführung (DGFP) provides educational seminars, publishes regular bulletins and updates, and facilitates the interchange of information amongst practitioners. One can see an escalation in the role from the dimension of heavy involvement with the education and development of practitioners, almost to the point of a licence to practise, at one end with a facilitative information sharing role at the other:

Attempts to professionalise   Facilitative
through certification, and   information sharing
accreditation   broad educational role

                    <-->
             IPM   SPF   ANDCP   DGFP

Generalisations made about whole countries in Europe without appreciating the subtleties of cultural understanding are likely to be wrong, so we must be cautious in applying our own interpretations of cultural differences. There are a number of commentators who have reported on national differences in HRM, for example by stressing a legalistic approach in Germany, or an intellectual and business emphasis in France (Lawrence 1991; Barsoux, and Lawrence 1990). There is a need to investigate the empirical evidence, to discover what educational and training activities regularly and typically occur to develop human resource managers in the main economies in Europe.

In this chapter we will analyse the data from the Price Waterhouse Cranfield Project and present the preliminary findings which our comparative study has revealed. Our particular focus was on the education and training of human resource practitioners in France, West Germany, Spain, Sweden and in the United Kingdom. Our starting point was our view that the higher education system in a country will not only influence the way the occupation of human resource specialist progresses, but may also help to explain the prevailing approaches adopted to managing the employment relationship. So following our presentation of a model for analysing the subject we present the data from twelve countries in the 1992 survey and then provide more detailed analysis of those five countries.

THE DEVELOPMENT OF THE SPECIALIST HUMAN RESOURCE OCCUPATION

The personnel management occupation is now well established, but over the years it has come to embrace many different fields of work ranging from welfare, industrial relations, employment management and applied social science disciplines (Tyson 1987). These origins are reflected in the various university study programmes in which personnel management is taught. The first specialised programme in the United Kingdom was started at the London School of Economics in the mid-1940s (Niven 1967), and in Sweden a basic university study programme in the area was created in the early 1980s when Uppsala University introduced the Human Resource Development and Labour Relations Study programme in order to effect the direction of personnel work in Sweden, and to enhance its scope (Lindberg and Wikander 1990; Wikander 1991).

The occupation has similar welfare origins in Europe and the United States and has evolved through various administrative and industrial relations activities, emerging as a separate occupational identity, where in some countries even a professional status is claimed based on the application of the social science disciplines to the management of the employment relationship (Watson 1977; Ritzer and Trice 1969; Tyson 1979). We must, of course, be cautious in generalising about this occupation, which is strongly influenced by the organisational context and therefore varies greatly within countries, according to the size of the organisation, the industry and the various philosophies of management adopted and is contingent upon an array of organisational variables (Legge 1978; Tyson and Fell 1986). The development of the function has also been affected by both world wars, and by political change. The war effort in the United Kingdom, the United States and in Germany, and the Occupation in France changed the nature of personnel work performed. After the Second World War, the Marshall Plan brought many management ideas from the United States to Europe. Similarly, the post-Franco period has seen new approaches to employee relations in Spain (Vicente 1993).

The present phase of evolution has seen 'personnel management' change from a concentration on operational activity towards an involvement with strategic objectives: reflected, arguably in the term 'human resource management'. In spite of the many different backgrounds of human resource specialists, assumptions are made about their capacity to contribute to the strategic advance of their businesses. Any such advances are likely to be within a broad European context rather than to be limited by national boundaries. One might anticipate therefore a need for human resource managers to obtain a European educational grounding as part of their formative development.

Variations in basic training and in education, with different educational systems and variations within company development programmes make common standards difficult to achieve. Yet there are similarities in the concerns of HR specialists and in the problems their companies face. There is enough common ground for an occupational language, comparative research and for international and European conferences on human resource management to be held which indicates that international comparisons are meaningful (Brewster and Tyson 1991). There are more and more programmes at undergraduate and postgraduate levels within the specialised HRM fields. In 1987 a survey showed 34 universities offering HRM programmes in West Germany, 3 in Austria and 8 in Switzerland (Ferring and Thom 1987). In the United Kingdom there are many institutions accredited by the IPM to offer courses granting membership of the IPM, and in France, whilst there are fewer specialised degrees, 21 Institute Universitaire de Technologie offer training in HRM and there are diploma courses at the Ecoles Supérieure de Commerce (ESC) and the Universities as well as some masters programmes. The ESC have all been expanding their management programmes, all of which contain some teaching in HRM. The burgeoning number of MBA programmes and diplomas in the United Kingdom should also be noted since they usually contain courses in HRM, organisational behaviour and industrial relations.

THE USEFULNESS OF COMPARISONS

The theoretical bases for these programmes differ, in the sense that there are different academic departments responsible for the programmes. In most countries, the cost-effectiveness and quality of higher education are debated. This debate is often about the risk of conflict between traditional academic training and vocational training towards a special professional area. It has also become clear that the conditions for university education have changed with respect to the expectations from the state, society and the students. The value of an academic training within any one area has to be related to the benefits the students and the employers obtain.

In view of the competition between different labour markets and also since there are growing cross cultural contacts it is even more necessary to understand and develop norms to make it possible to understand and compare the development within different professional fields. The discussion within the EC in Brussels about the transfer of academic credits supports the idea of evaluation and comparisons. The multinational corporations' recruitment policies result in students being selected from different national systems. This brings into focus the benefit in developing models for comparison when making policies and procedures for recruitment. The growing cooperation between countries makes it even more necessary to develop these models. 'It has become more clear, as research has progressed, that cross-national comparison and exchange in higher education will become more significant as globalization of corporations and regional cooperation among nations increase' (Harris 1991: 154).

FRAMEWORK

The objectives of higher education and its relation to the labour market and the influence of higher education on the labour market and vice versa have been frequently discussed in the last decades. There is in general a need for cross-national studies in the science of education. In particular our concern here is with higher education and the labour market. In many countries such as the United Kingdom and Sweden higher education faces changes and reforms. Cross-national studies then become potentially very important and have many implications for the assumptions that we hold.

As Bron-Wojciechowska, Kvarnström and Wikander (1991) point out:

There are two important goals of higher education that we think contradict or complement each other. The first of these is in the area of general academic education which serves to educate professionals in a given scientific discipline. Thus, higher education is meant to develop scientific disciplines by research and theory building and at the same time produce and reproduce intellectual elites. In such higher education a general scientific grounding is necessary as well as specialization in a given scientific discipline. The second is in professional academic education which seeks to educate specialists in different vocations to be able to serve society in the sphere of practice. Thus, higher education prepares well educated specialists for the labour market. In other words it can be described as a service to the labour market.

Bron-Wojciechowska *et al*. (1991) illustrate this as follows:

Two goals of higher education

General academic education
(professional in the scientific discipline)

*Contradiction or
complementarity in
higher education goals* }

Professional academic education
(vocational, to educate practitioners)

(Bron-Wojciechowska *et al.* 1991: 5)

In many countries this second goal was and is more or less explicitly formulated. In the last reform of Dutch higher education commentators stated that higher education institutions should be more labour market orientated and explore and respond to social needs and 'market forces'. On the other hand the Swedish Government in their discussions and in their proposal to the Swedish parliament have proposed a new system for higher education in Sweden (Ds 1992:1, Regeringens' proposition 1992–3:1). The decision has been that Swedish higher education will go from longer general market oriented study programmes to a scientific subject oriented system in high education. In the United Kingdom the research lead by Kogan (Boys *et al.* 1988) discussed the same issue in the context of higher education and the preparation for work.

As our main purpose is to compare different educational environments and programmes the most important theoretical issue is to find out what information is needed to make the comparisons relevant. A basis for this comes from the discussions of Dahllöf (1967a, 1967b, 1971, 1975) concerning the frame factors which influence the educational process. In different studies of higher education with different objectives the 'frame factor model' has been used, for example by Dahllöf (1969, 1975, 1984, 1989a), Franke-Wikberg and Johansson (1975), Elgqvist-Saltzman (1976, 1978), Löfgren (1978), and Willén (1978, 1981). The frame factor model gives the opportunity to classify the main components of the educational process. For this purpose it is adequate for us to say that the frames for a specific programme are not only: the total time at disposal, the programme structure, the human resources available, the material resources and rules for the allocation of resources but also the total context of the programme at a national level. Dahllöf (1991) has presented a model for the relations between society and the educational systems being evaluated that emphasises the relevance of the programme contents in relation to the general goals of a specific type of training. The total framework for the project is presented in Wikander (1991).

For our purpose we have chosen to construct a simplified model as the framework for our research as shown in Figure 3.1. Overall, in order to make a comparison between the education and training of HR managers and study programmes in HRM in different countries one must not only describe the outcomes of a programme in terms of academic attitudes by describing the actors, frames of reference and the processes. One must also consider the whole context including the labour market, employment laws and HRM careers.

In addition to utilising the data from the Price Waterhouse Cranfield Project the authors

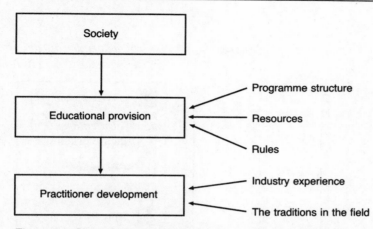

Figure 3.1 Simple model for evaluating the education and training of HR managers

of this chapter have more detailed research programmes, described in Tyson and Wikander (1992). The main objective for the total project is to describe the processes of personnel practitioner development in France, West Germany, Spain, Sweden and the United Kingdom and to discover through this comparison the divergence and convergence in the formal education and training approaches to practitioner development amongst countries which have growing economic ties. We seek to advance knowledge of educational processes, by testing a general theory of how educational courses can be analysed and compared, and discuss the influences of institutions on manager development. The research should assist in a curriculum review for those institutions providing education and training and suggest new frameworks for training and developing personnel practitioners, according to the variety of approaches discovered.

The relationship between the variables which operate at the education institution and company level need to be described and the inter-relationship of these influences has to be discovered. In this chapter we are working on the third level of analysis which means the personal development of the practitioner. Here we are considering how practitioners are trained or developed to do their jobs. We are interested in both the formal and informal means by which practitioners come to learn to be human resource specialists. The research areas include the individual's experience within industry, on the job and the coaching or mentoring activities experienced by the practitioners. Inevitably, this takes us into the realm of careers. We are comparing the 'objective' careers of our subjects (the work history) with their subjective career (the image of oneself in process) (Hughes 1937).

EDUCATIONAL PROFILES OF THE HR MANAGER

Data from the Price Waterhouse Cranfield Project on educational profiles show different patterns between the countries in the predominant qualifications for the senior human resource specialist, although most do have degree- or diploma-level qualifications. There is the largest frequency of HR managers with a diploma in Germany (24 per cent),

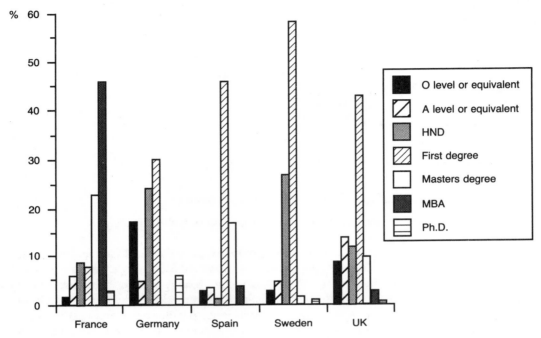

Figure 3.2 Highest level of educational qualifications achieved by senior practitioners in the organisation

Denmark (20 per cent), Finland (20 per cent) and Sweden (27 per cent). More than half of the respondents in the Netherlands (65 per cent), Sweden (58 per cent), and Turkey (55 per cent) have a first degree. In the Nordic countries a high proportion of managers have a masters degree (Denmark 23 per cent, Finland 52 per cent and Norway 38 per cent). The Netherlands also shows this high level of specialisation with 23 per cent having a masters degree. In Finland, there are also 15 per cent who have an MBA type qualification, an unusually high proportion for HR specialists. Figure 3.2 shows the highest level of educational qualifications for the countries in the five countries on which we focused.

When interpreting these figures we should note the difficulties there are in making direct comparisons between educational qualifications in different countries. The educational systems in each of the five countries are very different. In our research, we have tried to standardise by using the 7 levels found in the United Kingdom, as indicated in Figure 3.2. In France, 9 levels of academic attainment were identified: BEPC; Baccalaureat; DUT/ BTS; Licence; Maitrise; DESS/DEA; Diploma d'Ecole d'Ingenieur ou de Commerce; Doctorat; Autodidacte; and we have consequently taken the nearest United Kingdom equivalents. In Spain six levels were used by excluding the doctoral level of qualification. Given these provisos, the results show that the educational background is more varied in Germany and in the United Kingdom for human resource specialists. In Germany 17 per cent gave the equivalent of O level as their highest qualifications but in addition 6 per cent have a Ph.D. degree. A large proportion of respondents in Germany and Sweden have a

Diploma, and in Sweden, the majority of respondents have a first degree. Although in Spain and in the United Kingdom there appear to be more respondents with a Masters degree including the MBA than in Germany, this reflects the absence of the MBA in the German educational system, where there are a majority of respondents who have finished university.

The complete tables of the results are presented in Appendix III Table 1.6 where the profiles of the other countries included in the survey may be found. It is notable that Denmark, Finland, Norway and the Netherlands have a high proportion of HR managers with a Masters degree.

Responses on the subject of the first degree fall into three groups: those countries where business studies is the most common first degree for practitioners – Germany 45 per cent, Ireland 41 per cent, Turkey 35 per cent, Denmark 24 per cent and Norway 20 per cent; those countries where there was a strong social science bias in the first degree – Sweden 54 per cent, Portugal 24 per cent; and those where law was a common first degree subject – Spain 32 per cent, France 25 per cent and Portugal 31 per cent. Other countries showed mixed results, as in the case of the United Kingdom where the humanities, arts and languages were frequently cited (21 per cent), as first degree subjects. Figure 3.3 shows the results of the question which enquired about the academic field of study of the first degree for the HR specialists responding in the five countries.

There is a great deal of variety in the subjects studied amongst those of our respondents who have a first degree. The most notable finding here is that 54 per cent of Swedish

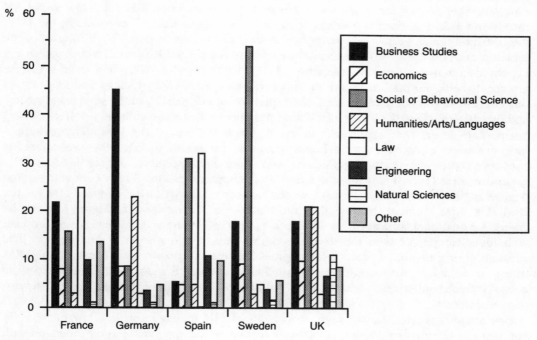

Figure 3.3 Academic field of first degree

respondents have studied social or behavioural sciences in their first degree. The educational system in Sweden has always been very centralised. The reform of higher education in Sweden in 1977 was intended to make university education more sensitive to the needs of the labour market. After 1977, study programmes within the social sciences were developed with centralised curricula. Within the area of personnel work, a general study programme called Human Resource Development and Labour Relations was established in 1983 at ten universities. The university departments maintained their scientific subject oriented courses parallel to the study programmes. There is a strong social science tradition in Sweden and this would be a characteristic area for those with an interest in personnel management to study. The Swedish labour market and the approach to labour relations has been subject to considerable change. There will be more individually and locally based negotiations in the future, which has resulted in the suggestion that the 'Swedish model' of industrial relations has collapsed. A move away from the more planned and regulated approach may generate more interest in human resource management from students who have been educated in different disciplines. It is perhaps significant that in 1993 the university system was decentralised, with no centrally decided curricula in the future, illustrating the continuous change to education.

In the United Kingdom and France there is a more heterogeneous picture. This may reflect the variety of educational provision available to be used as a preparation for a human resource role. In both countries it would not be unusual for someone to move into a senior human resource management post from a line management position as evidenced by the 9 per cent of HR practitioners with engineering degrees in France, and the 22 per cent in Law, and that 26 per cent have spent less than five years in an HR role. The variety of routes into HRM in France may also contribute to these results: these include the IUT, the ESC and the universities. The responses also indicate the 'expansion' of interest in the function since the early 1970s, both in France and in the United Kingdom, which now draws in people from many different disciplines. It was in 1969 that the ANDCP formed le Centre Universitaire de Formations à la Fonction Personnel (CIFFOP) which helped to generate this interest. In the United Kingdom, the expansion of HR activity in the service industries, and the changing face of industrial relations has encouraged more colleges to offer courses, but perhaps of greatest significance in this regard is the role of the IPM. By providing a 'post-graduate' diploma route in human resource management, the IPM has offered a conversion programme for humanities, and other non-specialist, degree holders. The generally lower level of education in the United Kingdom (around 30 per cent with no first degree as the highest qualification) also can be seen as a part of the raison d'être for the IPM. The IPM seems to be providing an educational service for non-degree holders, by giving a vocational education in the social sciences, economics, statistics and applied techniques for people who find themselves in a senior role without a first degree. The substantial proportion of humanities degrees reflects the possibilities a career in HRM offers to a student who would not be qualified to enter management in any technical capacity. Such students may wish to 'work with people' and believe that HRM is the nearest to their interests.

The Spanish results show a high proportion of HR managers with a law degree. By contrast the German respondents, although displaying the expected large proportion with higher degrees, were not especially legally educated. Since commentators have often described the German personnel function as being 'legalistic' (Lawrence 1991), this may seem surprising. However, where there are very well established rules and legal procedures to which all subscribe, the very extent of this acceptance removes the need for lawyers. By contrast, the Spanish constitution has been in existence since approved by a referendum in December 1978. Labour courts and industrial tribunals have been established: the Centre de Mediación, Albitraye y Conciliación (CMAC) and the Court for social issues, the Juzgado de lo social, and the Tribunal Superior de Justicia for appeals, with two further higher courts. However, most cases are settled at the CMAC level. New laws and systems are likely to provoke interest, and when one considers that 'in addition to the constitution, the Spanish civil code and the workers' statutes there are many Acts that regulate the application of the basic principles and laws to day to day situations' (Vicente 1993: 238), and that there are 13 different types of standard contracts, it is perhaps not surprising that a legal education is seen as beneficial.

The legal focus was much more common amongst Southern European countries in general: Spain (32 per cent), France (25 per cent) and Portugal (31 per cent).

OTHER FORMS OF DEVELOPMENT

The formal education received by those entering an occupation as practical and non-theoretical as management is only a grounding, and we believed therefore that we needed to understand how human resource specialists were developed within their organisations. We defined five forms of training. Short courses and seminars we defined as 'off-the-job training', with formal teaching sessions of one day or more. Job related projects we interpreted as participation within different kinds of on-the-job projects which are both work tasks but which are set up also with the intention of developing the managers. Job rotation is a well known technique for developing people by giving the managers different assignments or moving them through various functional areas. Formal coaching we defined as the manager's boss providing guidance and help in a structured, planned way, on the job. Mentoring, on the other hand we defined as the provision of guidance both job related and career related, outside the boss-subordinate relationship, usually by a senior colleague.

Off-the-job training is the most common training in all the countries. In Finland (90 per cent), Norway (90 per cent), the Netherlands (87 per cent), Sweden (90 per cent) and the United Kingdom (91 per cent) a high majority have received short courses or seminars. Around half of the respondents have worked with job related projects for personal development (Germany 47 per cent, Denmark 40 per cent, Finland 55 per cent, Ireland 53 per cent, Norway 55 per cent, the Netherlands 47 per cent, Sweden 66 per cent and the United Kingdom 59 per cent). In Turkey 42 per cent have been trained by job rotation and assignments for different work areas. Formal coaching by the line manager is common in Germany (30 per cent), Denmark (30 per cent), France (26 per cent) and the United Kingdom (27 per cent). Twenty-seven per cent of respondents in Denmark have had formal mentoring by a colleague, other than their immediate boss (see Figure 3.4). See Appendix III Table 1.8 for the complete result.

There are similar patterns throughout the five focus countries. Off-the-job training through courses and seminars are the most common forms of development for human

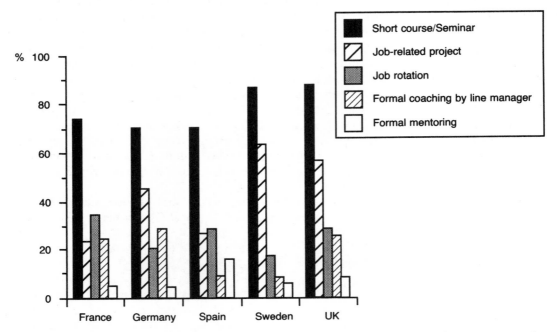

Figure 3.4 Training received from current or previous employers for the personnel management role

resource specialists. In Sweden and the United Kingdom short courses and seminars are most predominant (90 per cent and 91 per cent respectively). Another similarity between the United Kingdom and Sweden was the extensive use made of job related projects for personal development. In France, job rotation or assignments in different work areas were also the most common form of development after short courses and seminars.

Amongst the other differences we may note that formal coaching by line managers is most common in Germany (30 per cent), and that formal mentoring systems are most frequently found in Spain (17 per cent) by comparison with the other four countries. One possible explanation for this result is that 54 per cent of the Spanish respondents had been working in their personnel or training roles for five years or less. The total frequencies for these results are shown in Appendix III Tables 1.4 to 1.8, where it will be seen that 27 per cent of Danish managers have formal mentoring systems, a higher proportion than any of the other countries studied, the explanation again could be because 54.6 per cent of the Danish managers had five years or less personnel/training experience.

Perhaps the most significant finding from this question is the predominance of short courses and seminars in the development of HR staff. Off-the-job training may be more important for this group of managers because there is no other main source of expertise inside their organisations. There is also within all countries a need to be kept up to date on new legislation, new techniques and labour market changes. Different management styles may also be represented by the different approaches to learning adopted. We should be careful not to read too much into these differences, which are sometimes quite small, but there is evidence that the length of experience within the HR role is a key factor in the way HR staff are trained. It may also be that formal coaching sits more easily in some cultures than in others, for example where the power distance between managers is greater (using Hofstede's analysis), which encourages, for example, formal coaching rather than the more informal developmental relationships we might expect where the manager sees the superior as a friend.

PATTERNS AND AREAS FOR FURTHER RESEARCH

Whilst we have been concerned so far to search for national patterns in the data, we are aware that there may be other explanations of the differences. We have analysed the data to ensure that the sample sizes, and the characteristics of each sample are not distorting the results. When analysing these variables against organisational size, private sector, public sector, national and international organisation and the position or title of the respondents, we could find no statistically significant biases on the highest level of educational qualifications, academic field in first degree, and the other training received.

However, some differences in the populations should be noted. There were some differences in job titles which may or may not reflect differences in the work performed: in France the most senior personnel staff member was called Human Resource Director, in Germany the title Personnel Director, whilst in Spain both Personnel and Human Resource Director titles are equally reported. In Sweden the title Personnel Manager/ Officer is most frequently quoted, whilst the title Personnel Manager is still the most common in the United Kingdom (Guest and Hoque 1993).

Some of these differences reflect organisational-level differences which we must not forget in a study of this kind. For example private sector organisations within Germany use more short courses, job rotation, and mentoring but less job related projects, and formal coaching than public sector organisations. In the United Kingdom there is very little formal mentoring amongst those who are working in companies where the most senior personnel officer is given an administrative title. International companies revealed different approaches to development from national companies. International companies in France more frequently used job related projects for personal development, formal coaching and formal mentoring compared to the total in France. International companies in Germany used formal coaching, as did international companies in Sweden, which also adopted formal mentoring practices more frequently than other organisations responding in those countries. For UK international companies, more job rotation and more formal coaching occurs for HR staff. The continuing work on our project which entails conducting interviews with different levels of HR staff in all five countries may help to reveal more of the causes of different patterns at the organisation level of analysis.

There are clear patterns within some countries, but not in all. That there are patterns across national boundaries for example in off-the-job development, and in the heterogeneous fields of the first degree does show how the HR field of study is developing in Europe. All countries in the study have some form of professional association, but these associations play different roles in the education of HR practitioners. The educational profile in all five countries has shown some similarities, but the different country profiles show the saliency of the societal influence on systems. Our research has inevitably encountered the problems of making comparisons between qualifications, but there are signs of how different educational traditions such as the Swedish social science tradition have resulted in patterns of educational differences. The high proportion of managers with humanities degrees in Spain and the United Kingdom is likely to be an effect of the educational traditions in those countries also. The 'liberal arts' or general academic education from a university has an influence in the student's occupational choice: the various managerial occupations being one outlet. This helps to explain the need for professional associations, such as the United Kingdom's IPM to provide a more vocational education. The growing popularity of business degrees is already evident in some countries, and is one sign of the growth in managerial occupations. This may in turn result in new roles for the professional associations.

In this chapter we have outlined a simple model showing the influence of educational and institutional conditions, and we have argued that although some general patterns may be found, organisational variables such as whether the business is national or international, are also important. There is also evidence from the research that the standing of personnel functions within the enterprise may be contingent upon the education and training of the specialist personnel staff (Beaumont and Deaton 1986). In addition to organisational differences within countries, each country has developed human resource management from its own starting point, and our survey data is a brief picture, taken at one moment in time, whilst all five countries in our study are changing rapidly.

Although there are clear patterns in some countries, such as Germany and Sweden, we must be cautious about our interpretations. Much more research needs to be done. However, our conclusions may be helpful in showing the direction for further research. We believe there is sufficient evidence to indicate that the patterns within countries reflect the social, educational and institutional variables set out in our model. The different methods of professional development are a consequence in part of the various professional association influences, and of different managerial styles and perceptions of managerial work. The educational and training differences may well be causes of different managerial values.

From the data gathered so far, the differences between the north and the south of Europe warrant further investigation, to see whether these are based on different values. There are in addition contrasting orientations to human resource management which are also worthy of more investigation, perhaps at the organisation level of analysis, to see if there are clusters which bring together a strong preference for off-the-job training, with a theoretical stance, basing the human resource function on the social sciences, in contrast to an orientation of on-the-job development, with an administratively founded role, supported by business or law degrees. We hope our research has opened up this agenda for other researchers.

Our approach in this chapter has attempted to debate the issues, and to offer insights into the educational, institutional and organisational influences on the development of human resource managers in Europe. As such, our study has contributed to the debate on the significance of societal and organisational variables for the management of human resources and is one fruitful outcome from European comparisons.

REFERENCES

Barsoux, J. L. and Lawrence, P. (1990) *Management in France*, London: Cassell.

Beaumont, P. B. and Deaton, D. R. (1986) 'Correlates of specialisation and training among personnel managers in Britain', *Personnel Review* 15(2): 29–31.

Boys, C. Brennan, J., Henkel, M., Kirkland, J., Kogan, M. and Youll, P. (1988) *Higher Education and the Preparation for Work*, London: Jessica Kingsley Publishers.

Brewster, C. and Tyson, S. (1991) *International Comparisons in Human Resource Management*, London: Pitman.

Bron-Wojciechowska, A., Kvarnström, M. and Wikander, L. (1991) 'Cross-national studies: some comparative studies with a focus on design and methods and their application to studies of higher education and the labour market. Multi-national seminar on higher education and the labour market', Dept of Education, Uppsala University (mimeo).

Dahllöf, U. (1967a) *Skoldifferentiering och undervisningsförlopp*, Göteborg Studies in Educational Sciences 2, Stockholm: Almqvist & Wiksell.

Dahllöf, U. (1967b) 'Relevance and fitness analysis in comparative education', in U. Dahllöf (1967) *Skoldifferentiering och undervisningsforlopp*, Göteborg Studies in Educational Sciences 2, Stockholm: Almqvish & Wiksell.

Dahllöf, U. (1969) 'Ability grouping, content validity and curriculum process analysis', Project Compass 13, *Reports from the Institute of Education*, University of Göteborg 7.

Dahllöf, U. (1971) 'Relevance and fitness analysis in comparative education'. *Scandinavian Journal of Educational Research* 15: 101–21.

Dahllöf, U. (1975) 'Problems and pitfalls in assessing internal efficiency in higher education by means of mass statistics. Some experiences from Sweden', *Scandinavian Journal of Educational Research* 19: 175–89.

Dahllöf, U. (1984) 'An educational magpie: Student flow analysis and target groups for higher education reform in Sweden', *I Premfors* 1984: 114–35.

Dahllöf, U. (1989a) 'Doctoral studies and public policies affecting the labour market for Ph.Ds in Norway and Sweden', *Scandinavian Journal of Educational Research* 33: 165–84.

Dahllöf, U. (1989b) 'A three-dimensional approach to the planning of training programmes for the professions', *CREaction* 1989/2. 97–104.

Dahllöf, U. (1991) 'Towards a new model for the evaluation of teaching; an interactive process-centred approach', in Dahllöf *et al.* (1991) *Dimensions of Evaluation*, Report of the IMHE study group on evaluation in higher education, London: Jessica Kingsley Publishers.

Dahllöf, U., Harris, J., Shattock, M., Staropoli, A. and in't Veld, R. (1991), *Dimensions of Evaluation*, Report of the IMHE study group on evaluation in higher education, London: Jessica Kingsley Publishers.

Ds (1992) 1. *Fria universitet och högskolor*, Utbildningsdepartementet. Stockholm: Allmänna Förlaget.

Elgqvist-Saltzman, I. (1976) *Vägen genom universitetet* Ak.avh. Uppsala Studies in Education 1, Uppsala: Acta Universitatis Upsaliensis/Almqvist & Wiksell International.

Elgqvist-Saltzman, I. (1978) Uppföljning ar nya studerandegrupper vid universitet och hogskolor. Svenska problem och amemkanska erfarenheter. *Pedagogisk forskning i Uppsala 2*, Uppsala: Pedagogiska Institutionem.

Ferring, K. and Thom, N. (1987) *Personalwirtschaftliche Lehrstühle an den Wirtschaftsfakultäten in Deutschland, Österreich und der Schweiz*, Institut Für Berufs-und-Ausbildungsplanung Köln GmBH.

Franke-Wikberg, S. and Johansson, M. (1975), *Utvärdering av undervisning*, Lund: Studentlitteratur.

Guest, D. (1987)'Human resource management and industrial relations', *Journal of Management Studies* 24(5) 503–21.

Guest, D. and Hoque, K. (1993) 'The mystery of the missing human resource manager', *Personnel Management* (June): 40–1.

Harris, J. (1991) 'Cross-national comparison and exchange: higher education', in Dahllöf *et al.* (1991) *Dimensions of Evaluation, Report of The IMHE study group on evaluation in higher education*, London: Jessica Kingsley Publishers.

Hughes, E. C. (1937) 'Institutional office and the person', *American Journal of Sociology* 43 (November) 404–13.

Lawrence, P. (1991) 'The personnel function: an Anglo-German comparison', in C. Brewster and S. Tyson (eds.) (1991) *International Comparisons in HRM*, London: Pitman.

Legge, K. (1978) *Power, Innovation and Problem Solving in Personnel Management*, Maidenhead: McGraw-Hill.

Lindberg, L. and Wikander, L. (1990) 'Intressenterna om P-linjen. En riksutvärdering av Linjen för Personal- och arbetslivsfrågor vid den svenska hög-skolan, *Arbetsrapporter från Pedagogiska institutionen*, Uppsala University, 147.

Löfgren, J. (1978) *Yrkesteknisk högskoleutbildning 1975–1978. Erfarenheter från de två första försökomgångarna*. UHÄ-rapport 1978: 21, Stockholm: Universitets-och högskoleämbetet.

Niven, M. (1967) *Personnel Management 1913–1963*, London: IPM.

Regeringens proposition (1922–93):1. Universitet & högsolor. Frihet för kvalitet.

Ritzer, G. and Trice, H. M. (1969) *An Occupation in Conflict. A Study of the Personnel Manager*, Cornell University.

Teichler, U. (1989) 'Government and curriculum innovation in the Netherlands', in van Vught (ed.) (1989) *Governmental Strategies and Innovation in Higher Education*, London: Jessica Kingsley Publishers.

Tyson, S. (1979) 'Specialists in Ambiguity: the study of personnel managers as an occupation, Ph.D. University of London.

Tyson, S. (1983) 'Personnel management in its organisational context', in K. Thurley and S. Wood (1983) *Industrial Relations and Management Strategy*, Cambridge: Cambridge University Press.

Tyson, S. (1987) 'The management of the personnel function', *Journal of Management Studies* 24(5): 523–32.

Tyson, S. and Fell, A. (1986) *Evaluating the Personnel Function*, London: Hutchinson.

Tyson, S. and Wikander, L. (1992) 'Comparative Study of the Education and Training of Personnel Managers in Europe', Cranfield School of Management, Cranfield Institute of Technology and Dept of Education, Uppsala University, (mimeo).

Vicente, C. S. (1993) 'Human resource management in Spain', in S. Tyson *et al.* (eds) (1993) *Human Resource Management in Europe. Strategic Issues and Cases*, London: Kogan Page.

Watson, T. J. (1977) *The Personnel Manager*, London: Routledge & Kegan Paul.

Wikander, L. (1991) 'A comparative study of university study programmes in human resource development and personnel management in some countries', Dept of Education, Uppsala University, (mimeo).

Willén, B. (1978) *Högskolestudier på distans. En utvärdering av svensk försöksverksamhet*, Pedagogisk Forskning i Uppsala 3.

Willén, B. (1981), *Distance education at Swedish universities*, Ak. avh. Uppsala Studies in Education 16, Uppsala: Acta Universitatis Uppsaliensis/Almqvist & Wiksell International.

Chapter 4

Human resources and line management

Chris Brewster and Magnus Söderström[1]

There is evidence of a trend, in all aspects of management, to push responsibilities out from the centre towards the operational units of the organisation. The abrogation of responsibility for anything other than a coordinating and direction-giving role, combined with the 'empowerment' of local managers to take whatever decisions help them to achieve their objectives, has now become almost an orthodoxy.

At the same time, the role of the line manager is often seen as a touchstone of HRM (Mackay and Torrington 1986; Weiss 1988; Legge 1989). One of the features which it is argued distinguishes HRM from personnel management is the closer relationship of the former to the requirements of operational management. The role of the specialist then becomes much more one of advising and supporting line managers. There is, or there should be if this version of the concept is accepted, a trend from personnel specialists taking responsibility for their systems, towards line managers taking responsibility for the people they supervise. There has been much discussion recently in the literature about how far personnel work can be 'contracted out' (Torrington 1989; Clark and Clark 1990) or 'flexibilised' (Adams 1991; Griffiths 1989) or compartmentalised (Tyson 1987).

This chapter addresses these twin drives, towards decentralisation and devolvement, particularly in the context of the responsibility for HRM and issues within HRM and the resultant changes in the relationship of personnel specialists and line managers.

A note on terminology is necessary here. By decentralisation we mean the allocation out to more local parts of the organisation of tasks formerly undertaken centrally. By devolvement we mean the allocation of tasks formerly undertaken by the personnel specialists to line managers. (We use the phase 'devolvement' to distinguish this process from the implication of decentralisation and subsidiarily implied in the, usually political, use of the more correct 'devolution'.) These are separate, though related, forms of organisational change.

THE CHANGING ENVIRONMENT

Customers, competitors and technologies are no longer what they used to be. Product preference, brand loyalty, consumer behaviour are only stable and predictable for a limited collection of products and services, like perhaps water and garbage collection. Other products, which it had been assumed would have a lifecycle that would survive for generations, like beer, suddenly met new competitors, (not just foreign beers and beers without alcohol, but also moves to more wine drinking and the growth of drinking bottled water) and saw turnover and marketshare go down.

Internationalisation and globalisation imply that new competitors enter markets and prove less ready to respect the understandings between traditional competitors on prices and marketshare distribution. Moreover these competitors use more advanced technologies, have a lower cost price per product, ask lower prices from customers and still make more profit. They also invest more in research and development, are able to develop new products at a faster rate and are able to claim major market shares in high margin new product markets and still have healthier balance sheets as well.

Nor is this all; organisations find new suppliers able to sell them products and services better and cheaper than their own staff can provide, stimulating more frequent make-or-buy comparisons and decisions.

One noticeable trend of the 1990s will probably be the continuing movement in the labour force in most industrialised countries from traditional manufacturing towards organisations working with high-tech, competence, information and service as the main organisation-determining factors. This trend implies principally that the proportion of employees occupied within the service sector will increase to about 70 to 75 per cent of the total labour force in the middle of the 1990s in a number of Western countries. At the same time there is a dramatic change going on in the relative importance of various production factors within a growing number of companies and administrations, from the traditional factors of labour, capital and raw materials towards an increased role of the factor of competence (or, more traditionally, 'know how'). Drucker (1993) says, for example, that competence is no longer a resource, it has rapidly become *the* resource!

This means that competence now becomes still more interesting from a strategic and economic point of view, and that various human capital approaches will be more developed and utilised in the HRM field as well as an integrated part of operations and business development.

This kind of change on a macro level is the sum of significant changes at the micro level, in companies and other organisations, in terms of an increasing demand for adjustment and renewal. Kanawaty *et al.* (1989), for example, discern four factors of major importance here: the introduction of advanced technology, increased flexibility in production of goods and services, the changing role of the state *vis-à-vis* the enterprise, and internal work restructuring. Kanawaty *et al.* say that (1989: 294): 'The picture that emerges from this review is one of enterprises that are intensifying the search for greater operational flexibility.'

All these environmental developments also put pressure on productivity development, quality development and product development. The human resource department, therefore, has to devote more attention to manpower planning to foster productivity, performance appraisal to monitor quality and leadership styles, corporate culture and incentive policy to stimulate creativity and commitment to a high paced product development. Factors such as product development, new product introductions, changes in the production and sales mix also imply a need for people with skills that are different from the skills that were previously required. Flexibility and multiskilling and resultant training become increasingly important.

In less turbulent times policy making implied a theoretical process involving the formulation of objectives, means and time schedules on the basis of inventories of needs and possibilities, comparisons of costs and benefits and the systematic choice from a number of alternatives. According to traditional theory, organisations generally try to reduce uncertainty in the environment and within the organisation (see, e.g., March and Simon 1958; Thompson 1967; Ansoff 1978, 1982). Traditionally the objective in managing uncertainty was to make the world more predictable through long-range planning, formal structures, control and internal administration or, in other words, a question of improving internal rationality. Implementation of policies was a question of overcoming ordinary resistance to change; and evaluation was possible against needs and objectives that were still more or less the same.

It is perhaps almost inevitable that the implementers have always adapted the policies they deal with so that they achieve their own requirements whilst being able to report back to the policy makers that they have carried out the policy. This changes as change in the environment becomes more common. With increasing turbulence, needs and possibilities on which policies are based change rapidly, as do the costs and benefits of activities and the nature and number of policy alternatives. If inventories of needs and possibilities and other activities in the sphere of policy preparation take too much time, then actual policy making will take place on the basis of needs and possibilities that no longer exist. Those who are responsible for the implementation of policies created on this basis will realise that their efforts are less useful or useless and will start to develop their own policies, objectives, means and time schedules. A major disparity between the theory of the formal central organisation and the practice of the material decentral organisation might develop this way.

Organisations that critically review their policy making may realise they are unable to match the speed of environmental change. As long as policy making takes place at central and high hierarchical levels, reaching consensus on needs and possibilities, costs and benefits, alternatives and, on objectives, means and time schedules all takes too much time. And in those cases where organisations succeed in changing their central policies, frequently this flexibility is often interpreted as a lack of consistency and a lack of managerial control. Running through the policy making cycle at greater speed does not seem to be the answer to rapid environmental change. Nor does improving planning activities or spending more time on planning seem to be the answer: especially since environmental uncertainty and unpredictability are increasing. Globalisation of policies, concentration on the main and more stable objectives, implies giving up the aspiration to more detailed target setting and the possibility of monitoring and appraising results in relation to these more specific targets.

Since doing away with policy making altogether is not a serious alternative either, (nobody would believe you really stopped it, and shareholders or trade unions would immediately claim mismanagement!) organisations have tended to respond to fast environmental change with efforts to increase flexibility and above all decentralisation.

Decentralisation and devolvement have to be defined as parts of a new general strategic concept. Instead of looking at the environment as steady and predictable the aim is to improve the capacity of managing change and unclear conditions in the whole organisation. Instead of promoting internal rationality it has become necessary to underline external rationality in terms of market orientation and a more 'self-changing' organisational structure. Although the 'state of the art' today, probably, still can be simply expressed by saying that there is no 'best way of organising' it seems obvious that the new concept is based on unhierarchical, decentralised and more flexible structures as an alternative to traditional forms.

Decentralisation aims to formalise localised initiatives to overcome the shortcomings of slow central policies and reduce the number of persons, levels and organisations involved in the altering of policies that pertain to the local unit. Broadening the competences and responsibilities of decentralised management can give a powerful motivational injection and make it easier for individuals to identify themselves with their unit ('my business', 'our business'). By stipulating the need for self-reliance of the decentral unit, which will have its own balance sheet, profit and loss account and a clear profitability yardstick, (or comparable measures of efficiency in the public sector) it becomes easier to monitor and appraise decentral performance. Where this performance is unsatisfactory, decentralisation makes it easier to adapt organisational performance or to let the unit merge with the activities of other organisations or indeed to cut the non-performing unit out of the organisation. In one survey in the Netherlands (Petter *et al.* 1990) decentralisation proved to be a widespread phenomenon: 58.7 per cent of the respondents had gone through decentralisation processes during the 1985–90 period and 66.7 per cent expected more decentralisation during the 1990–95 period. (Centralisation had been experienced by 6.7 per cent and was expected by 12.9 per cent in the years to come.) In the past 5 years 34.2 per cent had seen no change, but for the next 5 years only 19.1 per cent expected no change. This is occurring in HRM too (Hoogendoorn and Brewster 1992). In HRM there is evidence of similar moves in the United Kingdom generally (Richards-Carpenter 1992; Kinnie 1990; Marginson *et al.* 1988) and in the public sector (Corby 1991). Similar trends have been discovered in Germany and Italy (Windolf 1989) in France (Baron 1993) and generally for Europe (Ferner and Hyman 1992).

There are tensions and risks here. Communication problems may easily arise if decentralisation is perceived as the freedom to stop communication within a group and to stop cooperation, loyalty and solidarity. So for instance liberalisation of purchasing policies might imply that purchase benefits are booked that are offset by losses in the rates of capital utilisation at sister companies within a group. Especially when we also look at the costs of a drop in the utilisation rate, (costs of negotiation, dismissals, image loss, loss of customers, loss of labour market status and productivity losses due to conflict), uncontrolled decentralisation and liberalisation may become a costly affair.

In passing, we note that on a rather different measure of 'decentralisation' to local subsidiaries from multinational corporation headquarters (rather than our measure of decentralisation within the national organisation) a number of earlier studies have found consistently that personnel was the least decentralised amongst the various functional areas of MNCs (Goehle 1980; Hedlund 1981; Schuit *et al*. 1981; Van den Bulcke and Halsberghe 1984; Young, Hood and Hamill 1985).

A NEW MODEL OR BACK TO THE CORE?

A general observation seems to be that decentralisation tends to mean new roles both for previous staff departments and for line management. Further, decentralisation obviously is a process more than a shift from one situation to another (Södergren 1992). However, it has become possible to identify three different roles for the remaining central HRM function in a decentralised organisation with varying contents and 'internal markets' as follows:

Role	*Related to*	*Contents*
Strategic	Top management, other companies etc.	Strategic planning coordination and support
Consultancy	Line management	Non-standardised consultancy services (within plans, agreements etc.)
Service/admin. support	Line management All employees	Standardised services, e.g. training, salaries, pensions, insurance, health care

Sometimes all roles and functions could be organised in the same department, other times there will be, for example, a small strategic group close to top management and other units for consultancy and administrative services. The role of line management in this model will primarily be as an 'internal customer' who demands services from the HR function according to their own operations, needs and conditions.

As decentralisation processes gather speed only a few tasks tend to survive centrally. If the central capacity available for these tasks is also limited then it forces a concentration on those tasks that are most important and cannot easily be decentralised. In HR terms such tasks could for instance be management development especially involving inter-national transfers (Dowling and Schuler 1990; Brewster 1991; Black, Gregerson and Mendenhall 1993); liaison with international bodies such as the EC, ILO and OECD; and tasks related to company-wide collective bargaining duties in countries where such negotiations are still common. It is also likely that strategic tasks like environmental scanning, competitor analysis and corporate comparisons of human resource policies will remain centralised, as will tasks that have to do with giving a central incentive to decentral policy development and evaluation of the quality of decentral human resource policies. Another task that might continue centrally is the provision of human resource information.

Where the responsibility for the personnel information system remains central, clear divisions of tasks are necessary for central and decentral inputs, download possibilities for central inputs, upload possibilities for decentral inputs, guarantees against illegal access and abuse of information and the use of expertise that is either centrally or decentrally available. An additional problem is that these identified 'most important' personnel tasks are not static, and will change over time (Hoogendoorn 1987; Towers Perrin 1992; Derr *et al*. 1992) The advantage of a serious decentralisation process is that the organisation no longer has to pretend that central and decentral human resource priorities are identical. Nor is it necessary to strike a compromise where central and decentral priorities seem to be inconsistent. A substantial loss of uniformity in HR policies within one company may occur. For personnel management this implies another task: to explain that central and decentral environment and organisation require different policies and to explain that pluriformity is not the same as injustice.

Studies in the United Kingdom in particular have found evidence of increased decentralisation (WIRS 1984; Marginson *et al*. 1988; Hendry and Pettigrew 1992). However, other commentators have argued that the survey evidence may not be able to reveal full details of a complex process and that, in practice headquarters may retain much more of a coordination and control function than is immediately evident (Purcell 1989; Kinnie 1990). The 1990 Workplace IR survey in the United Kingdom shows an increase in contacts with higher-level personnel managers (1993); and an IPM report showed 14 per cent of large United Kingdom companies recentralising their remuneration policies (IPM 1992).

THE EVIDENCE ON DECENTRALISATION

So where are HR policies in organisations determined? One of the central messages from our research is that, across Europe, the majority of organisations establish these policies at or above the national level. And the more directly the policy impinges upon immediate finances, the more likely the decisions are to be held at the top.

Inevitably the extent of this centralisation varies across the nation states. Eleven of the twelve countries in the 1992 survey have more than half of their organisations determining pay policy at the national HQ level (Appendix III Table 2.5). The country that does not have more than half of their organisations taking such decisions at national HQ level has, like one or two of the other countries, more than 1 in 10 organisations establishing pay policy at the international level. The result is that there is not one of the 12 countries that has more than 4 out of 10 organisations creating such policies at subsidiary or establishment level. In industrial relations only Denmark, France, Ireland and the United Kingdom had more than half the organisations establishing policy at subsidiary or establishment level. Workforce expansion and reduction policies are determined at national or international level in more than half the organisations in all countries except Denmark, Finland, the Netherlands, Sweden and the United Kingdom.

HR policies with less immediate financial implications are more likely to be decentralised. Most countries have a majority of organisations determining policy on recruitment and selection, training and development and health and safety at subsidiary or establishment level. The major exceptions are the Iberian countries – Spain and Portugal – where the majority of organisations keep even these decisions centralised. Finland and Turkey also tend to be rather more centralised and, perhaps significantly on the training and development issue, so does Germany.

There are some sectoral differences. There is no surprise in finding that the public sector has no 'international level' policy decisions; nor that it is more centralised at the national level than other sectors (Appendix III Table 2.5). Within this pattern however, there are some notable exceptions. For example in recruitment and selection and in training and development in Denmark, France and the Netherlands, the public sector is more decentralised than the private sector. The concentration of much research in industrial sociology, industrial relations and human resource management on the manufacturing sector – which is the most decentralised – may go some way towards explaining why our data shows that the decentralisation of human resource management policies is not as widespread as some commentators believe.

A recent article has built on the idea of contingent HRM (see Chapter 2) arguing that organisational lifecycle changes are a key determinant. The evidence, taken just from a small sample of British companies, shows that decentralisation may be a central feature of the 'retrenchment' stage (Hendry and Pettigrew 1992). Further exploration of our data may provide additional evidence here. Size differences are less significant (Appendix III Table 2.5).

DEVOLVEMENT

The other factor we consider is *devolvement*. By this we mean the degree to which HRM practice involves and gives responsibility to line managers rather than personnel specialists. There is an increasing recognition of this issue in the literature (see, e.g., Torrington 1989; Walker 1989; Schuler 1990, 1992; Freedman 1991). With the closer link between strategy development and human resource development, line managers are, theoretically, given a primary responsibility for HRM. It is argued that within the major areas of HRM (attracting, retaining, motivating and developing staff) the line manager needs to be aware of the synergy between human, financial and physical resources; for him or her, allocating time, money and energy to the development of subordinate staff is an investment in enhanced effectiveness and future success; and there is no way this responsibility can be picked up by the human resource manager. The HRM function is seen as playing the role of coordinator and catalyst for the activities of line managers – a 'management team player . . . working (jointly) with the line manager solving people-related business issues' (Schuler 1990: 51).

Devolvement is driven by both organisational and effectiveness criteria. Organisationally, it is now widely believed that responsibilities should be located with line management rather than specialist functions. For most organisations the most expensive item of operating costs is the employees. Hence, in cost or profit centre based organisations (in the private or public sectors), there is pressure to include the management of the human resource in line management responsibilities.

Effectively, it is only by motivating and committing the workforce that value can be added to other resources. It is line managers, not specialist staff functions, who are in frequent, often constant, contact with employees. For most employees it is their immediate superiors who represent the management of the company. Providing these managers with the authority and responsibility to control and reward their employees makes them more effective people managers. There is a general belief that these pressures 'are likely to intensify during the 1990s. For many organisations a key question will be: who should perform and control the P/HR functions that are so critical to organisational success – P/HR professionals or senior line managers' (Derr *et al.* 1992: 1).

There can, of course, be problems in devolvement as in decentralisation. Tasks are being taken away from specialists, with usually (see Chapter 3) appropriate training and skills and, crucially, with a concentration on this one area. They are being passed to managers who may well have little training or skill in the area and who are often uncomfortable or lack confidence in it, and who have myriad other responsibilities. Ideally, the transfer of responsibilities to line management would involve substantial commitment, preparation and support by personnel management: the appraisal of potential for an increase in job requirements; the registration of interest and motivation for such a broadening of responsibilities; the establishment of training activities to support new tasks; and the appraisal of performance for those who undertake new tasks and requirements. It is not certain, to say the least, that this occurs in all cases. Risks also occur if HR tasks are transferred to (managerial) employees who already have a full or more than full workload. In such a case the new tasks get a low priority from those who are now responsible; in effect, this may imply that devolvement equals a liquidation of tasks or, again, at least a serious loss in the quality of performance.

There is considerable case-study or small-scale survey evidence from many European countries that devolution of HRM to line managers is spreading. Space constrains our use of examples, but evidence from Sweden and the Netherlands is indicative. In Sweden as in many other Western countries personnel departments were originally organised during the 1950s, first in manufacturing and business companies and, later on, in the public sector. As most personnel managers came from a varied background – psychologists, social workers, retired army officers or union officials – they sometimes had difficulties to find and design their role.

Most often personnel departments therefore developed staff and specialist functions mainly on a central level for recruitment, training, local negotiations, manpower planning and work security. During this period the HR function of the line managers in general became restricted. Instead functional line management was emphasised where line managers took the responsibility for operations and technical issues only while most planning and administration lay upon central departments.

Later, during the 1970s, when a couple of new labour market laws were introduced a radical change in industrial relation policies took place, creating new demands on the personnel departments to act as the employer for all employees. The centralised model therefore became reinforced for a couple of years where line management still did not fully accept an HRM process.

However things changed in the 1980s when new management strategies were introduced. The theoretical basis for these strategies is to be found, from a general point of view, in e.g. Thompson (1967), Ansoff (1978) and Argyris and Schön (1978) but, more specifically, from the Swedish arena especially could be mentioned Normann (1983), who has developed the ideas of service management, and Beckérus *et al.* (1988), who explain ideas like a new 'doctrine of management'. In a summary of some studies of successfully changing companies in Sweden, Vedin *et al.* (1983) identified five preconditions for successful change, namely:

1 The presence of a basic and clear 'vision' or business idea for the whole organisation.
2 A properly working system for feed-back in the organisation.
3 A farseeing management and leadership.
4 An organisational structure which supported the vision and the management.
5 That basic human needs could be fulfilled in the organisation.

The net result of these changes in Sweden was an increase in the devolvement of HRM from personnel specialists to line management, with two major effects:

First, line management has received and developed more responsibility for HRM issues. This pattern is of course varying a lot, reflecting different kinds of business and operations but two models could be identified. The first one is that line managers on different levels have taken over most daily HRM procedures such as recruitment, training, assessment, determination of wages and salaries (within the frames of local agreements), health and security etc. Another model which has become quite popular, particularly in big companies and public bodies such as hospitals and health care, is that line managers have their own all round 'bare foot' HRM assistants, mainly young officials with a university background in HRM.

Second, the former HRM departments have become organised in a new way, focusing three different roles: the strategic role, the consultancy role and the internal service role. However varying in detail, this model has been introduced during the last years in manufacturing and service industries as well as in the public sector.

According to an empirical study which has been carried out at the Swedish IPF institute (Hedlund and Rolander 1990) there is an obvious trend away from an administrative and centralised HRM role towards more strategy and consultancy work for the HRM professionals together. The daily HRM work has, on the other hand, become more integrated in line operations and business. In the table below answers from 60 leading HRM directors in Swedish service industries and public sector show how they spent their time in 1990 compared to their judgements for 1992.

Different HRM roles	1990 (%)	1992 (%)
Strategic role	20	32.5
Consultancy role	32	37
Service/administrative role	48	30.5

In another current Swedish study decentralisation in 40 big private companies was analysed (Södergren 1992). The most conscious and explicit changes that took place in the decentralisation process, were changes in structures, formal responsibilities and control systems. Less evident, but even more important, says Södergren, were changes in working roles and competence patterns, factors that have not been highlighted in earlier research. The strongest pressure for change was reported amongst local managers who were typically responsible for the local business level. They met an increasing amount of 'indirect work' such as planning, HRM issues and administration (Södergren 1992: 324). Frequent examples were the budgets and accounting of the unit, human resource management, marketing and customer contacts, quality control, rationalisations, and business development. Consequently this meant a considerable change in role expectations and demands for new competences for most line managers. It also illuminates our discussion in this chapter in general that HRM is still becoming more integrated with operations and business in general.

In the Netherlands Petter *et al.* (1990) found that most of their respondents, the personnel and organisation managers of larger organisations, did not expect devolvement to be a success. A majority (73.8 per cent) were confident that line managers were interested in personnel tasks, although 22.7 per cent lacked this confidence. However another majority (77.3 per cent) thought that line management did not have the personnel management knowledge and skills to properly execute personnel tasks; only 16 per cent thought that these skills and knowledge were sufficiently available. Furthermore, 59.1 per cent thought that line management had not sufficient time to take responsibility for personnel tasks, whereas 33.8 per cent thought that time would not create a problem. Finally, readiness to give personnel tasks more priority was not expected by 62.6 per cent, while 29.3 per cent expected line management to be ready to do so.

A Dutch training firm that observed these survey results came to the optimistic conclusion that the absence of personnel management knowledge and skills among line managers could be the hole in the market they had been looking for. After a major mail-out and a response of less than 1 in 1,000 they concluded that line managers did not only have no time for personnel tasks, but even had no time for training to learn the skills needed!

THE EVIDENCE ON DEVOLVEMENT

One issue concerns the degree of responsibility that is being devolved. It is one thing for the personnel department to establish clear policies on how many and who to employ, how to recruit them, what procedures for selection should take place and then leave the interviews and choice between candidates to the line managers: quite another to leave the policy decisions to the line managers and have the personnel specialists responsible just for advertising the posts and setting up the interviews. Our survey was concerned with devolvement of policies.

We asked our respondents to identify the position of their own organisation on six issues: pay and benefits; recruitment and selection; training and development; industrial relations; health and safety; and workforce expansion or reduction. In each case organisations were rated according to whether primary responsibility for major policy decisions rested with line management; line management with personnel or HR department support; the personnel or HR function with line management support; or with the personnel or HR department alone. The resultant rankings were then conflated to provide an overall comparison. A country ranking was produced.[2] The methodology used was rather simple and begs a number of questions – it is presented here as a contribution to the debate rather than as a final word.

These broad rankings can be no more than indicative. The weakness of the rankings stems from two main sources – the methodological (see note 2 at the end of this chapter) and the perceptual. In the latter respect these are the views of senior HRM specialists about their relationship with the line on a series of issues. They encapsulate a good deal of complexity – different elements of industrial relations, to take one example, may be divided differently, different companies within the overall organisation may handle things differently and so on. It would have been valuable, too, if the results had included the views of equivalent line managers. Attempts to address these issues often show line managers as less than enthusiastic about their personnel departments (see e.g. Tissen 1991; Allen 1991; IBM/Towers Perrin 1989). More research is needed on this issue. Nevertheless, the rankings show clear country distinctions that are maintained over the three years of the survey. With all the problems, there is here a clear measure of at least differences in the way senior personnel specialists perceive devolvement across the various European countries. The advantages of this approach are that, whilst it loses some of the detail, it provides a simple means of analysis and generates a comparative rating of the various countries. The results show some fascinating variations.

Devolvement ranking for European countries

Least devolved   *Most devolved*

IRL   F   UK   E   N   D   NL   S   P   FIN   T   DK

Because these are relative rankings and not finite numbers it is not possible to compare across the years but it seems clear that the two '1990–1 only' countries – Switzerland and Italy – would take their places at opposite ends of this spectrum (Brewster and Holt Larsen 1992; Hoogendoorn and Brewster 1992). Italy is one of the least devolved countries: Switzerland is at the other end of the scale.

Several facts emerge. Starting at the most devolved and, Denmark is consistently ranked in that half of the spectrum on all issues and is most devolved on two issues. Note 2 to this chapter indicates that whichever measures of devolution are taken, Denmark retains this position. In 1991 Switzerland was amongst the four countries with most devolution on all issues with the exception of industrial relations, where the trend, as has been shown, is for countries to cluster at the less devolved end of the spectrum. Finland also tends to have most organisations consistently at the most devolved end, though it also has less devolution of industrial relations and, in this case, also of health and safety which in Finland is seen as a specialist area for personnel department expertise. Finland has moved considerably recently. More than 50 per cent of Finnish organisations report that they have increased line management responsibility in training and development and workforce expansion or reduction. More than a third have increased line responsibility in pay and benefits and recruitment and selection.

Turkey and Portugal come from a different tradition. Their relatively recent history of free enterprise and personnel management as an acknowledged specialism may indicate that in these cases the ranking owes more to a lack of line management trust in the personnel function than a wish by that function to push responsibility out to the line. This is supported by the findings on changes in responsibility. These are the only two countries to have more organisations reporting decreases in line management responsibility than increases (in workforce expansion and reduction and, in the case of Portugal, in industrial relations). On most issues there are almost as many organisations reporting decreases as increases. Clearly, this is a time of change for the personnel role in these countries, but not yet a time for an established trend.

Spain, which in some degree shares the problems of being a poorer, more recently democratic, nation is an interesting case. It shows perhaps the widest variation of focus of responsibilities, being, for example, at the least devolved end of the spectrum on recruitment and health and safety, in the middle on training and industrial relations and also on workforce expansion or reduction, and almost the most devolved on pay. Spain has been, as an economy, more successful than Turkey and Portugal and is establishing a respected personnel profession – the data reflects the country's ambivalent position. Note 2 to this chapter shows that if the measure of devolvement had been restricted to the 'line management only' criteria, Spain would be with Turkey and Portugal. However, in line with this analysis there is a consistent trend in Spain towards increased line management responsibility in all areas.

At the other end of the spectrum the United Kingdom and Ireland are, perhaps not surprisingly, close on nearly all issues. It is only on the question of workforce expansion or reduction that there is a separation, with Irish organisations more likely to have responsibility for that issue led by the HR function.

France is the country where organisations are least likely to allow 'line management only' responsibility for major policy decisions on HR issues. The division between functions (as well as the hierarchical divisions) seem to remain strong in France (Randlesome 1993). However there is a trend towards increasing line management responsibility, particularly in training and development.

Amongst the countries in the middle of this ranking it is worth noting Germany and Sweden. Germany has, on all issues, had amongst the fewest organisations devolving responsibility further to the line managers over the last three years and the highest number reporting 'no change'. This fits common stereotypes of German employers as conservative and stable (see, e.g., Randlesome 1993; Lawrence 1991). Sweden, by contrast, is the country reporting the greatest amount of change, with over 50 per cent of organisations reporting an increase in line management responsibility over the previous three years in all areas except industrial relations (39 per cent) and workforce expansion or reduction (46 per cent). There seems to be little doubt that in line with a new Government philosophy and greater decentralisation a new ethic of devolution has taken hold in Sweden. The size of organisation and the sector make some difference to the extent of devolution: but not that much (Appendix III Table 2.7). In this area, as in others, it is country that is the significant variable.

DEVOLVEMENT AND THE PERSONNEL DEPARTMENT

The devolvement of personnel issues to line managers is likely to be related to the size of the personnel department (see Table 4.1). This is unlikely to be an exact match because certain functions may stay with personnel departments, even in a devolved organisation. There may be a need, for example, to increase the capacity to train line managers in certain 'people skills', thus leading to more training specialists within the department. In general, however, there should be a correlation, and we tested to see if there was (Table 4.2).

Table 4.1 Percentage of functionaries per 1,000 employees

P	*IRL*	*E*	*NL*	*FIN*	*UK*	*N*	*D*	*S*	*T*	*F*	*DK*
17	16	14	13	11	10	10	9	9	7	6	6

Table 4.2 Percentage of personnel functionaries per 1,000 employees/devolvement rankings

Personnel:													
I[a]	P	IRL	E	NL	FIN	UK	N	D	S	CH[a]	T	F	DK
Devolvement:													
I[a]	IRL	F	UK	E	D	N	NL	S	T	P	FIN	CH[a]	DK

Note: [a] 1991 data

The devolvement rankings are no more than indicative (see Table 4.3). The proportion of personnel specialists is likely to be quite accurate: most senior HR specialists will have a good idea of how many people the organisation employs and how many of them are in the personnel department. An indication of these proportions for 1992 is given in Table 4.1. Within the continuum three broad groupings can be seen. One group, which (with the exception of Turkey) includes the poorer countries in the survey, has more than 1 in 8 people employed working in the personnel departments. A second, and the most typical, group has about 1 in 10 in personnel – this is the European average. A third smaller group has notably less than the average.

As might be anticipated, there are some clear regional groupings. The EC's Mediterranean countries (with the notable exception of France, which Filella (1991) also finds to be an exception) have a larger proportion of personnel specialists. If the Italian figures from 1991 are included this relationship remains true. Norway, Sweden and Finland are all close. However, again as indicated elsewhere, Denmark is distinct. Although not shown in these figures West Germany also fits one other stereotype in that personnel departments there have the lowest number of specialists, and therefore the highest number of administrators, in Europe (see Lawrence 1991; Randlesome 1993).

Set against the devolution rankings (see p. 61) the proportion of personnel functionaries shows quite a close match. In broad terms the assumption that there is a close linkage between the level of devolvement and the proportion of employees in the personnel department is borne out.

There are some discrepancies. Portugal has a considerable number of personnel functionaries. This in line with other information about the personnel profession in

Table 4.3 Devolvement rankings

	Least devolved											*Most devolved*
1991 (Brewster/Holt Larsen	I	UK	N	F	E	D	NL	S	CH	DK		
1992 (method A)	IRL	F	UK	E	N	D	NL	S	P	FIN	T	DK
(method B)	IRL	F	UK	E	D	N	NL	S	T	P	FIN	DK
(method C)	F	UK	NL	IRL	N	D	FIN	S	E	P	T	DK

Notes: Method: A = Brewster/Holt Larsen collation of rankings; B = Summation of 'HR' and 'HR with line' percentages; C = Summation of 'line only' percentages

Portugal which has a highly successful personnel management institute running one of the largest personnel management conferences in Europe (Mendes 1992). However, like the Spanish personnel profession, the Portuguese is struggling to achieve acceptance and trust; line managers play a significant role in Portuguese HRM. Finland is also anomalous: this may however be a function of the devolvement rankings. If one takes, for example, a simple measure of the extent to which line managers have full responsibility for HR practices then Finland moves to a comparable position in the middle of the rankings – close to Norway and Sweden, who stay in almost the same position whatever measure of ranking is used. The major discrepancy in the rankings concerns France which is at the least devolved end of the spectrum but reports comparatively small personnel departments.

These results illustrate that a high level of devolvement can occur in quite different (and not overlapping) situations. Thus, two organisations, one with a very positive and one with a very negative perception of HRM, might both be characterised by a high level of devolvement. The former organisation might find HRM too important to be dealt with by a central staff function, whereas the latter might find it a waste of resources in the first place to invest in human resources (or mistrust a central HRM function).

Interestingly, we find little evidence that organisations are providing any formal training to help their line managers to handle human resource issues. There is no clear correlation between the amount of training in human resource issues that managers have received and devolution. We identified the number of organisations that had trained at least a third of the managers in such HR techniques as performance appraisal, communications, delegation, motivation and team building.

In none of these topics are the numbers in any country which have done such training correlated with the devolution ranking. Denmark, for example, the most devolved country is amongst those countries where line managers are least trained: Norway and the United Kingdom have considerable numbers of organisations training over a third of their managers in HR techniques, even though they are amongst the least devolved (Table 4.4).

These somewhat conflicting results also raise different explanations. An obvious one is that line managers are just not being trained to undertake an HR role. There is statistical evidence, from the Netherlands, that this is the case in some instances (Hoogendoorn and Brewster 1991). The second is that the most devolved countries have established a situation where line managers are actually able to perform the HRM responsibility: consequently, there is no need for training. The third interpretation is that a manager who is actively undertaking the HRM task gets so much experiential learning that no formal training is needed. A fourth explanation, that the link is with *increases* in training has also received some support from this data (Hoogendoorn and Brewster 1992).

Table 4.4 Areas in which at least a third of managers trained (% organisations)

Country	DK	N	S	UK	F	E	I[a]	D	NL	CH[a]
Performance appraisal	19	64	77	71	47	31	45	34	51	69
Staff communication	43	58	56	54	53	48	49	50	52	69
Delegation	40	47	47	41	25	32	34	40	23	56
Motivation	44	46	47	47	32	48	47	67	47	76
Team building	27	33	27	50	28	34	29	24	35	39

Note: [a] 1991 data

CONCLUSION

The evidence here is that decentralisation and devolution are widespread trends across Europe. They are, however, trends that need to be read carefully in the national context; and it is important not to exaggerate them. Many European organisations are still centralised in many aspects of HRM. Furthermore, whilst devolution is extensive in some countries it is still a rarity in others. The concepts of pushing responsibility out from the centre, and from specialists to line managers, have by now achieved so much of the air of received wisdom that personnel and HR specialists often find themselves almost apologising for their expertise and their involvement. Perhaps they should have more confidence.

Our data is drawn from the central specialists themselves and therefore needs to be treated with caution. However, there seems to be little reason to doubt the findings:

1 That in most cases decentralisation is not so widespread as has sometimes been assumed.
2 That the most common pattern of responsibility is where line management and HR specialists share it.
3 That the extent of decentralisation and devolvement varies considerably by country.
4 That despite the trends towards decentralisation and devolvement HR specialists are required to determine and run HR policies effectively.

NOTES

1 Our colleague in the Netherlands, Jacob Hoogendoorn at Erasmus University, was instrumental in the development of some of the ideas in this chapter, and his contribution is gratefully acknowledged.
2 The rankings were established through the simple mechanism of adding together the percentages of organisations in each country who identified 'HR department' or 'HR department with line management' as having the primary responsibility for policies in the six areas. The resultant scores from addition of the 12 percentages in each country were then ranked in order down to the one with the lowest score, the 'most devolved'.

    This crude method is open to numerous questions, particularly about the weighting of the various areas and about whether the options chosen represent a fair view of devolvement. They show, first, the opinions of senior HR practitioners in the main (see Methodology Appendix) and, second, they count those areas in which they believe HR specialists take the lead.

    Alternative methods of ranking give marginally different orders. A ranking by collation of order in each area was used on the 1990–1 data (see Brewster and Holt Larson 1992). Table 4.3 shows that ranking, plus a similar methodology applied to the 1991–2 data. A third method, simply counting the percentages in which primary responsibility rests entirely with line management, is also shown in the table.

REFERENCES

Adams, K. (1991) 'Externalisation vs specialisation: what is happening to personnel?', *Human Resource Management Journal* 1(4): 40–54.
Allen, K. R. (1991) 'How middle managers view the function', *Personnel Management* June: 40–3.
Ansoff, S. (1978) *Strategic Management*, London: Macmillan.

Argyris, C. and Schön, D. A. (1978) *Organizational Learning: a Theory of Action Perspective*, Reading, Mass.: Addison-Wesley.

Baron, X. (1993) 'L'organisation des fonctions centrales de gestion des ressources humaines', *Revue française de Gestion* (Jan.–Feb.): 5–14.

Beckérus, Å. *et al.* (1988) *Doktrinshiftet*, Stockholm: FA-rådet & SvD.

Black, J. S., Gregerson, H. B. and Mendenhall, M. E. (1993) *Global Assignments*, San Francisco: Jossey-Bass.

Brewster, C. (1991) *The Management of Expatriates*, London: Kogan Page.

Brewster, C. and Holt Larsen, H. (1992) 'Human resource management in Europe: evidence from ten countries', *International Journal of Human Resource Management* (3)3: 409–34.

Clark, I. and Clark, T. (1990) 'Personnel management and the use of executive recruitment consultancies', *Human Resource Management Journal* 1(1): 46–62.

Corby, S. (1991) 'Civil service decentralisation: reality or rhetoric?' *Personnel Management*, February: 38–42.

Derr, C. B., Wood, J. D., Walker, M. and Despres, C. (1992) 'The emerging role of the HR manager in Europe', London: IPM Resource Report.

Dowling, P. and Schuler, R. S. (1990) *International Dimensions of Human Resource Management*, Boston Mass.: PWS-Kent.

Drucker, P. (1993) *Managing the Non-profit Organisation: Practices and Principles*, Oxford: Butterworth Heinemann.

Ferner, A. and Hyman, R. (1992) 'IR on the Continent: a model of co-operation?', *Personnel Management*, August: 32–4.

Filella, J. (1991) 'Is there a Latin model in the management of human resources?' *Personnel Review* 20(6): 14–24.

Francis, A. (1989) 'The structure of organisations', in Sisson, K. (ed.) (1989) *Personnel Management in Britain*, Oxford: Blackwell.

Freedman, A. (1991) *The Changing Human Resources Function*, New York: The Conference Board.

Goehle, D. G. (1980) 'Decision making in multinational corporations', University of Michigan research paper, Ann Arbor, MI.

Griffiths, W. (1989) 'Fees for "house" work: the personnel department as consultancy', *Personnel Management*, January: 36–9.

Hedlund, G. (1981) 'Autonomy of subsidiaries and formalisation of headquarters–subsidiary relations in Swedish MNCs', in L. Otterbeck (ed.) (1981) *The Management of Headquarters–Subsidiary Relations in Multinational Corporations*, Aldershot: Gower.

Hedlund, G. (1990) 'Who manages the global corporation? Changes in the nationality of Presidents of foreign subsidiaries of Swedish MNCs during the 1980s', *IIB/Stockholm School of Economics Working Paper 90/3*, Stockholm.

Hedlund, G. and Rolander, D. (1990) 'Action in hierarchies: new approaches to managing the MNC'; in C. A. Bartlett, Y. Doz and G. Hedlund (eds) *Managing the Global Firm*, London: Routledge.

Hendry, C. and Pettigrew, A. (1992) 'Patterns of strategic change in the development of human resource management', *British Journal of Management* 3: 137–56.

Hoogendoorn, J. (1987) 'Veranderende eisen aan personeelmanagement', in P. W. Maandblad (ed.) (1987) *Voor personeelmanagement en arbeidsverhoudingen*, Rotterdam.

Hoogendoorn, J. and Brewster, C. (1992) 'Human resource aspects of decentralisation and devolution', *Personnel Review* 21(1): 4–11.

Humble, J. (1988) 'How to improve the personnel service', *Personnel Management*, February: 30–3.

IBM/Towers Perrin (1989) *Competitive Advantage: a World-wide Human Resource Study*, New York: Towers Perrin.

IPM (1992) *Performance Management in the UK: an Analysis of the Issues*, London: IPM.

IRS Employment Trends (IRS ET) (1991) 'Devolving personnel management at the AA and Prudential Corporation', *IRS Employment Trends* 479: 4–9.

Kanawaty, G., Gladstone, A., Prokopenko, J. and Rodgers, G. (1989) 'Adjustment at the micro level', *International Labour Review* 128(3): 269–97.

Kinnie, N. (1990) 'The decentralisation of industrial relations? – recent research considered', *Personnel Review* 19(3): 28–34.

Lawrence, P. (1991) 'The personnel function: an Anglo-German comparison', in C. Brewster and S. Tyson (eds) (1991) *International Comparisons in Human Resource Management*, London: Pitman.

Legge, K. (1989) 'Human resource management: a critical analysis', in J. Storey (ed.) (1989) *New Perspectives on Human Resource Management*, London: Routledge.

Mackay, L. and Torrington, D. (1986), *The Changing Nature of Personnel Management*, London: Institute of Personnel Management.

March, J. G. and Simon, H. A. (1958) *Organizations*, New York and Chichester: Wiley.

Marginson, P., Edwards, P., Martin, R., Purcell, J. and Sisson, K. (1988) *Beyond the Workplace*, Oxford: Blackwell.

Mendes, P. (1992) 'A product of the country's history: Personnel management in Portugal', *Personnel Management*, June: 40–3.

Normann, R. (1983) *Service Management: Strategy and Leadership in Service Business*, New York and Chichester: Wiley.

Petter, J. H. L., Schuchman, E., van Voorneveld, H. and Yspeert, K., (1990) *Carrieres in PZ*, Report, Graduate School of Management, Rotterdam, Erasmus University.

Purcell, J. (1989) 'How to manage decentralised bargaining', *Personnel Management* 21(5): 53–5.

Randlesome, C. (ed.) (1993) *Business Cultures in Europe*, Oxford: Butterworth Heinemann.

Richards-Carpenter, C. (1992) 'Capitalising on devolution', *Personnel Management* 24(4): 59–61.

Schuit, J. *et al.*, (1981) *Centralisatie versus decentralisatie in internationale ondernemingen: een multifunctionele benadering*, Rotterdam: Erasmus University.

Schuler, R. S. (1990) 'Repositioning the human resource function: transformation or demise?' *Academy of Management Executive* 4(3): 49–60.

Schuler, R. S. (1992) 'Strategic HRM: linking people with the strategic needs of the business', *Organisational Dynamics*, Summer: 18–31.

Södergren, B. (1992) *Decentralise-ring*, Förändring i företag och arbetsliv, Stockholm School of Economics.

Thompson, J. D. (1967) *Organisations in Action*, New York: McGraw-Hill.

Tissen, R. (1991) *Mensen beter managen*, Deventer: Kluwer.

Torrington, D. (1989) 'Human resource management and the personnel function', in J. Storey (ed.) (1989) *New Perspectives on Human Resource Management*, London: Routledge.

Torrington, D. P. and Mackay, L. E. (1986) *The Changing Nature of Personnel Management*, London: IPM.

Towers Perrin (1992) *Priorities for Competitive Advantage: a worldwide human resource study*, London: Towers Perrin.

Tyson, S. (1987) 'The management of the personnel function', *Journal of Management Studies* September: 523–32.

Van den Bulke, D. and Halsberghe, E. (1984) *Employment Decision-making in Multinational Enterprises: Survey Results from Belgium*, Working Paper 32, Geneva: International Labour Office.

Vedin, B-Å *et al.* (1983), *Leda rätt*, Stockholm: SNS.

Walker, J. W. (1989) 'Human resource roles for the '90s', *Human Resource Planning* 12(1): 55–61.

Weiss, D. (1988) *La fonction ressources humaines*, Paris: Editions d'organisation.

Windolf, P. (1989) 'Productivity coalitions and the future of European corporatism', *Industrial Relations* 28(1): 1–20.

Young, S., Hood, N. and Hamill, J. (1985) *Decision Making in Foreign-owned Multinational Subsidiaries in the United Kingdom*, Working Paper 35, Geneva: International Labour Office.

Chapter 5

Recruitment and selection in Europe
Policies, practices and methods[1]

Françoise Dany and Véronique Torchy

Recruitment is crucial to an organisation in so far as it has important implications for organisational performance. Recruitment generates costs and conditions the current and future development of the organisation. It has therefore to be understood and analysed as a strategic act in all its implications.

The strategic impact of recruitment is great, since decisions have long-run consequences. This has a particular significance today where the labour turnover within organisations is decreasing because of dramatic unemployment problems. At the same time, the increasing complexity of certain jobs requires long learning periods (D'Iribarne 1989); lots of organisations consequently tend to recruit their personnel with a long-term perspective (Dany 1991). Even if the concept of a 'lifetime job' is tending to disappear, most employers contend with labour turnover in order to limitate the short(er) stays in their organisations.

With these considerations in mind, recruitment cannot be reduced to a choice of recruitment methods aimed at selecting the best candidate for a given job. This core concern of occupational psychologists is of importance but should not hide the other issues related to recruitment policies. In practice, the kind of recruitment policy an organisation chooses has to be coherent with its human resources management policy and with its business policy as a whole.

Organisations have to make decisions on a number of issues related to recruitment:

Decisions between short-term organisational needs and long-term organisational requirements

Some organisations hire people with the sole objective of filling a vacant position. Others hire people without knowing what they can offer them as a career start but knowing that they want to keep and develop them in the long term. The choice an organisation makes is not unchanging but varies according to the resources available on the external labour market.

Recruitment costs

Recruitment generates costs which are difficult to estimate but nevertheless high. Asked about their recruitment costs in 1988 (*Sciences et Vie Economie* 1988) Michelin estimated their annual recruitment costs were 12 million French francs and Hewlett Packard in France estimated 15 to 22 million French francs. Another study among ten big French organisations (Dany 1992) confirmed the importance of the financial aspect of recruitment and selection, highlighting that the hiring of a young manager cost about 50 000 French francs.

Recruitment costs in an organisation vary according to:

1 The organisation's image.
2 The ease with which it attracts candidates.
3 The kind of people it wants to hire (experienced managers, school-leavers, low qualified or highly qualified people).
4 The selectivity of recruitment.

Recruitment costs are difficult to estimate because they are numerous and because some of them (indirect costs and induced costs) are invisible. The following example has been elaborated with the collaboration of partner-organisations of the Groupe ESC Lyon (Dany 1992); it allows organisations to establish the different costs which are attributable to recruitment:

1 Indirect communication costs (milk rounds, partnership with business schools/universities, stages).
2 Structural costs of the personnel department (personnel costs, purchase of specific software, training of recruitment managers).
3 Variable costs related to the attraction of candidates (advertising, mailing etc.).
4 The examination of candidates (assessment centres, graphologic analyses when sub-contracted, pay-back of the candidates' travelling expenses, time spent by line managers interviewing candidates etc.).
5 Induced costs linked to the integration and the training of the selected candidates.

Decisions about the kind of profile the organisation is looking for

Does it want to hire relatively specialised workers who will be able to develop their expertise in a specific field or generalists a priori capable of moving from one job to another? This choice has to be coherent with the career management policy of the organisation.

Decisions about how to achieve the qualification level the organisation is looking for

Does it want to recruit low-qualified people and develop them through vocational training/reskilling? Does it want to recruit highly qualified people, assuming that they are best qualified to improve organisational performance? Decisions between an external recruitment policy on one hand and a policy relying on internal promotions on the other hand potentially have a substantial social impact. Indeed, the choice which is made affects:

1 The nature of the employer/employee relationship: is it a money-against-work relationship or a mutual commitment?
2 The social climate (potential conflicts between age groups and qualification groups).
3 The innovative ability of the organisation: the age pyramid, the different sub-cultures existing in an organisation can alter or favour the innovative ability of the organisation.

Decisions about the organisation of recruitment

How centralised should recruitment be? Decentralised recruitment policies and practices have the advantage of involving local line management whereas centralised recruitment policies are more efficient in so far as relationships with business schools/universities and coherence in career management are concerned.

European comparisons

We shall analyse here recruitment patterns existing in European organisations from twelve countries, determine the main existing or emerging trends, draw comparisons and then try to find out and account for convergences and divergences. This will allow practitioners to have reference points in the field – this being the main interest of leading a quantitative study. In analysing developments, we deliberately chose to focus on the country variable since:

1 The country reflects cultural peculiarities (Hofstede 1983; D'Iribarne 1985) or reveals specific societal structures (Maurice *et al.* 1982).
2 We want to challenge the existence of what the literature calls the European management model.

Before considering the findings, we would like to recall briefly certain weaknesses inherent in the questionnaire method that have an influence on the results obtained. The responses to some of the questions can be subjective in the sense that they reflect the personal opinion of the human resources manager answering the questionnaire (mainly open questions such as 'Which job categories do you currently find hardest to recruit?').

Some of the countries are more sensitive to the variable under consideration than others. The above results lead us to the conclusion that R&S issues can be looked at from a 'public sector/private sector' angle. We encourage researchers to determine other contingency variables that are relevant to the analysis of recruitment issues and understand how they can enrich results based on the country variable. (See also chapters on equal opportunity.)

Because the environment is complex and constantly evolving, it becomes difficult for an individual to have a global sight of what is happening in the organisation. The response to some questions can be influenced by the human resource manager's cognitive filters: (see Appendix II).

The status of our work is therefore not to bring unquestionable results to the fore but:

1 To bring new results on recruitment issues and challenge them with available results so as to take part in a cumulative process of knowledge production.
2 To define research hypotheses that correspond to recent and/or new tendencies which will have to be understood and explained.

In this chapter, we shall examine the following:

1 Recruitment issues through three key perspectives:
   (a) the organisation of the recruitment (centralisation vs decentralisation, main agents involved, temporal dimension);
   (b) the articulation between an external recruitment policy and promotion;
   (c) the recruitment methods and their raison d'être.
2 The possibility of accounting for different recruitment and selection models in Europe.

In order to examine national patterns we will follow the approach developed by Bournois, Chanchat and Roussillon (see Chapter 8) who applied Bertin's graphic model and correspondence analysis (Benseron *et al.*) to this area. (See below.)

Public sector vs private sector

Before concentrating on national comparisons we will briefly analyse the influence of public ownership. 'Country' is certainly not the only criterion that can be used to account for the contingency of policies and practices (Levy-Leboyer 1991). However, it has already proved to be relevant in the comparative analysis of compared HRM practices (Bournois and Torchy 1992; Bournois and Brewster 1991; Brewster and Holt Larsen 1992).

We examined here the relevance of the variable 'public sector' (national industries, other public corporations, public administrations) 'private sector' (private organisations) to the analysis of recruitment and selection policies and practices.[2] The chi-square test has been used for all the countries but can only be interpreted for some of them, the raw number of responding organisations belonging to the public sector being too low in some countries (the Netherlands, Turkey and Portugal), therefore generating a too low minimum expected frequency.

Table 5.1 analyses the responses to the following questions: With whom does the primary responsibility lie for major policy decisions on R&S? How far ahead do you plan staffing requirements? What proportion of your senior managers are recruited externally? Do you recruit to maintain current staff ratios? Have you introduced any of the following measures to aid recruitment (flexible working hours etc.)?

The main lessons which can be drawn from this analysis (Table 5.1) are the following ones:

Table 5.1 The public sector effect in recruitment and selection

	UK	F	S	E	DK	N	IRL	FIN
Recruitment policies								
Primary responsibility for R&S	*	ns	***	ns	**	**	ns	ns
Staffing requirements planning	***	*	***	ns	***	–	ns	ns
% of senior managers recruited externally	***	–	*	ns	**	***	*	*
R&S to maintain current staff ratios	***	–	–	ns	*	–	**	ns
Recruitment practices								
Flexible working hours	***	*	**	–	***	***	***	
Recruiting abroad	**	**	*	ns	*	**	–	*
Relaxed age requirements	–	*	–	**	**	–	–	–
Relaxed qualifications	***	–	**	–	–	***	ns	–
Relocation of company	–	ns	ns	ns	ns	ns	ns	ns
Retraining existing employees	–	*	–	ns	–	–	–	–
Training new employees	*	–	–	ns	–	*	–	–
Part-time work	***	***	–	ns	***	***	*	–
Job sharing	***	na	*	ns	***	***	***	na
Increased pay & benefits	***	–	–	**	***	***	*	–
Marketing the organisation's image	*	–	–	*	*	–	–	–

Notes: The following codes indicate that a specific R&S issue is dependent on the company statute (public sector vs private sector): *** 0.001 level of significance; ** 0.01 level of significance; * 0.5 level of significance, – no statistical indication of dependence, ns chi-square calculation impossible, na not applicable.

1 Recruitment practices are very much dependent on the 'public/private sector' variable as far as the use of flexible working practices (flexible working hours, job sharing, part-time work) to aid recruitment is concerned (16 out of the 20 possible tests).
2 Recruitment practices are not dependent on the 'public/private sector' variable as far as the use of training practices (retraining of existing employees, training of new employees) to aid recruitment is concerned (3 out of the 14 possible tests).
3 Recruitment policies are dependent on the 'public/private sector' variables (17 out of the 22 possible tests).

COUNTRIES GROUPED ACCORDING TO POLICIES, PRACTICES AND METHODS STUDIED

The organisation of recruitment and selection

The organisation of recruitment and selection can be analysed through three main items: are recruitment and selection policies centrally or decentrally determined? Who are the main agents responsible for recruitment and selection? What is the temporal dimension of recruitment?

Centralisation vs decentralisation

When the responding firm belongs to a larger entity (group, multinational, central administration etc.), recruitment and selection policies can be decided at its international

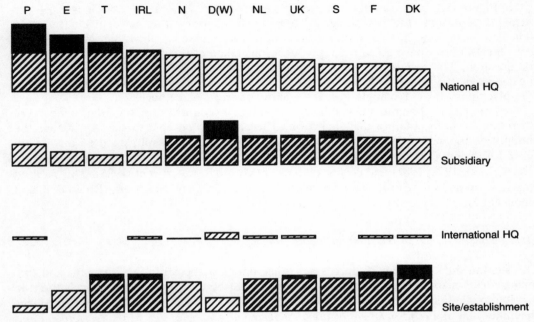

Figure 5.1 Level of decision for firms belonging to a larger entity (group, multinational, central administration, etc.)

headquarters (HQ), at its national head office, at subsidiary level or at company (site/establishment) level (see Chapter 4). On this particular point, practices vary enormously; for example, 68 per cent of Portuguese organisations take policy decisions at the national head office whereas only 23 per cent of Danish organisations do so. Complete results are displayed in Figure 5.1.

Countries can be grouped according to their dominant way of making decisions on R&S policies:

1 Group A, containing Denmark, France and the Netherlands, where an above average number of organisations decentralise recruitment to the site/establishment. Thus, if the differences between countries partly reflect the structural differences between firms due to the size of country (Denmark and the Netherlands have more small firms than France), it must be acknowledged here that other factors intervene.
2 Group B, with Spain, Ireland, Norway, Portugal, and Turkey, where an above average number of organisations make policy decisions on R&S at their national head office.
3 Group C, with the former West Germany and Sweden, where an above average number of organisations decentralise recruitment to the subsidiary.

International headquarters, if they exist, play an almost non-existent role in the determination of recruitment and selection policies in all the countries. R&S is certainly too remote an issue in the business policy implementation for international headquarters' experts to deal with.

On Figure 5.1 and on the following figures of the same type, the height of the rectangle represents the percentage of firms in the country that have given the reply indicated on the line. For example, 8 per cent of Portuguese (P) firms and 49 per cent of Danish (DK) firms have given the reply 'decisions taken at the site/establishment level' to the question. The rectangle is *thinly striped* if this percentage is less than the average for the countries; the *heavily striped* rectangle stands for the average percentage on each reply. The black part of the rectangle stands for above average percentages.

The lines (replies) on the one hand, and the columns (countries) on the other hand, were organised so as to obtain a diagonal form. The aim is to be able to see at a glance the similarities and differences between countries. To obtain this graph, we used a software named Tabview (Chauchat and Risson 1993), which combines Bertin's graphic method (Bertin 1973, 1977, 1981) and correspondence analysis (Benzecri *et al.* 1976). This method was first applied to European comparisons in this field by Bournois, Roussillon and Chouchet (see Chapter 8).

Main agents involved in recruitment issues

The sharing out of human resources activities among a specialised department and line management is an accepted fact throughout Europe (see Chapter 4). However, is the role distribution definitely set or is it evolving? The findings (displayed in Table 5.2) are explicit: they underline the *reinforcement of line management responsibilities in the recruitment and selection field*. Either line managers are confirmed in their role/responsibilities or their responsibilities for R&S issues are increased. A trend is common to all countries: there is almost no decrease in line management responsibilities.

Out of the three level alternative responses possible (increased, same, decreased), 1 means the majority of organisations in the country answered in this category, 2 indicates the second most common response, and 3 means this response was given by the lowest number of respondents.

Hence, the respective roles of line management and personnel specialists are changing with more HRM responsibilities being taken up by line managers (Table 5.2). This evolution is in accordance with the prediction of experts:

1 Weiss (1988) mentioned 'the tendency to have human resources managed by line managers'.
2 In a survey of personnel management in the UK, MacKay and Torrington (1986) found that traditional personnel activities such as recruitment, performance appraisal, employee relations were increasingly delegated to line managers.

Does this evolution mean that line managers become the sole agents responsible for decision making? Not at all. The primary responsibility for major policy decisions for R&S

Table 5.2 Devolution of R&S responsibilities to line management

	DW	DK	E	F	FIN	IRL	N	NL	P	S	T	UK
Increased responsibilities	2	2	2	2	2	2	1	2	2	1	2	2
Same responsibilities	1	1	1	1	1	1	2	1	1	2	1	1
Decreased responsibilities	3	3	3	3	3	3	3	3	3	3	3	3

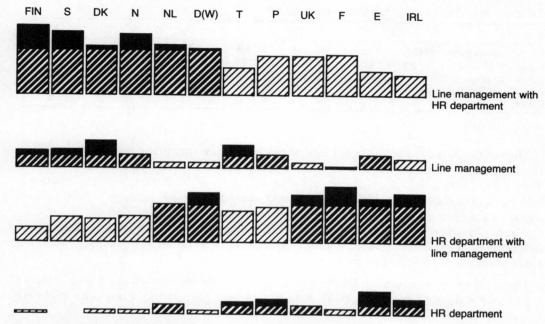

Figure 5.2 Primary responsibility for recruitment and selection issues

issues either lie with the 'HR Department supported by line management' or with 'line management supported by the HR Department'. Results can be visualised in Figure 5.2.

Very few organisations let the primary responsibility for R&S issues lie with 'line management' only or with the 'HR Department' only. Responsibilities for R&S issues are shared, but who – among line management and the HR department – is the istigator and who is the follower? Three groups emerge from the analysis:

1 A group gathering the Scandinavian countries, where the line management role is predominant.
2 A group gathering the UK, France, Spain and Ireland, where the HR Department role prevails.
3 An intermediary group where responsibilities are almost equally shared (the Netherlands, former West Germany, Turkey and Portugal).

Temporal dimension

What we call the temporal dimension of recruitment very much relates to manpower planning. Indeed, manpower planning can be based either on the continuation of what is currently done (the purpose of recruitment is then to perpetuate what the organisation is in terms of qualifications, profile, number of people employed) or on the will to adapt the personnel to organisational requirements. Recruitment is then based on the forecast of future skills requirements.

Table 5.3 Methods used for manpower planning (%)

	D	DK	E	F	FIN	IRL	N	NL	P	S	T	UK
Recruit to maintain current staff ratios	83	70	74	65	9	76	19	94	70	48	92	63
Forecast of future skill requirements	87	92	82	94	81	95	80	34	93	90	85	94
Sales/business or service forecasts	89	52	87	78	68	71	75	63	74	87	90	83
Analysis of labour markets	45	46	60	37	37	33	32	62	74	38	74	59
Other	7	9	5	6	5	7	6	8	2	5	3	5

The results displayed in Table 5.3 lead to the conclusion that many methods are used at the same time, with a predilection for the 'forecast of future skills requirements' method. They place recruitment at the heart of other HRM issues such as manpower planning, training and development, HRM strategy and even of business strategy. These various elements play a role, simultaneously or not (Bournois and Versaevel 1993).

When asked how far ahead they plan their staffing requirements, European organisations differentiate themselves clearly. Figure 5.3 encapsulates the survey results. Two main conclusions can be inferred from it:

1 The most usual time horizon for the planning of staffing requirements is a year. Human resource managers therefore think within a budget framework. Long-term planning vanishes as soon as it is compared to day-to-day practices.

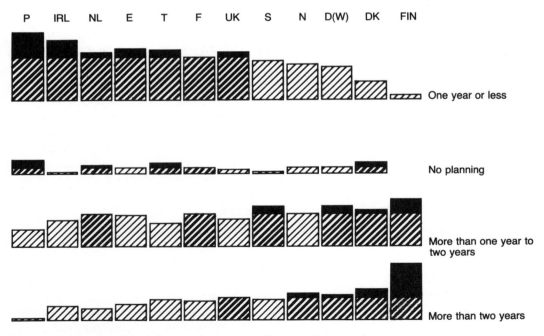

Figure 5.3 How far ahead do you plan your staffing requirements?

2 The horizon at which organisations plan their staffing requirements differs between the Scandinavian countries and the southern countries. There is a greater propensity to plan in the former whereas there seems to be no will to do so in the latter.

The alternative of external recruitment vs promotion

The Price Waterhouse Cranfield Project gives us a clear view of the alternative of external recruitment vs promotion in European organisations. We shall analyse it through four issues which will give the practitioner a better understanding of the internal and external personnel flows in European companies:

1 Which personnel categories are difficult to recruit?
2 Do companies recruit their top managers on the external labour market or do they favour people from the seraglio?
3 Which measures are introduced to aid recruitment: flexible working practices? training? advertising?
4 How are vacant positions filled? Is internal advertising used at the expense of recruitment agencies? Do organisations use the same methods for manual workers and for managers?
5 What are the job categories hardest to recruit?

When asked which job categories they find hardest to recruit (results displayed in Table 5.4), HR managers give widespread answers. Salient facts nevertheless emerge.

1 Numerous organisations mention they have no recruitment problems. The better provided organisations are Scandinavian (Danish, Finnish and Swedish, where 60 per cent and over mention no recruitment problems). The lesser provided organisations are French,[3] Spanish and German, where only 1 organisation out of 4 reports no recruitment problems. Let us note that there has been a dramatic increase in the number of organisations mentioning no recruitment problems during the three years of the survey.
2 There is a general lack of managers, except for Portugal and Turkey – they have other concerns. The questionnaire does not tell us if this is a quantitative lack or a qualitative one.
3 There is a general lack of skilled workers, even in the former West Germany (well known for its dual training system). The lack of qualified workers on the external labour market is a serious problem in countries like Portugal. Recruitment problems in Portuguese companies revolve around technical qualification problems: 'qualified professionals', 'information/technology', 'technicians', 'skilled manuals'. This pattern is to be found – to a lesser extent – in Turkey.
4 French companies find it difficult to recruit sales people. This can be explained in two different but related ways:
   (a) there is no management degree to train salespeople in France;
   (b) sales functions are often devalued in France. Social prestige is an important notion in French firms (Courpasson and Sarnin 1990) and the most prestigious functions – the ones young graduates hunt for – are marketing and finance; the French

Table 5.4 Job categories hardest to recruit (%)

	DW	DK	E	F	FIN	IRL	N	NL	P	S	T	UK
Management	24	28	32	17	22	25	10	17	3	25	8	13
Qualified professionals	8	17	13	6	10	14	11	11	11	19	4	27
Health and social	2	25	0	7	1	18	51	0	0	16	0	8
Engineers	11	5	9	14	0	15	7	5	8	13	15	14
Information technology	5	4	8	5	0	8	2	5	11	6	7	12
Technicians	5	2	12	17	0	1	1	15	20	4	14	5
Administrative/clerical	6	2	2	1	0	1	1	8	3	3	7	5
Sales and distribution	9	7	13	11	0	4	5	10	6	1	5	5
Skilled manuals	18	4	7	16	12	11	5	20	25	10	18	7
Manual	2	3	0	1	0	1	2	7	4	1	1	2
Foreign languages	1	2	3	1	0	1	0	0	1	0	13	0
No recruitment problems	24	65	23	28	74	44	44	18	16	60	46	35

educational system maintains the prestige scales between functions (Dany 1993). As Barsoux and Lawrence (1990) put it, there is a devaluation of functions not associated with cleverness and intellectualism in French organisations; and sales are considered to be a professional field for self-taught persons.

The difficulty of recruiting salespeople is also encountered in Spain.

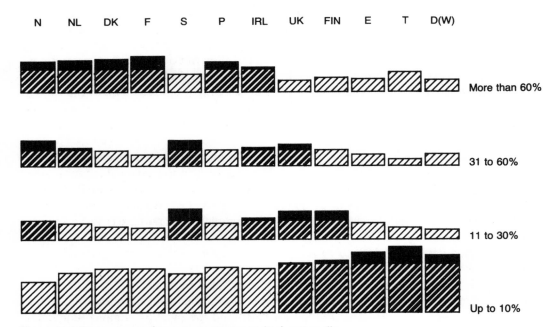

Figure 5.4 Percentage of top managers recruited externally

Senior managers: external or internal labour market?

Two patterns emerge from the analysis of Figure 5.4.

1 An external recruitment pattern: a large proportion of senior managers are recruited on the external labour market, even if the current staff are not neglected. French and Norwegian organisations follow this pattern. In France and Norway, one organisation out of three recruits more than 60 per cent of its senior managers on the external labour market.
2 An internal promotion pattern. In Spain, Turkey and former West Germany, 1 organisation out of 2 hires less than 10 per cent of its senior managers on the external labour market.

These two patterns are closely linked to career management policies, and particularly to high-flyer detection and development policies (Torchy 1992).

Practices set up in order to face recruitment problems

Organisations can adopt a variety of practices to deal with recruitment problems: flexible working practices, training practices etc. Let us see which practices they favour and if organisations introduce them separately or concomitantly.

1 Many practices are introduced at the same time (complete results are displayed in Table 5.5), underlining the fact that there are no simple answers to this complex issue.
2 The emphasis is very much on training, reskilling and development. Organisations use training as a leverage to help them face the lack of certain qualifications on the labour market. They provide training for new employees *and* retraining for existing employees. In some countries, too few managers are educated each year. This is the conclusion the Handy report (1987) arrived at about Great Britain:
   (a) most managers in the USA, Germany, France and Japan have been educated to a higher level than in the United Kingdom;
   (b) there is not yet a well-signposted and generally accepted route into business and management in the United Kingdom;
   (c) most of the 90,000 managers-to-be will either receive no formal introduction to the new elements of business and management or will wait till mid-career, at which stage over one-third will still receive nothing.
3 Fewer organisations have recourse to flexible working practices (flexitime, part-time), which can be accounted for, among other things, by different national legislations (see also discussion in Chapters 11 and 12 on flexibility and equal opportunities).

How are vacant positions filled?

Some outstanding results can be highlighted:

1 Among all the suggested methods (promotion, internal advertising, external advertising, word of mouth, recruitment agencies, search consultants, job centres, apprentices), few

Table 5.5 Practices introduced in order to aid recruitment (%)

	DW	DK	E	F	FIN	IRL	N	NL	P	S	T	UK
Flexible working hours	76	42	26	40	55	28	51	25	25	63	7	39
Recruiting abroad	16	13	13	16	9	35	27	14	14	15	5	20
Relaxed age requirements	54	13	52	27	26	25	29	52	48	27	29	40
Relaxed qualifications	12	9	46	22	16	10	10	26	50	25	33	21
Relocation of the company	3	3	13	4	5	2	2	2	10	3	2	7
Retraining existing employees	56	49	67	38	56	54	53	69	71	53	63	67
Training for new employees	58	59	64	73	59	51	61	71	65	39	62	68
Part-time work	67	31	17	30	27	33	45	33	12	30	2	53
Increased pay and benefits	47	32	52	37	26	32	35	47	67	23	34	44
Marketing the organisation's image	64	41	37	59	63	33	42	52	50	54	35	53

are neglected. Multiple methods are used at the same time. This can be linked to the fact that the horizon for manpower planning is usually a year. So, when there is a vacant position, there is not always someone nominated in the succession plan to take up the job!

2 National peculiarities such as the existence of job centres for managers in France (APEC Agence Pour l'emploi des Cadres) or the apprenticeship system in the former West Germany influence the results.

3 The word of mouth method is not an attribute solely of southern countries. It is a widely used technique in Spanish organisations to fill managerial vacant positions (Filella 1991) but also a widely used technique to fill vacant clerical and manual positions in all the countries surveyed.

4 The choice of methods differs according to the hierarchical level of the vacant position to be filled: the 'promotion + external advertising + internal advertising' trio prevails for managerial and clerical positions. Word of mouth appears to be a favoured method for manual positions.

5 As a consequence, it seems that there are no clear policy decisions on how vacant positions should be filled but a contingent mix of different methods, either turned outwards or inwards to find suitable candidates.

Recruitment methods and their *raison d'être*

The perspective that a European labour market will develop (Benayoun 1990; Thurley and Wirdenius 1991) reinforces the interest of challenging the specificity, relevance and acceptability of the recruitment methods used in European countries. Three points have to be kept in mind about the results on recruitment methods:

1 The use of certain recruitment methods (astrology, morpho-psychology etc.) is more or less taboo: organisations are not very enthusiastic about admitting their use.

2 Recruitment practices are complex and difficult to comprehend through the filter of written studies. The diversity of practices is such that the same concepts might cover different realities. What does 'interview' mean, structured or unstructured interview?

Table 5.6 Recruitment methods (%)

	DW	DK	E	F	FIN	IRL	N	NL	P	S	T	UK
Application form	96	48	87	95	82	91	59	94	83	na	95	97
Interview panel	86	99	85	92	99	87	78	69	97	69	64	71
Bio data	20	92[a]	12	26	48	7	56	20	62	69	39	8
Psychometric testing	6	38	60	22	74	28	11	31	58	24	8	46
Graphology	8	2	8	57	2	1	0	2	2	0	0	1
References	66	79	54	73	63	91	92	47	55	96	69	92
Aptitude test	8	17	72	28	42	41	19	53	17	14	33	45
Assessment centre	13	4	18	9	16	7	5	27	2	5	4	18
Group selection methods	4	8	22	10	8	8	1	2	18	3	23	13
Other	3	2	4	3	2	6	5	6	0	5	6	4

Note: [a] CV

What is a CV analysis? And what is a CV? An Italian CV does not look the same as a German one (Tixier 1987).

3 The examination of recruitment methods used to hire a manual worker, a technician, a 'technical' manager and a 'top manager' will differ.

Quantitative studies on recruitment methods have therefore to be examined very carefully. They are nevertheless interesting for the understanding of what is done in European organisations. Table 5.6 gives the survey results for this area. These findings are confirmed by other studies dedicated to the analysis of recruitment methods (Smith 1991).

Table 5.6 leads to three main conclusions:

1 Although 'the evidence for the predictive validity of handwriting analysis in personnel selection (and other) situations is not great' (Smith and Robertson 1986), graphology is used in 57 per cent of French firms. It is hardly ever used in the other countries.[4]
2 Assessment centres which are considered to be among the more valid techniques, are not widely used for recruitment purposes (except in the Netherlands). This however does not mean that they are not used at all, especially for career management purposes.
3 The 'classic trio' (Levy-Leboyer 1990) composed of 'application form + interviews + professional references' is *the* recruitment tool in all the countries. The scientific validity of these three methods is nevertheless questioned in numerous studies (see Table 5.7).

Table 5.7 Validity, cost and acceptability of selection methods

Method	Validity	Cost	Acceptability
Work sample	high	high	very good
Aptitude test	high	low	good
Assessment centre	high	high	very good
Cognitive test	high	low	good
Bio data	medium	medium	good
References	low	low	very good
Interviews	low	medium	very good
Personality test	low	low	low
Self-evaluation	low	low	low
Graphology	no validity	medium	good

Source: Levy-Leboyer 1990

The evaluation of a recruitment method can be based on its practicability, its sensitivity, its reliability and its validity (Table 5.7). Validity refers to the part of the systematic variance of a score which is unrelated to a particular inference (for example, test familiarity, bias, seniority) but related to a particular criterion (for example, ability, personality) (Smith and Robertson 1986). The essence of validity is the correctness of inferences and actions that can be based on it.

If some selection methods have a low validity and should be eliminated, a high validity does not imply that the method is systematically good; it has always to be used within a specific context. The above results raise important questions: how is it that the most commonly used recruitment methods are the ones with the lowest validity? How is it that they are still used? What can account for national peculiarities? Three elements can be brought to the fore:

1 *Validity is not often questioned by recruitment managers*. Practitioners are not always well aware of the scientific validity of the recruitment methods they use. Recruitment managers often base their choice on their personal feeling, on criteria of perceived validity, but also on cost efficiency and on practicability. They tend to use recruitment methods which are already used, and legitimate because of their perceived efficiency in the past.
2 *The impact is not always visible*. Many elements account for the acceptance of recruitment methods which are a priori not valid. The efficiency of a recruitment method is difficult to evaluate and few companies try to do so systematically. It is very difficult – in fact almost impossible – to evaluate the impact of 'false negatives' (rejected candidates who would have performed well). Moreover very few organisations possess criteria to evaluate their recruitment; they cannot distinguish between 'a good recruitment' and a 'not so good recruitment'. Only obvious failures of the system (resignations, people never integrated) are visible. Last but not least, the success of a newly recruited candidate is not only a function of the quality of recruitment; other factors such as organisational and interpersonal factors intervene. Besides, the evaluation of the success is made through subjective performance appraisal meetings.
3 *Recruitment methods are part of HRM as a whole*. Another factor may account for the disparity between available results on validity and actual practices: scientists and practitioners don't use the same criteria to evaluate recruitment methods. Numerous scientific studies try to analyse the utility/validity of recruitment methods in order to predict the performance in a given job. Recruitment has other objectives, depending on the career management policy of the organisation, on the state of relationships between the candidate and the organisation. The organisation may need to sell itself and certainly needs to evaluate the candidate's ability to be integrated in the organisation, to see if he/she is compatible with its value system. The wide use of interviews can then be justified by the opportunity it creates to discuss with the candidate about the job, about career perspectives and so on.

SETTING UP A TYPOLOGY OF THE DIFFERENT RECRUITMENT AND SELECTION MODELS IN EUROPE

We tried to answer one of our questions relating to the existence or not of a European management model by testing the main characteristics of the recruitment and selection policies/practices and methods. A certain frustration may arise from the fragmented results we obtained. The practitioner and the researcher are so eagerly looking for similarities that we cannot help setting up some groupings and working on a typology. The typology expounded here is a provisional conclusion, which means that it can be tested, explained and completed by further research.

We hoped to classify the 12 countries in homogeneous groups as far as the questions related to recruitment and selection issues are concerned. The results are displayed in Figure 5.5. To do our typology, we used Ward's algorithm (1963). (This method was first applied to this area by Bournois *et al.*, Chapter 8.) The computer:

1 Calculates the differences between the countries two by two (calculation done for each item and for all the questions).
2 Groups together the two countries that have the smallest difference.
3 Calculates the differences between the group of countries just constituted and each of the other countries and so on.

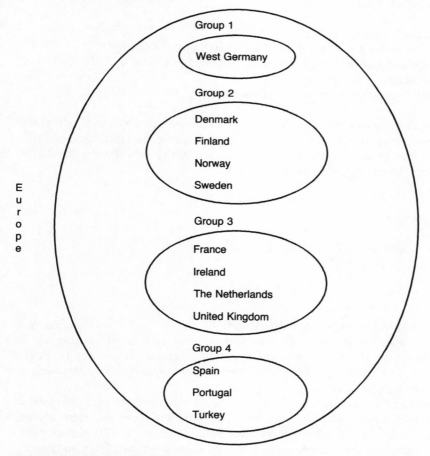

Figure 5.5 Typology of the different R&S models in Europe

The algorithm brings out at each step the grouping that maximises the within-group variance and consequently, minimises the between-groups variance. In doing so, we can infer that the groups obtained are homogeneous compared to the others. To begin with, there are the 12 countries, of which each forms a group in itself. Then there are 11 groups, then 10, and so on, until they are all linked together. These successive groupings can be represented by a 'tree': the 'trunk' is made up of the 12 countries all together; then this 'trunk' separates out into 'branches', becoming smaller and smaller until they represent only one country.

To work out the difference between two groups of countries, the algorithm calculates the mean of the replies of the countries of each group; to do this, it gives automatically the same weighting to each country. The typology obtained in following the above described method is a four-groups typology (a five-groups typology brought little more information, a three-groups typology brought much less information). The four-groups typology is therefore the more stable and the more interesting for us.

The typology reveals the four following groups:

1 Germany is in a group apart (Group 1).
2 The Scandinavian countries are together (Group 2) and close to Group 1.
3 The two English-speaking countries of the study are together (UK and Ireland), with France and the Netherlands (Group 3).
4 The southern countries form a group on their own (Group 4).

A set of leading features stands out for each group of countries but we cannot talk about specific features, since other groups may also include these same characteristics, but to a much lesser extent. The group by group analysis we are going to expound has to be understood within this determined statistical framework.

Group 1 (former West Germany)

The leading features which are to be found are as follows:

Practices

1 Germany makes recourse largely to apprenticeship to fill vacant clerical and professional jobs. This can be easily associated with the dual training system which prevails in Germany. This brings to the fore the hypothesis that societal factors are of prime importance (Maurice *et al.* 1982) in the determination of management practices such as recruitment and selection practices.
2 In order to facilitate the recruitment of scarce resources in their national labour market, German companies develop flexitime and part-time practices and neglect training and reskilling practices. This can be interpreted, within the German context, as a will to develop what has not yet been developed by the well-known German training system.

3 The categories most organisations find difficult to recruit are: engineers and qualified manual workers.

Policies

1 Recruitment and selection policies are, more than anywhere else, determined at the subsidiary level and less than anywhere else, determined at the 'site/establishment' level. This particular trend may reflect the way codetermination is organised in German companies

2 There are some countries in which line management responsibilities have decreased over the last three years in comparatively more organisations, even if the general trend is – as seen above – the increase of line management responsibilities regarding recruitment and selection issues. Germany is among the countries in which these responsibilities decreased most.

Group 2 (Denmark, Finland, Norway, Sweden)

The leading features which are to be found are as follows:

Practices

1 In these countries, there are less recruitment problems than anywhere else, except for health professionals; they constitute the personnel category hardest to recruit in Scandinavian countries.

2 Line managers are very much involved in the management of recruitment and selection. Line managers responsibilities increased over the last three years. Line management and the HR department are responsible for recruitment and selection issues, the HR department being supportive of line managers.

3 The Group 2 countries are characterised by a wide use of internal and external advertising to fill vacant clerical, manual and managerial jobs.

4 Flexible working hours are widely used to aid recruitment. Relaxed qualifications, relaxed age requirements, increased pay and benefits are less used than in any of the other groups.

5 The staffing requirements are planned, more often than the other groups, at two years' time. This feature particularly prevails in Finland (influence of the former USSR model).

Policies

The determination of recruitment and selection policies is done most of the time at the site/ establishment level and not at the national level.

Group 3 (France, Ireland, United Kingdom, the Netherlands)

The leading features which are to be found are as follows:

Practices

1 Recruitment agencies are used in the process of filling vacant positions of all sorts (clerical, professional/technical, managerial).
2 The Group 3 countries are characterised by the large number of methods they use in order to fill vacant professional/technical positions and by the low use of apprenticeship in order to fill vacant professional/technical and clerical positions.
3 France, Ireland, United Kingdom and the Netherlands are among the countries that have introduced the recruitment of foreigners more widely in order to find the people who are difficult to recruit in their home labour market.
4 Line management and the HR department are responsible for recruitment and selection issues, the line managers being supportive of HR department. Line managers rarely hold the sole responsibility for recruitment and selection issues.

Policies

The determination of recruitment and selection policies is done most of the time at the site/ establishment level and not at the national level.

Group 4 (Spain, Portugal, Turkey)

The leading features which are to be found are as follows:

Practices

1 What mainly characterises the organisations in this group is their difficulty in hiring technicians, IT professionals and people speaking foreign languages.
2 In order to facilitate the recruitment of scarce skills, they have introduced measures related to flexible working practices – flexitime, part-time – less than in any of the other countries but have largely introduced all the other possible measures suggested in the questionnaire i.e. relaxed qualifications requirements, relaxed age requirements, training for new employees, retraining for existing employees, increased pay and benefits, relocation of the organisation.
3 The staffing requirements are planned for the next year or even for a shorter length of time.
4 The southern countries are among the ones that use the least internal advertising to fill vacancies of all sorts.

5 Line management and the HR department are responsible for recruitment and selection issues, the line managers being supportive of HR department.

Policies

The determination of recruitment and selection policies is more than anywhere located at the national level and less than anywhere else located at the subsidiary level.

NOTES

1 We would like to thank J. H. Chauchat, Maître de Conférences, Université Lumière Lyon 2 and Professeur au Groupe ESC Lyon, for his help with the statistical part of our work and for his patience.
2 A CNPF survey points out that around 500,000 jobs are vacant in France. Even if French companies have less recruitment problems than in the previous years, 1 company out of 4 mentions difficulties to hire, in *L'Entreprise*, 85, November 1992.
3 Amado (1992) also strongly criticises the validity of graphology calling it a regressive and magic practice.

REFERENCES

Amado, G. and Deumic, C. (1991) 'Pratiques magiques et régressives en Gestion des Ressources Humaines', *Revue de Gestion des Ressources Humaines*, 1 (7): 16–27.
Barsoux, J. L. and Lawrence, P. (1990) *Management in France*, London: Cassell.
Benayoun, J. L. (1990) *Les Ressources Humaines en Europe*, Paris: HCE.
Benzecri, J. P. (1976) *L'analyse des données*, tomes 1 et 2, Paris: Dunod.
Bertin, J. (1973) *Sémiologie graphique*, Mouton: Gauthier-Villars, Pais La Haye (2nd edn).
Bertin, J. (1977) *Le graphique et le traitement graphique del'information*, Paris: Flammarion.
Bertin, J. (1981) *Graphics and Graphic Information Processing*, New York: Walter de Gruyter.
Bertin, J. (1983) *Semiology of Graphics: Diagrams, Network, Maps*, Wisconsin: University of Wisconsin.
Bournois, F. and Brewster, C. (1991) 'A European perspective on human resource management', *Personnel Review* 20(6): 4–13.
Bournois, F., Duval-Hamel J., Torchy V. and Tyson, S. (1993) *Glossaire Français–Anglais–Allemand du Management des Ressources Humaines*, Paris: Editions Eyrolles.
Bournois, F. and Torchy, V. (1992) 'Human resources management in financial services organisations: France and Britain compared', *European Management Journal* 10(3): 315–26.
Bournois, F. and Versaevel, B. (1993) 'Gestion stratégique des ressources humaines: une approche contingente à travers une typologie des grandes entreprises françaises', *Gestion 2000*, autumn: 33–58.
Brewster, C. and Holt Larsen, H. (1992) 'Human resource management in Europe: evidence from ten countries', *International Journal of Human Resource Management* 3 (3): 409–34.
Chauchat, J. H. and Risson, A. (1993) *Optimiser la représentation graphique des données: Tabview, un nouveau logiciel graphique combinant technique de J. Bertin et analyse de données*, LESA, Université Lumière Lyon 2.
Courpasson, D. and Sarnin, P. (1990) Scales of prestige and regulations in organisations', XIIth World Congress of Sociology, Madrid, 9–13 July.

Dany, F. (1991) 'L'évolution du marché de l'emploi cadre: les parcours professionnels des personnels qualifiés dans les trois années à venir', *Rapport IRE*, July.

Dany, F. (1992) 'Le coût du recruitment', *Document IRE* October.

Dany, F. (1993) 'Jeunes diplômés: pour de nouvelles pratiques de gestion des carrières', *Stratégies Ressources Humaines* 5 (spring): 14–23.

Filella, J. (1991) 'Is there a Latin model of human resource management?', *Personnel Review* 20(6): 14–23.

Handy, C., Gordon, C., Gow, I. and Randlesome, C. (1987) *The Making of Managers*, London: Pitman.

Hofstede, G. (1983) 'The cultural relativity of organisational practices and theories', *Journal of International Business Studies*, Fall: 75–89.

D'Iribarne, P. (1985) 'La Gestion à la française', *Revue française de Gestion* Jan.–Feb.: 5–13.

D'Iribarne, A. (1989) *La compétitivité, Défi social, enjeu éducatif*, Paris: Presse du CNRS.

Levy-Leboyer, C., (1990) *Evaluation du Personnel: quelles méthodes choisir?*, Paris: Editions d'Organisation.

Levy-Leboyer, C. (1991) Introduction à la *Revue Européenne de Psychologie Appliquée* 1(41): 5–8.

Mackay, L. and Torrington, D. (1986) *The Changing Nature of Personnel Management*, London: IPM.

Maurice, M. Sellier, F. and Silvester, J. J. (1982) *Politique d'Education et Organisation Industrielle en France et en Allemagne* Paris.

Smith, J. M. (1991) 'Recruitment and selection in the UK with some data on Norway', *Revue Européenne de Psychologie Appliquée*, 1: 27–34.

Smith, J. M. and Robertson, I. (1986) *The Theory and Practice of Scientific Staff Selection*,

Thurley, K. and Wirdenius, H. (1991) 'Will management become European?', *European Management Journal* 9(2): 127–34.

Tixier, M. (1987) 'Cultures nationales et Recutement', *Revue française de Gestion*, Sept.–Oct.: 59–68.

Torchy, V. (1992) 'La gestion et la détection des cadres à potentiel', *Document de Recherche, Département Management et Ressources Humaines*, Groupe ESC Lyon.

Ward, J. (1963) 'Hierarchical grouping to optimise an objective function', *Journal of American Statistical Association* 58: 236–4.

Weiss, D. (1988) *La Fonction Ressources Humaines*, Paris: Editions d'organisation.

Chapter 6

European experiments with pay and benefits policies

Jaime Filella and Ariane Hegewisch

INTRODUCTION

The equitable distribution of the benefits accruing to a firm from its successful performance within a market has been a perennial organisational problem. Capital, labour, management, competent technicians and professionals, administrators, adequate technology, energy, raw materials, have all contributed in some measure to the overall success of a firm in a society. It is but just that each should claim some share in the benefits obtained. Few would call this into question. The problem arises when an attempt is made to determine how much and in what way such benefits should be shared.

Originally, in the heyday of unrestrained capitalism, the relation between employer and employee was considered to be an economic contract; and indeed, it is. Gradually, however, in the course of this century, it has been explicitly recognised that individual people and organisations, large or small, have more at stake than a salary or a fair wage. Devoted workers contribute much more than can be equitably returned through a pay cheque; likewise, a dynamic organisation gives much more to the employees than the assurance of an hourly wage or a monthly salary.

At present, two fairly obvious conclusions seem clear: (1) that most people work for more than just money; and (2) that monetary rewards must be and will remain an integral and substantial part of what is to be distributed. Pay has always held a central position in any type of reward package.

In the present socio-economic system, organised work is the most common and, for most people, the only way in which they can earn their living. There is a value shared by most Europeans, that people have to *earn* their living. Such sentiments for example are expressed in the European Community Charter of the Fundamental Social Rights of

Workers (Title I, No. 5) which states that people must 'be assured of an equitable wage, i.e. a wage sufficient to enable them to have a decent standard of living' even if this must be read more like a programme for social cohesion in the face of potentially countervailing forces as a result of the completion of the Single European Market (Fina Sanglas 1992). Equity is also the issue in the only other area where European Community legislation deals with the field of remuneration, namely the equity between men's and women's pay, as expressed in Article 119 of the Treaty of Rome and several Directives since (see also chapter on equal opportunity policies).

However a brief comparison of pay distribution across Europe shows how diverse patterns and practices continue to be, not least as expressed in the reaction of policy makers in different EC member states to the principles expressed in the Social Charter. An examination of pay patterns across Europe shows wide differences in earnings dispersion for example with, in general, incomes differentials being smaller in the Scandinavian countries than in other parts of Europe (even if European countries display much greater regional similarity to each other than to Japan or the US for example) (Rowthorn 1992: 506). This also applies to the persistent gap between men's and women's wages – ranging from around 10 per cent in Denmark to over 30 per cent in the United Kingdom (IDS 1992a). Such differences cannot be reduced to varying industry structures across Europe. According to a study of earnings differentials in eight European Community countries in the late 1970s the impact on earning distributions of factors such as occupational qualifications, length of service or sex differed substantially between countries as did remuneration hierarchies in relation to manual and non-manual work (CERC 1988). The impact of these factors appears to be relatively constant over time, although the lack of more recent data makes it impossible to see whether there has been a greater trend towards convergence during the last decade. A similar lack of uniform relationships arises when examining the impact of bargaining structures on pay equality; as a general finding countries with highly centralised bargaining structures generally display greater wage equality than those where bargaining is fragmented. However Austria, a country with similarly centralised bargaining structures to the Scandinavian countries, shows one of the highest earning differentials in Europe: social and political pressures for narrower differentials went hand in hand with the development of centralised bargaining in Scandinavia but never did in Austria (Rowthorn 1992: 508). This highlights the 'strength of national specificity in the arrangements for managing and working' in Europe (Lane 1989: 292) and the persistent influence of cultural and institutional factors on outcomes in the pay field.

There is however in Europe, compared to other geographical areas, greater regulation and institutionalisation of pay bargaining. Most countries have some system of setting a wage floor, either directly through the fixing of minimum wages such as in Belgium, France, Greece, the Netherlands or Portugal, or indirectly by extending collective agreements to all workers in an industry or by legislating for quasi bargaining institutions in industries which are traditionally low paid and where it is traditionally difficult for workers to organise collectively, as in Ireland (Pond 1991; Brewster *et al.* 1992; IDS/ IPM 1992). There are also common historical trends across Europe, even if detailed outcomes vary. The 1960s and 1970s for example were characterised by trends for standardisation of pay structures, with an emphasis on grading structures and collectively agreed pay rates rather than individual bargaining. High inflation levels in several countries led to government intervention and (hotly contested) attempts to introduce incomes policies. Overall these years were a period in which differentials were flattened rather than widened (Marsden and Silvestre 1992).

During the 1980s and 1990s debates have increasingly been dominated by pressure for greater wage individualisation in order to improve economic efficiency and the functioning of labour markets. At the macro-economic level the arguments for greater wage individualisation linked into debates on the need for labour market flexibility with the argument that there was a strong causal link between unemployment and labour market rigidities. Of course such arguments remain heavily debated. There is evidence that countries with centralised bargaining systems and/or coordinated industrial relations systems have a better pay/jobs relationship than decentralised countries (Layard 1990; Soskice 1990; Dell'Aringa 1992). Oswald has argued that 'the existence of a going rate of pay is an important part of an efficiently functioning market economy' (1992: 6). Perhaps in practice the greater impetus to pay individualisation came in response to skill shortages in the second half of the 1980s rather than to unemployment earlier. Reasons for this changing climate are various: reflecting a move away from Fordist mass production type of economies, towards greater emphasis on knowledge based jobs, creativity and individual initiative and flexibility (although the extent of the 'decline of Fordism' remains debated, see, for example, Tolliday and Zeitlin 1992; Curry 1993); political changes, with a shift towards generally more conservative governments in Europe; and a shifting distribution of power between management and trade unions as a result of the recession.

These changes have also found their expression at the more micro level: our focus here. In the management literature in particular there has been a renewed emphasis on linking pay to performance. James (1989) notes a radical social-cultural change in favour of three interrelated trends: individual salary increases, merit/performance related pay and variability (both up and downwards) in pay rewards. Others, such as the director of employment of the Confederation of British Industries, argue that 'the vital link between pay and performance (productivity and profits) can best be made down the line while local managers are best placed to size up relevant labour market conditions' (Gilbert 1991: 1). Such policy prescriptions clearly have implications not only for trade union and bargaining structures but also for corporate control of pay outcomes, and for the relation of employees to line managers and to each other.

The aim of this chapter is to examine how far pressures towards individualisation and decentralisation of pay have been taken up at the organisational level across Europe. We begin by considering how far national or industry-wide pay agreements continue to be the norm and how far there has been a decentralisation. We will then examine the current levels of centralisation or decentralisation of pay policy decisions within organisations. Finally we take up the issue of variable and performance related pay. We draw on longitudinal data for those countries (France, Germany, Spain, Sweden and the United Kingdom) where developments were surveyed in three consecutive years.

LEVELS OF PAY DETERMINATION

Having argued that the last decade has seen greater emphasis on the decentralisation of pay bargaining the survey explored the levels at which pay bargaining takes place. (We did not ask respondents to assess the importance of the different levels.) A number of common trends emerge. As expected, the likelihood of national or industry wide bargaining in all countries apart from France increases as one moves down the organisational hierarchy from management to manual workers (Appendix III Table 4.1a to 4.1d). In France over a third of employers refer to national bargaining for managerial staff but only a quarter for manual staff – an expression of the continued importance of relatively rigid pay progression among managers based on age, educational background and length of service (IDS Focus 1989; Handy *et al.* 1988; Gordon 1993).

The results also show that regional bargaining, apart from Norway and Spain, is only used by a small minority of organisations. The Spanish results might reflect regional policy in Spain in so far as it grants a 25 per cent bonus for people living in the North African enclaves of Ceuta and Melilla, or in the outlying provinces of the Canary and the Balearic islands. Official Spanish statistics further suggest that, in terms of employees covered, regional sectoral bargaining is more important, covering just under 4 million workers, compared to 1.6 million workers covered by national sector agreements (Martinez Lucio 1992: 509). Regional bargaining is of course also an integral institutional part of the German industrial relations system; however given that levels of bargaining are much more circumscribed for organisations in Germany than elsewhere, leaving little formal choice once an organisation is part of the employers federation, the question about levels of bargaining was not included in the German questionnaire.

Another common theme across all countries where sufficient data exists is that national or industry-wide bargaining is more common in the public sector than in the private sector (with the notable exception of Sweden where private sector non-managerial employees are more likely to be covered by national bargaining than their counterparts in the public sector). Regarding the public sector, at least for the pay of manual workers, between 6 and 9 out of 10 employers across the sample negotiate at national or industry level. Given that much public sector reform has been targeted at cost reductions and budget controls it is perhaps not surprising that at least in the central European countries in the survey bargaining continues to be relatively centralised. However, there have been some trends towards decentralisation, particularly in the Nordic countries (Gustaffson 1990; Wise 1993) and the British Government, in its recent White Paper 'People, jobs and opportunities' stresses its determination to increase the move away from nationalised bargaining during the 1990s (IDS 1992b). A look at multi-employer bargaining in the private sector shows much greater diversity across countries. Details of bargaining levels are given in Appendix III Tables 4.1a to 4.1d. Since they show that bargaining levels are most likely to be above the organisational level for manual workers, and since much of the literature addresses bargaining levels in the private sector, the remainder of this section on bargaining levels concentrates upon manual workers in private sector organisations.

Multi-employer bargaining for private sector manual employees

Multi-employer bargaining at national or industry level is least common in France and the United Kingdom (with less than a quarter of employers involved); in the more southern economies of Portugal, Turkey and Spain between 4 and 5 out of 10 employers bargain at

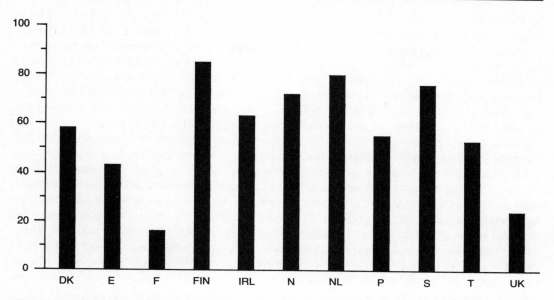

Figure 6.1 National/industry level negotiations for manual workers in the private sector (% of organisations)

this level whereas in the Nordic countries, Ireland and the Netherlands it involves between 6 and 8 out of 10 employers (see Figure 6.1).

In France and the United Kingdom, employers federations have been actively involved in trying to shift negotiations away from the national level (Shonfield 1992). In France for example the employers federation CNPF in 1984 made a policy decision to discontinue the issuing of central pay guidelines and similar policies were followed by industry based employers federations, such as the one for engineering (IDS Focus 1989). Employers' associations in the United Kingdom were not quite as interventionist, but there was a clear overall trend and one that was strongly supported by exhortation from Government. In the United Kingdom over the three years of the survey the number of private sector employers being involved in national or industry-wide negotiations for manual workers fell from 28 per cent to 12 per cent; the same however does not hold in France where no clear trend can be observed (Hegewisch 1991; 1992).

The move away from multi-employer bargaining has been much less marked in the Nordic countries, Ireland or the Netherlands. The results in the Scandinavian countries however mask some decentralisation from national central to industry-wide bargaining. Employers' federations in Sweden also argued that the existing system of national bargaining was too inflexible, that greater account needed to be taken of variations in productivity, labour requirements and export sensitivity of different industries. This approach was paralleled by the strategies of some of the skilled workers unions which were arguing for greater skill differentials. However, the old patterns of national bargaining have been rather resilient, and instead of showing a clear trend developments have been described as a 'continual see-sawing between centralised and industry bargaining' (Ferner and Hyman 1992: xxi). In Denmark the combination of a Conservative Government for much of the last decade with high levels of unemployment compared to the other Nordic countries has led to a greater weakening of central bargaining structures for white and blue collar unions and a more consistent trend towards industry or even company level bargaining (IDS/ IPM 1992). Ireland's traditionally centralised collective bargaining system has seen little movement towards decentralisation during the last decade (Prondzynsky 1992: 71), whereas, according to Visser (1992: 351) the persistently high level of national/ industry-wide bargaining in the Netherlands masks greater scope and flexibility for adjusting these at firm level. Thus similar levels of national/industry-wide bargaining are the outcome of quite different practices and developments during the last decade.

Developments are rather reversed in the remaining southern group of countries where democratic Governments have only comparatively recently encouraged the development of such centralised structures. In Spain for example, the number of organisations referring to multi-employer collective agreements have increased, from 32 per cent of organisations in the 1990 survey to 43 per cent in 1992 negotiating manual workers pay at the national level, thus continuing a trend towards centralisation of bargaining observed for the 1980s (Martinez Lucio 1992). In Portugal too the growth of multi-employer bargaining has been more recent, although the actual impact on working conditions and pay of employees is debated (Barreto 1992).

Company level and plant bargaining for manual workers

The survey shows that centralisation does not preclude bargaining at company level, indeed, the integration of different levels of bargaining is a formal part of some industrial relations systems. Thus company level bargaining is a significant part of most bargaining systems (Appendix III Table 4.1d). It is only in Denmark that this level of pay determination is virtually irrelevant. Denmark is interesting too in so far as the public sector has moved further in this direction than private sector employers. In Finland, France and Sweden negotiations at company level are clearly complementary to national/industry level negotiations; the likelihood of a private sector organisation negotiating at national level is not lower for companies who have company level arrangements than for those who do not. In Portugal, Spain, Turkey and the United Kingdom company level bargaining is more clearly a substitute for bargaining at higher levels. This is particularly so in the United Kingdom where companies bargaining at company level are less than half as likely as other private sector employers to also make reference to national or industry-wide wage determination.

In general pay determination at plant level is less likely than at company level, with the exception of the Netherlands and the United Kingdom (where equal numbers engage in them), and Finland (where they are more likely than company level negotiations). Plant level negotiations in the public sector continue to be rare. Whereas in Spain there has been a slight fall in the share of private sector employers negotiating at this level, from 26 per cent in 1990 to 18 per cent in 1992, the United Kingdom has seen an increase (from 29 per cent to 38 per cent during the same period), neither France nor Sweden have shown much change.

While national bargaining is generally more common among larger employers, size differences are much less in relation to company or plant bargaining. There is no systematic relationship between organisational size and levels of bargaining across countries (Appendix III Table 4.1d).

The proponents of plant and company level bargaining suggest that 'it can represent a deepening of the bargaining relationship between employers and their workforces' and thus 'create[s] greater scope for a more cooperative approach to employee relations'. (Hara *et al*. 1992: 198). The major reasons for the decentralisation of pay bargaining, according to a study of large British companies, were to gain more control over bargaining outcomes than was felt to be available with industry bargaining and to integrate pay bargaining with newly decentralised corporate structures (Walsh 1992). Increased cooperation between management and employees did not play a role; however, the ability to use pay bargaining at local level to 'buy' changes in working practices was rated highly. Decentralisation of bargaining to local levels puts heavy pressure on trade unions. They either have to put more officials into bargaining at a time when union membership in many countries, particularly those with high levels of establishment bargaining, has been falling; or rely on more local lay officials, with a consequent increase in the demand for training and research. However, employers found unions to be quick to adapt to the new situation in order to secure better deals for their members.

CORPORATE DECISION MAKING ON PAY POLICIES

The locus of responsibility for major policy decisions within corporations has, for the countries which have been surveyed over three consecutive years, remained virtually unchanged. This might of course hide a changing degree of flexibility within centrally issued guidelines over the period. Not surprisingly, given their direct budgetary impact, pay policy decisions are more likely to be made at national or international headquarter level than policy decisions in other areas of personnel management (see Chapter 4). Portugal, Spain and Turkey show the greatest proportion of organisations with pay policies being decided at national or international headquarters; by 8 out of 10 private employers (Appendix III Table 2.5a) (see Figure 6.2). This finding suggests the compound effect of two factors. There are the three economically weakest nations in the survey and a higher proportion of their large companies are multinationals with headquarters outside their territory.

In five of the countries in the study in 1992, Finland, Germany, Ireland, Norway and the United Kingdom the number of organisations where decision making is decentralised to below headquarters level involves more than 40 per cent of employers. In Finland, Germany and Norway this is likely to be an expression of the existing consultation and codetermination arrangements where the implementation of central framework agreements are negotiated locally. Bargaining at this level in the Scandinavian countries indeed is a major source of 'wage drift' and can effectively account for as much as half of the increases during the pay period (Ahlén 1989: 337; Johnson and Lange 1992: 421). Only in the United Kingdom is the localisation of decision making paralleled by a decentralisation of bargaining. Policy making has not been pushed down the system to the same extent as bargaining; in 4 out of 10 private sector organisations where pay for manual workers is determined at site level, pay policy decisions have been devolved to this level, too.

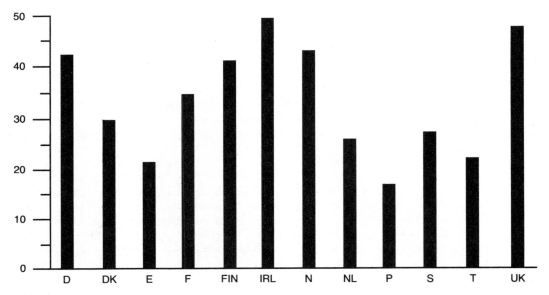

Figure 6.2 Decentralisation of pay policies to subsidiary or site/establishment level within the private sector (% of organisations)

The question of course is how real this decentralisation of bargaining decisions has been. Research from the United Kingdom in the 1980s suggests that, given continued headquarter control over bargaining outcomes, what we observe is 'establishment illusion' (Marginson *et al.* 1988: 251), with managers both in the corporate and local level drawing some benefits from an impression of establishment autonomy as a means of deflecting and managing trade union demands in the bargaining situation (Kinnie 1989: 32). At least some companies have reacted to the problems of decentralisation by reinforcing central guidelines and limits on the type of deals that could be negotiated (Walsh 1992: 10–11). The recession, and with it the need for tighter budgetary controls, also resulted in some recentralisation of policies. However, as we have pointed out elsewhere (Hegewisch 1991: 31), our survey findings reflect the assessment of trends by personnel managers at the highest corporate level who have less incentive than line managers to overestimate the level of decentralisation of decision making than plant managers and indeed, according to Marginson *et al.* (1988), were generally more likely to see decision making as centralised. The results cited here therefore are likely to reflect a real increase in decentralisation.

VARIABLE PAY

The last decade has not only seen a challenge to centralised bargaining structures but within these a push for greater flexibility of pay grades and structures. This is most directly evidenced by the number of organisations in the sample who increased the share of variable pay in the total reward package during the last three years, with hardly any organisations moving away from variable pay elements (Appendix III Table 4.a). Of course this common trend takes place against a widely differing base line of pay practices which influence the extent and definitions of variable pay in each country. Nevertheless, the fact that employers in Germany, Sweden and the United Kingdom appear to be moving in the same direction in spite of these differences makes the development even more remarkable.

Variable pay and labour market shortages

Variable pay increases are most widely spread in Portugal, with over two-thirds of employers having increased its share in the pay package. The fragmented nature of pay bargaining in Portugal arguably facilitates such processes; more importantly there has been an intense competition for staff, with labour shortages particularly acute in managerial and professional jobs and low levels of unemployment (IDS/IPM 1992: 193). Under such circumstances variable pay, the ability to react flexibly to demands by individual employees or applicants, becomes an important instrument in recruitment and retention. Indeed almost as many Portuguese organisations as have increased variable pay use the increased offer of pay and benefits in their recruitment campaigns, by far the highest level in the survey (Appendix III Table 3.2).

Least change in this area can be seen in Ireland, with less than a third of employers having moved towards variable pay, or responding to recruitment problems with higher pay levels. Pay increases in Ireland are circumscribed by the Program for Economic and Social Progress (PESP) which, for 1992, limited basic pay rises to 3 per cent (Gunnigle 1992); having a relatively well functioning incomes policy probably makes Ireland rather untypical in the general survey. This has not prevented some increase of variable pay, leading to the growth of earnings outstripping basic pay increases (IDS/IPM 1992: 137); with high birth rates, high rates of unemployment and a proportionately high number of graduates, labour market pressures have been more muted than elsewhere. Nevertheless, recruiters from other countries have began to turn to Irish graduates, and together with a long standing tradition of emigration, this has led to shortages in some areas (Gunnigle 1992: 281), leading employers to search for flexibility in the generally tight framework of PESP.

Such a correspondence between increases in variable pay and the offer of increased pay and benefits in recruitment can also be found in Germany, France, Norway, Spain and the United Kingdom. However this link is not universal in the sample. In the remaining Nordic countries and in Turkey a much higher share of organisations have increased variable pay than use pay increases as recruitment incentives. These are the countries in the survey with the highest share of organisations without recruitment problems (Appendix III Table 3.1). The continued increase of variable pay elements under such circumstances is perhaps an indication of more fundamental changes in the payment systems in those countries there.

The gradual fall in the number of firms reporting more variable pay in the total reward package and the steady increase of those reporting 'no change' shows an attitude of greater caution in 1992 than 1990 and suggests a sensitivity to the state of the labour market. In 1990 when unemployment in Sweden was below 2 per cent over 8 out of 10 Swedish employers had increased variable pay in the previous three years. By 1992, when the number of employers experiencing no recruitment problems had reached 60 per cent (doubling since the previous year) the proportion of organisations increasing variable pay had fallen to less than half. The change in Sweden may also reflect the impact of the Rehnberg Commission in 1991, 'which controls all pay negotiations in the country on behalf of the government' (Söderström and Syrén 1992: 509). (In so far as the question assesses developments in the previous three years, thus still covering the boom period, it is of course likely to be an overestimation of current activities.) France, the United Kingdom and, to a lesser extent, Spain have also seen a drop in the number of organisations having increased variable pay over the period, though not as steep as in the Swedish case. In Germany on the other hand there has been little change during the three years of the survey.

Variable non-monetary benefits

Flexibility in remuneration in response to recruitment problems extends also to non-monetary benefits. However by and large organisations are significantly less likely to have increased the share of fringe benefits in compensation packages (Figure 6.3). The largest differences in the preference for increased variable monetary over non-monetary rewards are observed in the Scandinavian countries and in France, which overall has the lowest change in benefit policies, an indication of the continued preference for hard cash in the French reward culture. Organisations in the Anglo-Germanic countries of central Europe tend to have more balanced policies in the total compensation package, between financial and non-financial rewards, more than organisations in Latin and Scandinavian countries.

  The evidence on non-monetary rewards confirms the cautionary trend over the three years of the survey observed in the case of variable pay: again proportionately fewer organisations say in 1992 that variable non-monetary benefits are increasing in relation to

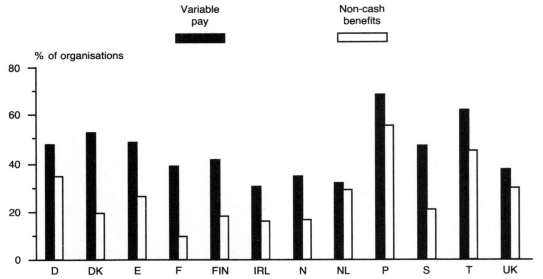

Figure 6.3 Increases in variable pay and non-cash benefits during the last three years (% of organisations)

other components in the total pay package than three years earlier. Here France joins Germany in being remarkably consistent over the period. Both countries show no difference in the proportions of organisatons indicating an increase or decrease or no change in the importance of non-monetary benefits in rewarding employees. On the other hand, the United Kingdom, Spain and Sweden note a trend indicating that fewer organisations offer such increases and more firms make 'no changes'.

INCENTIVE PAY

The survey in particular investigated the uptake of the following policies covered by general changes in 'variable pay': organisation level incentive schemes such as profit sharing and share options; individual and group bonus schemes; and merit or performance related pay.

Financial participation and profit sharing

One of the few areas where the European Community is attempting to influence practice in the remuneration area is on schemes for financial participation and profit sharing. In July 1991 the Commission issued a draft recommendation that member states should introduce legal and tax incentives, encouraging organisation level incentive schemes which are 'as close as possible to the employee and the enterprise'; it also sets out general principles such as the need to guard against payouts substituting for basic pay increases or the need to protect individual employees from compulsory membership in schemes. Overall however the recommendation 'refrains from efforts to harmonise national variants or reduce the existing diversity' (IDS/IPM 1992: xxvi). The moderate foray of the Community into this area is probably at least partly due to two rather distinct ideological origins of the organisation level financial participation debates. On the one hand this is promoted as a means of giving employees greater involvement, commitment and influence over key employer decisions, on the other as a means of binding employees more closely into the economic rationale of the individual company. Despite these arguments there is little hard evidence that financial participation and profit sharing achieve that objective. The Commission's own investigation of schemes in membership countries, the PEPPER Report (Commission of the EC 1991) for example, could not find 'overwhelming evidence of strong advantages'. A study of profit sharing schemes in British companies which investigated their impact on a range of factors from employee motivation to work performance concluded: 'On balance, however, there appeared to have been no widespread change in productivity and employee involvement practices stemming directly from the introduction of schemes' (Poole and Jenkins 1988: 32). The same study however found some positive impact on communication and employee satisfaction.

In view of this the low uptake of profit sharing or employee share option schemes in most European countries is perhaps not surprising. France is the only country with a persistently high uptake, across all staff groups, of profit sharing (Appendix III Tables 4.3a to 4.3d). Profit sharing (*interessement*) is a legal obligation on French companies with more than fifty employees and is designed (or at least intended) to prevent its use as a substitute for annually negotiated basic pay increases. (The fact that only 75 per cent of French private sector companies in the sample profess to have such schemes is an indication of rather loose compliance in the field of employment legislation in France; see also Chapter 12 on equal opportunities.)

The only other country where profit sharing is widely employed is Germany, where 6 out of 10 employers use it as part of managerial remuneration; for other staff groups the uptake in Germany, too, is much lower. One possible explanation for this is the predominance of medium size owner-managed companies with a long tradition of financial participation for senior managers (even if by now there is no difference in uptake between smaller and larger firms). While profit sharing in the Netherlands is not as widespread it is also comparatively popular with 3 out of 10 organisations offering it to all staff groups (and slightly more to managerial and professional staff) and is often introduced as part of collective agreements (hence its greater spread across staff groups). According to IDS/IPM (1992: 187) there is no uniform definition of what profit sharing in the Netherlands entails, with 'a number of company payments bearing no actual relationship to profits'. In the United Kingdom where profit sharing has received considerable attention in the last decade it nevertheless has not been introduced in more than a quarter of private sector organisations. In the remaining countries it applies to 1 in 8 or less employers.

Employee share options are even less widespread. In the United Kingdom almost 4 out of 10 employers provide these to managers, and almost 3 out of 10 in Ireland but much less elsewhere (Appendix III Tables 4.3a to 4.3d).

Individual and group bonus schemes

It is difficult to discern a clear pattern in the spread of bonus schemes across countries (Appendix III Tables 4.3a to 4.3d). We compared for example the uptake of individual bonus schemes with that of group bonus schemes (with much management literature in the 1980s promoting the latter as part of a greater emphasis on team working) (Table 6.1). In all countries (apart from Norway where the uptake of schemes in this area is very low) managerial staff are more likely to be in receipt of individual incentive than group incentive schemes; a less clear trend emerges for professional and technical workers although on balance across the countries they too are more likely to be covered by individual schemes. Clerical workers are most likely not to be covered at all, without any clear patterns for those countries where there is a significant uptake of schemes. And the pattern for manual workers is spread equally between a predominance of individual schemes, of group schemes and of an equal uptake of both.

Turning to geographic comparisons, in Germany and the Netherlands there is a clear preference for individual bonus schemes, and many more organisations than in the other countries make use of incentive schemes generally. Everywhere else the pattern is mixed. The introduction of either type of schemes, particularly for lower staff groups, is comparatively low in the Mediterranean countries in the survey – France, Portugal, Spain and Turkey, confirming the country cluster suggested in Filella (1991). But also in Sweden which makes much less use of incentive schemes than other Scandinavian countries. In line

Table 6.1 Individual vs group bonus: a comparison of uptake

Country	Managerial	Professional	Clerical	Manual
D	x	x	x	x
DK	x	x	=*	■
E	x	x	=*	=*
F*	x	x	n.a.	■
FIN	x	=	■	■
IRL	x	x	=	=
N	=	=	■	■
NL	x	x	x	x
P	x	x	=*	=
S	x	■	■	x*
T	x	x	=*	=
UK	x	x	■	■

Notes: Legend:
x   – Uptake of individual bonus schemes higher than of group bonus schemes
■   – Uptake of group bonus schemes higher than of individual bonus
=   – No or only small difference
*   – Less than 10 per cent of organisations have introduced either scheme
F* – French data from 1990; no separate data on clerical and professional staff

with common perceptions of the emphasis on group work Scandinavian countries make more use of group bonus: so does the United Kingdom.

Comparing trends over the three years of the survey, in the United Kingdom the uptake of both group and individual scheme for manual workers has marginally declined; in Germany the reverse has been true (for individual schemes, there is no discernible trend for group schemes). The British results confirm other research in this area; a study for the British Institute of Personnel Management for example found few new schemes had been introduced during the 1980s (Cannell and Long 1991). Where companies are moving away from schemes they gave as reasons that individual bonus and piece work encouraged employees to value quantity over quality, that it penalised skills (in so far as supervisors tend to give more difficult time consuming work to the more skilled workers who will not be adequately compensated), that schemes do not encourage initiative and often are accompanied by an inordinate amount of bureaucracy. Those organisations who abandoned individual piece work schemes for a move to cellular or team work found that in order for these changes to be successful they had to be accompanied by a range of other measures indicating a culture change or otherwise 'be doomed to failure', in the words of one British personnel director (Cannell and Long 1991: 59). However, a consistent minority are clearly keeping schemes and revising and updating them.

Performance related pay

Maybe the most interesting development in the area of variable pay is merit and performance related pay, not only because it tends to be more widely spread than other forms of variable pay (Appendix III Table 4.3a to 4.3d). The introduction of performance related pay presents a change (or at least an attempt to change) perceptions of fairness in remuneration – from reference to objective job related grading structures with an emphasis on seniority and general criteria such as qualification to reward on the basis of (mostly) individual performance (Murlis and Wright 1993: 6), a move towards a new *Leistungsgerechtigkeit* (justice of performance) (Lehmann 1993: 604).

In almost all countries this form of remuneration is most widely used in the managerial and professional/technical staff group, with uptake lower for the other groups. However there are a few notable exceptions to this general pattern. In Germany for example managers are least likely among the four staff categories to be subject to performance related pay; it appears that against the background of a long standing tradition of profit sharing as part of managerial remuneration the use of formal performance related pay schemes has not found much acceptance. The comparatively high uptake for the other groups on the other hand is also a reflection of particular collective agreements; the collective agreement for the metal industry for example includes provisions for appraisal linked pay increases (incidentally including the precise appraisal form to be used, thus giving companies little formal scope to develop their own policies in the area). Sweden on the other hand is also atypical in having twice as many organisations where manual workers are covered by schemes than organisations covering any other staff group. To some extent this is a result of the translation; there are no clear equivalents to merit/performance related pay in all other European countries. In Sweden (and in Denmark) the translation more closely reads as 'individually negotiated pay' and in this context the Swedish results reflect wage drift at company level. The highest uptake of performance related pay can be found in Portugal where, moreover, there is little difference between staff groups in uptake. As we mentioned previously, Portugal was also the country with the highest proportion of countries increasing variable pay and using an increase in pay and benefits in response to recruitment difficulties, suggesting once again a link to recruitment problems. As a respondent in the British IPM study put it: 'The system [of performance related pay] is only partly designed to motivate, and partly to give flexibility for rewarding achievement and recognising market rates' (Cannell and Long 1991: 60).

The use of performance related pay as a means of reacting to labour market trends is also confirmed by studies in France where performance awards in Paris were consistently higher than in the rest of the country, suggesting that this is at least partly a response to the higher cost of living there (IDS Focus 1989). Performance-related pay ('individualisation') in France is widely used for all staff levels; Marsden (1989) suggests that the spread of this practice is at least partly a reaction to the flattening of differentials at the beginning of the decade.

However, the theory of performance related pay rarely mentions these more mundane reasons for its introduction, concentrating instead on the presumed beneficial effect on motivation and performance management as a result of the introduction of schemes (see, for example, Lehmann 1993). These treatments underestimate the practical difficulties in objective setting and assessment and the fact 'that it is easier to measure action than effectiveness' (Cannell and Long 1991: 63). Little concrete evidence moreover for a (positive) effect on motivation exists (see, for example, Cannell and Long 1991; Marsden and Richardson 1992; Guest 1993). In countries such as the United Kingdom the introduction of performance related pay was promoted very strongly by senior policy makers in the private and public sector; as Murlis and Wright (1993 p.6) put it 'in retrospect top management, be they ministers or directors of major companies, sought to translate a simplistic motivational view into the way employees were paid and managed'.

Whatever the motivational impact of performance related pay it changes the relationship between the employee and the supervisor, reinforcing hierarchical patterns of management; a related aspect is of course its disciplining effect on line managers themselves by forcing them to pay greater attention to performance management (Hegewisch 1991). The changing responsibilities of line managers have been reviewed more extensively elsewhere in this book (see Chapter 4). Here we would just like to say that in spite of the responsibility put on line managers for pay issues by policies such as performance related pay, compared to other policy areas their increase in responsiblity is rather limited (with the exception of Sweden) (Appendix III Table 2.7). This might be an indication that line managers, given the financial implications of pay decisions, remain executors rather than policy initiators in the area.

Finally, and relatedly, performance related pay has major implications for trade unions and workplace representation. The decentralisation of collective bargaining to local levels leaves employee representatives with a formal role, indeed their role might be strengthened in the process. Merit and performance related pay individualises bargaining to such an extent that the role of the trade union in bargaining can be almost completely marginalised to that of support for individual employees in appeals procedures.

CONCLUSION

The purpose of this chapter was to orient the reader in an area of great importance and complexity. Pay is and will most certainly continue to be a central issue in any reward package as long as we remain in a society where people work for their livelihood, and aim for a decent one at that. But the issue is a complex one, too, particularly considering its effect on motivation and cooperation at work.[1] Human resource management experts have much work to do in this area. It is to their credit, however, that some progress is being made and acknowledged.

There are real pressures for change in remuneration systems in Europe. A combination of demographic and structural changes, economic uncertainty and unemployment and government and employer action have weakened the trade unions. Increasing, and increasingly international, competition is putting pressure on labour expenditure. New ideas and new fashions are developing. It is little wonder, therefore, that our evidence shows considerable change in remuneration issues across Europe; however, it also shows some areas of stability.

Change is apparent in particular in the moves towards the decollectivisation of pay. This may not always involve pay determination outside of union influence – in fact that remains very much in the minority (see also Chapter 9). It does mean a move towards pay determination at a lower level, increased variability of pay and, indeed, in some cases individual pay determination. This is not a uniform development. There are examples in all countries of organisations moving against the trend and in some countries the proportions moving against the European trend outweigh those following it. There is also some evidence from out data that in some cases these movements reflect stages of the economic cycle. Overall, however there is a clear trend away from central, large group pay determination towards decentralised, variable and more individually related pay.

This broad general conclusion has to be set in the European context. There is stability as well as change. Different European countries retain nationally distinct preferences in the forms of pay variability that they are likely to embrace, reflecting national tax and legislative arrangements, industrial relations traditions and deeper cultural values. Furthermore, on a continent-wide basis it remains true that Europe is distinct in having so many organisations where important aspects of pay are set above the organisational level. The history of economic development in Europe shows that, far from being a bar to economic development, this may well be, as we noted some economists arguing, a key to it. In terms of pay determination, despite the variety in systems and practice, despite the overall trend towards decentralisation and variability, Europe remains a region of the world where centralised pay determination remains an important component of employee relations for most organisations.

NOTE

1 This is not the place to enter into a full discussion on the motivational value of pay. Deci (1985; Deci and Ryan 1985) with his views on intrinsic and extrinsic motivation and Adams (1965) with his equity theory have said very valuable things on the matter.

REFERENCES

Adams, J. S. (1965) 'Inequity in social exchange', in L. Berkowitz (ed.) *Advances in Experimental and Social Psychology*, Vol. 2, New York: Academic Press.

Ahlén, K. (1989) 'Swedish collective bargaining under pressure: inter-union rivalry and incomes policies', *British Journal of Industrial Relations*, 27(3): 330–46.

Andersen, T., Kamp, M. and Larsen, H. H. (1992) 'Denmark', in C. Brewster, A. Hegewisch, L. Holden and T. Lockhart, (eds) (1992) *The European Human Resource Management Guide*, London: Academic Press.

Barreto, J. (1992) 'Portugal: industrial relations under democracy', in A. Ferner and R. Hyman (eds) (1992) *Industrial Relations in the New Europe*, Oxford: Blackwell Publishers.

Brewster, C., Hegewisch, A., Holden, L. and Lockhart, T. (eds) (1992) *The European Human Resource Management Guide*, London: Academic Press.

Cannell, M. and Long, P. (1991) 'What's changed about incentive pay?', *Personnel Management* October: 58–63.

CERC (1988) *Les structure de salaires dans la Communaute Economique Européenne*, Document du Centre d' Etude de Revenus et de Coûts no. 91, 4th trimestre, CERC, Paris.

Commission of the European Communities (1991) 'The Pepper Report: promotion of employee participation and enterprise results', *Social Europe*, Supplement 3/91.

Curry, J. (1993) 'The flexibility fetish: a review essay on flexible specialisations', *Capital and Class* 50 (summer): 99–126.

Deci, E. (1976). *Intrinsic motivation*. New York: Plenum Press.

Deci, E. L. and Ryan, R. M. (1985) *Intrinsic Motivation and Self-determination in Human Behaviour*, New York and London: Plenum Press.

Dell'Aringa, C. (1992) 'Industrial relations and the role of the state in EEC countries', in D. Marsden, (ed) (1992) *Pay and Employment in the New Europe*, Aldershot: Edward Elgar.

Ferner, A. and Hyman, R. (eds) (1992) *Industrial Relations in the New Europe*, Oxford: Blackwell.

Filella, J. (1991) 'Is there a Latin model in the management of human resources?', *Personnel Review* 20(6): 14–23.

Fina Sanglas, L. (1992) Preface, in D. Marsden (ed) (1992) *Pay and Employment in the New Europe*, Aldershot: Edward Elgar.

Gilbert, R. (1991) 'Pay bargaining in the UK – new approach needed?', mimeo, London: CBI.

Gordon, C. (1993) 'The business culture in France', in C. Randlesome *et al*. (1993) *Business Culture in Europe*, Oxford: Heinemann Professional Publishing (2nd edn).

Guest, D. (1993) 'Current perspectives on human resource management in the United Kingdom', in A. Hegewisch and C. Brewster (eds) (1993) *European Developments in Human Resource Management*, London: Kogan Page.

Gunnigle, P. (1992) 'Ireland', in C. Brewster, A. Hegewisch, L. Holden, and T. Lockhart, (eds) (1992) *The European Human Resource Management Guide*, London: Academic Press.

Gustaffson, L. (1990) 'Promoting flexibility through pay policies – experiences from the Swedish national administration', in OECD (1990) *Flexible Personnel Management in the Public Services*, Paris: OECD.

Handy, C., Gordon, C., Gow, I. and Randlesome, C (1988) *Making Managers*, London: Pitman.

Hara, R., Marsden, D. and Morin, J. (1992) 'Conclusion: pay policies for the Single European Market', in D. Marsden (ed.) (1992) *Pay and Employment in the New Europe* Aldershot: Edward Elgar.

Hegewisch, A. (1991) 'The decentralisation of pay bargaining: European comparisons'. *Personnel Review* 20(6): 28–35.

Hegewisch, A. (1992) 'European comparisons in reward policies: the findings of the first Price Waterhouse Cranfield Survey', in Public Finance Foundation (1992) *Public Sector Pay*, PPF discussion paper no. 43, London.

Income Data Service (IDS) (1992a) 'Equal pay–a distant goal?', *IDS European Report* 371 (November): I–VIII.

Income Data Service (IDS) (1992b) 'Local pay in the public sector', *IDS Study* 510 (July).

IDS Focus (1989) 'The European view', 53 (December).

IDS/IPM (1992) *Pay and Benefits: European Management Guides*, London: IPM.

James, M. C. (1989) 'Les moeurs et l'argent des moeurs: l'individualisation des rémunérations comme événement culturel dans l'entreprise', *Humanisme et entreprise* 177 (whole).

Johnson, P. and Lange K. (1992) 'Norway', in C. Brewster, A. Hegewisch, L. Holden, and T. Lockhart, (eds) (1992) *The European Human Resource Management Guide*, London: Academic Press.

Kinnie, N. (1989) 'The decentralisation of industrial relations? Recent research considered'; *Personnel Review* 19(3) 28–34.

Lane, C. (1989) *Management and Labour in Europe*, Aldershot: Edward Elgar.

Layard, D. (1990) 'How to end pay leapfrogging', Employment Institute, *Economic Report* 5 (5 July).

Lehmann, D. (1993) 'Leistung und Entgelt – eine mißverstandene Beziehung, Erwartungen, Erfahrungen und Grundhaltungen', *Personalführung* 7: 604–7.

Marsden, D. (1989) '*Developments of pay level patterns and flexibility in Western Europe*', paper to the Eighth World Congress of the International Industrial Relations Conference, Brussels.

Marsden, D. and Richardson, R. (1992) '*Motivation and performance related pay in the public sector: a case study of the Inland Revenue*', Centre for Economic Performance, Discussion Paper 75, London School of Economics.

Marsden, D. and Silvestre, J.-J. (1992) 'Pay and European integration', in D. Marsden (ed.) (1992) *Pay and Employment in the New Europe*, Aldershot: Edward Elgar.

Marginson, P., Edwards, P., Martin, P., Purcell, J. and Sisson, K. (1988) *Beyond the Workplace*, Oxford: Blackwell.

Martinez Lucio, M. (1992) 'Spain: constructing institutions and actors in a context of change', in A. Ferner and R. Hyman (eds) (1992) *Industrial Relations in the new Europe*, Oxford: Blackwell.

Murlis, H. and Wright, V. (1993) 'Remuneration', *Benefits and Compensation International* Jan.–Feb.: 5–10.

Oswald, A. (1992) *Pay Setting, Self-employment and the Unions: Themes of the 1980s*, Centre for Economic Performance, Discussion Paper 64, London: LSE.

Pond, C. (1991) 'International comparisons of low pay policies', in: J. Hawkins (ed.) (1991) *International Pay Policies*, Public Finance Foundation, Discussion Paper 39, London.

Poole, M. and Jenkins, G. (1988) 'How employees respond to profit sharing', *Personnel Management* July: 30–4.

Prondzynsky, F. (1992) 'Ireland: between centralism and the market', in A. Ferner and R. Hyman (eds) (1992) *Industrial Relations in the new Europe*, Oxford: Blackwell.

Rowthorn, R. E (1992) 'Centralisation, employment and wage dispersion', *Economic Journal*, 102 (May): 506–23.

Shonfield, D. (1992) 'The pay policies of large firms in Europe', in D,. Marsden (ed.) (1992) *Pay and employment in the new Europe*, Aldershot: Edward Elgar.

Söderström, M. and Syrén, S. (1992) 'Sweden', in C. Brewster, A. Hegewisch, L. Holden and T. Lockhart (eds) (1992) *The European Human Resource Management Guide*, London: Academic Press.

Soskice, D. (1990) 'Wage determination: the changing role of institutions in advanced industrial countries', *Oxford Review of Economic Policy* 6(4): 36–61.

Tolliday, S. and Zeitlin, J. (1992) *Between Fordism and Flexibility: the Automotive Industry and Its Workers*, Oxford and New York: Berg New York.

Visser, J. (1992) 'The Netherlands: the end of an era and the end of a system', in A. Ferner and R. Hyman (eds) (1992) *Industrial Relations in the New Europe*, Oxford: Blackwell.

Walsh, J. (1992) 'Managing fragmented pay bargaining: some UK evidence', *Personnel Review* 21(7): 3–13.

Wise, L. R. (1993) 'Wither solidarity? Transitions in Swedish public sector pay policy', *British Journal of Industrial Relations* 31(1): 73–95.

Chapter 7

Key issues in training and development

Henrik Holt Larsen

INTRODUCTION

With the increasing importance of organisations based on knowledge, service and hi-tech in the European Community, the training and development of employees is attracting increasing attention (Kleingartner and Anderson 1987; Tannenbaum and Yukl 1992). This reflects the fact that development of human resources has become a strategic factor – and a competitive advantage – for private enterprises and public agencies (Salaman 1992). To an increasing extent, production in companies has a non-material nature, and the development and selling of the 'products' requires an intensive use of high level human competencies. Organisations can only achieve their business objectives if the human resources possess not only the appropriate functional knowledge, skills and flexibility, but also personality characteristics considered to be vital for the specific work environment (Storey 1989; Blyton and Turnbull 1992).

The ongoing discussion of why and how human resource management has replaced the previously well established concept of personnel management is particularly relevant for – and to some extent caused by – the changing role of training activities in organisations. Thus, the increasing complexity of production and administrative systems requires not only an update of functional skills, but in addition the acquisition of qualitatively different areas of skills and knowledge like computer, planning and negotiation skills (Zuboff 1988). Second, there is an increasing pressure on individuals to assure that they are not only familiar with a fairly narrow functional area, but have a general understanding of the tasks and processes of the organisation and possess interpersonal skills (Goldstein and Gilliam 1990). Third, in knowledge based and service oriented organisations (in particular) the behaviour of the employees is in itself a competitive factor. Hence, organisations are increasingly concerned with the personality profile of the employees and keen to develop personality traits or attitudes believed to stimulate business activities and the success of the organisation. Finally, with the increasing emphasis on organisational culture there is a (deliberate or accidental) pressure on the individual to be familiar with and behave in accordance with fundamental cultural values of the organisation (Schein 1992).

There has, however, been a widespread disappointment in, and frustration with, the lack of implementation and effectiveness of many training activities (Noe and Ford 1992). This is caused by a number of factors. First of all, we have been suffering from a scarcity of operational methods to detect the training needs of individuals or groups of employees – and perhaps, intertwined with this, a lack of motivation to use the methods at our disposal. Second, whether training needs are analysed systematically or not, we have not been good at implementing the outcome of the training. The transfer process is extremely complex, and our understanding of potential barriers for transfer of learning to the job setting is insufficient (Baldwin and Ford 1988). Third, there has been a somewhat naive perception that learning takes place best in formalised training sessions (classroom settings) removed from the job. Thus, we have underestimated the importance and effectiveness of learning processes inherent in the job – so called experiential or action oriented learning processes (Revans 1982; MacNamara and Weekes 1982; McCall et al. 1988). Challenging tasks, special assignments, participation in cross-organisational activities as well as job rotation and job transfer are all examples of potentially powerful learning situations.

The close link between business strategy and human resource management, as well as the increasing focus on training and development and the revitalisation of experiential learning processes on the job all bring the human resource responsibility of the line manager into focus. Training and development should no longer be looked upon as an 'external' activity, disconnected from the business activities of the organisation. It should be considered a strategic investment in the professionalisation of the organisation. For the line manager, training and development is not an activity taking the employee away from the job, but enabling the person to do the job. The job becomes a setting for learning, and a synergy is created between job design and learning/development of the individual and the organisation (Argyris and Schön 1978; Hosking and Morley 1991; French and Bell 1990; Bushe and Shani 1991). However, there is still a widespread reluctance among line managers to undertake this active role in training and developing the employees. The line managers might not believe in the relevance or profitability of training, or they might feel uncomfortable with the pedagogical role. To the extent that human resource responsibility is devolved to the line managers, there is probably no alternative, however, for the line manager than to accept the training and development responsibility.

The survey analyses training and development practices in the following areas: the strategic role of training and development, the use of systematic methods for analysing training needs and effectiveness, the role of line managers in training and development as well as the actual volume of training in European organisations. Hence, the survey tests the hypothesis that training and development is getting an increasingly crucial role in public and private organisations, and that more and more resources are allocated to this area. The present chapter analyses the results relevant to training and development.

Table 7.1 Organisations: training and development objectives/spending

% organisations with training and development as main objective		% organisations spending more than 2% on training	
%	Country ranking	Country ranking	%
34	D	F	80
31	N	S	60
31	DK	T	47
30	S	D	43
26	NL	NL	40
25	F	IRL	40
25	T	P	39
24	P	FIN	36
22	UK	N	36
22	IRL	UK	26
19	E	DK	25
12	FIN	E	23

THE STRATEGIC ROLE OF TRAINING AND DEVELOPMENT

The respondents were asked about the *main objectives* of personnel or human resource management in the organisation over the next three years. In all participating countries except Finland training and development comes out as the highest rated objective for the next three years (Appendix III Table 2.1). In Table 7.1, the figures in the left column indicate the percentage of organisations rating training and development as the main objective.

The figures for training and development as main objectives are compared with the present level/volume of training. The right column indicates the percentage of companies spending more than 2 per cent of annual salaries and wages on training. This measure should only be considered as an approximate indication of the volume of training in each country. However, it makes a comparison with the figures for HR objectives interesting. Both columns of figures are ranked.

Comparing, on a national basis, the number of organisations who prioritise training and development with a high average expenditure, we find that there is no simple correlation. Countries such as Denmark and Norway, for example, have a below average level of present training, but put heavy emphasis on training as a future HRM objective. Denmark and Norway are known for a highly skilled work force, but have reacted to difficult financial circumstances by reducing training costs. Presumably, they expect a comeback in emphasis in the future.

Exactly the opposite is happening in France, Finland, Turkey, Ireland and – to a lesser extent – Sweden and Portugal. These countries are characterised by a high current level of training, but put less emphasis on training as a future HRM objective than Denmark or Sweden. There may be several reasons for this apparent downgrading of training: a previous intense training effort 'justifying' a brake, a financial crisis in business, a feeling that a (temporary) saturation point has been reached, or competition from other HRM issues. Such a downgrading of training might, however, make it difficult to meet the need for continuing development of employee competencies, caused by the turbulence in the business environment as well as the fast development of technology.

This warning also applies to countries like Spain and the United Kingdom who give relatively low priority to training and development – at present as well as in the near future. On the contrary, Germany is characterised by a high, stable level. Somewhat lower, but also stable, is the Netherlands.

THE TRAINING VOLUME

Table 7.2 shows the proportion of annual salaries and wages currently spent on training. Some of the figures were part of Table 7.1. More detailed figures are given in the Appendix, Table 5.1. The table shows considerable differences in the volume of training across Europe. With the exception of France, Sweden and the United Kingdom, all countries are characterised by having at least one third of the companies spending *less than 1 per cent* of the salary bill on training. There does not seem to be a geographical pattern in this. Sweden deviates from the other Nordic countries, France deviates from the other Southern European countries, and the United Kingdom deviates from its neighbour countries. France is known for having demanding legislation on training, effectively imposing on companies a requirement to spend at least 1.2 per cent of the salary bill on training. The nature of this policy as well as the strict enforcement of it also explains why the figure for 'Don't know' is so low.

It is interesting to note that 80 per cent of French companies and 60 per cent of Swedish companies spend *more than 2 per cent* of salaries and wages on training. In all other countries, the figure is around 40 per cent or below. This low figure is somewhat alarming, as it indicates that even in well driven and profit-making companies it is not taken for granted that one should put pressure on training. Also, it is disturbing that so many companies *do not know* how much they are spending on training. The percentage varies from 2 to 47 per cent, and there is no national correlation between the volume of training and knowledge about the training costs. Thus, 47 per cent of all Swedish companies do not

Table 7.2 Countries: salaries and wages (valid %)

	0.01–1.00	1.01–2.00	2.00–	Don't know
Germany	35	22	43	41
Denmark	39	36	25	25
Spain	50	27	23	21
France	1	18	80	2
Finland	32	30	36	18
Ireland	37	24	40	35
Norway	45	20	36	35
Netherlands	31	30	40	10
Portugal	30	31	39	25
Sweden	15	25	60	47
Turkey	33	20	47	44
UK	20	27	26	34

know how much is spent on training: but at the same time the general level of money spent on training is quite high in this country.

The survey provides data about the average *number of days* each employee receives each year. These figures are registered separately for each staff category (management, professional/technical staff, clerical staff and manual workers). Appendix III Tables 5.2a–d lists the percentage of the employees – for each staff category in each country – receiving more than three days of training per year.

The figures show that management and professional/technical staff roughly speaking receive the same number of days on training. Clerical workers get less training than this, and manual workers get even less training. The higher a person is placed in the organisational hierarchy, the more training the person tends to get. As there quite often is a correlation between level in the organisation and the person's education (volume and level), this means that the more education and training people have already got, the more they keep participating in training activities.

However, there are some national differences in this pattern. Whereas Germany, Denmark, Spain, France, Portugal, Sweden, and the United Kingdom all illustrate the correlation between organisational level and volume of training, Finland is characterised by a high training volume for clerical workers, and in Ireland, Norway and the Netherlands, manual workers are given relatively more training.

The Appendix clearly illustrates that employees in general spend a lot of time on training in Turkey, Spain and to a lesser extent in Portugal, Norway and Sweden. Least time spent on training is found in some of the traditionally powerful industrial states (the Netherlands, Germany and in particular the United Kingdom). Although it is a methodologically problematic procedure, the average ranking has been calculated and this is correlated with the training expenditure.

When we correlate the number of organisations in each country spending more than 2 per cent of the salary bill on training and the percentage of the employees (unweighted average for all categories) spending more than three days on training per year, surprisingly, there is not a very high correlation between training volume and training cost. Spain, Denmark and the United Kingdom are all spending relatively equal (and modest) financial resources on training, but vary a great deal in training volume. A large number of countries (including Portugal, Norway, Finland, Ireland, the Netherlands and Germany) all spend more money on training than the three countries mentioned above, but show the same variation in training days. Organisations in France are (as mentioned above) spending a very large proportion of the salary bill on training, but do no not seem to get 'value for money' in terms of training days. This finding raises some doubt about the way in which the training expenditures are actually calculated in France. Are employers there 'padding' their expenditure?

ANALYSIS OF TRAINING NEEDS

Effectiveness of training is usually believed to require a thorough diagnosis of training needs. Otherwise it is doubtful whether the training activity will provide the employee with the desired qualifications. However, in any organisational setting there are a number of factors making such a needs analysis difficult. In addition to pragmatic barriers like lack of time, resources and commitment, needs diagnosis suffers from the sheer complexity of the operation. Thus, an analysis of training needs should in principle reflect the future job situation (tasks and required competencies) rather than the present job-person match. Furthermore, it is very complex to assess the actual and/or potential capability of a person, as well as determining which training methods might be appropriate to meet the training need, i.e. provide the competencies in question.

The survey shows great differences in the extent to which companies systematically analyse the training needs of the employees. The most commonly used method of needs analysis is in most countries line management requests. More than 80 per cent of all organisations in all countries (except Finland) use this method often or always. This is in accordance with the fairly pronounced trend that line managers are to an increasing extent concerned with and willing to undertake a human resource responsibility. The role of the line manager will be dealt with in section 6 of this chapter, so at present we will just stress that line management requests play a dominant role compared to employee requests.

On the average, employee requests are used to only a moderate extent, but there are big variations from one country to another. Whereas, for example, 78 per cent of Dutch and 76 per cent of Danish organisations always or often use employee requests for training needs analysis, the similar figures for Germany and Portugal are 45 and 46 per cent. Considering how important the acceptance of and commitment to training is for the motivation of the individual, it is quite surprising that employees are not more intensively involved in the need assessment.

In general, performance appraisal is a commonly used tool for training needs analysis. In the United Kingdom, 52 per cent of the respondents 'always' use performance appraisal and 30 per cent 'often' use this method for training needs analysis. In almost all other countries performance appraisal is used less in this area (see Appendix III Table 5.5d). Although performance appraisal systems do vary in terms of how and how much the employees are involved in the appraisal of his or her own performance, the roles are usually pretty much those of assessor and an assessee. So, even in this case there is some question about the assessment of the training need by somebody other than the person in question.

The survey also asks the respondents to indicate whether training audits are used for need assessment. The figures vary a great deal from country to country. Whereas 67 per cent of respondents in Turkey always use training audits, the equivalent figure for Norway is 3 per cent. And whilst 54 per cent of the Swedish respondents never use training audits, the similar figure for Finland, Portugal and Turkey is 0 per cent. This response pattern may indicate cultural differences or may reflect some misinterpretation or ambiguity in the term itself.

Finally, the survey asks whether projected Business/Service plans are used for systematic training needs assessment. Given the strategic emphasis of the survey, this is a crucial question. The results indicate that more than 60 per cent of the respondents in the various countries 'always' or 'often' use business plans in training need analysis. Considering that the very same survey documents the problems involved in converting a business strategy into a personnel/HRM strategy, and a personnel/HRM strategy into work programmes, the quoted figures are surprisingly high. However, it is difficult to know how close an operational link there has to be between business plans and training needs analysis to make the respondents answer positively to this question.

Overall, the survey shows a very diverse picture across Europe in the extent to which systematic needs analysis is done, and if so by which methods. In addition to cultural and financial factors, the national differences can probably de explained by differences in the dominant purpose of training. The training might be aiming at a very 'job-close' acquisition of specific skills, it might be aiming at a more general attitudinal and ideological impact on the employees, or it might reflect a 'welfare' purpose where training almost becomes a fringe benefit. Depending on what the specific training purpose is, varying degrees and methods of needs analysis will be appropriate. The training purpose is to a high degree

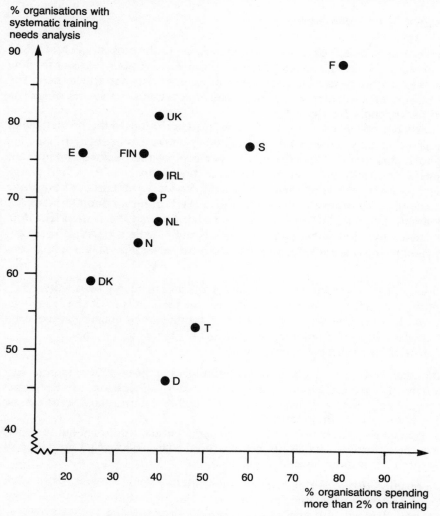

Figure 7.1 The correlation between training needs analysis and average training expenditure

determining – and determined by – the relative priority given to the various occupational groups in the organisation. This is discussed in the following section.

Rather surprisingly, there is no correlation at the national level between the degree of systematic need assessment and the actual volume of training. Although France scores high on both dimensions (need analysis and training volume), and Denmark is scoring low on both, some countries (like the United Kingdom and Spain) use systematic methods to analyse training need, but have fairly low levels of actual training. And the reverse: in Germany the training volume is high, although only half of the companies do systematic needs analysis. This appears from Figure 7.1.

THE EFFECTIVENESS OF TRAINING

Measuring – and ensuring – the effectiveness of training is one of the most difficult of HRM issues. With the increasing focus on and allocation of resources to various forms of training the need for documenting the return on investment in training costs has accelerated. The survey asked the respondents whether they monitor the effectiveness of their training. The results are shown in Appendix III Table 5.6.

The picture is fairly heterogeneous, but can be simplified according to the percentage of respondents claiming that they do actually monitor the effectiveness of their training. In the United Kingdom, Spain and Finland, some 80 per cent of the respondents monitor training effectiveness. In France and Ireland, the percentage is around 70. A fairly large group of countries, (Norway, the Netherlands, Portugal, Sweden and Turkey) have some 60 per cent respondents monitoring effectiveness, and at the bottom we find Germany (51 per cent) and Denmark (39 per cent). It is interesting to notice that the United Kingdom – which is characterised by a low volume of training – is right at the top with 82 per cent of the companies monitoring training effectiveness. There are several possible explanations for this:

1 A deliberate attempt not to initiate more training than can effectively be monitored.
2 A realisation of the fact that the less training initiated, the easier it is to do the follow-up.
3 A scarcity of financial resources setting a limit to the training volume and – at the same time – imposing heavy implementation requirements on trainers and trainees.
4 Loose criteria of what monitoring actually entails.

Responses are also likely to be affected by national differences in the criteria of monitoring. Hence, in Germany, for example there has been a lot of discussion of 'Personnel controlling'. Thus, possibly, German respondents have higher expectations, standards or awareness of what evaluation might entail.

Measurement of training effectiveness has to rest on a deliberate decision about the locus or level at which the effectiveness has to be measured. The following four types of effectiveness measurement in training can be defined:

1 The immediate reaction (like/don't like the training activity).
2 The actual, specific skills or competencies acquired during the training.
3 Subsequent, specific changes in job behaviour, caused by the training.
4 Long-term effect on the organisation.

Unfortunately, not very many organisations are able or willing to initiate evaluation at most or all of these levels. In most cases, the immediate reaction by the trainee is used as a pragmatic approximation for the effectiveness of training (Tannenbaum and Yukl 1992; Brinkerhoff 1989).

The survey asked the respondents whether they monitor the effectiveness in any of the following ways: tests, formal evaluation immediately after training and/or some months after the training, informal feedback from the line manager and informal feedback from the trainee (see Table 7.3). The percentage of companies using tests is fairly low across the board (with the exception of Turkey and to a lesser extent Ireland and the United Kingdom). This may be a reflection of the changing nature of training – with less and less training aimed at the type of skills that can easily be tested.

Formal evaluation immediately after training is heavily used (61 to 94 per cent), but a similar evaluation some months later scores considerably lower. This seriously restricts the opportunity to measure not only the immediate reaction and competencies acquired, but also visible changes in job behaviour – and eventually the performance of the organisation. Roughly speaking, the percentage of organisations doing formal evaluation decreases by a third or even half if we compare those doing it immediately after training to those including evaluations a few months after the training has taken place.

Informal feedback from the trainee and/or the line manager is extremely common, as most percentages are in the 1990s. The exception is Finland where only 60 per cent use the informal feedback as a systematic monitoring device, and Portugal where only 45 per cent of the respondents use informal feedback from the line manager, but 97 per cent use informal feedback from the trainee. If the response pattern in these two countries (or at least Finland) reflects a general scepticism as to whether informal feedback can be called a systematic evaluation method, the perception is fairly rational. Informal feedback (from line managers or the trainee) can probably (partly) be considered as an 'emergency exit' for HR functions not having the necessary skills or commitment to do proper training evaluation. However, one should not underestimate the value of an informal talk between the HR function and the manager or trainee as a tool to communicate and discuss the more sensitive and personal experiences during the training.

Table 7.3 Percentage of companies monitoring the effectiveness of training in the following ways

Country	Tests	Formal evaluation immediately after training	Formal evaluation some months after training	Informal feedback from: line manager	employee
Germany	32	70	33	89	92
Denmark	36	83	54	96	97
Spain	53	85	54	93	93
France	35	90	64	91	93
Finland	12	61	25	61	66
Ireland	49	84	50	99	99
Norway	24	70	29	95	97
Netherlands	65	64	45	98	99
Portugal	40	93	55	45	97
Sweden	46	88	39	92	93
Turkey	77	94	68	86	85
United Kingdom	46	89	70	98	98

As described, the results generally indicate that although measuring effectiveness of training is a high priority area, we are still looking for more valid, reliable and operational measures to do it. The United Kingdom scores very high on monitoring effectiveness in general, as well as utilising the various methods listed in the questionnaire. Finland also scores high on the general question, but is rather low on all the specific monitoring tools (tests, formal and informal evaluation). It is not very likely that Finnish respondents are using different tools than the ones presented in the questionnaire. Hence, it remains somewhat unexplained why there is a contrast between the heavy emphasis on monitoring effectiveness in general and the fairly modest use of the specific methods.

Implementation of training is not a process starting at the closing of the training activity and only (mainly) involving the trainee and the superior. Effective implementation starts long before the actual training and involves, in addition to the trainee and his or her superior, the peers, the subordinates (if any), the personnel/HRM function and the trainer. In fact, one can systematise this into a matrix, defining all the relevant actors along one side and crucial moments or events (long before, right before, during, right after and long after the training) along the other side. This is done in Figure 7.2.

Obviously, the effectiveness of training is enhanced if not only the training outcome is measured, but also the training need analysis is solid and systematic. Some interesting

		Time horizon				
		Long before	Right before	During	Right after	Long after
Functions involved	The trainee					
	The superior					
	The peers					
	The subordinates					
	The HRM function					
	The trainer					

Figure 7.2 The 'implementation of training' grid

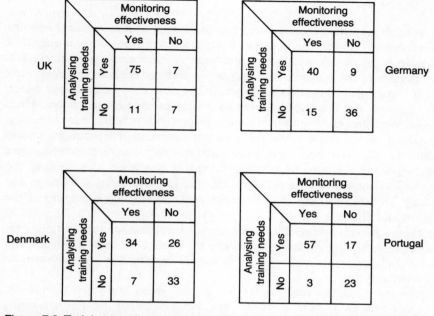

Figure 7.3 Training needs analysis vs training evaluation matrix for selected countries

results appear if one does cross tabulations of these two questions in the survey. In Figure 7.3 are shown 2 × 2 tables for a number of characteristic countries.

The United Kingdom is the 'model' for Europe, as 75 per cent of all respondents do both. Analysing the training need without monitoring effectiveness (11 per cent) is a fairly common and 'understandable' approach. One starts out with a careful need analysis but loses interest, tends to forget or just does not have the time to do the follow-up when the trainee returns from the training. The 7 per cent not doing a systematic needs analysis, but monitoring the effectiveness have an ironic desire to implement what was not very carefully decided or chosen in the first place.

Denmark shows far less discipline with only 34 per cent yes/yes. Twenty-six per cent are doing the systematic need analysis but tend to forget the implementation. One-third rely on intuition and good luck! Portugal is somewhere in between the United Kingdom and Denmark, and Germany is interesting in having a higher percentage of no/yes than yes/no.

In short, the survey documents that there are great variations across the board in terms of the intensity and the methods by which the effectiveness of training is evaluated. The survey mainly looks at post-training evaluation and does not detect the ways in which the pretraining environment (Tannenbaum and Yukl 1992) can influence training effectiveness. In this sense, the survey reflects a very pragmatic approach to training evaluation in the organisations. This is justified, as the aim of the survey is to test actual HRM practices. However, it does not test the (lack of) synergy between the various methods at various points of time: in other words the process aspect of effectiveness assessment.

THE ROLE OF THE LINE MANAGER

The training and development field clearly illustrates the trends in line manager responsibility for human resources. As the line manager is expected to ensure a given output of products or services from his or her area, the match between each employee and the job becomes of vital importance. The person as well as the job undergo continuous change and development, and it is part of the managerial responsibility to ensure a continuous match between the person and the job. This development has two significant consequences. First, decentralisation and devolvement of human resource responsibility to line managers has been generally encouraged, although there are a number of potential problems in this (Blyton and Turnbull 1992; Brewster and Holt Larsen 1992). Second, training and development becomes a crucial tool, as training is one of the ways of providing the employee with necessary, non-present qualifications for the job. Similarly, job design and development are ways of adjusting job characteristics to the needs and capability of the job holder (Hackman and Oldham 1980).

Across Europe there are very great differences in line management responsibility for training and development. It appears from Appendix III Table 2.6c that in Turkey and Portugal, the responsibility for training and development is devolved to line managers to a very considerable extent.

The same applies – to a slightly lesser extent – in the Nordic countries (Denmark, Sweden, Norway and Finland). On the contrary, line manager responsibility for training is very low in France, the United Kingdom and the Netherlands. Between these two extremes are Spain, Germany and Ireland. These differences are possibly caused by variations in national and managerial culture, the role of the line manager in general, the educational profile of the employees etc. However, the impact of each of these variables cannot be hypothesised and tested by the survey data.

Although there are quite substantial arguments for strong devolvement to the line manager, the devolvement of responsibility for training and development is actually *less pronounced* than the responsibility for other areas (see Chapter 4). Regardless of – or because of (?) – the low level of devolvement, there has been a net increase in line manager responsibility for training in all countries over the last three years. This increase is larger in the field of training and development than for any other area. So, although training and development is an area where a large number of organisations have increased the responsibility of line managers, this has happened against a background of low responsibility to date.

Comparing the actual level of line management responsibility with the net increase over the last three years provides an interesting picture (see Table 7.4).

Thus, in Sweden, Norway and Finland line management has experienced a very large increase in training responsibility which has brought line management responsibility up to a fairly high level. France, the United Kingdom and the Netherlands have also experienced a very high increase in devolvement, but the actual level is nevertheless very low. For France, this is thought-provoking, as France has a high level of spending on training. Presumably, the HR function is responsible for this vast volume of training. Turkey, Denmark and Portugal have all experienced very low increases in line management responsibility, but are already very high on this dimension which makes further increase

Table 7.4 Line manager responsibility for training and development/increase in responsibility

Line manager responsibility for training and development %	Country ranking	Increase in line manager responsibility over the last 3 years Country ranking	%
21	T	S	67
19	DK	N	56
18	P	F	55
16	S	E	53
14	FIN	FIN	51
14	N	NL	50
9	D	UK	46
9	E	IRL	43
7	IRL	DK	39
6	NL	T	20
4	UK	P	18
2	F	D	13

difficult. Spain, Ireland and the Netherlands have experienced substantial increases in devolvement, but are still characterised by a slightly low (below average) level of line management responsibility. Germany is characterised by the same actual level of devolvement, and there has only been a very modest increase over the last three years.

It should be added that although line management responsibility across Europe is lower for training than for pay, recruitment, health and safety and, in particular, workforce adjustments, the increase is larger for training responsibility than for any other functional area. Presumably this illustrates a realisation of the fact that line management involvement in training increases the effectiveness of the training. The difficulties in ensuring a transfer of the training outcome to the job environment has led to an increasing focus on so called experiential learning processes (Kolb 1984). The job situation is a potential learning situation and a talented utilisation of this potential provides the jobholder with an important set of learning experiences. Special tasks, cross-organisational assignments, job rotation and temporary assignments are all means of intensifying the challenges of a given job. This creates an experience-loaded work situation which provides good learning opportunities. The best example of experiential learning is management development on the job.

As this is dealt with in Chapter 8 we won't go into detail here, but just stress that the increase in line management involvement may be partially explained (caused) by the closer link between performing a job and benefiting from the spin-off effect in terms of learning. As line management is traditionally responsible for monitoring job performance, they also have the key to experiential learning on the job. More non-classroom type learning environments are created and more responsibility and actual training (learning) are undertaken by the line management. For the HR function it becomes increasingly difficult to overview (not to speak of control) the training and development activities of the organisation, as the training area is devolved to the line organisation where business strategy, job design and the human resource responsibility meet in a potentially synergetic crossroad.

PERSPECTIVES

The survey documents the high priority given to training and development in European companies. Considerable resources in terms of time and money are allocated to training purposes in all countries. With the exception of Finland, training and development is the highest ranking main objective of HRM over the next three years. This reflects the fact that the availability of human competencies is considered a must for organisational survival.

The survey stresses the importance of a close link between business strategies and HRM strategies. However, it also documents how difficult it is to establish such a link in practice. The turbulent business environment makes forecasts difficult, but without forecasting the likely or desired future development of the organisation, it is difficult to determine the future manpower requirements – in quantitative and/or qualitative terms. This is especially the case in service and knowledge based organisations with immaterial resources and products.

Even if an organisation succeeds in defining an operational HR strategy for training and development, this does not in itself ensure a successful implementation of training. As we have seen, the analysis of training needs is not always systematic, and specific training activities are undertaken without a specific plan for measuring the transfer and effectiveness of the training. This is not to say that non-systematic need assessment or incidental implementation unconditionally prevents a satisfactory training outcome. Thus, comprehensive training activities and fairly successful business development (in terms of long-term organisational survival) can be achieved with very intuitive decision making processes in the training area. The question is, however, whether this fairly successful HRM procedure is caused by or occurs in spite of the non-systematic approach to training issues.

One of the great challenges of training in working life is getting people acquainted with the organisational culture, accepting it and behaving according to it. To an increasing extent, organisations are driven by the fundamental values and assumptions, which add up and constitute the organisational culture (Schein 1992). Training cultural values and ensuring the implementation of these in the actual job behaviour of the employee is an almost unmanageable task. In fact, socialisation to an organisational culture is most effectively achieved through experiential learning on the job (McCall *et al.* 1988). This applies in particular to the management training and development area, as a vital ingredient of all management development is absorbing and radiating the cultural 'core' of the organisation.

With the increasing emphasis on training in most European countries there is an increasing need for costing the financial implications (costs and benefits) from training. The study shows that organisations find it difficult to monitor the effectiveness of training which among other things makes it difficult to assess the cost–benefit ratio. Human resource accounting is a method by which attempts are made to evaluate the financial consequences of human behaviour. However, this method has not reached a level of operationalisation enabling it to help monitoring the use of resources for training purposes.

As human resources become a key factor in the organisation, increasing demand is being put on the line manager to undertake the responsibility for people management. The survey has shown that although at present line management is not always performing this role to a very high extent, line management responsibility for human resources is increasing. One can anticipate that the ability and willingness to undertake this responsibility will become an ultimative requirement for promotion to managerial positions. This creates a need for training programmes and other types of development by which the (potential) line manager can become acquainted with the new role. In that regard it is interesting to notice that the survey also enquired about main training requirements in the organisation in the coming years. Here, people management and supervision ranks fairly high among the alternatives given.

The ultimate objective for the training and development area is to create a synergy between the training and development of the individual employee, development of the business strategies and plans, and development of the organisation. Such a coordinated effort will not only maintain the key role of human resources, but also enable the organisation to emphasise strategic human resource development as a competitive (comparative) factor.

REFERENCES

Argyris, C. and Schön, D. A. (1978) *Organizational learning: a Theory of Action Perspectives*, Reading, Mass.: Addison-Wesley.

Baldwin, T. T. and Ford, J. K. (1988) 'Transfer of training: a review and directions for future research', *Personnel Psychology* 41: 65–105.

Blyton, P. and Turnbull, P. (eds) (1992), *Reassessing Human Resource Management*, London: Sage Publications.

Brewster, C. and Holt Larsen, H. (1992) 'Human resource management in Europe: evidence from ten countries', *International Journal of Human Resource Management* 3(3): 409–34.

Brinkerhoff, R. O. (1989) *Evaluating Training Programs in Business and Industry*, San Francisco: Jossey-Bass.

Bushe, G. R. and Shani, A. B. (1991) *Parallel Learning Structures*, Reading, Mass.: Addison-Wesley.

French, W. L. and Bell, C. H., Jr (1990) *Organization Development*, Englewood Cliffs, NJ: Prentice-Hall (2nd edn).

Goldstein, I. and Gilliam, P. (1990) 'Training systems in the year 2000', *American Psychologist* 45: 134–43.

Hackman, J. R. and Oldham, G. R. (1980) *Work Redesign* Reading, Mass.: Addison-Wesley.

Hosking, D. M. and Morley, I. E. (1991) *A Social Psychology of Organizing*, New York: Harvester Wheatsheaf.

Kleingartner, A. and Anderson, C. S. (1987) *Human Resource Management in High Technology Firms*, Lexington: Lexington Books.

McCall, M. W., Lombardo, M. M. and Morrison, A. M. (1988) *The Lessons of Experience*, Lexington, Mass.: Lexington Books.

MacNamara, M. and Weekes, W. H. (1982) 'The action learning model of experiential learning for developing managers', *Human Relations* 35: 879–902.

Noe, R. A. and Ford, J. K. (1992) 'Emerging issues and new directions for training research', in G. R. Ferris and K. M. Rowland (eds) (1992) *Research in Personnel and Human Resource Management*, Vol. 10, Greenwich, Conn.: JAI Press.

Revans, R. W. (1982) *The Origins and Growth of Action Learning*, Lund: Studentlitteratur.

Salaman, G. (ed.) (1992) *Human Resource Strategies*, London: Sage.

Schein, E. H. (1992) *Organizational Culture and Leadership*, San Francisco: Jossey-Bass (2nd edn).

Storey, J. (ed.) (1989) *New Perspectives on Human Resource Management*, London: Routledge.

Tannenbaum, S. and Yukl, G. (1992) 'Training and development in work organizations', in M. R. Rosenzweig and L. W. Porter (eds) (1992) *Annual Review of Psychology*, Vol. 43: 399–441, Palo Alto, Cal.: Annual Reviews Inc.

Zuboff, S. (1988) *In the Age of the Smart Machine*, Oxford: Heinemann.

Chapter 8

Training and management development in Europe

Frank Bournois, Jean-Hugues Chauchat and Sylvie Roussillon

In this chapter our aim is to describe how executives are trained and how their career development is managed in European companies. The European single market is now a reality but studies carried out in this field are still all too rare. Very little work has been done in comparing different European approaches and what we mostly hear are comments on the practices of certain large organisations which are frequently mentioned in the press.

We shall make comparisons between firms from a dozen different countries. In doing this, we are automatically giving more importance to the variable 'country'. It must be emphasised that the 'country' is certainly not the only criterion that can be used to differentiate an organisation. Its size, the type of market it is active in, the technological system it uses, are variables that are just as important. Yet we have decided to proceed on the basis of comparing different countries because, in the field of executive career management, it is the national culture and the size of the firm (to a lesser degree), that seem to be the contingency factors that best explain the differences between the firms (Bournois 1991a).

We shall devote ourselves here to examining the management training and career development of executives, since a number of studies show that this theme figures among the main concerns of firms for the future. The survey commissioned by the EAPD (European Association of Personnel Directors) is another indication of the importance of this subject for human resource managers and for top management in general (EAPD 1990).

As we have already stressed in other publications, it seems hazardous to us for a human resource manager to set about working out systems of European human resource management (intra-European mobility, Euro-managers' career development, etc.), without a sufficient knowledge of the realities of human resource management at a national level and without being well aware of the similarities and differences between the countries, which is the concern of international comparisons in human resource management. The conceptual and methodological pitfalls, which we shall not go into here, are many (Brewster and Tyson 1991) and we agree with Begin (1992: 380) when he defines a human resource management system as: 'all HRM structures, processes, policies and policy effects at the societal and organisational level of a particular country.'

THE UNDERLYING PROBLEMS

Out of the 500 largest firms in the world (based on turnover) in 1989, 120 were Japanese, 152 were American and 149 belonged to one of the member countries of the EC. Without meaning to spark off a traditional polemic between management researchers, the question must be asked, whether, because of internationalisation and the single European market in particular, training and development policies and practices will converge. As far as the converging of human resource management problems is concerned, some consider that the problems and their solutions will be the same in Japan, in Europe and in the United States due to the similar development taking place in technology, demography, economics and industry (for example, the 'power-slide' from the employers to the employees) (Doyle 1990). It is this marked tendency towards convergence that often justifies developing management methods that are uniform, compatible and valid in all situations and in all countries.

Another line of thought, to which the seminal works of Hofstede contributed (1983), attempts to demonstrate the impact that national culture has (through the political, economic and legal systems) on the particular forms that management, motivation and work organisation take. Thus, Brewster (1988) showed clearly that the selection criteria for expatriates are not the same in Europe and in the United States, since in Europe there are more criteria and also that the failure rate for the expatriation experience is lower. Recent research has brought out the fact more and more that the human resource management systems in Europe are the product of very different political and historical contexts from those of the USA (Brewster and Bournois 1991) and, furthermore, that the greatest caution must be observed in interpreting social systems when one embarks on the delicate task of international comparisons (Brewster and Tyson 1991).

On this question of the degree of convergence of policies and practices in human resources management, we share the view of our two last-quoted colleagues when they write:

It would be presumptuous to draw conclusions about this debate. Undoubtedly, there are elements of, particularly, economic and business life which are now less disparate than they were. It is equally true that the deep-rooted and 'sticky' nature of cultural differences must not be overlooked and is likely to mediate the effects of convergence. In general terms, it is clear that researchers who focus on the content of management tend to find similarities; researchers who focus on process tend to identify cultural variations. Our inability to agree on terminology and the paucity of our evidence make any better summary impossible (pp. 4–5).

Figure 8.1 Different levels of analysis

We think that over and above the 'process versus content' difference, there is perhaps another way of interpreting these problems: the observation level (see Figure 8.1). In fact, what one claims when describing a management system 'globally', may be not so easily justified and need certain adjustments when observed from a closer level (for example, the human resource management level in general, the recruitment level in particular, and the recruitment methods level even more specifically). We shall now examine this full spectrum as it concerns one of the main items of human resource management: management training and development – MT&D.

With reference to human resource management, Filella identifies three cultural sub-models within Europe: the Latin model (France, Spain, Italy), the Central Model (Germany, the United Kingdom, the Netherlands and Switzerland) and the Nordic Model (Denmark, Sweden, Norway) (Filella 1991). He emphasises above all the characteristics of the Latin countries: the importance of the oral tradition, the modernisation of the human resources departments and 'the presence of subtle political structures . . . unconsciously nurturing a docile and dependent attitude towards authority' (p 23).

What is the situation in the field of management training? In the area of organisational sciences in general and in human resource management in particular, the current theories are influenced by American values which tend to misinterpret social phenomena (Cox and Cooper 1985); these theories often advocate universal precepts, except in the case of certain authors (Boyacigiller and Adler 1991) who give warning as we do (Bournois and Chauchat 1990) about the need to adopt particular approaches taking into account specific factors such as the size of the firm, its type of strategy, the sector the firm is in, the different populations concerned in the firm, and so on.

COUNTRIES GROUPED ACCORDING TO THE PRACTICES STUDIED

Every industrialist who has worked with partners beyond his national frontiers knows just how much the definition of the term executive can vary from country to country. Even though it is easy enough to identify the managerial category (representing about 10 per cent of the population in the industrial sector), it is not always easy to define it. A great number of variants exist: in France where this population represents a particularly prestigious social category; in Germany, where many make their career within the same firm; the United Kingdom, where there is no precise definition and where the level of initial training is not usually considered to be high (Dopson *et al.* 1992). A brief glance at these different countries shows, for example, that in France, large firms do not produce their own legitimate top managerial authority, in contrast to what happens in Germany. That is why specialists (Bauer and Bertin-Mourot 1992) write that 'unless you consider that the quality of the top managers contributes little to explaining the performance of a firm and that the way of producing top managers contributes little to the quality of those top managers, you have there one of the fundamental reasons for the differences in performance between French and German firms'.

And so, with the idea of exploring this theme as fully as possible, we have established these three main guidelines:

1 The decision making levels.
2 Training procedures.
3 Career management procedures.

Figure 8.2 gives the outline of our investigation process. Thus, we are following a process of careful observation, theme by theme. In the following account, we shall call the group

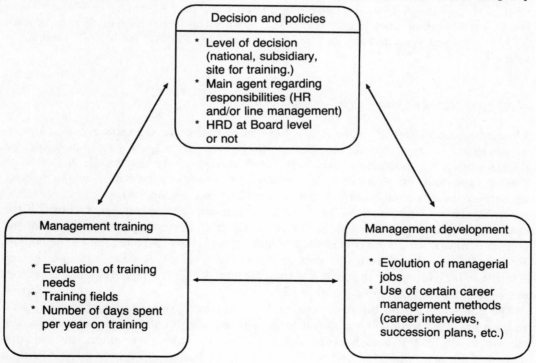

Figure 8.2 Model of investigation

of countries in which the replies are superior to the average of all the countries studied, Group AA (above average). In the same way, Group BA (below average) includes the countries in which the replies are inferior to the average of all the countries studied. We shall base our analysis on the results obtained by the Price Waterhouse Cranfield Project for the year 1992.

Decision making

Level of decision

For firms belonging to a larger entity (group, multinational, central administration, etc.), training and development policies can be decided at company level, subsidiary level or at the national head office. On this point, practices vary enormously: 7 per cent of the German firms take policy decisions on the work site, compared to 44 per cent of French firms.

Decisions taken at site/establishment level

1 Above average: F, DK, IRL, T, N, S.
2 Below average: D, P, E, NL.

Over and above the structural differences between firms due to the size of the country (Denmark and the Netherlands have more small firms than Germany or France) these results would certainly not please those analysts who deal in stereotypes: France, known for its centralised bureaucracy compared to Germany, well known for its codetermination within firms.

Main agent regarding training and development decisions

The sharing out of human resource activities among the specialised services and the chain of command is an accepted fact throughout Europe. Two groups can, however, be distinguished: the countries in which the staff managers are responsible for decision making, and those in which it is the hierarchy who above all decides on the policies concerning the direct subordinates (Roussillon 1991) (see Figure 8.3).

On Figure 8.3, the height of the rectangle represents the percentage of firms in the country that have given the reply indicated on the line. For example, 38 per cent of the German firms (D) and 3 per cent of the Swedish firms (S) have given the reply 'The Human Resources Department' to this present question. The rectangle is white if this percentage is less than the average for the countries and grey and black if it is higher. Here the average per cent is between 12 per cent and 13 per cent.

The lines (replies) on the one hand, and the columns (countries) on the other, were reorganised so as to obtain a diagonal form. The aim is to be able to see at a glance the similarities and differences between the countries. To obtain this graph, we used the software Tabview (Chauchat and Risson 1993), which combines Bertin's graphic method (Bertin 1973, 1977, 1981, 1983) and correspondences analysis (Benzecri 1976).

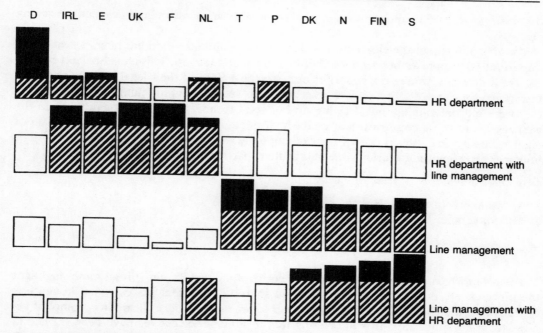

Figure 8.3 Who is mainly responsible for decisions regarding training and career development?

HRD at Board level or not

We consider, along with other writers in the strategic management of human resources field (Fombrun *et al.* 1984) that the presence of the human resource manager on the Board of directors must be taken as a sign of the importance given to this function and consequently, to the sub-activities of HRM as training and career management.

Human Resources Director present on Board

1 Above average: F, S, E, N, FIN.
2 Below average: D, T, NL, IRL, P, UK, DK.

Training procedures

Evaluation of training needs

Training is the major objective of European firms (Holden and Livian 1992) and this fact has not varied during the last three years whereas the budget devoted to it keeps on increasing. The strategic decision makers also consider training and management development as a major objective for the next ten years with the emphasis on perceiving the different legal environments and understanding the differences between the markets. They often stress the prime importance of executive mobility and investment in executive training (Day 1989).

Training and career development is a delicate issue and attention has been drawn to the important discrepancies between the theory and the application. This issue not only reveals the great diversity among the countries but also the weight of their legal systems and their traditions: for example, French law insists on firms spending a minimum of 1.2 per cent of the wage bill on training and drawing up budgets. Hence, the fact that France is in the avant-garde of those countries that regularly evaluate training needs is rather the result of legal necessity than the proof of an exceptionally advanced social awareness. So, it is important to view the different practices in their particular contexts (see Chapter 7).

Systematic evaluation of training needs

1 Above average: F, UK, S, FIN, E, IRL.
2 Below average: D, T, DK, N.

Training fields

The fields in which at least a third of the executives followed training programmes highlight the preferences and the enthusiasms that are shared in different places, even though it is obvious that the challenges facing firms are the same everywhere (flexibility, competitiveness, team building, etc). It is interesting that in Finland executives have been trained in all of these themes. And apart from this particular case, Figure 8.4 shows clearly the

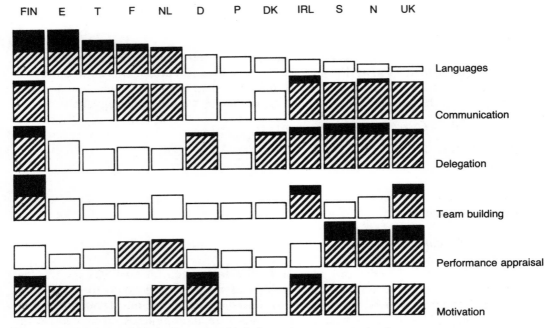

Figure 8.4 Fields in which at least one-third of managers were trained

emphasis put on team building in the United Kingdom and Ireland, on motivation in Germany and on delegation in Norway and Sweden. While a number of specialists highlight the role played by languages in European integration, the very wide spread of the answers to this subject shows the lack of development of certain countries (see Figure 8.4).

Number of days spent per year on training

The quantitative aspect of the preceding question is brought out by this fact. The efforts made by Spanish firms stand out and correspond to the economic revival that this country is engaged in. Here again, in interpreting the data caution is the watchword: when a country goes in for on-the-job training (and this applies to Germany in many ways), it is very difficult to calculate the total time spent on it.

More than five days training per year for managers

1 Above average: E, UK, S, T, N, FIN.
2 Below average: NL, P, D, IRL.

MANAGEMENT DEVELOPMENT PRACTICES

Evolution of managerial jobs

Career management and the techniques associated with it depend on the notion one has of managerial functions and their development. Two very different groups stand out: the countries in which executive posts are supposed to become increasingly specialised and those in which they are increasingly held to be of a generalist nature. The different education systems are, in many cases, both the origin and the result of these representations: the origin, because this conception depends, of course, on the qualities of the executives already in the firm and the level of satisfaction within the firm with the training programmes on offer at that time. It is clear that, in the course of time, these attitudes will lead to very different types of work organisation and styles of innovation (Hosking and Anderson 1992).

Managerial jobs become more specific

1 Above average: F, N, FIN, T, E, NL.
2 Below average: DK, S, IRL, UK, P, D.

Use of principal career management methods

At this point we shall consider how firms can best develop their managerial resources and on what information career development decisions should be based. One thing is obvious at the outset: in spite of the very different types of relationship that exist between the various levels in the hierarchy (Shaw 1990), the performance appraisals supplied by the hierarchy represent quite clearly in all countries the first source of information for career management (86 per cent of the firms in the Netherlands and Sweden, 85 per cent in the United Kingdom, 75 per cent in Germany, etc.).

A second practice that proves to be fairly widespread is that of succession plans: set up in about one-third of the firms interviewed. Alternative organisation charts that result from these succession plans are supposed to assure that the best candidates reach the top and some people even recommend that the hierarchy should be rewarded when it does in fact facilitate access to the top by the best candidates. The Germans have a particular penchant for these methods (48 per cent use them) which they consider to be 'strategic' (Leupold 1987: 52) in so far as they contribute to keeping the firm's management stable.

A quarter of the firms studied go in for job rotation which enables executives to be observed and so to justify the impressions the firm has formed about their managerial qualities. It should also be brought out that less than 20 per cent of the firms use international assignments as a means of career development for their executives. Barham (1992), after interviewing internationally oriented top managers, speaks of two types of basic ability essential in this field: active abilities and personal abilities such as cognitive complexity, emotional energy and psychological maturity. It is surely rather surprising that there is so little interest shown in carrying out international assignments at a time when the single European market stands in even greater need of multicultural management abilities. In view of these findings, we should perhaps not draw so much attention (Scullion 1992) to the fact that firms try to identify executive potential as early as possible so as to give foreign assignments accordingly. In the same way, we may question the pressure put on those in charge of subsidiaries to identify the high-fliers whose talent will guarantee the success of the subsidiary or of the parent company (Lennox 1992). Apart from these few general tendencies, we think it important to deal with the much less widespread practices. An analysis of existing high-flier management schemes shows that there is far from being a set of common criteria. As shown in Figure 8.5, the concern to pilot high-flier managers varies from country to country. This sometimes reflects the importance that some countries give to their elite (c.f. France, which is high on Hofstede's power distance scale) and sometimes the desire to give equal recognition to all talent (McCall et al., 1988) which seems to be the case in Sweden). When the practice does exist, the three stages already identified by our colleague Derr (1988) in the executive high-flier career development pattern seem to be in evidence almost everywhere: first, they are chosen, and entrusted with test assignments; then specific assignments help their development, and finally, they pass through particular posts and follow certain training programmes.

It is also interesting to observe that assessment centres are used to varying degrees in different countries. They are practically unknown in France, Denmark, Norway and Portugal, where they are considered as importations from American and English companies. This does not mean that high-flier potential is not identified in these countries. As we have shown elsewhere, in some countries the techniques for detecting potential are all-important (assessment centres are one such technique), whereas in other countries, it is the development process that counts: the importance of the degree of performance in the present post, the number of people participating in the choice of the 'potential high-flier' (Bournois and Roussillon 1992). In such countries as France, it is clearly realised that the techniques used are far from infallible, and the assessment centres, however sophisticated

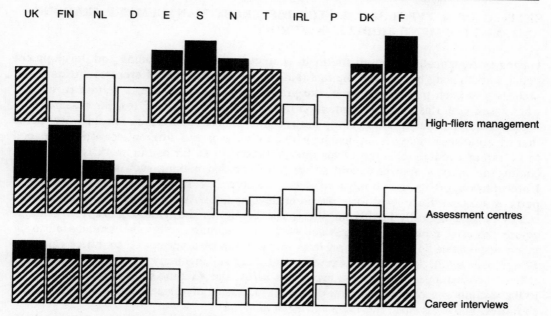

Figure 8.5 The use of certain practices in executive career management in Europe

they may be, can at times be manipulated by those making the assessments (Blackman and Smith 1989). This of course means that such a process is only relatively reliable. These few pertinent comments explain in part why it is not the countries where the interest in high-flier executives is the greatest that assessment centres are used the most (eg. see Norway and Finland on Figure 8.5).

Up until now, we have discussed the performance interviews between the hierarchy and the executive without actually addressing the process of career interviews between human resource management and the executive himself. There again, important variations are observed, including those between countries geographically and culturally close: it is used up to 78 per cent in Denmark and only in 14 per cent of the cases in Sweden and Norway.

These few short analyses of management practices lead us to make two important interim observations:

1 Analysing a firm's management practices theme by theme does not lead to an automatic grouping together of countries; on the contrary, the grouping varies greatly according to the subjects treated. An example of this is seen in Figure 8.5: even though the United Kingdom can be grouped together with Denmark when it comes to the use of career interviewing, they no longer belong together when it comes to the use of assessment centres.

2 One must be careful to guard against linking in any way the use of a certain management practice with the performance-ratings of a particular human resources management system, and even less with the performance of a firm at the economic level; a temptation succumbed to by a number of authorities.

SETTING UP A TYPOLOGY OF THE DIFFERENT MANAGEMENT TRAINING AND DEVELOPMENT MODELS IN EUROPE

Having systematically reviewed the main characteristics of the training and development policies and having highlighted the fact that the grouping of the different countries varied according to each particular theme, the practitioner might well feel a certain frustration when faced with this mass of fragmented facts resulting from this European research.

Our colleague Martin Hilb (1992) has recently published an article on the very theme that we are discussing here but dealing with another year and different countries. We tend to be rather cautious of some of his interpretations in so far as our work is based on a contingent analysis approach, and so we have avoided making such statements as 'the Eurocentric approach is the most advanced because . . .' which may imply that there is perhaps an ideal 'European' form of career development. We are rather sceptical when it comes to systematically identifying the characteristics of the 'global' European manager whose extensive cultural awareness and well tried language ability had already led to his being responsible for ambitious projects in the firms of a variety of countries (Gerevas 1991; Lobel 1990). At the very time when European homogeneity is being more and more talked about as a reality, studies carried out across the Atlantic show evidence (contrary to the assumptions of their authors) of certain increasing divergencies within industrialised countries, above all since the 1970s (Craig *et al*. 1992).

In spite of this confused situation, we have tried in all the work we have done on the different training and development themes, to discover if it is possible to group certain countries together.

We were hoping to be able to classify the 12 countries in homogeneous groups as far as the questions relating to executive training and development were concerned. We have used Ward's algorithm (1963). The computer:

1 Calculates the differences between the countries two by two (by the sum of the squares of the differences of the percentages of the responses for each item and for all the questions).
2 Groups together the two countries that have the smallest difference.
3 Calculates the differences between the group of countries that it has just constituted and each of the other countries, and so on.

This algorithm brings out at each step the grouping that maximises the within-groups variance and, consequently, minimises the between-groups variance. In this way, groups of countries that are homogeneous in each group and different from one group to the next are obtained.

To begin with, there are the 12 countries, of which each one forms a group in itself. Then there are 11 groups, then 10, and so on, until they are all linked together. These successive groupings can be represented by a 'tree': the 'trunk' is made up of the 12 countries all together; then this 'trunk' separates out into 'branches', becoming smaller and smaller, until they represent only one country.

To work out the difference between two groups of countries, the algorithm calculates the mean of the replies of the countries of each group; to do this, it gives automatically the same weighting to each country (as in the American Senate – but not as in the European Parliament!). This is justified by the fact that we are taking the variable 'country' as a basis.

It must be noted here that once the questions have been selected (in this case, all the questions describing the training and development of executives in firms), the computer carries on alone, without any intervention on our part. Thus, the typology that we are presenting here is, in this sense, quite 'objective'. This resultant tree (Figure 8.6) reveals five groups of countries in which we notice that:

1 Germany is a group apart (Group 1).
2 The Latin countries in the south (Spain and Portugal) are together (Group 3).
3 The 'English-speaking' countries (Ireland, the United Kingdom and the Netherlands) are together in the same sub-group (Group 4).
4 Norway and its neighbour Sweden (Group 5) have many points in common.
5 Group 2 is a hybrid group in which France, Finland and Denmark seem to be relatively close.

So, as Figure 8.6 shows, a set of leading features stands out for each bloc of countries. But we cannot, for all that, talk about specific features, since the other blocs may also include these same characteristics, but to a much lesser degree.

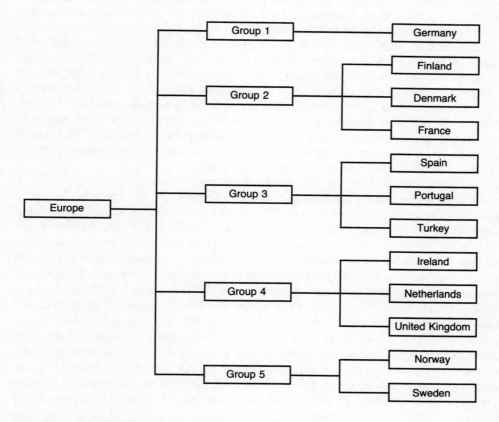

Figure 8.6 Tree showing five groups of countries

1 In Germany, where, more than anywhere else, the human resource director is not a member of the Board of directors (the chairman and managing director often embody this role), the central office of the human resource management department is chiefly concerned with policy interpretation because of its role as mediator between management, employees and the works council (Gaugler and Wiltz 1992: 223). The executives are for the most part trained in the field of motivation and succession plans are the most used means for executive career management. In the vast majority of German firms, executive posts are becoming more comprehensive and general, which has a very real effect on the organisation linking the education system and the ongoing training schemes.

2 The group Finland, Denmark and France is, to our mind, a slightly hybrid group. France, because of its central geographical position in Europe is sometimes thought of as a southern France (close to the Latin countries) and a northern France (having certain features of the English or German speaking countries). In the same way, and without putting its national identity into question, Danish specialists maintain that 'the culture of the country is strongly influenced by its neighbours : the United Kingdom, Germany and the other nordic countries' (Andersen *et al.* 1992: 81). Executive training and career development practices are not often radically different from those of the other blocs except for three points: decisions tend to be taken at the level of the workplace and the executive function is seen as becoming more and more specialised.

3 The group Spain, Portugal and Turkey, wrongfully called Latin since Turkey is part of this group, contains firms whose important decisions are taken, more than in other countries, at the national head-office level. Executives follow training courses that are much longer than elsewhere (58 per cent of the employees spend more than five days on training courses each year). Language training accounts for the largest investment in time and effort while the other themes are on the whole less preferred. The most frequently used techniques for career development are foreign assignments, planned job rotation and career plans. It must not be forgotten that these countries are economically weaker than most of the other states in our survey (Filella 1991).

4 The United Kingdom, Ireland and the Netherlands make up a coherent Anglo-Saxon group with certain important features in common: policies are, on the whole, worked out at human resource management head-office level but in constant liaison with on-the-spot executives. The average time spent by executives on training programmes is less than elsewhere. However, these countries show a marked preference for communication, information and team building seminars. This corresponds to the results obtained in their study by Berger and Watts (1992) which brought out the main differences between the French and the English in their working methods: the French use analytical strategies to get blocked situations moving again, whereas the English bring more behavioural and communication techniques into play. As far as career development methods are concerned, performance appraisal (interview and information exchanges between the executive and his chain of command) and assessment centres are the most used. From our attempts to explain the differences between the French and the British in their use of assessment centres (Bournois and Roussillon 1992), it became clear that the former are more concerned with the process of career development, whereas the latter give more weight to the method and its feasibility.

5 The Scandinavian bloc made up of Norway and Sweden, has its own distinctive

characteristics. The human resource director is a member of the Board of directors in 78 per cent of the cases (compared to 30 per cent for the German group, 45 per cent for the 'Anglo-Saxon' group, 52 per cent for the Latin group and 65 per cent for the hybrid group). Training and development decisions are above all the responsibility of the hierarchy in cooperation with the specialised entity. The training seminars are quite markedly based on performance evaluation, delegation and communication. It should be noted here that performance evaluation is both the main objective of training and the main technique used in career management. As in Germany, it is noticeable that executive functions are becoming more and more polyvalent and require a wide scope of knowledge and know-how.

Thus we can say as our main conclusion that in training and development, the grouping of the countries varies according to the particular theme under consideration. Nevertheless, if an overall view of this area is required, it is possible to divide the countries into five blocs. These blocs are not made up in the way we are used to when we think of people management – that is, the Latin countries, the Germanic countries and the 'Anglo-Saxon' countries. But they are not all that different either.

This research should interest the scientific community and professional practitioners in several ways:

1 As Harris and Feild point out (1992), the risks involved in manager development programmes are many and can lead to serious lack of efficiency if they are not carefully thought out. We recommend a contingent approach if more or less shared national habits are to be considered. If a firm, in the context of its Europeanisation strategy, wishes to shun national differences or reduce them to a minimum, then the need to base executive career management on the corporate culture becomes all the more important. This will mean that individual opportunities and development opportunities for the firm as a whole can be followed through (Tijmstra and Casler 1992).

2 Our research was concerned with the management population in the wider sense of the term, and such specific studies as those done by Staehle and Schirmer (1992), could prove to be more relevant to the training and development needs of lower-level and middle-level managers: the need for social skills, strategic knowledge and knowledge of languages vary according to the responsibilities inherent in each function.

3 In view of the vast transformations taking place in the ex-communist countries and in particular the privatisation process, it would be useful to define as clearly as possible what is happening and to identify the different driving forces of change in the field of executive development – the importance of the time factor, a description of previous practices, etc, (Naguy 1992). In the same way, the disappearance of regulations and administrative procedures implies new behaviour patterns that managers have not yet developed: an entrepreneurial attitude, ability to take risks, the necessity of justifying one's legitimacy as a manager on other grounds than the authority given by bureaucratic rules (Hertz 1991).

4 Since our aim was to adopt a comparative approach based on a vast corpus of data, we have concentrated essentially on the macro level. Our epistemological position in human resource management research has led us to observe closely what happens at the meso level (the firm considered as an organisational individual) (Bournois and Livian 1993).

We must now have access to more clinical research done on comparative and international HRM. What we have so far is insufficient, with the exception of a few examples (c.f. the work of McKinlay and Starkey (1992), on the policies of Ford and the practices of HRM in the United States and in Europe which show the importance of political considerations linked to the careers and personalities of the top managers). At this point we must take the micro level into consideration, that is to say, the individual: for example, what makes the difference in any given firm or in any given culture, between the so-called 'careerists' and the others (Feldman and Weitz 1991). Clinical approaches which can contribute greatly (Kerr 1991) when their scientific status is clearly established, should not be rejected for the simple reason (now outdated in any case) that they do not lend themselves to sound generalisations (Eisenhardt 1989).

REFERENCES

Andersen, T., Kamp, M., Holt Larsen, H., La Cour, C., Svendsen, L. and Kiel, O., 'Denmark', in C. Brewster, A. Hegewisch, L. Holden, and T. Lockhart (eds) (1992) *The European Human Resource Management Guide*, London: Academic Press.

Barham, K. (1992) 'Overseas assets', *International Management* 47(9): 56–9.

Bauer, M. and Bertin-Mourot, B. (1992) 'Les 200 en France et en Allemagne; deux modèles contrastés de détection-sélection-formation de deirigeants de grandes entreprises', document, Paris: CNRS–Heidrick & Struggles.

Begin, J. (1992) 'Comparative human resource management', *The International Journal of Human Resource Management* 3(3): 379–408.

Benzecri, J. P. (directed by) (1976) *L'analyse des données tomes 1 and 2*, Paris: Dunod.

Berger, M. and Watts, P. (1992) 'Management development in Europe', *Journal of European Industrial Training* 6(6): 13–21.

Bertin, J. (1973) *Sémiologie Graphique*, Mouton, Gauthier-Villars, Paris: La Haye, (2nd edition).

Bertin, J. (1977) *La graphique et le Traitement de Graphique de l'Information*, Paris: Flamarion.

Bertin, J. (1981) *Graphics and Graphic Information Processing*, New York: Walter de Gruyter.

Bertin, J. (1983) *Semiology of Graphics: diagrams, network, maps* Wisconsin: University of Wisconsin Press, reprinted by Books on Demand, University Microfilms International, 1987.

Blackman, R. and Smith, D. (1989) 'Decision-making in a management assessment centre', *Journal of the Operational Research Society* 40(11): 953–60.

Bournois, F. (1991a) *La gestion des cadres en Europe*, Paris: Editions Eyrolles.

Bournois, F. (1991b) 'Gestion des RH en Europe: données comparées', *Revue française de Gestion* (March–May): 68–83.

Bournois, F. (1992a) 'Human Resource Management in France', in C. Brewster *et al.* (eds) (1992) *The European Human Resource Management Guide*, London: Academic Press.

Bournois, F. (1992b) 'The impact of 1993 on management development in Europe', *International Studies of Management and Organization* 22(1): 7–29.

Bournois, F. and Chauchat, J.-H. (1990) 'Managing managers in Europe', *European Management Journal* 8(1): 3–18.

Bournois, F. and Livian, Y. (1993) 'Les nouvelles perspectives de la recherche', in J. Brabet (ed.) *Repenser la gestion des resources humaines*, Paris: Economica.

Bournois, F. and Metcalfe, P. (1991) 'Human resource management of executives in Europe: structures, policies and techniques', in C. Brewster, and S. Tyson, (eds) *International Comparisons in Human Resource Management*, London: Pitman.

Bournois, F. and Roussillon, S. (1992) 'Detection and management of high potential managers in large French companies: discourse and reality', *Human Resource Management Journal* 3(1): 37–56.

Boyacigiller, N. and Adler, N. (1991) 'The parochial dinosaur: organizational science in a global context', *Academy of Management Review* 16(2): 262–90.

Brewster, C. (1988) 'Managing expatriates', *International Journal of Manpower* 9(2); 17–20.

Brewster, C. and Bournois, F. (1991) 'Human resource management: a European Perspective', *Personnel Review* 20(6): 4–13.

Brewster, C. and Tyson, S. (1991) *International Comparisons in Human Resource Management*, London: Pitman.

Chauchat, J. H. and Risson, A. (1993) 'Optimiser la représentation graphique des données: TABVIEW, un nouveau logiciel graphique combinant technique de J. Bertin et analyse des données', LESA, Université Lumière – Lyon 2.

Cox, C. and Cooper, C. (1985) 'The irrelevance of American organizational sciences to the UK and Europe', *Journal of General Management* 11(2): 27–34.

Craig, C., Douglas, S. and Grein, A. (1992) 'Patterns of convergence and divergence among industrialized nations: 1960–1988', *Journal of International Business Studies* (fourth quarter): 773–87.

Day, D. (1989) 'Towards 1992: a strategy for training, *Long Range Planning*, 22(6): 48–54.

Derr, C. B. (1988) 'Managing high potentials in Europe: some cross cultural findings', *European Management Journal* 5(2): 72–80.

Derr, C. B. (1988) *Managing the New Careerists*, San Francisco: Jossey Bass.

Derr, C. B., Candace, J. and Toomey, E., (1988) 'Managing high-potential employees: current practices in thirty-three US corporations', *Human Resource Management* 27(3): 273–90.

Dopson, S., Risk, A. and Stewart, R. (1992) 'The changing role of the middle manager in the United Kingdom', *International Studies of Management & Organization* 22(1): 40–53.

Doyle, F. (1990) 'People-power: the global human resource challenge for the 90s', *Columbia Journal of World Business* 25(1): 36–45.

EAPD (1990) (Association Européenne des Directeurs de Personnel), 'L'Europe est en mouvement', Lausanne: document IMD.

Eisenhardt, K. (1989) 'Building theories from case study research', *Academy of Management Review* 14(4): 532–50.

Feldman, D. and Weitz, B. (1991) 'From the invisible hand to the gladhand: understanding a careerist orientation to work', *Human Resource Management* 30(2): 237–57.

Filella, J. (1991) 'Is there a Latin model in the management of human resources?', *Personnel Review* 20(6): 14–23.

Fombrun, J., Tichy, N. and Devanna, M.-A. (1984) *Strategic Human Resource Management*, New York: John Wiley & Sons.

Gaugler, E. and Wiltz, S. (1992) 'Federal Republic of Germany', in C. Brewster, A. Hegewisch, L. Holden and T. Lockhart (eds) (1992) *The European Human Resource Management Guide*, London: Academic Press.

Gerevas, R. (1991) 'The search for an elusive new breed of global manager', *Human Resources Professional* 3(4): 53–5.

Harris, S. and Feild, H. (1992) 'Realizing the "potential of high-potential" management development programmes', *Journal of Management Development* 11(1): 61–70.

Hertz, D. (1991) 'Developing management skills in Eastern Europe', *Journal of European Business* 3(1): 60–1.

Hilb, M. (1992) 'The challenge of management development in Western Europe in the 1990s', *The International Journal of Human Resource Management* 3(3): 575–84.

Hofstede, G. (1983) 'The cultural relativity of organizational practices and theories', *Journal of International Business Studies*, (fall): 75–89.

Holden, L. and Livian, Y. (1992) 'Does strategic training policy exist? Evidence from ten European countries', *Personnel Review* 21(1): 12–23.

Hosking, D. M. and Anderson, N. (1992) *Organizational Change and Innovation – Psychological Perspectives and Practices in Europe*, London: Routledge.

Kerr, S. (1991) 'Assessing development needs at executive level: a case study', *Journal of European Industrial Training* 15(9): 3–9.

Kovach, B. (1986) 'The derailment of fast-track managers', *Organizational Dynamics* (fall): 41–8.

Lennox, R. (1992) 'Wither the country manager?', *Business Quarterly* 56(4): 16–19.

Leupold, J. (1987) *Management Development*, Landsberg am Lech: Verlag Moderne Industrie.

Lobel, S. (1990) 'Global leadership competencies: managing to a different drumbeat', *Human Resource Management* 29(1): 39–47.

McCall, M., Lombardo, M. and Morrison, A. (1988) *The Lessons of Experience – How Successful Executives Develop on the Job*, Toronto: Lexington Books.

McKinlay, A. and Starkey, K. (1992) 'Strategy and human resource management', *The International Journal of Human Resource Management* 3(3): 435–50.

Martinet, A. C. (1990) *Epistémologies et sciences de gestion*, Paris: Economica.

Naguy, S. (1992) 'Historical background of management development in central and eastern Europe', *Review of Business* 13(4): 10–12.

Roussillon, S. (1991) 'Développer les compétences de ses collaborateurs', *Revue Personnel*, (321): 15–21.

Schein, E. H. (1978) *Careers Dynamics: Matching Individual and Organizational Needs*, Reading, Mass.: Addison-Wesley.

Schein, E. H. (1984) 'Culture as an environmental context for careers', *Journal of Occupational Behavior* 5: 71–81.

Scullion, H. (1992) 'Attracting management globetrotters', *Personnel Management* 24(1): 28–32.

Shaw, J. (1990) 'A cognitive categorization model for the study of intercultural management', *Academy of Management Review* 15(4): 626–45.

Staehle, W. and Schirmer, F. (1992) 'Lower-level and middle-level managers as the recipients and actors of human resource management', *International Studies of Management & Organization* 22(1): 67–79.

Tijmstra, S. and Casler, K. (1992) 'Management learning for Europe', *European Management Journal* 10(1): 30–8.

Vickerstaff, S. (ed.) (1992) *Human Resource Management in Europe*, London: Chapman & Hall.

Ward, J. (1963) 'Hierarchical grouping to optimize an objective function', *Journal of American Statistical Association* 58: 236–44.

Chapter 9

European industrial relations
Change and continuity

Patrick Gunnigle, Chris Brewster and Mike Morley

INTRODUCTION

A feature of the industrial relations literature over the last few years has been the suggestion that workplace industrial relations has undergone extensive change (Baglioni 1990; Due *et al.* 1991; Bridgeford and Stirling 1991). The last decade witnessed large-scale change in the social, political, legal and economic climate of many European countries, resulting in changes in the nature of the relationship between Governments, businesses and trade unions. Commentaries often focus on contentions such as the suggestion that the role of trade unions has diminished and that there is increased adoption of human resource management (HRM) approaches, often seen as anti-union. There is also a suggestion that there is convergence of industrial relations, particularly within the EC.

This chapter considers evidence of these trends. It investigates a number of key aspects of industrial relations at the level of the employing organisation as a means of evaluating developments in the nature and conduct of industrial relations. In particular, it examines:

1 Levels of trade union membership in organisations across Europe.
2 The extent and nature of trade union recognition.
3 The locus of policy determination in industrial relations.

EXAMINING CHANGE IN INDUSTRIAL RELATIONS

In the last decade the nature and context of industrial relations in Europe has undergone several major changes. As Baglioni (1990) suggests:

All countries, though not all precisely at the same time, faced the need to overcome recession and simultaneously preserve or improve the efficiency of their economies. While Government policy makers were concerned principally with recouping lost output, curing inflation and trimming budget deficits, private firms engaged in sweeping complicated industrial restructuring, designed chiefly to improve competitiveness through technological innovation, new, more advanced products, and new standards for the utilisation of labour.

Similarly, Bridgford and Stirling (1991) point out that:

Structural shifts in labour markets, movements of capital into different sectors and the alterations of patterns of ownership have taken place alongside the introduction of organisational strategies which are moving from industrial relations to human resource management.

During the 1980s it became evident that although a pluralist tradition existed in many organisations, there was evidence of an emergent workplace industrial relations style, one aspect of which was a management focus that was more unitarist in perspective. This approach placed the emphasis on dealing with individual employees and adopted what are often termed HRM techniques such as elaborate communications mechanisms, career development, employee involvement initiatives and performance related pay. It was an approach in which employers sought to treat employees as resources to be developed and utilised in the most cost-effective way possible.

In the bulk of Western European countries, industrial relations in most larger organisations has traditionally been based on pluralist principles, with reliance on collective bargaining as the primary vehicle for resolving differences between employers and employees. In this approach, trade unions assume a key role, representing employees in interactions and/or in bargaining with employers, or their representative associations. Manifestations of the pluralist tradition include relatively well developed collective bargaining institutions at establishment, industry and/or national level, and industrial relations as a key role for the personnel function.

However, despite the broad similarities and the common movements that have occurred in the labour market context, it is widely recognised that industrial relations in Europe differs significantly from country to country and that the extent and nature of change varies considerably. As Due *et al.* (1991) point out:

It is interesting to note that the trend towards convergence in European labour markets does not appear to have been very prevalent. Most of today's member states have thus been members of the Community for 20–30 years, sharing in many fields the same market and technological base, without producing any general homogenisation of industrial relations.

Perhaps the fundamental reason for this lack of convergence may lie in the fact that industrial relations is contextually bound, existing within a cultural, social, structural and most importantly of all, a political web. Such divergence points to a number of important issues. Key questions concern the extent to which governments recognise trade unions as social partners, and the way in which trade unions are organised to relate to Governments. This is to some degree a political question: one would expect, for example, union participation in national discussion in a country such as France, where there is a socialist president, and might have lesser expectations of that in countries with more centre or centre-right governments. It is arguable however that this is not a simple correlation. Unions are indeed 'out in the political cold' in countries such as the Netherlands and the United Kingdom, but are still seen as relevant by Conservative Governments in, for example, Germany and Italy. It has been argued that in many European countries conservatism has a strong 'social catholic' element which includes an acceptance of clear collective rights (Ferner and Hyman 1992). However, what operates successfully in one country may not be appropriate for another and, while importation of specific features of one system may occur, a blanket approach to the transposition of complete industrial relations systems onto pre-existing ones appears limited.

A variety of reasons have been advanced for the differences that exist: referring to country size (Poole 1986); economic concentration (Stephans 1990) or directly to political factors (Przeworski and Spague 1986). Excellent papers by Visser (1991, 1992) have tested levels of unionisation and found a variety of factors are required for full explanation. Visser also found that although union membership is subject to variation, countries tend not to change relative to one another, so that the rank ordering of countries' membership levels tends to stay the same.

Against these findings it is apposite to set the 'convergence' thesis, which argues that the effects of increasing internationalisation in general, and the role of the European Community in particular, will eventually give rise to an increasing similarity of industrial relations in Europe. The argument has, perhaps, three related strands: internationalism; the impact of the European Community; and the development of human resource management.

The internationalism of business and the role of multinational corporations (MNCs) has been addressed in numerous texts. Staehle (1986), for example, argues that the development of internationally operating MNCs requires that trade unions and international organisations develop coordinated approaches.

The impact of the European Community has also been the focus of much comment and indeed, particularly in the United Kingdom with that Government's 'opt-out' of the social chapter of the Maastricht Treaty, a focus of intense political debate. The effects of the Single European Market on industrial relations have been carefully assessed by Due *et al.* (1991). The European trade unions have argued that they must, necessarily, involve a degree of convergence of industrial relations (Fodeul *et al.* 1992; Coldrick 1990).

The development of human resource management has been seen as an international trend, even if only by implication in the many texts which ignore the national context (for critiques see Poole 1981; Hendry and Pettigrew 1990; Boxall 1992). It has been argued that HRM is 'anti-union and anti-collective bargaining' (Beaumont 1991), that HRM is 'a wolf in sheep's clothing' (Kennoy 1990) and that HRM and trade unionism are 'incompatibles' (Cradden 1992). However, it has been suggested that HRM can be seen in a specifically European context (see Chapter 1, and Brewster 1993a, 1993b) and this would include a form of HRM that involves managements working with trade unions.

These three trends – the internationalisation of business, the influence of the EC and the development of an internationally applicable HRM approach – could be creating a new pressure for the convergence of industrial relations in Europe. This chapter presents new evidence, drawn from a major study of employing organisations, to examine union membership, recognition and influence in an attempt to shed light upon this issue.

TRADE UNION MEMBERSHIP

Across Europe, it is apparent that there are substantial differences in the extent to which employees belong to trade unions. Recent OECD figures on trade union density highlight large differences, with density ranging from a low of 12 per cent in France to a high of 73 per cent in Denmark (Table 9.1). We tested this data at organisational level, in companies employing 200 or more employees, to collect the data shown in Table 9.2 below.

While the results broadly reflect national membership statistics, they also reveal the spread of union membership within responding organisations. Thus in three EC member

Table 9.1 Union density in EC countries (1988)

	%
Denmark	73.2
Belgium	53.0
Ireland	52.4
Luxembourg	49.7
UK	41.5
Italy	39.6
Germany	33.8
Portugal	30.0
Netherlands	25.0
Greece	25.0
Spain	16.0
France	12.0

Source: OECD *Employment Outlook*, Paris 1991

Table 9.2 Proportion of employees in trade unions

	0%	1–25%	26–50%	51–75%	76+%	Don't know
Switzerland[a]	19	39	15	10	6	10
Germany (W)	2	33	24	19	8	12
Denmark	0	3	9	25	60	3
Spain	0	58	9	5	5	16
France	8	74	8	3	1	4
Finland	0	2	3	15	77	2
Ireland	12	3	7	20	51	5
Italy[a]	2	27	35	28	8	1
Norway	3	8	6	18	64	0
Netherlands	2	50	22	10	5	11
Portugal	1	25	16	24	27	7
Sweden	0	1	4	10	85	0
Turkey	15	2	7	23	53	0
UK	16	22	20	23	15	4

Note: [a] Switzerland and Italy 1990–1 data

states (Denmark, Ireland and Portugal), over half of the responding organisations report union membership in excess of 50 per cent. A particularly high incidence of union membership occurs in Denmark, where 60 per cent of organisations surveyed indicate that more than 75 per cent of their employees are union members. Similarly, 51 per cent of Irish companies report union membership in excess of 75 per cent. By contrast, the results from both France and the Netherlands reveal that a significantly high proportion of organisations have union membership levels of less than 25 per cent (82 per cent and 52 per cent respectively).

Data from previous years indicates a remarkable stability in this picture (Table 9.3). In the five countries for which there is data available for three successive years, the predominant impression is of very little change: the percentage of organisations reporting membership in each category (0/1–25 per cent of workforce/26–50 per cent etc), remains within a point or two in each successive year. There is evidence of a small trend towards increased levels of union membership in Spanish organisations: otherwise the pattern is one of remarkable stability.

Table 9.3 Proportion of employees in trade unions: three-year comparisons

%	Germany 1990	'91	'92	Spain 1990	'91	'92	France 1990	'91	'92	Sweden 1990	'91	'92	UK 1990	'91	'92
0	2	3	3	3	4	0	8	9	8	0	0	0	18	16	16
1–25	37	34	32	62	59	58	73	73	74	1	0	1	22	20	22
26–50	15	23	25	13	17	9	10	9	8	4	3	4	19	18	20
51–75	15	17	19	6	7	5	3	3	3	13	10	10	24	24	23
76–100	9	10	8	2	2	5	1	1	1	83	85	85	15	18	15
Don't know/ Missing	22	12	12	14	11	16	5	4	4	0	1	0	2	3	4

The national variations would appear to have a stronger explanatory power than organisational size and industrial sector (Table 9.4). (See also Appendix III Table 6:1). The data suggests that levels of trade union membership do not vary significantly with organisation size, indicating that, at least for organisations with over 200 employees, the level of union membership is independent of organisational size. However, there is evidence to suggest the existence of a relationship between levels of trade union membership and the sector within which the organisation operates (production/construction; services; public).

At the national level, differences in union membership have been linked with a variety of factors: centralisation of wage bargaining; a larger public sector and more leftist Governments (MacInnes 1987). Our data collected at organisational level partially supports these propositions as they relate to union membership. However, union membership per se is only a part of the picture: 'Numbers are important but not all important' (Ferner and Hyman 1992).

TRADE UNION RECOGNITION

A second major issue addressed by the survey was that of trade union recognition by employers. In some ways it is arguable that the issue of recognition is much more critical

Table 9.4 Rights of association, trade union recognition and bargaining in various countries

France	Freedom to join a trade union is a constitutional right and is also provided for in the Labour Code (Article L411–5). Individuals also have right not to join and therefore there is no legal basis for the closed shop. Under the Auroux Law (1982) the presence of a trade union in a company obliges the employer to bargain annually on pay, working time, training and the right of expression, but there is no obligation to come to an agreement.
Germany	The right to join a trade union is guarenteed under the 1949 Basic Law. Individuals also have right not to join and therefore the closed shop is illegal. An association has constitutional protection and has the right to engage in collective bargaining.
Ireland	There is no statutory obligation for an employer to recognise a trade union for bargaining purposes. However, in practice, employers usually recognise and negotiate with unions if they are representative of the employees or a particular section of employees. Under case law (*Becton Dickinson Ltd* v. *Lee*, 1973), a trade dispute concerning union recognition was held to be a valid dispute.
Italy	Freedom of association is enshrined in the Workers' Statute (1970). While the law recognises employees' right to belong to a trade union and the right to strike, it does not require the parties to bargain or to sign agreements. Generally though, employers will typically recognise a trade union and negotiate with it.
Netherlands	There is little general statutory regulation of trade unions and trade unions may be established by employees under the general principles of freedom of association. There is no closed shop. There is no statutory obligation for collective bargaining or any similar procedure in the Netherlands.
Portugal	Article 55 of the Constitution recognises trade union freedom and gives workers the right to belong, or not to belong to a trade union. Unions are free to exercise their rights within the enterprise and sign binding collective agreements, provided they are registered with the Minister for Labour.
Spain	The 1978 Constitution enshrines the right of association, further clarified in the Trade Union Freedoms Law (1985). Trade unions have a legal personality and are answerable for acts carried out by duly established organs acting within their competence, but not for the individual acts of union members, unless they are acting on behalf of the union.
Denmark	Employees are free to join or not to join a trade union. Also under case law, employees have a legal right to be members of organisations relevant to the exercise of their occupation.
Finland	Government plays a central role in the bargaining process. Collective agreements are often national and are entered into at the union/employer association level. Such agreements must normally also be applied to employers who do not belong to a negotiating employer association.
United Kingdom	In general, employees are free to establish and run trade unions as they see fit. There is nothing in United Kingdom legislation that prevents an employer from recognising a trade union, or from concluding a collective agreement. It is for the parties to a collective agreement to decide themselves whether their arrangements should be legally enforceable between them.

Sources: Brugess, P. (ed.) Industrial Relations Incomes Data Services, Institute of Personnel Management, 1991; Commission of the European Communities, Second Report from the Commission to the Council on the application of the Community charter of the fundamental social rights of workers., Office for Official Publications of the European Communities, 1992

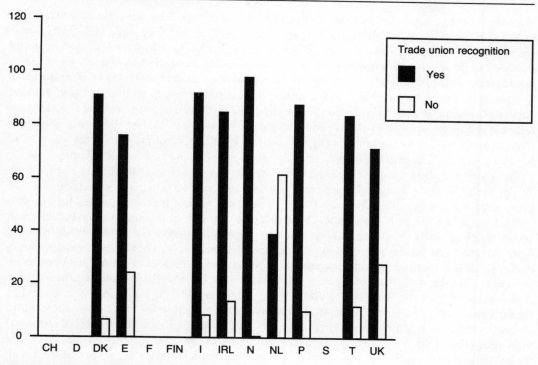

Figure 9.1 Trade union recognition (organisation level)

to industrial relations than union membership itself. It is, after all, only when employers recognise trade unions, and agree to deal with them, that the practical results of industrial relations accrue. Given that the practice in Europe is to cover entire groups of employees, recognition will usually cover greater numbers than would be indicated by membership figures alone (Figure 9.1).

The findings here reflect, to some degree, membership statistics. However, while trade union membership has declined in many countries, union recognition is holding up. Union recognition also varies far less across countries than does membership. Of central importance is the overall proportion of employers recognising trade unions: in most countries more than 7 out of 10 of all organisations with 200 or more employees, and considerably higher in many. Even in a country such as the United Kingdom, where union membership has decreased drastically in the last decade, and with an employer supported government committed to reducing union power, still 7 out of every 10 employers of this size negotiate with trade unions. Our data supports other surveys in the United Kingdom which show that there does not seem to have been a concerted effort to de-recognise trade unions (Gregg and Yates 1993). The evidence from the third Workplace Industrial Relations Survey in the United Kingdom shows change, but no clear alternative to traditional systems of collective bargaining (Millward *et al.* 1992) and Storey (1992) argues that traditional industrial relations and HRM practices can exist side by side in the same organisation.

Trade union recognition was not explored in all countries. The question was not asked in Sweden and Germany where trade union recognition is virtually universal, particularly amongst organisations of more than 200 employees. Colleagues involved in managing the research in these countries felt that in such circumstances a question would not yield useful information and would lead to a loss of credibility in the research instrument. The question was not asked in France or Switzerland either. Union membership and recognition in these countries is by no means as widespread as in Sweden or Germany, but here local colleagues felt that the question was likely to generate a negative reaction and so it was not included. Data is available for two countries (Spain and the United Kingdom) over three years, and for three others (Denmark, Norway and the Netherlands) over two years (Table 9.5).

The evidence shows, again, a remarkable stability in the United Kingdom picture with 71 per cent, 72 per cent and 71 per cent of organisations recognising trade unions for the three successive years 1990, 1991 and 1992. There are almost identical figures for the two years 1991 and 1992 in Norway and Denmark also, though at a much higher level. Spain shows a trend towards an increasing number of organisations recognising trade unions: from 61 per cent to 73 per cent to 75 per cent. Conversely, the Netherlands shows a decrease in the number of organisations recognising trade unions from 43 per cent to 39 per cent. Clearly, with only two years' data this has to be interpreted with caution, but it is doubtless significant that the number of organisations dealing with unions is on either figure lower for the Netherlands than for any other country for which we have data. Overall, these are remarkably high figures, particularly in an international context, indicating that many employers continue to maintain the institutional structure which supports workplace industrial relations. The evidence from this data suggests that the much vaunted predictions of the terminal decline, or even death, of the trade union movement seem, to say the least, much exaggerated.

Trade union recognition varies across sectors, but the variation is less marked than the variation in union membership (Appendix III Table 6.2). Across countries, the public sector was consistently found to have a slightly higher frequency of trade union recognition than that of other sectors. Notable examples include Ireland (100 per cent), Portugal (100 per cent) and Denmark (94 per cent). On the issue of size, the results point to the existence of a positive relationship in Denmark, Spain, Ireland and the United Kingdom between trade union recognition and the number of people employed. No such relationship was found to exist in any of the other countries surveyed. Part of the explanation for this slightly unexpected conclusion must lie in the legal requirements for recognition which apply in some European countries.

TRADE UNION INFLUENCE

Assessing union influence is an altogether more complex task. Unlike membership or recognition, inflence is largely perceptual (if two parties believe one is influential, then that one will be influential, regardless of how an objective observer of the 'power balance' might assess the position). Furthermore, any discussion will be affected by national cultures and expectations. This section, therefore, is presented with the above caveats. In the survey, no attempt was made to measure any absolute standards of influence. It was decided that

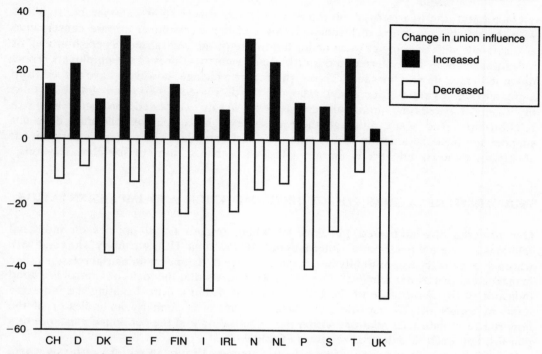

Figure 9.2 Change in trade union influence (organisation level)

the most reliable data would be obtained from estimates of the change of influence within each organisation on a simple scale. HR directors were asked whether they thought the influence of trade unions on their organisation had increased, decreased or remained the same over the last three years (Figure 9.2).

Three key findings emerge from the data. First, there was a spread of trends with at least some organisations reporting increases, no changes, and decreases in all countries. Second, in most countries, a majority of organisations have seen no change in union influence over the last three years. Third, the data indicates that there is no single trend across Europe: the 'withering away of union influence' thesis is not supported by the evidence. Thus, countries which in other trade union respects report similar data, like Spain and Portugal, here show differences. Twelve per cent of Portuguese organisations report increased union influence, but 41 per cent report it to be decreased; whilst in Spain 14 per cent report a decrease, but in 33 per cent of organisations union influence has increased (Figure 9.2).

Table 9.5 Trade union influence: three-year comparisons (% organisations: valid)

%	Germany			Spain			France			Sweden			UK		
	1990	'91	'92	1990	'91	'92	1990	'91	'92	1990	'91	'92	1990	'91	'92
Increased	26	25	23	38	44	33	9	7	8	25	29	11	6	4	4
Decreased	7	10	9	13	12	14	46	46	41	10	21	29	49	52	54
Same	67	65	67	49	44	54	46	47	51	66	59	61	45	44	42

Once again, the figures over the three years of our survey show considerable stability, with the notable exception of Sweden. In Sweden the accession of a more conservative government, with ongoing debates about the future of the centralised 'Swedish model' of industrial relations are reflected in our data. Each year two-thirds of the employers report union influence staying the same. Those who report a change, however, have moved from a greater than 2:1 ratio of increased as opposed to decreased (1990) to an almost 1:3 ratio in favour of decreasing union influence (1992). Again we tested for sector and size relationships. And again, although there is some slight correlation, the data does not support any facile assumption that these are critical variables. The pattern is very mixed: clearly the national influence is considerably greater than sectoral or size considerations.

INDUSTRIAL RELATIONS POLICY DETERMINATION AND IMPLEMENTATION

Our research also addressed the issue of where organisational policies on industrial relations are mainly determined (international HQ; national HQ; subsidary; site) and with whom does primary responsibility lie for major policy decisions on industrial relations (line management or HR department). Filella (1991) suggests that the locus of control is a good indicator of the importance of the HR department within a firm. Isolating the industrial relations aspect of HR activities, the locus of control is similarly an indicator of the importance of industrial relations within the organisation and the continued existence of a pluralist approach to industrial relations (Table 9.6).

Overall the results suggest that there is no common European pattern as far as where policy decisions on industrial relations are made. Our evidence on this issue is broadly consistent with earlier analyses based on country-level data (Blyth 1987; Calmfors and Driffil 1988), although some of the variations within and between these analyses would reinforce the point that 'there has been great variation between countries in the nature and

Table 9.6 Where policy decisions on industrial relations are mainly determined

	International HQ	National HQ central personnel	Subsidiary service dept/division	Site/ establishment local offices
Switzerland[a]	12	51	28	9
Germany (W)	6	43	39	12
Denmark	2	40	42	17
Spain	2	61	14	24
France	2	35	26	36
Finland	0	51	15	34
Ireland	3	44	11	41
Italy[a]	5	73	12	10
Norway	2	57	23	18
Netherlands	7	45	26	23
Portugal	8	64	25	3
Sweden	1	51	29	19
Turkey	0	60	10	30
UK	2	37	28	32

Note: [a] Italy and Switzerland 1990–1 data

extent of decentralisation of industrial relations' (Ferner and Hyman 1992). The connotations of the term 'decentralisation' are very different in the various countries of course (Ferner and Hyman 1992), and decentralised structures do not always reflect decentralised authority (Kinnie 1990). However, with the exception of France and the United Kingdom, policy decisions on industrial relations in all other countries are made at HQ level (either international, or national) in over 40 per cent of cases, pointing to the relatively centralised nature of this activity. A high degree of centralisation is especially evident in some southern European countries, with 63 per cent of such decisions being made at HQ level in Spain and 72 per cent in Portugal. This range of centralisation may be very important, especially given the widespread moves towards decentralisation in Europe in the early 1990s. There is at very least an argument to be made that links centralisation of industrial relations to better economic performance (Henley and Tsakalotos 1992); or perhaps the extremes of centralisation or decentralisation with better economic performance (Freeman 1988).

On the issue of whether line or staff managers have responsibility for major policy decisions on industrial relations, no distinct pattern emerges, and the findings suggest differing approaches to the sharing of responsibility in this area (Table 9.7). However, confirming Filella's observations from earlier Price Waterhouse Cranfield data (Filella 1991), shared responsibility between the HR department and line management emerges as the most commonly adopted approach to decision making on industrial relations policy issues. More fundamentally, where shared responsibility does occur, the findings indicate that responsibility is ascribed to the HR department in a greater number of cases across all countries than is ascribed to line management in consultation with HR, again pointing to the continued centralised nature of this activity. This result is further augmented in Figure 9.3.

Table 9.7 Responsibility for major policy decisions on industrial relations

	Line management	Line management in consultation with HR department	HR department in consultation with line management	HR department
		Shared responsibility		
Switzerland[a]	10	13	27	49
Germany (W)	37	22	20	16
Denmark	20	21	30	26
Spain	15	17	41	20
France	2	14	37	46
Finland	7	24	32	31
Ireland	8	19	43	22
Italy[a]	1	1	35	59
Norway	7	15	35	40
Netherlands	9	38	31	19
Portugal	29	14	20	17
Sweden	7	17	47	28
Turkey	25	16	19	28
UK	4	24	48	20

Note: [a] Italy and Switzerland 1990–1 data

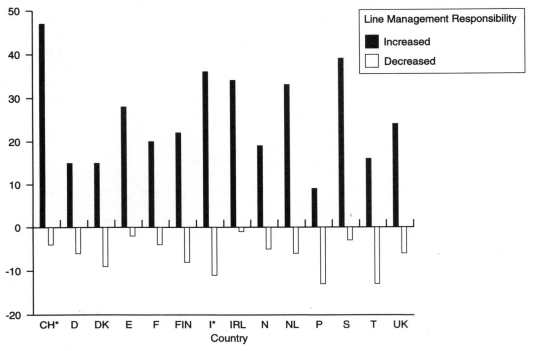

Figure 9.3 Industrial relations: change in line management responsibility
Note: * 1990–91 data

A significant percentage of respondents from EC member states (ranging from 9 per cent in Portugal to 34 per cent in Ireland) suggest that line management responsibility for industrial relations has increased over the period. Significantly smaller percentages are recorded for decreased line management responsibility in this area. Results range from a 1 per cent decrease in Ireland to a 13 per cent decrease in Portugal. Overall, across Europe, it is evident that the increase in line management responsibility for industrial relations outweighs the decreases.

Interestingly, and perhaps somewhat surprisingly, the data shows that it is the service sector which tends to be most likely to place responsibility for industrial relations outside the local establishment or site (i.e. at national or HQ level). Furthermore, although in general two-thirds of all European organisations retain HR responsibility for industrial relations, it is the service and public sectors which are more likely to have a significant HR department involvement: the production sector is most likely to give more responsibility to line management. Responsibility for industrial relations has not changed for two-thirds of organisations: where it has changed, however, it is most likely that line management responsibility has increased. It has increased in 2 out of every 10 private sector organisations and in 3 out of every 10 public sector organisations.

In general there appears to be limited size influence here. In Germany it is the smaller organisations (within our scope) which have increased line management responsibility for industrial relations most. Elsewhere, there is evidence that in some countries it is the largest companies which have increased line management responsibility most. Overall however, size does not appear to be a major variable.

DISCUSSION: CHANGE AND CONTINUITY

The new empirical data presented in this chapter leads us to give tentative support to the notion that European industrial relations is not yet, at least, converging. Our evidence is limited by the form in which it was collected but it is none the less a substantial and rich source of information, filling a gap at the level of international comparisons between organisational practices. A key finding from the survey is the reinforcement that national differences remain more significant than sector or size variables.

On the issue of trade union membership within EC member states, there has been a reduction; but also a degree of continuity over the last decade. In relation to trade union recognition, the data reveals that in most EC member states, and despite such large membership differences, 7 out of every 10 employers across most sectors recognise trade unions. This finding is particularly significant as it contradicts the popular trade union decline argument. With respect to trade union influence, this chapter suggests that in most countries, a majority of organisations have seen no change in influence over the last three years, a finding which is again at variance with the 'withering away of union influence' thesis. While industrial relations policy determination remains a relatively centralised activity, shared responsibility, between the personnel/human resource department and line management, emerges as the most commonly adopted approach to decision making on industrial relations policy issues.

Our survey cannot address the differing connotations that issues such as trade unionism itself, membership, recognition and influence have across different countries. Thus, in preparing this chapter, we have had to take as read the fact that, for instance, trade unions in Scandinavia typically adopt a much wider role involving a close involvement in social security and other systems well beyond the workplace. Similarly, the importance of union membership varies with the relevance of other, sometimes legally defined, means of employee representation within the workplace: recognition may be carefully defined in law or, as in the United Kingdom, simply de facto; and influence can be exercised at a range of levels from individual, work group, through a variety of collective bargaining arrangements (Towers 1992). These differing connotations simply serve to reinforce the importance of country level distinctions and the distance that we remain from any convergence of European industrial relations.

Our data is also limited by the fact that it is an international survey which aimed at obtaining substantial numbers of responses across a variety of different countries. Questioning was, therefore, restricted. In particular, our data is, as we have indicated, drawn from senior personnel/human resource practitioners at the top level of often complex organisations. There would seem to be no obvious reason why their answers to the survey questions should not be well informed, but further research is needed to establish whether line managers or trade union representatives would give different answers.

Overall, the data presented here must lead one to reject the 'post-modernist' hypothesis

(Lash and Urry 1988; Boreham 1992) that we are moving to a new paradigm of work relationships and employer–employee interactions. Certainly, the context of industrial relations in Europe is changing, but there is a strong sense of continuity. National influence explains many of the variants of industrial relations in Europe. Unions may be under some pressure, but they are not in terminal decline and continue to play a significant role in industrial relations across Europe.

REFERENCES

Baglioni, G. (1990) 'Industrial relations in Europe in the 1990s', in G. Baglioni and C. Crouch (ed) (1990) *European Industrial Relations: the Challenge of Flexibility*, London: Sage.

Beaumont, P. B. (1991) 'Trade unions and HRM', *Industrial Relations Journal* 22(4): 300–8.

Boxall, P. F. (1992) 'Strategic human resource management: beginnings of a new theoretical sophistication', *Human Resource Management Journal* 2(3): 60–79.

Boreham, P. (1992) 'The myth of post-Fordist management: work organisation and employee discretion in seven countries', *Employee Relations* 14(2): 13–25.

Bridgford, J. and Stirling, J. (1991) 'Britain in a social Europe: industrial relations in 1992', *Industrial Relations Journal* 22(4): 263–72.

Calmfors, L. and Driffil, J. (1988) 'Bargaining structures, corporatism and macroeconomic performance', *Economic Policy* 6 (April): 13–22.

Coldrick, P. (1990) 'Collective bargaining in the new Europe', *Personnel Management* (October): 58–62.

Cradden, T. (1992) 'Trade unionism and HRM: the incompatibles?' *Irish Business and Administrative Research Journal* 13: 37–48.

Due, J., Madsen, J. and Jensen, C. (1991) 'The social dimension: convergence or diversification of industrial relations in the Single European Market?', *Industrial Relations Journal* 22(2): 85–103.

Ferner, A. and Hyman, R. (1992) *Industrial Relations in the New Europe*, Oxford: Blackwell.

Filella, J. (1991) 'Is there a Latin model in the management of human resources?', *Personnel Review* 20(6): 14–23.

Fodeul, D., Fajertag, G. and Denis, J. (1992) *Collective Bargaining in Western Europe in 1991 and Prospects for 1992*, Brussels: European Trade Union Institute.

Freeman, R. B. (1988) 'Labour market institutions and economic performance', *Economic Policy* 6 (April): 63–80.

Gregg, P. and Yates, A. (1993) 'Changes in wage setting arrangements and trade union pressure in the 1980s', *British Journal of Industrial Relations* 31; 383–409.

Hendry, C. and Pettigrew, A. (1990) 'HRM: an agenda for the 1990s', *International Journal of Human Resource Management* 1(1): 3–8.

Henley, A. and Tsakalotos, E. (1992) 'Corporatism and the European labour market after 1992', *Personnel Review* 19(3): 28–34.

Kennoy, T. (1990) 'HRM: a case of the wolf in sheep's clothing', *Personnel Review* 19: 3–9.

Kinnie, N. (1990) 'The decentralisation of industrial relations? Recent research considered', *Personnel Review* 19(3): 28–34.

Lash, S. and Urry, J. (1988) *The End of Organized Capitalism*, Cambridge: Polity Press.

MacInnes, J. (1987) *Thatcherism at Work*, Milton Keynes: Open University Press.

Millward, N., Stevens, M., Stuart, D. and Haws, W. (1992) *Workplace Industrial Relations in Transition*, Aldershot: Dartmouth.

Poole, M. (1986) *Industrial Relations: Origins and Patterns of National Diversity*, London: Routledge & Kegan Paul.

Przeworski, A. and Spague, J. (1986) *Paper Stones: a History of Editorial Socialism*, Chicago: University of Chicago Press.

Staehle, W. H. (1986) 'Industrial relations and Europe's multinationals', in K. Macharzina and W. H. Staehle (eds) (1986) *European Approaches to Human Resource Management*, Berlin: Walter de Gruyter.

Stephans, J. D. (1990) 'Explaining cross-national differences in union strength in bargaining and welfare', paper read to the Twelfth World Congress of Sociology, Madrid, 9–13 July.

Storey, J. (1992) *Developments in the Management of Human Resources*, Oxford: Blackwell.

Towers, B. (1992) 'Collective bargaining levels', in B. Towers (ed.) (1992) *A Handbook of Industrial Relations Practice*, London: Kogan Page.

Visser, J. (1991) 'Trends in union membership', *Employment Outlook* 1991, Paris: OECD.

Visser, J. (1992) 'Union organisation: why countries differ', paper read to the Eleventh World Congress of the IIRA, Sydney.

Chapter 10

Employee communication and participation

Chris Brewster, Ariane Hegewisch, Lesley Mayne and Olga Tregaskis

Textbooks on human resource management give a central place to employee communication. Mahoney and Deckop (1986) for example identify a shift away from communication through collective channels to more direct communication with employees as individuals as a key component in HRM. They also argue that communication should be aimed increasingly at the task of changing employee interests from a narrow concern with job satisfaction to a broader concern with the company as a whole and used to develop a coherent organisational culture. Similarly, Beaumont (1992) in his review of American debates on HRM highlights predictions of more extensive internal communications; however he argues that this is, partly, with the aim of facilitating more individual participation in task related decisions.

The growth of attention to human resource management and to organisational culture has tended to raise the profile of the subject of communication with employees. In Europe legislative requirements for the provision of information to employees have in some countries required all companies operating there to have Board level policies on this subject. The European Community has put forward proposals to require internationally operating companies within the EC to institute 'worker participation'. These have been extremely controversial, being opposed particularly by several national employers associations and groups of US MNCs. This chapter addresses the topic of that controversy by considering the position of European legislation and the evidence from our survey about developments in communication at the organisational level before attempting to assess whether higher levels of legislative requirement for employee communication and participation are in fact correlated with higher levels of communication to employees.

THE SOCIAL PARTNERS AND CONSULTATION

Industrial relations and employee relations are different in each European country. This truism is only worth repeating here because it is so frequently ignored. The differences are not just in the structure and functioning of the institutions, the historical developments, the labour markets – remarkable as these have been and are – but also in the philosophy which underpins relationships in employing organisations. From the beginning the European Community adopted the philosophy shared by the original six founding members that representative trade unions not only have a legitimate role in industry and commerce, but are more generally a positive contribution towards the wider democracy that was defended at such cost during the Second World War. These views are widely shared throughout the larger Community that has since developed, but there is a difference in emphasis. For many in Europe the implication of the legitimacy of trade unions is captured in the concept of them as 'social partners', with a role and a purpose within employing enterprises certainly, but also with a wider role within the society. Hence the acceptance accorded to the Communist Party affiliated trade unions throughout much of the post-war period in many European countries. During the cold war era commentators in the United States of America in particular found it difficult to understand how such bodies could be seen as acceptable associates in industry. This reflects American misunderstanding of the nature of these trade unions to some extent, of course, but more fundamentally it reflects a different European philosophy. For the Europeans, there is no assumption that disagreement involves illegitimacy: even those who disagreed totally with the trade unions rarely argued that they should be restricted or repressed. There are still many in Europe who would share a conflictual and antagonistic view of industrial relations, arguing that employers and trade unions are opposite sides in the employment relationship with one side only succeeding at the expense of the other. This view, however, is a minority one. Even in the United Kingdom, where such opinions are perhaps more widespread and where there has been since 1979 a Government which took such a stance, this is still a position that is far from universal, particularly at the workplace.

Legislation with regard to information, consultation and participation in enterprise decision making varies considerably throughout Europe (Brewster *et al*. 1992; Cressey *et al*. 1987; Gold and Hall 1992). It is on this variety that the European Commission is attempting to build a Community wide requirement for participation within international organisations. The legislative provision varies between states not just in extent, but also in form. In the United Kingdom for example the only requirement is for employers to provide, in their annual report to shareholders, details of any steps they have taken to improve communication and consultation with their workforce. Other countries have legislation which requires the establishment of separate bodies to receive information. Thus, such separate bodies are the statutory works councils mandatory in Belgium, France, Luxembourg and the Netherlands, Germany, Greece, Portugal and Spain (Gold and Hall 1992; EIRR 1990; Brewster *et al*. 1992).

Some European countries have requirements for employee representation on company Boards. Again the details of which size of organisation and which sectors require such representation varies. The employee representation also varies in the proportion of seats, the way that they are filled and their powers. Forms of employee representation are required in Denmark, Germany, France, Finland, Luxembourg and Sweden.

Between the extremes of almost no legislation and employees on the Board are a range of legislative requirements for trade unions to be given information (from that which they need to carry out collective bargaining in the United Kingdom; to a right to be informed about and to negotiate changes on a very wide array of managerial actions in Sweden). There are also legislative requirements for information to be given to employee representative groups such as the *groupe d'expression directe* in France and the *consiglio de fabbrica* and *consiglio dei delegati* in Italy.

On the basis of an assessment of these different degrees of legal requirements it is possible to place the main European countries into categories based on the extent of their legal requirements for information, consultation and participation. In the highly regulated group will be found Germany, Denmark, the Netherlands and Sweden. In the medium regulated group will be found France, Spain, Italy, Norway and Portugal. Finally, in the less regulated group are Ireland and the United Kingdom. (See, for a broader view of the legislation on participation in the specific context of the introduction of technological change Gill and Krieger 1992.)

Legal requirements for information communication and participation

In relation to the countries covered by the survey we have the following groups:

1 *Highly regulated*. Germany, Denmark, the Netherlands, Finland, Sweden.
2 *Medium regulated*. France, Italy, Norway, Portugal, Spain.
3 *Less regulated*. Ireland, UK.

EUROPEAN COMMUNITY LEGISLATION

It is against this background that the European Community is considering supranational legislation designed to apply to larger and particularly to international organisations.

The role of the social partners was considerably enhanced by the initiatives introduced by Jacques Delors at the beginning of his Presidency of the Commission in the mid-1980s. These initiatives, dubbed *l'espace social*, focused on discussions between the social partners as a way out of the stalemate in social policy in which the EC found itself. This initiative, which led to the Social Charter and the Social Action Programme, placed the social partners firmly at the centre of EC thinking on these issues.

The effect of these developments has been that the trade unions in particular are seen as much more than just another interest group. It is against this background that the proposals for employee consultation should be examined. It is fundamental to the current majority opinion in the EC that the 'big project', the Single European Market, must have a social as well as an economic side. And important in that concept is the requirement for some form of consultation, participation or industrial democracy within employing organisations.

The history of these proposals dates back to the early 1970s; the Fifth Directive, itself the result of a long and complex procedure, was first presented to the Council in 1972

(Brewster and Teague 1989). The current position, still unresolved, still developing, has only been reached after long and tendentious debate. What is certain is that the proposals will eventually result in some form of EC required procedures for consultation with representatives of employees in, at least, the larger organisations; that the proposals are likely to have been modified (the unions would argue 'watered down') to the point where they are unremarkable and acceptable to most employing organisations across Europe; and that whatever the eventual proposals are they will be challenged in the European Court. It is also worth noting here that this movement towards some required form of consultation with employee representatives is already underway; there are now clear requirements for such consultation in several health and safety and collective dismissal provisions. The focus of attention however is on the specific consultation requirements of the Social Action Programme.

There are at present a variety of consultation proposals on the Commission's table. Those which will have most widespread applicability come under the resurrected Fifth Directive. There are also important provisions in the Schedule attached to the proposals for a European Company Statute.

The Fifth Directive

The Fifth Directive must be one of the most argued over and debated pieces of legislation of all time. For more than a quarter of a century thousands of administrators and politicians have devoted millions of words to the Directive. If time and effort spent were proportional to outcome, the eventual Directive would be one of the clearest and most easily understood laws ever. We cannot be certain that this will the case.

In its present form the Directive will apply to public limited liability companies throughout the Community which employ at least 1,000 people. It will require that every such company, or to be precise every such company in which a majority of employees do not oppose such participation, adopt one of four forms of what it calls *worker participation*. In brief, these forms are as follows:

1 Employees nominate between one-third and one-half of a supervisory Board. In the case of half representation the final say would always rest with the shareholder's representative. This is a replication of the system currently in operation amongst larger organisations in certain sectors of the German economy.

2 Employee representatives to form one-third to one-half of a single Board, as supervisory, non-executive members. Where members of the supervisory Board are co-opted, employees will have equal rights with shareholders to object to nominees. This proposal is based on the Dutch system.

3 Employees participate through the establishment of a separate body (such as a works council) which has the same rights of consultation and information as a supervisory Board.

4 Any other system agreed by collective bargaining provided only that it corresponds to the principles of and provides rights commensurate with the previous options. Member states would have to provide for one of the other options to apply if the collective bargaining failed to produce an agreed solution.

It is still unclear exactly how the Commission proposes to implement these systems in countries where there is no supervisory Board structure, although it has been stated that provided the separation between executive and non-executive directors is maintained there is no reason why all the options should not be available.

The European Company Statute

The proposal for a specifically European form of company incorporation was revived in 1988 as part of the debate about the Single European Market. The concept is that companies which meet certain conditions should be able to operate as European organisations independent of particular national bases. They would receive significant fiscal and legal advantages. Associated with the European Company Statute would be a requirement for the 'European' company to consult with its employees, in forms which reflect the Fifth Directive proposals.

These proposals have been the subject of intense debate, argument and lobbying. Some national employers associations, such as the British, have mounted carefully planned and well funded attacks on the proposed Directives. Groups of US multinationals have done the same. Some governments and trade union groups have advanced equally spirited support for the proposals. The issue revolves around philosophical issues of the rights of managements and employees and the essentially empirical question of whether greater levels of legal requirement in the area of communication and participation lead to higher levels of communication and participation in practice.

FINDINGS

Increase in communication

The survey allows for a broad evaluation of changes in amount of communication and in channels of communication. The clearest and most striking finding is that throughout Europe employers are reporting an increase in communication with employees. These increases are found in a majority of organisations in nearly all countries and across all methods of communication.

The highest increases have been in direct communication: either orally (in Denmark, Finland, France, Ireland, Sweden and the United Kingdom) (Figure 10.1) or via written communication (France, Sweden and the United Kingdom) (Figure 10.2). Most countries show a considerable proportion of organisations increasing both forms of direct communication and, indeed, hardly any organisations have decreased these forms of communication. Given this almost universal trend there is little surprise in finding that sectoral differences are minimal. Size of employment has little impact either, though there is some indication that larger organisations are more likely to have increased written communication to employees. MNCs are, once size differences have been discounted, no more likely than the average to have increased both kinds of communication.

This increase in communication is likely to be, at least in part, a result of developments

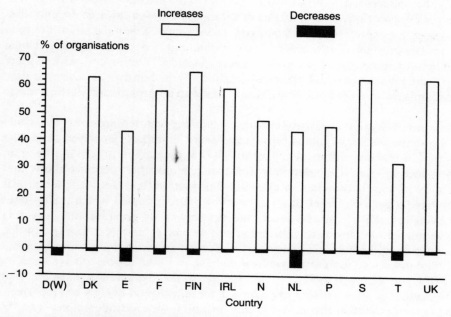

Figure 10.1 Verbal communication direct to employees

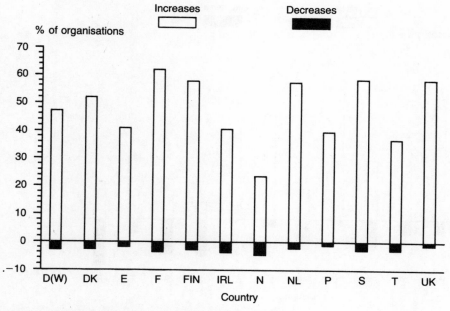

Figure 10.2 Written communication direct to employees

in practicality. The widespread moves towards smaller workplaces (which has occurred even within larger organisations) and the equally widespread moves towards decentralisation of managerial autonomy have encouraged face-to-face communication between management and employees. Furthermore, new technology, in the form of personal computers and 'mailmerge' systems, allows managers to send all employees 'personalised' copies of letters, memos, reports and other information. That, however, is no more than an enabling mechanism and is only one contributory factor to an explanation of the findings here.

There is also a possibility that legislative changes, including even requirements to include evidence about communication in annual reports, have had an impact. However during the time-scale covered in this data (three years before 1990 at the earliest) there has been no widespread introduction of new legislation in Europe. It is possible, perhaps likely, that there is an element of wishful thinking, or even self-delusion, in the responses. Senior HR specialists may have a genuine belief that information is being passed which reality does not support. Even in such a case, however, the proportion of organisations reporting increases in communication here is so substantial and so widespread as to render this as, at best, only a partial explanation. Furthermore, evidence from another recent substantial survey reports that employee representatives also believe communication to have been on the increase (Gill and Krieger 1992). At least part of the explanation must be that employers have made a positive decision to provide more information directly to employees.

The increased use of collective channels of communication, such as trade unions or works councils, is less. Contrary to some predictions, however, this area too has increased or at

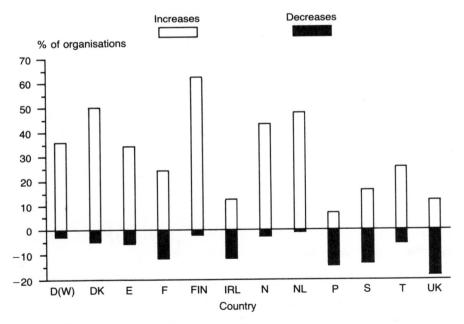

Figure 10.3 Communication through collective channels

least has not been cut back significantly. In half of the countries surveyed more than one-third of organisations have increased their use of collective channels of communication (Figure 10.3) and in the majority of the countries the number of organisations cutting back their use of collective channels is well below 10 per cent; cutbacks are highest in the United Kingdom – but even here are still less than 20 per cent. It appears that rather than displacing collective channels, organisations are concentrating on supplementing them with more direct links with employees.

There are few distinguishable sectoral differences here. Across Europe the average increases in communication through representative staff bodies are broadly similar across sectors though a slightly lower proportion of organisations increasing their use of staff representative bodies is found in the private sector than the public sector (Appendix III Table 6.4a). Decreases tend to be higher in the manufacturing sector, and lower in the public sector. MNCs on average are more likely to have decreased their use of collective channels than other large employers. This is particularly so for MNCs in the United Kingdom and Ireland. However there are no significant differences in responses between MNCs and other large employers in Germany and France. The overall picture here then is one of a substantial proportion of organisations increasing direct communication with employees and a smaller, though still substantial, proportion increasing communication through representative bodies.

FORMAL BRIEFINGS

Much of EC legislation as well as HRM literature on the role of communication, places emphasis on information about the organisation's strategy and financial results in order for employees or their representatives to be more fully involved in the organisation. The data on briefings about strategy is presented in Appendix III Table 6.5a.

Whether employees are formally briefed on strategic issues or not strongly depends on their place in the company hierarchy and on their country. Taking an analogy from the 'glass ceiling' referred to in much of the equal opportunities literature, one can here speak of a 'glass floor'. Hierarchically there is a consistent pattern in every country that whilst managers are nearly always briefed on strategy the proportion of organisations briefing other staff groups becomes increasingly smaller the further down the organisation one looks. In no country do more than half the organisations provide briefing on strategy for manual workers. The Nordic countries are more likely to provide this information to the lower levels of their organisations (between a quarter and a half of the organisations in Denmark, Norway, Sweden and Finland brief clerical and manual workers on strategy). In Germany, Spain, Portugal and Turkey less than one-fifth of organisations provide such briefings for these levels. Organisational size or sector have little impact on practices (Appendix III Table 6.5a). Whether organisations are MNCs or are indigenous makes little difference.

The evidence on briefing about financial performance shows a similar pattern (Appendix III Table 6.5b). However the hierarchical 'slope' varies much more between countries. In general, organisations in Europe are more likely to brief employees on financial performance than on strategy. In the Nordic countries, in particular, more than half the organisations provide financial information for all employees. There are some interesting changes in the country ranking of information provision. Thus, whilst organisations in Germany are least likely to brief manual or clerical workers about strategy they are (with the United Kingdom and France) most likely – after organisations in the Nordic countries – to brief them about financial performance. Spain, Ireland and Turkey are against the trend, with fewer organisations briefing lower level employees on financial performance than on strategy. The size of organisation has no significant impact on these figures (Appendix III Table 6.5b). Sector has a marked impact, with the public sector less likely to provide financial information (Appendix III Table 6.5b). MNCs show some greater likelihood to provide information at each level and particularly at the lower levels.

The figures throw an interesting light on the question of legislative provision for consultation and communication. There is little difference, regarding strategic or financial information, between countries such as Germany where extensive rights for participation and consultation are given to employee representatives, and countries such as the United Kingdom where there are few legislative obligations in this area. One might anticipate that where there is a legislative requirement to give information to employee representatives there might be a 'trickle down' effect so that all employees are in the event given more information. Alternatively, it could be expected that where information is required to be given to representatives by law, then such information might in practice be carefully controlled and restricted, so as not to provide potentially sensitive data to the representatives. From our data there appears to be no correlation between legislative provisions and information given: either positive or negative. Employers are no more likely to give such information, or indeed not to give it, where there is a legislative requirement than where there is none. Clearly this requires further investigation.

The relationship between legislation on the provision of information to employee representatives and communication with employees remains open. However the evidence supports those who would argue that HRM as a concept is being increasingly adopted in Europe and that HRM would include greater communication with employees. It does not support those who would argue that this should be done through individual communication at the expense of collective channels.

The data also leaves open the question of whether employees are actually interested in receiving financial or strategic information about their organisation and whether the results of our survey are not partly the result of employers responding to a lack of interest from subordinate employees. Attitude and communication surveys frequently show employees wanting information of direct concern to their job and their immediate working environment, and that their preferred means of receiving this information is through their line manager.

The evidence from elsewhere (Mulder 1971; Hespe and Wall 1976; IDE 1981; Drenth and Koopman 1984; McCarthy 1989) is that in general employees want to participate in areas where they have direct experience, but in other areas are both unwilling, and sometimes incapable, of participating. 'A major problem is that many employees when offered the responsibility of participation, choose not to become involved' (McCarthy 1989: 115). This can be seen to apply in the formal employee director or works council role as much as elsewhere (see Brannen *et al.* 1976 and Batstone *et al.* 1983 for the United Kingdom; Mulder 1971 for the Netherlands; Hildebrandt 1989 for West Germany). It has long been argued that participation succeeds or fails on the basis of employee competence and that the conditions for successful participation are 'motivated competence', (Heller 1992: 84).

In general there is a question as to whether organisations, and indeed line managers, have the wish – and the ability – to present financial and strategic information in a way that is relevant and interesting. Staff communication skills are now a major feature in management competence and in the majority of organisations in all countries, with the exception of Portugal and Denmark, at least a third of managers have received training in this field. Still, in summary, it appears from the survey that much of the increased information flow continues along traditional lines and traditional topics and remains within management rather than being an indication of a major shift towards new human resource management practices.

UPWARD COMMUNICATION

So far this chapter has concentrated on 'downward' communication, from employer to employee; while the particular form of some of these channels might be designed to invite comment or participation from employees, these channels are largely 'one-way'. Given the increasingly important role of employee involvement the survey also covered the major means of upward communication through which employers ascertain the opinions of their employees. The data on upward communication is presented in Appendix III Table 6.6.

By far the most frequently used method of upward communication is via an immediate superior. More than 9 out of 10 organisations across Europe, irrespective of size, sector or ownership of company, identify the line manager as a key channel of upward communication.

Collective channels, communication through trade unions or works councils, are a close second in all countries apart from Portugal, emphasising again the continuing importance of trade unions, work councils and consultation bodies and the dual approach to communication. Irrespective of changes in trade union membership or influence, between 8 and 9 out of 10 organisations see this as an integral part of upward communication. Across Europe public sector organisations are more likely to use this method than private sector organisations. Apart from Portugal, where large organisations are much more likely to use collective channels, size of employment makes little difference to responses. MNCs are marginally less likely than other large employers to use this form of upward communication; however even in the United Kingdom and Ireland, where differences are most marked, over 7 out of 10 MNCs are making use of this method (Figure 10.4).

After communication through an immediate supervisor or representative body, the next most popular form of upward communication is regular workforce meetings. Here larger national differences are apparent. Regular workforce meetings are most popular in Denmark, Finland, Germany, France, Ireland and the United Kingdom where at least two-thirds of employers hold them. In countries such as Germany and France monthly workforce meetings are a legal obligation in organisations with works councils. However, this is not the case in other countries. Of course, how real or effective such legally required meetings are – and whether they even take place – is a separate question: once again this

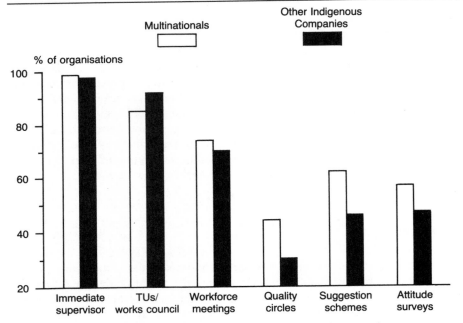

Figure 10.4 Upward channels of communication (European average)

suggests that legislation as such is not the major determinant of organisational practice in this field. In Sweden and Spain workforce meetings are much less popular and are being used by less than half of employers. Size breakdown and company status showed no significant difference in the use of this measure; however the private sector is more likely to use regular meetings than the public sector.

National variations are even more marked when we consider the use of other measures such as suggestion schemes, quality circles or attitude surveys. Suggestion schemes for example are not very popular in the Mediterranean countries, being used by less than a third of employers in Portugal and Spain, and less than a fifth in France. In Germany and Sweden on the other hand two-thirds of employers have such schemes. Suggestion schemes are significantly more likely to be used in MNCs than large indigenous employers (see Figure 10.4). There were no significant differences between sectors.

Arguably the primary use of quality circles is not upward communication but the use of teams of employees to work on particular problems. Given their membership across hierarchy and their aim of increasing participation and involvement they were nevertheless included in this part of the survey. Across Europe this is the least widespread method of communication, with only Turkish employers stating that they use it in more than 4 out of 10 organisations. The high uptake of quality circles in Turkey is probably due to the large numbers of MNCs and manufacturing companies in the Turkish sample. The use of quality circles is markedly lower in the Scandinavian countries, ranging from 14 per cent in Norway to 19 per cent in Denmark. Elsewhere the uptake varies between a fifth and a third of employers. Across Europe it is private sector rather than public sector employers, MNCs rather than indigenous employers and large rather than small employers who have introduced quality circles.

Attitude surveys are the most systematic means of establishing employee opinions, even if they are generally limited to an agenda set by the employer and are thus complementary to means in which employees spontaneously pass on grievances or opinions. Attitude surveys are most popular in Sweden (62 per cent) and Finland (54 per cent) but are virtually unused in the Netherlands (10 per cent). As with suggestion schemes there were no marked sectoral differences, or, perhaps surprisingly, differences between private and public sector employers. Given the sophistication and expense of attitude surveys it is not surprising that they are more commonly used by larger employers, or by MNCs compared to indigenous employers (see Figure 10.4).

This brief review does not allow us an evaluation of the relative weighting of different methods, nor of change in their relative importance. The 'line manager' or trade unions as a communication channel, may be part of proactive and planned communication strategy, or may be part of more reactive practices, constituting in the main fall-back options. Nevertheless the survey shows that both of these are almost universally accepted as part of upward communication. It also shows that, irrespective of national legislation, workforce meetings are widely used. Beyond this, however, policies differ widely between countries, with little systematic sectoral differences across them, suggesting that this is an area considerably influenced by cultural and historical preferences.

RESPONSIBILITY FOR FORMULATING POLICY ON STAFF COMMUNICATIONS

Given the increased volume of communication within organisations and the potential new demands placed on organisations by the EC the coordination and development of communication policies in organisations becomes increasingly important. The responsibility for formulating policy on staff communication varies markedly by country (Appendix III Table 6.7). In all countries except the Netherlands, Portugal and Sweden it is most likely to rest with the HR or personnel department. The Swedish results – with the public relations department as likely as the personnel department to have responsibility, are due to a broader formulation of this question in the translation in the Swedish survey. The Netherlands and Portugal are unusual in that organisations are more likely to give this responsibility to line managers than to the personnel specialists. Line managers also play a significant role in Germany, Denmark and Norway with a third or more of organisations in those countries allocating responsibility here to the line. These results of course reflect the views of HR specialists; it would be interesting to compare these to the views of line managers and public relations specialists, but that is an area that is as yet unresearched.

There is little sectoral variation here, although the service sector is somewhat more likely to allocate responsibility to the PR department (Appendix III Table 6.7). It is also noticeable that it is the larger organisations who are more likely to give responsibility to public relations specialists. Perhaps more importantly smaller organisations are significantly more likely to allocate responsibility for staff communications policy to line management

(Appendix III Table 6.7). By contrast, MNCs are less likely to allocate responsibility to the PR department or the line; more likely to allocate it to the personnel specialists.

CONCLUSIONS: COMMUNICATION IN EUROPEAN AND NATIONAL CONTEXT

In communications policy as in other areas of HR strategy, one important overall finding is the correlation of organisations with country, and the lack of significant correlation with size of organisation, sector or ownership. In one sense at least this finding is only remarkable in that the relative paucity of internationally comparative research based on significant numbers has tended to obscure it. Another recent survey based on thousands of respondents across Europe (Gill and Krieger 1992) has come to similar conclusions. Research drawn from smaller numbers or based in only one or a few countries has tended to emphasise sectoral or size variation and missed the crucial significance of country.

There are some general trends operating, irrespective of country, across Europe. The main trend is towards an increase in communication with employees, particularly marked in the case of individual communication but not excluding collective channels. There is also clear evidence of a slope towards a 'glass floor' in information given about strategy and financial performance. The further down the hierarchy, the less likely one is to be given such information. The gradient of the slope varies by country with a broad north–south correlation. Organisations in the Nordic countries are most likely to pass information down the hierarchy, the Mediterranean countries least likely to do so. Country differences are most likely to be found in the area of 'upward' communication and the particular mechanism that is chosen.

Finally, it is clear that although national differences are the most significant correlation with communication to employees, there is no simple link between communication and national legislation. Our data indicates that the link is more complex. Differences, in particular, of managerial style, trade union organisations, educational levels and other factors undoubtedly play a part. There will be an interesting debate with the theorists of corporatism and of national culture, but from our data alone there is little doubt that the relationship of the extent and form of communication with national boundaries is far from straightforward.

REFERENCES

Bamberg, U., Dizekak, S., Hindrichs, W., Matens, H. and Peter, G. (1984) Praxis der *Unternehmensmitbestimmung nach dem Mitbestimmungsgesetz 76: ein Problemstudie*, Dusseldorf: Hans-Bockler-Stiftung.

Batstone, E., Ferner, A., and Terry, M. (1983) *Unions on the Board*, Oxford: Blackwell.

Beaumont, P. (1992) 'Trade Unions and HRM' *Industrial Relations Journal* 22(4): 300–308.

Brannen, P., Batstone E., Fatchett, D., and White, P. (1976) *The Worker Directors: A Sociology of Participation*, London: Hutchinson.

Brewster, C., Hegewisch, A., Holden, L. and Lockhart T. (eds) (1992) *The European Human Resource Management Guide*, London: Academic Press.

Brewster, C. and Teague, P. (1989) *European Community Social Policy*, London: IPM.

Cressy, P., di Martino, V., Bolle de Bal, M., Treu, T. and Trayanor, K. (1987) *Participaton Review: a Review of Foundation Studies on Participation*, Dublin: European Foundation for the Improvement of Liviing and Working Conditions.

Drenth, P. and Koopman, P. (1984), 'A contingency approach to participative leadership: how good?', in J. Hunt, D.-M. Hosking, C. Schjriesheim and R. Stewart, (eds) (1984) *Leaders and Managers: International Perspectives on Managerial Behaviour and Leadership*, (New York: Pergamon Press.

EIRR Report 4 (1990) *Employee Participation in Europe*, London: Eclipse Publications.

Gill, C. and Krieger, H. (1992) 'The diffusion of participation in new information technology in Europe: survey results', *Economic and Industrial Democracy* 13: 331–58.

Gold, M. and Hall, M. (1992) *European Level Information and Consultation in Multinational Companies: An Evaluation of Practice*, Dublin: European Foundation for the Improvement of Living and Working Conditions.

Heller, F. A. (ed.) (19XX) *Decision Making and Leadership*, Cambridge: Cambridge University Press.

Hespe, G. and Wall, T. (1976) 'The demand for participation among employees', *Human Relations* 29: 411–28.

Hildebrandt, E. (1989), 'From codetermination to comanagement: the dilemma confronting works councils in the introduction of new technologies in the machine building industry,' in C. Lammers,and G. Szell (eds) (1989) *International Handbook of Participation in Organizations*, Vol. 1 Oxford: Oxford University Press.

IDE (Industrial Democracy in Europe Research Group) (1981) *Industrial Democracy in Europe*, Oxford: Oxford University Press.

Kissler, L. (1989) 'Codetermination research in the Federal Republic of Germany: a review', in C. Lammers and G. Szell (eds) (1989) *International Handbook of Participation in Organizations*, Vol. 1 Oxford: Oxford University Press.

Mahoney, T. and Deckop (1986) 'Evolution of concept and practice in personnel administration/human resource management', *Journal of Management* 12(2): 223–41.

McCarthy, S. (1989) 'The dilemma of non-participation', in C. Lammers and G. Szell (eds) (1989) *International Handbook of Participation in Organizations*, Vol. 1 Oxford: Oxford University Press.

Mulder, M. (1971) 'Power equalization through participation', *Administrative Science Quarterly* 16: 31–8.

Chapter 11

Flexible working practices
The controversy and the evidence[1]

Chris Brewster, Ariane Hegewisch and Lesley Mayne

The subject of flexible working patterns has been the source of considerable comment and much controversy for some years. The spread of what the European Community refers to as 'atypical' working patterns is now widely recognised and attracting the attention of personnel specialists and other managers, trade unions, national governments and the European Community as well as academics.

Much of what has been called 'management writing on flexibility' has been criticised for being 'characterised by a consistent style of global prophesying, sweeping generalisation from very limited evidence, economic or technical determinism and an assumption of a radical break with the past' (Pollert 1988b). By basing this chapter on carefully collected, representative data covering all sectors of the economy we seek to overcome these cited shortcomings.

Flexible working patterns are now the focus of much commentary. Amongst managements in particular the drive towards more flexible working has reached almost the status of an orthodoxy. Over the last decade many assumptions about working time have been broken down. In fact, the 'standard' 9 a.m. to 5 p.m., 5 days a week permanent employment contract has never been universal; what has happened is that non-standard patterns have spread extensively in recent years – causing a re-evaluation. Associated with this development is the breaking of the assumed links within organisations between tasks and jobs. Until recently most managers saw a direct relationship between the two: less work meant less jobs; more work, more jobs. This relationship is now seen as much less direct. More work may or may not mean more jobs – there is a considerable range of ways other than direct employment in which the work might be covered. At the furthest extreme the work can be subcontracted, so that the organisation achieves the extra work without any increase in numbers employed. Other options (part-time work, short-term contracts, home working and so on) may involve different numbers of people, for different periods of time or employed in different formats. These options are now more widespread, more complex and more difficult to evaluate and to manage. What is contentious is the precise meaning of this growth and its impact within and beyond employing organisations.

Part of the problem is definitional; it is therefore worth clarifying the precise limits of this chapter's focus: on developments at the level of the employing organisation. Most comparative information in the field of flexible working (with the notable other exception of a study by the European Foundation, Bielenski *et al.* 1992) derives from research data collated by international organisations such as the European Commission, the ILO or the OECD. These tend to have a fairly strong labour market perspective, thus concentrating more on changes in the workforce than directly on policy decisions by employing organisations. The major source of European data on numerical flexibility for example is the European Labour Force Survey (LFS) which is now carried out annually in all EC member states (see Hakim 1991, for a more detailed discussion of the LFS). The LFS is a survey of employees' working patterns and thus is only indirectly capable of identifying changing employer practices. The LFS is only carried out in those countries that have already joined the European Community; given the pending enlargement of the EC this limits its use for European comparisons.

The employer's perspective on flexible working has been taken up in Britain in several surveys in the second half of the 1980s (Atkinson 1985; NEDO 1986; ACAS 1988; Marginson *et al.* 1988a; McGregor and Sproull 1992; Hunter and McInnes 1992) which try to establish the extent, nature and motivation for changing employment practices and whether, as sometimes claimed, a fundamental shift towards a more strategic use of flexible labour had taken place. The 'strategic shift' debates were much less dominant in other European countries and as a result there are few comparable studies. Research in the field elsewhere in Europe concentrates more on the employment effect of flexible working, that is whether deregulation of employment protection and more flexible working encourage organisations to create additional employment (see, for example, Boyer 1990; Büchtemann 1991; Treu 1992).

This chapter analyses changes in flexible working patterns from the point of view of the employing organisation across Europe. We focus on internationally comparative data in the areas of what may be broadly defined as working time and contract flexibility, though we do deal briefly with task flexibility. The subject of what has been termed the 'financial flexibility' involved in variable pay patterns is dealt with in Chapter 6. The issues that are the focus here include 'those aspects of working time that allow variability which lie at the heart of temporal flexibility' (Blyton 1992).

This chapter therefore examines the advantages and disadvantages of flexibility in general and then examines some of the differing forms of flexibility: part-time working; non-permanent employment, other evidence on variable working hours; and we also examine briefly the evidence on task flexibility. In each section we note the definitional issues inevitably involved in international research, outline the currently available labour market data on levels of flexible working and then draw on our data to examine its uptake at organisational level, changes in the recent past and explanations for the international variation in patterns of flexibility. A final section addresses the issue of managerial strategies.

ADVANTAGES AND DISADVANTAGES

Advantages and disadvantages of flexibility vary, of course, depending upon the perspective that is taken, and even upon the individual instances that are examined. This broad overview is therefore written in the context that in any one case examples will be found of crude exploitation by employers and of employees insisting upon flexible contracts despite opposition from employers. What is attempted here is a summary of all the main advantages and disadvantages for employers and employees.

Since the focus is on these two parties, it is worth addressing briefly the 'Continental Europe' debate about the social benefits and costs of flexibility. There has been an argument in much of Europe for deregulation of the employment relationship and indeed in the United Kingdom, and elsewhere, changes to the law – unfavourable to employees – have been introduced (Blanpain and Köhler 1988; Büchtemann 1989). However, Europe remains an area where legal protection against dismissal, for example, is much greater than that found in the United States (Grenig 1991) and it has been argued that the extreme effects of deregulation have not materialised even if there has been a considerable increase in the numbers of employees on flexible contracts (Baglioni and Crouch 1990). 'Most European governments (with the major exception of the United Kingdom) have not adopted a policy of outright deregulation but have promoted concerted measures to increase the flexibility of the labour market' (Treu 1989: 501). Often the measures are based on tripartite consultation.

Behind deregulation and promotion of flexibility lies the assumption that Europe has a set of institutional rigidities which make it more difficult for its business to operate effectively or to compete in world terms. Therefore, it is argued, increasing flexibility in the labour market will increase efficiency and, inter alia, lead to increases in employment. Linked to this argument is the assumption that the continuing high levels of unemployment in most of Europe in the early and mid-1980s were at least partly due to employers' fear of making permanent appointments in the face of economic uncertainty and the high costs of redundancies (Berg 1989). However national evidence available, for example, from Germany (Büchtemann, 1991) shows no obvious correlations in practice.

Advantage for employers

The advantages of flexible working to employers appear clear. The large number of organisations that are using flexible working patterns, and using them in increasing numbers, do not do so on a whim or a fad. Flexible working patterns allow managements to respond to ever greater pressures for cost-effectiveness both through reducing costs and improving effectiveness. Since work rarely comes in neat $7\frac{1}{2}$ hour, more or less permanent, packages, to employ people in that way must have built in surplus costs and inefficiencies. Flexible patterns enable managers to match work provision closely to work demands.

There are additional advantages for managers. Flexible working patterns provide a greater focus on the work rather than the job. The requirements of flexible working often force management to establish clearer performance targets and undertake closer and more realistic performance monitoring. Work can be varied easily – by such devices as extending or reducing part-time hours, renewing fixed-term contracts or changing shift patterns. Workers on non-standard contracts are often more productive as, for example, part-time workers suffer less end-of-the-day fatigue and short-term employees can work under high pressure knowing that it will be for a limited period. Flexible employment patterns involve less absenteeism – it is easier for shift-workers and part-timers to arrange medical or dental visits outside working hours. On top of these benefits to managers, flexible workers are less likely to join trade unions and that is often seen as an additional plus point. There are also potential advantages in the capacity of flexible work to attract or retain skilled and trained personnel who otherwise – through family commitments for example – would be unable to join the workforce. In addition to their skills these groups can sometimes bring new thinking into the organisation. Such workers can also be cheaper: home workers require fewer overhead costs; in some countries many part-timers fall outside national insurance requirements; short-term contract workers are rarely included in pension schemes or other fringe benefits.

Advantages for employees

There is, according to a line of research (Social Europe 1991; Wareing 1992), a significant number of flexible workers who prefer to work in their current pattern. This no doubt includes some people who are justifying to themselves the employment pattern that they have, in reality, been forced to accept. It will also include other people who have deliberately and enthusiastically chosen to adopt these flexible work patterns. These might be people who have made decisions about balancing work, income and other aspects of their lives in a less typical way; people who do not want to tie themselves to organisations for long periods of time (for reasons of temperament, or because their skills are so marketable that they can increase their salary with each career move); or people who are combining one job with other work ('poetry' for instance). At the same time there are, of course, many people involved in flexible working patterns who would prefer to be working a more normal '9 to 5', permanent employment pattern. They are working flexible patterns as a consequence of being unable to find work on the kind of employment contract they would prefer.

There is a view that there are additional advantages to employees of flexible working beyond those of career choice or just getting at least some kind of job. Flexible work patterns can be seen as 'family friendly'. There are many parents who would argue that part-time, shift or home working allows them to spend more time with their children; there are other carers, of children or elderly or disabled people, who are unable to work in a 'typical' pattern and therefore can only work if non-standard hours are available.

Disadvantages for employers

There has been, perhaps, less focus on the disadvantages, but these are just as real. For employers, there are real problems involved in the effective management of a more flexible workforce; it is administratively more complicated and raises important issues concerning the challenge to managerial skills and assumptions about such issues as recruitment, pay systems, training and work organisation. Furthermore, recent research has shown that, despite the general assumption that flexible working is cheaper, a detailed breakdown of all costs shows that in some cases flexible workers are more expensive overall than typical workers (Nollen 1992). In some instances there will also be important issues concerning negative reactions by individuals and groups of employees. A final, but by no means unimportant, topic is that of the commitment of flexible workers. By definition, these are employees who have a lesser time commitment to the organisation – and often (even if not always, Simkin and Hillage 1992) a lesser psychological commitment too. This raises questions of enthusiasm, motivation, confidentiality and trust: closely related to this are important issues of communication between managerial and non-managerial employees (Hunter and McInnes 1992).

Disadvantages for employees

For employees, too – and perhaps more obviously – flexible working can be disadvantageous. It is, of course, less well paid both on a total and often on a pro rata basis. Flexible working brings a lower income.

There are further disadvantages. Part-time work, temporary work and subcontract workers are less likely to receive training and promotion. This is a key issue both of policy (the EC social policy has as one key objective trying to ensure equal treatment here) and of practice (the administration and cost of ensuring equal treatment are high). It is clear that flexible workers are often disadvantaged, as is the fact that involvement in key decisions is difficult and, much exacerbated in the case of some forms of flexible working, social interaction can be much reduced. Overall, the 1987 EC Labour Force Survey found an average of 30 per cent of men working part-time 'involuntarily', (ranging from 4 per cent in Luxembourg to 54 per cent in Ireland) and 10 per cent of women (ranging from 6 per cent in Germany to just over 30 per cent in Portugal, Spain and Italy) working part-time 'involuntarily'. Temporary jobs are frequently taken because no permanent work is available: in nearly 70 per cent of cases for men and 50 per cent for women. Generally the levels of involuntary non-permanent work are highest in those countries which have high levels of non-permanent employment, such as the more southern economies (Commission of the EC 1990).

The social costs of flexibility receive, perhaps, less attention. The existence of large numbers of employees with low pay, periods out of work and a lesser commitment to benefits and training from their employers will put pressures on local, national and European Community levels of government. Arguably if increased employment was created this would partly compensate for this, but the evidence for such job-creation effects is thin.

In equally broad terms, differing forms of flexible working patterns throw additional costs onto the state system. Thus, temporary employment contracts will involve the state in subsidising periods between employment and, perhaps, in establishing the contact between employer and prospective employee. Some part-time, and other flexible contract, workers will be in receipt of governmental support whilst in employment. In each of these cases the state bears additional costs which enable those forms of flexible working patterns to exist. Arguably there may be more long-term costs in terms of increasing social differentiation, large numbers of vulnerable workers and increasing individual disadvantage. This may well involve, for example, issues such as pensions, where the lack of occupational pension provisions for many atypical workers will throw additional burdens on the state in years to come.

Following this brief consideration of broad advantages and disadvantages, we now turn to evidence of developments in the major areas of non-standard employment. We begin by discussing part-time and non-permanent employment, as two of the most extensive and most discussed areas of flexible working. Then we examine overtime working, followed by a discussion of other more 'conventional' forms of flexible working: shift and weekend work and we then consider two newer forms of flexibility: annual hours and home working, and end with a brief discussion of the evidence from our survey of a strategic shift of intent from employers in this area.

PART-TIME WORKING

Part-time employment is playing an increasingly important role in Europe. One in seven people in the European Community is working part-time, and part-time employment has been the major area of employment growth during the last decade. However, definitions of part-time work and, even taking that into account, the levels of part-time work, vary greatly between different European countries. There are also variations in the treatment of part-time workers in legal and social security systems. European comparisons are made difficult by the lack of uniform statistical definitions of part-time working in Europe (see Konle-Seidl *et al.* 1990; Bruegel and Hegeuisch 1994).

In most European countries employment rights, such as protection against unfair dismissal or maternity leave, for example, apply irrespective of the hours of work of an employee. The United Kingdom, the Netherlands, Norway and Ireland (in Ireland the hours threshold to full employment rights was recently reduced from 18 to 8 per week) limit access to legal employment rights to employees who work for longer than a defined minimum number of hours per week; they thus give lower legal employment protection to at least a section of part-time workers. There is currently some debate as to whether this fully meets EC legislative requirements. Some part-timers also face discrimination with regard to social security benefits. An exemption from national insurance contributions (and therefore services) applies below a certain income in Denmark, Germany, Ireland and the United Kingdom; in the other countries services and contributions are pro rata (Konle-Seidl *et al.* 1990). This is an issue that has exercised the European Community: EC draft Directives would, if passed, ensure that part-timers have equality with full-timers, but at present these Directives are stalled.

The level of part-time employment

The share of part-time as a proportion of total employment differs greatly between countries. Broadly, there is a north–south divide. Part-time employment is highest now in

Table 11.1 The share of part-time employment in Europe

Country	% of workforce
Belgium	10.2
Denmark	23.4
Finland[a]	8.0
France	12.1
Germany (W)	13.4
Greece	4.4
Ireland	7.5
Italy	5.7
Luxembourg	6.9
Netherlands	31.7
Norway[b]	25.0
Portugal	5.9
United Kingdom	21.7
Sweden[c]	23.0

Source: Eurostat; [a] 1992 Statistics Finland; [b] Statistical Arbok Oslo 1991; [c] Statistical Abstract Stockholm 1991

the Nordic countries (with the exception of Finland). Within the EC, part-time work is highest in the Netherlands where, after very rapid growth during the last decade, by the end of the 1980s over 30 per cent of the labour force, and 6 out of 10 women, worked part-time. Denmark, Norway, Sweden and the United Kingdom also have an overall part-time share of over 20 per cent, with more than 4 out of 10 women working part-time. At the other end of the spectrum are the southern and more agricultural countries such as Greece, Portugal, Spain and to some extent Italy, and Ireland, where part-time employment is well below 10 per cent of all employment (see Table 11.1).

The north–south split is confirmed if we look, using our data, at the number of organisations who employ part-time workers. Thus in Portugal, Turkey and Spain there are more than 50 per cent of organisations which do not use any part-time workers at all. In Denmark, Germany, Norway, the Netherlands and the United Kingdom this proportion is less than 10 per cent (see Figure 11.1).

Amongst the organisations with at least some part-timers, we find that Denmark, Norway, Sweden and the United Kingdom have a comparatively high level of organisations where at least 20 per cent of the workforce work part-time (see Figure 11.2). However, the number of employers who use only very small proportions of part-timers, less than 1 per cent of the workforce, is much higher in the United Kingdom than in the other countries with a high or medium share of part-time employment: 29 per cent in the United Kingdom against 5 per cent in Sweden and 11 per cent in West Germany and Norway. Thus in the United Kingdom there appears to be a greater concentration of part-time employment amongst a relatively limited number of organisations whereas in other countries there is a more even spread of part-time employment. The likely explanations for this would include the origin of the drive for part-time working – led in Scandinavia and Germany by the right (legal or conventional) of women to work part-time, whereas in the United Kingdom the drive has been from employers who, in particular sectors, have required part-time work to enable them more easily to match work requirement with labour availability.

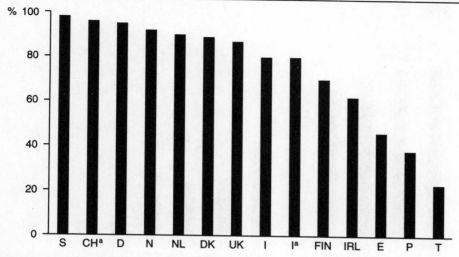

Figure 11.1 Percentage of organisations employing part-timers, 1992
Note: ª Data from 1991 survey

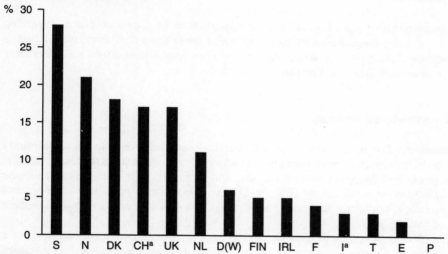

Figure 11.2 High part-time users (% of organisations where part-timers are at least 20% of the workforce)
Note: ª Data from 1991 survey

This analysis is confirmed when we look at sectoral differences in part-time use: the British manufacturing industry shows a lower level of part-time employment than Danish, German, Norwegian, Dutch and Swedish manufacturing (see Figure 11.3); while differences are less marked in the service industry, there is a greater polarisation between low and high part-time users than in the other economies with a high share of part-time employment. Patterns for the public sector, the sector which traditionally employs the greatest number of part-time workers, are similar in Britain and the Scandinavian countries.

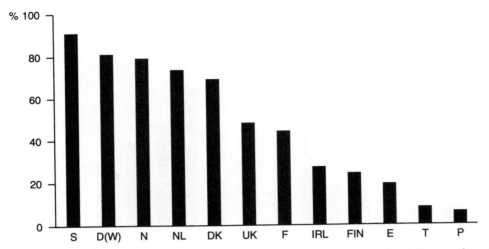

Figure 11.3 Percentage of manufacturing organisations where level of part-time workers is more than 1% of the workforce

Part-time employment is proportionately more important in smaller workplaces (Wareing 1992). However, among medium and large employers of at least 200 employees, that is among the employers included in our survey, there is no consistent correlation between size and high or low part-time use (Appendix III Table 7.2a).

The growth of part-time employment

Apart from Denmark, Portugal and Greece all countries within the European Community saw a growth in the relative share of part-time employment in their workforces during the 1980s. The size of this increase was generally less than 2.5 per cent, except in the Netherlands with an increase of 10 per cent. In Greece the share of part-time employment dropped by 2 per cent, while in Denmark and Portugal there was a more marginal decline (Commission of the EC 1992).

Since the late 1980s differences in growth rates at organisational level have become more marked (see Figure 11.4). In our most recent survey in countries such as the Netherlands, Germany and the United Kingdom between 4 and 5 out of 10 employers increased their employment of part-time workers during the preceding three years; in France, Ireland and Norway this proportion is more than a quarter of all employers. Comparisons between this and the survey of the previous year show the impact the recession of the early 1990s had in reducing the proportion of employers who increased part-time employment; in the United Kingdom the proportion fell from 48 per cent to 39 per cent and in the Netherlands from 58 per cent to 49 per cent, for example. However, even with the recession, it is the increasing employment of part-timers that is levelling off rather than a fall in absolute terms. The number of employers who say they decreased part-time employment is below 10 per cent everywhere, apart from Sweden and Denmark; there the number of employers increasing part-time employment are smaller than those who decreased it.

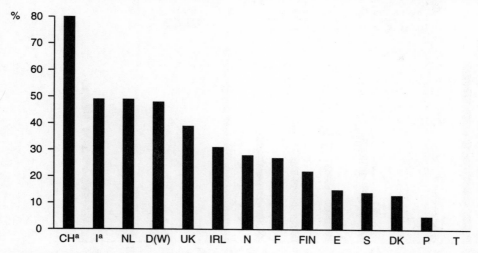

Figure 11.4 Organisations having increased their employment of part-time workers during the three years up to 1992
Note: [a] Data from 1991 survey

In sectoral terms, Germany, Norway and the Netherlands share a pattern in which growth in the percentage of organisations using part-time work has been marked in the public sector, less in the service sector and least in manufacturing (Figure 11.5). These are all countries where growth has been higher than the European average. The data may partly reflect a response to public sector financial constraints in these countries. In most of the other countries, where the growth in part-time work has been lower, it has tended to be concentrated in the service sector. In these countries part-time employment is not seen as a cheaper labour option, so public sector restraints have not been translated into such extensive increases in part-time work.

A dominance of large employers among organisations increasing part-time employment is found in the United Kingdom, Germany, Ireland and the Netherlands. Elsewhere size differences are less clear or not significant in explaining the distribution of growth. A complex of different factors come together in explanations of national differences in the level and growth rates of part-time employment; they include the share of the service sector in employment; the link between part-time and female employment; the availability of child care; labour market policies and the relationship to recruitment.

Part-time employment is generally more pronounced in private and public services. Across Europe we find that there is a broad positive correlation between the share of the workforce in services and proportions working part-time, although the pattern is not uniform (Bruegel and Hegewisch 1994). Part-time work is a female domain, although there are quite substantial differences between countries in this respect (Commission of the EC 1992). The majority of part-time workers in all countries are women, an issue explored in more detail in Chapter 12.

In summary, part-time employment is becoming more important across Europe, but there continue to be major national differences in growth rates and levels of part-time

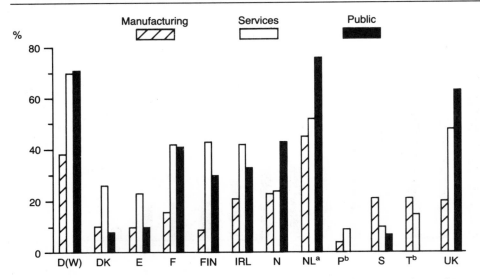

Figure 11.5 Sectoral differences in the % of organisations which increased part-time employment during the three years up to 1992
Notes: [a] Public sector figures from 1991 survey; [b] Public sector sample insufficient

employment. No single factor explains these variations; they are multi-causal. The trend towards an increased use of part-time work however is widespread.

NON-PERMANENT (TEMPORARY/CAUSAL/FIXED TERM EMPLOYMENT)

In this section we will use the term 'non-permanent' employment to cover any form of employment other than permanent open ended contracts, 'temporary' in the narrower use of direct temporary, casual or agency employment. To some extent temporary and 'fixed term' contracts are substitutes, and which is used most heavily in a country depends largely on legal and quasi-legal regulations and national expectations; therefore the two forms are considered jointly in this section.

Temporary work in Europe plays a lesser role in the overall labour market than part-time employment and its growth during the 1980s is less dramatic; however, as with part-time employment, levels and growth rates of non-permanent employment vary substantially across Europe.

Legal approaches to non-permanent employment

Some form of non-permanent employment is permitted in all European countries although the extent and form of regulation varies greatly (see, for example, Brewster *et al.* 1992). At one end of the spectrum are countries such as Denmark, Ireland or the United Kingdom where regulation is minimal and where there are no restrictions on the length, repetition or type of non-permanent contract. At the other end are countries with fairly stringent restrictions such as Italy, Greece and Luxembourg. Countries like Spain fall in the middle: there, conditions for fixed term contracts are much broader and include the launch of a new product or the hiring of new employees and employment creation in general. EC action here has included passing two Directives (Health and Safety of Temporary Workers, Proof of Employment Relationships) which came into effect at the end of 1992. Whilst these will increase costs for some employers, their main effect is to consolidate current provision. Two Directives on working conditions and benefits would have the same equality provision for non-permanent as 'part-time' workers and have been more controversial.

The level of non-permanent employment

The level of non-permanent employment in the workforce varies greatly across Europe. In general it is the poorer countries of the European Community which have the highest levels of employees on such contracts. Non-permanent employment is highest in southern countries such as Greece, Portugal and Spain where the percentage of the workforce is over 15 per cent and lowest in Luxembourg, Belgium and Italy at around 5 per cent. The differences are even more marked when male and female levels of temporary employment are separated out: for men in 1989 this was lowest at 3.1 per cent of the workforce in Belgium and highest at 24.5 per cent in Spain; and for women, temporary employment is lowest in Luxembourg at 4.2 per cent and highest in Spain at 31 per cent (Commission of the EC 1992). Temporary employment through agencies is the most regulated and least significant category of non-permanent employment across Europe. Even though the number of agency temps in Germany and the Netherlands more than tripled between 1982 and 1988, in neither country did their total number in 1988 exceed 100,000 (Marshall 1989).

At organisational level our data shows that the use of non-permanent employment is widespread: used by 8 or 9 out of every 10 employers in all countries except Denmark and Turkey. The 'wealth divide' however is clearer when we look at the share of those organisations in each country which are high temporary/casual or fixed term users (those where at least 10 per cent of the workforce are on such contracts); in Spain, Portugal, Turkey and the Netherlands more than one-fifth of organisations are 'high users'. The level of fixed term use in the Netherlands is also high and has been explained by Dutch experts as a response to employment legislation which makes redundancy and dismissal very difficult but allows the extensive use of fixed term employment as a long-term probation period (Hoogendoorn et al. 1992).

The comparative use of non-permanent employment in the public and private sectors varies considerably by country, with no consistent pattern across Europe (Appendix III Tables 7.2b and 7.2c).

Growth during the last decade

Growth rates for non-permanent employment varied substantially during the 1980s, increasing rapidly in some countries while remaining at a low level or declining in others

(OECD 1991). The largest increases occurred in France, where the proportion of non-permanent employment for both men and women more than doubled between 1983 and 1989 (to 9.4 per cent of the female and 7.8 per cent of the male workforce); Ireland, Greece and the Netherlands also show positive increases (Commission of the EC 1992).

At the end of the 1980s most economies in Europe were comparatively strong. This was reflected in the number of organisations in 1991 which had increased their employment of temporary/casual or fixed term employees: 40 per cent or more in France, Germany, Italy, Norway, Spain, Switzerland and the United Kingdom. In 1992 the impact of the recession has clearly made itself felt and similarly high levels of increases are now only found in Ireland, Germany and the Netherlands. No clear international differences emerge in terms of sectoral patterns. Only in the United Kingdom and Ireland has the public sector increased its use of temporary/casual employment significantly more than other sectors. However, for fixed term employment, Germany, Finland, the Netherlands and Sweden also have a markedly greater share of public sector organisations who have increased their use of these forms of contract (Appendix III Tables 7.1f and 7.1g).

Explaining national differences

Unemployment, more than legislative or sectoral differences, appears to be the biggest factor in explaining national differences in levels of non-permanent employment. Unemployment in Europe is highest in the southern economies and Ireland, as is non-permanent employment; much of this is linked to agriculture and tourism (where the average size of employment is small and thus is not reflected in our survey). During the early 1980s several governments encouraged an increase in temporary employment as a response to unemployment by easing legislative constraints (in Spain in 1977 and 1984; in Belgium, France, Germany and the Netherlands in 1985). It has been estimated that 40 per cent to 50 per cent of new hirings in Germany and France are now on fixed term contracts; however commentators dispute that this has led to no net job growth (Marshall 1989). Overall the levels of non-permanent employment in Europe continue to differ greatly. However, independently of the existing levels of use a substantial share of employers in almost all countries has increased the use of these forms of employment since the late 1980s.

OVERTIME

Overtime is an area where international comparisons become particularly difficult – compounded as they are by legal, definitional and cross-national factors. (See Brewster et al. 1992.) The controversial EC Directive on working time at least provides a European wide basic provision. Overtime is generally limited by law in most European countries. More than 48 hours per week are worked by less than 5 per cent of the workforce in all European countries with the exception of Ireland (8.3 per cent) and the United Kingdom (15.9 per cent) (Watson 1992). The United Kingdom is by far the highest user of what is an expensive and less productive form of working (Spink 1989). In general European terms, overtime working is spread across all sectors of the economy and all sizes of organisation.

Our data shows a reduction in the use of overtime in the United Kingdom, Finland, Ireland and Spain (see Figure 11.6). In Denmark, France, Sweden and Portugal about equal proportions of employers are increasing and decreasing their use of overtime. However, in Germany, Norway and the Netherlands there is still a significantly greater proportion of organisations increasing their use of overtime than decreasing it. There are differences in sectoral trends in Spain (production reducing the use of overtime, services and the public sector increasing it), France (with more organisations increasing its use in the production sector; more decreasing its use in services and broadly equal numbers increasing and decreasing in the public sector) and Sweden (where only the service sector has more organisations decreasing its use). Elsewhere the sectors tend to show similar patterns. There is no correlation between increases or decreases in the use of overtime and the size of organisation.

Overtime is more than just a means towards a flexible matching of work demand to work provision. At organisational level, there are significant implications for, as instances, productivity, cost and industrial relations. Overtime is less productive: it is difficult for employees to maintain high levels of commitment and enthusiasm through a long working period. A lot of overtime is unpaid, but in Europe where overtime is paid it usually attracts a premium rate: sometimes as much as two or three times the normal rate. So, overall, overtime may be less productive and more costly. Where it is used as a means of covering emergencies and shortages it is clearly, none the less, a positive tool for management. In many cases, however, there is evidence that overtime can become built-in and institutional: this appears to be particularly often the case in the United Kingdom.

In terms of industrial relations, overtime work has always been a contentious issue. In most countries the trade unions wish to restrict overtime, since it is argued that it brings

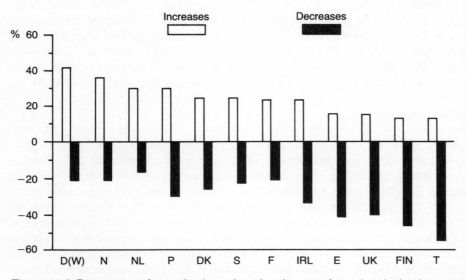

Figure 11.6 Percentage of organisations changing the use of overtime in the three years up to 1992

potential health problems and limits the possibility of extra employment. However, there is often a tension between the union officials and their members, who would prefer the short-term benefit of the premium rated extra hours of work. Increasing economic recession and unemployment have, on our data as well as other evidence, led to a decline in the use of overtime and, perhaps, focused its use more clearly on its immediate flexibility benefit.

Overtime is and can be used as a form of flexibility. The data show, however, that overtime is used considerably more in some countries than in others and that the impact of recession has slowed, but not universally reduced its growth. The EC Directive, trade union concerns and the potential inefficiencies make it clear that overtime is an issue which will continue to be of importance for many managements across Europe.

OTHER VARIABLE TIME OPTIONS

There are, of course, a wide variety of other flexible employment patterns available – some of them very new and very imaginative. Our research examined several of the more widely used options. With some limited exceptions, however, these are less widespread, and perhaps less challenging to traditional patterns than part-time and non-permanent employment. For this reason, we summarise some of the main points of our findings here rather than report on them in detail. (Detailed analysis is available in Brewster *et al.* 1993.)

Shiftworking

Shiftworking covers a wide variety of working practices: 'double day' shifts (with two shifts run each day); night shifts; three-shift systems, to keep plant going continuously; twilight shifts (regular early evening shifts, often on part-time hours); weekend shifts or continuous shiftwork where services have to be provided around the clock, each day of the week (as in the health service, transport or hotels, for example). Increasingly, now, employers are developing new shift patterns with varying working hours or 'split' shifts to match work time more closely to work environments. Traditionally, in manufacturing the extension of the working day into the evening or night is most common but this might also include an extension of the standard working week into the weekend, as is already common in services and chemical process industries.

Shiftworking is not a particularly new form of working; it is essential in some industries where equipment, services and production processes must continue on a 24-hour cycle. Examples as diverse as newspaper production, public transport and utilities, food production and delivery and hospital and emergency services illustrate the need for continuous production and services. New technology, as well as debates over work sharing and working time reductions, have put shiftworking into the limelight during the 1980s. Ever more expensive technology has increased competitive pressures on employers to extend operating hours and increase productivity; at the same time working time reductions for the individual employee were facilitated by introducing new shift patterns which extended plant utilisation and gave management greater flexibility in working time arrangements (Blyton 1992; Bielenski *et al.* 1993). A key development in recent years has been the spread of shiftworking to industries, such as telephone sales and banking, where it has not been used previously.

Concern with the impact on employees' health and social welfare of changing working patterns, new shift arrangements and work during unsocial hours led the European Commission to introduce the draft Directive on working time in 1990; the Directive was adopted in 1993 and will be implemented by 1996. As the Directive is formulated as a health and safety measure, based on Article 118 of the Treaty of Rome, it was adopted by qualified majority voting. Limits on night work and requirements for periods of rest once a week would have obvious implications for many shiftworking patterns, particularly some of the newer and more varied patterns now operating. The implementation of the Directive would require some legislative adjustments in most Community member states, particularly in the United Kingdom which currently has no working time legislation.

It is not easy to get comparable figures on the incidence of shiftworking among employees in Europe. Our research shows that across Europe shiftworking (paid and unpaid) is a widespread practice; only in Denmark, Finland, the Netherlands and Sweden are there less than 80 per cent of organisations who do not use any form of shiftworking (the lowest level of use being in Sweden with 26 per cent of organisations not using any shiftworking) (Appendix III Table 7.1b). It is clear from our evidence that growth in shiftworking is correlated with national economic performance; growing most strongly in countries which have been impacted less by the recession, growing least in those worst hit. Shiftworking is an area of work that has seen some increases in use since the mid to late 1980s albeit not as strongly as contract flexibility. While shiftworking is important in certain service industries its stronghold remains in production.

Weekend work

The introduction of weekend working potentially increases the competitiveness of industry as well as allowing employers to tap new sources of labour. However, these economic pressures are legally restricted. In nearly all European countries weekly rest periods are provided for by law. The provisions for time off and rest periods normally include Sunday and, in some cases, Saturday. In Spain and Portugal one and a half days' rest are guaranteed by legislation. In many countries the working week is organised over five days providing two rest days. In most cases, when work is carried out on Sundays (or public holidays), legislation gives the right to compensatory time the following week and in some countries special monetary compensation is paid for Sunday work. In countries where Sunday is specified as a day off, however, there are normally exemptions which permit Sunday opening or operation for certain enterprises. In Belgium, France and Italy collective agreements can derogate from legislation.

The subject of weekend working is an emotive one and the introduction or extension of weekend working often brings problems, particularly in manufacturing industries where the workforces are traditionally more likely to be male and covered by collective agreements. Trade unions in several European countries have argued vigorously against increases in weekend working.

In a recent survey of flexible working practices in the private sector in 9 European countries Saturday working was the most common form of non-standard working, with an estimated 13 per cent of private sector employees regularly working Saturdays (Bielenski *et al.* 1993); comparable figures are not available for Sunday working which is much less common across Europe.

Most employers in our research use weekend working. At one end, only 6 per cent of organisations in the United Kingdom do not use weekend working at all, ranging up to 35 per cent in the Netherlands. Across Europe however there is evidence of a modest if steady increase in the use of weekend working, although in none of the countries in the survey have more than a fifth of organisations increased their use of this working arrangement in the previous three years.

Subcontracting

Subcontracting is 'the displacement of an employment contract by a commercial one as a means of getting a job done' (Atkinson and Meager 1986a). Unlike most other forms of flexible working discussed in this report subcontracting might not necessarily involve 'non-standard' forms of employment from the worker's point of view. They might be a permanent full-time employee in the contractor firm.

In all major West European countries there is a marked increase or steady uptake in subcontracting. Only a minority of organisations in the public or private sectors in any country have decreased the use of subcontracting. In West Germany, 41 per cent of all organisations surveyed in our research indicate that subcontracting has increased. In Spain, France, Ireland, Turkey and the United Kingdom 30 per cent or more of all organisations have increased their use of subcontracting. There appears to be generally less uptake of subcontracting in the Nordic countries and the Netherlands than in other parts of Europe. Subcontracting is not used in 44 per cent of Dutch or Swedish organisations (Brewster *et al.* 1993).

Annual hours

We now turn to two new forms of employment, annual hours and home working, which have been much discussed in countries such as Germany, the United Kingdom or Sweden. However, evidence on both of these suggest that increases so far remain limited to a small number of employers.

An annual hours contract has been defined as where the employee works an agreed number of hours across the year disposed according to agreement or to the demands of the employer (Brewster and Connock 1985; Hutchinson 1993). Such arrangements work most effectively where regular variations in demand can be foreseen (Brewster *et al.* 1993; Pickard 1991).

An annual hours contract attempts to overcome the problem of mismatch between employee working time and the hours required to cover workload by allowing available working hours to be rescheduled over the year in order to match output or demand. By allowing managers to match the available manpower resources more closely to business needs, costs can be significantly reduced through the elimination of additional labour, inefficient overtime and reduced stock levels. Some organisations report unexpected benefits not initially foreseen such as reduced absence rates, improved motivation and industrial relations (Hutchinson 1993).

For employees annual hours are normally associated with a higher level of guaranteed earnings, more time off and a greater predictability and stability. However, setting the correct level of annual hours in the first instance can be a problem, and for this reason the system can be unsuitable for businesses with unpredictable demand (Pickard 1991). The system can also be inflexible in adapting to recessionary times. The disadvantages for employees include a loss of earnings through overtime, rostered holidays, and the use of 'reserve' or extra hours which are 'owed' by the employee to the company.

Such contracts are in a growing minority. Our data confirms that this trend is upward. The bulk of interest in the United Kingdom occurred in the public sector with 19 per cent of organisations reporting an increase compared to 8 per cent in the public sector. Similar comparisons across Europe show much variation, significant increases occur in the private sector in the Netherlands. Scandinavia shows an overall decrease in their use. The situation in the Netherlands is almost totally reversed with almost one-third of organisations increasing their use of annual hours (Appendix III see Table 7.1d). The size of organisation does not seem to be a critical variable nor surprisingly does sector. Although the spread of annual hours is not as widespread as discussion would imply, the use of such schemes seems to be increasing.

Home working

Home working can be broken down into two major areas, that of 'traditional' home work and that of 'teleworking'. Home working, in our definition, includes employees who are working from home for a wage or salary, mainly for one employer. This is the most common definition of home working although some researchers (for example, Hakim 1987a) broaden the definition to include people who are working *from* home (as against *at* home), such as small business men or consultants. These occupy quite a different place in the labour market and, more importantly for the purposes of this chapter, their employment presents different issues for management, more akin to subcontracting. (See Phizacklea and Wolkowitz 1990 for a critical discussion of the implications of different definitions.)

In 1986 respondents to a survey on the long-term implications of IT in the United Kingdom forecast a proportion of between 10 and 15 per cent of the skilled workforce engaged in telework in 1995 increasing to 15 to 20 per cent by the year 2010 (NEDO 1986). So far, however, there has been little sign of such a dramatic increase. Data from our research shows home working involves less than 1 per cent of the workforce in the vast majority of organisations in all countries. Contrary to prediction there has been little sign of any increase over the last three years; small general increases can be found only in the Scandinavian countries. Private sector employers have hardly moved at all in this direction and, if anything, it has been the public sector which has been more enthusiastic in taking up home working. (Appendix III Table 7.1h).

This being the case the question is raised as to why more people in more organisations have not moved to home working. The answer may have something to do with a lack of awareness on the part of employers and employees; with the technological costs which are only now coming down significantly and beginning to turn a technical opportunity into an economic one; or with fears of exploitation of home workers. It is more likely, however, that the claimed benefits are not so great as at first assumed and are outweighed by two more substantial issues. The first is that managers are reluctant to lose the contact with, and control of, staff that comes from face to face meetings: home working does generate problems of creating and maintaining the effective liaison and coordination between staff that are often critical to successful performance. The second is that home working is not all fun – home workers often feel isolated and alienated, missing the social contact that work provides.

TASK FLEXIBILITY: A BATTLE THAT IS WON?

The discussion so far has been of working time and contractual flexibility. Significant moves have also been made in the area of task flexibility. For many years jobs in Europe have tended to be closely circumscribed, bound by detailed job descriptions. The consequence was a workforce unwilling to broaden their work or change it: at least, they were unwilling to do so unless there was a pay inducement. In the past many European countries, particularly the northern ones, carried the managerial process of the division of labour to great lengths. Jobs were increasingly tightly defined and qualifications carefully specified. Trade unions and professional associations jealously guarded the boundaries in many cases. In the United Kingdom and Ireland, particularly 'demarcation disputes' where unions fought to protect job boundaries were common in the 1960s and 1970s. Throughout Europe job categories are defended by law, particularly in the case of the professions and in socially defined service areas such as policing: in some countries occupational groups such as management or the public sector (the French *cadre*, the German *Beamten*) have legally defined job categories.

The requirements of flexibility are challenging these boundaries. The increasing speed of technological change, and the requirements of cost-efficiency, have raised questions concerning whether individuals could continue to refuse to work beyond their job boundaries or refuse entry to 'their' work to others. To a considerable degree these boundaries have been broken down, particularly at the lower levels of the organisational hierarchy (Bamber 1989; Boyer 1990). It seems to be at the highest levels that there is most resistance to flexibility.

Our data on task flexibility shows less evidence of any clear-cut trends than the evidence on temporal (or for that matter financial, see Chapter 6) flexibility. As a general rule, across Europe managerial roles are tending to become more specific in a greater number of countries and wider/more flexible in only a few: notably, Germany (61 per cent organisation), Sweden, (59 per cent), the United Kingdom (45 per cent) and Ireland (42 per cent). Elsewhere, France, Finland and Norway have more than half their organisations reporting managerial jobs have been made more specific (55 per cent, 52 per cent and 52 per cent of organisations respectively); with the Netherlands, Portugal and Turkey all showing almost equal proportions of organisations making managerial jobs more specific, staying the same, and becoming more flexible.

Nationally the evidence is of widening jobs in all areas in Sweden and the United Kingdom; and of widening jobs in all areas except management in Finland and Norway. German organisations tend to report jobs being made wider/more flexible at all levels in the hierarchy but with a higher proportion not changing at the lower, clerical and manual levels. The southern European countries have a majority of countries reporting no change, or sometimes reporting a split between those making jobs wider and those making them more specific. Of course in all countries there are some organisations making extensive increases of flexibility at the lower levels of the organisation. In the clerical area, for example, there is also case-study evidence of change (Juul 1993).

As we move down the hierarchy the tendency not to have had any major change in the three years to 1992 grows, so that this is the predominant pattern in ten of the twelve countries for manual workers. Only in Sweden do around half of the organisations (48 per cent) report a widening of manual jobs: Finland (44 per cent) is the only other country reporting more 'widening' than 'no change'. However, in only a few cases are manual jobs being made more specific (less than 25 per cent of organisations in all countries report this).

The evidence, overall, may be that there is already considerable task flexibility within European organisations and that it continues to grow. The slower growth of flexibility at managerial level may reflect continued resistance to job widening and job changes at this level. The variety of movement here is also perhaps testament to a continuing debate about the best way to organise managerial jobs and it may also reflect a desire to specify the outcomes of managerial work rather more clearly.

FLEXIBILITY: A STRATEGIC APPROACH?

The academic discussion of human resource flexibility at the level of the firm has been led by British commentators, starting with the work of Atkinson (1984a, 1984b, 1985) Atkinson and Meager (1986a, 1986b) and attacks on the concept led by Pollert (1987, 1988a, 1991). The model of the 'flexible firm' put forward by Atkinson focused on the type of contracts offered by employers and proposed a differentiation between a core workforce of full-time, permanent employees, for whom functional flexibility was seen to be appropriate; and a peripheral workforce of part-time, temporary and subcontract workers for whom numerical flexibility was relevant. A further development adds in the concept of 'distancing', which includes even more peripheral, non-employment relationships such as franchising, self-employment, home working, networking and subcontracting. In keeping with British experience at the time Atkinson's model attaches little importance to financial flexibility, only mentioning 'assessment-based pay systems' as a means of facilitating numerical or functional flexibility.

The attacks on the model have argued that it is not a new theory; that there is little evidence that the growth in flexibility is more than a reflection of a sectoral shift to the service sector; that the core/peripheral distinction is not useful; and that it confuses analysis with prescription. A central plank of the attack on the flexible firm concept has been an argument that there is no evidence that employers have manpower strategies: that they are merely reacting in an opportunistic fashion.

In the flexible firm debate various authors have argued that managerial motives of reducing costs are fundamental to a flexibility strategy (Piore and Sabel 1985) or are evidence that there is no such strategy (Pollert 1987, 1991). Rubery (1988) has pointed out that a coherent managerial strategy in this area may be merely a spin-off from some wider strategy. Other authors have attempted to identify whether there was a relationship between different forms of flexibility, such that employers might be seen to be developing a 'full set' of peripheral workers, or setting use of one type against another (Hakim 1985; Blanchflower and Corry 1987; Casey 1991). Authors who have used this approach through some form of survey include Marginson *et al.* 1988b; Wood and Smith 1989; Hakim 1990; IRS 1990; Hunter and MacInnes 1992; McGregor and Sproull 1992. Most of the commentators here have failed to find evidence of written, or worked through strategies aimed at the creation of a core/peripheral workforce per se and have concluded that there is, therefore, no strategy.

Our research tested some of these propositions. The results show hardly any correlation between either the use, or changes in the use, of flexibility and managerial strategies: neither corporate, nor personnel or HR strategy, nor the presence of an HR director at Board level were significantly correlated with organisations which showed greater use of flexibility. Nor were they significantly correlated with change, increase or decrease, in the use of the various forms of flexible working that have been examined here.

Overall, this shows that a planned move towards flexibility is, at the least, not linked to any formal, written or unwritten, strategic approach to HRM. The absence of correlation needs to be qualified in four respects. There is some evidence that there may be a limited correlation between strategies and flexibility in France (almost alone of all the European countries). There is some evidence of a limited correlation between subcontracting and corporate strategy in a few countries. There is some evidence that the use of larger numbers of temporary or casual workers is correlated with personnel or HR strategies in a few countries. Finally, within the context of an overall lack of correlation between flexibility and strategy, it does seem that if there is a link, it is more likely to be with the presence of corporate strategies than with the existence of personnel or HR strategies. This bears out the point made by such commentators as Piore and Sabel (1985) and Rubery (1988), that the drive for flexibility is a response to financial constraints rather than being human resource management driven.

Our data does not, of course, imply that within this clear evidence of an absence of strategy there may not be individual firms who have conscious, well thought out and effective strategies. Those who have undertaken research at the case-study level have been inclined to be cautious about denying an absence of any link between flexibility and strategy: though finding little evidence of simplistic core/peripheral strategies, by linking manpower policies directly to wider managerial policies, they do tend to find evidence of strategies of a more incremental kind (O'Reilly 1992; Collinson *et al.* 1990; Geary 1992). A recent article, based on work carried out in the 'late 1980s', found that employers were often dealing with qualitative rather than quantitative assessments, balancing costs against 'behavioural consequences', such as timekeeping, absenteeism and loyalty. In that context they argue that:

> a truly corporate strategy for manpower is something of a chimera . . . Rather it was the business strategy which really mattered at corporate level, governed very much by the competitive forces at work in the 1980s, and its demands had to be satisfied by the lower levels of management . . . if this meant attempting to reduce labour costs by adopting or extending the use of non-standard contracts, they would do so
>
> (Hunter and MacInnes 1992)

The issue of employer strategies is bedevilled by different views of how such strategies would be manifested. The extent to which managerial adoption of flexibility can be characterised as 'strategic' as opposed to 'opportunistic' may be largely a question of how formalistic a strategy one searches for. There are clearly other cases where organisations have taken up aspects of flexibility for purely opportunistic reasons: to recruit particular workers or overcome 'headcount' restrictions, for example. There are organisations who have developed conscious and coherent strategies for increasing the number and kind of flexible contracts. These, however, are a minority and it is in this sense that it is possible to argue that flexible working is not, in general, a strategic response by management.

However, the strategy literature has moved on. Since the late 1970s Mintzberg (1978, 1987a, 1987b) and others (Quinn 1980; Pascale 1984; Child 1985; Pearson 1990) have argued that in practice strategy is rarely so formalised. Usually it 'emerges' as a consistent pattern of behaviour over time in response to particular stimuli. Clearly survey data is not the best way to establish such patterns (Morris and Wood 1991), but in so far as our evidence sheds light on the debate, it does seem to support the argument that on this definition at least there is a managerial strategy of flexibility.

CONCLUSION

Several key facts emerge. The first, and perhaps the most important, is that despite the different legal, cultural and labour traditions around Europe there is a clear general trend amongst employers across the different sectors towards increasing their use of flexibility. This trend varies by country, sector and size and has been slowed by the impact of the recession. It is, nevertheless, a clear and largely consistent development. Reasons for this undoubtedly lie mainly in the pressure on employers to utilise more cost-effective human resource management and the way in which flexible working practices enable them to match labour provision more closely to work requirements and hence to reduce unit labour costs. That flexibilisation also has other advantages is an additional bonus.

Second, the data presented here shows that the largest growth recently has been in the use of part-time, temporary and fixed term contracts. There has been a lower increase in the use of other aspects of flexibility such as shift or weekend working, overtime and subcontracting. In these areas, too, there is a small but more noticeable number of organisations who have reduced their use of these forms of flexibility. The growth in tele- and home working is so small as to raise questions about why the predicted boom has simply not materialised. This is presumably because those making the predictions failed to take account of the social elements involved in work: the value of face-to-face meetings and the psychological benefits of interactions with colleagues which are largely lost in home working.

Third, our data shows the impact of the recession. This has, of course, had differing effects throughout Europe. It is, in general, northern Europe, though less perhaps in Germany and the Netherlands, that has been more severely hit. The fact that the recession has slowed down the adoption of what is often argued to be cost-reducing strategies should give pause for thought for those arguing for a strategic approach to flexibility. Either managements are unconvinced that flexible labour does in fact lead to greater cost-effectiveness; or the pressures of the recession are such that managers are being forced to behave in a reactive manner, irrespective of cost-effectiveness. Of course, the dichotomy between strategy and opportunism is a false one: it would be a strange strategy indeed that ignored opportunities or failed to respond to unforeseen problems. However, if the cost-effectiveness of flexibility in general is accepted, then being forced away from that track does not fit neatly with a strategic approach to human resource issues.

A fourth summary point concerns the impact of labour market regulation and deregulation. There is little conclusive evidence from our data that the lower degree of regulation of the labour market in the United Kingdom has put Britain in a qualitatively different position from most other European countries. This may be misleading: if it is, for example, easier to dismiss employees in the United Kingdom, especially within the first two years of employment, then some employers may opt for 'informal' short-term contracts and just not tell employees that they expect a time limit on their contract (Rubery 1989; Casey 1991). Having taken all this into account, however, there seems to be little correlation between legal regulation and the attraction of, and movement towards, flexibility. Within each set of national laws and national contexts there are differences in the way different sectors and even, perhaps more starkly, different organisations use flexibility. It is thus perhaps, as Horrell and Rubery (1991) argue, that organisational cultures, experiences and expectations play a major role in determining labour use patterns.

NOTE

1 The evidence in this chapter is largely based on analysis carried out for the United Kingdom's Institute of Personnel Management and published as *Flexible Working Patterns in Europe*, Brewster, C., Hegewisch, A., Lockhart, T. and Mayne, L., 1993, London: IPM.

REFERENCES

Advisory, Conciliation and Arbitration Service (1988) *Labour Flexibility in Britain: the 1987 ACAS Survey*, London: ACAS.
Atkinson, J. (1984a) *Flexibility, Uncertainty and Manpower Management*, IMS Report 89, Brighton.
Atkinson, J. (1984b) 'Manpower strategies for flexible organisations', *Personnel Management* August: 28–31.
Atkinson, J. (1985) 'Flexibility: planning for the uncertain future', *Manpower Policy and Practice* 1 (summer): 26–9.

Atkinson, J. and Meager, N. (1986a) 'Is flexibility just a flash in the pan?', *Personnel Management* September: 26–9.

Atkinson, J. and Meager, N. (1986b) *New Forms of Work Organisation*, IMS Report 121, Brighton.

Baglioni, G. and Crouch, C. (eds) (1990) *European Industrial Relations: the Challenge of Flexibility*, London: Sage.

Bamber, G. J. (1989) *Job flexibility: Some International Comparisons and Hypotheses about the Dynamics of Work Organisation*, paper for the Eighth World Congress of the International Industrial Relations Association, Brussels, September.

Berg, A. M. (1989) 'Part time employment: a response to economic crisis'?, in S. Rosenberg (ed.) (1989) *The State and the Labor Market*, New York: Plenum.

Bielenski, H. *et al.*, (1993) 'New forms of work and activity: a survey of experiences at establishment level in eight European countries', *European Foundation for the Improvement of Working and Living Conditions*, working paper, Dublin.

Blanchflower, D. and Corry, B. (1987) 'Part-time employment in Great Britain: an analysis using establishment data', *Department of Employment*, Research Paper 57.

Blanpain, R. and Köhler, E. (eds) (1988) *Legal and Contractual Limitations to Working Time in the European Community Member States*, Deventer: Kluwer.

Blyton, P. (1992) 'Flexible times? recent developments in temporal flexibility', *Industrial Relations Journal* 23(1): 26–36.

Boyer, R. (ed.) (1989) *The Search for Labour Market Flexibility: the European Economy in Transition*, Oxford: Oxford University Press.

Boyer, R. (1990) 'The impact of the Single Market on labour and employment', *Labour and Society* 15(7): 109–42.

Brewster, C. and Connock, S. (1985) *Industrial Relations: Cost-effective Strategies* London: Hutchinson Business Books.

Brewster, C. and Spink, R. (1989) 'Overtime: a perennial problem', *Modern Management*, 4: 16–18.

Brewster, C., Hegewisch, A., Holden, L. and Lockhart, T. (1992) *The European Human Resource Management Guide*, London: Academic Press.

Brewster, C., Hegewisch, A., Lockhart, T. and Mayne, L. (1993) *Flexible Working Patterns in Europe*, London: Institute of Personnel Management.

Brewster, C., Hegewisch, A. and Mayne, L. (1993) 'Trends in HRM in western Europe', in Kirkbride, P. (ed.) (1993) *Human Resource Management in the New Europe of the 1990s*, London: Routledge.

Bruegel, I. and Hegewisch, A. (1994) 'Flexibilisation and Part-time Employment in Europe', in Brown, R. and Crompton, R. (eds) *The New Europe: Economic Restructuring and Social Exclusion*, London: UCL Press.

Büchtemann, C. (1991) 'Does (de-) regulation matter? Employment protection and temporary work in the Federal Republic of Germany', in G. Standing and V. Tokman (eds.) *Towards Social Adjustment*, Geneva: ILO.

Casey, B. (1991) 'Survey evidence on trends in "non-standard" employment', in A. Pollert (ed.) (1991) *Farewell to Flexibility?*, Oxford: Basil Blackwell.

Child, J. (1985) 'Managerial strategies, new technology and the labour process', in D. Knights, H. Willmott, and D. Collinson, (eds) (1985) *Job Redesign: Critical Perspectives and the Labour Process*, Gower: Aldershot.

Collinson, D., Knights, D. and Collinson, M. (1990) *Managing to Discriminate*, London: Routledge.

Commission of the EC (1990) *Employment in Europe*, Luxembourg: Office for Official Publications of the European Community.

Commission of the EC (1992) 'The position of women on the labour market: trends and developments in the 12 member states', *Women of Europe* supplement 36.

Geary, J. F. (1992) 'Employment flexibility and human resource management: the case of three American electronics plants', *Work, Employment and Society* 6(2): 251–70.

Grenig, J. E. (1991) 'The dismissal of employees in the United States', *International Labour Review* 130(5–6): 569–81.

Hakim, C. (1985) *Employers' Use of Outwork* Department of Employment Research Paper 44, London: HMSO.

Hakim, C. (1987a) *Homebased Work in Britain: A Report on the 1981 Homeworking Survey*, Department of Employment, Research Paper 60, London: HMSO.

Hakim, C. (1987b) 'Trends in the flexible workforce', *Employment Gazette*, December: 549–60.

Hakim, C. (1990) 'Core and periphery workers in employers' workforce strategies: evidence from the 1987 ELUS survey', *Work, Employment and Society* 4(2): 157–88.

Hakim, C. (1991) 'Cross-national comparative research on the European Community: the EC Labour Force Surveys', *Work, Employment and Society* 5(1): 101–17.

Hoogendoorn, J.. Haima van der Wal, T. and Spitsbaard, T. (1992) 'The Netherlands', in C. Brewster, A. Hegewisch, L. Holden, and T. Lockhart, *The European Human Resource Management Guide*, London: Academic Press.

Hunter, L. and MacInnes, J. (1992) 'Employers' and labour flexibility: the evidence from case studies', *Employment Gazette* June: 307–15.

Hutchinson, S. (1993) 'Annual hours working in the UK', Institute of Personnel Management, *Issues in People Management Series*, 5, May.

IRS (1990) 'Temporary working 2; how employers use temporary workers', *IRS Employment Trends* 469: 5–14.

Juul, I. (1993) 'Human resource management: two Danish projects and the development of personnel and job competence', in P. Cressey (ed.) *Developments in European Human Resource Management*, European Foundation for the Improvement of Living and Working Conditions, Working Paper no. WP/93/42/EN, Dublin.

Konle-Seidl, R., Ullman, H. and Walwei, U. (1990) 'The European social space: atypical forms of employment and working hours in the EC', *International Social Securities Review* 43(2): 151–87.

Marginson, P., Edwards, P. K., Martin, J., Purcell, J. and Sisson, K., (1988a) *Beyond the Workplace: Managing Industrial Relations in the Multi Establishment Enterprise*, Oxford: Blackwell.

Marginson, P., Edwards, P. K., Purcell, J. and Sissons, K. (1988b) 'What do corporate officers really do?', *British Journal of Industrial Relations* 26: 229–45.

Marshall, A. (1989) 'The sequel of unemployment: the changing role of part time and temporary work in Western Europe' in G. Rodgers, and J. Rodgers, (ed.) (1989) *Precarious Work*, Geneva: ILO.

McGregor, A. and Sproull, A. (1992) 'Employers and the flexible workforce', *Employment Gazette* May: 225–34.

Mintzberg, H. (1978) 'Patterns in strategy formation', *Management Science* 24(9): 934–48.

Mintzberg, H. (1987a) 'Crafting strategy', *Harvard Business Review* (July–August): 66–75.

Mintzberg, H. (1987b) 'Strategy concept: five Ps for strategy', *California Management Review* 30(1): 11–24.

Morris, T. and Wood, S., (1991) 'Testing the survey method: continuity and change in British Industrial Relations', *Work, Employment and Society* 5(2): 259–82.

Nedo (1986) *Changing Work Patterns: a Report by the IMS*, London: HMSO.

Nollen, S. D. (1992) 'The cost-effectiveness of contingent labour', *Proceedings, 9th World Congress* (Communications Abstracts) Geneva: International Industrial Relations Association.

OECD (1991) *Employment Outlook*, Paris.

O'Reilly, J. (1992) 'Where do you draw the line? Functional flexibility, training and skill in Britain and France', *Work, Employment and Society* 6(3): 369–96.

Pascale, R. (1984) 'Perspectives on strategy: the real story behind Honda's success' *California Management Review* 26(3): 47–72.

Pearson, G. (1990) *Strategic Thinking*, London: Prentice Hall.

Phizacklea, A. and Wolkowitz, C. (1990) 'Homeworking in the 90s: a case study in Coventry (United Kingdom)', paper delivered at the World Congress of Sociology, Madrid.

Pickard, J. (1991) 'Annual hours: a year of living dangerously?' *Personnel Management*, August: 39–43.

Piore, M. J. and Sabel, C. F. (1985) *The Second Industrial Divide: Possibilities for Prosperity*, New York: Basic Books.

Pollert, A. (1987) 'The flexible firm: a model in search of reality (or a policy in search of a practice)?', *Warwick Papers in Industrial Relations* 19.

Pollert, A. (1988a) 'Dismantling flexibility', *Capital and Class*, 34: 42–75.

Pollert, A. (1988b) 'The 'flexible firm': fixation or fact?', *Work, Employment and Society* 2(3): 281–316.

Pollert, A. (ed.) (1991) *Farewell to Flexibility?*, Oxford: Basil Blackwell.

Quinn, J. (1980) *Strategies for Change: Logical Incrementalism*, Homewood, ICC: Richard D. Irwin.

Rubery, J. (ed.) (1988) *Women and Recession*, London: Routledge & Kegan Paul.

Rubery, J., (1989) 'Precarious forms of work in the UK', in G. Rodgers and J. Rodgers (eds) (1989) *Precarious Work*, Geneva: ILO.

Spink, R. and Brewster, C. (1989) 'Overtime: a perennial problem', *Modern Management* 4: 16–18.

Simkin, C. and Hillage, J. (1992) 'Family friendly working: new hope or old hype?', Brighton: IMS.

Social Europe, *Working Time, employment and production capacity; reorganisation/reduction of working time*, supplement 4/91, DGV European Commission.

Treu, T. (1989) 'Introduction: new trends in working time arrangements', in A. Gladstone *et al.* (eds) *Current Issues in Labour Relations: An International Perspective*, Berlin and New York: de Gruyter.

Treu, T. (1992) *Participation in Public Policy: the Rise of Trade Unions and Employers Associations*, Berlin and New York: W. de Gruyter.

Wareing, A. (1992) 'Working arrangements and patterns of working hours in Britain', *Employment Gazette* March: 88–100.

Watson, G. (1992) 'Hours of work in Great Britain and Europe: evidence from the United Kingdom and European Labour Force surveys', *Employment Gazette* November: 539–57.

Wood, D. and Smith, P. (1989) *Employers' Labour Use Strategies First Report on the 1987 Survey*, Department of Employment Research Paper 63, London: HMSO.

Chapter 12

Equal opportunities policies in Europe

Ariane Hegewisch and Lesley Mayne

The issue of equal opportunities has a high profile in Europe. It is, however, a culturally bound term, having different connotations in different countries. The European Community has, until recent often traumatic events have raised new problems in the public consciousness, restricted its view to the removal of discrimination between men and women. From the British side of the English Channel such an approach seems to miss important areas of equal opportunities for disabled people and, particularly, for people from the 'ethnic minority communities'. In this chapter we take a more Anglicised approach, addressing all three areas, even if in order to ensure comparability, we will put greater emphasis on equality measures for women. In line with the theme of this book, and the source of our data, our focus is on the policies and practices of employing organisations.

In this chapter, therefore, we examine briefly the legal framework for equal opportunities in Europe. We provide evidence to show that both for the topics where the EC and the associated countries have accepted a common legal framework, and for those where they have not, there remain substantial national differences in organisational practice as the extent of discrimination or equality in the labour market. We do this by considering in turn the extent to which employers monitor or target in recruitment the disabled, ethnic minorities and women; the extent to which they monitor training and promotion in their workforce and have introduced programmes to overcome barriers to women's employment. As part of this consideration, we examine the special role of two particular groups of employers – US multinational corporations (MNCs) and the public sector.

THE LEGISLATIVE FRAMEWORK FOR EQUAL OPPORTUNITIES IN EUROPE

Equality legislation in Europe is most clearly developed in the field of gender discrimination. The principle of non-discrimination in employment between men and women was incorporated in 1957 in the founding treaty of the European Community. Article 119 of the Treaty of Rome puts an obligation on member states to 'ensure and subsequently maintain the application of the principle that men and women should receive equal pay for equal work'. The motivation for its inclusion was less a concern with social justice and equal opportunities than an attempt to prevent 'social dumping' and ensure fair competition by eliminating the cost advantage enjoyed by the French textile industry through paying very low and unequal wages to its female employees (Hörburger 1990: 25). Whatever the original motivation of policy makers Article 119 gave all women in the EC a direct legal right to claim equal pay, irrespective of national legislation, even if it was not until the late 1960s that this right was first claimed by (Belgian) women workers. Article 119 also served as the basis for several equal treatment Directives from the mid-1970s to the mid-1980s, most importantly the 1976 Equal Treatment Directive, which provides EC member states with a comparable legislative base in areas such as equal pay for work of equal value (comparable worth), equal treatment in employment and training, occupational social security and self-employment (Brewster and Teague 1989). The equal treatment Directives led to the framing of national legislation in member states, most of which until then were mainly guided by a general non-discrimination clause in their constitutions. In the Nordic countries outside of the EC comparable legislation was passed in the late 1970s as a result of public concern with the continued under-representation of women in the political sphere and in more senior positions in employment.

Equality legislation is mainly framed in terms of protecting individuals from discrimination and firmly based in the concept of equal treatment, rather than on creating equality by remedying past discrimination. In other words equality legislation generally does not oblige employers to introduce equality measures, with some notable exceptions. Under French legislation of 1983 (introduced partly in response to the 1976 EC Equal Treatment Directive) for example, employers have to prepare annual equality audits which detail the distribution of recruitment, training and promotions, wages, job categories, terms and conditions by gender; if these show an imbalance between male and female employees they have to introduce measures to achieve greater equality (Ministere du Travail et de la Participation 1983). In practice, however, low levels of enforcement ensure that French employers are largely left free to ignore these regulations. While not providing for such a blanket obligation, Italian legislation since 1991 has provided regional equality offices with powers to demand similar action from employers (EIRR 1991). Outside the European Community Swedish organisations, too, since the late 1970s have been obliged to show what measures they are taking to increase equality between men and women. In Britain equal opportunity policies at organisational level are guided by a statutory Code of Practice; the Equal Opportunities Commission (and the Commission for Racial Equality) have the powers to impose a positive action programme on organisations once direct or indirect discrimination has been proven.

Within national legislation there are also important differences in the extent to which they allow for positive discrimination rather than positive action. The use of quotas as part of equality programmes for women, for example, is illegal in the United Kingdom but is legal in the Netherlands where it has been incorporated into some collective agreements; the preferential treatment of women is also possible in some German Federal states (Povall and Langkau-Herrmann 1991: xxi).

Protection against racial discrimination in employment

There is no comparable European framework in the field of race discrimination (see Forbes and Mead 1992 for a full discussion of legislative provisions in this area in EC member states). Within the EC the issue of discrimination on the basis of race or ethnic background is only dealt with indirectly through the right of EC citizens to work on an equal footing in other Community states (Article 7 of the Treaty of Rome). Thus this provides some protection to Portuguese workers in Germany but not to Turkish workers there; the legislation as such is focused on the 'migrant worker'. Arguably many people who came as migrant workers in the 1960s and 1970s – the high point of labour migration – have now de facto become immigrants. There are also major differences between the EC states in the extent to which citizenship is granted on the basis of birth or residence (as in the United Kingdom) or on the basis of parentage (as in Germany). It is thus possible for first generation children of immigrants to be citizens of one state, whilst third generation children of immigrants fail to be citizens of another state. There are also implications for those who have never lived in the EC but are children of EC member state citizens. Equally important is the fact that the legislation fails to recognise discrimination against black or ethnic minority EC citizens because of their racial or ethnic background. There are pressures within the EC to introduce framework legislation here but so far this has not produced any results. The preamble to the Social Charter (which was signed by governments of all Community member states apart from the United Kingdom in 1989) mentions the need to 'combat every form of discrimination, including discrimination on the basis of sex, colour, race, opinions and beliefs' but no further reference to race discrimination is made in the proposals for legislative action which make up the associated Social Action Programme which aims to implement the Charter. Resolution 31 in the (narrowly adopted) Report by the Committee of Inquiry into Racism and Xenophobia, passed by the European Parliament in 1990, also obliged the Community to, by March 1991, prepare a draft Directive on the protection from discrimination as a result of race, membership of an ethnic group, religion or regional or national status (Ford 1991: 153); so far this has not been acted on. Thus there is no comparable right to protection from direct or indirect discrimination on the basis of race across all European countries.

Only a minority of European countries have passed explicit race discrimination legislation. The British Race Relations Act (1976), broadly written to parallel British sex discrimination legislation and reflecting the predominance of a US race relations approach in Britain since the 1950s, and the French decree of 17 August 1982 remain isolated examples. In most European countries, whether EC or EFTA, legislation is limited to general non-discrimination clauses in their constitutions; as Forbes and Mead (1992: 14) point out, the refusal of most governments to introduce primary legislation in the field, and thus overcome the 'lack of specificity and practical force' of constitutional non-discrimination clauses is rather contradictory given that all governments agreed to the need for primary legislation in relation to gender discrimination.

Discrimination on the basis of disability

For discrimination on the basis of disability there is a similar absence of a general legislative framework at EC level, though recently the social and professional integration of disabled people has become one of the aims of the EC Social Chapter. Following the Second World War and attempts to provide employment for injured or disabled servicemen, most countries operate quotas for the employment of people with disabilities. No European country in or outside of the EC however so far has followed the United States by providing the right not to be discriminated on the basis of disability.

This brief overview of legislation shows that the European Community has led to a common framework in the field of gender legislation across Europe but that in other areas of discrimination, whether or not as a direct consequence of EC framework legislation, this has not happened. It is however likely that the common legal concepts of discrimination developed in the field of gender will influence the approaches to discrimination on the basis of race, ethnicity or disability, once a sufficient commonality of purpose is developed across the European institutions.

Legislation is of course not the only way of affecting national practice. Labour market and vocational training measures arguably also play an important contribution. The European Community has had successive 'action programmes' providing or supporting research, training and systems aimed at increasing equality for women, migrant and disabled workers. Such programmes are also common in the non-EC Nordic states, and to some extent it can be assumed that they provide a common framework for approaching equality. In other words, we are concerned here not so much with an evaluation of the effectiveness of a legislative approach to discrimination (which has been done elsewhere, see, for example, Mazey 1988; Rubery 1992; Whitehouse 1992) but with the development of common concepts and approaches which might influence organisational practices on equal opportunities.

LABOUR MARKET INEQUALITY IN EUROPE

Women

The European Community then provides a common statutory framework for equal opportunities for women and is influencing practices directly, to some extent, through various social action programmes. However a brief look at major indicators of labour market equality across Europe shows that after more than a quarter of a century of gender equality legislation, horizontal and vertical occupation segregation and pay inequality continue to be major characteristics of women's labour market experience across Europe (Rubery and Fagan 1993; Rubery 1988; Commission of the EC 1992; Income Data Service 1992). As Mazey (1988: 63) points out 'the socio-structural causes of sex discrimination lie beyond the reach of existing Equality Directives'.

Table 12.1 Women's labour force participation and share of civilian employment in Europe

	Labour force participation (1989)	Share of civilian employment (1991)	% of women working part-time (1990)[a]
Denmark	87.9	46.3	38
Finland[b]	62.0[h]	47.0[c]	10
France	73.2	43.0	23
Germany	63.4	41.2	33
Ireland	45.0	33.9	18
Italy	55.8	35.3	10
Netherlands	58.2	36.4	61
Norway	62.3[h]	45.3[d]	43
Portugal	69.9	44.8	9
Spain	47.9	32.8	12
Sweden	85.0[e]	47.9[f]	47
UK	72.7	43.3	43

Source: Eurostatistik 1993, no. 1
Notes: [a] EC Commission 1992; [b] 1990 from Statistics Sweden 1990; [c] Share of total economically active population, ILO Yearbook of Market Statistics 1992; [d] Statistical Arbok, Oslo 1991; [e] OECD Employment Outlook 1991, quoted in Nätti (1992), p. 5; [f] Statistical Abstracts Stockholm 1991; [h] 1992, the proportion of economically active women between 15 and 74 years

Across these common general patterns there continue to be major differences in women's position in the labour market between countries, particularly regarding the overall share of women in the workforce, levels of labour force participation, and levels of part-time employment (Table 12.1). While there are broad differences along a north–south divide, with participation rates and part-time employment greatest in the northern parts of Europe and lowest in the Mediterranean countries, neither of these factors operate on a simple continuum (Bruegel and Hegewisch 1994). To select some indicators of women's position in the labour market to make the point: women's participation rates may be high with low levels of part-time employment as in the case in Finland, France and Portugal; and they might be low with high levels of part-time employment, such as in the case of the Netherlands which has the highest level of part-time employment across all of Europe.[1]

Starting from such differences in employment patterns during the last decade most European countries have seen a growth in female participation rates and an increasing share of women in the labour force (even if that has not necessarily resulted in a commensurate increase in the number of paid hours worked by women (Hakim 1993; Jonung and Persson 1993)). So far this has not led to either a narrowing of occupational segregation (Rubery and Fagan 1993) or to a diminishing of the other major indicator of labour market inequality, the pay gap between men and women (IDS 1992). However, other commonly shared trends in the labour market, such as a projected increase in the number of managerial and professional jobs and demographic changes, leading to a decline in the numbers of young people entering the workforce, have increased the pressures on employers to use their workforces more effectively. This has highlighted the issues of discrimination and measures needed to overcome the 'underutilisation' of women workers (Pollert and Rees 1992). Policy makers, the women's movement and, increasingly, trade unions are adding to the pressures on employers to address this issue.

Ethnic background and disability

In a minority of countries such as Britain or the Netherlands such pressures to address labour market discrimination also included the situation of black and ethnic minority workers. In other countries such as Germany this has not been the case; as for example Nüse (1992: 28) points out: 'It is surprising how little mention was made of the theme of the employment of foreigners in public declarations or in response to direct requests by employers federations or chambers of trade and industry who nowadays constantly lament the shortage of apprentices and employees' (our translation).

The concentration of the EC on gender equality, and the absence of explicit legislation and indeed even collated data in many of the European countries, make comparisons of the position of black and ethnic minority workers difficult. Apart from the absence of strong policy commitment this also indicates a much greater problem of definition and grouping in the case of racial and ethnic groupings, particularly for the purpose of international comparison, than in the gender area. However, evidence from selected country surveys (for example Phizacklea 1983; Brown 1984; Castle 1984; Bruegel 1989; *Employment Gazette* 1991; Schultze 1992; Bell 1993) suggests that inequality along racial lines continues to be a major feature of European labour markets, as expressed, for example, in rates of unemployment and average pay levels. As Bovenkerk *et al.* (1991: 377) point out: 'Corresponding migration movements have been processed differently in many countries and produce marked analogies as well as striking dissimilarities in their social, economic and political consequences.'

The general absence of comprehensive statistics on the position in employment applies even more strongly to people with disabilities, who continue not to be fully integrated into employment.

ORGANISATION LEVEL EQUAL OPPORTUNITIES

Our concern here is to examine patterns of organisational level activities in the field of equal opportunities. We are concerned with measures introduced by employers which address the under-representation of certain groups in their workforce, or, in the words of the Commission of the EC's guide on equal opportunities for women in employment (1988), any measure 'which allows an organisation to identify and eliminate any discrimination in its employment policies and practices, and to put right the effects of past discrimination' (Commission of the EC 1988: 10). There has been much debate in the literature on employment discrimination of the potentially limited nature of equal opportunities policies and anti-discrimination approaches (see, for example, Whitehouse 1992); Forbes and Mead (1992: 2) however have argued that equal opportunity policies can act as an important change agent which can have a broader impact on social and political processes.

In our review we have selected a number of indicators for organisation level equal opportunities policies. These include monitoring of the composition of the workforce in recruitment, training and promotion. Workforce monitoring, at least in Anglo-American approaches to equality programmes, is an essential part of identifying discrimination or under-representation in the workforce and in measuring progress where positive action programmes have been introduced (EOC and CRE Codes of Practice; Meager and Metcalf 1988; Wilkinson 1992). A question on groups targeted in recruitment was included both as a proxy for an economic rationale for employers and as a potential positive action measure in itself. The remaining indicators are particularly concerned with policy measures designed to overcome barriers to women's full participation in employment given that this is the area of greatest activity across Europe; these include the offer of flexible working practices, part-time employment and job sharing as an incentive in recruitment; training for women returners; parental leave, career breaks and workplace childcare. These of course do not present a comprehensive list of possible equality measures; but our survey does provide substantial new comparative data to supplement that which is already available. In this section we will begin by reviewing the evidence on employers' activities in monitoring their workforces according to disability, followed by a look at activities in relation to ethnic minority employees and will then turn to workforce monitoring in relation to gender and evidence on the positive action measures for women mentioned above.

WORKFORCE MONITORING AND TARGETED RECRUITMENT

People with disabilities

Several countries in the survey operate a quota system for the employment of people with disabilities (IDS/IPM 1991; Brewster *et al.* 1992); where a quota system exists all organisations should be monitoring the share of people with disabilities in recruitment. Yet in none of the countries is monitoring a universal practice; outside of Turkey or the United Kingdom where between 6 and 7 out of 10 employers comply, less than half of all employers monitor recruitment for the share of people with disabilities (Appendix III Table 2.13a). Monitoring is particularly low in the four Nordic countries where 1 in 10 or fewer employers follow this course. Both Turkey and the United Kingdom operate a quota system but so do Germany, France and the Netherlands with substantially lower proportions of employers complying; indeed quotas and fines are considerably higher in Germany than in the United Kingdom, yet while there is greater activity in Germany than in most other countries, it is nevertheless much lower than in the United Kingdom. While fines in Turkey are high too, enforcement is generally said to be as low as in the other countries – thus higher policing of quotas is not an explanation. Employers in Turkey as elsewhere claim that a lack of suitable applicants is their major problem with the fulfilment of quotas.

A low level of applicants could be overcome by the introduction of special recruitment efforts; yet no more than between a tenth and a quarter of employers target people with disabilities in recruitment (Appendix III Table 3.3), another strong indicator for the absence of strong enforcement of these provisions. These figures also throw doubts on the practical effects of the high level of responses in Germany and the United Kingdom; few organisations fulfil the legally set quotas; yet less than a quarter of those monitoring recruitment in relation to disability in the United Kingdom and less than half of those organisations in Germany make active efforts to attract disabled applicants.

The monitoring of recruitment and selection decisions is only the first step in an equality programme; it is probably also the most ambiguous one given that organisations often have reasons other than equality for establishing these details, such as the avoidance of fines in case of underfulfilment of the quota. A better and fuller indicator of equality programmes is whether the monitoring includes the provision of training and/or promotions. Only a minority of organisations in any country establish such a full programme of monitoring for people with disabilities. Indeed Germany, Turkey and the United Kingdom, the countries where recruitment monitoring was highest, have a lower share of employers monitoring training provisions than the Netherlands or Finland, and in no country are more than a fifth of employers involved. Monitoring of promotions is even less frequent; only in the United Kingdom is it done by more than a sixth of employers; elsewhere it is less than one-tenth of organisations.

Black and ethnic minority employees

There are no legal obligations to monitor the recruitment of ethnic minority staff and less than one in ten employers outside Germany, the Netherlands and the United Kingdom have introduced policies in this area. In the United Kingdom the majority of employers monitor the share of ethnic minorities, more than twice as many as in the Netherlands (25 per cent) and Germany (21 per cent) (Appendix III Table 2.13a).

This is an area in which terminology and definitions are notoriously complex (Hammar 1985: 12; Bovenkerk *et al.* 1991). The term 'ethnic minorities', for example, is so far only readily accepted in the United Kingdom and the Netherlands; in the survey the closest commonly recognised translation of the term 'ethnic minority' into German is *Ausländer*, or foreigner. Since in Germany this is the commonly used official term for both migrant and immigrant workers (Räthzel 1991: 32) it is of course not possible to be sure that the term is always understood to refer to what the British would call 'ethnic minorities'.[2] Problems in this area arose not only from terminology: in France, one of the few countries in the survey with explicit race discrimination legislation, French respondents at the piloting stage felt that questions about the monitoring or targeting of ethnic minorities might cause offence and raise concerns about civil liberties, highlighting a different awareness and approach to equality issues there.

It is clear at least that if immigration and racial background are considered jointly the higher proportions of employers monitoring the share of ethnic minorities in recruitment in the United Kingdom and particularly the Netherlands are not due to a higher share of ethnic minority people in the workforce. Migrants, immigrants and political refugees are now a significant presence in almost all European countries, and the share of ethnic minorities in France and Germany, for example, is higher than in the Netherlands or the United Kingdom. These latter are also the only two countries where a significant minority of employers have targeted ethnic minorities in recruitment; elsewhere such action is only taken by between 1 per cent and 7 per cent of employers (Appendix III Table 3.3).

As in the case of people with disabilities employers may have other than equal opportunities motives for monitoring recruitment, such as the checking of work permits. Again it is only in the Netherlands and the United Kingdom that more than one in ten employers monitor training or promotions (Appendix III Tables 2.13b and 2.13c).

Women

The monitoring of the share of women in recruitment is a much more evenly spread practice across Europe, reflecting EC activities in this field. Again the uptake of this measure is highest in the United Kingdom with slightly over half of employers doing it; only in Denmark and Finland are less than a fifth of employers involved in such activity, in most other countries this is done by at least a third of all organisations (Appendix III Table 2.13a).

Arguably, equalities monitoring might be linked directly to attempts at overcoming recruitment difficulties. As shown in Table 12.1 labour force participation of women in countries such as Germany, the Netherlands and the United Kingdom continues to be lower than in the Nordic countries. More importantly perhaps women in these three countries continue to have a markedly different pattern of labour force attachment than men, due to a break from paid work when they have young children; hence they can be seen as a potential source of labour. In the Nordic countries, France and Portugal the reverse holds: high levels of participation make women a less obvious 'reserve army of labour'. Such pressures or reasons for turning to women are much less likely in countries such as Ireland or Spain where low female participation goes hand in hand with high levels of unemployment.

Recruitment targeting is of course a policy one would expect to be affected by the recession. By early 1992, the time of the last survey, the Nordic countries and the United Kingdom had moved into a recession while this was not yet the case in France, the Netherlands or Portugal. While Germany, too, had not yet fully entered the recession reunification and the resulting inflow of East German workers into the West German labour market had however lessened recruitment problems there.

Thus comparing the share of organisations who targeted women in recruitment in 1991 and 1992 for those countries included in both years of the survey, we can observe a drop in this activity, particularly in Germany, Sweden and the United Kingdom. There has been virtually no corresponding change in the number of organisations monitoring recruitment. This might be taken as evidence of a concern with equal opportunities which goes beyond a short-term business rationale; such policies, once in place, are less likely to change even if their practical effect in periods of low or no recruitment is likely to be marginal.

Turning now to the relationship between the two policies: Figure 12.1 shows that there is no simple national correlation between monitoring and targeting of women in recruitment. In Germany, France and Finland there is a rough correspondence: a comparable share of organisations within each country follow such policies; however in Ireland, Norway, Sweden, Turkey and the United Kingdom employers are much more likely to monitor than to target women in recruitment, perhaps supporting the above argument that monitoring procedures outlast recruitment pressures; whereas the reverse is true in the Netherlands and Spain.

As in the case of disabled or ethnic minorities employees, generally fewer organisations monitor training provision or promotions. The continued under-representation of women in management and their continued unequal access to training (see, for example, EOC 1991 in relation to training in the United Kingdom) provide ample evidence of inequality. Nevertheless, compared to monitoring practice regarding the other two groups of potential or existing employees, a much higher proportion of organisations monitor these three areas

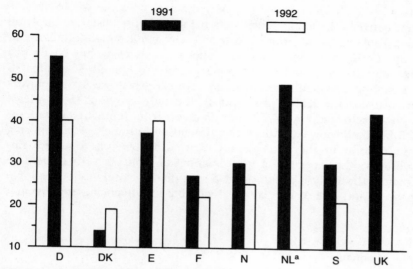

Figure 12.1 Targeted recruitment of women, 1991 and 1992 (% of organisations)
Note: ᵃ Dutch responses private sector only

for women. The low use of monitoring in France, by only a fifth of employers, given the above mentioned obligation to produce annual equality audits, highlights the lack of enforcement of this legislation.

Danish organisations are among the least likely to monitor, in spite of a strongly organised women's movement and much emphasis on equality in the workplace. Denmark is also the country within the European Community with the lowest pay gap between men and women. The low level of monitoring shows both the continued hostility of Danish employers and trade unions to institutionalised means of regulating workplace relations, and that an absence of direct equal opportunities programmes is not necessarily a sign of a lower commitment to equality.

EQUALITY MONITORING IN AMERICAN MNCs

The measures chosen in the survey as indicators of equality programmes reflect a particular institutional approach to equality in the workplace. Workforce monitoring is a standard prerequisite for companies qualifying for public contracts under the American federal contract compliance programme; such measures have been part of US civil rights legislation since the late 1960s. The proportionately greater uptake of equality monitoring particularly in Ireland and the United Kingdom might reflect the linguistic and cultural influences of North American practices.

Given the federal contract compliance programme most of the home-based operations of multinationals are likely to have a workforce monitoring system; however an analysis of US multinationals in France, Germany, Ireland and the United Kingdom (the countries where the sample is large enough for separate analysis) shows that on the whole there is no significant difference between the likelihood of national and US organisations applying monitoring policies (see Table 12.2). In France US MNCs are significantly more likely to monitor recruitment though in the other areas they appear to be as willing as French organisations to ignore national legislation. In Germany and the United Kingdom US MNCs conform to national patterns (compared to other British private sector employers they are however more active in the field of promotions). It is only in Ireland that, at least compared to other private sector employers, US MNCs divert from the national pattern. The proportions of US MNCs having introduced recruitment and promotions monitoring are (except on training) closer to the equivalent United Kingdom based subsidiaries than to the Irish averages; this suggests a coordination of policies across the two countries. However, overall the analysis shows that US subsidiaries closely follow national practices, confirming the importance of the 'country' variable in influencing employment practices.

The public sector factor in equality

Another factor highlighted in Table 12.3 is that results for the private sector tend to lie below the national average, particularly in Ireland and the United Kingdom. Indeed a closer look at the share of private and public sector employers who introduce equality monitoring shows that public sector employers are significantly more likely to have done this than private sector employers in most (though not all) countries (Table 12.3) (see Appendix III Tables 2.13a for frequency results).

Table 12.2 The monitoring of women's share of the workforce in recruitment, training and promotions in Europe (% of organisations)

	Recruitment	Training	Promotions
France			
National average	22[a]	20	21
Private sector	20[a]	20	22
US MNCs (n=57)	33	21	28
Germany			
National average	32	18	12
Private sector	31	17	11
US MNCs (n=57)	39	21	16
Ireland			
National average	40	28	32
Private sector	26[a]	25[a]	16[b]
US MNCs (n=34)	44	32	41
UK			
National average	53	25	32
Private sector	45	22	29[a]
US MNCs (n=130)	49	25	40

Note: [a] significant at 0.05 level; [b] significant at 0.01 level

Table 12.3 Public/private sector differences in the introduction of gender monitoring of the workforce in relation to recruitment, training and promotions

	Recruitment	Training	Promotions
Euro average	>**	>**	>**
Denmark	>*	>*	>**
Finland	>–	>n	>*
France	>–	>–	>–
Germany	>**	>**	>*
Ireland	>*	>*	>**
Netherlands[a]	>**	>**	>*
Norway	>**	>–	>–
Sweden	>–	>–	>*
UK	>**	>*	>**

Notes: > Public sector greater uptake than private sector;* Significant at 0.05 level; ** Significant at 0.01 level; – not significant
[a] 1991 data because the Dutch public sector response rate in 1992 was low

In all countries in the sample women are more likely than men to be employed in the public sector and the growth of public sector employment has been an important factor in women's increasing labour force participation (Commission of the European Communities 1992). However, this has not led to equality in employment for women in the public sector (see, for example, Commission of the European Communities 1992: 19; Leyenaar 1991; Langkau-Herrmann and Sessar-Karpp 1991; Sinkkonen and Hänninen-Salmelin 1991; Campos e Cunha 1993). For example, women remain under-represented at the highest levels of public administration only holding 5.9 per cent of positions at this level on average in the European Community countries even if this figure hides substantial variations across Europe (European Institute of Public Administration 1988).

As can be seen from Table 12.3 the public sector as an employer has generally been more active in trying to address such inequality. In so far as these measures are expressing a rather bureaucratic approach to equality they might also fit in more easily with the more rule oriented personnel tradition in the public sector. Social and political pressures for greater equality for women and for more representative public administration in general in the late 1970s led to a focus on the public sector as an employer. Thus in Norway, for example, quotas for women were introduced into public administration in the late 1970s, the tradition of quotas however is not strong in Norway and at least ten years later Norwegian public sector employers are still not generally active in this area (Laegreid 1990: 42). However, quotas or not, this pressure has resulted in some positive results as for example, in Finland, where during the 1980s the share of women among senior officials and managers in the public sector rose from 13 per cent to 21 per cent (Hänninen-Salmelin and Petäjäniemi 1993). In some countries social pressure has also resulted in the setting up of equalities units in local government; particularly in the United Kingdom and Germany. In Germany in 1990 500 local authorities had equalities units, responsible for internal personnel as well as aspects of service delivery (Povall and Langkau-Herrmann 1991) even if these were often undermined in their effectiveness by lack of resources, authority and overall political support (Meuser 1989). The relatively positive environment for equality policies for women in the public sector is however threatened by developments in other areas of public sector human resources policies, particularly through the increasing trend towards non-permanent employment and subcontracting, as well as the growth in decentralisation of budgets and managerial decision making processes (Hegewisch 1993).

Given the much lower uptake of policy related to ethnic minorities or people with disabilities, a similarly broad ranging comparison between public and private sector employers is not possible here. In the Netherlands and the United Kingdom a similar pattern holds, however. Research in Germany suggests that, at least regarding ethnic minorities, public sector employers have been even less active than private sector ones (Bell 1993).

Comparing monitoring activities in different fields

Given greater social and political pressures for women's equality one would expect employers to be more active in the gender field. Two points emerge from a comparison of patterns between monitoring in the three fields of inequality we examined. In relation to employees with disabilities or ethnic minority employees a higher share of organisations (in those countries who do anything at all in the area) are likely to monitor training provisions than promotions. This is likely partly to reflect the focus on a lack of relevant qualifications in the discussions on the underrepresentation of ethnic minority or disabled workers in better paid jobs. It may also partly reflect public sponsorship of training programmes and, in countries such as Finland, France and Germany (in relation to people with disabilities), a more general concern with training and training administration. The very low level of promotion monitoring outside of the United Kingdom is probably also a reflection of the very low share of people from both groups in positions that are part of a career/promotion track in organisations. In the area of gender monitoring the reverse is true, with marginally more organisations monitoring promotions than training. This is probably a reflection of the dominance in much of the discussions on women's equality of the 'glass ceiling' or lack of access of women to managerial positions.

The second point worth noting is the lack of integration between different areas of equality policy, as evidenced by the many organisations who are active in the field of gender but not in the other two areas. In the United States the monitoring of training and promotions of ethnic minorities in the workforce has equal standing with gender monitoring. This is not the case in Europe, apart perhaps from the Netherlands and the United Kingdom. And even in these countries the different numbers of organisations who are active in one or the other area suggests that equality policy is not integrated.

POLICIES AIMED AT OVERCOMING BARRIERS TO WOMEN'S EMPLOYMENT

We turn now from the emphasis on monitoring to European comparisons of equality measures, particularly those aimed at facilitating women's paid employment. These have been described as 'family friendly' employment policies; that is policies that recognise that women carry most domestic responsibilities and facilitate a combination of employment with a domestic timetable, and thus particularly address women with children or caring responsibilities. However, such flexible working arrangements can also be said to support rather than challenge the traditional domestic division of labour, 'making it easier for women to carry the "double load" of paid work and domestic commitment' (Pollert and Rees 1992: 4). Consequently they remain rather contested; one argument being that instead of concentrating on making it easier for women to cope with existing inequalities it is the role of public policy to create broader conditions for equality, involving changes in working practices for both men and women. Nevertheless in the absence of such more fundamental changes employers may react to existing constraints on women's ability to participate in paid work by offering 'family friendly' employment patterns of this kind to enhance/improve their recruitment and retention chances. We will examine in turn the offer of flexible working hours, part-time employment and job sharing, training courses for women returners, parental leave and career breaks and finally workplace childcare.

Flexible working hours, part-time employment and job sharing

The offer of flexible working hours as part of a recruitment effort is certainly popular across Europe. This is particularly so in Finland, Germany, Norway and Sweden where such practices are offered by between half and three quarters of employers, and in Denmark, France, and the United Kingdom where 4 out of 10 organisations provide it. The offer of flexible employment practices is lowest in Portugal, Spain and Turkey (Appendix III Table 3.2). One needs to add a word of caution here. In some countries, particularly in the United Kingdom, the common understanding of the term 'flexible working hours' is partly linked to women's employment and responses to skill shortages, that is to opening up employment to people who are unable to work the standard fixed working day. This is by no mean the case everywhere. French employers for example suggested that flexible working hours were a response to general 'value' changes and demands from male and female employees for greater flexibility/control over their working day – not particularly linked to domestic timetables; to some extent this is also true in Germany where the practice is more widely spread than elsewhere in Europe. Without an in depth analysis of male and female uptake of the offer of flexible working hours it is of course not possible to be sure whether, irrespective of the perceptions of French personnel managers, the practice is not more relevant to women than men (or whether, conversely, British men have used it to gain greater flexibility). Furthermore, as we note in Chapter 11, the drive for flexibility may well come from employer demands for the fuller utilisation of resources or a more cost-effective use of human resources. Our concern here is with the implications for women.

   Part-time employment is used most widely as a means of encouraging recruitment in Germany (by two-thirds of employers) and the United Kingdom (by over half of employers). A survey of middle managers in Germany shows that over a quarter of male middle managers would like the opportunity to work a 30-hour week (Authenrieth 1993: 535). Currently, however, few male employees, particularly in more professional and responsible jobs, are likely to find employers offering this opportunity. Part-time employment as a recruitment tool is clearly linked to women's work and in all European countries the large majority of part-timers are female. The countries with the strongest use of part-time employment as a recruitment aid, Germany and the United

Kingdom, also have amongst the lowest levels of public childcare provision, made worse in Germany by a school day which ends at midday (if not before). Once women have children labour force participation rates drop from over 80 per cent (only women in Denmark are more likely to work) to less than a third for women with young children. In Germany (though not the United Kingdom) participation rates remain below 50 per cent even for women with children of the age of 7 to 15 (Joshi and Davies 1992: 561). In such a situation working hours that fit in with the nursery or school day can enhance the labour supply. However, almost the same situation applies in the Netherlands where women's working lives are marked by similar breaks for childcare; yet part-time employment is only used as a recruitment tool by a third of employers. Possibly this is due to the high level of part-time employment, with 60 per cent of women and over 30 per cent of the workforce working part-time already, and there thus being less obvious scope for further expansion. In Denmark and Sweden existing levels of part-time employment are high but, more importantly perhaps, children hardly make a dent in women's participation rates, reflecting high levels of childcare provision. Norway on the other hand also has high levels of part time employment, higher than Denmark and Sweden, but a more traditional division between working women with and without children.

The countries least likely to use part-time employment as a recruitment tool are generally, and unsurprisingly, those with the lowest levels of part-time employment. They span countries such as Finland, France and Portugal with relatively high levels of female participation (and in the case of the former two high levels of childcare) and countries such as Spain and Turkey with low levels of female participation.

Job sharing

Across Europe the quality of part-time work varies, particularly regarding the levels of jobs that are available to part-time workers and the typical hours of part-time jobs (see Chapter 11). Thus, for example, in the Netherlands and Germany a higher share of part-time workers are in professional jobs than in the United Kingdom (Rubery and Fagan 1993). Nevertheless, it is a concern common to much of the debates on part-time employment across Europe that part-time work offers comparably less access to promotion, training and career development more generally. In the United Kingdom one of the responses to this problem has been the development of job sharing policies – opening jobs with promotion and career development prospects to people wishing to work part-time by sharing one job between two people. The United Kingdom with over a third of employers, has the widest uptake of job sharing, and the comparatively high level in Ireland (over a quarter) is possibly a reflection of the sharing of professional debates and concepts in the field of personnel management between the two countries (Appendix III Table 3.2). In Norway and Sweden, too, job sharing is beginning to be discussed as a means of opening professional and managerial jobs to part-time workers; actual uptake, that is, people sharing jobs rather than organisations offering the opportunity to share jobs, remains very low. In the Netherlands and Denmark, while the concept is starting to enter equal opportunities debates, organisations so far have not responded in significant numbers (Hegewisch et al 1993). However, job sharing is another concept that does not translate easily across Europe and does not have clear gender/equal opportunities connotations in all European countries. In Finland, France and Germany the concept is understood more narrowly as two people being held jointly responsible for the job they share (that is, also for the absences of their job sharing partner for example) and under that definition it is illegal; thus the question was not included in the questionnaire in those countries.

Training courses for women returners

Another measure particularly relevant in countries where women's working lives are disrupted by childcare are training courses for women who have had a break in employment and want to return to paid work. Such measures were much discussed in the late 1980s in the United Kingdom and Ireland as part of employers' responses to demographic changes in the labour markets (see, for example, CBI 1988), and the concept is also a familiar part of the equality 'menu' in Germany. Between a sixth and a quarter of organisations in these countries provide such training courses. In countries such as Denmark, France, Norway or Sweden extended breaks for childcare are less common and the concept of a 'women returner' is virtually unknown. In Spain and Turkey women's participation rates fall steeply when they have children, but given the general situation of the labour market, there is little pressure on employers to make efforts at accommodating or attracting women back into paid employment.

Parental leave provisions

Parental leave provisions are even harder to compare meaningfully because of the varying levels of statutory regulation across Europe. Thus only a sixth of Swedish employers provide enhanced maternity leave, but since legislation on maternity leave in Sweden entitles women to 15 months of leave, 12 months of which will be paid at the statutory benefit rates (of about 90 per cent of average earnings) Swedish working mothers are hardly disadvantaged compared to working mothers in other countries (Söderström and Syrén 1992). In the United Kingdom on the other hand over one in four employers enhance statutory maternity leave; however statutory maternity leave provisions are much lower: they are restricted according to length of service and provide low levels of pay, thus there is much more scope for enhancement (Appendix III Table 4.4a to 4.4d).

Similar arguments apply to paternity leave (Appendix III Table 4.4a to 4.4d). In countries such as Ireland, Portugal or the United Kingdom there is no statutory entitlement to paternity leave; in most of the other countries part of the 'maternity' leave may, in law, be shared between the mother and the father (Brewster et al. 1992; IDS/IPM 1991). Statutory provisions are highest in the Nordic countries. In Finland, for example, fathers are entitled to 6 to 12 days leave around the time of the birth, and 170 days of the paid 'maternity leave' of 281 days can be taken by either the father or the mother. Only a minority of fathers take their full paternity leave around the time of birth; however numbers have steadily increased from only 12 per cent in 1978 when the legislation was passed to 40 per cent in 1990 (Hänninen-Salmelin and Petäjäniemi 1993). The number of men who make use of their full entitlement of the extended leave period is only 3 per cent. Similar trends can also be found in Sweden where, apart from a period solely applying to the mother, leave can be taken by either the mother or the father. Women continue to be much more likely to take up the leave or make use of their rights to reduced working hours; however, as in Finland, the number of men taking these rights has risen steadily since the late 1970s (Statistics Sweden 1990).

Overall, in all countries, with the exception of Denmark and Portugal, organisations are more likely to have enhanced maternity leave provisions than provide better conditions for fathers. Apart from this there seems to be no common standard across Europe. Countries with high statutory provisions are not less likely to have a high share of organisations enhancing benefits than countries with low statutory provisions. Rather than organisations 'equalling up' varying national provision it seems that a legal provision is likely to reflect an existing cultural interest in maternity and paternity benefits and make organisations more aware of parents needs in the area.

Career break schemes

Where mothers take additional leave beyond statutory maternity provisions, a frequent occurrence particularly in those countries with low childcare provision and short leave arrangements, they will often break their employment contract. This often leads to a loss of seniority and other benefits related to continuity of employment. For employers it can mean the loss of an experienced and committed employee, and thus of considerable expenditure given the need to recruit, induct and train a replacement. Thus the concept of a career break, of providing extended unpaid leave with some guarantee of employment at the end has gained prominence in countries such as Germany and the United Kingdom. In both countries such schemes have been particularly pioneered in banking and in the public sector; the concept itself is not used simply as an extended maternity leave period but, at least as a model, involves some continued professional contact and arrangement for periodic attendance at training courses or holiday cover to ensure that professional skills are kept up to date. The survey results show that the organisations providing such schemes still remain in a minority in both countries (Appendix III Tables 4.4a to 4.4d).

The concept of a career break in the Anglo-German sense is much less common elsewhere; arguably women in other countries with statutory leave periods of up to two years might also benefit from such schemes. However, in the Scandinavian countries the concept is virtually unknown; in the Latin countries such as France, Portugal and Spain career break schemes are understood as sabbaticals – that is as leave that can be taken for childcare, but also for other reasons; for these reasons the survey results are not directly comparable.

Childcare

One of the largest barriers to women's full participation in employment is the lack of affordable childcare, particularly for young children. Here provisions vary greatly across the EC (see Moss 1990; Joshi and Davies 1992). Given the high cost of providing workplace childcare, one might expect that it will not be a widespread organisational measure anywhere. This is borne out by the survey results (Appendix III Tables 4.4a to 4.4d). However, the lack of publicly provided childcare under these circumstances has resulted in a comparatively high number of Portuguese and British employers (15 per cent and 11 per cent respectively) providing workplace childcare (Appendix Tables 4.4a–d). In the United Kingdom in the late 1980s, against the background, then, of labour market shortages, the lack of childcare and its effect on women was much debated, leading to initiatives from some large employers, such as the Midland Bank, for example. Discussions in Germany were similar, but have resulted in much less employer based initiatives, possibly due to the fact that provision for over threes in Germany is better than in either Portugal or the United Kingdom. In Turkey also, comparatively high proportions of organisations (14 per cent) provide workplace childcare. Organisations where more than 50 per cent of the workforce are female are legally obliged to provide creches. In contrast Norway, the country with the highest level of workplace childcare (up to a quarter of organisations) already has a fairly comprehensive public childcare system.

Public sector employers are also more likely to provide childcare than private sector organisations. This is particularly so in the Netherlands (with 7 per cent of private sector and 50 per cent of public sector organisations providing this in 1991) and the United Kingdom (with 3 per cent and 33 per cent respectively) but also in Ireland, Germany and Portugal.

CONCLUSIONS

This review of the evidence on employers' equality measures shows that there are strong country differences. As one would perhaps expect differences in family friendly policies are linked to women's labour market position and the public availability of childcare as well as levels of skills shortages at the time. Thus the highest efforts to target women in recruitment, provide flexible working hours or part-time work were made in Germany and the United Kingdom where women with children continue to have a very different working cycle to men, or to women without children. This is also the case in Spain or Turkey; however, in these countries there is much less labour market pressure on employers to actively encourage or enable women to work.

There is however no clear national correlation between the introduction of equality monitoring and women's labour market position or women's equality in the workplace and provisions vary greatly, irrespective of legislation. Equality monitoring is aimed at the improvement of women's position once they are employed, not at creating the pre-conditions for their paid employment. In the countries with the best labour market infrastructure and the highest female participation rates (the Nordic countries and France) such measures are not more widespread than in Germany, Ireland or the United Kingdom. Indeed in Denmark, the country within the European Community with the greatest share of working women and the smallest pay gap, monitoring is almost insignificant, an indication perhaps of a general hostility towards institutional regulations in the field of employee relations, including equal opportunities.

This raises the issue of the role of legislation in generating greater equality. A comparison of organisation level equality measures for women has shown that the common legislative framework in Europe has not led to a harmonisation of employers' activities. There is, moreover, no clear link at national level between a strong legislative framework and the uptake of equality practices at organisational level, or indeed with labour market equality more generally. This is most strongly demonstrated in the case of France which is the only country where there are statutory obligations on employers to introduce some of the equality measures examined here, yet where uptake, in the absence of strict enforcement or social pressure, remains low but female participation rates are high. Indeed, given the continued inequality of women in employment, as demonstrated in terms of their low share of managerial positions, persistent pay gaps and the rigid occupational segregation between men and women's work across Europe, the question is whether such legislation has had any positive impact on women's actual position or 'whether [it] seems to have had more of an impact on women's attitudes, making them conscious of their rights, than as an instrument of the advancement of women' (Hämminen-Salmelin and Petäjäniemi 1993). This confirms a point made in the context of equal pay legislation in particular, that equality legislation has generally been introduced in advance of generally accepted social practice (Eyraud 1993: 1). Equality for women seems greatest in those countries where there is the strongest institutional emphasis on labour market regulation and equality (irrespective of gender), not those where sex discrimination legislation is most developed (Rubery 1992; Whitehouse 1992).

European Community legislation provides a common framework in the field of women's equality and in much of Europe equal opportunities measures at the organisational level continue to focus mainly on the position of women. In the field of racial discrimination or discrimination against people with disabilities there is much greater national diversity in approach. While there clearly is no unilinear correlation between this and the absence of a common European framework on employment discrimination in these fields the comparatively lower level of diversity in the gender field suggests, perhaps points to, the importance of European level activity in contributing at least to a closer understanding of the issues involved.

NOTES

1 Jonung and Persson (1993) and Hakim (1993) suggest that, because of part-time work and 'family friendly' employment legislation, 'market work' or actual hours of paid employment are a better indicator for international comparisons than participation rates. Jonung and Persson show that women friendly policies (such as extended maternity leave during which women continued to be counted as in the workforce) lead to an overestimation of changes in the division of labour between men and women. Nevertheless in as far as participation rates measure the share of women who are actively, even if marginally, involved in paid employment we believe that it remains an important factor for international comparisons.
2 As Bovenkerk et al. (1991: 385) point out: 'An explicit content analysis of the variations of descriptive terms between countries would then offer a splendid starting point to study specificity' of the treatment of ethnic minorities in each country.

REFERENCES

Autenrieth, C. (1993) 'Frauen auf dem Weg ins Management: Ergebnisse einer Studie', *Personalführung* 6: 534–5.

Bell, D. (1993) 'Strukturelle Defizite bei der Beschäftigung ausländischer Arbeitnehmer und Arbeitnehmerinnen im öffentlichen Dienst', *WSI- Mitteilungen* 3: 173–8.

Bovenkerk, F., Miles, R., Verbunt, G. (1991) 'Comparative studies of migration and exclusion on the grounds of "race" and ethnic background in Western Europe: a critical appraisal', *International Migration Review* 25(2): 375–91.

Brewster, C. and Teague, P. (1989) *European Community Social Policy*, London: IPM.

Brewster, C., Hegewisch, A., Holden, L. and Lockhart, T. (1992) *The European Human Resource Management Guide*, London: Academic Press.

Brown, C. (1984) *White and Black in Britain*, London: Policy Studies Institute.

Bruegel, I. (1989) 'Sex and race in the labour market', *Feminist Review* 32(Summer): 49–68.

Bruegel, I. and Hegewisch, A. (1994) 'Flexibilisation and part time work in Europe', in: R. Brown and R. Compton (eds) (1994) *A New Europe? Economic Restructuring and Social Exclusion* London: UCL Press.

Campos e Cunha, R. (1993) 'Women in business and management: Portugal', in M. J. Davidson and C. Cooper (eds) (1993) *European Women in Business and Management*, London: Paul Chapman.

Castle, S. (ed.) (1984) *Here for Good: Western Europe's New Ethnic Minorities*, London: Pluto Press.

Commission of the European Communities (1988) *Positive Action: Equal Opportunities for Women in Employment; A Guide*, Luxembourg: Commission of the EC, Directorate General V.

Commission of the European Communities (1992) 'The position of women in the labour market: trends and developments in the twelve member states of the European Community 1983–1990', *Women of Europe* supplement 36.

Confederation of British Industry (1988): *Workforce 2000: An Agenda for Action*, London: CBI.

EIRR (1991) 'Italy: law on positive action', *European Industrial Relations Review* 208(May): 22–3.

Employment Gazette (1991) 'Ethnic origin and the labour market', Department of Employment, February: 59–72.

Equal Opportunities Commission (1991) *Women and Training: a Review*, Research Discussion Series, 1, Manchester: EOC.

Eyraud, F. (1993) 'Equal pay: an international overview', in F. Eyraud (ed.) (1993) *Equal Pay Protection in Industrialised Market Economies: in Search of Greater Effectiveness*, Geneva: ILO.

European Institute of Public Administration (1988) *Women in Higher Public Service*, Maastricht.

Forbes, I. and Mead, G. (1992) *Measure for Measure: a Comparative Analysis of Measures to Combat Racial Discrimination in the Member Countries of the EC*, Department of Employment, Research Series 1.

Ford, G. (1991) *Fascist Europe: the Rise of Racism and Xenophobia*, London: Pluto Press.

Gillmeister, H. (1992) 'Die Verdrängung ausländischer Arbeitnehmer folgt keinem Naturgesetz', *Die Mitbestimmung*, 38(8): 14–17.

Hakim, K. (1993) 'The myth of rising female employment' *Work, Employment and Society* 7(1): 97–120.

Hammar, T. (ed.) (1985) *European Immigration policy: A Comparative Study* Cambridge: Cambridge University Press.

Hänninen-Salmelin, E. and Petäjäniemi, T. (1993): 'Women managers, the challenge to management?', in N. Adler and D. Izraeli (eds) *Competitive Frontiers: Women Managers in a Global Economy*; Cambridge, USA: Blackwell.

Hegewisch, A. (1993) 'Gleichstellungspolitik – Entwicklungen im Personalmanagement in Europa', in G. Hausen and K. Krell (eds) *Frauenerwerbstätigkeit; Deutsch-deutsche Ansichten*, Munich: Rainer Hampp Verlag.

Hegewisch, A., Brewster, C, and Sirnes, C. (1993) *Equal Opportunities Policies in European Health Service Employment*, Cranfield: Cranfield School of Management (report commissioned by Oxford Regional Health Authority on behalf of the NHSME Women's Unit).

Hörburger, H. (1990) *Europas Frauen fordern mehr*, Marburg: SP-Verlag Norbert Schüren GmbH.

Income Data Services/Institute of Personnel Management (1991) *Terms & Conditions of Employment*; European Management Guides, London: IPM.

Income Data Services (1992) 'Equal pay – a distant goal?', *IDS European Report*, 371, (November): I–VIII.

Jonung, C. and Persson, I. (1993) 'Women and market work: the misleading tale of participation rates in international comparisons', *Work, Employment and Society* 7(2): 259–74.

Joshi, H. and Davies, H. (1992) 'Day care in Europe and mothers' forgone earnings', *International Labour Review* 132(6): 561–79.

Laegreid, P. (1990) 'Changes in Norwegian public personnel policy', in OECD (1990) *Flexible Personnel Management in the Public Service*, Public Management Studies, Paris: OECD.

Langkau-Herrmann, M. and Sessar-Karpp, E. (1991) 'Women in public administration in the Federal Republic of Germany', *Women and Politics* 11(4): 55–68.

Leyenaar, M. (1991) 'Women in public administration in the Netherlands', *Women and Politics* 11(4): 41–54.

Lockhart, T. and Brewster, C. (1992) 'Human resource management in the European Community', in C. Brewster, A. Hegewisch, L. Holden and T. Lockhart (eds) (1992) *The European Human Resource Management Guide*, London: Academic Press.

Mazey, S. (1988) 'European Community action on behalf of women: the limits of legislation', *Journal of Common Market Studies* 27(1): 63–84.

Meager, N. and Metcalf, H. (1988) 'Equal opportunities policies: tactical issues in implementation', *IMS Reports* 156, Brighton: Institute of Manpower Studies.

Meuser, M. (1989) *Gleichstellung auf dem Prüfstand: Frauenförderung in der Verwaltungspraxis*, Pfaffenweil: Centaurus.

Ministere du Travail et de la Participation (1983) *Guide pratique pour la promotion de l'emploi féminin dans l'entreprise*, Paris.

Moss, P. (1990) 'Parents at Work', in P. Moss and N. Fonda (eds) (1990) *Work and the Family*, London: Temple Smith.

Nätti, J. (1992) 'Part time employment in the Nordic countries: a trap for women?', paper for International Working Party on Labour Market Segmentation Conference, Cambridge, July.

Nüse, J.-C. (1992) 'Natürlich werden von den neuen Zuwanderern ganz andere Qualifikationen erwartet als von den Arbeitsimmigranten der 60ger Jahre', *Die Mitbestimmung* 39(8): 28–32.

Phizacklea, A. (ed.) (1983) *One way ticket*, London: Routledge.

Pollert, A. and Rees, T. (1992) *Equal Opportunities and Positive Action in Britain: Three Case Studies*, Warwick Papers in Industrial Relations, Coventry: IRRU, University of Warwick.

Povall, M. and Langkau-Herrmann, M. (eds) (1991) '*Equal Opportunity Development for Women in Local Government: an Anglo German Perspective*', London: Anglo German Foundation.

Räthzel, N. (1991) 'Germany: one race, one nation?', *Race & Class* 32(3): 31–48.

Rubery, J. (ed.) (1988) *Women and Recession*, London: Routledge.

Rubery, J. (1992) 'Pay, gender and the social dimension to Europe', *British Journal of Industrial Relations* 30(4): 605–21.

Rubery, J. and Fagan, C. (1993) 'Occupational segregation of women and men in the European Community'. *Network of Experts on the Situation of Women in the Labour Market*, Commission of the European Communities, Equal Opportunities Unit (synthesis report).

Schultze, G. (1992): Väter und Söhne; *Die Mitbestimmung*, 38(8): 18–20.

Sinkkonen, S. and Hänninen-Salmelin, E. (1991) 'Women in public administration in Finland', *Women and Politics* 11(4): 69–84.

Söderström, M. and Syrén, S. (1992) 'Sweden', in C. Brewster, A. Hegewisch, L. Holden and T. Lockhart (eds) (1992) *The European Human Resource Management Guide*, London: Academic Press.

Unit for Equal Opportunity Statistics (1990) *Women and Men in Sweden; Equality of the Sexes 1990*, Stockholm: Statistics Sweden.

Whitehouse, G. (1992) 'Legislation and labour market gender inequality: an analysis of OECD countries', *Work Employment and Society*, 6(1): 65–86.

Wilkinson, B. (1992) 'Implementing equal opportunities', *Equal Opportunities Review* Nov.–Dec.: 25–30.

Chapter 13

EC social policy and European human resource management

Paul Teague

INTRODUCTION

Social policy has been a source of deep friction inside the EC for the past decade or so. At root the issue has been controversial because it is a central part of the debate about what is the most appropriate social model for Europe in the 1990s and beyond. On the one hand, the United Kingdom Government and European employers want to make the Community labour market more flexible by curtailing government interventions in the economy. On the other hand, the Commission and some member states simply regard social policy as an extension of the model of welfare capitalism that has dominated national economies in Europe since the Second World War. The ideological clash between these two views has led to heated and exasperated negotiations. No clear victor has yet emerged from these exchanges. Thus the prospect is that EC social policy will continue to be a source of controversy.

This chapter examines some of the key issues surrounding the EC social policy debate. The first section outlines the (uneven) development of EC social policy, particularly with regard to EC labour law and a social dialogue at Community level. Then a discussion takes place of how EC social policy should be interpreted. The argument here is that the Commission has attempted to establish a Community labour market regime governed by a symbiotic dynamic so that the EC centre and member states can co-exist. However, this symbiotic dynamic has yet to emerge in practice and as a result EC social policy has been dominated by an obscuration effect. The final section uses evidence from the Price Waterhouse Cranfield survey to support this thesis.

THE EVOLUTION OF SOCIAL POLICY

Virtually no clause of an interventionist kind was included in the Treaty of Rome on social policy matters. Big aspirational objectives were laid down for the participating countries to increase the living standards of their citizens and work towards closer economic and social systems. But no specific programmes or policies were tied to these objectives, thereby ensuring that the various countries were not shackled to unrealistic or over ambitious commitments. Most social policy measures contained in the treaty were linked to the key goal of creating the free movement of labour. For instance, a social fund was established to ease the problems of social integration when people moved from one national labour market to another. An obligation to maintain the broad equivalence in holiday entitlements and to guarantee equal pay for equal work as well as proper health and safety standards were the only explicit positive social policies set down. All in all, the treaty reflected the consensus at the time that market integration alone would bring prosperity and employment.

In the following decade, employment policy played a marginal role in the integration project. Initiatives were launched on such things as health and safety and training provision, but these were small scale and were mainly concerned with increasing communication between national labour market bodies. Regulating the employment relationship continued to be firmly embedded in the national context. At the end of the 1960s, however, the integration agenda began to change. By this stage, the Common Market had reached an awkward point. On the one hand, the experiment of creating a new pan-European economic arrangement had been quite successful. Most of the 'negative' integration objectives of the Treaty of Rome had been achieved. But on the other hand, the Common Market was widely regarded as a remote institution, unrelated to the general economic and political affairs of the member states. Important political leaders such as Willy Brandt regarded this situation as undesirable. As a result, they started to argue for a Common Market with a 'human face'. To achieve this goal more 'positive' integration programmes were deemed to be necessary. Developing European level social policies was seen as a particularly important route to deepen the political and societal foundations of the Community. At the 1972 Paris Summit, the now nine member states officially endorsed this view by declaring themselves as committed to a social union as to an economic union (Brewster and Teague 1989).

From the 1970s onwards, the Commission has attempted to expand the EC's role in social policy in a number of ways. Probably the most important dimension has been efforts to introduce Community legislation on employment topics (Hepple 1990). Table 13.1 below lists the labour laws that have been passed by the member states. Most of the Directives were passed in the 1970s when the member states were more disposed to increasing the Community's presence in the European labour market. The nature of the Directives reveal that the Community was attempting to respond to the more pressing concerns in the labour market at the time. Thus the statutes on equal opportunities reflected the growing social consensus that legal penalties should be incurred by employers who discriminated against women. In addition, the workers' rights legislation was a response to the large scale redundancies and industrial restructuring programmes that were occurring in almost every member state. By fostering a resonance between labour market

Table 13.1 EC social policy Directives

Equal opportunities
1 *Equal Pay Directive 1975* Obliged member states to abolish all discrimination between the pay of men and women arising from their laws, regulations and administrative provisions and to take the measures necessary to ensure the principle of equal pay for work of equal value is applied.
2 *Equal Treatment Directive 1976* Concerned with promoting equal treatment for women as regards access to employment, vocational training, promotion and working conditions.
3 *Social Security Directive 1978* Designed to eliminate from social security schemes all discrimination based on sex, either directly or indirectly by reference in particular to marital or family status.
4 *Social Security Directive 1986* Established for the first time international social security standards for private sector occupational schemes.

Workers rights
1 *Collective Redundancies 1978 (amended 1991)* Obliged companies who were enacting redundancies to give workers, and their representatives, at least thirty days' notice.
2 *Transfer of Undertakings Directive 1978* Established the automatic transfer of workers rights in instances of mergers and takeovers and the right of workers representatives in companies employing more than fifty people to be informed in writing at least two months prior to the transfer.
3 *Insolvency Directive 1980* Required institutions to be set up at the member state level to pay workers' outstanding claims which arose from their employment relationship before the employer ceased to meet his obligations.
4 *Atypical Workers and Health and Safety 1991* Required agency workers and those on fixed term contracts to be informed of job risks and receive appropriate training. Authorities to be informed of allocation of temporary workers to potentially risky jobs.
5 *Employment Contracts Directive* Detailed contracts to be given to workers to provide them with 'more security, a better idea of their rights, and more mobility within the Community'.

dynamics and its institutional initiatives, the Community was attempting to establish itself as a legitimate actor in systems of employment regulation.

The 1970s was a relatively good decade for those who wanted to see social legislation being enacted by the Community. But it should be pointed out that the Commission had failures as well as successes. A proposal to introduce a common model of employee involvement was rejected by the member states as seeking too much harmonisation. Twenty years later, and after the initial proposal has been watered down enormously, the member states still remain reluctant to adopt the scheme. This suggests that real limits exist to any project aimed at increasing the uniformity of industrial relations systems inside the Community. Another proposal – the infamous Vredeling Directive – to establish information and consultation procedures inside multinational corporations also went aground after a highly effective world-wide campaign by these enterprises.

As shown in Table 13.1 few new social policy Directives, and none of any consequence, were passed during the 1980s, reflecting the stalemate that had crept into this area of Community activities (Teague 1989). To a large extent, this immobilism was caused by the British Government's unrelenting opposition to EC social policy proposals. For instance, in the early 1980s, the Commission brought forward a family of initiatives on the organisation and regulation of working time but the United Kingdom Government, by using or threatening to use its veto inside the Council of Ministers, was successful in blocking these initiatives. However, the Community's legal authority on labour market questions did increase during this period as a result of specific rulings by the European Court of Justice. Because clauses of the Treaty of Rome are regarded as primary Community legislation, these can be used to challenge existing practices or laws of a member state. Equal opportunities interest groups started to use Article 119 on equal pay and equal work to bring cases before the European Court of Justice in the hope that the decisions made would strengthen existing national equality measures. By and large, this practice was successful as many member states were obliged to introduce stronger anti-discrimination legislation as a result of certain decisions made by the Court of Justice.

Overall, however, by the mid-1980s EC social policy had become a highly contested issue. On the one hand, the Commission was eager to expand the Community's repertoire of employment measures, whilst on the other, the United Kingdom Government was firmly opposed to any such move (Gold 1992). This clash reached a climax in the debate about whether or not a social dimension should be grafted onto the programme to complete the internal market. To counter-balance some of the liberalising initiatives of the programme, the Commission proposed that a Social Charter be adopted setting out a range of employment rights that the member states should uphold. Predictably, the United Kingdom Government strongly resisted this proposal. The final curtain has yet to come down on this clash, but it appears that the other eleven member states have ostracised the United Kingdom on the matter. They have signed the Social Charter and an accompanying action programme which have been embodied in the Social Protocol to the Maastricht Treaty.

Although somewhat weaker than the original Commission proposals, the Social Protocol commits the eleven signatories to qualified majority voting on a number of labour market issues. In particular the protocol allows qualified majority voting on: (1) activities to improve the working environment, including health and safety; (2) working conditions, for instance, the length of the working week or holiday entitlements; (3) information and consultation of workers; (4) equal opportunities and the integration of people excluded from the labour market. Unanimous voting is still in place for all other issues, including social security, termination of employment, the representation and collective defence of the interests of workers (including codetermination) and employment conditions for third country nationals.

Another feature of the protocol is that effectively it focuses on individual rights and not on collective rights. Paragraph (6) of Article 2 stipulates that the question of pay, the right to strike or the right to impose lock-outs will remain outside the scope of Community action. Heavy intervention in these areas is ruled out as it ran the danger of disrupting locally established and finely tuned arrangements which structure power relations between national employers and trade unions. Overall, however, the Commission is hoping that the protocol will free up the log jam in EC social policy (Butt Philip 1992). Already, a new Directive on employment contracts has been adopted which aims to ensure 'transparency' in the employment relation in all member states and to assist plans for Europe-wide labour mobility. Other new pieces of legislation include the working time proposals originally blocked by the United Kingdom in the early 1980s. Thus the Community is set to increase its portfolio of labour market statutes in the 1990s.

THE SOCIAL DIALOGUE APPROACH

The second pillar to EC social policy has been attempts at obtaining a meaningful dialogue between the social partners at Community level (Grahl and Teague 1991). Activity in this area started in the late 1960s. At that time, the Commission encouraged the setting up of industrial sector committees, comprised of the representatives of European trade union and employer organisations. The envisaged purpose of these committees was to assist the Commission in developing employment policies for individual industries. In addition it was anticipated that once up and running the committees would conclude European collective agreements on working conditions, training strategies and so on. Just how these arrangements would relate to national level collective bargaining was subtly avoided: and, in the event, this highly sensitive question never had to be addressed as these committees failed to realise early expectations. Only one of the committees was able to conclude a collective agreement, but this fell short of existing national provisions. For the most part, the sector committees were unable to develop a role for themselves and as a result discussions lacked direction and purpose. Relatively quickly, many of the committees fell into abeyance. Some even stopped meeting, whilst others came together infrequently. As a result, by the early 1980s many of these committees were more or less defunct.

In 1985 when Jacques Delors became President of the Commission, the project for a European level exchange between trade unions and employers was resurrected under the title of a social dialogue. Delors calculated that a way out of the deadlock on EC social legislation would be to base future draft Directives on agreements reached by trade unions and employers at Community level. In other words the social partners would become the initiators of EC labour laws. European employers were opposed to performing such a role and would only agree to partake in a renewed social dialogue if it had no relationship with the legal dimension to EC social policy. This condition was accepted and as a result the Val Duchesse talks got under way. The exact purpose and status of these talks were not established, but they did produce a number of 'Joint Opinions'. Although not having any impact on national level collective bargaining, these talks were none the less significant as they increased contact and trust between the social partners at the European level. An indication of the new trust relations came in 1992 when the social partners agreed that the 'social dialogue' should be more directly connected to the formulation of EC employment policies. In 1993, the employees and unions further agreed to re-appraise the rules and procedures governing the social dialogue at European level, particularly with regard to how it could more effectively influence national collective bargaining.

Alongside this promotion of a dialogue between the 'peak' European organisations of trade unions and employers, an attempt was made to rejuvenate the European sector committees. This time however these organisations were not overburdened with grand plans. Instead the purpose of the committees was seen as encouraging an exchange on developments within respective industries and to suggest topics for research and deeper investigation to the Commission. Overall the rejuvenation strategy has been successful for most of European sector committees are now meeting regularly once again. Moreover, the dialogue in the committees is now more purposeful and a number of important if small innovations have occurred.

In the draft Maastricht Treaty the Commission imposes a more formalised arrangement for the social dialogue (Gold and Hall 1992). First of all, Article 3(3) obliges the Commission to formally consult the social partners before proposing any new social policy initiative. Should the social partners wish the subject under discussion to be governed by a European collective agreement then the Commission must do its utmost to accommodate this preference. Article 4(1) suggests that the social dialogue could lead to 'contractual agreements, including legislation' should both sides so desire. If any Community level agreements are concluded, then Article 4(2) lays down a procedure whereby it can be enacted in the member states by a Council Decision, which is a powerful legal instrument. Thus, the Maastricht Treaty establishes the legal framework for European collective bargaining should employers and unions want to initiate such a practice. The current social dialogue has certainly been strengthened recently but it still falls a long way short of institutionalised Community level bargaining. At the same time, relationships between European trade unions and employers are now cordial, thus making further progress in this area a distinct possibility.

EC SOCIAL POLICY: SYMBIOTIC INTENT, OBSCURATION EFFECT

An ill-assorted collection of views exist about EC social policy. One perspective is that instruments like the Social Charter place new burdens on business, thereby causing higher unemployment and reduced competitiveness (Addison and Siebert 1992). An alternative outlook is that the much vaunted social dimension to the 1992 programme has turned out to be an empty arrangement unable to effectively guarantee labour and employment rights (Streeck 1992). Clearly, more nuanced views exist about the role and potential of EC social policy between these two extremes. Nevertheless, these sharply contrasting views have dominated the debate on the issue. To a large extent, this is due to the huge influence of the supranational/intergovernmental framework on discussions about European integration. Such a framework encourages an assessment of EC policies in terms of whether they involve new powers for the Community centre or if they ensure national control over the integration process.

Whether all the complexities associated with deepening economic and political ties between the member states can be captured by this approach is open to question. Certainly it has not been very helpful in shedding light on the dynamics underpinning EC social policy. In the early 1970s, it was probably accurate to suggest that a strong harmonising and centralising logic underscored many draft Commission proposals for the labour market. But for more than a decade now the Commission and other key actors in the social policy arena have eschewed this 'monolithic harmonisation' approach. Measures that would cause far reaching change to national industrial relation systems are now regarded as inappropriate and unnecessary. At the same time, the Commission does not want EC social policy to be reduced to a range of innocuous and symbolic initiatives which characterise the labour codes of other international organisations like the *OECD Guidelines on Multinationals*. Only the weakest of links are seen as existing between these measures and national industrial relations systems.

Thus the Commission wants neither a maximalist nor a minimalist EC labour market regime, but some type of hybrid system. Such an arrangement would fall between federalism, implying some form of supranationalism at Community level, and intergovernmentalism, ensuring that the member states would continue to have an effective say over the direction of policy. From this perspective, EC social policy is about developing initiatives that allow for a degree of national autonomy within a common European system.

In other words, connections between the Community and member states would be governed by a symbiotic dynamic that would allow EC labour market measures to mesh with existing national industrial relations systems.

Perhaps this symbiotic dynamic can be better explained with the help of the strategic choice framework developed by Kochan, Katz and McKersie (1986). According to these authors, industrial relations systems can be regarded as comprising three institutional tiers. At the top level, Government, employers and unions are involved in strategic decision making. In the middle tier, the various parties are engaged in more functional matters such as collective bargaining or the development of human resource policies. The bottom tier largely consists of workplace personnel policies and their impact on individual employees. Inside the EC, such industrial relations systems have been mainly national in character. If a maximalist social dimension were to be introduced a new fourth European institutional tier would be grafted on to different national frameworks. The institutional linkages between the pre-existing three levels would in all likelihood have to be uprooted and recast to accommodate the new European dimension. As a result the EC would have a pervasive influence on all aspects of industrial relations activity. However, an EC social policy based on a symbiotic dynamic would not have such a far reaching impact. Certainly it would involve a new Community institutional structure becoming attached to national industrial relations systems. But such an arrangement would not trigger any sudden or abrupt changes to existing interrelationships among activities. Any changes that may occur would be gradual and incremental. More specifically, EC labour market policies would influence national industrial relations systems in three main ways. One is through approximation measures which aim at getting the member states to pursue broadly similar employment policies within their own peculiar institutional structures. In other words the aim is to establish a degree of policy uniformity in the context of institutional diversity. Most EC social policies fall under the approximation banner. Indeed the Social Action Programme is embedded in this line of thinking. For example, a good many of the proposals set out to deepen the information and consultation flows between national labour market institutions. These can be seen as an attempt to ensure that a cross-national policy learning process can begin on social policy topics. With regard to legal provision, few of the new proposed Directives aim at creating supranational EC legislation. Health and safety is perhaps the only area where heavy Community legal interventions may materialise. Other proposals aim at only paralleling existing national legislation or encouraging small change so as to introduce greater consistency between the different labour law regimes. All in all, the approximation function is about ensuring that employment policies across the Community display a common purpose (Vogel-Polisky and Vogel 1991).

A second way national industrial relations systems may be influenced is through policies aimed at reducing spillovers that arise from the integration progress. Certain political and economic interactions between the member states may produce tensions which Community intervention might be required to resolve (Pochet 1991). For example, EC measures may be necessary to reduce the tension between the Community objective of the free movement of labour and national labour market rules, like the non-recognition of diplomas gained in other member states, which creates obstacles to mobility. Initiatives in this mould are fairly benign and command wide support. But there are some proposed EC social measures designed to reduce perceived 'negative spillovers' that have proved more contentious. For instance, in the social action programme there is a proposal for a Directive on the external aspects of part-time and temporary staff. If passed, this piece of legislation would forbid companies in one member state employing part-time employees from another member state on terms and conditions that are the norm in the person's domestic economy but fall below the norm in the economy where they would be working. Such a practice is seen as a form of social dumping because enterprises are deliberately manipulating cost differences between the member states in a way that puts downward pressure on established social provision. The draft Directive has caused considerable disagreement amongst the member states and an argument has erupted about whether national action would be equally as effective as an EC measure in preventing such commercial practice.

Another matter that is proving controversial is whether Community action is needed to close the emerging gap between the mainly national boundaries to industrial relations systems and the growth in European level decision making by enterprises. One argument is that the asymmetry limits employee influence over decisions that could directly affect their livelihoods. Over the years the Commission has been sympathetic to this view since it has produced a number of draft Directives which would oblige transnational companies to create formal information and consultation procedures on a Europe-wide basis. The latest proposal is the draft European Works Council Directive. So far the Community has not adopted any policy in this area, reflecting a lack of agreement amongst the member states on the issue. Some member states fear that EC legislation on information and consultation procedures in multinational companies may open the door for centralising and harmonising social policies. The Commission has responded to these anxieties by putting forward proposals that are relatively weak (Streeck 1992). Nevertheless, uneasiness remains in some European capitals about the matter.

These problems about the extent to which the Community should address labour market spillover effects from the integration process show that the symbiotic model for EC social policy is not without its problems. Attempting to create EC social policies that reduce the lack of coterminous arrangements between the member states and the regional integration system in the labour market area is going to be difficult. In some cases the tensions created by asymmetries in the integration process will require immediate redress by the member states. For example, if the Community liberalises airways then it will be obliged to establish Europe-wide standards in certain employee relations matters such as pilot hours. But resolving other tensions, although important, will be less pressing. As a result, they may become irritants on the social policy agenda, festering relations between the member states. Recent thinking inside the Commission suggests that the Community should accept that as a result of negative labour market spillover effects arising from the integration process an aspect of EC social policy will always be a contested terrain. In this context, rather than assuming such problems can be easily resolved, the most prudent course may be to establish widely agreed rules and procedures to handle such potentially conflictual matters. Overall, however, a question mark must remain about whether the symbiotic model of EC social policy can effectively redress negative spillovers.

A third way a symbiotic social policy could influence national industrial relations systems is through what might be termed orientation agreements (Wedderburn 1990). The thinking here is that since the Community is removed from the day-to-day pressures of ground level employee relations or employment policy formation, it may be better placed to initiate discussion on more strategic and forward looking aspects of labour market governance. For instance, discussion could be promoted amongst labour market actors about the relationhsip between system-wide and firm specific training, or the nature and governance of work organisation in the next century. The basic idea is that dialogue at Community level could help generate new ideas about the type of changes that are required to accommodate the production and technological innovations occurring in European industry.

All in all, the symbiotic framework for EC social policy is about encouraging a common social model for the EC without disrupting too much the rules and interrelationships that underpin domestic labour market arrangements. The hope is that strong and transparent synergies would be created between the national and Community levels so that EC discussions on social policy would have a direct influence on national labour markets. Whether the Commission will be able to put this scenario into practice is an open question. Certainly the past history of EC social policy is not an encouraging omen. For Community employment policies have failed to mesh coherently with national labour market systems. Take, for instance, EC social legislation. Some Directives have a direct and strong impact on national level industrial relations, whereas others are relatively innocuous. In between, there are Directives on which confusion exists about the exact legal position. On other fronts, the record is not much better. Schemes to promote a social dialogue between European trade unions and employers and to establish dense communities amongst national labour market institutions have had limited success. All in all, the relationship between the Community centre and the member states on employment questions is untidy and haphazard. As a result, rather than being driven by a symbiotic dynamic, EC social policy currently appears to be overshadowed by an obscuration effect.

THE 'OBSCURATION' EFFECT

A number of factors account for this obscuration effect. First of all, the essentially intergovernmental decision making process of the Community makes it difficult to develop tidy labour market policies. In the absence of supranational decision making, Community policies normally take the form of package deals between the member states (Wallace 1991). This is to ensure that an initiative does not fall foul of the veto process in the European Council whereby a recalcitrant member state can slow Community action to a standstill. Thus in reality, Community policies and measures are more often than not the outcome of awkward and convenient compromises between competing positions held by the member states. Against this background, creating arrangements that properly address labour market issues and which, at the same time, push forward the symbiotic goal of strengthening the regional integration system while providing for national autonomy is clearly a herculean task. In the 1980s the Commission was not only unable to introduce a symbiotic element into EC social policy, but also failed to get package deals on employment questions. For the most part, this failure can be explained by the United Kingdom Government's complete opposition to Community level labour market interventions. But the general point is that an incongruity appears to exist between the symbiotic social policy project and the political characteristics of EC decision making. Whether the proposals contained in Maastricht are sufficient to redress this shortcoming is another open question.

Second, the legal system of the Community contributes to the haze surrounding EC social policy. To overcome the problem of legal diversity in national industrial relations systems, most EC social legislation takes the form of Directives. This instrument allows member states to introduce Community law in a manner which accords with their own legal custom and practice and any relevant national statutes. In many instances, this procedure has failed to ensure that the contents of Directives are incorporated within national law either correctly or comprehensively. Evidence suggests that some member states use their control over the ports of entry through which Community law is implemented domestically to change or distort the contents of Directives. A further problem is that uncertainties exist about the exact status of a Directive as a legal instrument. Thus, it is unclear in what circumstances Directives have, in Euro legal jargon, direct applicability – the situation where Community law takes precedence over parallel national law. Moreover, confusion exists about whether Directives which have direct applicability can be enforced in the public sector of member state economies. In combination these imperfections have served to reduce the impact of Community labour legislation. In broader terms, they have prevented a coherent legal dimension emerging to EC social policy.

A third obstacle in the way of symbiotic integration to sustain such a dynamic in the area of social policy has been the relative absence of the necessary supporting structures. For the most part, the EC institutional framework for social policy and national labour market institutions remain relatively disconnected, making collaborative efforts between the two levels difficult. The lack of established and organic linkages between national and Community institutions in the social policy area reduces the scope for mutual reinforcing mechanisms between the two levels.

Overall, a series of institutional weaknesses stands in the way of the enactment of a symbiotic EC social policy. As a result, the Community presence in the European labour market is fragmented and disjointed. In the areas of equal opportunities and health and safety legislation, Community legislation has a direct influence on national industrial relations system. In other spheres, EC measures only parallel national labour market provision and it is hard to decipher how one level relates to the other. Yet another group of EC social policies, particularly those relating to training and employment, are really best described as symbolic since they have no real impact on national arrangements. Thus, EC labour market policy is not guided by a symbiotic dynamic but overshadowed by an obscuration effect.

HUMAN RESOURCE MANAGERS AND EC SOCIAL POLICY

The portrayal of EC social policy as being more or less detached from the institutional tiers of national industrial relations systems is substantiated by the Price Waterhouse Cranfield survey on European Human Resource Management. For the overriding conclusion from the survey evidence is that most human resource managers are untroubled by developments such as the Social Charter and other envisaged EC labour market measures. Overall most companies and HRM staff appear to hold the view that the Community has a modest and uninfluential role in national or Europe-wide industrial relations matters. Thus when companies in different European countries were asked how they kept abreast of EC initiatives and developments the overwhelming majority suggested that they simply followed the general media's coverage of such events. Only a tiny faction thought developments at the Community centre were sufficiently important to warrant having a specialist employee permanently based in Brussels. Appendix III Table 8.2 details the overall responses to this question. As can be seen, a sizeable minority did partake in special events and used specialised briefing sessions to remain informed of EC social policy. Nevertheless, the clear message from this table is that most companies do not regard the Community as a strategic site for industrial relations or human resource management activity.

Appendix III Table 8.3 which details company responses to specific proposals associated with the EC Social Charter really only reinforces this message. When asked whether the Social Charter would require change to existing personnel policies the majority of firms said that it would either involve no change or minor change. A large number of enterprises responded by saying that they did not fully know, whilst only a handful of employers thought that the Charter would precipitate major revisions. A similar pattern of responses was made by the companies when asked about the likely impact of proposed legislation on a-typical employment, health and safety, equal treatment of men and women and procedures for consultation and participation of employees. Most organisations thought that only small revisions, if any at all, would be needed to comply with the proposed Directives. A sizeable group of organisations withheld judgement, whilst a small minority thought that the implementation of the proposals would cause far reaching change.

Beneath this broad picture, there are more nuanced findings. German employers were the least concerned about the enactment of new EC social policy Directives. No more than 3 per cent of organisations thought that any of the proposed new laws would have a significant impact on their operations. To a large extent, this situation reflects the fact that most of the proposals fall short of existing German regulations. At the other end of the spectrum, Spanish enterprises were the most anxious about the potential implications of EC social policy in the future. Overall 28 per cent of the organisations canvassed thought that major changes would be required if the Social Charter was implemented in full; 29 per cent thought that the draft atypical work Directives would oblige major change. The same figure for health and safety was 53 per cent; for equal treatment it was 23 per cent and for the consultation and information initiative it was 40 per cent. What probably accounts for this concern amongst Spanish employers is that they may anticipate that participation in the new Europe will require a more formal system of labour market regulation than currently is in place domestically.

Responses from United Kingdom employers display a degree of inconsistency. On the one hand, about a quarter of the organisations thought that the Social Charter could cause root and branch change. Yet a much smaller fraction regarded the specific proposals for legislation as menacing, apart from the information and consultation initiative. Perhaps this inconsistency can be explained by the gap that sometimes exists between the political opposition of some United Kingdom companies to EC social policy and the minimal impact many of the existing or proposed policies would be likely to have on their organisation. Obviously, across the countries surveyed more concern was expressed about certain proposals than others. In Ireland for example, enterprises were more worried about the consultation and information initiative than any other proposal. A plausible explanation for this is the high proportion of foreign companies in the Irish economy which may be slightly concerned about the proposal being the first step to EC-wide collective bargaining. With regard to Portugal, virtually no enterprise was worried about the equal treatment area, although a significant number of them expressed uneasiness about health and safety matters. Again this imbalance in responses owes a great deal to existing national labour market circumstances. Whereas Portuguese equal opportunities laws are tough, health and safety regulations are relatively under-developed.

The major impact of EC proposals – bar some amendments in information on redundancies which will affect all organisations – will be on MNCs with more than 1,000 employees. Not surprisingly, the proportion of organisations unsure about the effects of EC proposals is lower among this group. Across Europe, only one-quarter of MNCs believe that they would be significantly affected by the proposals; more than half of MNCs believe the proposals would make little or no difference to their practice. However there are marked national differences here, with MNCs in the United Kingdom, Ireland and Spain being particularly concerned and varying significantly in their response from other large employers in their country. Elsewhere MNCs reacted like other employers.

Beyond this, the data shows a private sector/public sector split with more organisations in the public sector answering 'don't know' to the question about EC social policy and fewer expecting any major change (Appendix III Tables 83a–e). Given current proposals this is as one would expect. Overall two aspects of the survey stand out. One is the relatively small number of organisations which thought that the Social Charter in its entirety or in specific areas would oblige them to make major changes. The other is the relatively large group which did not know whether the Charter or any of the specific proposals identified in the questionnaire would involve change. On this latter point, employers may be unconcerned about the external legal and political environment, being more interested in commercial and market developments: an explanation which would accord with the concept of 'internalisation' whereby enterprises attempt to disconnect themselves from external non-market institutional influences, particularly in the employee relations field. Another possibility is that the employers regarded EC social policy as irrelevant and simply did not bother paying attention to the adoption of the Social Charter and other related developments. The high number of respondents who thought they had nothing to fear from a social dimension to the EC lends weight to this last thesis. Certainly the survey suggests that a widespread indifference exists in the commercial world to EC social policy, suggesting that the Community is not yet a credible industrial relations actor.

CONCLUSION

Perhaps the main conclusion from the above discussion is that although EC social policy is politically controversial, its impact on ground level human resource management across the member states is minimal. This apparent paradox can be explained relatively easily. For the most part, Community labour market interventions lack influence because of the untidy nature of the integration process. At any one time, the integration process consists of both centrifugal and centripetal dynamics which reduces the scope for effective decision making at the Community centre. Moreover, transparent and smooth working connections have yet to emerge between the Community centre and the member states. In combination these two factors have considerably reduced the potential of EC social policy.

At the same time, this area is politically controversial because it touches directly the debate in every member state about the future model of social development in Europe. Faced with high unemployment and an increasing competitiveness challenge from the Far East and elsewhere, there is a growing recognition that changes are required to elements of the welfare model of capitalism that has dominated economic life in Europe for nearly half a century. But the exact form, and the extent of such changes, is a matter of deep dispute. On a Europe wide basis, EC social policy has been embroiled in this debate, therefore, making it unsurprising that it will be a controversial area. In the absence of radical institutional change, this paradox about EC social policy will remain. Politicians will continue to disagree over EC social policy and human resource managers will continue to remain relatively untroubled by such interventions.

REFERENCES

Addison, J. and Siebert, S. (1992) 'The Social Chapter: whatever next', *British Journal of Industrial Relations* 30(4): 495–515.

Brewster, C. and Teague, P. (1989) *EC Social Policy and the UK*, London: IPM.

Butt Philip, A. (1992) 'The strengthening of the social dimension, *Journal of European Social Policy* 2(2): 237–42.

Danthine, J. P., Bean, C., Bernholz, P. and Malihnand, L. (1990) *European Labour Markets: a long run view*, Economic Papers, Brussels, Commission of the European Communities.

European Institute of Public Administration (1991) *Subsidiarity: the Challenge of Change*, Maastricht: EIPA.

Gold, M. (1992) 'Social policy: the UK and Maastricht', *National Institute Economic Review* (February): 95–103.

Gold, M. and Hall, M. (1992) *European Level Information and Consultation in Multinationals*, an Evaluation of Practice, European Foundation for the Improvement of Living and Working Conditions.

Grahl, J. and Teague, P. (1991) 'The European Social Charter and labour market regulation', *Journal of Public Policy* 11(2): 207–32.

Hepple, B. (1990) 'European labour law', in R. Blanpain (ed.) *Comparative Labour Law and Industrial Relations in Industrialised Market Economies*, Vol. 1, Boston: Kluwer.

Kochan, T., Katz, H. and McKersie, R. (1986) *The Transformation of American Industrial Relations*, New York: Basic Books.

Marsden, D. and Silvestre, J. J. (1992) 'Pay and European Integration', in David Marsden (ed.) *Pay and Employment in the New Europe*, London: Edward Elgar.

Solow, R. (1989) *The Labour Market as a Social Institution*, Oxford: Basil Blackwell.

Soskice, D. (1988) 'Industrial relations and unemployment: the case for flexible corporatism', in J. A. Kregal, E. Matzuer and A. Roncaglia (eds) *Barriers to Full Employment*, London: Macmillan.

Streeck, W. (1992) 'The social dimension of the European economy', University of Wisconsin-Madison, duplicate.

Teague, P. (1989) *The European Community: the social dimension*, London: Kogan Page.

Teague, P. and Grahl, J. (1992) *Industrial Relations and European Integration*, London: Lawrence & Wishart.

Vogel-Polsky, E. and Vogel, J. (1991) *L'Europe Sociale 1993: Illusion Alibi ou Réalité*, Brussels: Editions de l'Université Libre de Bruxelles.

Wallace, W. (1991) *The Transformation of Western Europe*, London: RIIA/Pinter.

Wedderburn, Lord (1990) *The Social Charter, European Company and Employment*, London: Institute for Employment Rights.

Methodology of the Price Waterhouse Cranfield Project

Chris Brewster, Ariane Hegewisch, Lesley Mayne and Olga Tregaskis

Our research has taken the form of an international comparative survey of organisational policies and practices in human resource management across Europe. Whilst data on European labour markets is far from comprehensive and is open to considerable criticism, it is, in general, available to researchers. However, little data exists which allows a systematic analysis of European trends in human resource management policies and practices within employing organisations.

Available comparable labour market statistics, such as the EC labour force survey, are broad in their approach to employment, concentrating more on the type and size of employment than on aspects of human resource management or personnel policy within organisations. The study of personnel policies on the other hand is usually limited to case studies and, whilst the importance of case studies to an accurate understanding of human resource management is clear, it was felt that these needed to be complemented with a wider survey approach which could establish whether the case studies are representative or generalisable. Since case studies often concentrate on larger, more 'advanced' companies, generalisation from their practice might give a false impression of the general state of the art in the field.

Human resource management in most European countries is strongly influenced by the national legal and institutional framework, even if, as some observers stress, organisations across Europe are faced with common economic and structural changes which appear to elicit similar responses in personnel management strategies (Grahl and Teague 1991; Gaugler 1988; Brewster 1994). It was felt that a primary frame of reference for analysis should be organisational level data collected on a national basis.

In order to obtain an accurate picture of trends it was decided to carry out an annual

Table AI.1 Countries surveyed

1989–90	1990–1	1991–2	1993
Germany (West)	Germany (West)	Germany (West)	
Spain	Spain	Spain	
France	France	France	
Sweden	Sweden	Sweden	
UK	UK	UK	
	Denmark	Denmark	
	Netherlands	Netherlands	
	Norway	Norway	
	Switzerland		
	Italy		
		Finland	
		Ireland	
		Portugal	
		Turkey	
			Austria
			Czech Rep
			Greece
		Germany (East)	Germany (East)

survey, repeating it as often as possible, and certainly for the three years for which Price Waterhouse and Cranfield had committed themselves to the project. This gave us the opportunity to establish trends in the original five countries and also to widen the survey each year, as explained in the introductory chapter. The full list of countries in the survey is given in Table AI.1.

The research had two particular objectives: first to monitor over time the impact of the increasing 'Europeanisation' of business on specific human resource management practices in Europe. This Europeanisation is of course most plainly manifested in the EC countries and the single European market, though it is not limited to those countries as an examination of the links between Scandinavia or Switzerland and the EC would show. We were interested in whether such Europeanisation would lead to a harmonisation of personnel policies. We also wanted, originally, to assess whether there were significant differences in trends in EC and EFTA member states. Given the recent application of many of EFTA countries to join the EC and even before that, to align their legislation with the EC, this last point became more marginal.

The second objective was to establish how far there had been a shift in personnel policies towards 'strategic human resource management'. The conceptual issues this raises are discussed in Chapter 2. Here it suffices to note that a functional definition of human resource management was taken. In other words the survey was designed to establish how far personnel policies are planned, coherent and interactive with corporate strategies; how far there has been a shift towards greater flexibility and individualisation of the employment relationship; and what developments are taking place in areas such as recruitment, training and remuneration and employee relations. Of course, whilst 'thin/broad' survey data (that gains an overview of a range of organisational practices) is indispensable in establishing representativeness and comparisons it is an inappropriate methodology for establishing the practical reality of process and behaviour at the operational level (Morris and Wood 1991;

Brewster, Gill and Richbell 1983). For that purpose the 'deep/narrow' case study is more relevant. The objective here was, however, to provide the wider range of internationally comparable evidence about particular policies and practices that have been seen as relevant to the concept of HRM.

Our evidence was gathered from the corporate top of each organisation. As noted in a review of the data available from the British workplace industrial relations survey (WIRS), a focus on workplaces, particularly small workplaces, has disadvantages. On some definitions HRM is the stuff of head offices and boardrooms or at the very least of large workplaces; in adopting such a low threshold, it could be argued, WIRS excludes serious discussion of 'state of the art' developments (Sisson 1993: 202).

METHODOLOGICAL CONCERNS

Conducting such a survey as this has raised a number of interesting issues which have had to be addressed at each stage. An initial question concerns the level of analysis and, related to this, the nature of the conclusions that can be drawn. A simple example would be the question of reward structures within two organisations in different countries. A comparison of pay rates is uninformative without detailed knowledge of purchasing power, lifestyles, cultural issues, state social security provisions, working hours and working lifetime details and so on, for each country. Comparisons of pay structures – to what extent are systems or remuneration limited to performance or what is the differential from the top to the bottom of the organisation – whilst still flawed, may be more valid.

To some extent independent of the choice of levels of analysis, there is the question of subject matter. This is intrinsically related to the nationality issue: certain issues will be 'live' and controversial in some societies, unacknowledged or unremarkable in others. Studies of industrial relations, for example, might focus on strikes and disputes in a transatlantic context; but on dispute resolution and conciliation in a Pacific Basin analysis (Brewster and Tyson 1991). Researchers deal with this problem in a variety of ways. Some choose to compare societies which may be said to have broad cultural similarities; others undertake joint research programmes; and some choose to stand outside the cultural context, comparing societies which are beyond their own cultural upbringing.

This leads us directly to the choice of countries to compare. There are arguments for choosing countries which are, in as many ways as possible, as similar as can be. If the distorting effects of very different population sizes, industrial segmentation, wealth, infrastructure and cultural values can be diminished, then genuine differences in national human resource management style can be more clearly identified. The counter-argument suggests that it is precisely the differences between societies which illuminate and challenge the unacknowledged assumptions in the way organisations obtain and deal with their human resources. In our survey, given its aims of geographical as well as thematic breadth, these questions mainly relate to the interpretation of results.

In either case, the role of the researcher is problematic. Each particular researcher will bring to the task of comparative study a particular set of cultural assumptions and a particular degree of knowledge and expertise. The cultural assumptions will not only give the researcher easier access to understanding of his or her own society – and make understanding of other societies more difficult – but is also likely to affect the researcher's choice of subject matter and 'intellectual style'. The degree of knowledge of societies is fundamental to understanding the behaviour of people within employing organisations in those societies. Joint research is clearly one way to try to handle this issue.

In the event we had to make decisions (and compromises) in a number of areas: they relate to the design of the questionnaire; its distribution; the representativeness of the responses; and data preparation and analysis.

QUESTIONNAIRE DESIGN

In designing research tools for international comparisons, researchers then are faced with a dilemma: should they insist on the gathering of information using an identical measuring instrument – at the risk of 'losing' or misunderstanding data from different cultural contexts; or should the design be adapted to take account of national differences – and put at risk the comparability of the study? It was decided that, as the focus of the research was international comparability, a questionnaire that was, as far as possible, identical would be used in all countries. The questionnaire design was preceded by several bilateral or multilateral international discussions in order to identify major issues of interest and priority. To overcome the potential British bias in the design of the questionnaire the faculty at Cranfield worked closely with academic partners in each of the participating countries (see introductory chapter). This close partnership provided vital knowledge of national practices and debates. Therefore allowing broader indicators of HR policy and practices to be adopted without compromising national interpretation. The draft question-naire was tested with personnel managers in those countries. The issues chosen for coverage were:

1 HR departments and HR strategy.
2 Recruitment policies.
3 Pay and benefits policies.
4 Training policies and evaluation.
5 Contract and working hours flexibility.
6 Industrial relations and employee communication.
7 Responses and attitudes to the approaching single European market.

The potential conflict over the areas covered also extended to the design and sequence of the questions. For example, in such a functional area as staff categories it was necessary to reflect the habitual national categories and accept a lack of uniformity between countries. Thus in recognition of the usual German practice the group manual workers was split into two – skilled (*Facharbeiter*) and semi- and unskilled workers (the figures in the appendix relate to the former category).

Other differences arose from the different levels of regulation through employment legislation. 'Job sharing', for example, is more narrowly defined in several European countries than in the United Kingdom and under that more narrow definition is sometimes illegal. Similarly, some countries prohibit private recruitment agencies, or provide an automatic right to trade union recognition, and therefore questions asking whether private recruitment agencies are utilised or whether trade unions are recognised would simply make little sense to respondents in those countries. Another problem presented itself in the design of questions on equal opportunities policies. In Britain and the Netherlands, such discussions are generally concerned with addressing discrimination against women, ethnic minorities and people with disabilities. In France on the other hand, even though the proportion of black and ethnic minorities in the workforce is very similar, a reference to ethnic minority people was not included because the French partners of the project felt that such a question would raise concerns over civil liberties. Such issues were addressed by slight variations between national versions of the survey.

It was important in standardising the questionnaire to ensure the 'correct' translation into each relevant language. The draft questionnaire was developed in English. In order to ensure uniformity the questionnaire for each country was first translated and adapted into the other languages and then re-translated into English (Brislin 1976; Brislin, Lonner and Thorndike 1973; Hofstede 1980). The translation was tested with personnel directors to ensure that the terms and questions were comprehensible. Translation however is not merely a technical process: it again highlights cultural differences. Take, for example, the case of differentiating between the mission statement and corporate strategy. Whilst the more advanced business leaders would be familiar with the terms, an exact literal translation (where there is no direct correspondence to a commonly used national term) would often give terms which were unfamiliar to the majority of respondents in a particular country. It was decided to avoid, as far as possible, detailed explanatory notes: they make the questionnaire look overly complicated and reduce response rates. Eventually, in some countries compromise terminology (plus brief notes in some cases) were used. In Germany further difficulties arose in relation to public sector terminology and special public sector translations had to be prepared to take this into account.

The translation problems were minimised, though not overcome, by our objective of identifying, wherever possible, hard data rather than attitudinal information. The number of open ended questions was limited to two, on the future strategic objectives of the personnel function (Appendix III Table 2.1) and on problem areas in recruitment (Appendix III Table 3.1). These were coded in each country according to a framework developed mainly in the first year of the survey by analysing responses from the five countries included then (with 70 sub-categories for each variable). The results in the appendix reflect a regrouping of these in broad categories.

The survey at least to some extent relied on 'self-definition' and therefore to a certain extent reflects the evaluation of the respondent. The comparatively high levels of activity in the field of training assessment and evaluation, for example, are likely to be yet another expression of the paradox that has confounded British researchers on training practices for a while: that there seems to be a persistent discrepancy between what organisations say they are doing on training and the actual training efforts that can be observed on the ground (Keep 1989). Another example is flexible working. In Britain and Germany discussion of this issue has been closely linked to demographic change and the reintegration of women into the labour market. In France on the other hand, where demographic discussions are much less prevalent, flexible working is seen as a response to general changes in lifestyle, not particularly linked to female labour force participation. Thus, even if the questions are identical, respondents will interpret them within their given cultural and legal context. This reaffirms the point made above that the primary frame of reference for the interpretation of results has to be the national context.

The research instrument underwent a series of drafts and piloting exercises, involving the European partners, in order to overcome the types of issues outlined above. The resulting questionnaire was therefore a compromise: like all questionnaires. In this case the usual compromises between depth and length, between subjects in the instrument and between the subjects and the demographic data, were multiplied by adding different cultural assumptions from each country.

The primary frame of reference for the interpretation of results has to be the national context. With this in mind it was decided to set up a panel of experts in each country to discuss their national results. It was felt that these national panels would add a further dimension to the research findings by providing qualitative comment and opinion setting the data into the national context. Each panel consisted of HR specialists from organisations within each of the major industrial sectors.

In the first year, the outcomes of these national discussions were used to feed into an international panel of experts. The primary aim of this group was to assess the national information in terms of its meaning and implications at a European level. The international panel consisted of selected national panel members from each country and was chaired by M. Armand Mella, then president of the European Association of Personnel Managers (EAPM). Once again the panel was selected to reflect a cross-section of the major industrial classifications across Europe, including the public sector. Unlike the national panels these subsequent discussions were conducted in English, therefore, all members needed to have a good working knowledge of English, or access to an interpreter if necessary. The expansion of the number of countries in subsequent years unfortunately made the gathering of similar panels too expensive and complex.

DISTRIBUTION

The survey was aimed at establishing trends in the development of personnel policies. We wanted responses from personnel specialists at the organisational level. Research in Germany, for example, suggests that the threshold for a specialist personnel function lies with a couple of hundred employees (Semlinger and Mendius 1989); thus only organisations employing at least 200 people were included. In some countries such as Denmark, the Netherlands or Spain, this definition excludes at least half of the working population, in others such as Sweden or the United Kingdom the small firms sector is less significant. However, the study of smaller employers would require a different questionnaire design which was not within the scope of this project. Therefore, national organisational size distributions have to be taken into account when cross-cultural comparisons are made.

Responsibility for the distribution of the questionnaire within each country lay with the local partner schools. This involved approaching organisations by means of publicly available mailing lists personalised, in most instances, to the head of the personnel function or the CEO. Compared to surveys conducted within one country, international surveys require greater flexibility and more compromise in the establishment of appropriate databases. There are no internationally representative sources at the organisational level and therefore all such surveys will require a degree of adaptability to what is possible. It was found that the listings which claim to be Europewide in such publications as sector directories are often partial and/or biased by a focus on or absence of representation from one or more countries. In addition, listings from mailing list companies are not as comprehensive as they may first appear. Coverage varies greatly across countries and lists which are perfectly adequate in the United Kingdom for example proved patchy in other countries such as Italy. There was also a problem with public sector coverage. The final problem was that of cost; the costs of commercial or governmental lists were very high in some countries.

The design of mailing lists thus proved a similar task to the design of the questionnaire in terms of having to take account of local conditions and using the best available list in each country. In several countries this involved cooperation from the national personnel management association. At one level this might be seen to constitute a source of bias; including only those firms who are, by the nature of their membership of a professional association, likely to be more interested in the field. To some extent this is a general problem with postal surveys, as respondents cannot be forced to reply, those more interested or positive about their practices are more likely to respond; this is illustrated by a British respondent saying 'sorry, we are in the middle of redundancies – not in the mood to fill in the questionnaire'. At another level as the survey is directed at organisations with at least a degree of formalisation in their HR policies and practices, this is less of a drawback. The important question concerns the nature and coverage of the membership lists.

Personnel management associations can be corporately or individually based depending on country. In those countries with individual memberships care had to be taken to avoid duplication. In the case of France the INSEE, the government statistical office, mailing list was used in combination with the ANDCP (the French Personnel Managers Association). In Finland the national company register, which covered 95 per cent of all companies in Finland employing over 199 people, was used to select a sub-sample. However, this database only included service and industrial sector organisations. Finish public sector organisations addresses were more difficult to obtain and multiple sources had to be used. In the United Kingdom the primary mailing list was obtained from a private mailing list company specialising in the development of such data bases. This allowed personnel managers to be identified by industrial sector thus ensuring a representative sample of organisations from each. However, in order to increase sample size this list was supplemented by a Price Waterhouse client list and Cranfield School of Management's own database of about 6,000 organisations. These together covered 80 per cent of organisations of the required size. A similar procedure was adopted by ESADE in Spain. Once again care had to be taken to protect against duplication. Ireland also bought in a specially tailored sample frame from a private organisation, as did Germany. In countries such as Denmark, Switzerland, Italy, Turkey, Norway and Sweden the national personnel management organisations provided access to their membership lists. However, in Italy the personnel management association mailed out the questionnaires themselves in order to protect the anonymity of their members.

Public sector employment, in the sense of public administration covering central and local government, health and higher education, accounts for a substantial share of total employment in different European countries. Therefore it was important to ensure public administration was properly represented in the survey. In countries such as Denmark, Ireland, Norway, Sweden and the United Kingdom public and private sector personnel management are reasonably well integrated; there is only one professional body for personnel management and there is an overlap in training courses and educational routes. Integration is also reflected in the composition of mailing lists and generally it was not necessary to supplement mailing lists. This was not the case in Finland, Germany, France, Italy, Portugal, Turkey or Spain. In Finland the national company register, which covered the private sector, was supplemented with a variety of independent listings of health care, ministry, state owned public utilities, telecommunication operations and road administration organisations. In Germany individual local authorities will only participate in surveys if these have been approved by the relevant local authority federations. Therefore a sample of organisations were selected from lists provided by the local authority federations. The federations did not support the annual repetition of the survey; without the official support the public sector response in the second year was negligible. In the third year a limited degree of support was secured from the federations and this was supplemented by national handbook listings for public sector education and health organisations. There was a similar, if not as formalised, experience in the Netherlands. While the overall Dutch response rate fell somewhat between the 1991 and 1992 surveys the public sector response rate collapsed completely in the second year. In Portugal, Turkey, Italy and Spain the attainment of listings of public sector organisations proved more difficult again. Consequently, responses from this sector in these countries were low.

Countries used the same basic mailing lists each year, with some refinements. Selection of participants from the mailing lists varied in each country depending on the information available. Ideally each mailing list would have contained all the companies employing over 199 people broken down by industrial sector for each country. While identifying the relevant organisational size was not particularly problematic, often the industrial classification of an organisation could be. At HQ level many organisations may cover several sectors. The assessment of the representativeness of the list in terms of the population of organisations within a country was also difficult. Nevertheless, national samples were selected randomly and where possible stratified proportionate to the size of the national industrial sectors. The impact of this compromise on the representativeness of the data is discussed in the next section.

RESPONSES

Over 15,000 responses from organisations were received in the three years of the survey. The response rate for the first year of the survey was highest at 22 per cent; during the second and third years this fell to 17 per cent, while the number of countries participating rose, Table AI.2. The drop in the overall response rate between the first and the second year however largely reflects a drop in the British response rate when a decision was made not to send a second mailing of the questionnaire to non-respondents. In the first year of the survey the second mail out resulted in an increase of respondents by about a third. Nevertheless, the national and overall decline in response rates suggest that an annual

Table AI.2 Three-year survey response rates

Year	Sample	Returns	Response rate (%)	Usable responses
1989–90	25,200	5,682	22	5,098
1990–1	32,200	5,511	17	5,449
1991–2	33,100	5,507	17	4,684
Total	90,500	16,700	18	15,231

survey may be too frequent. Support from companies is likely to be stronger if they are approached on a biennial basis instead.

Figure AI.1 outlines the response rates obtained from each country over the survey period. While Table AI.3 highlights more specifically the number of usable responses. Clearly the numbers participating each year vary quite dramatically within each country while the response rate remains relatively constant or in some instances actually increases. The reason for this lies in the refinement of the sampling frame used. Mailing lists in some countries proved to be less than fully up to date or accurate. A common problem was that organisations which employed over 200 employees when the list was drawn up may have fallen below that total by the time the survey was conducted. Therefore, following the first year many of these were eliminated. As a result the sample size for the following years decreased. For example, in Sweden during the first year 330 companies participated, falling

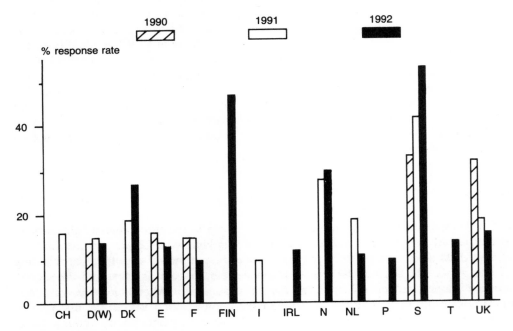

Figure AI.1 Survey sample response rate

Table AI.3 Usable responses across countries

Country	1990	1991	1992
CH	–	230	–
D(W)	502	933	884
DK	–	478	330
E	367	297	265
F	1,357	988	651
FIN	–	–	225
I	–	199	–
IRL	–	–	140
N	–	303	280
NL	–	223	128
P	–	–	93
S	330	295	322
T	–	–	123
UK	2,542	1,503	1,243

to 322 in 1992. In contrast, the response rate increased from 33 per cent to 53 per cent. A similar pattern can be seen in France. Follow-up contact and second mail outs were carried out en masse in the first year of the survey only. However, the sample size was considered large enough in most countries not to warrant this extra expense in both manpower and finances during the latter years. Out of date mailing lists also meant that although the overall number of questionnaires returned remained relatively constant the number of usable responses varied more markedly (Table AI.2). This again was largely a result of the decrease in organisations' employee numbers over the years due in part to the recesssion. Thus, decreasing the number of usable responses from organisations employing 200 or more employees.

There has been no significant change in the distribution of companies by industrial sector or size over the duration of the survey. The sample shows around half of the responses from the production sector each year, and around a quarter each for the service sector and the public sector, (Figure AI.2). The results of the significance test comparing the sector distribution for each year are reported in Table AI.4. Size analysis of the sample across all countries showed that one-third of organisations employed between 200 and 499 people. A further quarter employed between 500 and 999 with 1 in 10 employing 5,000 or more (Figure AI.3). Once again no significant difference was found in the size distribution across the three years (Table AI.5).

Given the sample profile and its consistency across years, the next important phase is to assess its representativeness against the target population. On an individual country level this is by no means an easy task. The difficulty in obtaining appropriate population parameters at cross-national level are multiplied. This is due largely to the lack of availability of statistics across all countries, and in cases where statistics are available, the lack of comparability. In this instance we required organisational level data for both EC and EFTA member countries. This we derived from two sources namely national statistical offices and Eurostat. As the sample data was not found to differ significantly year to year, the figures from the 1992 survey only are used here to assess representativeness. Sector comparisons were based on the NACE system of industrial classification (Nomenclature

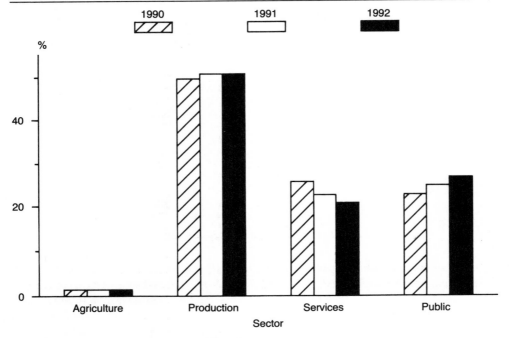

Figure AI.2 Survey sample industry classification

Table AI.4 Significance results for industry classification

Year	DF	Chi-square	Significance value	Level	Result
1990–1	2	0.571	0.752	0.05	NS
1990–2	2	1.803	0.406	0.05	NS
1991–2	2	0.339	0.884	0.05	NS

Table AI.5 Significance results for size distribution

Year	DF	Chi-square	Significance value	Level	Result
1990–1	4	0.611	0.962	0.05	NS
1990–2	4	1.217	0.875	0.05	NS
1991–2	4	0.139	0.998	0.05	NS

Activitie Classification pour les Economic). This is the Classification of Economic Activities introduced by the European Commission in an attempt to collate statistical information on the labour market across countries. It has now been adopted by most European countries. The classification system covers 10 broad divisions namely: agriculture (0); water and energy (1); extraction and processing of non-energy producing mineral and derived products, chemical industry (2); metal manufacture, mechanical, electrical and instrument engineering (3); other manufacturing industries (4); building and civil engineering (5); distributive trades, hotels, catering, repairs (6); transport and communication (7); banking and finance, insurance and business services, renting (8); other services (e.g. public

Figure AI.3 Survey sample size distribution

administration, education, health, personal) (9). As with most such listings the manufacturing sector is rather overspecified and the public service sector conglomerated. Subcategories of sector 9 were used, giving 15 classifications in all.

For analysis purposes these 10 divisions were collapsed into: Agriculture (division 0); Production (divisions 1–5); Services (divisions 6–8) and Public (division 9). Table AI.6 shows the percentage of organisations within both the sample and nationally, classified by sector (Table AI.6).

Table AI.6 Sample and population figures for industry distribution for each country (%)

Country	Sample				Population			
	Agr.	Pro.	Serv.	Pub.	Agr.	Pro.	Serv.	Pub.
CH	1	47	37	15	na	49	51	na
D(W)	0	69	24	7	<1	61	39	na
DK	2	36	24	38	<1	31	23	44
E	0	59	36	5	0	45	26	29
F	2	58	24	16	<1	58	36	6
FIN	1	54	27	18	1	58	38	3
I	0	62	28	10	0	78	22	na
P	4	58	27	11	0	76	21	3
S	3	39	25	33	2	45	20	33
UK	1	47	27	25	0	41	31	27

Notes: Agr. = Agriculture; Pro. = Production; Serv. = Service; Pub. = Public
Sources: Eurostat 1992; National Statistical Office Data 1989, 1990, 1991

Population estimates

The figures available from such bodies as the national statistical offices and Eurostat are only population estimates. While they are currently the best available they are, nevertheless, not without error. Sisson, Waddington and Whitson (1992) highlighted some of the problems in the use of such data. The particular difficulty in trying to obtain population estimates for the current research is that statistics are needed for different countries at the organisational level, i.e. company numbers. Unfortunately this is not the type of information that is collected easily or indeed given a high priority within countries. In addition where data are available they are not necessarily comparable due to the level at which they are collected. For example, data are collected at both the 'establishment' and 'enterprise' level. The first generally constitutes a single workplace or unit; the second a legal unit. Furthermore, an enterprise may be part of or a subsidiary of a larger organisation. In general the definition of establishment and enterprise does not cause particular problems in companies employing less than 499 people. Organisations employing more than this will tend to have approximately four establishments per enterprise. Based on this assumption Eurostat have converted, where necessary, establishment data into enterprise figures. Thus the figures reported above for Italy, Spain, France and Portugal are based on the number of enterprises. The information used here has been based on enterprise numbers available from Eurostat or the national statistical offices. One problem with the population estimates used is that the year in which the information was collected varies from 1989 to 1992 and other comparative data may not be available for direct comparisons at the same time periods.

In Norway and Ireland statistics are limited to the manufacturing sector, while in Turkey and the Netherlands sector statistics were not available – hence their exclusion from this table. Of the remaining ten countries comparisons were made between estimated population parameters and the sample data. The results of the chi-square test of significance for each of these countries is displayed in Table AI.7. With the exception of Portugal (the only country with less than 100 organisations participating) and Germany, there were found to be no significant difference between the sample and population figures at the 0.05 level. If the sample and national figures across countries are collated to achieve a European average and subsequently tested for differences the results indicate no significant difference between the sector make up of the sample compared with the sector make up of the population, Table AI.8.

A similar exercise was conducted to assess the size distribution of the sample in comparison with population estimates. Again data which were available at the time has been incorporated in Figure AI.4. This has resulted in the exclusion of Turkey, Norway, the Netherlands, Switzerland, Ireland, Finland and Germany. A brief glance at this Figure shows a clear discrepancy in nearly all countries between the sample and national data. The sample figures for each country show an under-representation of companies employing between 200 and 499 people, compared to the underlying national distribution. If these figures are again collated to achieve a European average there are 36 per cent of organisations employing 200–499 people in our sample, compared with 67 per cent in the population

Table AI.7 Significance results for industry distribution in each country

Country	DF	Chi-square	Significance value	Level	Result
CH[a]	1	1.961	0.161	0.05	NS
D(W)[a]	1	7.104	0.008	0.05	SIG
DK	3	2.631	0.452	0.05	NS
E[a]	1	0.067	0.796	0.05	NS
F[a]	1	4.560	0.030	0.02	NS
FIN[a]	1	1.323	0.250	0.05	NS
I[a]	1	4.700	0.030	0.02	NS
P	2	28.280	0.000	0.05	SIG
S	2	2.061	0.357	0.05	NS
UK	2	1.542	0.462	0.05	NS

Notes: If cell expectancy is less than 5 no comparisons made; [a] Production and service sectors compared only due to lack of appropriate population figures of small sample numbers in other sectors

Table AI.8 Sample and European sector distribution (%)

Sector	Europe	Sample
Agriculture	>1	1
Production	54	53
Services	31	29
Public	15	18

Note: Chi-square 0.748, df 2, not significant at the 0.05 level

Table AI.9 Distribution of organisations by size of employment: European statistics compared with sample statistics

No. of employees	Average % of organisations	
	Europe	Sample
200–499	67	36
500+	33	64

Note: Significance results: chi-square 43.464, df 1, significant at the 0.05 level

figures (Table AI.9). As with other surveys of this kind, the sample over represents the number of large organisations.

What about the non-respondents? To date the discussion has centred around the profile of the sample. However, if we want to generalise the results to the population overall it is important that respondents do not significantly differ from non-respondents. As it is not always feasible to ask non-respondents to fill in a questionnaire to test differences, we need to use an approximation or estimate of non-respondents. This, it is suggested, can be found in the form of late respondents. Oppenheim (1968: 34) points out that late respondents are most likely to be the closest approximation of non-respondents accessible to researchers. Therefore to establish if differences exist between those who responded and those who did not we can test the differences between early and late respondents. Consequently, the first

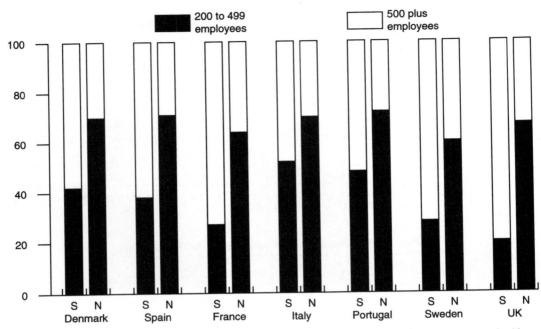

Figure AI.4 Distribution of organisations by size of employment (national figures compared with sample figures)
Notes: S = sample %; N = national %
Sources: Eurostat 1992; National Statistical Office 1989, 1990, 1991

and last 10 per cent of questionnaires returned in each country were compared, on key questions, using the chi-square test of significance. No significant differences were found.

DATA PREPARATION AND ANALYSIS

All questionnaires when completed were forwarded to the national business school or university in each country. Open ended responses to questions were coded for analysis using a coding structure developed jointly by the partners. It was felt more appropriate for this procedure to be conducted at national level to avoid misclassification of responses through inaccurate language translations. Only at this stage were the questionnaires returned to the United Kingdom.

The questionnaire format changed a little each year to incorporate new issues in European HRM or to improve questions which proved not to work so well when the analysis was conducted. Therefore it was important that the data could be compared across countries but also that no information was lost for each country. This meant the aggregation of the data had to be designed to account for these two analytical needs.

The statistical package for social scientists (SPSS) was used for both analysis and data entry purposes. This allowed the data to be subjected to a wide range of univariate and multivariate procedures appropriate for data of this nature. Each partner school consequently received a disk with the full national data; access to the international database was created via electronic mail.

CONCLUSIONS

This research is, like all other research, far from perfect. Mistakes have been made and opportunities missed. Overall, however, the project has been remarkably successful in generating the most extensive body of internationally comparative, broadly representative, data on organisational level HRM in Europe ever collated. We believe firmly that such data has to be interpreted by, or at least in collaboration with, experts in each country. That belief has been fundamental to the success of our network and its continuing programmes or research. We would encourage other researchers to work with us to illuminate our data further.

The next section of the book contains details of the raw frequency counts to enable others to interpret and even challenge the commentaries provided in the rest of the book.

REFERENCES

Brewster, C. (1994) 'Human resource management in Europe: reflection of or challenge to the American concept?', in P. Kirkbride (ed.) *Human Resource Management in Europe*, London: Routledge.

Brewster, C., Gill, C. and Richbell, S. (1983) 'Industrial relations policy: a framework for analysis', in K. Thurley and S. Wood (1983) *Industrial Relations and Management Strategy*, Cambridge: Cambridge University Press.

Brewster, C. and Tyson, S. (1991) *International Comparisons in Human Resource Management*, London: Pitman.

Brislin, R. W. (1976) (ed.) *Translation Applications and Research*. New York: Gouldner Press.

Brislin, R. W., Lonner, W. J. and Thorndike, R. M. (1973) *Cross-cultural Research Methods*, London: Wiley-Interscience.

Gaugler, E. (1988) 'Human resource management: an international comparison', *Personnel*. August: 24–30.

Grahl, J. and Teague, P. (1991) 'Industrial relations trajectories and European human resource management', in C. Brewster and S. Tyson (eds) (1991) *International Comparisons in Human Resource Management*, London: Pitman.

Hofstede, G. (1980) *Cultures Consequences: International Differences in Work Related Values*, Beverley Hills: Sage.

Keep, E. (1989) 'Corporate training strategies: the vital component', in J. Storey (ed.) (1989) *New Perspectives on Human Resource Management*, London: Routledge.

Morris, T. and Wood, S. (1991) 'Testing the survey method: continuity and change in British industrial relations', *Work, Employment and Society* 5: 259–82.

Oppenheim, A. N. (1968) *Questionnaire Design and Attitude Measurement*, London: Open University Book Set. Heinemann Educational Books Ltd, p. 34.

Semlinger, K. and Mendius, H. G. (1989) 'Personalplanung und Personalentwicklung in der gewerblichen Wirtschaft', Rationalisierungskuratorium der Wirtschaft, unpublished.

Sisson, K. (1993) 'In search of HRM', *British Journal of Industrial Relations* 31(2): 201–10.

Sisson, K., Waddington, J. and Whitson, C. (1992) 'The size of capital flows in the European Community', *Warwick Papers in Industrial Relations* 38.

Questionnaire (1992)

HOW TO COMPLETE
THIS QUESTIONNAIRE

This questionnaire is designed to make completion as easy and fast as possible. In tests, it took a maximum of 30 minutes to complete. Most questions can be answered by simply ticking boxes. Very little information will need to be looked up.

Wherever it says "**you**" in the questionnaire please answer from the point of view of your organisation.

"**Organisation**" means your firm, subsidiary or, if you are in a head office, the group in which you work. For the public sector it refers to the specific local or health authority, government department, etc.

"**Part of a larger group**" refers to subsidiaries, firms with branch plants or the parent company of a group. For central government departments the "larger group" is the civil service as a whole.

The questionnaire has been adapted for simultaneous use by private and public sector employers in 10 European countries; some questions may therefore be phrased in a slightly unfamiliar way.

THANK YOU FOR YOUR HELP

SECTION I: HUMAN RESOURCES/ PERSONNEL DEPARTMENT STRUCTURE

1. Does your organisation have a personnel or human resource management department/manager?

	Yes	No
	☐ 1	☐ 2

(If no, please go to question 10)

2. If YES, what is the job title of the most senior personnel or human resources manager?

    A. Personnel director ☐ 1

    B. Human resources director ☐ 2

    C. Personnel manager/officer/head of department ☐ 3

    D. Human resources manager/officer/head of department ☐ 4

    E. Other, please specify _____

3. Are you the most senior personnel or human resources manager?

	Yes	No
	☐ 1	☐ 2

    If NO, please give your title: _____

4. If you work as a personnel/training specialist, how long have you worked in a role with specialist personnel and/or training responsibility? (If not, please go to question 9)

    A. Less than 1 year ☐ 1

    B. 1 – 5 years ☐ 2

    C. More than 5 years ☐ 3

5. What is the highest level of educational qualifications you have attained? (Tick one box only)

    A. O level or equivalent   □ 1   B. A level or equivalent   □ 2

    C. HND   □ 3   D. First degree (B.A., B.Sc., etc)   □ 4

    E. Masters Degree (M.Sc., etc)   □ 5   F. MBA   □ 6

    G. Ph.D. (or other doctorate)   □ 7

6. If you have a first degree in what academic field did you study? (Tick main one only)

    A. Business Studies   □ 1   B. Economics   □ 2

    C. Social or Behavioural Sciences   □ 3   D. Humanities/Arts/ Languages   □ 4

    E. Law   □ 5   F. Engineering   □ 6

    G. Natural Sciences   □ 7

    H. Other (please specify) _____

7. What professional qualifications have you obtained?

    A. Diploma in Personnel Management (including IPM Membership)   □ 1

    B. IPM membership without a diploma   □ 2

    C. Other professional qualifications (eg. accountancy/teaching)   □ 3

        please specifiy _____

8. What other training have you received from your current or previous employer for the personnel management role you perform? (Please tick as many as applicable).

    A. Short courses/ seminars   □ 1

    B. Job-related projects for personal development   □ 2

    C. Assignment to different work areas/job rotation   □ 3

    D. Formal coaching by line manager   □ 4

    E. Formal mentoring by superior outside work area   □ 5

9. Does the head of the personnel or human resources function have a place on the main board of directors or equivalent?

	Yes	No
	☐ 1	☐ 2

10. If NO, who on the board or equivalent has responsibility for personnel issues?

A. Chief executive/Managing director   ☐ 1

B. Administrative director   ☐ 2

C. Finance director   ☐ 3

D. Company secretary   ☐ 4

E. Production director   ☐ 5

F. Worker director   ☐ 6

G. Other, please specify _____

11. Approximately how many people are employed in the personnel function (including wage administration and training)?

In total: _____

Professional staff only: _____

12. From where was the most senior personnel or human resources manager recruited?

A. From within the personnel department   ☐ 1

B. From non-personnel specialists in your organisation   ☐ 2

C. From personnel specialists from outside of the organisation   ☐ 3

D. From non-personnel specialists from outside of the organisation   ☐ 4

SECTION II: HUMAN RESOURCE STRATEGY

1. What are the main objectives of personnel or human resource management in your organisation over the next 3 years? (Please list up to 3)

    A. _____

    B. _____

    C. _____

2. Does the organisation have a:

	Yes, written	Yes, unwritten	No	Don't know
A. Mission statement	☐ 1	☐ 2	☐ 3	☐ 4
B. Corporate strategy	☐ 1	☐ 2	☐ 3	☐ 4
C. Personnel/ HR management strategy	☐ 1	☐ 2	☐ 3	☐ 4

3. **If you have a corporate strategy,** at what stage is the person responsible for Personnel/Human Resources involved in its development? (If not, please go to next question)

    A. From the outset   ☐ 1

    B. Consultative   ☐ 2

    C. Implementation   ☐ 3

    D. Not consulted   ☐ 4

4. **If you have a personnel/HR management strategy,** is it translated into work programmes and deadlines for the personnel function? (If not, please go to next question)

        Yes   No

        ☐ 1   ☐ 2

5. **If your organisation is part of a larger group of companies/divisions, etc.,** please indicate where policies on the following are mainly determined. (If not, please go to next question)

Private Sector ➤	International HQ	National HQ	Subsidiary	Site/Establishment
Public Sector ➤		Central personnel	Service dept/division	Local offices
A. Pay & benefits	☐ 1	☐ 2	☐ 3	☐ 4
B. Recruitment & selection	☐ 1	☐ 2	☐ 3	☐ 4
C. Training & development	☐ 1	☐ 2	☐ 3	☐ 4
D. Industrial relations	☐ 1	☐ 2	☐ 3	☐ 4
E. Health & safety	☐ 1	☐ 2	☐ 3	☐ 4
F. Workforce expansion/reduction	☐ 1	☐ 2	☐ 3	☐ 4

6. With whom does the primary responsibility lie for major policy decisions on the following issues?

	Line management	Line management in consultation with HR dept	HR department in consultation with line management	HR department
A. Pay & benefits	☐ 1	☐ 2	☐ 3	☐ 4
B. Recruitment & selection	☐ 1	☐ 2	☐ 3	☐ 4
C. Training & development	☐ 1	☐ 2	☐ 3	☐ 4
D. Industrial relations	☐ 1	☐ 2	☐ 3	☐ 4
E. Health & safety	☐ 1	☐ 2	☐ 3	☐ 4
F. Workforce expansion/reduction	☐ 1	☐ 2	☐ 3	☐ 4

7. Has the responsibility of line management changed over the last 3 years for any of the following issues?

	Increased	Same	Decreased
A. Pay & benefits	☐ 1	☐ 2	☐ 3
B. Recruitment & selection	☐ 1	☐ 2	☐ 3
C. Training & development	☐ 1	☐ 2	☐ 3
D. Industrial relations	☐ 1	☐ 2	☐ 3
E. Health & safety	☐ 1	☐ 2	☐ 3
F. Workforce expansion/reduction	☐ 1	☐ 2	☐ 3

8. Is the performance of the personnel department systematically evaluated?

Yes	No	Don't know	No personnel department
☐ 1	☐ 2	☐ 3	☐ 4

9. **If Yes,** are any of the following criteria used? (If no, please go to next question)

	Yes	No
A. Number of employees per personnel staff member	☐ 1	☐ 2
B. Cost of personnel function per employee	☐ 1	☐ 2
C. Numbers recruited	☐ 1	☐ 2
D. Numbers trained	☐ 1	☐ 2
E. Performance against budget	☐ 1	☐ 2
F. Performance against objectives	☐ 1	☐ 2
G. Feedback from line management	☐ 1	☐ 2

H. Other, please specify_____

10. Do you carry out manpower planning?

	Yes	No
	☐ 1	☐ 2

11. **If Yes,** do you use any or several of the following methods? (If no, please go to next question)

	Yes	No
A. Recruit to maintain current staff ratios	☐ 1	☐ 2
B. Forecast of future skill requirements	☐ 1	☐ 2
C. Sales/Business or service forecasts	☐ 1	☐ 2
D. Analysis of labour markets	☐ 1	☐ 2
E. Other, please specify_____		

12. Do you collect and use any of the following categories of data on the workforce for manpower planning?

	Yes	No
A. Staff turnover	☐ 1	☐ 2
B. Age profile	☐ 1	☐ 2
C. Qualifications & training	☐ 1	☐ 2
D. Absence levels	☐ 1	☐ 2

13. In response to skill shortages, demographic changes or equal opportunities issues, do you monitor the numbers of the following in your workforce with regard to recruitment, training and/or promotion?

	Recruitment	Training	Promotion	Don't know
A. People with disabilities	☐ 1	☐ 2	☐ 3	☐ 4
B. Women	☐ 1	☐ 2	☐ 3	☐ 4
C. People from ethnic minorities	☐ 1	☐ 2	☐ 3	☐ 4

14. How far ahead do you plan your staffing requirements? (Please tick one only)

    A. 1 year or less   ☐ 1

    B. More than 1 year to 2 years   ☐ 2

    C. More than 2 years   ☐ 3

    D. No planning   ☐ 4

15. Which, if any, of your personnel/HR functions are aided by computerised information systems? (Please tick as many as applicable)

    A. No computerised personnel information system   ☐ 1

    B. Individual employee records   ☐ 1

    C. Pay and benefit administration   ☐ 1

    D. Absences and leave   ☐ 1

    E. Manpower planning   ☐ 1

    F. Recruitment and selection   ☐ 1

    G. Training and development   ☐ 1

    H. Performance appraisal   ☐ 1

    I. Job evaluation   ☐ 1

    J. Industrial relations   ☐ 1

    K. Other, please specify_____

If you ticked more than one of the above, are the computerised information systems you use fully integrated?

    L. Fully integrated   ☐ 1

    M. Partially integrated   ☐ 2

    N. Not integrated   ☐ 3

SECTION III: RECRUITMENT

1. Which job categories do you currently find hardest to recruit? (Please list up to three)

   A. _____

   B. _____

   C. _____

   D. No recruitment problems   ☐ x

2. Have you introduced any of the following measures to aid recruitment?

		Yes	No
A.	Flexible working hours	☐ 1	☐ 2
B.	Recruiting abroad	☐ 1	☐ 2
C.	Relaxed age requirements	☐ 1	☐ 2
D.	Relaxed qualifications requirements	☐ 1	☐ 2
E.	Relocation of the company	☐ 1	☐ 2
F.	Retraining existing employees	☐ 1	☐ 2
G.	Training for new employees	☐ 1	☐ 2
H.	Part-time work	☐ 1	☐ 2
I.	Job sharing	☐ 1	☐ 2
J.	Increased pay/benefits	☐ 1	☐ 2
K.	Marketing the organisation's image	☐ 1	☐ 2
L.	Other, please specify _____		

3. Have you specifically targeted any of the following in your recruitment process?

		Yes	No
A.	The long-term unemployed	☐ 1	☐ 2
B.	Older people	☐ 1	☐ 2
C.	People with disabilities	☐ 1	☐ 2
D.	People from ethnic minorities	☐ 1	☐ 2
E.	Women	☐ 1	☐ 2
F.	School leavers	☐ 1	☐ 2

4. How, in general, are vacant positions filled? (Please tick as many as applicable)

		Managerial	Professional Technical	Clerical	Manual
A.	From amongst current employees	☐ 1	☐ 2	☐ 3	☐ 4
B.	Advertise internally	☐ 1	☐ 2	☐ 3	☐ 4
C.	Advertise externally	☐ 1	☐ 2	☐ 3	☐ 4
D.	Word of mouth	☐ 1	☐ 2	☐ 3	☐ 4
E.	Use of recruitment agencies	☐ 1	☐ 2	☐ 3	☐ 4
F.	Use of search/selection consultants	☐ 1	☐ 2	☐ 3	☐ 4
G.	Job centres	☐ 1	☐ 2	☐ 3	☐ 4
H.	Apprentices	☐ 1	☐ 2	☐ 3	☐ 4
I.	Other, please specify _____				

5. Approximately what proportion of your senior managers are recruited externally?

A.	Up to 10%	☐ 1
B.	11 – 30%	☐ 2
C.	31 – 60%	☐ 3
D.	More than 60%	☐ 4

6. Please indicate which, if any, of the following selection methods are **regularly** used in your organisation.
    (Please tick as many as applicable)

Application forms	☐ 1	References	☐ 6
Interview panel	☐ 2	Aptitude test	☐ 7
Bio data	☐ 3	Assessment centre	☐ 8
Psychometric testing	☐ 4	Group selection methods	☐ 9
Graphology	☐ 5		

Others, please specify _____

SECTION IV: PAY AND BENEFITS

1. At what level(s) is basic pay determined? (Please tick as many as applicable for each category of staff)

	Managerial	Professional Technical	Clerical	Manual
A. National/industry-wide collective bargaining	☐ 1	☐ 2	☐ 3	☐ 4
B. Regional collective bargaining	☐ 1	☐ 2	☐ 3	☐ 4
C. Company/division, etc.	☐ 1	☐ 2	☐ 3	☐ 4
D. Establishment/site	☐ 1	☐ 2	☐ 3	☐ 4
E. Individual	☐ 1	☐ 2	☐ 3	☐ 4
F. Other, please specify				

2. Has there been a change in the share of the following in the total reward package in the last 3 years?

	Yes, increased	Yes, decreased	No	Don't know
A. Variable pay	☐ 1	☐ 2	☐ 3	☐ 4
B. Non-money benefits	☐ 1	☐ 2	☐ 3	☐ 4

3. Do you offer any of the following incentive schemes?
    (Please tick as many as applicable for each category of staff)

	Managerial	Professional Technical	Clerical	Manual
A. Employee share options	☐ 1	☐ 2	☐ 3	☐ 4
B. Profit sharing	☐ 1	☐ 2	☐ 3	☐ 4
C. Group bonus schemes	☐ 1	☐ 2	☐ 3	☐ 4
D. Individual bonus/commission	☐ 1	☐ 2	☐ 3	☐ 4
E. Merit/performance related pay	☐ 1	☐ 2	☐ 3	☐ 4

4.   Do you offer any of the following benefits to parents? Please tick as many as applicable for each category of staff (but only if provision is **in excess of statutory requirements***).

	Managerial	Professional Technical	Clerical	Manual
A. Workplace childcare	☐ 1	☐ 2	☐ 3	☐ 4
B. Childcare allowances	☐ 1	☐ 2	☐ 3	☐ 4
C. Career break scheme	☐ 1	☐ 2	☐ 3	☐ 4
D. Maternity leave*	☐ 1	☐ 2	☐ 3	☐ 4
E. Paternity leave	☐ 1	☐ 2	☐ 3	☐ 4

F.   Other, please specify _____

SECTION V: TRAINING AND DEVELOPMENT

1. Approximately what proportion of annual salaries and wages is currently spent on training?

    _____ %   Don't know

                                                       ☐ x

2. How many days training per year does **each employee** in each staff category below receive on average?

                                                       Don't know

    A. Management   _____ days per year per employee   ☐ x

    B. Technical/Professional   _____ days per year per employee   ☐ x

    C. Clerical   _____ days per year per employee   ☐ x

    D. Manual   _____ days per year per employee   ☐ x

3. Has the money spent on training per employee (allowing for inflation) over the last three years increased or decreased for the following categories of staff?

	Increased	Same	Decreased	Don't know
A. Management	☐ 1	☐ 2	☐ 3	☐ 4
B. Professional/Technical	☐ 1	☐ 2	☐ 3	☐ 4
C. Clerical	☐ 1	☐ 2	☐ 3	☐ 4
D. Manual	☐ 1	☐ 2	☐ 3	☐ 4

4. Do you systematically analyse employee training needs?

                                           Yes   No

                                           ☐ 1   ☐ 2

5. **If Yes,** are any of the following methods used? (If no, please go to next question)

	Always	Often	Sometimes	Never
A. Analysis of projected business/service plans	☐ 1	☐ 2	☐ 3	☐ 4
B. Training audits	☐ 1	☐ 2	☐ 3	☐ 4
C. Line management requests	☐ 1	☐ 2	☐ 3	☐ 4
D. Performance appraisal	☐ 1	☐ 2	☐ 3	☐ 4
E. Employee requests	☐ 1	☐ 2	☐ 3	☐ 4
F. Other, please specify				

6. Do you monitor the effectiveness of your training?

Yes	No	Don't know
☐ 1	☐ 2	☐ 3

7. **If Yes,** is it monitored in any of the following ways? (If no, please go to next question)

	Yes	No
A. Tests	☐ 1	☐ 2
B. Formal evaluation immediately after training	☐ 1	☐ 2
C. Formal evaluation some months after training	☐ 1	☐ 2
D. Informal feedback from line managers	☐ 1	☐ 2
E. Informal feedback from trainees	☐ 1	☐ 2
F. Other, please specify		

8. In which, if any, of the following areas have at least a third of your managers been trained?
(Please tick as many as applicable)

    A. Performance appraisal   ❏ 1

    B. Staff communication   ❏ 1

    C. Delegation   ❏ 1

    D. Motivation   ❏ 1

    E. Team building   ❏ 1

    F. Foreign languages   ❏ 1

9. Do you provide training courses to update the skills of women returners?

	Yes	No
	❏ 1	❏ 2

10. Do you regularly use any of the following?

	Yes	No
A. Formal career plans	❏ 1	❏ 2
B. Performance appraisal	❏ 1	❏ 2
C. Annual career development interviews	❏ 1	❏ 2
D. Assessment centres	❏ 1	❏ 2
E. Succession plans	❏ 1	❏ 2
F. Planned job rotation	❏ 1	❏ 2
G. "High flier" schemes for managers	❏ 1	❏ 2
H. International experience schemes for managers	❏ 1	❏ 2

11. Which areas do you think will constitute the main training requirements in your organisation in the next 3 years? (Please tick **no more than 3**)

    A. Business administration and strategy   ❏ 1

    B. Computers and new technology   ❏ 2

    C. Health and safety and the work environment   ❏ 3

    D. Manufacturing technology   ❏ 4

    E. Marketing and sales   ❏ 5

    F. People management and supervision   ❏ 6

    G. Customer service skills   ❏ 7

    H. Management of change   ❏ 8

    I. Quality   ❏ 9

    J. Languages   ❏ 10

    K. Other, please specify _____

SECTION VI: EMPLOYEE RELATIONS

1. Approximately what proportion of staff in your organisation are members of a trade union?

    A. 0%   ☐ 1

    B. 1 – 25%   ☐ 2

    C. 26 – 50%   ☐ 3

    D. 51 – 75%   ☐ 4

    E. 76 – 100%   ☐ 5

    F. Don't know   ☐ 6

2. Do you recognise trade unions for the purpose of collective bargaining?

	Yes	No
	☐ 1	☐ 2

3. If you recognise any trade unions, has their influence on this organisation changed over the last three years?

	Yes, increased	No, decreased	No, the same
	☐ 1	☐ 2	☐ 3

4. Has there been a change in how you communicate major issues to your employees?

	Yes, increased	No, decreased	No, the same
A. Through representative staff bodies (eg trade unions)	☐ 1	☐ 2	☐ 3
B. Verbally, direct to employees	☐ 1	☐ 2	☐ 3
C. Written, direct to employees	☐ 1	☐ 2	☐ 3

    D. Other, please specify_____

5. Which employee categories are formally briefed about the strategy and financial performance of your organisation?

		Strategy	Financial performance
A.	Management	☐ 1	☐ 2
B.	Professional/Technical	☐ 1	☐ 2
C.	Clerical	☐ 1	☐ 2
D.	Manual	☐ 1	☐ 2

6. By what method(s) do your employees communicate their views to management?

		Yes	No
A.	Through immediate superior	☐ 1	☐ 2
B.	Through trade unions or works councils	☐ 1	☐ 2
C.	Through regular workforce meetings	☐ 1	☐ 2
D.	Through quality circles	☐ 1	☐ 2
E.	Through suggestion box(es)	☐ 1	☐ 2
F.	Through an attitude survey	☐ 1	☐ 2
G.	No formal methods	☐ 1	☐ 2
H.	Other, please specify _____		

7. Who has the main responsibility for formulating policy on staff communication? (Please tick one only)

A.	Human Resource/ Personnel department	☐ 1
B.	Public relations department	☐ 2
C.	Marketing department	☐ 3
D.	Line management	☐ 4
E.	Other, please specify _____	

SECTION VII: FLEXIBLE WORKING PATTERNS

1. Has there been a change in the use of any of the following working arrangements over the last 3 years?

	Increased	Same	Decreased	Not used	Don't know
A. Weekend work	☐ 1	☐ 2	☐ 3	☐ 4	☐ 5
B. Shift work	☐ 1	☐ 2	☐ 3	☐ 4	☐ 5
C. Overtime	☐ 1	☐ 2	☐ 3	☐ 4	☐ 5
D. Annual hours contracts	☐ 1	☐ 2	☐ 3	☐ 4	☐ 5
E. Part-time work	☐ 1	☐ 2	☐ 3	☐ 4	☐ 5
F. Temporary/casual	☐ 1	☐ 2	☐ 3	☐ 4	☐ 5
G. Fixed-term contracts	☐ 1	☐ 2	☐ 3	☐ 4	☐ 5
H. Homebased work	☐ 1	☐ 2	☐ 3	☐ 4	☐ 5
I. Government training schemes (eg YTS, ET)	☐ 1	☐ 2	☐ 3	☐ 4	☐ 5
J. Subcontracting	☐ 1	☐ 2	☐ 3	☐ 4	☐ 5

2. Please indicate the approximate proportion of your workforce who are on the following contracts.

	Less than 1%	1–10%	11–20%	More than 20%	Don't know
A. Part-time	☐ 1	☐ 2	☐ 3	☐ 4	☐ 5
B. Temporary/casual	☐ 1	☐ 2	☐ 3	☐ 4	☐ 5
C. Fixed-term	☐ 1	☐ 2	☐ 3	☐ 4	☐ 5
D. Homebased work	☐ 1	☐ 2	☐ 3	☐ 4	☐ 5
E. Government training scheme (eg YTS, ET)	☐ 1	☐ 2	☐ 3	☐ 4	☐ 5

3. Has there been a **major** change in the specification of jobs in your organisation over the last three years?

	Management	Professional Technical	Clerical	Manual
A. Jobs made more specific	☐ 1	☐ 2	☐ 3	☐ 4
B. No major change	☐ 1	☐ 2	☐ 3	☐ 4
C. Jobs made wider/more flexible	☐ 1	☐ 2	☐ 3	☐ 4
D. Don't know	☐ 1	☐ 2	☐ 3	☐ 4

SECTION VIII:
THE EUROPEAN COMMUNITY

1. Has your organisation developed a business and/or human resources strategy in response to the Single European Market?

	Yes, written	Yes, unwritten	No
A. Business Strategy	☐ 1	☐ 2	☐ 3
B. Human Resources Strategy	☐ 1	☐ 2	☐ 3

2. How does your organisation keep abreast of EC initiatives and developments? (Tick as many as applicable)

A. Through a specialist or team responsible for EC matters within the organisation ☐ 1

B. Through a specialist based in Brussels ☐ 1

C. By participating in local employers/trade organisation events ☐ 1

D. Through IPM briefings/local personnel management association ☐ 1

E. By following general media ☐ 1

F. Other please specify _____

3. Would the full implementation of the EC Social Charter require a change in your personnel policies in any of the areas below?

	Major change	Minor change	No change	Don't know
A. Working hours/shifts	☐ 1	☐ 2	☐ 3	☐ 4
B. Use of part-time, temporary, fixed-term contracts	☐ 1	☐ 2	☐ 3	☐ 4
C. Health and safety	☐ 1	☐ 2	☐ 3	☐ 4
D. Equal treatment of men and women	☐ 1	☐ 2	☐ 3	☐ 4
E. Procedures for consultation and participation of employees	☐ 1	☐ 2	☐ 3	☐ 4

SECTION IX:
ORGANISATIONAL DETAILS

1. Please indicate the main sector of industry or services in which you operate.

    A. Agriculture, hunting, forestry, fishing   ☐ 1

    B. Energy and water   ☐ 2

    C. Chemical products; extraction and processing of non-energy minerals   ☐ 3

    D. Metal manufacturing; mechanical, electrical and instrument engineering; office and data processing machinery   ☐ 4

    E. Other manufacturing, (eg food, drink and tobacco; textiles; clothing; paper, printing & publishing; processing of rubber and plastics, etc.)   ☐ 5

    F. Building and civil engineering   ☐ 6

    G. Retail and distribution; hotels; catering; repairs   ☐ 7

    H. Transport & communication (eg rail, postal services, telecoms, etc.)   ☐ 8

    I. Banking; finance; insurance; business services (eg consultancies, PR and advertising, law firms, etc.)   ☐ 9

    J. Personal, domestic, recreational services   ☐ 10

    K. Health services   ☐ 11

    L. Other services (eg television and radio, R&D, charities, etc.)   ☐ 12

    M. Education (including universities and further education)   ☐ 13

    N. Local government   ☐ 14

    O. Central government   ☐ 15

    P. Other, please specify _____

2. Approximately how many people are employed by your organisation?

    A. In total   _____

    B. Part-time   _____

3. Please indicate the approximate share of each of the following employee categories in your organisation.

                                                                          None

    A. Management   _____ %   ☐ 1

    B. Professional/Technical   _____ %   ☐ 1

    C. Clerical   _____ %   ☐ 1

    D. Manual   _____ %   ☐ 1

                    Total: 100   %

4. **If your organisation is part of a larger group of companies/divisions, etc.,** approximately how many people are employed by the whole group? (If not, please go to next question.)

                                                                          Don't know

    A. In the UK   _____   ☐ 1

    B. World-wide, including the UK   _____   ☐ 1

5. Has the total number of your employees increased or decreased **in excess of 5%** in the last 3 years?

    A. Increased   ☐ 1

    B. No change   ☐ 2

    C. Decreased   ☐ 3

6. **If your workforce has decreased by more than 5%,** which of the following methods were used? (If your workforce has not decreased, please go to next question.)

    A. Voluntary redundancies   ☐ 1

    B. Compulsory redundancies   ☐ 1

    C. Early retirement   ☐ 1

    D. Natural wastage   ☐ 1

    E. Other, please specify_____

7. Please indicate the organisation's turnover or revenue budget (public sector) in the last financial year.

£ _____ million(s)

Don't know/not available   ☐ x

8. What percentage of the last financial year's turnover or revenue budget was accounted for by labour costs? Please complete one of the following.

A. Turnover   _____ %

B. Revenue budget (for public sector) _____ %

C. Don't know/not available   ☐ x

9. Apart from normal seasonal variations, how has the demand for the main product or service of your organisation altered over the last 3 years?

A. Increased   ☐ 1

B. No change   ☐ 2

C. Decreased   ☐ 3

10. How would you describe the market(s) for your organisation's products or services?

A. Local   ☐ 1

B. Regional   ☐ 2

C. National   ☐ 3

D. European   ☐ 4

E. World-wide   ☐ 5

11. Has your organisation been involved in a major change of ownership, such as major acquisition(s), take-over(s) or merger(s) in the last 3 years?

A. Yes   ☐ 1

B. No   ☐ 2

12. Is your organisation:

    A. Public limited company (PLC)   ☐ 1

    B. Trust/friendly society/cooperative   ☐ 2

    C. Other private sector organisation   ☐ 3

    D. State owned industry (trading)   ☐ 4

    E. Other state owned corporation   ☐ 5

    F. Public administration (local/central government, health, education)   ☐ 6

    G. Other, please specify _____

13. Is your organisation:

    A. Corporate headquarters of an international group   ☐ 1

    B. Corporate headquarters of a national group   ☐ 2

    C. Subsidiary/division of a larger group   ☐ 3

    D. Independent single site organisation   ☐ 4

    E. Independent company with more than one site   ☐ 5

    F. Headquarters of a national/local government service   ☐ 6

    G. Health authority   ☐ 7

    H. Other, please specify _____

14. Where are the corporate headquarters of your organisation? (Please refer to ultimate parent company if your organisation is part of a larger group.)

Denmark	☐ 1	Republic of Ireland	☐ 6	Sweden	☐ 11
France	☐ 2	Spain	☐ 7	Switzerland	☐ 12
Germany	☐ 3	UK	☐ 8	Other Non-EC Europe	☐ 13
Italy	☐ 4	Other EC Europe	☐ 9	USA	☐ 14
The Netherlands	☐ 5	Norway	☐ 10	Japan	☐ 15

Other, please specify _____

Appendix III

Tables

Note: For ease of reading the numbering of the tables in this appendix corresponds directly to the numbering of the questions in the questionnaire (Appendix II). In a small number of cases questions are not directly comparable across countries, and a table of results has therefore not been included.

All figures in the following tables are simple column percentages based on the total number of responding organisations in 1992 (see Tables A to C). All percentages are rounded to the nearest full per cent.

The following country abbreviations are used in the tables:

b(w)	West Germany	N	Norway
DK	Denmark	NL	Netherlands
E	Spain	P	Portugal
F	France	S	Sweden
FIN	Finland	T	Turkey
IRL	Ireland	UK	United Kingdom

The following abbreviations are used in the tables:

Pu	Public sector (nationalised industries, health, education, public administration)
Pr	Private sector
<1	Organisations with 200–999 employees
>1	Organisations with 1,000 and more employees
(+1)	Multiple choice, responses in table are independent variables
ni	Question not included in country survey
n	Number of organisations
*	Less than 20 organisations (public sector)

OVERVIEW: NUMBER OF ORGANISATIONS

Table A: Number of organisations across countries

	D(W)	DK	E	F	FIN	IRL	N	NL	P	S	T	UK
Number of organisations	884	330	260	651	225	140	280	128	93	322	123	1243

Table B: Number of public and private organisations across countries

	D(W)		DK		E		F		FIN		IRL		N		NL		P		S		T		UK	
	Pu	Pr	Pu	Pr	Pu	Pr	Pu	Pr	Pu	Pr	Pu	Pr	Pu	Pr	Pu	Pr	Pu	Pr	Pu	Pr	Pu	Pr	Pu	Pr
Number of organisations	103	703	129	192	16	236	111	487	62	136	40	88	103	118	2	123	13	73	137	168	16	102	314	795

Table C: Number of organisations employing less than 1000 or 1000 or more employees

	D(W)		DK		E		F		FIN		IRL		N		NL		P		S		T		UK	
	<1	>1	<1	>1	<1	>1	<1	>1	<1	>1	<1	>1	<1	>1	<1	>1	<1	>1	<1	>1	<1	>1	<1	>1
Number of organisations	538	341	219	111	165	94	382	268	145	80	107	32	196	78	102	26	71	22	161	158	77	46	551	680

SECTION I : HUMAN RESOURCES/PERSONNEL DEPARTMENT STRUCTURE

Table 1.1: Percentage of organisations having a personnel or human resource management department/manager

Country

	D(W)	DK	E	F	FIN	IRL	N	NL	P	S	T	UK
Yes	97	88	95	99	78	86	93	96	96	98	99	96
No	3	12	5	1	22	13	5	4	4	1	1	3

Private and public sector

	D(W)		DK		E		F		FIN		IRL		N		NL		P		S		T		UK	
	Pu	Pr	Pu	Pr	Pu	Pr	Pu	Pr	Pu	Pr	Pu	Pr	Pu	Pr	Pu	Pr	Pu	Pr	Pu	Pr	Pu	Pr	Pu	Pr
					*										*		*				*			
Yes	99	97	95	84	88	96	100	98	86	81	82	88	95	94	100	96	92	96	99	98	100	99	100	96
No	1	3	5	16	12	4	0	2	14	19	18	12	5	6	0	4	8	4	1	2	0	1	0	4

Less than 1,000 or greater than or equal to 1,000 employees

	D(W)		DK		E		F		FIN		IRL		N		NL		P		S		T		UK	
	<1	>1	<1	>1	<1	>1	<1	>1	<1	>1	<1	>1	<1	>1	<1	>1	<1	>1	<1	>1	<1	>1	<1	>1
Yes	96	99	84	96	93	99	98	99	72	93	86	91	93	99	95	100	94	100	98	99	99	100	95	99
No	4	1	16	4	7	1	2	1	28	7	14	9	7	1	5	0	6	0	2	1	1	0	5	1

Table 1.2: Job title of the most senior personnel or human resources manager. (Valid %)

Country	D(W)	DK	E	F	FIN	IRL	N	NL	P	S	T	UK
Personnel Director	78	16	29	15	18	18	20	11	25	29	67	36
HR Director	9	1	42	42	42	8	1	3	32	1	3	12
Personnel mgr/officer	6	54	14	18	3	55	56	69	17	66	2	39
HR mgr/officer	2	2	3	6	<1	10	1	8	4	1	2	5
Other	5	26	7	15	36	8	9	6	15	4	25	9

Public/Private

	D(W)		DK		E*		F		FIN		IRL		N		NL*		P*		S		T*		UK	
	Pu	Pr	Pu	Pr	Pu	Pr	Pu	Pr	Pu	Pr	Pu	Pr	Pu	Pr	Pu	Pr	Pu	Pr	Pu	Pr	Pu	Pr	Pu	Pr
Personnel Director	70	79	8	22	21	31	15	16	21	21	12	21	7	26	0	11	10	31	21	37	69	68	39	35
HR Director	15	9	1	3	43	44	41	41	44	49	3	10	0	2	0	3	40	31	0	2	0	4	11	12
Personnel mgr/officer	2	6	55	54	21	15	17	20	3	2	68	49	61	55	100	69	30	19	75	58	13	1	37	40
HR mgr/officer	7	1	1	3	0	4	11	7	2	0	3	14	1	0	0	7	0	0	0	4	6	1	3	6
Other	6	5	35	18	15	6	16	16	30	28	14	6	14	7	0	6	20	15	4	2	18	22	10	7

Less than 1,000 or greater than or equal to 1,000 employees

	D(W)		DK		E		F		FIN		IRL		N		NL		P		S		T		UK	
	<1	>1	<1	>1	<1	>1	<1	>1	<1	>1	<1	>1	<1	>1	<1	>1	<1	>1	<1	>1	<1	>1	<1	>1
Personnel Director	86	68	11	23	30	32	16	15	10	34	16	23	11	44	7	27	25	32	14	44	78	50	20	48
HR Director	5	16	2	2	40	52	39	47	45	38	7	17	1	1	3	4	25	64	0	2	3	4	9	13
Personnel mgr/officer	3	9	56	51	21	4	21	14	4	2	59	40	60	45	76	54	25	0	82	50	1	1	54	26
HR mgr/officer	2	3	2	3	4	3	3	9	0	1	1	10	1	1	0	8	0	1	0	0	2	1	6	4
Other	3	4	29	21	5	9	15	17	41	25	7	10	11	5	6	7	4	3	3	4	17	9	11	9

Table 1.3: Did the most senior personnel or human resources manager respond to this questionnaire?

Country	D(W)	DK	E	F	FIN	IRL	N	NL	P	S	T	UK
Yes	ni	70	68	78	74	67	75	77	75	74	70	61
No	ni	22	28	20	26	21	19	19	18	24	29	35

Public/Private (* E * NL * P * T)

	D(W)		DK		E		F		FIN		IRL		N		NL		P		S		T		UK	
	Pu	Pr	Pu	Pr	Pu	Pr	Pu	Pr	Pu	Pr	Pu	Pr	Pu	Pr	Pu	Pr	Pu	Pr	Pu	Pr	Pu	Pr	Pu	Pr
Yes	ni	ni	67	72	69	68	73	79	79	70	52	72	74	76	50	79	61	75	74	78	69	71	58	62
No	ni	ni	28	14	19	28	27	19	21	29	35	15	19	17	50	19	31	16	26	22	25	28	40	34

Less than 1,000 or greater than or equal to 1,000 employees

	D(W)		DK		E		F		FIN		IRL		N		NL		P		S		T		UK	
	<1	>1	<1	>1	<1	>1	<1	>1	<1	>1	<1	>1	<1	>1	<1	>1	<1	>1	<1	>1	<1	>1	<1	>1
Yes	ni	ni	70	70	67	70	86	67	77	66	67	67	74	78	83	61	75	77	83	67	73	65	67	56
No	ni	ni	16	26	28	28	12	31	23	34	18	31	18	19	15	39	18	23	15	32	26	33	27	42

ni question not included in country

Table 1.4: Length of time personnel specialists have worked in that role. (Valid %)

Country	D(W)	DK	E	F	FIN	IRL	N	NL	P	S	T	UK
Less than one year	4	6	8	3	3	4	5	7	4	1	2	2
One to five years	19	29	30	22	16	20	24	27	10	16	12	17
More than 5 years	60	40	37	74	78	52	62	62	21	76	85	73
Not applicable	17	25	25	1	3	24	10	4	64	7	1	8

Public/Private (* E * NL * P * T)

	D(W)		DK		E		F		FIN		IRL		N		NL		P		S		T		UK	
	Pu	Pr	Pu	Pr	Pu	Pr	Pu	Pr	Pu	Pr	Pu	Pr	Pu	Pr	Pu	Pr	Pu	Pr	Pu	Pr	Pu	Pr	Pu	Pr
Less than one year	7	4	6	5	0	8	7	2	2	3	7	3	5	5	0	7	0	5	1	1	6	2	2	2
One to five years	28	18	22	32	50	28	36	18	17	17	27	17	31	20	0	28	7	11	18	14	12	12	21	16
More than 5 years	50	61	44	39	12	39	57	78	77	76	35	58	56	64	100	61	15	22	71	80	81	85	72	73
Not applicable	15	17	27	24	37	24	0	1	3	4	30	21	8	12	0	4	77	62	10	5	0	1	5	9

Less than 1,000 or greater than or equal to 1,000 employees

	D(W)		DK		E		F		FIN		IRL		N		NL		P		S		T		UK	
	<1	>1	<1	>1	<1	>1	<1	>1	<1	>1	<1	>1	<1	>1	<1	>1	<1	>1	<1	>1	<1	>1	<1	>1
Less than one year	4	4	6	4	7	8	3	2	3	2	6	0	5	3	8	4	6	0	1	1	4	2	2	2
One to five years	18	19	29	28	31	29	23	21	17	16	19	22	26	18	23	42	13	11	18	20	12	13	21	14
More than 5 years	56	65	37	47	33	44	72	77	79	77	51	56	58	70	66	50	17	36	72	80	86	83	66	78
Not applicable	22	10	27	22	28	19	2	1	3	2	24	22	10	10	4	4	65	64	7	8	1	0	11	5

Table 1.6: Area of degree studied by personnel/human resource manager. (Valid %)

Country	D(W)	DK	E	F	FIN	IRL	N	NL	P	S	T	UK
Business Studies	45	24	6	22	14	41	37	21	11	18	35	18
Economics	9	11	5	8	5	1	2	0	13	9	24	10
Social/Behavioural sciences	9	16	31	16	13	16	12	9	24	54	6	21
Humanities/Arts/languages	24	4	5	3	3	15	15	32	2	3	4	21
Law	3	23	32	25	15	1	6	26	31	5	12	3
Engineering	4	2	11	10	13	8	8	3	4	4	5	7
Natural Sciences	1	0	1	1	2	8	3	0	0	2	1	11
Other	6	21	10	14	5	8	18	9	13	6	14	9

Public/Private

	D(W)		DK		E *		F		FIN		IRL		N		NL *		P *		S *		T *		UK	
	Pu	Pr	Pu	Pr	Pu	Pr	Pu	Pr	Pu	Pr	Pu	Pr	Pu	Pr	Pu	Pr	Pu	Pr	Pu	Pr	Pu	Pr	Pu	Pr
Business Studies	24	45	9	36	10	6	16	23	9	32	40	38	33	35	0	21	0	11	16	20	50	34	15	19
Economics	9	10	13	10	0	5	12	8	9	7	0	2	3	0	0	0	20	11	10	9	33	23	8	11
Social/Behavioural sciences	3	10	28	5	20	32	13	18	14	24	5	21	16	12	0	9	20	23	56	51	0	6	20	22
Humanities/Arts/languages	27	24	0	7	0	6	4	2	9	2	30	11	15	16	0	32	0	3	3	2	0	3	26	19
Law	9	2	36	15	70	28	34	23	18	14	0	0	10	6	0	26	40	34	8	2	8	13	5	2
Engineering	3	4	0	3	0	12	11	11	25	17	15	6	2	13	0	3	20	3	3	7	8	3	4	8
Natural Sciences	0	1	0	0	0	1	0	1	2	3	0	13	3	3	0	0	0	0	2	2	0	1	11	12
Other	24	4	15	24	0	10	10	14	14	1	10	6	18	15	0	9	0	14	2	8	0	0	11	7

Less than 1,000 or greater than or equal to 1,000 employees

	D(W)		DK		E		F		FIN		IRL		N		NL		P		S		T		UK	
	<1	>1	<1	>1	<1	>1	<1	>1	<1	>1	<1	>1	<1	>1	<1	>1	<1	>1	<1	>1	<1	>1	<1	>1
Business Studies	50	39	26	21	6	6	22	24	28	10	39	45	38	36	16	33	15	0	14	21	37	33	21	16
Economics	9	9	9	14	2	9	8	9	11	2	0	5	3	0	0	0	12	18	6	12	27	19	11	9
Social/Behavioural sciences	8	9	15	16	32	30	17	15	13	25	20	10	11	14	4	22	24	27	56	51	3	10	24	20
Humanities/Arts/languages	18	29	3	5	3	9	4	2	4	6	17	10	15	14	36	22	3	0	2	3	7	0	19	22
Law	3	4	23	25	30	34	24	27	18	25	2	0	6	7	32	11	27	46	6	4	8	17	3	3
Engineering	4	3	2	2	13	9	9	13	16	22	7	10	7	9	4	0	6	0	6	4	2	10	5	8
Natural Sciences	0	2	0	0	0	1	0	1	4	0	7	10	2	5	0	0	0	0	1	3	2	0	0	12
Other	7	5	23	18	15	3	17	10	5	10	7	10	19	16	8	11	15	0	8	3	15	11	8	9

Table 1.8: Training received by personnel/human resource managers from current or previous employers. (+)

Country

	D(W)	DK	E	F	FIN	IRL	N	NL	P	S	T	UK
Short courses/seminars	74	80	73	77	90	78	90	87	45	90	77	91
Job–related projects	46	40	28	25	55	53	55	47	23	66	33	59
Assignments/job rotation	22	26	30	36	37	32	35	17	12	19	42	30
Formal coaching by Line Mgr.	29	30	10	26	11	17	16	9	8	9	15	27
Formal mentoring by superior outside	5	27	17	6	7	13	11	6	9	7	7	9

Public/Private

* (E)   * (NL)   * (P)   * (T)

	D(W)		DK		E		F		FIN		IRL		N		NL		P		S		T		UK	
	Pu	Pr	Pu	Pr	Pu	Pr	Pu	Pr	Pu	Pr	Pu	Pr	Pu	Pr	Pu	Pr	Pu	Pr	Pu	Pr	Pu	Pr	Pu	Pr
Short courses/seminars	12	80	43	54	5	92	18	75	26	61	26	55	38	42	0	13	14	71	42	53	19	22	27	64
Job–related projects	10	82	44	53	6	92	15	75	26	58	19	66	34	44	50	55	10	71	43	53	75	66	26	64
Assignments/job rotation	13	80	45	51	4	90	13	82	27	64	24	62	32	47	100	83	10	91	45	52	69	58	20	70
Formal coaching by Line Mgr.	13	81	33	64	8	92	10	84	32	56	33	63	27	41	100	91	14	86	33	58	94	83	20	67
Formal mentoring by superior outside	15	80	44	52	2	98	10	87	39	56	17	61	23	45	100	94	13	88	23	77	81	95	25	66

Less than 1,000 or greater than or equal to 1,000 employees

	D(W)		DK		E		F		FIN		IRL		N		NL		P		S		T		UK	
	<1	>1	<1	>1	<1	>1	<1	>1	<1	>1	<1	>1	<1	>1	<1	>1	<1	>1	<1	>1	<1	>1	<1	>1
Short courses/seminars	58	42	65	35	60	40	59	41	65	35	74	26	70	30	81	19	71	29	51	49	59	41	43	57
Job–related projects	51	49	59	41	58	42	55	45	62	38	70	30	63	37	73	27	62	38	49	51	58	42	40	60
Assignments/job rotation	43	57	61	39	58	42	53	47	64	36	67	33	68	32	86	14	82	18	48	52	67	33	34	66
Formal coaching by Line Mgr.	49	51	75	25	76	24	59	41	44	56	75	25	73	27	75	25	57	43	52	48	63	37	47	53
Formal mentoring by superior outside	55	45	68	32	68	32	62	38	33	67	72	28	68	32	88	12	75	25	32	68	38	62	44	56

Table 1.9: Percentage of organisations where the head of personnel/HR function has a place on the main board.

Country	D(W)	DK	E	F	FIN	IRL	N	NL	P	S	T	UK
Yes	30	49	73	84	61	44	71	42	46	84	37	49
No	67	39	23	12	38	38	24	54	46	15	60	47

Public/Private

	D(W)		DK		E		F		FIN		IRL		N		NL		P		S		T		UK	
					*										*		*				*			
	Pu	Pr	Pu	Pr	Pu	Pr	Pu	Pr	Pu	Pr	Pu	Pr	Pu	Pr	Pu	Pr	Pu	Pr	Pu	Pr	Pu	Pr	Pu	Pr
Yes	11	33	53	48	56	72	80	85	64	59	35	44	71	71	0	43	38	48	81	86	31	39	54	49
No	76	64	40	37	31	24	17	11	34	40	45	38	24	23	100	53	46	45	18	12	69	59	43	47

Less than 1,000 or greater than or equal to 1,000 employees

	D(W)		DK		E		F		FIN		IRL		N		NL		P		S		T		UK	
	<1	>1	<1	>1	<1	>1	<1	>1	<1	>1	<1	>1	<1	>1	<1	>1	<1	>1	<1	>1	<1	>1	<1	>1
Yes	28	31	47	54	67	80	82	87	64	55	39	59	70	76	40	50	46	45	78	91	35	41	43	54
No	67	64	42	37	26	19	14	10	35	44	43	28	24	22	57	42	44	54	21	8	62	56	51	43

Table 1.10: Percentage of organisations with someone other than the personnel/HR manager on the board with responsibility for personnel issues. (Valid %)

Country	D(W)	DK	E	F	FIN	IRL	N	NL	P	S	T	UK
Chief executive/MD	26	63	43	35	9	70	26	60	44	22	62	60
Administrative Director	20	9	9	15	17	0	12	2	13	52	12	7
Finance Director	3	8	9	6	7	13	18	15	4	8	2	9
Company Secretary	0	0	12	23	0	3	4	0	7	2	0	3
Production Director	2	1	4	4	1	0	0	8	2	2	0	5
Worker Director	7	2	1	1	0	0	3	4	0	2	2	0
Other	10	17	21	15	7	15	38	11	15	12	21	15

Public/Private	D(W)		DK		E*		F		FIN		IRL		N*		NL*		P*		S		T*		UK	
	Pu	Pr	Pu	Pr	Pu	Pr	Pu	Pr	Pu	Pr	Pu	Pr	Pu	Pr	Pu	Pr	Pu	Pr	Pu	Pr	Pu	Pr	Pu	Pr
Chief executive/MD	38	23	29	35	6	13	4	5	8	12	30	37	13	1	50	35	0	25	4	3	38	44	24	30
Administrative Director	3	22	7	3	6	3	2	2	13	18	0	0	3	3	0	2	0	8	9	8	25	5	6	2
Finance Director	1	3	1	6	6	3	1	1	3	10	0	0	0	12	0	8	0	3	0	2	0	2	1	5
Company Secretary	0	0	0	0	0	6	7	3	0	0	15	3	2	1	0	0	15	1	1	0	0	0	0	2
Production Director	0	2	0	1	6	1	0	1	0	2	0	2	0	0	0	5	0	0	0	1	0	1	0	4
Worker Director	0	8	1	1	0	0	0	0	0	0	0	0	0	1	0	2	0	0	0	1	2	2	0	0
Other	32	8	11	7	19	6	5	1	11	3	13	7	10	10	50	50	4	31	11	4	19	11	11	0

Less than 1,000 or greater than or equal to 1,000 employees	D(W)		DK		E		F		FIN		IRL		N		NL		P		S		T		UK	
	<1	>1	<1	>1	<1	>1	<1	>1	<1	>1	<1	>1	<1	>1	<1	>1	<1	>1	<1	>1	<1	>1	<1	>1
Chief executive/MD	27	22	34	29	66	81	7	3	8	11	36	28	7	6	36	27	21	23	4	3	39	46	32	58
Administrative Director	23	14	6	4	16	6	2	2	16	21	0	0	3	4	2	0	9	0	14	0	9	7	3	26
Finance Director	2	3	6	2	4	1	2	0	9	3	0	5	5	4	11	0	3	0	2	1	3	0	7	4
Company Secretary	0	1	0	0	0	3	3	3	0	0	7	3	1	1	0	0	1	9	0	2	0	0	2	2
Production Director	2	1	1	1	4	1	3	0	2	0	2	0	0	0	6	0	0	1	1	0	0	0	4	1
Worker Director	1	16	1	2	1	1	0	0	0	0	0	0	1	0	2	4	0	0	1	1	3	0	0	0
Other	11	10	6	13	6	6	2	2	3	10	9	7	9	10	4	15	14	18	3	1	17	9	6	8

Table 1.11a: People employed in the personnel function (including wage administration and training).

Country	D(W)	DK	E	F	FIN	IRL	N	NL	P	S	T	UK
1 – 5	36	51	29	25	22	41	49	46	43	23	34	18
6 – 10	27	22	20	29	36	24	22	26	17	23	31	23
11 – 25	19	16	28	25	22	20	19	14	16	27	15	27
26 or more	13	7	16	16	11	9	7	9	15	21	14	27

Public/Private

	D(W)		DK		E *		F		FIN		IRL		N		NL *		P *		S		T *		UK	
	Pu	Pr	Pu	Pr	Pu	Pr	Pu	Pr	Pu	Pr	Pu	Pr	Pu	Pr	Pu	Pr	Pu	Pr	Pu	Pr	Pu	Pr	Pu	Pr
1 – 5	18	38	37	60	6	31	9	30	24	51	20	52	45	53	0	45	38	47	9	32	12	37	8	22
6 – 10	31	27	24	20	25	19	23	30	21	14	17	25	28	20	50	25	0	22	21	23	25	31	20	24
11 – 25	24	19	21	13	44	26	41	20	29	17	25	18	13	20	0	15	15	11	34	22	31	14	32	24
26 or more	22	11	11	4	25	15	22	15	16	10	27	1	9	5	50	9	31	12	29	15	19	13	36	23

Less than 1,000 or greater than or equal to 1,000 employees

	D(W)		DK		E		F		FIN		IRL		N		NL		P		S		T		UK	
	<1	>1	<1	>1	<1	>1	<1	>1	<1	>1	<1	>1	<1	>1	<1	>1	<1	>1	<1	>1	<1	>1	<1	>1
1 – 5	56	4	68	16	45	2	35	11	52	17	49	12	63	12	56	4	38	0	41	4	48	11	36	4
6 – 10	33	19	18	30	28	5	37	17	19	17	29	9	21	26	28	15	22	0	32	13	36	22	38	11
11 – 25	7	40	6	34	14	50	21	30	16	35	13	44	11	38	12	27	11	32	18	36	7	30	18	34
26 or more	1	32	1	17	4	36	2	36	5	24	4	28	2	19	1	42	1	59	3	40	7	26	4	45

Table 1.11b: Professional staff employed in the personnel function (including wage administration and training).

Country	D(W)	DK	E	F	FIN	IRL	N	NL	P	S	T	UK
1 – 5	78	59	25	60	47	54	33	65	52	30	51	46
6 – 10	9	11	10	16	25	8	9	8	8	14	12	17
11 – 25	3	5	7	9	1	2	6	8	8	15	8	13
26 or more	2	2	4	5	5	4	1	4	3	7	2	9

Public/Private	D(W)		DK		E *		F		FIN		IRL		N		NL *		P *		S		T *		UK	
	Pu	Pr	Pu	Pr	Pu	Pr	Pu	Pr	Pu	Pr	Pu	Pr	Pu	Pr	Pu	Pr	Pu	Pr	Pu	Pr	Pu	Pr	Pu	Pr
1 – 5	75	79	54	60	25	24	57	62	60	63	30	59	33	34	50	63	15	54	30	27	19	55	39	50
6 – 10	14	8	15	8	0	10	16	14	10	12	7	11	12	7	0	8	8	8	19	12	12	12	21	14
11 – 25	7	3	5	4	6	8	7	8	6	2	5	1	0	9	50	7	23	6	20	11	12	12	18	11
26 or more	0	2	2	1	1	4	9	4	5	0	7	1	1	1	0	4	0	3	12	2	0	3	3	9

Less than 1,000 or greater than or equal to 1,000 employees	D(W)		DK		E		F		FIN		IRL		N		NL		P		S		T		UK	
	<1	>1	<1	>1	<1	>1	<1	>1	<1	>1	<1	>1	<1	>1	<1	>1	<1	>1	<1	>1	<1	>1	<1	>1
1 – 5	89	61	66	45	34	8	76	37	70	50	57	41	36	24	76	15	61	23	42	18	70	20	71	26
6 – 10	1	20	4	24	5	18	12	21	9	19	6	19	7	15	6	15	1	27	13	16	4	26	9	22
11 – 25	0	8	1	13	4	14	3	17	1	9	1	6	3	13	2	31	1	27	7	23	4	15	1	23
26 or more	0	5	1	4	0	11	<1	12	0	4	2	9	0	4	2	11	0	14	1	12	1	1	1	15

Table 1.12: Source of recruitment of senior personnel/human resource manager.

Country	D(W)	DK	E	F	FIN	IRL	N	NL	P	S	T	UK
Within personnel dept.	22	18	24	16	20	15	15	23	32	20	33	25
Non–personnel within org.	25	34	26	23	30	35	25	16	22	17	20	16
Personnel specialists outside	38	25	41	46	31	34	30	51	34	47	38	47
Non specialists outside	10	20	3	13	15	8	25	7	11	14	7	9

Public/Private

	D(W)		DK		E		F		FIN		IRL		N		NL		P		S		T		UK	
	Pu	Pr	Pu	Pr	Pu	Pr	Pu	Pr	Pu	Pr	Pu	Pr	Pu	Pr	Pu	Pr	Pu	Pr	Pu	Pr	Pu	Pr	Pu	Pr
					*										*		*				*			
Within personnel dept.	35	20	26	12	38	23	16	15	22	17	20	10	11	18	50	23	39	32	22	19	44	33	28	24
Non–personnel within org.	40	22	30	38	19	26	33	19	29	30	50	27	23	26	0	17	31	18	16	18	25	20	11	18
Personnel specialists outside	14	42	22	28	38	42	28	51	31	32	15	45	29	30	0	50	23	38	46	48	25	38	52	45
Non specialists outside	9	11	19	20	6	3	21	11	13	18	18	9	33	23	50	6	0	11	14	13	6	8	6	9

Less than 1,000 or greater than or equal to 1,000 employees

	D(W)		DK		E		F		FIN		IRL		N		NL		P		S		T		UK	
	<1	>1	<1	>1	<1	>1	<1	>1	<1	>1	<1	>1	<1	>1	<1	>1	<1	>1	<1	>1	<1	>1	<1	>1
Within personnel dept.	20	25	16	22	18	36	12	21	12	32	12	25	12	23	22	27	30	41	18	22	29	41	19	30
Non–personnel within org.	26	23	37	28	24	28	22	24	35	21	37	25	29	15	17	15	21	23	20	14	18	22	17	15
Personnel specialists outside	36	42	24	28	45	33	49	42	30	34	34	37	27	38	55	35	35	32	44	50	44	28	51	44
Non specialists outside	12	6	19	22	4	1	14	10	19	9	8	6	28	18	5	15	11	4	15	13	8	6	9	8

Table 2.1: The main objectives of personnel or human resource management department over the next three years

Country	D(W)	DK	E	F	FIN	IRL	N	NL	P	S	T	UK
Personnel function	7	19	8	8	2	11	12	8	7	14	5	12
Manpower planning	4	2	16	14	2	4	4	6	4	7	6	5
Recruitment	11	5	3	4	3	5	4	8	3	3	12	7
Pay and benefits	3	4	6	5	8	4	4	3	5	4	6	9
Job evaluation	1	2	1	4	0	0	1	5	1	0	3	1
Training/Development	34	31	19	25	12	22	31	26	24	30	25	22
Performance appraisal	2	4	2	3	0	2	2	4	0	1	2	2
Employee relations	10	10	18	18	20	19	6	12	5	9	7	12
Efficiency	5	10	8	20	19	20	11	16	10	8	12	18
Workforce adjustment	5	3	4	3	8	1	4	1	8	8	8	2
Working time	3	0	0	0	0	0	0	0	1	0	0	0
Health and safety	1	1	2	1	2	4	4	2	2	3	1	1
Single European Market	2	1	1	1	0	1	1	0	1	1	1	1
Organisational development	6	7	5	4	5	6	9	10	9	11	3	6

Private and public sector

	D(W)		DK		E*		F		FIN		IRL		N		NL*		P*		S		T*		UK	
	Pu	Pr	Pu	Pr	Pu	Pr	Pu	Pr	Pu	Pr	Pu	Pr	Pu	Pr	Pu	Pr	Pu	Pr	Pu	Pr	Pu	Pr	Pu	Pr
Personnel function	6	4	25	14	3	9	10	7	1	2	11	9	18	11	33	8	6	9	19	11	0	6	18	10
Manpower planning	5	5	1	3	21	17	11	15	1	3	3	5	4	4	0	7	11	3	5	8	8	5	5	6
Recruitment	12	11	2	7	0	3	3	4	4	3	6	5	3	4	0	6	6	9	3	3	15	13	5	7
Pay and benefits	8	9	2	5	9	6	2	4	14	7	1	6	4	5	3	3	0	7	2	6	10	10	6	9
Job evaluation	2	1	1	3	3	1	5	4	0	1	1	0	0	1	5	4	0	2	0	0	0	4	1	1
Training/Development	32	36	29	34	27	20	23	26	12	19	27	21	33	34	33	27	50	26	29	32	40	30	19	24
Performance appraisal	3	2	4	4	3	2	2	3	0	1	1	2	2	2	4	4	0	1	0	1	0	0	2	2
Employee relations	9	11	10	10	10	18	20	18	29	22	13	23	6	6	0	13	0	6	6	7	8	13	13	13
Efficiency	3	6	10	9	3	9	13	11	22	26	18	18	10	3	13	15	12	12	10	8	10	12	17	19
Workforce adjustment	6	5	3	2	0	4	6	2	11	9	3	1	3	5	0	1	0	1	9	5	15	9	2	3
Working time	0	4	0	0	0	0	0	0	1	1	0	0	0	0	0	0	0	0	0	0	0	0	0	0
Health and safety	1	1	1	1	0	1	1	1	1	3	3	4	7	2	2	0	3	1	5	2	0	1	1	1
Single European Market	1	2	0	2	3	3	0	1	0	0	1	1	1	1	0	0	0	1	1	1	1	1	0	1
Organisational development	12	6	10	5	9	9	5	4	4	4	10	4	8	14	10	10	6	12	10	12	3	3	8	6

Table 2.1 (cont): The main objectives of personnel or human resource management department over the next three years

Less than 1,000 or greater than or equal to 1,000 employees

Country	D(W) <1	D(W) >1	DK <1	DK >1	E <1	E >1	F <1	F >1	FIN <1	FIN >1	IRL <1	IRL >1	N <1	N >1	NL <1	NL >1	P <1	P >1	S <1	S >1	T <1	T >1	UK <1	UK >1
Personnel function	3	7	18	22	9	8	8	7	2	3	10	3	13	15	10	6	10	6	14	15	7	3	11	13
Manpower planning	5	4	2	1	19	14	14	15	3	2	3	2	4	7	6	8	3	9	9	5	7	7	5	6
Recruitment	12	11	5	6	2	3	4	4	3	4	6	6	4	2	6	8	9	0	4	2	13	13	7	6
Pay and benefits	8	9	5	3	6	8	4	3	9	8	5	8	4	5	4	0	6	6	4	4	4	7	9	9
Job evaluation	1	1	3	0	1	0	4	3	1	0	0	0	1	1	3	6	2	0	0	0	0	2	1	1
Training/Development	36	34	32	30	20	21	25	26	17	17	23	20	37	32	25	33	32	23	32	29	28	33	23	21
Performance appraisal	2	1	4	4	3	2	4	2	1	0	2	1	2	3	4	3	0	6	6	10	1	3	9	0
Employee relations	12	10	10	10	19	21	19	16	22	26	19	19	6	7	12	12	6	6	6	8	3	0	12	12
Efficiency	6	5	10	9	9	8	11	12	24	21	19	22	13	10	16	15	10	13	10	8	14	11	19	17
Workforce adjustment	5	5	2	3	4	4	2	5	10	9	1	2	4	5	0	0	9	11	9	9	9	7	2	3
Working time	3	3	0	0	0	0	0	0	0	0	0	0	0	1	0	0	1	0	0	0	0	0	0	0
Health and safety	1	3	2	1	0	2	1	1	2	1	5	0	5	2	3	0	3	2	4	3	2	0	1	1
Single European Market	1	3	1	0	0	1	1	1	0	0	1	1	0	1	0	0	0	0	2	0	0	1	1	1
Organisational development	7	6	6	9	5	8	3	5	5	7	13	8	11	9	10	8	8	19	9	12	2	5	5	7

Table 2.2a: Percentage of organisations with a mission statement

Country	D(W)	DK	E	F	FIN	IRL	N	NL	P	S	T	UK
Yes, written	42	71	40	37	83	57	78	35	60	83	20	63
Yes, unwritten	35	15	38	20	10	11	9	9	24	11	24	9
No	10	6	9	34	1	23	9	26	10	5	26	20
Don't know	2	3	4	1	0	1	2	7	1	0	7	1

Private and public sector

	D(W) Pu	D(W) Pr	DK Pu	DK Pr	E* Pu	E Pr	F Pu	F Pr	FIN Pu	FIN Pr	IRL Pu	IRL Pr	N Pu	N Pr	NL* Pu	NL Pr	P* Pu	P Pr	S Pu	S Pr	T Pu	T Pr	UK Pu	UK Pr
Yes, written	32	43	57	79	38	40	32	37	86	82	45	62	63	90	50	34	61	88	78	88	13	20	63	62
Yes, unwritten	12	39	19	12	56	36	21	20	10	10	15	10	13	6	0	11	15	26	13	10	6	27	7	10
No	9	10	12	2	2	6	37	35	2	1	22	21	19	2	26	50	15	0	7	0	44	6	22	20
Don't know	1	3	2	3	0	4	4	3	0	0	2	1	2	1	50	6	0	0	1	1	1	6	1	2

Less than 1,000 or greater than or equal to 1,000 employees

	D(W) <1	D(W) >1	DK <1	DK >1	E <1	E >1	F <1	F >1	FIN <1	FIN >1	IRL <1	IRL >1	N <1	N >1	NL <1	NL >1	P <1	P >1	S <1	S >1	T <1	T >1	UK <1	UK >1
Yes, written	39	45	76	60	37	49	32	45	85	57	56	82	76	82	30	50	53	86	82	86	16	26	58	67
Yes, unwritten	37	32	14	17	37	37	24	16	10	7	8	22	11	3	10	11	25	18	14	8	26	20	9	8
No	12	7	3	12	11	11	4	36	1	24	16	7	13	7	0	13	32	0	5	4	23	30	22	18
Don't know	2	2	2	2	4	3	3	1	1	0	2	0	2	1	7	8	0	1	0	0	1	9	2	1

Table 2.2b: Percentage of organisations with a corporate strategy

Country

Country	D(W)	DK	E	F	FIN	IRL	N	NL	P	S	T	UK
Yes, written	41	57	40	42	78	54	83	61	42	85	29	70
Yes, unwritten	41	22	33	43	10	24	7	27	34	10	42	16
No	12	10	16	8	5	12	5	3	11	4	11	8
Don't know	2	3	4	1	1	2	0	1	4	0	7	2

Private and public sector

	D(W)		DK		E *		F		FIN		IRL *		N *		NL *		P *		S		T *		UK	
	Pu	Pr	Pu	Pr	Pu	Pr	Pu	Pr	Pu	Pr	Pu	Pr	Pu	Pr	Pu	Pr	Pu	Pr	Pu	Pr	Pu	Pr	Pu	Pr
Yes, written	31	43	39	70	50	39	34	43	73	85	40	58	76	88	100	60	46	42	84	85	44	28	72	69
Yes, unwritten	42	40	24	21	19	34	37	46	8	10	30	20	9	6	0	28	23	36	9	10	12	47	9	19
No	21	11	20	3	25	16	15	6	10	1	15	12	9	3	3	0	23	8	4	4	19	8	13	5
Don't know	1	2	2	2	6	4	4	1	1	0	1	2	0	0	0	1	1	0	4	0	1	0	2	2

Less than 1,000 or greater than or equal to 1,000 employees

	D(W)		DK		E		F		FIN		IRL		N		NL		P		S		T		UK	
	<1	>1	<1	>1	<1	>1	<1	>1	<1	>1	<1	>1	<1	>1	<1	>1	<1	>1	<1	>1	<1	>1	<1	>1
Yes, written	40	41	61	49	32	54	40	46	79	76	52	59	82	86	58	73	37	59	81	88	26	35	63	75
Yes, unwritten	39	43	21	23	32	33	46	39	10	7	23	25	7	6	31	11	32	41	12	8	43	39	19	14
No	14	9	6	16	20	9	7	8	6	6	14	6	5	5	4	0	0	14	5	3	10	11	9	6
Don't know	2	2	2	2	6	0	2	1	1	0	3	0	1	0	1	0	6	0	1	0	8	4	3	1

Table 2.2c: Percentage of organisations with a Personnel/HR management strategy

Country

Country	D(W)	DK	E	F	FIN	IRL	N	NL	P	S	T	UK
Yes, written	18	72	37	34	52	41	71	44	34	73	29	50
Yes, unwritten	42	20	41	52	29	34	16	33	41	24	41	24
No	32	4	16	10	14	15	9	13	14	3	18	19
Don't know	2	1	0	0	1	9	0	1	3	0	1	1

Private and public sector

	D(W)		DK		E *		F		FIN		IRL *		N *		NL *		P *		S		T *		UK	
	Pu	Pr	Pu	Pr	Pu	Pr	Pu	Pr	Pu	Pr	Pu	Pr	Pu	Pr	Pu	Pr	Pu	Pr	Pu	Pr	Pu	Pr	Pu	Pr
Yes, written	13	18	30	44	44	37	33	33	55	50	33	46	68	74	50	43	39	33	79	70	13	30	54	48
Yes, unwritten	41	42	38	31	31	41	58	52	24	32	43	30	17	17	50	33	15	45	19	27	25	45	19	26
No	41	32	17	18	25	16	6	12	18	13	13	16	11	5	0	14	46	11	2	4	38	13	22	19
Don't know	2	2	3	2	0	<1	0	<1	0	2	0	0	0	1	0	1	0	4	0	0	0	1	<1	1

Less than 1,000 or greater than or equal to 1,000 employees

	D(W)		DK		E		F		FIN		IRL		N		NL		P		S		T		UK	
	<1	>1	<1	>1	<1	>1	<1	>1	<1	>1	<1	>1	<1	>1	<1	>1	<1	>1	<1	>1	<1	>1	<1	>1
Yes, written	14	23	40	35	28	55	27	44	47	62	42	44	70	76	40	58	30	50	60	86	29	28	41	57
Yes, unwritten	41	45	33	27	43	33	58	43	30	25	32	37	17	15	35	27	39	45	37	11	40	41	26	23
No	37	25	17	18	20	8	11	9	19	8	17	9	9	8	15	8	18	4	3	3	17	20	23	15
Don't know	2	2	2	4	1	0	0	0	1	1	0	0	1	0	1	0	4	0	0	0	1	0	1	1

Table 2.3: Personnel/HR department involvement in corporate strategy (Valid %)

Country	D(W)	DK	E	F	FIN	IRL	N	NL	P	S	T	UK
From the outset	55	47	54	54	48	50	65	50	42	56	45	53
Consultative	25	31	25	27	23	31	24	36	30	31	9	32
Implementation	10	15	18	16	10	10	9	10	18	8	33	9
Not consulted	10	7	4	3	7	9	3	3	10	6	13	7

Private and public sector

	D(W)		DK		E *		F		FIN *		IRL		N		NL *		P *		S		T *		UK	
	Pu	Pr	Pu	Pr	Pu	Pr	Pu	Pr	Pu	Pr	Pu	Pr	Pu	Pr	Pu	Pr	Pu	Pr	Pu	Pr	Pu	Pr	Pu	Pr
From the outset	64	53	52	45	64	53	67	51	57	52	50	51	61	68	50	50	56	41	54	58	33	46	61	50
Consultative	27	25	31	30	27	26	16	29	26	27	29	30	27	23	0	36	33	25	29	33	0	11	30	32
Implementation	5	11	12	16	9	17	16	17	14	12	18	9	10	7	50	10	11	21	8	7	33	33	6	10
Not consulted	4	11	5	9	0	4	1	3	4	9	4	11	2	2	0	4	0	13	9	3	33	11	4	8

Less than 1,000 or greater than or equal to 1,000 employees

	D(W)		DK		E		F		FIN		IRL		N		NL		P		S		T		UK	
	<1	>1	<1	>1	<1	>1	<1	>1	<1	>1	<1	>1	<1	>1	<1	>1	<1	>1	<1	>1	<1	>1	<1	>1
From the outset	53	57	47	49	50	57	50	60	53	57	46	64	62	71	52	46	48	40	52	60	36	59	47	57
Consultative	24	26	31	30	28	21	31	21	25	30	33	24	26	17	33	46	14	36	32	31	13	3	33	31
Implementation	10	10	14	16	16	21	15	18	13	9	11	8	9	7	10	8	33	12	9	6	38	27	11	7
Not consulted	13	7	8	5	5	1	4	1	10	4	4	11	2	4	4	0	5	12	8	3	13	12	9	5

Table 2.4: Organisations with a personnel/HR strategy and translate it into work programmes etc. for personnel function (Valid %)

Country	D(W)	DK	E	F	FIN	IRL	N	NL	P	S	T	UK
Yes	62	50	74	64	67	73	64	48	72	56	65	70
No	38	50	26	36	11	27	36	52	28	44	35	30

Private and public sector

	D(W)		DK		E *		F		FIN		IRL		N		NL *		P *		S		T *		UK	
	Pu	Pr	Pu	Pr	Pu	Pr	Pu	Pr	Pu	Pr	Pu	Pr	Pu	Pr	Pu	Pr	Pu	Pr	Pu	Pr	Pu	Pr	Pu	Pr
Yes	62	62	48	51	71	75	62	65	85	86	72	73	54	72	0	49	44	75	56	57	50	66	71	70
No	38	38	52	49	29	25	38	35	15	14	28	27	46	28	100	51	56	25	44	43	50	34	29	30

Less than 1,000 or greater than or equal to 1,000 employees

	D(W)		DK		E		F		FIN		IRL		N		NL		P		S		T		UK	
	<1	>1	<1	>1	<1	>1	<1	>1	<1	>1	<1	>1	<1	>1	<1	>1	<1	>1	<1	>1	<1	>1	<1	>1
Yes	56	71	44	62	65	87	59	72	82	91	76	63	63	66	42	70	77	69	51	60	61	71	66	73
No	44	29	56	38	35	13	41	29	18	9	24	37	37	34	58	30	23	31	49	40	39	29	34	27

Table 2.5a: Where policies on pay and benefits are mainly determined in organisations which are part of a larger group (Valid %)

Country

	D(W)	DK	E	F	FIN	IRL	N	NL	P	S	T	UK
International HQ	11	5	14	12	5	11	5	11	12	2	6	9
National HQ (central)	47	57	65	58	60	54	64	61	68	63	76	53
Subsidiary (Service dept/division)	34	31	9	19	15	8	18	15	15	22	4	19
Site/Establishment (Local offices)	8	8	13	12	21	27	12	13	5	14	14	18
n=	534	256	131	489	135	100	169	93	41	253	70	826

Private and public sector

	D(W) Pu	D(W) Pr	DK Pu	DK Pr	E Pu	E Pr	F Pu	F Pr	FIN Pu	FIN Pr	IRL Pu	IRL Pr	N Pu	N Pr	NL Pu	NL Pr	P Pu	P Pr	S Pu	S Pr	T Pu	T Pr	UK Pu	UK Pr
International HQ	2	12	0	9	0	14	9	12	0	7	0	16	2	8	0	11	0	14	3	0	0	7	3	10
National HQ (central)	75	44	53	60	80	65	80	54	67	50	93	36	90	49	0	63	50	69	56	73	100	71	86	44
Subsidiary (Service dept/division)	19	36	38	23	10	9	5	22	12	19	3	10	3	29	100	13	50	11	25	17	0	5	6	24
Site/Establishment (Local offices)	4	8	8	7	10	12	5	12	21	24	4	39	5	14	0	13	0	6	16	10	0	17	5	23
n=	47	454	107	141	110	118	56	394	42	74	28	62	58	77	2	91	4	35	99	142	10	58	178	578

Less than 1,000 or greater than or equal to 1,000 employees

	D(W) <1	D(W) >1	DK <1	DK >1	E <1	E >1	F <1	F >1	FIN <1	FIN >1	IRL <1	IRL >1	N <1	N >1	NL <1	NL >1	P <1	P >1	S <1	S >1	T <1	T >1	UK <1	UK >1
International HQ	9	13	6	3	13	14	10	13	4	6	14	0	4	7	15	15	12	13	1	3	8	3	8	10
National HQ (central)	40	55	52	65	60	71	51	67	53	71	47	77	59	73	62	60	64	87	50	75	83	70	44	61
Subsidiary (Service dept/division)	40	28	33	26	11	7	24	13	20	8	9	9	20	14	15	18	0	27	18	5	3	18		21
Site/Establishment (Local offices)	12	4	9	6	16	7	15	7	24	15	30	14	16	5	14	10	6	0	23	4	18	10	30	8
n=	284	250	163	91	75	56	265	219	82	53	78	22	112	56	72	20	33	8	131	122	40	30	374	452

Table 2.5b: Where policies on recruitment and selection are mainly determined in organisations which are part of a larger group

Country	D(W)	DK	E	F	FIN	IRL	N	NL	P	S	T	UK
International HQ	7	3	0	3	1	4	2	3	3	1	0	3
National HQ (Central)	35	23	59	28	19	42	36	33	68	28	51	31
Subsidiary (Service dept/division)	43	25	17	27	27	16	29	30	23	36	12	30
Site/Establishment (Local offices)	16	49	23	43	54	39	32	34	8	35	38	37
n=	534	256	131	489	135	100	169	93	41	253	70	826

Private and public sector

	D(W)		DK		E		F		FIN		IRL		N		NL		P		S		T		UK	
	Pu	Pr	Pu	Pr	Pu	Pr	Pu	Pr	Pu	Pr	Pu	Pr	Pu	Pr	Pu	Pr	Pu	Pr	Pu	Pr	Pu	Pr	Pu	Pr
					*										*		*				*			
International HQ	0	8	2	4	0	0	0	4	0	1	0	7	2	3	0	3	0	3	0	1	0	1	1	2
National HQ (Central)	83	28	5	36	60	61	20	28	16	20	75	29	37	35	0	33	0	74	30	25	88	44	38	28
Subsidiary (Service dept/division)	9	48	11	35	30	17	11	29	23	22	14	11	26	31	0	31	100	14	36	37	10	12	23	32
Site/Establishment (Local offices)	8	17	82	24	10	22	66	40	61	57	11	53	35	31	100	33	0	9	33	37	10	44	39	37
n=	47	454	107	141	10	118	56	394	42	74	28	62	58	77	2	91	4	35	99	142	10	58	178	578

Less than 1,000 or greater than or equal to 1,000 employees

	D(W)		DK		E		F		FIN		IRL		N		NL		P		S		T		UK	
	<1	>1	<1	>1	<1	>1	<1	>1	<1	>1	<1	>1	<1	>1	<1	>1	<1	>1	<1	>1	<1	>1	<1	>1
International HQ	6	7	3	3	0	0	2	4	0	2	5	0	1	5	3	5	3	0	1	1	0	0	1	4
National HQ (Central)	30	41	25	20	57	63	24	32	17	21	39	55	33	43	32	35	66	75	18	38	46	57	28	33
Subsidiary (Service dept/division)	43	42	29	19	13	23	29	24	26	28	14	23	30	29	29	35	23	25	38	34	13	10	24	35
Site/Establishment (Local offices)	20	10	44	58	29	14	45	40	57	49	42	23	37	23	36	25	9	0	44	28	41	33	47	29
n=	284	250	163	91	75	56	265	219	82	53	78	22	112	56	72	20	33	8	131	122	40	30	374	452

Table 2.5c: Where policies on training and development are mainly determined in organisations which are part of a larger group

Country

	D(W)	DK	E	F	FIN	IRL	N	NL	P	S	T	UK
International HQ	11	3	4	4	2	5	4	9	3	1	3	5
National HQ (Central)	49	27	52	28	18	37	39	37	62	31	52	37
Subsidiary (Service dept/division)	33	28	23	25	25	20	27	26	28	38	13	29
Site/Establishment (Local offices)	7	42	22	44	55	38	31	28	8	30	31	29
n=	534	256	131	489	135	100	169	93	41	253	70	826

Private and public sector

	D(W)		DK		E *		F		FIN		IRL		N *		NL *		P *		S		T *	
	Pu	Pr	Pu	Pr	Pu	Pr	Pu	Pr	Pu	Pr	Pu	Pr	Pu	Pr	Pu	Pr	Pu	Pr	Pu	Pr	Pu	Pr
International HQ	4	11	0	6	0	4	4	3	0	3	0	8	2	5	0	9	0	0	0	2	0	4
National HQ (Central)	83	46	7	43	40	54	20	28	17	17	57	29	41	36	0	37	0	63	31	28	60	49
Subsidiary (Service dept/division)	9	36	22	32	40	21	11	28	19	23	25	15	30	26	0	26	100	26	35	41	30	11
Site/Establishment (Local offices)	4	7	72	19	20	21	66	40	64	58	18	48	27	33	100	27	0	9	33	29	10	36
n=	47	454	107	141	10	118	56	394	42	74	28	62	58	77	2	91	4	35	99	142	10	58

Less than 1,000 or greater than or equal to 1,000 employees

	D(W)		DK		E		F		FIN		IRL		N		NL		P		S		T		UK	
	<1	>1	<1	>1	<1	>1	<1	>1	<1	>1	<1	>1	<1	>1	<1	>1	<1	>1	<1	>1	<1	>1	<1	>1
International HQ	8	15	3	3	3	6	2	5	0	4	0	6	4	6	7	15	3	0	1	2	5	0	4	6
National HQ (Central)	46	53	27	28	47	60	24	32	16	21	33	50	32	51	35	45	61	62	18	42	46	61	32	40
Subsidiary (Service dept/division)	36	29	33	20	23	22	29	21	27	23	19	27	30	20	28	20	29	25	40	37	15	11	23	34
Site/Establishment (Local offices)	10	4	37	49	27	13	45	42	57	52	41	23	34	24	31	20	6	13	41	20	33	29	40	20
n=	284	250	163	91	75	56	265	219	82	53	78	22	112	56	72	20	33	8	131	122	40	30	374	452

Table 2.5d: Where policies on industrial relations are mainly determined in organisations which are part of a larger group

Country

	D(W)	DK	E	F	FIN	IRL	N	NL	P	S	T	UK
International HQ	1	2	2	2	0	3	2	7	8	1	0	2
National HQ (Central)	37	40	61	35	51	44	57	45	64	51	60	37
Subsidiary (Service dept/division)	49	42	14	26	15	11	23	26	25	29	10	28
Site/Establishment (Local offices)	12	17	24	36	34	41	18	23	3	19	30	32
n=	534	256	131	489	135	100	169	93	41	253	70	826

Private and public sector

	D(W) Pu	D(W) Pr	DK Pu	DK Pr	E Pu	E Pr	F Pu	F Pr	FIN Pu	FIN Pr	IRL Pu	IRL Pr	N Pu	N Pr	NL Pu	NL Pr	P Pu	P Pr	S Pu	S Pr	T Pu	T Pr	UK Pu	UK Pr
					*								*		*		*				*			
International HQ	0	6	0	3	0	2	4	2	0	0	0	5	2	1	1	0	0	9	1	1	0	0	1	3
National HQ (Central)	67	43	28	50	88	61	31	35	56	41	75	31	83	42	0	46	50	63	54	49	64	58	48	34
Subsidiary (Service dept/division)	31	40	47	36	0	15	11	29	17	14	4	10	9	33	50	25	50	25	25	32	18	9	23	29
Site/Establishment (Local offices)	2	11	25	11	13	22	55	35	27	45	21	54	7	25	50	22	0	3	20	18	18	33	29	34
n=	47	454	107	141	10	118	56	394	42	74	28	62	58	77	2	91	4	35	99	142	10	58	178	578

Less than 1,000 or greater than or equal to 1,000 employees

	D(W) <1	D(W) >1	DK <1	DK >1	E <1	E >1	F <1	F >1	FIN <1	FIN >1	IRL <1	IRL >1	N <1	N >1	NL <1	NL >1	P <1	P >1	S <1	S >1	T <1	T >1	UK <1	UK >1
International HQ	4	7	1	2	1	2	2	3	0	0	4	0	1	4	6	10	7	13	1	2	0	0	1	3
National HQ (Central)	38	54	35	48	57	67	30	41	47	59	39	64	52	68	44	50	57	87	35	66	53	70	32	41
Subsidiary (Service dept/division)	43	34	45	36	15	13	28	25	14	16	10	14	24	20	26	25	32	0	35	24	10	10	23	32
Site/Establishment (Local offices)	15	7	19	14	28	18	41	32	39	26	47	23	23	9	25	15	4	0	30	9	38	20	43	24
n=	284	250	163	91	75	56	265	219	82	53	78	22	112	56	72	20	33	8	131	122	40	30	374	452

Table 2.5e: Where policies on health and safety are mainly determined in organisations which are part of a larger group

Country

	D(W)	DK	E	F	FIN	IRL	N	NL	P	S	T	UK
International HQ	4	4	2	4	0	1	2	7	8	1	0	6
National HQ (Central)	36	28	50	19	36	41	48	34	64	49	31	39
Subsidiary (Service dept/division)	44	37	18	23	25	16	26	33	21	32	16	25
Site/Establishment (Local offices)	16	32	31	55	39	42	24	27	8	18	53	30
n=	534	256	131	489	135	100	169	93	41	253	70	826

Private and public sector

	D(W) Pu	Pr	DK Pu	Pr	E* Pu	Pr	F Pu	Pr	FIN Pu	Pr	IRL Pu	Pr	N Pu	Pr	NL* Pu	Pr	P* Pu	Pr	S Pu	Pr	T* Pu	Pr	UK Pu	Pr
International HQ	0	5	0	5	0	2	4	4	0	0	0	0	2	3	0	7	0	9	0	1	0	0	1	8
National HQ (Central)	34	36	10	42	60	50	16	20	41	31	61	34	57	43	0	34	50	66	59	42	10	32	44	37
Subsidiary (Service dept/division)	57	43	39	35	20	18	7	25	15	25	7	15	22	29	0	33	50	17	28	35	30	14	22	26
Site/Establishment (Local offices)	9	16	51	17	20	30	73	52	44	44	32	50	19	26	100	26	0	9	13	22	60	54	33	30
n=	47	454	107	141	141	10	118	56	42	74	28	62	58	77	2	91	4	35	99	142	10	58	178	578

Less than 1,000 or greater than or equal to 1,000 employees

	D(W) <1	>1	DK <1	>1	E <1	>1	F <1	>1	FIN <1	>1	IRL <1	>1	N <1	>1	NL <1	>1	P <1	>1	S <1	>1	T <1	>1	UK <1	>1
International HQ	4	5	4	3	1	2	5	2	0	0	1	0	2	4	6	10	7	13	0	2	0	0	5	6
National HQ (Central)	31	42	28	28	44	57	17	21	33	42	40	46	43	57	33	35	64	62	36	62	31	31	31	45
Subsidiary (Service dept/division)	45	42	36	38	15	21	25	20	27	22	12	32	28	21	32	35	19	25	34	30	15	17	23	27
Site/Establishment (Local offices)	20	11	32	32	39	20	53	57	40	36	47	23	27	18	29	20	10	0	31	7	54	52	40	22
n=	284	250	163	91	75	56	265	219	82	53	78	22	112	56	72	20	33	8	131	122	40	30	374	452

Table 2.5f: Where policies on workforce expansion/reduction are mainly determined in organisations which are part of a larger group

Country	D(W)	DK	E	F	FIN	IRL	N	NL	P	S	T	UK
International HQ	12	5	7	12	0	16	5	11	5	1	6	7
National HQ (Central)	42	30	58	39	40	42	49	29	68	35	59	32
Subsidiary (Service dept/division)	35	49	13	22	26	12	24	25	23	41	10	30
Site/Establishment (Local offices)	11	16	22	27	34	30	23	35	5	23	25	31
n=	534	256	131	489	135	100	169	93	41	253	70	826

Private and public sector

	D(W)		DK		E		F		FIN		IRL		N		NL		P		S		T		UK	
	Pu	Pr	Pu	Pr	Pu	Pr	Pu	Pr	Pu	Pr	Pu	Pr	Pu	Pr	Pu	Pr	Pu	Pr	Pu	Pr	Pu	Pr	Pu	Pr
International HQ	4	13	0	9	0	7	4	13	0	13	23	14	2	4	0	11	0	6	0	2	0	7	0	9
National HQ (Central)	87	37	18	39	60	59	45	38	45	28	31	31	62	40	0	30	33	69	40	30	40	61	35	31
Subsidiary (Service dept/division)	6	39	63	38	20	13	16	23	21	31	8	18	16	30	0	25	67	20	38	45	30	7	29	30
Site/Establishment (Local offices)	4	11	19	14	20	22	36	26	33	41	39	14	21	26	100	34	0	6	22	23	30	25	36	30
n=	47	454	107	141	10	118	56	394	42	74	28	62	58	77	2	91	4	35	99	142	10	58	178	578

Less than 1,000 or greater than or equal to 1,000 employees

	D(W)		DK		E		F		FIN		IRL		N		NL		P		S		T		UK	
	<1	>1	<1	>1	<1	>1	<1	>1	<1	>1	<1	>1	<1	>1	<1	>1	<1	>1	<1	>1	<1	>1	<1	>1
International HQ	11	13	7	2	7	7	11	13	0	13	18	5	4	7	10	15	6	0	1	2	10	0	8	6
National HQ (Central)	39	46	31	28	53	64	34	44	36	45	38	59	49	48	32	20	59	100	26	42	51	70	27	35
Subsidiary (Service dept/division)	35	34	45	56	15	11	25	19	27	25	10	18	23	25	22	35	28	0	40	44	13	7	23	36
Site/Establishment (Local offices)	15	7	17	14	25	18	30	24	37	30	34	18	25	20	36	30	6	0	34	12	26	23	42	23
n=	284	250	163	91	75	56	265	219	82	53	78	22	112	56	72	20	33	8	131	122	40	30	374	452

Table 2.6a: Primary responsibility for major policy decisions on pay and benefits

Country

Country	D(W)	DK	E	F	FIN	IRL	N	NL	P	S	T	UK
Line Management	8	23	32	9	17	9	9	6	29	5	33	5
Line Management with HR department	39	31	40	45	39	12	29	29	42	40	21	21
HR Department with line management	44	35	25	37	27	36	46	40	18	51	19	51
HR Department	8	9	3	7	13	33	12	22	8	5	16	18

Private and public sector

Private and public sector	D(W)		DK		E *		F		FIN		IRL		N		NL *		P *		S		T *		UK	
	Pu	Pr	Pu	Pr	Pu	Pr	Pu	Pr	Pu	Pr	Pu	Pr	Pu	Pr	Pu	Pr	Pu	Pr	Pu	Pr	Pu	Pr	Pu	Pr
Line Management	8	8	21	23	*		16	7	10	21	3	12	4	14	50	5	62	19	6	4	44	31	2	5
Line Management with HR department	32	40	29	32	38	32	38	47	39	40	15	12	19	34	0	31	8	49	43	39	13	22	16	24
HR Department with line management	33	46	36	35	25	25	27	39	26	27	25	40	49	44	50	40	0	23	49	52	13	21	45	53
HR Department	22	5	12	8	0	4	11	6	18	11	35	29	22	6	0	21	8	8	2	6	0	18	26	14

Less than 1,000 or greater than or equal to 1,000 employees

Less than 1,000 / ≥ 1,000 employees	D(W)		DK		E		F		FIN		IRL		N		NL		P		S		T		UK	
	<1	≥1	<1	≥1	<1	≥1	<1	≥1	<1	≥1	<1	≥1	<1	≥1	<1	≥1	<1	≥1	<1	≥1	<1	≥1	<1	≥1
Line Management	10	4	31	8	40	17	10	7	19	11	6	9	10	6	4	12	35	9	4	4	35	28	7	3
Line Management with HR department	40	37	28	35	37	40	45	45	39	43	14	6	28	28	28	39	44	36	37	44	22	20	22	20
HR Department with line management	43	46	32	42	21	33	37	38	25	31	38	31	43	53	44	23	16	27	52	48	14	26	48	53
HR Department	6	11	9	11	1	7	5	9	13	14	28	47	13	9	23	19	3	23	6	3	17	15	18	18

Table 2.6b: Primary responsibility for major policy decisions on recruitment and selection

Country	D(W)	DK	E	F	FIN	IRL	N	NL	P	S	T	UK
Line Management	8	25	13	3	17	10	13	6	14	18	22	6
Line Management with HR department	42	46	24	39	63	21	56	47	38	59	27	38
HR Department with line management	44	22	40	51	14	45	24	35	33	23	29	43
HR Department	5	5	22	6	3	15	5	9	15	0	13	10

Private and public sector

	D(W)		DK		E *		F		FIN		IRL		N		NL *		P *		S		T *		UK	
	Pu	Pr	Pu	Pr	Pu	Pr	Pu	Pr	Pu	Pr	Pu	Pr	Pu	Pr	Pu	Pr	Pu	Pr	Pu	Pr	Pu	Pr	Pu	Pr
Line Management	8	8	33	19	31	11	2	3	18	16	5	14	10	12	50	6	39	10	29	8	44	18	7	5
Line Management with HR department	28	44	38	51	13	25	40	39	63	65	23	21	44	65	0	48	46	34	56	63	19	28	38	40
HR Department with line management	50	44	19	25	25	41	44	53	11	15	33	49	33	17	50	34	8	38	15	29	13	33	38	44
HR Department	13	4	9	3	25	22	13	5	2	2	23	10	9	3	0	9	8	18	0	0	0	14	13	9

Less than 1,000 or greater than or equal to 1,000 employees

	D(W)		DK		E		F		FIN		IRL		N		NL		P		S		T		UK	
	<1	>1	<1	>1	<1	>1	<1	>1	<1	>1	<1	>1	<1	>1	<1	>1	<1	>1	<1	>1	<1	>1	<1	>1
Line Management	9	5	23	27	17	5	4	2	16	18	10	9	12	13	5	12	17	5	9	26	23	20	7	5
Line Management with HR department	42	42	46	47	25	20	41	35	60	70	20	22	52	67	47	46	37	41	56	61	26	36	36	40
HR Department with line management	44	45	24	19	38	46	48	56	17	10	50	31	28	15	37	23	31	41	33	13	28	42	42	43
HR Department	4	8	6	5	19	27	6	6	3	3	11	28	6	3	10	8	16	14	1	0	10	17	11	10

Table 2.6c: Primary responsibility for major policy decisions on training and development

Country

	D(W)	DK	E	F	FIN	IRL	N	NL	P	S	T	UK
Line Management	9	19	9	2	14	7	14	6	18	16	21	4
Line Management with HR department	20	43	23	32	50	17	46	34	30	55	21	27
HR Department with line management	31	26	50	57	26	54	31	46	37	26	32	57
HR Department	39	9	15	8	4	13	5	13	12	3	11	10

Private and public sector

	D(W)	DK		E		F		FIN		IRL		N		NL		P		S		T		UK	
	Pr	Pu	Pr	Pu	Pr	Pu	Pr	Pu	Pr	Pu	Pr	Pu	Pr	Pu	Pr	Pu	Pr	Pu	Pr	Pu	Pr	Pu	Pr
Line Management	5	26	15	19	19	1	3	13	15	5	9	10	14	0	6	23	14	24	10	38	17	4	4
Line Management with HR department	15	35	48	19	24	23	34	48	51	18	16	36	57	50	34	39	30	54	58	25	21	27	26
HR Department with line management	27	23	28	31	50	61	55	27	26	48	56	40	25	0	46	31	38	21	29	13	35	52	59
HR Department	51	15	6	25	15	14	6	2	4	13	14	10	1	50	11	8	14	1	3	0	13	13	8

Less than 1,000 or greater than or equal to 1,000 employees

	D(W)		DK		E		F		FIN		IRL		N		NL		P		S		T		UK	
	<1	>1	<1	>1	<1	>1	<1	>1	<1	>1	<1	>1	<1	>1	<1	>1	<1	>1	<1	>1	<1	>1	<1	>1
Line Management	10	6	22	14	12	5	2	2	15	13	7	6	15	13	4	12	21	9	10	22	21	22	6	3
Line Management with HR department	21	18	43	43	27	18	30	34	48	54	16	19	42	58	36	27	30	32	55	57	22	20	24	28
HR Department with line management	33	28	26	26	44	60	55	59	25	29	57	50	33	26	44	50	31	55	31	20	26	41	58	56
HR Department	33	48	9	12	15	15	11	5	4	1	12	16	7	1	15	4	14	5	4	1	14	4	10	11

Table 2.6d: Primary responsibility for major policy decisions on industrial relations

Country	D(W)	DK	E	F	FIN	IRL	N	NL	P	S	T	UK
Line Management	37	20	15	2	7	8	7	9	29	7	25	4
Line Management with HR department	22	21	17	14	24	19	15	38	14	17	16	24
HR Department with line management	20	30	41	37	32	43	35	31	20	47	19	48
HR Department	16	26	20	46	31	22	40	19	17	28	28	20

Private and public sector

	D(W)		DK		E*		F		FIN		IRL		N		NL*		P*		S		T*		UK	
	Pu	Pr	Pu	Pr	Pu	Pr	Pu	Pr	Pu	Pr	Pu	Pr	Pu	Pr	Pu	Pr	Pu	Pr	Pu	Pr	Pu	Pr	Pu	Pr
Line Management	25	39	16	23	19	15	3	2	5	6	3	11	3	9	0	9	23	32	13	2	38	23	2	4
Line Management with HR department	13	23	16	23	0	18	23	12	18	26	20	19	7	18	50	39	15	12	22	16	19	17	23	25
HR Department with line management	31	19	40	24	38	41	40	37	36	30	43	40	38	36	50	29	15	22	46	49	19	20	43	50
HR Department	22	15	28	24	19	21	33	48	31	35	20	23	48	34	0	19	8	21	19	33	0	30	28	17

Less than 1,000 or greater than or equal to 1,000 employees

	D(W)		DK		E		F		FIN		IRL		N		NL		P		S		T		UK	
	<1	>1	<1	>1	<1	>1	<1	>1	<1	>1	<1	>1	<1	>1	<1	>1	<1	>1	<1	>1	<1	>1	<1	>1
Line Management	37	36	25	10	19	<1	3	2	5	6	8	6	7	6	8	12	34	14	5	9	30	17	6	3
Line Management with HR department	22	22	23	16	18	16	13	15	26	21	19	15	14	15	34	54	13	18	16	20	14	20	21	26
HR Department with line management	20	21	25	41	40	42	36	37	30	40	42	50	33	42	33	19	21	18	46	48	18	20	48	47
HR Department	16	16	23	30	15	31	46	46	35	26	22	19	42	33	22	8	11	36	33	23	23	35	19	21

Table 2.6e: Primary responsibility for major policy decisions on health and safety

Country

	D(W)	DK	E	F	FIN	IRL	N	NL	P	S	T	UK
Line Management	11	37	10	12	6	15	16	9	18	24	20	13
Line Management with HR department	39	27	20	25	24	21	30	40	28	30	20	32
HR Department with line management	36	20	37	35	31	44	34	34	18	27	18	37
HR Department	12	13	28	26	33	14	16	14	29	19	29	15

Private and public sector

	D(W)		DK		E *		F		FIN		IRL		N		NL *		P *		S		T *		UK	
	Pu	Pr	Pu	Pr	Pu	Pr	Pu	Pr	Pu	Pr	Pu	Pr	Pu	Pr	Pu	Pr	Pu	Pr	Pu	Pr	Pu	Pr	Pu	Pr
Line Management	8	12	34	39	25	9	7	13	5	6	10	17	9	21	0	9	15	18	26	21	25	19	10	13
Line Management with HR department	32	39	21	31	19	20	25	24	19	26	23	20	30	29	50	42	31	27	27	35	25	19	32	33
HR Department with line management	36	37	23	18	25	39	31	36	36	29	33	47	35	36	0	34	23	18	33	23	13	20	34	37
HR Department	19	11	19	10	19	28	33	25	29	37	20	11	21	11	50	13	8	34	14	21	13	32	16	14

Less than 1,000 or greater than or equal to 1,000 employees

	D(W)		DK		E		F		FIN		IRL		N		NL		P		S		T		UK	
	<1	>1	<1	>1	<1	>1	<1	>1	<1	>1	<1	>1	<1	>1	<1	>1	<1	>1	<1	>1	<1	>1	<1	>1
Line Management	13	9	38	34	11	7	12	11	6	5	15	13	17	15	9	12	23	5	22	26	22	17	14	11
Line Management with HR department	40	37	27	28	19	21	24	25	23	28	19	28	27	36	41	39	31	18	30	31	18	24	30	33
HR Department with line management	34	39	20	19	40	34	34	36	28	39	44	41	35	32	33	35	16	27	23	30	18	17	37	37
HR Department	11	14	13	14	25	34	26	27	39	24	16	9	16	14	16	8	27	36	25	12	27	33	14	16

Table 2.6f: Primary responsibility for major policy decisions on workforce expansion/reduction

Country	D(W)	DK	E	F	FIN	IRL	N	NL	P	S	T	UK
Line Management	11	35	21	10	25	15	10	13	15	18	28	10
Line Management with HR department	37	40	35	38	52	26	33	50	31	46	28	53
HR Department with line management	35	16	36	35	12	40	32	28	23	28	27	26
HR Department	15	7	7	15	6	12	19	6	27	7	7	7

Private and public sector

	D(W)		DK		E *		F		FIN		IRL		N *		NL *		P *		S		T *		UK	
	Pu	Pr	Pu	Pr	Pu	Pr	Pu	Pr	Pu	Pr	Pu	Pr	Pu	Pr	Pu	Pr	Pu	Pr	Pu	Pr	Pu	Pr	Pu	Pr
Line Management	5	13	40	32	31	20	16	9	15	31	8	19	3	16	50	13	23	14	24	11	38	25	7	10
Line Management with HR department	30	37	28	46	19	36	36	39	50	52	20	30	18	40	0	51	31	30	46	48	19	29	49	56
HR Department with line management	42	35	19	50	44	35	27	36	19	9	35	40	41	32	0	29	15	22	21	34	13	29	29	25
HR Department	20	14	12	4	0	8	19	14	7	5	20	6	29	8	50	4	23	30	7	7	6	8	9	7

Less than 1,000 or greater than or equal to 1,000 employees

	D(W)		DK		E		F		FIN		IRL		N		NL		P		S		T		UK	
	<1	>1	<1	>1	<1	>1	<1	>1	<1	>1	<1	>1	<1	>1	<1	>1	<1	>1	<1	>1	<1	>1	<1	>1
Line Management	14	8	34	36	24	17	12	8	25	24	16	9	11	6	12	19	20	0	12	24	26	30	10	9
Line Management with HR department	37	37	42	36	37	30	40	36	51	54	27	28	30	41	48	58	35	18	46	48	29	26	50	56
HR Department with line management	34	38	17	15	31	43	33	37	12	16	42	31	34	27	31	15	17	41	34	21	26	28	28	25
HR Department	14	16	6	9	7	7	13	18	7	3	8	22	18	22	7	0	24	36	7	6	8	7	8	7

Table 2.7a: Percentage change in responsibility of line management for pay and benefits over the last three years

Country

	D(W)	DK	E	F	FIN	IRL	N	NL	P	S	T	UK
Increased	18	30	34	35	38	12	33	18	18	64	27	26
Same	72	60	62	58	55	81	59	69	68	34	59	65
Decreased	8	8	3	4	6	3	4	10	9	2	5	7

Private and public sector

	D(W)		DK		E *		F		FIN		IRL		N		NL *		P *		S		T *		UK	
	Pu	Pr	Pu	Pr	Pu	Pr	Pu	Pr	Pu	Pr	Pu	Pr	Pu	Pr	Pu	Pr	Pu	Pr	Pu	Pr	Pu	Pr	Pu	Pr
Increased	18	17	50	16	25	35	29	36	47	29	13	10	42	26	100	17	8	19	76	57	44	25	39	21
Same	70	73	45	70	70	60	62	57	47	62	83	81	55	61	0	71	62	70	24	39	31	62	56	69
Decreased	4	9	4	11	0	4	3	4	5	8	0	5	1	7	0	10	8	8	0	4	6	5	3	8

Less than 1,000 or greater than or equal to 1,000 employees

	D(W)		DK		E		F		FIN		IRL		N		NL		P		S		T		UK	
	<1	>1	<1	>1	<1	>1	<1	>1	<1	>1	<1	>1	<1	>1	<1	>1	<1	>1	<1	>1	<1	>1	<1	>1
Increased	21	14	28	32	36	32	35	34	35	43	12	9	30	41	17	23	16	27	56	72	33	17	21	30
Same	69	78	64	54	58	66	57	58	48	59	80	88	62	50	73	58	73	50	41	25	51	72	69	62
Decreased	9	7	7	10	4	2	3	4	5	9	4	0	5	4	10	12	7	14	3	2	5	4	8	6

Table 2.7b: Percentage change in responsibility of line management for recruitment and selection over the last three years

Country

	D(W)	DK	E	F	FIN	IRL	N	NL	P	S	T	UK
Increased	17	32	38	38	45	30	49	43	20	64	16	31
Same	72	56	55	52	46	61	43	52	60	35	59	59
Decreased	10	10	5	7	7	5	5	5	18	1	15	8

Private and public sector

	D(W)		DK		E *		F		FIN		IRL		N		NL *		P *		S		T *		UK	
	Pu	Pr	Pu	Pr	Pu	Pr	Pu	Pr	Pu	Pr	Pu	Pr	Pu	Pr	Pu	Pr	Pu	Pr	Pu	Pr	Pu	Pr	Pu	Pr
Increased	24	16	44	23	38	38	44	36	53	35	18	32	60	40	100	41	15	19	70	60	13	17	42	27
Same	67	74	47	63	50	55	45	54	39	55	68	62	33	47	0	54	62	62	29	39	50	59	49	63
Decreased	8	10	8	12	6	5	5	7	9	5	9	10	5	8	0	5	15	19	1	2	13	16	7	8

Less than 1,000 or greater than or equal to 1,000 employees

	D(W)		DK		E		F		FIN		IRL		N		NL		P		S		T		UK	
	<1	>1	<1	>1	<1	>1	<1	>1	<1	>1	<1	>1	<1	>1	<1	>1	<1	>1	<1	>1	<1	>1	<1	>1
Increased	18	16	32	32	37	39	36	40	43	49	29	34	45	60	39	43	20	23	61	67	16	17	42	27
Same	70	74	58	53	54	56	53	51	48	43	61	63	46	35	52	54	62	55	37	31	56	63	62	57
Decreased	10	9	9	12	6	3	7	5	8	8	7	0	7	1	5	4	17	23	1	2	16	13	9	7

Table 2.7c: Percentage change in responsibility of line management for training and development over the last three years

Country	D(W)	DK	E	F	FIN	IRL	N	NL	P	S	T	UK
Increased	13	39	53	55	51	43	56	50	18	67	20	46
Same	78	49	45	38	40	53	37	42	66	31	59	44
Decreased	7	10	2	3	7	1	4	7	14	2	10	8

Private and public sector

	D(W)		DK		E		F		FIN		IRL		N		NL		P		S		T		UK	
	Pu	Pr	Pu	Pr	Pu	Pr	Pu	Pr	Pu	Pr	Pu	Pr	Pu	Pr	Pu	Pr	Pu	Pr	Pu	Pr	Pu	Pr	Pu	Pr
Increased	12	14	53	28	44	54	63	52	60	44	30	45	62	54	100	50	8	19	71	66	13	21	51	44
Same	81	78	40	56	50	44	32	41	32	48	63	52	32	36	0	43	69	66	28	30	50	60	41	46
Decreased	4	7	5	14	0	2	1	4	5	7	3	1	4	5	0	7	15	14	1	4	13	10	6	8

Less than 1,000 or greater than or equal to 1,000 employees

	D(W)		DK		E		F		FIN		IRL		N		NL		P		S		T		UK	
	<1	>1	<1	>1	<1	>1	<1	>1	<1	>1	<1	>1	<1	>1	<1	>1	<1	>1	<1	>1	<1	>1	<1	>1
Increased	14	11	36	45	45	66	54	56	49	58	39	53	52	67	45	69	16	27	63	72	21	17	41	50
Same	75	83	53	41	51	33	39	37	44	34	56	47	41	28	47	23	68	59	35	26	53	70	47	42
Decreased	8	5	10	11	2	1	3	4	6	8	2	0	5	1	8	4	14	14	2	3	13	3	4	6

Table 2.7d: Percentage change in responsibility of line management for industrial relations over the last three years

Country	D(W)	DK	E	F	FIN	IRL	N	NL	P	S	T	UK
Increased	14	15	28	20	22	34	19	32	9	39	16	24
Same	77	73	63	71	68	59	72	61	59	58	59	67
Decreased	6	9	2	4	8	1	5	6	13	3	13	6

Private and public sector

	D(W)		DK		E		F		FIN		IRL		N		NL		P		S		T		UK	
	Pu	Pr	Pu	Pr	Pu	Pr	Pu	Pr	Pu	Pr	Pu	Pr	Pu	Pr	Pu	Pr	Pu	Pr	Pu	Pr	Pu	Pr	Pu	Pr
Increased	15	14	25	7	19	29	29	18	27	17	35	30	24	17	50	32	0	10	54	29	6	18	29	22
Same	78	77	67	79	56	63	64	73	65	71	58	62	69	71	50	61	54	63	45	67	63	58	64	68
Decreased	3	7	7	9	6	2	2	3	5	7	0	2	3	8	0	6	0	15	1	4	6	15	4	6

Less than 1,000 or greater than or equal to 1,000 employees

	D(W)		DK		E		F		FIN		IRL		N		NL		P		S		T		UK	
	<1	>1	<1	>1	<1	>1	<1	>1	<1	>1	<1	>1	<1	>1	<1	>1	<1	>1	<1	>1	<1	>1	<1	>1
Increased	16	11	12	19	22	38	20	20	21	23	32	38	18	22	29	39	9	9	31	48	18	13	21	27
Same	74	83	76	69	68	54	72	71	68	69	59	59	73	71	63	54	58	64	65	51	53	70	68	65
Decreased	8	4	8	9	2	2	3	6	9	8	8	2	5	4	7	4	14	9	4	1	16	9	9	4

Table 2.7e: Percentage change in responsibility of line management for health and safety over the last three years

Country	D(W)	DK	E	F	FIN	IRL	N	NL	P	S	T	UK
Increased	16	18	32	33	15	57	40	50	13	57	20	39
Same	77	75	63	62	78	38	54	45	72	41	58	57
Decreased	3	4	2	1	6	1	2	5	11	2	11	3

Private and public sector

	D(W)		DK		E *		F		FIN		IRL		N		NL *		P *		S		T *		UK	
	Pu	Pr	Pu	Pr	Pu	Pr	Pu	Pr	Pu	Pr	Pu	Pr	Pu	Pr	Pu	Pr	Pu	Pr	Pu	Pr	Pu	Pr	Pu	Pr
Increased	9	18	23	14	25	33	32	34	15	11	68	49	44	38	50	50	15	12	64	51	13	22	37	39
Same	83	77	73	78	69	62	62	62	82	80	28	46	52	53	50	45	62	73	34	46	50	58	58	56
Decreased	3	4	2	6	0	2	2	1	1	2	0	2	2	3	0	5	0	14	1	2	2	6	3	3

Less than 1,000 or greater than or equal to 1,000 employees

	D(W)		DK		E		F		FIN		IRL		N		NL		P		S		T		UK	
	<1	>1	<1	>1	<1	>1	<1	>1	<1	>1	<1	>1	<1	>1	<1	>1	<1	>1	<1	>1	<1	>1	<1	>1
Increased	16	17	15	24	29	37	36	30	11	19	54	69	40	40	47	58	13	14	52	63	17	26	34	42
Same	77	77	78	68	66	56	59	65	79	78	41	31	54	55	48	35	70	77	47	35	58	57	61	53
Decreased	4	3	4	5	1	3	1	2	2	9	2	0	3	0	5	4	4	0	2	2	2	12	3	3

Table 2.7f: Percentage change in responsibility of line management for workforce expansion/reduction over the last three years

Country	D(W)	DK	E	F	FIN	IRL	N	NL	P	S	T	UK
Increased	16	28	33	25	51	25	19	39	15	46	20	30
Same	73	64	60	63	40	70	74	56	63	49	46	63
Decreased	9	4	4	7	8	1	2	5	17	5	23	5

Private and public sector

	D(W)		DK		E *		F		FIN		IRL		N		NL *		P *		S		T *		UK	
	Pu	Pr	Pu	Pr	Pu	Pr	Pu	Pr	Pu	Pr	Pu	Pr	Pu	Pr	Pu	Pr	Pu	Pr	Pu	Pr	Pu	Pr	Pu	Pr
Increased	22	14	38	20	25	34	36	23	55	46	25	22	14	19	100	37	0	16	54	38	6	23	39	27
Same	68	74	57	71	50	60	46	66	36	44	65	76	80	71	0	58	62	64	42	57	38	47	55	66
Decreased	5	10	2	6	19	3	10	7	8	9	5	0	2	3	0	4	23	16	3	5	31	22	4	5

Less than 1,000 or greater than or equal to 1,000 employees

	D(W)		DK		E		F		FIN		IRL		N		NL		P		S		T		UK	
	<1	>1	<1	>1	<1	>1	<1	>1	<1	>1	<1	>1	<1	>1	<1	>1	<1	>1	<1	>1	<1	>1	<1	>1
Increased	16	15	27	32	28	45	24	26	59	47	26	17	12	35	37	42	14	18	42	49	14	30	39	35
Same	71	76	66	62	65	50	65	60	31	44	69	78	82	56	60	42	66	55	52	47	49	41	67	60
Decreased	10	7	5	4	4	4	6	9	9	8	2	0	2	3	3	12	16	23	6	3	25	20	7	31

Table 2.8: Percentage of organisations where the performance of the personnel department is systematically evaluated

Country

	D(W)	DK	E	F	FIN	IRL	N	NL	P	S	T	UK
Yes	23	29	50	43	41	35	45	39	40	42	47	46
No	72	60	45	53	42	51	44	54	45	55	46	48
Don't know	3	5	3	3	4	4	5	4	8	4	3	2
No personnel dept	1	4	2	0	13	7	1	2	5	0	0	2

Private and public sector

	D(W) Pu	Pr	DK Pu	Pr	E* Pu	Pr	F Pu	Pr	FIN Pu	Pr	IRL Pu	Pr	N Pu	Pr	NL* Pu	Pr	P* Pu	Pr	S Pu	Pr	T* Pu	Pr	UK Pu	Pr
Yes	23	23	21	33	94	49	39	44	36	44	18	39	31	57	0	39	0	45	36	45	50	48	45	46
No	75	72	71	52	6	46	56	51	52	40	70	45	55	36	100	53	85	38	61	50	38	45	52	48
Don't know	2	4	3	7	0	3	2	3	2	4	5	2	2	8	0	5	8	8	3	4	13	2	1	3
No personnel dept	0	1	2	5	0	2	2	0	0	10	3	11	2	1	0	2	0	7	0	1	0	0	0	3

Less than 1,000 or greater than or equal to 1,000 employees

	D(W) <1	>1	DK <1	>1	E <1	>1	F <1	>1	FIN <1	>1	IRL <1	>1	N <1	>1	NL <1	>1	P <1	>1	S <1	>1	T <1	>1	UK <1	>1
Yes	20	28	27	31	41	68	39	47	37	49	36	34	43	50	36	50	37	50	37	44	40	59	43	49
No	74	70	57	65	52	31	56	49	44	41	49	53	45	44	60	27	45	46	58	54	52	35	48	48
Don't know	5	2	6	3	4	1	3	2	3	3	4	3	7	1	3	12	10	0	4	3	4	2	3	2
No personnel dept	2	0	6	0	2	0	0	0	15	6	8	3	2	0	1	4	6	5	0	1	0	0	4	0

Table 2.9: Criteria used to evaluate performance of the personnel dept. (Valid %) (+)

Country

	D(W)	DK	E	F	FIN	IRL	N	NL	P	S	T	UK
Nos of employees per staff	52	38	71	59	22	39	35	44	52	32	59	44
Function cost per employee	35	29	65	44	18	35	35	33	50	37	68	45
Numbers recruited	60	34	79	66	13	49	31	54	78	31	73	54
Numbers trained	62	47	85	74	24	69	40	47	89	28	73	68
Performance against budget	81	78	95	84	38	91	83	75	84	97	74	90
Perf. against objectives	36	96	97	85	38	94	96	86	90	87	89	90
Feedback from line mgmt	73	87	71	53	33	75	87	83	86	84	65	96

Private and public sector

	D(W)		DK		E *		F		FIN		IRL		N		NL *		P *		S		T *		UK	
	Pu	Pr	Pu	Pr	Pu	Pr	Pu	Pr	Pu	Pr	Pu	Pr	Pu	Pr	Pu	Pr	Pu	Pr	Pu	Pr	Pu	Pr	Pu	Pr
Nos of employees per staff	60	50	63	31	75	70	55	62	54	50	57	32	37	34	0	44	0	53	47	19	100	58	43	42
Function cost per employee	22	34	25	30	64	65	43	44	42	44	17	39	28	36	0	32	100	44	38	35	100	65	45	45
Numbers recruited	74	57	25	37	83	78	68	65	38	25	33	42	35	28	0	54	100	78	41	24	100	72	60	53
Numbers trained	74	60	44	47	73	86	91	69	71	58	50	67	35	40	0	47	100	91	39	22	100	70	66	68
Performance against budget	86	81	53	87	83	97	81	85	88	97	67	97	63	86	0	75	100	81	100	94	100	70	81	94
Perf. against objectives	33	36	91	97	87	98	70	88	79	97	89	97	96	95	0	85	100	96	84	90	100	89	94	97
Feedback from line mgmt	58	75	92	86	62	72	56	52	83	81	67	88	88	81	0	85	0	92	91	82	100	63	87	89

Less than 1,000 or greater than or equal to 1,000 employees

	D(W)		DK		E		F		FIN		IRL		N		NL		P		S		T		UK	
	<1	>1	<1	>1	<1	>1	<1	>1	<1	>1	<1	>1	<1	>1	<1	>1	<1	>1	<1	>1	<1	>1	<1	>1
Nos of employees per staff	40	66	35	43	62	80	53	67	56	48	31	60	30	46	43	47	57	43	23	41	53	70	41	46
Function cost per employee	31	39	26	35	65	65	39	51	41	43	33	50	32	41	31	36	62	29	32	42	65	73	46	45
Numbers recruited	54	66	29	42	77	81	64	69	27	31	48	50	28	40	62	40	79	75	22	39	63	90	51	57
Numbers trained	56	68	46	50	79	90	76	71	51	69	72	57	41	39	52	40	95	75	20	38	61	92	67	68
Performance against budget	78	85	81	74	94	96	83	85	93	90	91	81	84	81	76	73	75	100	97	98	85	67	91	90
Perf. against objectives	39	32	97	94	97	96	84	86	95	88	92	92	96	97	91	73	91	90	85	90	81	96	96	90
Feedback from line mgmt	71	75	87	87	63	80	54	52	81	80	72	89	81	97	83	85	86	88	78	89	40	90	89	90

Table 2.10: Percentage of organisations who carry out manpower planning

Country	D(W)	DK	E	F	FIN	IRL	N	NL	P	S	T	UK
Yes	87	73	86	65	89	83	45	74	77	81	81	74
No	12	25	14	32	8	15	49	21	20	19	17	24

Private and public sector

	D(W)		DK		E		F		FIN		IRL		N		NL		P		S		T		UK	
	Pu	Pr	Pu	Pr	Pu	Pr	Pu	Pr	Pu	Pr	Pu	Pr	Pu	Pr	Pu	Pr	Pu	Pr	Pu	Pr	Pu	Pr	Pu	Pr
					*										*		*				*			
Yes	86	87	71	75	94	85	60	65	87	90	85	82	42	46	50	74	77	81	74	89	100	80	68	76
No	11	13	27	24	6	15	36	33	7	10	15	16	54	46	50	21	15	19	26	11	0	18	28	22

Less than 1,000 or greater than or equal to 1,000 employees

	D(W)		DK		E		F		FIN		IRL		N		NL		P		S		T		UK	
	<1	>1	<1	>1	<1	>1	<1	>1	<1	>1	<1	>1	<1	>1	<1	>1	<1	>1	<1	>1	<1	>1	<1	>1
Yes	84	91	75	70	83	90	61	71	88	93	82	88	47	42	75	73	76	82	83	81	78	87	71	76
No	15	9	23	29	17	10	36	27	11	4	16	13	48	51	21	23	23	14	17	19	20	13	26	22

Table 2.11: Percentage of organisations using manpower planning methods. (Valid %) (+)

Country

	D(W)	DK	E	F	FIN	IRL	N	NL	P	S	T	UK
Recruit to maintain current staff ratios	84	70	74	65	9	76	19	94	70	48	92	63
Forecast of future skill requirements	86	92	82	94	81	95	80	34	93	90	85	94
Sales forecasts	88	52	87	78	68	71	75	63	74	87	90	83
Analysis of labour markets	45	46	60	37	37	33	32	62	74	38	74	59

Private and public sector

	D(W)		DK		E		F		FIN		IRL		N		NL		P		S		T		UK	
	Pu	Pr	Pu	Pr	Pu	Pr	Pu	Pr	Pu	Pr	Pu	Pr	Pu	Pr	Pu	Pr	Pu	Pr	Pu	Pr	Pu	Pr	Pu	Pr
Recruit to maintain current staff ratios	89	82	79	64	*		59	64	11	82	93	63	11	23	100	93	*		45	50	*		76	56
Forecast of future skill requirements	84	86	91	93	79	83	97	94	91	93	96	94	79	81	0	36	100	92	94	88	100	85	94	94
Sales forecasts	65	91	16	64	64	90	83	76	79	81	36	78	74	75	0	65	0	78	94	84	100	89	68	87
Analysis of labour markets	41	45	38	49	50	62	35	37	42	47	25	27	32	30	0	62	0	81	47	30	0	76	70	57

Less than 1,000 or greater than or equal to 1,000 employees

	D(W)		DK		E		F		FIN		IRL		N		NL		P		S		T		UK	
	<1	>1	<1	>1	<1	>1	<1	>1	<1	>1	<1	>1	<1	>1	<1	>1	<1	>1	<1	>1	<1	>1	<1	>1
Recruit to maintain current staff ratios	83	85	70	69	72	75	67	64	10	8	75	80	20	16	92	100	69	73	52	43	93	91	63	62
Forecast of future skill requirements	85	88	92	93	76	92	93	96	91	92	95	96	78	84	36	30	91	100	86	93	84	87	94	94
Sales forecasts	88	86	58	37	84	94	74	82	76	82	70	81	71	85	66	50	74	75	89	88	84	100	84	83
Analysis of labour markets	41	51	43	52	56	66	30	47	39	47	22	73	29	37	60	71	77	100	49	29	79	64	54	64

Table 2.12: Percentage of organisations collecting the following categories of data on the workforce for manpower planning. (+)

Country	D(W)	DK	E	F	FIN	IRL	N	NL	P	S	T	UK
Staff turnover	71	58	66	64	89	69	69	94	61	81	50	82
Age profile	77	67	68	70	88	59	66	83	77	80	45	73
Qualifications & training	62	74	77	77	88	72	79	80	74	73	70	66
Absence levels	54	48	63	46	83	65	76	87	80	70	44	64

Private and public sector

	D(W)		DK		E*		F		FIN		IRL		N		NL		P*		S		T*		UK	
	Pu	Pr	Pu	Pr	Pu	Pr	Pu	Pr	Pu	Pr	Pu	Pr	Pu	Pr	Pu	Pr	Pu	Pr	Pu	Pr	Pu	Pr	Pu	Pr
Staff turnover	78	69	53	63	62	67	56	66	95	89	67	68	61	80	100	94	23	67	79	83	25	56	79	83
Age profile	82	76	66	69	69	68	74	69	89	89	65	57	48	79	100	82	61	81	87	75	42	45	73	74
Qualifications & training	67	61	67	78	75	78	75	77	89	92	72	71	76	82	50	81	69	75	71	76	87	69	59	67
Absence levels	39	54	46	51	69	63	50	46	93	81	67	63	74	80	100	86	77	81	74	67	37	45	67	64

Less than 1,000 or greater than or equal to 1,000 employees

	D(W)		DK		E		F		FIN		IRL		N		NL		P		S		T		UK	
	<1	>1	<1	>1	<1	>1	<1	>1	<1	>1	<1	>1	<1	>1	<1	>1	<1	>1	<1	>1	<1	>1	<1	>1
Staff turnover	65	80	57	60	63	73	61	69	89	92	66	70	69	69	93	96	58	73	79	84	48	54	80	84
Age profile	74	82	68	67	61	79	67	75	88	90	69	57	65	68	83	81	73	91	74	87	43	48	67	77
Qualifications & training	59	67	76	69	72	87	77	77	90	90	71	75	79	79	79	85	75	73	71	77	66	76	64	67
Absence levels	53	54	48	49	65	62	48	43	81	91	66	65	78	73	87	85	77	86	67	75	40	50	68	61

Table 2.13a: Percentage of organisations monitoring the following in the workplace with regards to recruitment. (+)

Country	D(W)	DK	E	F	FIN	IRL	N	NL	P	S	T	UK
People with disabilities	39	8	14	34	11	28	6	28	8	8	72	60
Women	35	15	25	22	18	40	38	33	33	41	34	53
People from ethnic minorities	21	4	3	0	4	3	5	25	7	6	8	53

Private and public sector

	D(W)		DK		E*		F		FIN		IRL		N		NL		P*		S		T*		UK	
	Pu	Pr	Pu	Pr	Pu	Pr	Pu	Pr	Pu	Pr	Pu	Pr	Pu	Pr	Pu	Pr	Pu	Pr	Pu	Pr	Pu	Pr	Pu	Pr
People with disabilities	58	37	12	5	31	13	41	33	13	9	50	18	8	5	50	28	8	8	11	7	81	71	77	54
Women	48	32	21	12	13	27	25	22	16	15	55	34	51	34	0	32	0	4	47	37	50	32	72	45
People from ethnic minorities	6	24	2	5	0	3	ni	ni	5	2	3	1	2	8	0	24	0	7	8	4	0	10	72	46

Less than 1,000 or greater than or equal to 1,000 employees

	D(W)		DK		E		F		FIN		IRL		N		NL		P		S		T		UK	
	<1	>1	<1	>1	<1	>1	<1	>1	<1	>1	<1	>1	<1	>1	<1	>1	<1	>1	<1	>1	<1	>1	<1	>1
People with disabilities	39	40	6	11	13	6	9	17	7	15	25	41	5	9	24	42	8	4	7	10	75	67	55	65
Women	34	36	12	20	22	32	20	24	17	23	37	53	36	44	31	39	31	41	33	50	36	30	46	59
People from ethnic minorities	21	23	4	4	3	2	ni	ni	3	3	3	3	5	6	25	27	8	0	6	6	13	0	44	60

ni question not included in country

Table 2.13b: Percentage of organisations monitoring the following in the workplace with regards to training.(+)

Country	D(W)	DK	E	F	FIN	IRL	N	NL	P	S	T	UK
People with disabilities	10	1	6	12	18	11	6	21	2	4	11	17
Women	19	11	15	20	14	28	26	21	19	34	15	25
People from ethnic minorities	7	1	2	0	3	1	4	17	3	3	7	18

Private and public sector

	D(W)		DK		E		F		FIN		IRL		N		NL		P		S		T		UK	
	Pu	Pr	Pu	Pr	Pu	Pr	Pu	Pr	Pu	Pr	Pu	Pr	Pu	Pr	Pu	Pr	Pu	Pr	Pu	Pr	Pu	Pr	Pu	Pr
People with disabilities	15	9	2	1	6	7	19	11	24	15	15	6	9	5	50	20	0	3	6	2	19	10	17	17
Women	34	17	16	7	13	15	22	20	18	10	43	23	34	25	0	20	8	21	39	29	25	14	29	23
People from ethnic minorities	1	8	0	1	0	2	ni	ni	7	2	3	0	2	5	0	16	0	3	5	2	0	7	22	17

Less than 1,000 or greater than or equal to 1,000 employees

	D(W)		DK		E		F		FIN		IRL		N		NL		P		S		T		UK	
	<1	>1	<1	>1	<1	>1	<1	>1	<1	>1	<1	>1	<1	>1	<1	>1	<1	>1	<1	>1	<1	>1	<1	>1
People with disabilities	9	12	1	0	5	10	4	9	16	19	10	13	6	8	24	12	3	0	3	4	9	13	17	17
Women	16	25	11	21	14	17	16	25	13	16	24	47	24	31	21	19	17	27	29	40	10	22	23	26
People from ethnic minorities	7	7	1	2	2	0	ni	ni	4	3	3	1	3	5	20	8	4	0	2	4	7	4	16	20

ni question not included in country

Table 2.13c: Percentage of organisations monitoring the following in the workplace with regards to promotion.(+)

Country	D(W)	DK	E	F	FIN	IRL	N	NL	P	S	T	UK
People with disabilities	5	0	3	6	2	7	1	8	1	2	5	17
Women	14	15	17	21	13	33	27	20	18	35	8	34
People from ethnic minorities	3	0	1	0	2	1	1	11	3	1	2	24

Private and public sector

	D(W)		DK		E		F		FIN		IRL		N		NL		P		S		T		UK	
	Pu	Pr	Pu	Pr	Pu	Pr	Pu	Pr	Pu	Pr	Pu	Pr	Pu	Pr	Pu	Pr	Pu	Pr	Pu	Pr	Pu	Pr	Pu	Pr
People with disabilities	10	5	0	0	13	2	11	5	2	2	15	2	1	1	50	7	0	0	1	1	6	5	23	14
Women	33	11	23	9	13	18	20	22	16	9	53	27	30	28	0	20	22	0	42	30	6	8	40	31
People from ethnic minorities	0	4	0	0	0	1	ni	ni	7	1	3	0	0	2	0	10	0	3	1	1	0	2	34	20

Less than 1,000 or greater than or equal to 1,000 employees

	D(W)		DK		E		F		FIN		IRL		N		NL		P		S		T		UK	
	<1	>1	<1	>1	<1	>1	<1	>1	<1	>1	<1	>1	<1	>1	<1	>1	<1	>1	<1	>1	<1	>1	<1	>1
People with disabilities	5	5	0	0	2	3	18	17	3	1	5	13	1	1	6	15	0	1	2	2	5	4	16	18
Women	11	20	9	14	30	26	18	26	12	16	30	50	23	36	16	35	17	23	29	43	7	11	28	39
People from ethnic minorities	4	3	0	0	1	1	ni	ni	2	3	1	0	1	0	12	8	4	0	1	1	3	0	19	28

ni question not included in country

Table 2.14: The length of time ahead organisations plan their staffing requirements

Country	D(W)	DK	E	F	FIN	IRL	N	NL	P	S	T	UK
One year or less	32	19	48	41	5	57	34	44	63	38	47	44
More than one < two years	38	34	30	32	43	25	31	32	17	37	23	27
More than two years	24	28	15	19	51	14	24	11	2	20	20	22
No planning	6	11	6	7	0	3	6	9	14	3	11	5

Private and public sector

	D(W)		DK		E *		F		FIN		IRL		N		NL *		P *		S		T *		UK	
	Pu	Pr	Pu	Pr	Pu	Pr	Pu	Pr	Pu	Pr	Pu	Pr	Pu	Pr	Pu	Pr	Pu	Pr	Pu	Pr	Pu	Pr	Pu	Pr
One year or less	16	34	6	27	37	49	39	43	2	7	63	54	33	36	50	43	77	66	31	44	56	46	31	48
More than one < two years	30	38	30	37	37	30	33	32	45	50	22	25	26	34	0	33	0	19	31	44	19	25	28	26
More than two years	47	21	40	20	25	14	25	16	53	41	12	16	26	23	0	11	0	3	32	8	25	19	29	19
No planning	6	6	15	8	0	6	3	8	0	0	2	3	7	4	0	10	15	11	4	3	0	11	8	5

Less than 1,000 or greater than or equal to 1,000 employees

	D(W)		DK		E		F		FIN		IRL		N		NL		P		S		T		UK	
	<1	>1	<1	>1	<1	>1	<1	>1	<1	>1	<1	>1	<1	>1	<1	>1	<1	>1	<1	>1	<1	>1	<1	>1
One year or less	34	28	24	10	57	34	44	38	7	2	59	50	33	35	46	35	62	68	44	33	45	50	52	37
More than one < two years	36	39	35	32	27	35	30	33	40	50	24	28	33	27	30	39	16	23	32	43	29	13	25	28
More than two years	21	28	25	35	8	27	15	23	52	46	12	19	23	27	10	15	1	5	19	20	14	28	15	28
No planning	6	4	10	12	8	3	9	4	1	0	3	3	6	5	10	8	18	0	3	3	12	9	6	5

Table 2.15: Percentage of organisations where the personnel/HR function is aided by computer. (+)

Country	D(W)	DK	E	F	FIN	IRL	N	NL	P	S	T	UK
No computerised system	5	2	2	1	2	9	8	14	1	1	8	9
Individual employee records	61	82	89	91	94	71	73	77	86	95	87	80
Pay and benefit admin	95	96	99	99	99	80	94	98	95	99	90	85
Absences and leave	77	74	84	81	77	66	74	87	80	91	59	59
Manpower planning	20	25	40	23	35	28	25	39	19	34	26	37
Recruitment and selection	18	15	40	14	20	30	16	26	22	18	20	30
Training and development	27	34	43	63	59	41	31	35	29	40	20	46
Performance appraisal	17	9	38	10	15	23	7	23	27	6	18	22
Job evaluation	10	8	23	10	21	7	5	32	10	8	2	16
Industrial relations	0	34	12	4	22	9	14	8	5	50	13	5

Private and public sector

Country	D(W)		DK		E *		F		FIN		IRL		N *		NL *		P *		S		T *		UK	
	Pu	Pr	Pu	Pr	Pu	Pr	Pu	Pr	Pu	Pr	Pu	Pr	Pu	Pr	Pu	Pr	Pu	Pr	Pu	Pr	Pu	Pr	Pu	Pr
No computerised system	6	5	2	2	0	2	0	1	0	2	5	12	7	7	0	15	8	0	0	1	19	7	7	9
Individual employee records	56	60	79	83	94	89	89	91	97	94	73	69	66	80	100	76	62	90	94	95	75	89	79	80
Pay and benefit admin	93	95	96	96	100	99	100	98	100	99	77	80	95	94	100	96	85	97	99	99	81	91	81	86
Absences and leave	59	78	82	68	81	84	80	80	82	79	67	64	74	75	100	87	61	82	88	92	38	63	56	59
Manpower planning	18	20	28	23	56	40	16	23	45	28	32	27	19	31	0	37	8	22	39	30	12	28	46	33
Recruitment and selection	14	19	7	21	56	39	17	13	42	18	43	21	16	16	50	24	23	22	19	17	19	21	32	29
Training and development	31	27	19	44	44	44	62	62	71	54	35	39	19	41	50	34	15	30	41	41	19	20	38	49
Performance appraisal	9	18	5	12	44	38	11	10	19	13	10	26	19	1	100	21	0	34	6	5	6	21	16	25
Job evaluation	3	11	5	10	31	23	7	10	23	22	5	9	0	7	50	32	0	11	6	9	0	3	14	18
Industrial relations	0	0	55	19	13	13	5	3	27	21	10	8	15	9	0	7	8	6	74	32	14	0	4	6

Country	D(W)		DK		E		F		FIN		IRL		N		NL		P		S		T		UK	
Less than 1,000 or greater than or equal to 1,000 employees	<1	>1	<1	>1	<1	>1	<1	>1	<1	>1	<1	>1	<1	>1	<1	>1	<1	>1	<1	>1	<1	>1	<1	>1
No computerised system	6	3	2	1	2	1	1	0	1	1	10	6	8	6	15	11	1	0	1	1	9	6	12	6
Individual employee records	57	67	80	85	86	95	88	94	94	97	66	91	68	86	75	89	86	86	92	97	84	91	73	85
Pay and benefit admin	94	97	96	96	98	100	98	99	99	100	79	84	94	96	98	100	95	98	98	100	88	94	81	88
Absences and leave	75	80	72	79	79	90	78	85	75	82	64	75	72	78	85	87	78	86	88	93	56	65	55	62
Manpower planning	17	25	24	26	28	62	18	29	26	52	23	47	20	40	36	42	16	32	31	38	21	35	24	48
Recruitment and selection	10	31	12	21	32	52	7	24	13	31	25	47	15	20	26	27	17	36	14	23	16	26	20	38
Training and development	17	42	32	40	28	68	57	72	53	73	35	59	30	36	33	42	20	59	34	45	13	33	38	53
Performance appraisal	14	20	9	10	32	48	8	13	15	18	23	22	6	8	24	19	21	46	9	3	13	26	20	24
Job evaluation	8	14	6	10	18	31	5	16	18	25	7	6	5	5	32	31	10	9	7	8	1	4	11	21
Industrial relations	0	0	27	48	8	19	3	4	21	23	16	7	12	17	10	0	4	9	42	59	11	7	3	7

Table 2.15a: Percentage of organisation using fully integrated computer systems (Valid %)

Country	D(W)	DK	E	F	FIN	IRL	N	NL	P	S	T	UK
Fully integrated	27	31	26	39	21	27	31	25	34	26	34	27
Partially integrated	48	60	66	52	67	50	60	51	55	71	53	50
Not integrated	25	9	8	5	5	24	9	24	12	3	13	23

Private and public sector

	D(W)		DK		E		F		FIN		IRL		N		NL		P		S		T		UK	
	Pu	Pr	Pu	Pr	Pu	Pr	Pu	Pr	Pu	Pr	Pu	Pr	Pu	Pr	Pu	Pr	Pu	Pr	Pu	Pr	Pu	Pr	Pu	Pr
					*										*		*				*			
Fully integrated	27	27	42	25	25	26	43	40	24	28	15	32	23	39	50	22	40	34	23	30	27	34	24	29
Partially integrated	36	49	51	65	63	66	53	55	71	68	67	38	66	57	50	53	20	57	74	66	64	53	52	51
Not integrated	37	24	7	10	13	7	4	5	5	4	18	30	11	4	0	25	40	7	3	4	9	13	24	21

Less than 1,000 or greater than or equal to 1,000 employees

	D(W)		DK		E		F		FIN		IRL		N		NL		P		S		T		UK	
	<1	>1	<1	>1	<1	>1	<1	>1	<1	>1	<1	>1	<1	>1	<1	>1	<1	>1	<1	>1	<1	>1	<1	>1
Fully integrated	30	26	29	36	27	25	44	36	24	22	25	34	29	35	24	28	38	20	27	26	35	33	26	28
Partially integrated	41	58	58	61	64	69	50	60	72	71	49	48	61	58	50	56	52	65	67	73	52	55	48	52
Not integrated	31	16	13	3	9	6	6	4	4	7	26	17	10	7	26	16	11	15	6	1	14	13	27	20

Table 3.1: Job categories hardest to recruit. (Valid %)

Country	D(W)	DK	E	F	FIN	IRL	N	NL	P	S	T	UK
Management	24	28	32	17	22	25	10	17	3	25	8	13
Qualified professionals	8	17	13	6	10	14	11	11	11	19	4	27
Health and Social	2	25	0	7	1	18	51	0	0	16	0	8
Engineers	11	5	9	14	0	15	7	5	8	13	15	14
Information Technology	5	4	8	5	0	8	2	5	11	6	7	12
Technicians	5	2	12	17	0	1	1	15	20	4	14	5
Administrative/Clerical	6	2	2	1	0	1	1	8	3	3	7	5
Sales and Distribution	9	7	13	11	0	4	1	10	6	1	5	5
Skilled Manual/Crafts	18	4	7	16	12	11	5	20	25	10	18	7
Manual	2	3	0	1	0	1	2	7	4	1	1	2
Specified by qualifications	5	1	1	4	0	0	0	2	0	1	0	1
Foreign Languages	1	2	3	1	0	1	0	0	1	0	13	0

	D(W)	DK	E	F	FIN	IRL	N	NL	P	S	T	UK
No Recruitment problems	24	65	23	28	74	44	44	18	16	60	46	35

Country	D(W)		DK		E		F		FIN		IRL		N		NL		P		S		T		UK	
Private and public sector					*										*		*				*			
	Pu	Pr	Pu	Pr	Pu	Pr	Pu	Pr	Pu	Pr	Pu	Pr	Pu	Pr	Pu	Pr	Pu	Pr	Pu	Pr	Pu	Pr	Pu	Pr
Management	21	27	19	34	44	31	35	13	16	33	11	32	3	27	0	19	0	4	21	32	22	8	5	17
Qualified professionals	6	9	13	22	15	12	4	6	9	14	23	12	9	16	20	11	6	13	26	14	11	4	41	18
Health and Social	10	<1	53	3	0	<1	18	5	31	0	51	3	84	0	0	0	0	0	24	9	0	0	21	2
Engineers	14	11	1	8	4	9	11	15	9	6	0	18	2	17	0	5	6	8	10	16	0	18	9	18
Information Technology	5	5	4	4	7	8	3	5	9	8	11	8	0	0	4	0	12	10	7	4	0	8	9	13
Technicians	13	4	3	1	19	11	13	19	0	2	0	1	0	1	0	16	35	22	2	7	11	16	3	6
Administrative/Clerical	15	5	5	0	0	2	2	1	0	3	0	7	1	1	20	7	0	3	3	1	0	9	6	5
Sales and Distribution	9	9	0	12	4	14	1	12	3	6	0	16	0	15	20	10	0	8	1	1	11	0	5	7
Skilled Manual/Crafts	5	21	1	7	7	7	11	18	22	16	0	3	1	12	40	20	41	28	4	15	33	4	<1	10
Manual	1	3	1	4	0	0	1	0	3	6	3	1	1	5	0	7	0	4	4	1	0	1	3	3
Specified by qualifications	2	6	0	1	0	0	3	5	0	0	0	0	0	0	2	0	0	0	1	0	0	0	0	1
Foreign Languages	0	1	0	3	0	3	1	2	6	5	0	1	1	0	0	0	0	0	1	0	11	13	0	1

	D(W)		DK		E		F		FIN		IRL		N		NL		P		S		T		UK	
	Pu	Pr	Pu	Pr	Pu	Pr	Pu	Pr	Pu	Pr	Pu	Pr	Pu	Pr	Pu	Pr	Pu	Pr	Pu	Pr	Pu	Pr	Pu	Pr
No Recruitment problems	21	24	63	66	13	24	29	29	66	75	48	45	26	62	0	19	15	16	51	67	41	69	29	37

Table 3.1 (cont): Job categories hardest to recruit. (Valid %)

Country	D(W)		DK		E		F		FIN		IRL		N		NL		P		S		T		UK	
Less than 1,000 or greater than or equal to 1,000 employees	<1	>1	<1	>1	<1	>1	<1	>1	<1	>1	<1	>1	<1	>1	<1	>1	<1	>1	<1	>1	<1	>1	<1	>1
Management	26	26	29	27	32	34	15	19	26	30	26	18	10	11	16	23	3	3	23	29	5	16	12	14
Qualified professionals	8	10	23	10	12	14	5	6	13	16	16	9	12	13	9	16	12	15	18	22	6	2	26	28
Health and Social	1	3	19	37	<1	0	9	4	6	16	17	21	53	56	0	0	0	0	8	25	0	0	2	12
Engineers	11	12	6	5	7	12	13	15	6	9	11	27	8	8	5	7	10	6	17	10	16	16	16	14
Information Technology	3	8	3	5	9	6	4	6	4	7	6	12	1	2	5	2	11	15	8	4	3	14	10	13
Technicians	5	7	0	5	15	6	18	17	0	2	1	3	1	1	16	9	19	32	8	1	12	21	6	4
Administrative/Clerical	5	9	1	5	2	2	1	1	4	0	1	0	0	0	9	2	3	3	2	2	9	7	7	4
Sales and Distribution	10	8	8	3	13	13	10	10	6	5	6	0	5	6	9	14	7	3	3	0	6	5	7	3
Skilled Manual/Crafts	22	12	5	3	8	6	18	13	24	9	14	3	7	1	22	14	30	21	16	4	25	11	11	5
Manual	3	1	3	2	1	0	3	1	9	6	1	3	1	2	6	7	4	3	1	1	2	0	3	2
Specified by qualifications	5	5	1	0	<1	3	3	5	0	0	0	0	0	0	2	5	0	0	0	1	1	0	0	1
Foreign Languages	<1	1	3	3	2	5	2	1	4	7	3	0	0	0	0	0	1	0	0	0	17	9	<1	<1
No Recruitment problems	26	22	64	67	20	28	28	29	77	70	42	50	46	40	19	19	20	5	60	62	43	50	36	33

Table 3.2: Percentage of organisations which have introduced any of the following measures to aid recruitment.(+)

Country

	D(W)	DK	E	F	FIN	IRL	N	NL	P	S	T	UK
Flexible working hours	76	42	26	40	55	28	51	25	25	63	7	39
Recruiting abroad	16	13	13	16	9	35	27	14	14	15	5	20
Relaxed age requirements	54	13	52	27	26	25	29	52	48	27	29	40
Relaxed qualifications	12	9	46	22	16	10	10	26	50	25	33	21
Relocation of the company	3	3	13	4	5	2	2	2	10	3	2	7
Retrain existing employees	56	49	67	38	56	54	53	69	71	53	63	67
Training for new employees	58	59	64	73	59	51	61	71	65	39	62	68
Part–time work	67	31	17	30	27	33	45	33	12	30	2	53
Job sharing	ni	15	6	ni	ni	27	24	13	7	30	29	35
Increased pay/benefits	47	32	52	37	26	32	35	47	67	23	34	44
Marketing the organisation's image	64	41	37	59	63	33	42	52	50	54	35	53

Private and public sector

	D(W)		DK		E *		F		FIN		IRL		N		NL *		P *		S		T *		UK	
	Pu	Pr	Pu	Pr	Pu	Pr	Pu	Pr	Pu	Pr	Pu	Pr	Pu	Pr	Pu	Pr	Pu	Pr	Pu	Pr	Pu	Pr	Pu	Pr
Flexible working hours	87	73	58	31	25	26	43	38	61	49	45	20	70	36	0	26	39	21	71	56	0	8	76	27
Recruiting abroad	7	17	7	17	19	13	5	19	3	12	23	38	36	19	0	15	1	15	9	20	6	5	25	18
Relaxed age requirements	61	52	6	18	31	53	15	31	27	24	28	23	32	26	0	54	31	53	25	29	13	32	42	39
Relaxed qualifications	14	11	12	8	44	45	17	25	16	15	0	15	20	2	0	27	39	52	31	19	35	25	31	18
Relocation of the company	3	4	4	1	6	13	4	4	6	6	3	2	2	1	0	2	2	10	1	4	0	2	5	7
Retrain existing employees	52	57	50	48	69	67	44	37	55	57	50	56	59	50	0	69	54	78	51	54	56	64	67	67
Training for new employees	56	58	58	59	63	64	64	74	60	65	33	56	70	60	0	71	46	70	32	44	63	61	72	66
Part–time work	79	65	47	21	13	16	46	25	29	24	40	29	68	27	0	33	8	11	30	30	0	2	83	42
Job sharing	ni	ni	26	8	0	6	ni	ni	ni	ni	58	10	40	10	0	14	0	8	31	24	25	29	78	19
Increased pay/benefits	25	49	47	23	31	55	37	37	27	24	10	38	59	15	50	47	0	81	25	21	19	36	59	38
Marketing the organisation's image	66	65	47	37	19	40	57	59	68	65	23	37	44	39	0	53	23	58	55	54	19	36	56	51

Table 3.2 (cont): Percentage of organisations which have introduced any of the following measures to aid recruitment.(+)

Country	D(W)		DK		E		F		FIN		IRL		N		NL		P		S		T		UK	
Less than 1,000 or greater than or equal to 1,000 employees	<1	>1	<1	>1	<1	>1	<1	>1	<1	>1	<1	>1	<1	>1	<1	>1	<1	>1	<1	>1	<1	>1	<1	>1
Flexible working hours	74	78	37	52	29	20	38	43	48	65	24	41	49	58	26	27	24	27	61	65	3	13	30	47
Recruiting abroad	13	20	14	11	13	13	16	16	5	14	36	31	26	30	13	19	13	18	12	16	3	9	15	24
Relaxed age requirements	53	55	11	16	55	47	30	24	22	28	24	25	26	35	54	42	48	50	29	24	33	22	39	40
Relaxed qualifications	15	7	10	9	29	40	22	22	19	10	11	6	8	15	26	27	49	50	20	29	31	35	22	21
Relocation of the company	3	5	3	4	13	13	3	6	4	6	3	0	1	4	3	0	11	5	3	3	4	0	6	8
Retrain existing employees	56	56	45	57	69	65	36	42	52	63	57	47	49	63	67	69	69	77	53	52	61	67	70	64
Training for new employees	48	72	58	60	60	70	69	78	55	68	52	47	60	65	72	65	59	82	39	40	62	61	69	67
Part-time work	66	69	26	41	20	12	29	33	26	29	39	44	43	50	32	35	14	5	31	30	1	2	45	60
Job sharing	ni	ni	12	20	8	4	ni	ni	ni	ni	20	38	23	26	15	8	8	9	0	28	26	33	27	42
Increased pay/benefits	49	42	27	41	55	47	39	44	26	23	33	25	35	35	45	54	68	64	23	21	34	35	45	43
Marketing the organisation's image	57	75	39	45	31	49	57	62	58	76	32	34	38	53	51	54	54	54	47	60	34	37	47	57

ni question not included in country

Table 3.3: Percentage of organisations which have targeted any of the following in their recruitment process.(+)

Country	D(W)	DK	E	F	FIN	IRL	N	NL	P	S	T	UK
The long–term unemployed	16	20	9	12	5	6	6	27	46	3	13	7
Older people	12	4	10	4	2	12	2	6	19	3	1	18
People with disabilities	15	4	8	22	2	8	2	26	12	2	18	18
People from ethnic minorities	18	3	3	ni	2	1	1	25	7	5	2	17
Women	40	19	40	21	11	20	25	45	46	21	7	33
School leavers	65	29	70	62	43	32	16	55	83	4	4	35

Private and public sector

	D(W)		DK		E		F		FIN		IRL		N		NL		P		S		T		UK	
	Pu	Pr	Pu	Pr	Pu	Pr	Pu	Pr	Pu	Pr	Pu	Pr	Pu	Pr	Pu	Pr	Pu	Pr	Pu	Pr	Pu	Pr	Pu	Pr
The long–term unemployed	19	16	32	13	19	17	17	11	11	2	8	5	8	6	50	27	31	52	4	2	19	13	11	7
Older people	13	11	3	4	6	11	1	5	3	2	18	9	2	3	0	7	15	21	4	3	0	1	16	17
People with disabilities	32	12	6	3	19	7	27	21	2	2	15	5	5	0	100	25	23	10	1	2	6	19	31	12
People from ethnic minorities	4	20	0	4	13	3	ni	ni	2	2	0	0	1	2	50	25	15	6	7	3	6	3	32	11
Women	57	38	26	14	31	43	19	22	15	8	23	18	36	18	50	45	23	51	24	17	6	7	48	28
School leavers	77	62	23	33	70	69	62	58	45	49	35	32	22	10	0	57	54	88	7	2	6	4	38	34

Less than 1,000 or greater than or equal to 1,000 employees

	D(W)		DK		E		F		FIN		IRL		N		NL		P		S		T		UK	
	<1	>1	<1	>1	<1	>1	<1	>1	<1	>1	<1	>1	<1	>1	<1	>1	<1	>1	<1	>1	<1	>1	<1	>1
The long–term unemployed	16	16	16	28	11	3	12	11	5	5	7	3	6	5	27	27	51	32	3	3	13	13	6	8
Older people	15	8	4	3	13	5	4	4	1	4	13	6	2	1	8	6	24	5	4	2	1	0	19	17
People with disabilities	14	17	1	9	7	9	21	23	3	3	8	6	2	3	25	31	14	5	1	6	16	22	14	21
People from ethnic minorities	19	16	3	3	3	3	ni	ni	2	0	1	0	1	1	23	35	9	0	4	6	3	2	9	24
Women	40	42	16	24	44	36	21	22	8	15	20	22	22	33	42	54	51	32	19	23	5	9	27	38
School leavers	61	70	25	37	62	62	60	65	43	48	37	16	15	18	54	64	86	73	4	4	4	4	30	39

ni question not included in country

Table 3.5: Proportion of senior managers recruited externally.

Country	D(W)	DK	E	F	FIN	IRL	N	NL	P	S	T	UK
Up to 10%	49	38	51	38	45	38	27	35	39	34	55	42
Eleven to 30%	10	13	16	12	25	19	18	16	15	27	11	25
Thirty–one to 60%	11	15	11	12	14	17	24	17	15	22	7	19
More than 60%	12	30	13	32	14	23	28	29	27	17	18	12

Private and public sector

	D(W)		DK		E		F		FIN		IRL		N		NL		P		S		T		UK	
	Pu	Pr	Pu	Pr	Pu	Pr	Pu	Pr	Pu	Pr	Pu	Pr	Pu	Pr	Pu	Pr	Pu	Pr	Pu	Pr	Pu	Pr	Pu	Pr
Up to 10%	59	47	28	45	56	50	36	38	58	35	40	38	16	34	0	37	39	40	31	34	63	55	31	47
Eleven to 30%	14	9	14	11	6	17	12	12	21	25	10	22	9	23	50	15	8	16	19	33	6	12	22	27
Thirty–one to 60%	7	12	16	14	25	10	14	11	8	18	10	20	28	24	0	17	0	18	25	20	6	7	29	14
More than 60%	3	14	39	24	6	13	32	33	11	18	32	18	44	16	0	29	31	26	22	13	0	19	16	10

Less than 1,000 or greater than or equal to 1,000 employees

	D(W)		DK		E		F		FIN		IRL		N		NL		P		S		T		UK	
	<1	>1	<1	>1	<1	>1	<1	>1	<1	>1	<1	>1	<1	>1	<1	>1	<1	>1	<1	>1	<1	>1	<1	>1
Up to 10%	48	48	39	35	46	61	35	42	40	55	35	33	26	29	34	38	41	32	36	31	60	46	42	43
Eleven to 30%	7	13	15	8	19	11	10	15	24	21	19	19	19	15	13	27	14	18	23	31	6	17	20	29
Thirty–one to 60%	19	14	10	24	13	7	12	12	14	13	18	16	24	23	17	19	14	18	18	25	6	6	21	16
More than 60%	13	11	31	29	15	10	37	24	18	8	26	9	28	28	33	12	28	23	22	12	21	13	15	10

Table 3.6: Selection methods regularly used by organisations.(+)

Country

	D(W)	DK	E	F	FIN	IRL	N	NL	P	S	T	UK
Application forms	96	48	87	95	82	91	59	94	83	15	95	97
Interview panel	86	99	85	92	99	87	78	69	97	69	64	71
Bio data	20	92	12	26	48	7	56	20	62	69	39	8
Psychometric testing	6	38	60	22	74	28	11	31	58	24	8	46
Graphology	8	2	8	57	2	1	0	2	2	0	0	1
References	66	79	54	73	63	91	92	47	55	96	69	92
Aptitude test	8	17	72	28	42	41	19	53	17	14	33	45
Assessment centre	13	4	18	9	16	7	5	27	2	5	4	18
Group selection methods	4	8	22	10	8	8	1	2	18	3	23	13

Private and public sector

	D(W) Pu	D(W) Pr	DK Pu	DK Pr	E Pu	E Pr	F Pu	F Pr	FIN Pu	FIN Pr	IRL Pu	IRL Pr	N Pu	N Pr	NL Pu	NL Pr	P Pu	P Pr	S Pu	S Pr	T Pu	T Pr	UK Pu	UK Pr
Application forms	99	98	44	52	81	87	94	94	84	85	92	91	49	69	100	94	92	82	7	20	81	97	98	96
Interview panel	85	89	98	98	81	86	90	92	100	99	98	82	89	66	100	68	92	97	76	62	63	65	99	60
Bio data	18	81	89	92	25	11	32	24	34	54	0	7	60	54	0	20	39	66	74	64	6	44	4	9
Psychometric testing	8	8	16	53	56	60	22	21	74	82	13	37	4	16	0	32	46	59	16	31	0	10	36	52
Graphology	1	10	2	3	0	8	31	63	2	2	0	1	0	0	0	2	0	3	0	0	0	0	0	1
References	54	71	74	81	6	58	74	73	49	70	88	92	90	93	50	47	15	62	94	97	44	73	97	90
Aptitude test	23	17	10	23	69	71	35	25	36	48	33	48	11	23	100	52	8	19	6	20	50	31	44	46
Assessment centre	21	15	1	6	13	19	8	9	6	19	2	8	2	5	50	27	0	1	5	5	13	3	16	20
Group selection methods	70	7	14	4	19	22	13	10	10	9	5	9	1	0	0	3	23	19	2	4	31	23	16	13

Country

Less than 1,000 or greater than or equal to 1,000 employees

	D(W) <1	D(W) >1	DK <1	DK >1	E <1	E >1	F <1	F >1	FIN <1	FIN >1	IRL <1	IRL >1	N <1	N >1	NL <1	NL >1	P <1	P >1	S <1	S >1	T <1	T >1	UK <1	UK >1
Application forms	97	98	47	51	87	86	95	93	81	81	92	99	58	62	94	92	85	77	13	16	96	93	97	96
Interview panel	87	92	99	100	84	87	92	93	100	97	84	94	80	72	68	69	96	100	72	68	62	67	66	75
Bio data	20	22	90	94	10	16	22	32	47	53	7	3	52	68	17	31	62	64	69	67	33	50	5	10
Psychometric testing	6	9	37	40	51	78	18	27	69	83	26	41	10	13	29	39	45	100	20	30	4	15	42	49
Graphology	9	8	2	3	9	4	56	60	2	1	0	3	0	0	2	4	1	5	0	0	0	1	1	1
References	70	68	80	76	55	52	73	72	62	60	92	88	93	90	48	46	63	27	95	96	71	65	93	92
Aptitude test	16	20	14	24	69	77	29	26	39	49	42	44	15	30	54	50	9	46	16	11	25	46	42	47
Assessment centre	10	25	4	5	18	18	8	8	15	18	9	7	4	6	25	35	1	5	4	7	1	9	10	25
Group selection methods	7	10	8	7	21	25	10	10	12	3	9	7	2	1	2	8	13	36	4	3	23	22	10	16

Table 4.1a: The level at which basic pay is determined for managers (+)

Country	D(W)	DK	E	F	FIN	IRL	N	NL	P	S	T	UK
National/industry-wide collective bargaining	ni	37	14	35	20	33	35	28	29	57	6	28
Regional collective bargaining	ni	4	3	3	2	0	16	na	1	9	1	2
Company/division, etc.	ni	28	25	56	40	28	22	39	41	31	35	47
Establishment/site	ni	5	8	10	9	15	12	15	5	7	16	17
Individual	ni	53	75	28	66	40	57	49	48	52	28	41
			*					*	*	*		

Private and public sector

	D(W)		DK		E		F		FIN		IRL		N		NL		P		S		T		UK	
	Pu	Pr	Pu	Pr	Pu	Pr	Pu	Pr	Pu	Pr	Pu	Pr	Pu	Pr	Pu	Pr	Pu	Pr	Pu	Pr	Pu	Pr	Pu	Pr
National/industry-wide collective bargaining	ni	ni	75	11	25	12	68	27	29	3	80	11	64	15	50	29	54	22	55	56	13	4	79	7
Regional collective bargaining	ni	ni	8	2	0	2	1	3	5	1	0	0	28	7	na	na	0	1	13	5	0	0	1	1
Company/division, etc.	ni	ni	35	23	6	27	19	64	39	49	12	36	15	29	50	38	23	48	30	31	25	37	22	56
Establishment/site	ni	ni	5	5	6	9	6	11	10	12	2	17	12	12	50	38	0	5	4	11	25	16	10	20
Individual	ni	ni	19	77	50	76	8	34	55	80	10	55	28	78	50	39	0	55	51	52	0	32	17	51

Less than 1,000 or greater than or equal to 1,000 employees

	D(W)		DK		E		F		FIN		IRL		N		NL		P		S		T		UK	
	<1	>1	<1	>1	<1	>1	<1	>1	<1	>1	<1	>1	<1	>1	<1	>1	<1	>1	<1	>1	<1	>1	<1	>1
National/industry-wide collective bargaining	ni	ni	30	49	13	15	31	42	18	21	30	44	36	33	28	35	21	35	57	58	8	2	19	35
Regional collective bargaining	ni	ni	4	4	3	1	2	3	1	4	0	0	14	19	na	na	0	5	4	13	0	0	1	2
Company/division, etc.	ni	ni	25	33	22	31	56	56	41	43	29	22	18	32	39	35	42	36	26	35	35	35	46	48
Establishment/site	ni	ni	5	5	10	5	10	10	12	6	16	13	12	12	39	35	6	5	7	7	14	20	22	12
Individual	ni	ni	58	44	75	76	30	25	70	60	44	31	57	56	39	39	48	50	55	47	29	26	43	39

ni question not included in country

Table 4.1b: The level at which basic pay is determined for professional and technical staff (+)

Country

	D(W)	DK	E	F	FIN	IRL	N	NL	P	S	T	UK
National/industry–wide collective bargaining	ni	48	29	29	35	40	54	47	30	54	6	32
Regional collective bargaining	ni	8	8	7	2	2	19	ni	1	6	2	2
Company/division, etc.	ni	21	33	46	47	24	20	39	47	24	45	44
Establishment/site	ni	13	17	24	23	17	16	21	4	12	20	22
Individual	ni	42	47	18	43	31	38	33	42	34	23	27

Private and public sector

	D(W)		DK		E*		F		FIN		IRL		N		NL*		P*		S		T*		UK	
	Pu	Pr	Pu	Pr	Pu	Pr	Pu	Pr	Pu	Pr	Pu	Pr	Pu	Pr	Pu	Pr	Pu	Pr	Pu	Pr	Pu	Pr	Pu	Pr
National/industry–wide collective bargaining	ni	ni	72	28	21	29	66	9	47	15	82	14	84	31	100	45	54	23	47	59	0	6	87	9
Regional collective bargaining	ni	ni	8	8	6	8	2	9	6	1	0	3	28	12	ni	ni	0	1	9	4	0	2	1	2
Company/division, etc.	ni	ni	33	13	12	34	13	53	42	56	12	31	11	28	0	39	23	56	24	24	38	47	17	54
Establishment/site	ni	ni	5	18	12	18	12	28	26	27	2	20	10	19	0	39	0	5	9	14	25	19	6	28
Individual	ni	ni	18	58	25	48	4	21	32	56	2	45	20	49	0	40	0	48	36	32	0	29	5	36

Less than 1,000 or greater than or equal to 1,000 employees

	D(W)		DK		E		F		FIN		IRL		N		NL		P		S		T		UK	
	<1	>1	<1	>1	<1	>1	<1	>1	<1	>1	<1	>1	<1	>1	<1	>1	<1	>1	<1	>1	<1	>1	<1	>1
National/industry–wide collective bargaining	ni	ni	39	65	24	39	24	36	32	35	33	59	51	60	45	54	21	59	52	58	5	7	21	40
Regional collective bargaining	ni	ni	9	6	7	9	7	8	2	3	2	3	17	23	ni	ni	0	5	4	8	0	4	2	3
Company/division, etc.	ni	ni	17	30	30	36	49	43	46	49	26	16	16	30	39	35	49	41	20	28	44	46	44	44
Establishment/site	ni	ni	11	17	19	14	22	27	23	24	19	13	16	15	35	39	6	0	9	15	18	22	28	17
Individual	ni	ni	46	32	51	40	19	16	46	40	34	22	36	39	39	39	50	39	36	31	20	24	30	24

ni question not included in country

Table 4.1c: The level at which basic pay is determined for clerical staff (+)

Country	D(W)	DK	E	F	FIN	IRL	N	NL	P	S	T	UK
National/industry-wide collective bargaining	ni	53	46	29	85	55	65	77	44	66	10	33
Regional collective bargaining	ni	8	17	7	4	7	22	ni	1	8	2	5
Company/division, etc.	ni	19	31	45	22	25	16	33	40	28	42	39
Establishment/site	ni	13	19	27	23	17	14	16	5	12	19	29
Individual	ni	35	16	15	18	17	27	12	19	35	17	17

Private and public sector

	D(W)		DK		E*		F		FIN		IRL		N		NL*		P*		S		T*		UK	
	Pu	Pr	Pu	Pr	Pu	Pr	Pu	Pr	Pu	Pr	Pu	Pr	Pu	Pr	Pu	Pr	Pu	Pr	Pu	Pr	Pu	Pr	Pu	Pr
National/industry-wide collective bargaining	ni	ni	78	37	31	48	66	20	82	83	92	37	90	48	100	76	54	41	59	70	25	8	90	12
Regional collective bargaining	ni	ni	6	9	6	18	3	8	11	2	0	10	29	18	ni	ni	0	1	14	4	0	3	2	6
Company/division, etc.	ni	ni	31	11	25	32	13	51	24	21	12	33	11	22	0	33	23	47	28	29	25	45	15	48
Establishment/site	ni	ni	6	17	19	19	14	31	23	28	5	21	9	12	0	33	0	7	11	12	25	19	8	38
Individual	ni	ni	16	48	6	6	4	18	20	21	0	25	8	40	0	33	0	20	37	32	0	21	2	22

Less than 1,000 or greater than or equal to 1,000 employees

	D(W)		DK		E		F		FIN		IRL		N		NL		P		S		T		UK	
	<1	>1	<1	>1	<1	>1	<1	>1	<1	>1	<1	>1	<1	>1	<1	>1	<1	>1	<1	>1	<1	>1	<1	>1
National/industry-wide collective bargaining	ni	ni	44	70	43	54	24	37	81	91	52	60	63	69	78	73	35	73	65	67	8	13	21	44
Regional collective bargaining	ni	ni	9	6	18	16	7	7	3	6	7	6	20	27	ni	ni	0	5	5	11	1	4	4	6
Company/division, etc.	ni	ni	16	23	30	33	49	39	21	21	24	25	15	21	33	31	45	23	23	34	44	39	40	39
Establishment/site	ni	ni	11	17	21	14	24	32	24	24	18	16	14	12	33	31	7	0	7	16	14	26	36	24
Individual	ni	ni	41	23	19	12	15	15	19	19	19	9	31	18	33	31	20	18	38	31	17	14	21	14

ni question not included in country

Table 4.1d: The level at which basic pay is determined for manual staff (+)

Country

	D(W)	DK	E	F	FIN	IRL	N	NL	P	S	T	UK
National/industry-wide collective bargaining	ni	64	43	25	86	71	80	80	55	73	55	41
Regional collective bargaining	ni	18	20	7	7	8	25	ni	2	10	26	6
Company/division, etc.	ni	15	26	36	16	18	16	29	34	27	15	29
Establishment/site	ni	7	18	25	23	13	11	14	3	10	6	30
Individual	ni	13	3	11	13	6	17	9	15	18	7	7

Private and public sector

	D(W)		DK		E		F		FIN		IRL		N		NL		P		S		T		UK	
	Pu	Pr	Pu	Pr	Pu	Pr	Pu	Pr	Pu	Pr	Pu	Pr	Pu	Pr	Pu	Pr	Pu	Pr	Pu	Pr	Pu	Pr	Pu	Pr
National/industry-wide collective bargaining	ni	ni	75	58	31	43	61	16	82	85	87	63	91	72	100	80	54	55	69	76	69	53	89	24
Regional collective bargaining	ni	ni	7	25	6	21	3	8	11	7	2	12	27	25	ni	ni	0	3	14	7	0	30	2	8
Company/division, etc.	ni	ni	29	6	25	26	12	41	23	14	10	25	19	19	0	29	23	40	29	26	6	50	14	36
Establishment/site	ni	ni	5	8	19	18	11	30	23	26	5	18	9	8	0	29	0	4	7	12	0	7	12	38
Individual	ni	ni	15	11	0	3	4	12	13	15	0	8	10	22	0	29	16	0	20	16	0	9	1	10

Less than 1,000 or greater than or equal to 1,000 employees

	D(W)		DK		E		F		FIN		IRL		N		NL		P		S		T		UK	
	<1	>1	<1	>1	<1	>1	<1	>1	<1	>1	<1	>1	<1	>1	<1	>1	<1	>1	<1	>1	<1	>1	<1	>1
National/industry-wide collective bargaining	ni	ni	60	73	40	48	20	32	80	95	69	78	77	86	81	77	49	73	71	76	48	65	28	52
Regional collective bargaining	ni	ni	21	13	21	17	7	5	8	6	7	13	24	30	ni	ni	1	5	7	13	29	22	6	7
Company/division, etc.	ni	ni	12	21	24	30	39	31	17	16	17	25	13	22	23	23	37	27	22	33	14	15	29	30
Establishment/site	ni	ni	6	9	21	13	22	30	26	20	13	16	11	12	30	23	4	0	7	12	5	7	36	26
Individual	ni	ni	14	11	4	2	10	12	13	14	7	7	17	17	30	23	14	18	22	13	9	7	9	6

ni question not included in country

Table 4.2a: Organisations where there has been a change in the share of variable pay in the total reward package.

Country	D(W)	DK	E	F	FIN	IRL	N	NL	P	S	T	UK
Yes, increased	49	54	49	40	42	31	36	33	69	48	63	38
Yes, decreased	4	3	4	7	5	4	4	6	5	3	3	7
No	43	36	43	50	50	58	50	56	24	45	24	49
Don't know	0	3	1	2	2	2	5	4	2	3	1	3

Private and public sector

	D(W)		DK		E		F		FIN		IRL		N		NL		P		S		T		UK	
	Pu	Pr	Pu	Pr	Pu	Pr	Pu	Pr	Pu	Pr	Pu	Pr	Pu	Pr	Pu	Pr	Pu	Pr	Pu	Pr	Pu	Pr	Pu	Pr
Increased	47	50	83	34	50	49	48	40	48	40	25	35	34	41	50	33	77	69	43	53	44	65	49	35
Decreased	1	4	0	5	6	4	2	8	3	7	0	8	4	3	0	7	8	6	2	4	0	4	4	8
No	49	42	10	54	44	44	49	52	47	50	65	54	48	50	50	55	15	25	51	41	38	23	41	51
Don't know	0	0	1	4	0	1	1	1	2	4	5	1	9	3	0	5	0	0	4	2	6	0	4	3

Less than 1,000 or greater than or equal to 1,000 employees

	D(W)		DK		E		F		FIN		IRL		N		NL		P		S		T		UK	
	<1	>1	<1	>1	<1	>1	<1	>1	<1	>1	<1	>1	<1	>1	<1	>1	<1	>1	<1	>1	<1	>1	<1	>1
Increased	50	48	47	69	45	55	40	41	39	49	28	44	35	39	30	42	70	73	46	49	61	67	31	44
Decreased	4	4	4	3	4	4	7	6	6	4	4	6	5	3	7	4	6	5	3	3	4	2	7	6
No	42	43	42	24	48	37	52	50	53	43	62	41	51	49	58	46	25	23	49	43	23	24	55	43
Don't know	0	0	4	1	1	1	1	3	2	4	2	3	6	1	4	8	0	0	2	4	1	1	3	3

Table 4.2b: Organisations where there has been a change in the share of non–money benefits in the total reward package.

Country	D(W)	DK	E	F	FIN	IRL	N	NL	P	S	T	UK
Increased	36	20	27	10	19	16	17	30	56	21	46	30
Decreased	5	6	3	5	11	3	10	8	3	18	8	5
No	55	61	56	73	61	68	59	55	31	51	33	57
Don't know	0	6	2	2	2	3	6	2	10	3	2	3

Private and public sector

	D(W)		DK		E		F		FIN		IRL		N		NL		P		S		T		UK	
	Pu	Pr	Pu	Pr	Pu	Pr	Pu	Pr	Pu	Pr	Pu	Pr	Pu	Pr	Pu	Pr	Pu	Pr	Pu	Pr	Pu	Pr	Pu	Pr
Increased	30	36	19	21	25	26	14	10	18	21	0	25	15	16	100	29	56	63	22	20	25	48	41	25
Decreased	2	6	5	7	6	3	3	6	8	15	0	3	3	17	0	8	0	3	4	4	0	10	1	7
No	58	54	67	63	56	55	66	75	68	57	83	62	60	56	0	55	44	34	63	42	50	30	50	61
Don't know	0	0	0	6	0	5	2	2	0	4	5	2	9	4	0	3	0	0	3	4	6	1	5	3

Less than 1,000 or greater than or equal to 1,000 employees

	D(W)		DK		E		F		FIN		IRL		N		NL		P		S		T		UK	
	<1	>1	<1	>1	<1	>1	<1	>1	<1	>1	<1	>1	<1	>1	<1	>1	<1	>1	<1	>1	<1	>1	<1	>1
Increased	39	32	22	16	26	29	10	10	18	20	17	19	18	13	25	30	57	50	19	22	51	37	30	30
Decreased	5	6	7	5	2	4	5	6	12	9	3	3	8	14	9	4	2	10	17	18	7	11	6	5
No	52	59	58	65	58	51	73	74	63	59	69	63	58	62	60	35	41	14	51	52	29	41	58	57
Don't know	0	0	6	5	1	2	3	3	2	4	3	3	8	4	0	0	4	3	1	2	3	4	3	3

Table 4.3a: Percentage of organisations offering the following incentive schemes for managers.(+)

Country	D(W)	DK	E	F	FIN	IRL	N	NL	P	S	T	UK
Employee share options	11	ni	11	12	13	28	14	18	8	10	1	37
Profit sharing	60	6	17	70	14	15	5	38	29	18	11	26
Group bonus schemes #	3	7	9	34	13	16	10	7	11	12	7	25
Individual bonus/commission#	48	20	36	44	36	28	12	59	18	26	20	32
Merit/performance related pay#	21	54	56	70	31	51	15	21	60	12	52	65

Private and public sector

	D(W)		DK*		E		F		FIN		IRL		N		NL*		P*		S		T*		UK	
	Pu	Pr	Pu	Pr	Pu	Pr	Pu	Pr	Pu	Pr	Pu	Pr	Pu	Pr	Pu	Pr	Pu	Pr	Pu	Pr	Pu	Pr	Pu	Pr
Employee share options	1	13	ni	ni	0	14	4	14	10	18	0	40	2	26	0	19	0	8	0	18	0	1	1	54
Profit sharing	16	67	0	9	6	18	34	78	21	14	0	20	1	5	0	38	0	33	7	26	6	13	5	35
Group bonus schemes#	10	2	4	9	6	10	23	37	10	7	5	21	4	17	0	7	0	12	4	20	0	8	7	32
Individual bonus/commission#	41	48	5	29	12	38	24	49	26	47	7	38	1	20	100	59	0	20	6	43	0	22	9	41
Merit/performance related pay#	16	21	38	65	69	55	47	74	26	37	27	64	7	21	0	21	15	64	9	14	19	58	68	64

Less than 1,000 or greater than or equal to 1,000 employees

	D(W)		DK		E		F		FIN		IRL		N		NL		P		S		T		UK	
	<1	>1	<1	>1	<1	>1	<1	>1	<1	>1	<1	>1	<1	>1	<1	>1	<1	>1	<1	>1	<1	>1	<1	>1
Employee share options	9	14	ni	ni	12	11	9	15	12	16	28	28	12	17	17	23	7	9	11	9	1	0	30	43
Profit sharing	61	59	6	4	19	14	69	72	15	13	15	13	6	5	35	46	31	22	15	20	13	9	33	28
Group bonus schemes#	2	3	7	8	4	18	34	35	10	10	17	9	11	8	8	4	10	14	12	12	4	11	22	27
Individual bonus/commission#	49	47	21	16	31	44	43	47	31	45	27	31	12	12	61	54	20	14	27	25	16	26	33	32
Merit/performance related pay#	19	25	52	58	49	66	65	77	30	33	54	47	14	17	20	27	54	82	11	13	46	63	58	71

ni question not included in country   # French results are for 1990

Table 4.3b: Percentage of organisations offering the following incentive schemes for professional and technical staff.(+)

Country	D(W)	DK	E	F	FIN	IRL	N	NL	P	S	T	UK
Employee share options	9	ni	5	3	11	16	13	12	7	7	0	29
Profit sharing	20	3	11	68	18	12	4	38	22	12	6	21
Group bonus schemes#	7	6	5	30	27	15	13	9	12	11	6	18
Individual bonus/commission#	67	16	32	34	29	22	10	59	19	3	15	27
Merit/performance related pay#	40	51	59	60	33	44	16	25	61	9	53	52

Private and public sector

	D(W)		DK		E		F		FIN		IRL		N		NL		P		S		T		UK	
	Pu	Pr	Pu	Pr	Pu	Pr	Pu	Pr	Pu	Pr	Pu	Pr	Pu	Pr	Pu	Pr	Pu	Pr	Pu	Pr	Pu	Pr	Pu	Pr
Employee share options	2	10	ni	ni	0	5	1	4	10	14	0	21	2	24	0	12	0	8	0	12	0	0	1	42
Profit sharing	8	22	0	6	6	11	32	76	26	18	0	15	1	5	0	37	0	23	8	15	6	6	6	27
Group bonus schemes#	14	6	3	8	12	5	20	32	21	25	7	18	4	23	0	10	0	14	4	18	0	7	6	23
Individual bonus/commission#	38	71	9	19	6	34	20	37	16	40	2	30	2	16	100	60	0	23	0	5	0	16	9	34
Merit/performance related pay#	18	43	43	57	56	59	39	63	34	35	17	55	8	22	50	25	15	68	9	8	31	58	35	59

Less than 1,000 or greater than or equal to 1,000 employees

	D(W)		DK		E		F		FIN		IRL		N		NL		P		S		T		UK	
	<1	>1	<1	>1	<1	>1	<1	>1	<1	>1	<1	>1	<1	>1	<1	>1	<1	>1	<1	>1	<1	>1	<1	>1
Employee share options	6	12	ni	ni	7	2	3	4	11	11	16	16	11	15	13	8	6	9	9	5	0	5	25	32
Profit sharing	18	22	3	4	9	14	67	69	15	25	12	9	5	4	37	39	21	23	9	15	5	7	19	22
Group bonus schemes#	7	8	6	7	4	7	30	28	26	31	16	9	14	10	8	15	11	14	12	11	3	11	16	18
Individual bonus/commission#	69	64	16	14	31	32	31	36	26	35	20	25	10	9	57	69	21	14	4	2	14	17	28	26
Merit/performance related pay#	38	42	50	53	55	64	56	65	29	38	45	38	17	14	24	35	55	82	10	8	51	57	52	53

ni question not included in country   # French results are for 1990 and include administrative staff

Table 4.3c: Percentage of organisations offering the following incentive schemes for clerical staff.(+)

Country	D(W)	DK	E	F	FIN	IRL	N	NL	P	S	T	UK
Employee share options	8	ni	5	3	11	10	13	10	5	8	0	26
Profit sharing	11	3	9	68	17	12	4	32	20	16	4	19
Group bonus schemes	6	4	2	ni	33	12	11	6	7	12	3	14
Individual bonus/commission	52	6	4	ni	13	11	3	36	7	1	6	7
Merit/performance related pay	35	49	42	ni	27	27	10	22	59	7	48	42

Private and public sector

	D(W)		DK		E *		F		FIN		IRL		N		NL *		P *		S		T *		UK	
	Pu	Pr	Pu	Pr	Pu	Pr	Pu	Pr	Pu	Pr	Pu	Pr	Pu	Pr	Pu	Pr	Pu	Pr	Pu	Pr	Pu	Pr	Pu	Pr
Employee share options	2	10	ni	ni	0	5	<1	4	10	13	0	16	2	24	0	11	0	7	0	14	0	0	<1	37
Profit sharing	4	12	0	5	6	9	35	75	26	18	0	15	1	4	0	32	0	22	7	22	6	4	6	24
Group bonus schemes	11	5	1	6	6	1	ni	ni	31	29	5	15	4	18	0	6	0	8	4	20	0	4	5	19
Individual bonus/commission	29	55	8	3	0	4	ni	ni	10	16	7	13	1	4	100	37	0	8	0	2	6	5	5	8
Merit/performance related pay	15	39	41	55	44	41	ni	ni	27	27	5	36	4	13	50	22	15	66	6	8	31	52	21	50

Less than 1,000 or greater than or equal to 1,000 employees

	D(W)		DK		E		F		FIN		IRL		N		NL		P		S		T		UK	
	<1	>1	<1	>1	<1	>1	<1	>1	<1	>1	<1	>1	<1	>1	<1	>1	<1	>1	<1	>1	<1	>1	<1	>1
Employee share options	6	12	ni	ni	6	3	3	4	10	11	11	11	11	15	11	8	4	9	10	6	0	0	23	27
Profit sharing	8	15	3	4	7	13	67	70	15	24	12	12	4	4	30	39	20	23	13	18	4	4	17	21
Group bonus schemes	5	7	4	5	1	2	ni	ni	28	43	14	31	9	11	6	4	4	14	13	11	3	4	15	14
Individual bonus/commission	50	55	4	10	2	7	ni	ni	15	10	10	12	3	4	33	50	6	9	1	1	4	9	6	8
Merit/performance related pay	33	38	50	48	42	39	ni	ni	24	29	16	16	10	10	22	27	54	77	7	8	47	50	44	40

ni question not included in country

Table 4.3d: Percentage of organisations offering the following incentive schemes for manual staff.(+)

Country	D(W)	DK	E	F	FIN	IRL	N	NL	P	S	T	UK
Employee share options	7	ni	4	4	10	10	13	10	5	7	1	23
Profit sharing	10	2	8	57	16	11	4	31	19	13	3	17
Group bonus schemes#	14	18	3	25	43	17	15	7	10	27	13	25
Individual bonus/commission#	30	9	3	17	8	13	7	35	10	6	10	17
Merit/performance related pay#	32	24	30	41	24	12	10	27	57	26	18	21

Private and public sector

	D(W)		DK		E		F		FIN		IRL		N		NL		P		S		T		UK	
	Pu	Pr	Pu	Pr	Pu	Pr	Pu	Pr	Pu	Pr	Pu	Pr	Pu	Pr	Pu	Pr	Pu	Pr	Pu	Pr	Pu	Pr	Pu	Pr
					*								*		*		*		*		*			
Employee share options	3	8	ni	ni	0	5	0	4	10	12	0	16	2	24	0	11	0	7	0	11	0	1	1	33
Profit sharing	4	11	0	4	6	8	31	64	26	16	0	13	1	4	0	30	0	20	6	18	6	3	11	20
Group bonus schemes#	11	15	3	27	6	3	17	28	40	41	12	20	6	25	0	7	0	12	13	40	38	10	37	23
Individual bonus/commission#	15	33	8	8	0	0	12	19	2	11	7	17	1	12	100	35	0	11	4	8	19	8	27	13
Merit/performance related pay#	8	36	29	20	37	27	29	43	27	23	2	18	5	15	50	27	15	64	21	30	19	19	9	26

Less than 1,000 or greater than or equal to 1,000 employees

	D(W)		DK		E		F		FIN		IRL		N		NL		P		S		T		UK	
	<1	>1	<1	>1	<1	>1	<1	>1	<1	>1	<1	>1	<1	>1	<1	>1	<1	>1	<1	>1	<1	>1	<1	>1
Employee share options	5	11	ni	ni	5	2	3	3	10	10	11	6	11	15	11	8	4	9	8	4	1	0	21	23
Profit sharing	8	14	2	2	5	12	55	60	13	24	11	9	4	4	29	35	18	23	10	15	3	4	17	18
Group bonus schemes#	13	15	19	14	2	4	27	23	34	59	16	22	14	15	8	4	9	14	30	25	9	20	24	27
Individual bonus/commission#	28	34	8	10	2	3	17	18	10	4	12	16	7	5	31	50	11	5	6	5	7	15	13	20
Merit/performance related pay#	30	35	23	25	27	20	39	44	23	24	14	6	12	6	27	31	56	59	23	30	20	15	24	19

ni question not included in country   # French results are for 1990

Table 4.4a: Percentage of organisations who offer the following parental benefits to managers (+)

Country	D(W)	DK	E	F	FIN	IRL	N	NL	P	S	T	UK
Workplace childcare	2	3	1	3	4	4	20	4	12	3	11	11
Childcare allowances	2	ni	9	12	ni	1	7	20	ni	ni	4	3
Career break scheme	7	1	15	19	6	23	4	5	41	ni	5	17
Maternity leave	11	17	25	51	35	38	28	31	4	15	38	43
Paternity leave	8	8	12	32	33	9	25	19	15	11	19	29

Private and public sector

	D(W)		DK		E *		F		FIN		IRL		N *		NL *		P *		S *		T		UK	
	Pu	Pr	Pu	Pr	Pu	Pr	Pu	Pr	Pu	Pr	Pu	Pr	Pu	Pr	Pu	Pr	Pu	Pr	Pu	Pr	Pu	Pr	Pu	Pr
Workplace childcare	8	1	4	3	0	1	7	2	10	3	12	0	24	17	50	3	23	8	4	3	13	12	33	3
Childcare allowances	3	2	ni	ni	25	7	25	9	ni	ni	2	0	7	6	0	0	ni	ni	ni	ni	0	5	7	2
Career break scheme	14	5	2	1	37	12	45	13	7	4	65	5	4	5	0	5	77	31	ni	ni	6	5	35	10
Maternity leave	23	8	2	2	44	22	43	79	44	29	31	52	26	33	50	29	15	1	26	6	50	37	81	29
Paternity leave	20	6	2	2	25	10	66	24	40	27	10	9	26	24	100	16	31	12	20	4	13	21	47	21

Less than 1,000 or greater than or equal to 1,000 employees

	D(W)		DK		E		F		FIN		IRL		N		NL		P		S		T		UK	
	<1	>1	<1	>1	<1	>1	<1	>1	<1	>1	<1	>1	<1	>1	<1	>1	<1	>1	<1	>1	<1	>1	<1	>1
Workplace childcare	0	5	1	7	1	1	1	5	1	10	1	13	16	30	2	12	7	27	3	4	3	26	2	19
Childcare allowances	1	4	ni	ni	7	12	9	16	ni	ni	1	0	5	13	15	42	ni	ni	ni	ni	3	7	2	4
Career break scheme	3	14	2	0	7	27	14	27	5	2	19	34	4	4	0	23	37	55	ni	ni	3	9	6	26
Maternity leave	7	17	16	15	19	34	47	57	34	36	36	44	28	27	27	46	3	9	8	22	35	43	34	51
Paternity leave	4	14	6	9	7	19	26	42	32	35	7	13	25	26	17	27	13	23	6	16	18	20	21	34

ni question not included in country

Table 4.4b: Percentage of organisations who offer the following parental benefits to professional and technical staff (+)

Country

	D(W)	DK	E	F	FIN	IRL	N	NL	P	S	T	UK
Workplace childcare	2	3	2	3	4	4	24	4	12	3	13	11
Childcare allowances	2	ni	11	12	ni	1	7	20	ni	ni	6	3
Career break scheme	9	2	20	19	10	23	6	5	44	ni	5	17
Maternity leave	13	17	34	51	38	40	27	36	4	13	46	43
Paternity leave	9	8	14	32	36	9	25	20	16	10	22	29

Private and public sector

	D(W) Pu	Pr	DK* Pu	Pr	E Pu	Pr	F Pu	Pr	FIN Pu	Pr	IRL Pu	Pr	N Pu	Pr	NL* Pu	Pr	P* Pu	Pr	S* Pu	Pr	T Pu	Pr	UK Pu	Pr
Workplace childcare	8	1	4	3	0	2	7	2	10	3	12	0	34	17	50	3	23	8	4	3	19	13	33	3
Childcare allowances	3	2	ni		31	9	26	9	ni		2	0	6	7	0	21	ni		ni		0	7	7	2
Career break scheme	20	7	5	1	50	16	44	13	11	8	65	6	4	6	0	6	85	34	ni		6	5	35	10
Maternity leave	28	10	2	27	56	32	77	44	45	32	52	33	33	24	50	35	15	1	22	5	62	44	80	29
Paternity leave	24	7	2	11	25	12	64	24	40	30	30	10	26	23	100	17	31	14	17	4	19	24	46	21

Less than 1,000 or greater than or equal to 1,000 employees

	D(W) <1	>1	DK <1	>1	E <1	>1	F <1	>1	FIN <1	>1	IRL <1	>1	N <1	>1	NL <1	>1	P <1	>1	S <1	>1	T <1	>1	UK <1	>1
Workplace childcare	0	5	1	7	2	2	1	5	1	10	1	13	20	35	2	12	7	27	3	4	3	30	2	19
Childcare allowances	1	4	ni		10	13	10	16	ni		1	0	5	13	15	42	ni		ni		5	7	2	4
Career break scheme	4	17	3	1	13	30	15	25	9	11	19	38	4	6	1	23	41	54	ni		3	9	6	26
Maternity leave	9	20	17	15	28	45	48	57	37	39	37	47	27	27	31	54	3	9	6	20	46	46	34	51
Paternity leave	5	15	7	9	10	18	26	41	34	37	7	16	24	26	17	31	13	27	4	15	23	20	22	34

ni question not included in country

Table 4.4c: Percentage of organisations who offer the following parental benefits to clerical staff (+)

Country	D(W)	DK	E	F	FIN	IRL	N	NL	P	S	T	UK
Workplace childcare	2	3	2	3	5	4	18	5	13	3	14	11
Childcare allowances	2	ni	16	14	ni	0	6	20	ni	ni	7	3
Career break scheme	8	2	16	15	11	30	3	2	44	ni	6	14
Maternity leave	12	18	42	54	38	41	28	39	4	16	48	43
Paternity leave	9	8	15	33	36	9	25	20	16	12	22	28

Private and public sector

	D(W)		DK		E *		F		FIN		IRL		N		NL *		P *		S		T *		UK	
	Pu	Pr	Pu	Pr	Pu	Pr	Pu	Pr	Pu	Pr	Pu	Pr	Pu	Pr	Pu	Pr	Pu	Pr	Pu	Pr	Pu	Pr	Pu	Pr
Workplace childcare	8	1	4	3	0	2	7	2	11	3	12	0	20	17	50	4	23	10	2	3	19	14	33	3
Childcare allowances	3	2	ni	ni	31	14	30	10	ni	ni	0	0	6	6	0	21	0	0	ni	ni	0	9	7	2
Career break scheme	18	6	5	1	1	18	31	11	13	8	70	12	2	4	0	2	92	34	ni	ni	6	7	32	7
Maternity leave	27	10	3	28	56	41	82	46	45	32	55	34	34	25	50	37	15	1	26	7	62	47	80	29
Paternity leave	24	6	2	12	25	13	66	25	44	30	10	8	26	24	100	17	31	14	21	4	19	24	46	21

Less than 1,000 or greater than or equal to 1,000 employees

	D(W)		DK		E		F		FIN		IRL		N		NL		P		S		T		UK	
	<1	>1	<1	>1	<1	>1	<1	>1	<1	>1	<1	>1	<1	>1	<1	>1	<1	>1	<1	>1	<1	>1	<1	>1
Workplace childcare	0	5	1	7	2	3	1	5	1	11	1	13	14	27	2	15	9	27	1	4	4	30	2	18
Childcare allowances	1	4	ni	ni	14	18	10	19	ni	ni	0	0	5	10	15	42	ni	ni	ni	ni	8	7	2	4
Career break scheme	16	3	3	2	12	23	13	18	10	11	25	47	4	1	0	11	42	50	ni	ni	4	11	6	21
Maternity leave	8	20	19	15	38	48	50	58	37	39	38	50	28	27	34	58	3	9	9	22	48	48	33	50
Paternity leave	5	15	9	7	11	20	27	43	36	38	7	16	25	26	17	31	13	27	7	16	23	20	21	34

ni question not included in country

Table 4.4d: Organisations who offer the following parental benefits to manual staff (+)

Country

	D(W)	DK	E	F	FIN	IRL	N	NL	P	S	T	UK
Workplace childcare	2	3	2	2	5	4	18	4	15	3	14	10
Childcare allowances	2	ni	14	9	ni	0	6	18	ni	ni	9	3
Career break scheme	5	2	20	16	10	22	3	6	44	ni	7	12
Maternity leave	11	9	38	43	37	36	28	37	4	15	48	38
Paternity leave	7	4	14	28	36	9	25	19	16	12	23	26

Private and public sector

	D(W) *		DK		E *		F		FIN		IRL		N *		NL *		P *		S		T *		UK	
	Pu	Pr	Pu	Pr	Pu	Pr	Pu	Pr	Pu	Pr	Pu	Pr	Pu	Pr	Pu	Pr	Pu	Pr	Pu	Pr	Pu	Pr	Pu	Pr
Workplace childcare	8	1	3	3	0	2	7	1	11	3	12	0	21	17	50	3	23	12	2	3	19	14	31	2
Childcare allowances	3	2	ni	ni	31	13	25	5	ni	ni	0	0	6	6	0	20	ni	ni	ni	ni	0	11	5	1
Career break scheme	12	4	4	0	50	16	42	10	13	7	50	9	2	4	0	7	92	34	ni	ni	6	7	29	5
Maternity leave	21	9	2	14	56	37	76	36	45	31	50	29	34	25	50	36	15	1	26	5	63	47	77	23
Paternity leave	19	5	2	5	25	12	60	20	44	29	10	8	26	24	50	17	31	14	21	4	19	24	44	19

Less than 1,000 or greater than or equal to 1,000 employees

	D(W)		DK		E		F		FIN		IRL		N		NL		P		S		T		UK	
	<1	>1	<1	>1	<1	>1	<1	>1	<1	>1	<1	>1	<1	>1	<1	>1	<1	>1	<1	>1	<1	>1	<1	>1
Workplace childcare	0	4	1	6	2	3	1	3	1	11	1	13	14	28	2	12	11	27	1	4	4	30	2	16
Childcare allowances	1	4	ni	ni	11	18	6	13	ni	ni	0	0	5	10	13	42	ni	ni	ni	ni	11	7	2	3
Career break scheme	2	10	1	2	13	29	13	21	9	11	19	34	4	1	1	27	42	50	ni	ni	4	11	3	18
Maternity leave	7	16	10	7	34	46	41	47	37	39	32	47	28	27	32	58	3	9	9	21	49	46	28	46
Paternity leave	4	13	4	4	11	16	22	36	35	38	7	16	24	26	16	31	13	27	7	6	25	20	18	32

ni question not included in country

SECTION V: TRAINING AND DEVELOPMENT

Table 5.1: The approximate proportion of annual salaries and wages currently spent on training (Valid %)

Country

	D(W)	DK	E	F	FIN	IRL	N	NL	P	S	T	UK
0.01 – 0.50	19	9	18	0	7	10	23	7	15	1	8	12
0.51 – 1.00	18	30	32	1	25	27	22	24	15	14	25	21
1.01 – 2.00	22	36	27	18	30	24	20	30	31	25	20	27
2.01 – 4.00	21	15	11	45	24	22	17	27	21	24	10	23
4.01 or more	21	10	12	35	12	18	19	13	18	36	37	17
Don't know (non valid)	41	25	21	2	18	35	35	10	25	47	44	34

Private and public sector

	D(W) Pu	D(W) Pr	DK Pu	DK Pr	E Pu	E Pr	F Pu	F Pr	FIN Pu	FIN Pr	IRL Pu	IRL Pr	N Pu	N Pr	NL Pu	NL Pr	P Pu	P Pr	S Pu	S Pr	T Pu	T Pr	UK Pu	UK Pr
0.01 – 0.50	32	17	13	3	10	19	0	0	9	4	13	8	33	7	0	6	12	13	3	0	13	7	18	11
0.51 – 1.00	19	19	35	25	27	31	6	<1	34	23	39	22	28	17	100	23	25	15	18	12	50	30	25	20
1.01 – 2.00	22	22	31	43	54	24	31	16	29	34	13	29	15	24	0	31	12	36	13	34	25	20	26	28
2.01 – 4.00	8	24	0	16	0	12	32	49	20	25	22	22	13	22	0	26	37	17	23	15	0	13	15	24
4.01 or more	21	18	6	13	9	13	31	35	7	14	13	20	11	30	0	13	12	19	42	29	12	30	15	16
Don't know (non valid)	17	45	30	19	13	22	4	1	11	21	33	36	22	46	50	10	21	27	55	42	44	45	37	33

Less than 1,000 or greater than or equal to 1,000 employees

	D(W) <1	D(W) >1	DK <1	DK >1	E <1	E >1	F <1	F >1	FIN <1	FIN >1	IRL <1	IRL >1	N <1	N >1	NL <1	NL >1	P <1	P >1	S <1	S >1	T <1	T >1	UK <1	UK >1
0.01 – 0.50	18	22	6	13	5	28	0	0	9	5	7	17	21	28	8	0	19	5	0	3	13	6	10	14
0.51 – 1.00	20	13	30	28	29	37	2	<1	23	34	26	25	25	12	24	20	17	11	13	17	31	35	24	19
1.01 – 2.00	24	19	38	34	20	35	22	13	30	32	28	13	21	16	31	30	29	37	26	23	25	17	29	25
2.01 – 4.00	16	26	16	14	10	13	49	39	25	24	21	25	17	16	24	35	19	26	21	28	5	25	20	25
4.01 or more	22	19	10	12	14	10	26	48	15	5	18	21	16	28	12	15	17	21	40	29	14	33	20	17
Don't know (non valid)	43	37	29	18	27	12	2	2	15	21	28	22	34	39	11	8	34	5	41	53	43	46	31	36

Table 5.2a: Average days training per year for managers. (Valid %)

Country	D(W)	DK	E	F	FIN	IRL	N	NL	P	S	T	UK
0.01 – 1.00	3	2	6	4	2	4	3	16	10	1	2	7
1.01 – 3.00	28	20	11	23	20	23	18	32	10	12	19	28
3.01 – 5.00	35	38	22	32	30	36	31	30	27	36	19	36
5.01 – 10.00	27	32	36	31	34	32	33	18	33	36	20	22
10 .00 and above	6	9	26	10	14	4	15	4	18	15	41	7
Don't know (non valid)	35	39	26	20	24	31	51	33	38	41	22	39

Private and public sector * * * * *

	D(W)		DK		E		F		FIN		IRL		N		NL		P		S		T		UK	
	Pu	Pr	Pu	Pr	Pu	Pr	Pu	Pr	Pu	Pr	Pu	Pr	Pu	Pr	Pu	Pr	Pu	Pr	Pu	Pr	Pu	Pr	Pu	Pr
0.01 – 1.00	10	2	0	3	10	5	7	3	2	2	12	2	5	2	0	16	25	8	0	1	0	2	8	7
1.01 – 3.00	32	28	19	20	0	11	22	24	21	21	24	22	11	17	0	33	0	13	6	16	33	27	30	28
3.01 – 5.00	25	36	31	41	20	22	45	30	31	37	24	41	30	31	0	29	37	28	34	39	50	25	34	37
5.01 – 10.00	27	28	39	28	50	37	22	32	31	34	36	32	46	31	0	19	37	31	41	33	17	29	23	22
10 .00 and above	7	6	11	8	20	25	5	10	14	7	4	3	8	19	100	3	0	20	18	11	0	18	5	7
Don't know (non valid)	35	35	40	38	25	27	21	20	26	22	35	30	61	44	50	33	31	37	48	37	19	23	53	34

Less than 1,000 or greater than or equal to 1,000 employees

	D(W)		DK		E		F		FIN		IRL		N		NL		P		S		T		UK	
	<1	>1	<1	>1	<1	>1	<1	>1	<1	>1	<1	>1	<1	>1	<1	>1	<1	>1	<1	>1	<1	>1	<1	>1
0.01 – 1.00	3	4	2	2	2	8	4	3	1	4	5	0	2	4	18	6	11	7	1	0	3	0	6	8
1.01 – 3.00	29	29	20	19	11	11	26	19	19	22	21	31	19	16	34	19	9	14	17	9	20	33	31	26
3.01 – 5.00	34	38	37	41	22	22	32	32	30	31	41	19	30	32	25	56	29	29	33	41	37	19	34	37
5.01 – 10.00	29	24	33	29	35	40	29	35	37	29	29	44	33	36	18	19	31	36	37	33	23	30	21	23
10 .00 and above	6	6	9	10	30	19	8	11	14	14	4	6	16	12	5	0	20	14	12	17	17	19	8	6
Don't know (non valid)	33	37	37	42	34	14	22	17	15	35	27	44	50	56	32	35	42	23	37	46	23	20	36	42

Table 5.2b: Average days training per year for professional and technical staff. (Valid %)

Country	D(W)	DK	E	F	FIN	IRL	N	NL	P	S	T	UK
0.01 – 1.00	9	3	2	3	2	3	2	8	6	6	3	7
1.01 – 3.00	43	21	17	28	19	27	16	26	18	18	17	29
3.01 – 5.00	27	34	22	32	37	32	27	35	28	31	10	33
5.01 – 10.00	17	36	32	30	28	30	38	27	26	38	26	24
10 .00 and above	5	7	28	7	11	9	17	4	24	8	44	8
Don't know (non valid)	34	39	24	20	22	33	51	32	37	44	21	40

Private and public sector

	D(W)		DK		E*		F		FIN		IRL		N*		NL*		P*		S*		T*		UK	
	Pu	Pr	Pu	Pr	Pu	Pr	Pu	Pr	Pu	Pr	Pu	Pr	Pu	Pr	Pu	Pr	Pu	Pr	Pu	Pr	Pu	Pr	Pu	Pr
0.01 – 1.00	5	9	1	3	0	1	5	3	2	1	0	4	6	0	0	8	22	3	4	6	0	5	8	6
1.01 – 3.00	55	41	25	18	11	18	20	31	19	22	33	26	14	11	0	27	11	20	14	19	33	18	28	29
3.01 – 5.00	22	27	35	32	11	24	36	31	30	47	38	33	31	28	100	34	33	26	20	37	11	27	30	35
5.01 – 10.00	10	18	34	37	56	30	32	29	39	23	24	30	33	41	0	27	22	22	48	32	33	30	27	24
10 .00 and above	7	5	4	9	22	27	7	1	9	7	5	7	17	20	0	4	11	26	14	5	22	20	5	7
Don't know (non valid)	35	35	42	36	31	25	19	22	26	21	38	33	60	42	50	32	23	37	50	42	13	22	54	35

Less than 1,000 or greater than or equal to 1,000 employees

	D(W)		DK		E		F		FIN		IRL		N		NL		P		S		T		UK	
	<1	>1	<1	>1	<1	>1	<1	>1	<1	>1	<1	>1	<1	>1	<1	>1	<1	>1	<1	>1	<1	>1	<1	>1
0.01 – 1.00	10	7	5	0	0	3	4	3	1	2	3	0	2	0	10	0	6	7	8	2	3	7	7	7
1.01 – 3.00	43	44	21	22	16	18	33	23	19	22	30	19	15	19	29	13	19	13	22	14	26	14	32	26
3.01 – 5.00	23	33	30	40	21	25	32	32	40	39	34	25	28	22	35	40	31	20	33	33	23	25	30	36
5.01 – 10.00	19	12	38	30	31	33	27	34	30	24	24	50	38	41	22	47	17	47	33	45	26	39	24	24
10 .00 and above	5	4	6	8	32	21	4	8	12	12	9	6	17	19	5	0	28	13	9	6	23	14	8	8
Don't know (non valid)	33	36	37	42	31	13	22	19	14	34	30	44	50	54	30	35	41	23	38	52	22	20	36	44

Table 5.2c: Average days training per year for clerical staff. (Valid %)

Country

	D(W)	DK	E	F	FIN	IRL	N	NL	P	S	T	UK
0.01 – 1.00	32	13	10	11	5	19	12	16	10	15	9	24
1.01 – 3.00	45	41	30	39	8	47	44	47	31	39	16	43
3.01 – 5.00	14	32	26	26	33	22	28	27	23	33	17	20
5.01 – 10.00	7	13	22	18	34	11	16	7	17	13	17	9
10.00 and above	2	1	13	5	20	1	1	3	19	1	41	4
Don't know (non valid)	39	40	25	21	22	32	53	32	38	44	23	42

Private and public sector

	D(W)		DK		E*		F		FIN		IRL		N		NL*		P*		S		T*		UK	
	Pu	Pr	Pu	Pr	Pu	Pr	Pu	Pr	Pu	Pr	Pu	Pr	Pu	Pr	Pu	Pr	Pu	Pr	Pu	Pr	Pu	Pr	Pu	Pr
0.01 – 1.00	43	30	4	18	22	10	9	11	11	10	17	21	17	7	0	16	11	11	14	14	25	11	24	24
1.10 – 3.00	32	45	41	39	0	33	38	41	36	34	46	44	40	46	0	46	22	34	27	48	38	29	46	44
3.01 – 5.00	11	15	29	35	33	25	23	28	34	37	29	21	40	21	100	28	44	14	42	27	13	27	18	20
5.01 – 10.00	9	7	25	5	33	21	23	16	11	17	8	8	3	25	0	8	0	20	16	10	13	18	8	9
10 .00 and above	4	2	0	2	11	11	7	3	7	2	0	0	0	0	0	0	22	20	0	0	0	16	4	4
Don't know (non valid)	37	40	42	38	31	38	26	19	24	21	33	33	60	47	50	32	23	23	49	42	13	25	54	37

Less than 1,000 or greater than or equal to 1,000 employees

	D(W)		DK		E		F		FIN		IRL		N		NL		P		S		T		UK	
	<1	>1	<1	>1	<1	>1	<1	>1	<1	>1	<1	>1	<1	>1	<1	>1	<1	>1	<1	>1	<1	>1	<1	>1
0.01 – 1.00	32	31	12	15	11	10	12	10	9	10	22	7	14	4	16	13	9	13	14	17	10	20	27	22
1.01 – 3.00	46	45	43	37	27	35	44	34	33	39	45	60	44	46	46	47	24	47	42	38	33	24	43	43
3.01 – 5.00	13	16	31	33	28	22	25	29	34	33	20	27	26	33	27	33	30	7	34	29	30	20	19	20
5.01 – 10.00	8	7	12	13	23	21	17	21	20	14	12	7	15	17	7	7	12	27	9	17	10	24	7	12
10 .00 and above	2	2	1	2	11	13	3	6	3	4	1	0	1	0	4	0	24	7	1	1	17	0	4	3
Don't know (non valid)	38	40	38	42	32	15	22	19	15	33	28	44	52	56	31	31	42	23	40	49	23	23	37	46

Table 5.2d: Average days training per year for manual staff. (Valid %)

Country	D(W)	DK	E	F	FIN	IRL	N	NL	P	S	T	UK
0.01 – 1.00	44	20	12	17	22	14	17	11	24	16	12	26
1.01 – 3.00	34	34	32	39	49	40	35	46	24	38	16	38
3.01 – 5.00	13	30	22	20	22	20	25	26	18	27	16	20
5.01 – 10.00	6	13	20	18	6	26	19	11	24	16	18	11
10 .00 and above	3	3	15	7	2	3	4	6	11	3	38	4
Don't know (non valid)	42	44	25	20	24	33	55	34	41	46	20	44

Private and public sector

	D(W)		DK		E*		F		FIN		IRL		N		NL*		P*		S		T*		UK	
	Pu	Pr	Pu	Pr	Pu	Pr	Pu	Pr	Pu	Pr	Pu	Pr	Pu	Pr	Pu	Pr	Pu	Pr	Pu	Pr	Pu	Pr	Pu	Pr
0.01 – 1.00	45	45	32	12	17	12	13	19	23	22	29	11	14	14	0	10	25	25	16	19	18	19	46	22
1.01 – 3.00	27	32	39	30	33	32	37	39	48	49	47	35	41	35	0	46	25	22	36	39	36	27	39	39
3.01 – 5.00	18	13	18	37	17	22	22	20	20	23	28	20	21	26	0	27	50	16	33	24	18	23	8	22
5.01 – 10.00	9	6	11	14	33	20	28	16	2	5	6	33	21	20	0	11	0	25	13	15	9	14	4	12
10 .00 and above	0	4	0	7	0	15	6	5	45	1	0	2	3	4	0	6	12	0	2	4	18	17	2	4
Don't know (non valid)	38	43	50	40	44	25	16	22	24	24	33	33	64	49	100	33	39	41	51	43	6	23	59	38

Less than 1,000 or greater than or equal to 1,000 employees

	D(W)		DK		E		F		FIN		IRL		N		NL		P		S		T		UK	
	<1	>1	<1	>1	<1	>1	<1	>1	<1	>1	<1	>1	<1	>1	<1	>1	<1	>1	<1	>1	<1	>1	<1	>1
0.01 – 1.00	51	36	21	18	14	9	19	13	23	18	16	8	19	10	12	6	21	29	20	12	14	25	27	26
1.01 – 3.00	27	42	33	34	39	27	44	32	48	51	36	46	37	29	44	50	29	14	33	45	32	29	39	38
3.01 – 5.00	16	8	31	26	13	30	18	23	22	20	20	15	22	38	28	25	17	21	30	22	22	21	19	22
5.01 – 10.00	6	8	11	16	21	20	14	24	6	6	26	23	19	19	11	13	25	21	14	17	16	7	11	12
10 .00 and above	0	8	4	5	13	14	5	8	1	4	2	8	4	5	5	6	8	14	3	3	16	18	5	3
Don't know (non valid)	40	44	42	50	33	13	21	17	17	35	29	44	53	62	34	31	47	23	42	52	22	17	37	49

Table 5.3a: Changes in the amount spent on training for managers, per employee (allowing for inflation)

Country	D(W)	DK	E	F	FIN	IRL	N	NL	P	S	T	UK
Increased	54	48	58	56	38	57	47	58	61	60	48	61
Same	25	38	26	34	41	23	29	24	14	28	18	23
Decreased	2	7	5	5	14	8	10	6	7	6	3	9
Don't know	16	4	8	3	6	10	9	9	14	5	16	7

Private and public sector

	D(W)		DK		E*		F		FIN		IRL		N		NL*		P*		S		T*		UK	
	Pu	Pr	Pu	Pr	Pu	Pr	Pu	Pr	Pu	Pr	Pu	Pr	Pu	Pr	Pu	Pr	Pu	Pr	Pu	Pr	Pu	Pr	Pu	Pr
Increased	68	52	50	47	63	57	61	53	32	35	53	61	51	44	50	58	69	62	62	58	44	49	64	59
Same	21	25	38	39	19	27	31	36	48	43	23	23	26	33	0	24	15	14	25	30	19	19	20	24
Decreased	3	2	5	9	5	9	4	5	5	7	9	10	6	7	6	0	8	6	6	5	6	6	5	10
Don't know	6	18	4	4	8	8	4	3	10	2	13	9	7	11	50	8	0	15	4	6	13	17	10	6

Less than 1,000 or greater than or equal to 1,000 employees

	D(W)		DK		E		F		FIN		IRL		N		NL		P		S		T		UK	
	<1	>1	<1	>1	<1	>1	<1	>1	<1	>1	<1	>1	<1	>1	<1	>1	<1	>1	<1	>1	<1	>1	<1	>1
Increased	49	62	48	51	46	77	57	55	35	43	57	59	46	50	55	73	59	68	56	63	44	54	58	63
Same	27	21	36	41	32	18	33	34	42	41	19	31	32	23	27	11	14	14	34	23	18	17	24	21
Decreased	2	2	9	4	7	3	4	5	19	6	6	10	10	9	6	4	3	18	5	6	4	2	10	7
Don't know	19	12	5	4	12	1	3	3	2	7	7	10	8	11	8	12	18	0	4	6	20	11	6	8

Table 5.3b: Changes in the amount spent on training for professional and technical staff, per employee (allowing for inflation)

Country	D(W)	DK	E	F	FIN	IRL	N	NL	P	S	T	UK
Increased	56	46	64	58	40	52	43	59	62	35	50	54
Same	22	40	22	30	35	23	31	24	11	37	19	28
Decreased	3	8	5	4	20	7	10	4	10	6	2	9
Don't know	16	4	7	3	5	13	10	8	14	9	15	7

Private and public sector

	D(W)		DK		E*		F		FIN		IRL		N		NL*		P*		S		T*		UK	
	Pu	Pr	Pu	Pr	Pu	Pr	Pu	Pr	Pu	Pr	Pu	Pr	Pu	Pr	Pu	Pr	Pu	Pr	Pu	Pr	Pu	Pr	Pu	Pr
Increased	70	54	45	45	75	64	62	57	42	37	40	58	43	46	50	58	69	63	30	38	50	51	52	54
Same	18	23	41	41	6	23	29	31	35	36	27	21	30	31	0	25	23	10	37	38	19	20	30	28
Decreased	3	2	7	8	9	5	1	4	11	24	10	4	9	11	0	4	8	8	5	5	6	2	6	10
Don't know	6	18	4	4	6	6	4	3	10	2	15	12	9	14	50	7	0	15	10	8	13	16	10	6

Less than 1,000 or greater than or equal to 1,000 employees

	D(W)		DK		E		F		FIN		IRL		N		NL		P		S		T		UK	
	<1	>1	<1	>1	<1	>1	<1	>1	<1	>1	<1	>1	<1	>1	<1	>1	<1	>1	<1	>1	<1	>1	<1	>1
Increased	53	62	44	50	56	79	59	58	35	50	51	59	45	39	57	69	61	68	39	31	47	57	52	54
Same	23	21	41	40	26	16	30	30	39	29	20	31	30	33	27	15	11	9	37	37	20	17	26	29
Decreased	2	3	8	6	6	2	2	5	22	13	9	0	10	9	4	4	6	23	6	5	4	0	10	8
Don't know	18	12	4	4	10	1	3	3	3	6	14	9	9	11	7	12	18	0	6	11	18	11	6	9

Table 5.3c: Changes in the amount spent on training for clerical staff, per employee (allowing for inflation)

Country	D(W)	DK	E	F	FIN	IRL	N	NL	P	S	T	UK
Increased	33	37	53	49	31	48	32	53	55	37	37	43
Same	35	47	31	37	43	30	39	32	17	46	24	37
Decreased	4	10	6	7	22	9	15	4	9	10	6	10
Don't know	18	4	7	3	4	11	10	7	16	6	16	8

Private and public sector

	D(W)		DK		E*		F		FIN		IRL		N		NL*		P*		S		T*		UK	
	Pu	Pr	Pu	Pr	Pu	Pr	Pu	Pr	Pu	Pr	Pu	Pr	Pu	Pr	Pu	Pr	Pu	Pr	Pu	Pr	Pu	Pr	Pu	Pr
Increased	51	34	47	31	56	52	59	46	35	30	45	48	36	29	50	52	85	57	43	32	44	36	42	43
Same	36	39	38	53	25	32	34	39	36	43	30	30	36	47	0	33	8	18	41	50	25	26	38	37
Decreased	3	5	8	12	6	6	3	8	19	24	13	7	14	12	0	4	8	8	9	11	0	7	7	11
Don't know	10	22	4	4	6	7	4	3	8	2	2	11	12	11	8	50	0	18	6	6	13	17	10	7

Less than 1,000 or greater than or equal to 1,000 employees

	D(W)		DK		E		F		FIN		IRL		N		NL		P		S		T		UK	
	<1	>1	<1	>1	<1	>1	<1	>1	<1	>1	<1	>1	<1	>1	<1	>1	<1	>1	<1	>1	<1	>1	<1	>1
Increased	32	44	35	41	45	65	49	50	30	35	47	47	36	23	53	54	55	55	40	33	35	41	45	42
Same	40	36	48	44	34	27	38	35	43	43	27	44	37	42	30	35	14	27	44	49	23	26	35	38
Decreased	4	5	10	9	7	4	7	7	25	14	11	0	13	18	4	8	4	6	11	9	9	4	11	9
Don't know	23	15	4	5	10	1	3	3	2	6	6	11	9	10	7	8	18	21	5	6	19	11	6	9

Table 5.3d: Changes in the amount spent on training for manual staff, per employee (allowing for inflation)

Country	D(W)	DK	E	F	FIN	IRL	N	NL	P	S	T	UK
Increased	15	35	42	49	37	44	36	64	48	41	40	38
Same	35	40	29	23	40	28	37	21	16	35	24	33
Decreased	3	5	4	5	15	7	11	3	8	8	4	9
Don't know	22	6	7	2	4	12	10	6	18	7	15	9

Private and public sector

	D(W)		DK		E*		F		FIN		IRL		N		NL*		P*		S		T*		UK	
	Pu	Pr	Pu	Pr	Pu	Pr	Pu	Pr	Pu	Pr	Pu	Pr	Pu	Pr	Pu	Pr	Pu	Pr	Pu	Pr	Pu	Pr	Pu	Pr
Increased	31	37	34	36	66	41	57	48	36	39	30	51	37	37	50	63	46	51	36	45	50	37	28	42
Same	27	29	44	37	13	30	28	23	40	37	37	23	35	38	0	22	18	16	41	31	31	24	42	31
Decreased	4	2	7	4	6	4	6	3	4	6	10	6	10	12	0	3	8	8	9	7	0	5	11	9
Don't know	9	11	5	8	8	6	6	4	8	2	12	12	14	12	50	6	15	18	7	6	6	16	12	7

Less than 1,000 or greater than or equal to 1,000 employees

	D(W)		DK		E		F		FIN		IRL		N		NL		P		S		T		UK	
	<1	>1	<1	>1	<1	>1	<1	>1	<1	>1	<1	>1	<1	>1	<1	>1	<1	>1	<1	>1	<1	>1	<1	>1
Increased	31	44	35	35	33	56	48	51	37	40	42	53	40	27	62	73	45	59	43	38	40	39	41	36
Same	28	28	38	42	31	27	24	21	41	39	26	34	36	40	22	19	14	23	32	40	20	30	30	35
Decreased	2	3	4	6	6	1	6	1	16	11	8	0	10	12	4	0	0	7	9	9	4	4	10	9
Don't know	20	13	6	6	10	1	2	3	2	6	13	9	8	8	6	8	24	0	6	6	17	11	6	10

Table 5.4: Organisations who systematically analyse employee training needs

Country

	D(W)	DK	E	F	FIN	IRL	N	NL	P	S	T	UK
Yes	46	59	76	88	76	73	64	67	70	77	53	81
No	51	39	23	10	23	25	32	28	27	20	39	18

Private and public sector

	D(W)		DK		E *		F		FIN		IRL		N		NL *		P *		S		T *		UK	
	Pu	Pr	Pu	Pr	Pu	Pr	Pu	Pr	Pu	Pr	Pu	Pr	Pu	Pr	Pu	Pr	Pu	Pr	Pu	Pr	Pu	Pr	Pu	Pr
Yes	51	46	50	66	80	76	88	87	77	72	58	76	65	65	100	66	62	71	77	77	56	54	74	84
No	49	52	47	34	20	24	10	10	21	27	40	20	32	33	0	29	38	26	19	21	25	40	25	15

Less than 1,000 or greater than or equal to 1,000 employees

	D(W)		DK		E		F		FIN		IRL		N		NL		P		S		T		UK	
	<1	>1	<1	>1	<1	>1	<1	>1	<1	>1	<1	>1	<1	>1	<1	>1	<1	>1	<1	>1	<1	>1	<1	>1
Yes	39	58	58	61	69	91	86	90	70	88	68	91	64	64	67	69	62	96	73	82	52	54	78	82
No	58	40	40	37	31	9	11	8	30	10	29	9	33	30	28	23	35	0	16	44	44	30	20	17

Table 5.5a: Training needs analysed through projected business/service plans. (Valid %)

Country

	D(W)	DK	E	F	FIN	IRL	N	NL	P	S	T	UK
Always	35	24	45	36	17	30	30	24	23	21	34	30
Often	32	29	33	28	23	28	41	28	44	46	40	32
Sometimes	28	37	15	22	13	28	29	34	33	31	14	35
Never	5	11	7	15	4	14	1	14	0	3	11	4

Private and public sector

	D(W)		DK		E *		F		FIN		IRL		N		NL *		P *		S		T *		UK	
	Pu	Pr	Pu	Pr	Pu	Pr	Pu	Pr	Pu	Pr	Pu	Pr	Pu	Pr	Pu	Pr	Pu	Pr	Pu	Pr	Pu	Pr	Pu	Pr
Always	25	35	16	27	22	47	38	36	26	33	18	34	32	31	0	25	17	17	21	20	50	31	20	33
Often	30	34	34	27	11	34	34	24	39	42	23	30	33	45	0	28	46	46	49	45	50	41	27	33
Sometimes	37	26	38	37	33	13	17	24	24	22	29	27	35	22	100	33	37	37	29	32	0	16	46	31
Never	7	5	12	9	33	6	12	16	10	3	29	9	0	1	0	14	0	0	0	1	0	3	13	7

Less than 1,000 or greater than or equal to 1,000 employees

	D(W)		DK		E		F		FIN		IRL		N		NL		P		S		T		UK	
	<1	>1	<1	>1	<1	>1	<1	>1	<1	>1	<1	>1	<1	>1	<1	>1	<1	>1	<1	>1	<1	>1	<1	>1
Always	39	31	25	25	39	53	31	41	22	42	31	27	33	22	19	36	19	36	19	22	41	28	30	30
Often	33	31	36	16	34	32	26	30	32	21	29	27	36	53	35	11	50	27	48	45	41	39	32	32
Sometimes	23	32	31	46	18	11	24	18	22	21	25	36	30	24	30	44	31	36	31	31	6	22	35	34
Never	6	6	9	13	9	5	18	11	8	5	15	9	1	0	17	6	0	0	3	2	12	11	3	4

Table 5.5b: Training needs analysed through training audits. (Valid %)

Country	D(W)	DK	E	F	FIN	IRL	N	NL	P	S	T	UK
Always	35	21	13	9	24	22	3	37	54	0	67	20
Often	36	46	20	16	27	27	10	38	30	2	21	34
Sometimes	24	31	24	37	20	38	40	19	16	19	13	39
Never	5	2	43	38	<1	14	48	6	0	29	0	8

Private and public sector *

	D(W) Pu	D(W) Pr	DK Pu	DK Pr	E Pu	E Pr	F Pu	F Pr	FIN Pu	FIN Pr	IRL Pu	IRL Pr	N Pu	N Pr	NL Pu	NL Pr	P Pu	P Pr	S Pu	S Pr	T Pu	T Pr	UK Pu	UK Pr
Always	33	34	23	19	0	14	13	9	31	38	0	27	4	2	50	36	57	54	0	0	78	64	12	22
Often	37	36	45	46	29	21	10	17	47	31	41	25	13	5	50	38	43	28	2	1	11	23	33	34
Sometimes	21	25	32	30	0	26	37	36	22	29	47	31	53	34	0	20	0	17	26	12	11	11	48	36
Never	8	4	0	4	71	39	40	38	0	1	12	16	29	59	0	6	0	0	17	40	0	0	7	8

Less than 1,000 or greater than or equal to 1,000 employees

	D(W) <1	D(W) >1	DK <1	DK >1	E <1	E >1	F <1	F >1	FIN <1	FIN >1	IRL <1	IRL >1	N <1	N >1	NL <1	NL >1	P <1	P >1	S <1	S >1	T <1	T >1	UK <1	UK >1
Always	34	36	23	16	13	14	12	7	35	32	22	22	4	0	35	42	51	60	0	0	68	65	23	18
Often	35	37	42	52	21	19	14	18	32	44	28	28	9	12	38	42	30	30	1	2	15	30	32	34
Sometimes	24	24	34	26	21	28	34	41	33	23	35	44	38	44	23	5	19	10	19	20	17	4	36	40
Never	7	3	1	7	46	39	40	35	0	2	15	6	49	44	5	11	0	0	27	31	0	0	9	8

Table 5.5c: Training needs analysed through line management requests. (Valid %)

Country	D(W)	DK	E	F	FIN	IRL	N	NL	P	S	T	UK
Always	38	31	50	67	33	28	29	32	48	27	48	31
Often	52	54	44	28	30	52	62	50	39	59	33	51
Sometimes	11	15	5	5	7	19	8	17	13	14	19	18
Never	0	0	1	0	0	1	1	1	0	0	0	0

Private and public sector *

	D(W) Pu	D(W) Pr	DK Pu	DK Pr	E Pu	E Pr	F Pu	F Pr	FIN Pu	FIN Pr	IRL Pu	IRL Pr	N Pu	N Pr	NL Pu	NL Pr	P Pu	P Pr	S Pu	S Pr	T Pu	T Pr	UK Pu	UK Pr
Always	33	37	20	36	46	51	66	65	42	50	29	29	26	37	50	33	14	53	30	24	80	44	31	30
Often	51	51	59	51	31	44	26	30	42	42	49	48	65	57	0	51	57	35	56	61	20	35	49	53
Sometimes	16	11	13	20	15	5	8	4	13	7	20	17	9	5	50	16	29	12	14	14	0	22	20	17
Never	0	0	0	0	0	1	0	0	0	2	1	0	0	1	0	1	0	0	0	0	0	0	0	0

Less than 1,000 or greater than or equal to 1,000 employees

	D(W) <1	D(W) >1	DK <1	DK >1	E <1	E >1	F <1	F >1	FIN <1	FIN >1	IRL <1	IRL >1	N <1	N >1	NL <1	NL >1	P <1	P >1	S <1	S >1	T <1	T >1	UK <1	UK >1
Always	30	45	31	31	38	62	65	69	48	46	28	30	28	32	26	55	50	43	26	29	41	60	30	32
Often	55	49	55	51	52	36	30	27	41	46	52	52	64	58	53	36	35	48	61	57	41	20	51	51
Sometimes	15	7	14	18	8	2	6	4	10	8	18	18	8	8	19	9	15	10	14	14	19	20	18	17
Never	0	0	0	0	2	0	0	0	1	0	1	0	2	1	1	0	0	0	0	0	0	0	0	0

Table 5.5d: Training needs analysed through performance appraisal. (Valid %)

Country	D(W)	DK	E	F	FIN	IRL	N	NL	P	S	T	UK
Always	36	24	27	30	10	38	30	38	28	30	54	52
Often	23	36	33	38	26	38	41	37	21	45	31	30
Sometimes	22	30	29	26	25	18	25	21	40	24	14	15
Never	19	10	11	6	3	6	4	5	12	1	2	2

Private and public sector

	D(W)		DK		E		F		FIN		IRL		N		NL		P		S		T		UK	
	Pu	Pr	Pu	Pr	Pu	Pr	Pu	Pr	Pu	Pr	Pu	Pr	Pu	Pr	Pu	Pr	Pu	Pr	Pu	Pr	Pu	Pr	Pu	Pr
Always	40	36	13	30	11	29	25	30	7	20	14	48	26	32	0	39	0	32	29	31	0	56	37	56
Often	26	21	43	33	33	34	33	40	34	39	50	29	37	45	0	37	40	19	45	46	67	29	33	30
Sometimes	23	22	36	26	44	27	30	25	56	37	27	18	28	19	0	21	40	40	25	21	33	13	25	13
Never	11	21	9	12	11	10	10	12	2	4	9	4	9	3	0	3	8	20	0	2	0	2	5	1

Less than 1,000 or greater than or equal to 1,000 employees

	D(W)		DK		E		F		FIN		IRL		N		NL		P		S		T		UK	
	<1	>1	<1	>1	<1	>1	<1	>1	<1	>1	<1	>1	<1	>1	<1	>1	<1	>1	<1	>1	<1	>1	<1	>1
Always	34	38	23	27	26	27	29	32	14	17	38	37	30	32	38	38	23	42	35	28	52	57	56	49
Often	22	23	38	31	29	38	37	39	38	40	38	37	50	50	36	44	26	8	43	46	31	30	25	35
Sometimes	27	18	28	33	33	24	28	24	43	40	19	16	12	21	21	19	42	33	21	27	14	13	17	14
Never	17	21	11	9	12	11	11	6	6	5	7	3	6	6	6	0	10	17	2	0	3	0	2	2

Table 5.5e: Training needs analysed through employee requests. (Valid %)

Country	D(W)	DK	E	F	FIN	IRL	N	NL	P	S	T	UK
Always	12	16	18	35	15	9	10	26	10	11	26	14
Often	32	60	36	38	36	45	52	52	36	48	28	40
Sometimes	50	25	43	26	19	43	38	21	48	42	46	46
Never	7	0	3	1	0	4	0	1	5	1	0	0

Private and public sector

	D(W)		DK		E		F		FIN		IRL		N		NL		P		S		T		UK	
	Pu	Pr	Pu	Pr	Pu	Pr	Pu	Pr	Pu	Pr	Pu	Pr	Pu	Pr	Pu	Pr	Pu	Pr	Pu	Pr	Pu	Pr	Pu	Pr
Always	11	11	21	14	0	19	49	32	29	19	9	8	6	14	0	27	0	9	9	9	44	23	15	13
Often	17	34	65	58	39	37	42	37	36	58	57	39	56	50	0	53	29	36	58	43	33	27	46	37
Sometimes	65	48	14	28	46	42	10	31	36	23	35	48	38	36	100	19	71	49	32	49	22	50	39	50
Never	7	7	0	0	0	15	2	0	0	0	0	5	0	0	0	1	0	6	1	0	0	0	0	0

Less than 1,000 or greater than or equal to 1,000 employees

	D(W)		DK		E		F		FIN		IRL		N		NL		P		S		T		UK	
	<1	>1	<1	>1	<1	>1	<1	>1	<1	>1	<1	>1	<1	>1	<1	>1	<1	>1	<1	>1	<1	>1	<1	>1
Always	10	14	15	18	14	22	30	42	18	29	7	12	13	4	22	38	11	10	10	10	30	21	14	14
Often	25	39	62	55	34	40	40	35	52	51	43	48	51	54	57	38	38	33	49	49	27	29	38	41
Sometimes	59	40	23	27	48	37	29	22	30	20	47	32	36	42	20	24	46	52	41	41	42	50	48	45
Never	6	7	0	0	5	1	1	0	0	0	3	8	0	0	0	0	5	5	0	1	0	0	0	0

Table 5.6: Percentage of organisations who monitor the effectiveness of training.

Country

	D(W)	DK	E	F	FIN	IRL	N	NL	P	S	T	UK
Yes	50	39	80	71	78	73	60	65	57	58	58	82
No	41	57	14	23	18	20	20	26	38	31	24	13
Don't know	4	4	3	2	3	3	3	4	2	7	6	2

Private and public sector

	D(W)		DK		E *		F		FIN		IRL		N		NL *		P *		S		T *		UK	
	Pu	Pr	Pu	Pr	Pu	Pr	Pu	Pr	Pu	Pr	Pu	Pr	Pu	Pr	Pu	Pr	Pu	Pr	Pu	Pr	Pu	Pr	Pu	Pr
Yes	50	51	28	45	75	80	62	72	76	79	75	70	57	65	0	67	54	56	54	60	63	57	80	83
No	37	47	66	51	19	14	31	22	23	17	18	21	22	17	100	24	46	37	34	30	25	24	16	12
Don't know	6	4	4	3	0	3	5	2	2	2	5	2	5	2	0	4	0	3	7	7	0	7	2	2

Less than 1,000 or greater than or equal to 1,000 employees

	D(W)		DK		E		F		FIN		IRL		N		NL		P		S		T		UK	
	<1	>1	<1	>1	<1	>1	<1	>1	<1	>1	<1	>1	<1	>1	<1	>1	<1	>1	<1	>1	<1	>1	<1	>1
Yes	43	62	39	38	75	89	69	72	77	84	69	84	60	59	65	69	51	77	52	64	61	52	80	84
No	48	30	56	57	17	9	24	22	20	13	22	9	20	21	27	23	42	23	36	26	23	24	15	12
Don't know	4	4	4	4	4	1	2	2	3	2	4	0	3	4	3	8	3	0	7	8	2	2	2	2

Table 5.7a: Percentage organisations monitoring through tests. (Valid %)

Country	D(W)	DK	E	F	FIN	IRL	N	NL	P	S	T	UK
Yes	32	36	53	35	12	49	24	65	40	46	77	46

Private and public sector

	D(W)		DK		E		F		FIN		IRL		N		NL		P		S		T		UK	
					*										*		*				*			
	Pu	Pr	Pu	Pr	Pu	Pr	Pu	Pr	Pu	Pr	Pu	Pr	Pu	Pr	Pu	Pr	Pu	Pr	Pu	Pr	Pu	Pr	Pu	Pr
Yes	51	28	35	34	63	51	38	33	15	15	33	54	30	21	0	67	0	42	27	53	75	76	28	52

Less than 1,000 or greater than or equal to 1,000 employees

	D(W)		DK		E		F		FIN		IRL		N		NL		P		S		T		UK	
	<1	>1	<1	>1	<1	>1	<1	>1	<1	>1	<1	>1	<1	>1	<1	>1	<1	>1	<1	>1	<1	>1	<1	>1
Yes	26	39	28	48	45	61	21	48	16	15	57	36	22	28	62	75	36	50	41	48	67	92	41	49

Table 5.7b: Percentage organisations monitoring through formal evaluation immediately after training. (Valid %)

Country	D(W)	DK	E	F	FIN	IRL	N	NL	P	S	T	UK
Yes	70	83	85	90	61	84	70	64	93	88	94	89

Private and public sector

	D(W)		DK		E		F		FIN		IRL		N		NL		P		S		T		UK	
					*										*		*				*			
	Pu	Pr	Pu	Pr	Pu	Pr	Pu	Pr	Pu	Pr	Pu	Pr	Pu	Pr	Pu	Pr	Pu	Pr	Pu	Pr	Pu	Pr	Pu	Pr
Yes	58	72	70	89	86	85	93	81	75	79	77	87	68	68	0	66	86	91	86	94	100	93	90	88

Less than 1,000 or greater than or equal to 1,000 employees

	D(W)		DK		E		F		FIN		IRL		N		NL		P		S		T		UK	
	<1	>1	<1	>1	<1	>1	<1	>1	<1	>1	<1	>1	<1	>1	<1	>1	<1	>1	<1	>1	<1	>1	<1	>1
Yes	63	77	80	91	79	92	87	93	76	85	88	72	75	61	60	78	89	100	88	88	93	95	86	91

Table 5.7c: Percentage organisations monitoring through formal evaluation some months after training. (Valid %)

Country	D(W)	DK	E	F	FIN	IRL	N	NL	P	S	T	UK
Yes	33	54	54	64	25	50	29	45	55	39	68	70

Private and public sector

	D(W)		DK		E		F		FIN		IRL		N		NL		P		S		T		UK	
	Pu	Pr	Pu	Pr	Pu	Pr	Pu	Pr	Pu	Pr	Pu	Pr	Pu	Pr	Pu	Pr	Pu	Pr	Pu	Pr	Pu	Pr	Pu	Pr
					*										*		*				*			
Yes	32	34	54	54	20	56	71	61	24	36	50	52	22	28	100	45	50	53	32	44	100	67	70	70

Less than 1,000 or greater than or equal to 1,000 employees

	D(W)		DK		E		F		FIN		IRL		N		NL		P		S		T		UK	
	<1	>1	<1	>1	<1	>1	<1	>1	<1	>1	<1	>1	<1	>1	<1	>1	<1	>1	<1	>1	<1	>1	<1	>1
Yes	30	37	50	58	53	54	59	71	29	41	50	54	30	28	44	54	50	63	50	31	62	83	67	73

Table 5.7d: Percentage organisations monitoring through informal feedback from line managers. (Valid %)

Country	D(W)	DK	E	F	FIN	IRL	N	NL	P	S	T	UK
Yes	89	96	93	91	61	99	95	98	45	92	86	98

Private and public sector

	D(W)		DK		E		F		FIN		IRL		N		NL		P		S		T		UK	
	Pu	Pr	Pu	Pr	Pu	Pr	Pu	Pr	Pu	Pr	Pu	Pr	Pu	Pr	Pu	Pr	Pu	Pr	Pu	Pr	Pu	Pr	Pu	Pr
					*										*		*				*			
Yes	88	89	97	96	100	93	86	92	81	76	100	98	92	97	100	98	100	100	94	92	67	87	96	99

Less than 1,000 or greater than or equal to 1,000 employees

	D(W)		DK		E		F		FIN		IRL		N		NL		P		S		T		UK	
	<1	>1	<1	>1	<1	>1	<1	>1	<1	>1	<1	>1	<1	>1	<1	>1	<1	>1	<1	>1	<1	>1	<1	>1
Yes	89	88	99	92	93	93	94	88	79	77	100	96	95	96	97	100	100	100	90	93	81	93	97	98

Table 5.7e: Percentage organisations monitoring through informal feedback from trainees. (Valid %)

Country	D(W)	DK	E	F	FIN	IRL	N	NL	P	S	T	UK
Yes	92	97	93	93	66	99	97	99	97	93	85	98

Private and public sector

	D(W)		DK		E	F		FIN		IRL		N		NL		P		S		T		UK	
	Pu	Pr	Pu	Pr		Pu	Pr	Pu	Pr	Pu	Pr	Pu	Pr	Pu	Pr	Pu	Pr	Pu	Pr	Pu	Pr	Pu	Pr
Yes	90	92	100	95	*	92	92	87	81	100	98	94	100	99	100	100	97	95	90	67	87	98	98

Less than 1,000 or greater than or equal to 1,000 employees

	D(W)		DK		E		F		FIN		IRL		N		NL		P		S		T		UK	
	<1	>1	<1	>1	<1	>1	<1	>1	<1	>1	<1	>1	<1	>1	<1	>1	<1	>1	<1	>1	<1	>1	<1	>1
Yes	92	93	97	95	92	94	93	91	86	84	100	96	97	98	99	100	96	100	90	94	79	93	97	98

Table 5.8: Percentage organisations where at least a third of managers have been trained in the following areas.(+)

Country	D(W)	DK	E	F	FIN	IRL	N	NL	P	S	T	UK
Performance appraisal	34	19	31	47	42	43	64	51	32	77	36	71
Staff communication	50	43	48	53	61	65	58	52	28	56	45	54
Delegation	40	40	32	25	47	44	47	23	19	47	24	41
Motivation	67	44	48	32	61	62	46	47	27	47	34	47
Team building	24	27	34	28	68	49	33	35	27	27	27	50
Foreign languages	20	17	48	33	49	15	8	28	18	11	37	6

Private and public sector

	D(W)		DK		E		F		FIN		IRL		N		NL		P		S		T		UK	
	Pu	Pr	Pu	Pr	Pu	Pr	Pu	Pr	Pu	Pr	Pu	Pr	Pu	Pr	Pu	Pr	Pu	Pr	Pu	Pr	Pu	Pr	Pu	Pr
					*								*		*		*				*			
Performance appraisal	50	31	19	18	25	31	43	47	32	46	28	47	59	66	50	51	23	33	84	73	19	38	71	71
Staff communication	46	50	42	43	44	49	51	54	60	61	63	63	54	64	0	51	23	30	57	55	63	43	44	57
Delegation	44	38	42	38	13	33	25	24	47	45	50	40	52	42	0	23	15	22	53	44	31	23	34	42
Motivation	57	68	42	45	44	49	21	34	60	65	58	63	35	54	50	46	31	27	41	51	19	37	36	51
Team building	28	24	19	32	38	34	23	28	68	68	45	55	32	31	0	34	15	30	29	24	6	30	40	54
Foreign languages	4	23	7	23	44	50	14	39	47	50	18	11	3	9	0	29	8	19	5	16	25	40	1	7

Less than 1,000 or greater than or equal to 1,000 employees

	D(W)		DK		E		F		FIN		IRL		N		NL		P		S		T		UK	
	<1	>1	<1	>1	<1	>1	<1	>1	<1	>1	<1	>1	<1	>1	<1	>1	<1	>1	<1	>1	<1	>1	<1	>1
Performance appraisal	28	42	18	22	25	44	43	53	39	46	45	38	60	73	48	62	25	54	72	84	30	46	66	75
Staff communication	45	57	39	51	42	62	51	55	63	58	65	66	58	58	50	58	20	55	53	60	40	52	54	53
Delegation	36	47	38	43	24	48	23	27	44	49	43	50	49	42	21	31	16	32	42	52	21	28	41	40
Motivation	62	74	42	47	42	62	30	36	63	35	59	72	50	39	45	54	21	46	43	50	26	48	50	45
Team building	19	33	23	35	25	51	25	33	66	67	59	47	30	40	33	39	23	41	56	25	25	30	50	50
Foreign languages	19	22	20	12	46	52	32	33	43	58	17	9	7	10	29	27	11	41	17	6	43	28	7	4

Table 5.9: Percentage organisations that provide training courses to update the skills of women returners.

Country	D(W)	DK	E	F	FIN	IRL	N	NL	P	S	T	UK
Yes	15	2	6	8	13	15	3	9	0	7	4	24
No	79	95	86	89	83	76	90	89	93	89	75	72

Private and public sector

	D(W)		DK		E *		F		FIN		IRL		N		NL *		P *		S		T *		UK	
	Pu	Pr	Pu	Pr	Pu	Pr	Pu	Pr	Pu	Pr	Pu	Pr	Pu	Pr	Pu	Pr	Pu	Pr	Pu	Pr	Pu	Pr	Pu	Pr
Yes	35	12	2	2	0	6	9	7	10	14	13	13	2	3	0	10	0	0	6	7	0	5	37	19
No	58	83	93	95	94	86	90	90	86	84	87	81	90	97	100	88	100	92	88	90	69	78	60	77

Less than 1,000 or greater than or equal to 1,000 employees

	D(W)		DK		E		F		FIN		IRL		N		NL		P		S		T		UK	
	<1	>1	<1	>1	<1	>1	<1	>1	<1	>1	<1	>1	<1	>1	<1	>1	<1	>1	<1	>1	<1	>1	<1	>1
Yes	12	21			2	10	4	7	9	13	13	15	13	3	3	19	0	0	5	8	4		18	28
No	83	73			94	82	89	91	87	86	81	78	72	91	90	81	92	96	91	87	79		78	67

Table 5.10: Percentage organisations who regularly use the following. (+)

Country	D(W)	DK	E	F	FIN	IRL	N	NL	P	S	T	UK
Formal career plans	11	12	30	8	11	17	18	20	30	19	15	25
Performance appraisal	56	41	55	63	57	65	69	86	66	86	62	85
Annual career development interviews	41	78	33	75	50	41	14	45	20	0	16	57
Assessment centres	10	3	11	8	23	7	4	14	3	9	5	19
Succession plans	47	23	30	20	30	33	43	24	26	41	55	43
Planned job rotation	12	28	23	10	30	33	25	24	40	12	33	19
"High flier" schemes for managers	18	32	38	46	11	11	34	25	16	43	28	28
International experience schemes for managers	7	14	18	14	21	20	14	17	30	23	24	18

Private and public sector

	D(W)		DK		E *		F		FIN		IRL		N *		NL *		P *		S		T *		UK	
	Pu	Pr	Pu	Pr	Pu	Pr	Pu	Pr	Pu	Pr	Pu	Pr	Pu	Pr	Pu	Pr	Pu	Pr	Pu	Pr	Pu	Pr	Pu	Pr
Formal career plans	13	10	7	15	19	31	18	6	11	11	8	25	14	22	50	19	31	29	11	26	6	6	17	28
Performance appraisal	68	53	29	48	56	55	48	65	39	67	45	75	59	76	100	86	54	69	89	83	69	62	80	88
Annual career development interviews	20	43	68	83	6	35	74	75	45	54	23	48	8	19	50	44	8	23	0	0	6	19	50	57
Assessment centres	18	8	1	5	13	11	8	8	26	24	5	8	4	5	0	15	0	3	7	11	0	0	17	22
Succession plans	31	49	3	27	25	30	14	23	31	33	10	44	28	52	0	24	0	32	31	49	63	55	13	54
Planned job rotation	17	11	23	32	13	22	10	10	23	34	43	32	17	32	0	24	31	41	4	18	38	33	17	19
"High flier" schemes for managers	6	21	17	42	38	38	41	49	8	13	3	15	24	43	0	27	0	21	34	50	13	30	24	30
International experience schemes for managers	3	8	1	23	0	20	9	15	15	27	8	25	6	18	0	18	8	34	14	30	0	28	4	23

Less than 1,000 or equal to 1,000 employees

	D(W)		DK		E		F		FIN		IRL		N		NL		P		S		T		UK	
	<1	>1	<1	>1	<1	>1	<1	>1	<1	>1	<1	>1	<1	>1	<1	>1	<1	>1	<1	>1	<1	>1	<1	>1
Formal career plans	8	15	10	16	21	48	7	10	6	18	19	16	17	22	15	35	27	41	18	20	8	28	19	30
Performance appraisal	53	61	42	39	46	69	59	69	53	63	69	53	65	80	86	85	81	82	79	93	58	67	83	87
Annual career development interviews	37	47	77	79	28	43	70	83	47	55	42	44	12	21	42	54	20	23	0	0	14	20	48	60
Assessment centres	6	16	3	5	8	17	6	12	21	28	7	6	4	6	14	15	1	9	6	12	5	4	9	28
Succession plans	45	50	24	14	22	43	16	27	29	31	32	41	40	49	25	19	23	36	36	47	52	59	37	47
Planned job rotation	9	17	32	22	16	33	7	13	28	35	37	22	25	26	22	35	39	41	14	10	33	33	16	22
"High flier" schemes for managers	12	28	31	34	28	56	35	61	10	13	12	9	33	37	21	46	14	23	37	47	25	33	18	36
International experience schemes for managers	5	11	16	11	13	28	9	20	17	28	20	22	12	18	17	19	27	41	22	23	20	33	14	21

Table 5.11: Areas which organisations think will constitute the main training requirements in the next 3 years.

Country	D(W)	DK	E	F	FIN	IRL	N	NL	P	S	T	UK
Business administration and strategy	15	13	13	28	ni	8	17	9	13	16	16	9
Computers and new technology	13	18	17	9	ni	15	13	12	20	11	18	12
Health and safety and the work environment	2	4	5	4	ni	14	9	11	7	6	4	8
Manufacturing technology	5	4	7	5	ni	5	3	5	8	3	9	4
Marketing and Sales	9	7	12	5	ni	4	7	8	13	10	14	5
People management and supervision	24	13	13	21	ni	18	17	20	10	16	11	19
Customer service skills	10	7	8	4	ni	8	6	11	1	3	5	12
Management of change	9	14	7	12	ni	13	15	9	12	16	6	15
Quality	10	15	12	8	ni	12	12	14	15	13	10	14
Languages	2	4	5	4	ni	2	1	2	2	5	6	2
			*					*	*		*	

Private and public sector	D(W)		DK		E		F		FIN		IRL		N		NL		P		S		T		UK	
	Pu	Pr	Pu	Pr	Pu	Pr	Pu	Pr	Pu	Pr	Pu	Pr	Pu	Pr	Pu	Pr	Pu	Pr	Pu	Pr	Pu	Pr	Pu	Pr
Business administration and strategy	23	13	16	11	23	12	33	27	ni	ni	8	9	19	16	17	9	14	13	18	16	12	17	12	8
Computers and new technology	18	12	21	16	23	17	13	11	ni	ni	22	12	15	10	0	13	31	18	11	10	31	17	13	11
Health and safety and the work environment	2	3	5	3	8	5	4	4	ni	ni	20	12	13	6	17	11	11	7	9	3	10	3	6	8
Manufacturing technology	1	6	1	6	2	8	2	6	ni	ni	2	6	1	4	0	5	0	10	1	5	7	9	<1	5
Marketing and Sales	5	9	2	10	0	13	3	5	ni	ni	1	6	3	12	17	8	0	15	7	12	19	13	2	6
People management and supervision	24	24	14	13	10	13	22	21	ni	ni	18	17	20	16	17	20	23	8	16	17	10	11	18	19
Customer service skills	19	9	7	7	4	8	2	4	ni	ni	7	9	6	5	0	11	0	1	4	3	5	5	15	12
Management of change	6	10	17	13	10	7	13	12	ni	ni	12	14	15	14	0	10	11	11	19	13	0	6	17	14
Quality	2	12	15	15	15	12	7	9	ni	ni	8	13	8	8	33	13	9	16	10	15	5	11	14	13
Languages	1	3	1	1	4	4	1	4	ni	ni	3	2	<1	2	2	2	0	1	4	5	2	7	1	1

ni question not included in country

Table 5.11 (cont): Areas which organisations think will constitute the main training requirements in the next 3 years.

Country	D(W)		DK		E		F		FIN		IRL		N		NL		P		S		T		UK	
Less than 1,000 or greater than or equal to 1,000 employees	<1	>1	<1	>1	<1	>1	<1	>1	<1	>1	<1	>1	<1	>1	<1	>1	<1	>1	<1	>1	<1	>1	<1	>1
Business administration and strategy	13	17	13	13	13	14	25	31	ni	ni	9	7	16	18	9	9	11	20	17	15	15	18	8	11
Computers and new technology	14	11	18	18	18	17	10	8	ni	ni	15	17	13	13	13	10	19	23	12	10	20	15	11	12
Health and safety and the work environment	3	2	4	4	7	3	4	4	ni	ni	14	16	9	8	13	5	8	3	6	6	3	4	9	7
Manufacturing technology	6	4	4	3	8	4	6	3	ni	ni	4	5	3	2	5	4	8	6	4	3	11	6	5	2
Marketing and Sales	9	8	8	4	13	12	5	5	ni	ni	4	3	7	7	6	14	14	11	10	10	15	12	6	5
People management and supervision	24	25	13	14	12	14	22	21	ni	ni	18	19	17	18	21	16	11	6	16	17	11	12	19	19
Customer service skills	11	10	6	9	7	10	4	4	ni	ni	7	12	6	8	9	18	2	0	2	5	4	7	12	13
Management of change	7	12	14	15	7	8	11	13	ni	ni	14	12	15	14	9	12	11	16	13	18	4	9	14	17
Quality	11	9	15	16	11	14	9	7	ni	ni	13	8	13	10	14	12	15	13	14	11	9	11	14	13
Languages	2	3	5	4	5	4	4	4	ni	ni	2	2	1	1	2	0	2	2	5	4	7	5	2	2

ni question not included in country

Table 6.1: Percentage of organisations with the following proportion of staff who are members of a trade union.

Country	D(W)	DK	E	F	FIN	IRL	N	NL	P	S	T	UK
0%	3	0	0	8	0	12	3	2	1	0	15	16
One to 25%	32	3	58	74	2	3	8	50	25	1	2	22
Twenty–six to 50%	25	9	9	8	3	7	6	22	16	4	7	20
Fifty–one to 75%	19	25	5	3	15	20	18	10	24	10	23	23
Seventy–six to 100%	8	60	5	1	77	51	64	5	27	85	53	15
Don't know	12	3	16	4	2	3	0	11	7	0	0	4

Private and public sector

	D(W)		DK		E		F		FIN		IRL		N		NL		P		S		T		UK	
	Pu	Pr	Pu	Pr	Pu	Pr	Pu	Pr	Pu	Pr	Pu	Pr	Pu	Pr	Pu	Pr	Pu	Pr	Pu	Pr	Pu	Pr	Pu	Pr
0%	2	2	0	0	0	0	1	10	0	0	0	18	0	5	0	2	0	1	0	1	6	17	1	21
One to 25%	43	28	0	5	50	60	74	74	0	4	0	3	0	11	100	48	8	29	0	2	0	2	5	28
Twenty–six to 50%	18	26	0	16	13	9	13	6	0	4	0	10	1	8	0	22	8	15	1	5	6	6	32	16
Fifty–one to 75%	12	21	8	34	0	5	6	2	10	18	10	22	14	23	0	11	39	22	2	16	6	27	35	18
Seventy–six to 100%	8	9	88	42	13	4	2	1	85	73	85	40	84	52	0	4	39	25	97	75	81	48	20	13
Don't know	17	12	4	3	25	14	3	4	3	1	5	2	2	0	0	12	8	7	0	0	0	0	33	0

Less than 1,000 or greater than or equal to 1,000 employees

	D(W)		DK		E		F		FIN		IRL		N		NL		P		S		T		UK	
	<1	>1	<1	>1	<1	>1	<1	>1	<1	>1	<1	>1	<1	>1	<1	>1	<1	>1	<1	>1	<1	>1	<1	>1
0%	3	1	0	0	0	0	0	11	0	4	0	14	2	0	0	1	0	1	0	0	14	15	22	10
One to 25%	32	31	3	2	58	62	73	75	3	0	4	6	49	50	9	31	1	5	1	1	0	4	23	22
Twenty–six to 50%	23	27	11	6	9	11	7	9	1	5	7	9	6	4	24	15	17	14	4	3	7	7	16	23
Fifty–one to 75%	20	18	26	22	4	5	3	4	14	18	19	22	17	21	10	11	25	18	12	8	31	9	22	24
Seventy–six to 100%	8	8	57	67	5	4	1	1	18	74	52	59	63	67	6	0	0	18	83	87	44	67	14	16
Don't know	12	13	3	3	19	19	9	4	0	2	3	3	0	0	10	19	6	9	0	0	0	0	3	4

Table 6.2: Percentage of companies recognising trade unions for the purpose of collective bargaining.

Country

	D(W)	DK	E	F	FIN	IRL	N	NL	P	S	T	UK
Yes	ni	90	75	ni	ni	84	97	39	87	ni	83	71
No	ni	7	24	ni	ni	14	1	61	10	ni	12	28

Private and public sector

	D(W)		DK		E		F		FIN		IRL		N		NL		P		S		T		UK	
	Pu	Pr	Pu	Pr	Pu	Pr	Pu	Pr	Pu	Pr	Pu	Pr	Pu	Pr	Pu	Pr	Pu	Pr	Pu	Pr	Pu	Pr	Pu	Pr
					*										*		*		*		*			
Yes	ni	ni	92	89	94	72	ni	ni	ni	ni	100	76	99	94	0	42	100	86	ni	ni	94	81	91	65
No	ni	ni	5	9	6	27	ni	ni	ni	ni	0	20	0	1	100	58	0	11	ni	ni	0	14	8	34

Less than 1,000 or greater than or equal to 1,000 employees

	D(W)		DK		E		F		FIN		IRL		N		NL		P		S		T		UK	
	<1	>1	<1	>1	<1	>1	<1	>1	<1	>1	<1	>1	<1	>1	<1	>1	<1	>1	<1	>1	<1	>1	<1	>1
Yes	ni	ni	90	91	67	86	ni	ni	ni	ni	81	97	95	100	35	58	86	91	ni	ni	82	85	64	77
No	ni	ni	8	5	31	14	ni	ni	ni	ni	17	3	1	0	65	42	11	5	ni	ni	14	9	35	22

ni question not included in country

Table 6.3: Percentage of organisations reporting a change in the influence of trade unions over the last three years. (Valid %)

Country

	D(W)	DK	E	F	FIN	IRL	N	NL	P	S	T	UK
Increased	23	13	33	8	18	10	32	25	12	11	26	4
Decreased	9	36	14	41	24	23	16	14	41	29	10	54
Same	67	51	54	51	57	66	52	60	47	61	64	42

Private and public sector

	D(W)		DK		E		F		FIN		IRL		N		NL		P		S		T		UK	
	Pu	Pr	Pu	Pr	Pu	Pr	Pu	Pr	Pu	Pr	Pu	Pr	Pu	Pr	Pu	Pr	Pu	Pr	Pu	Pr	Pu	Pr	Pu	Pr
					*										*		*		*		*			
Increased	28	23	19	8	19	34	12	6	23	17	10	9	38	29	0	25	8	12	13	10	20	26	7	2
Decreased	9	10	28	42	13	13	39	42	29	22	18	28	15	17	0	16	31	44	30	27	0	11	52	57
Same	63	68	53	50	69	53	49	52	48	62	73	63	48	54	0	29	61	44	57	63	80	63	40	41

Less than 1,000 or greater than or equal to 1,000 employees

	D(W)		DK		E		F		FIN		IRL		N		NL		P		S		T		UK	
	<1	>1	<1	>1	<1	>1	<1	>1	<1	>1	<1	>1	<1	>1	<1	>1	<1	>1	<1	>1	<1	>1	<1	>1
Increased	23	24	11	15	32	33	6	10	16	23	11	7	34	27	23	31	13	9	12	10	22	32	4	4
Decreased	10	8	36	36	12	15	44	40	28	17	22	27	14	22	13	25	41	41	22	35	11	8	52	56
Same	66	68	53	49	55	52	54	47	61	57	67	67	52	51	65	44	46	50	65	55	67	60	44	40

Table 6.4a: Percentage organisations reporting a change in the use of representative staff bodies for communicating major issues to employees.

Country	D(W)	DK	E	F	FIN	IRL	N	NL	P	S	T	UK
Increased	36	52	34	24	62	12	43	49	8	16	25	12
Decreased	3	5	6	12	2	12	3	1	15	14	7	19
Same	53	43	47	53	33	51	49	46	45	65	46	52

Private and public sector

	D(W)		DK		E		F		FIN		IRL		N		NL		P		S		T		UK	
	Pu	Pr	Pu	Pr	Pu	Pr	Pu	Pr	Pu	Pr	Pu	Pr	Pu	Pr	Pu	Pr	Pu	Pr	Pu	Pr	Pu	Pr	Pu	Pr
Increased	50	35	66	39	31	34	41	21	66	63	13	11	45	42	100	48	8	7	18	15	31	23	17	10
Decreased	1	4	2	6	13	6	7	14	2	2	5	15	3	3	0	1	0	19	14	14	0	8	16	20
Same	42	54	30	50	56	46	50	55	29	34	73	42	48	50	0	46	62	43	61	67	50	47	62	48

Less than 1,000 or greater than or equal to 1,000 employees

	D(W)		DK		E		F		FIN		IRL		N		NL		P		S		T		UK	
	<1	>1	<1	>1	<1	>1	<1	>1	<1	>1	<1	>1	<1	>1	<1	>1	<1	>1	<1	>1	<1	>1	<1	>1
Increased	36	35	49	53	36	32	25	24	61	65	12	13	44	41	53	31	6	14	21	12	25	26	13	12
Decreased	3	3	5	5	5	5	10	16	3	1	9	22	2	5	0	4	16	14	9	18	7	7	16	20
Same	50	58	43	39	45	49	53	53	35	30	49	59	48	51	44	54	45	46	67	62	46	48	50	53

Table 6.4b: Percentage organisations reporting a change in the use of direct verbal methods to communicate major issues to employees.

Country	D(W)	DK	E	F	FIN	IRL	N	NL	P	S	T	UK
Increased	47	65	43	58	66	58	47	43	45	63	33	63
Decreased	3	1	5	2	2	1	1	7	1	1	3	1
Same	45	34	43	31	29	30	47	43	39	33	43	31

Private and public sector

	D(W)		DK		E		F		FIN		IRL		N		NL		P		S		T		UK	
	Pu	Pr	Pu	Pr	Pu	Pr	Pu	Pr	Pu	Pr	Pu	Pr	Pu	Pr	Pu	Pr	Pu	Pr	Pu	Pr	Pu	Pr	Pu	Pr
Increased	36	50	62	63	44	44	51	60	73	60	48	65	42	51	0	45	46	45	63	63	25	33	59	65
Decreased	3	2	2	1	0	1	1	2	0	3	3	0	2	2	0	7	0	1	1	1	0	4	1	2
Same	55	43	33	32	56	42	42	29	24	35	43	23	50	46	50	42	31	41	33	33	50	42	35	30

Less than 1,000 or greater than or equal to 1,000 employees

	D(W)		DK		E		F		FIN		IRL		N		NL		P		S		T		UK	
	<1	>1	<1	>1	<1	>1	<1	>1	<1	>1	<1	>1	<1	>1	<1	>1	<1	>1	<1	>1	<1	>1	<1	>1
Increased	48	45	63	63	46	39	60	55	61	73	59	56	46	50	42	46	41	59	62	64	29	39	61	64
Decreased	2	4	1	1	5	5	2	3	2	3	1	0	0	2	8	4	0	1	0	1	1	5	0	2
Same	43	48	33	32	42	44	27	37	33	24	30	28	47	47	44	39	45	18	34	31	44	41	32	31

Table 6.4c: Percentage organisations reporting a change in the use of direct written methods to communicate major issues to employees.

Country	D(W)	DK	E	F	FIN	IRL	N	NL	P	S	T	UK
Increased	47	54	41	62	57	41	24	58	40	58	37	59
Decreased	3	3	2	4	2	4	5	2	1	3	3	1
Same	43	43	46	27	36	41	58	38	41	36	44	36

Private and public sector

	D(W)		DK		E *		F		FIN		IRL		N		NL *		P *		S		T *		UK	
	Pu	Pr	Pu	Pr	Pu	Pr	Pu	Pr	Pu	Pr	Pu	Pr	Pu	Pr	Pu	Pr	Pu	Pr	Pu	Pr	Pu	Pr	Pu	Pr
Increased	45	47	60	47	44	41	69	59	55	57	30	47	19	28	100	58	39	40	60	55	6	40	64	57
Decreased	2	2	2	3	0	2	5	4	3	2	3	5	7	3	0	0	0	1	4	2	6	3	0	1
Same	49	43	36	45	44	44	24	29	39	36	58	34	59	58	0	38	46	40	31	40	44	45	33	37

Less than 1,000 or greater than or equal to 1,000 employees

	D(W)		DK		E		F		FIN		IRL		N		NL		P		S		T		UK	
	<1	>1	<1	>1	<1	>1	<1	>1	<1	>1	<1	>1	<1	>1	<1	>1	<1	>1	<1	>1	<1	>1	<1	>1
Increased	43	53	48	60	37	50	58	66	59	56	41	44	27	17	62	42	37	50	56	61	31	48	54	63
Decreased	3	2	2	3	2	1	1	2	2	4	4	6	6	3	1	4	1	0	0	3	4	2	2	0
Same	44	42	45	34	46	43	29	25	35	35	41	41	55	65	35	50	42	36	38	32	48	37	39	33

Table 6.5a: Percentage organisations with the following employee categories formally briefed about the strategy of their organisations.(+)

Country	D(W)	DK	E	F	FIN	IRL	N	NL	P	S	T	UK
Management	94	95	96	86	98	94	96	97	94	96	82	91
Professional/Technical	31	53	58	44	87	65	65	73	53	46	43	59
Clerical	13	40	17	28	50	42	51	28	18	44	17	33
Manual	7	26	12	20	42	41	50	27	16	38	15	28

Private and public sector

	D(W)		DK		E *		F		FIN		IRL		N		NL *		P *		S		T *		UK	
	Pu	Pr	Pu	Pr	Pu	Pr	Pu	Pr	Pu	Pr	Pu	Pr	Pu	Pr	Pu	Pr	Pu	Pr	Pu	Pr	Pu	Pr	Pu	Pr
Management	97	94	92	97	88	96	82	87	100	97	93	93	95	97	100	96	77	99	96	96	88	81	90	92
Professional/Technical	26	31	59	50	50	59	44	46	86	87	50	70	53	74	50	73	39	55	36	54	44	44	56	58
Clerical	12	13	47	36	13	18	29	29	45	47	28	49	35	63	0	29	8	22	39	36	19	17	28	34
Manual	2	8	31	23	13	12	23	21	39	40	23	52	38	59	0	28	8	19	36	38	19	14	22	29

Less than 1,000 or greater than or equal to 1,000 employees

	D(W)		DK		E		F		FIN		IRL		N		NL		P		S		T		UK	
	<1	>1	<1	>1	<1	>1	<1	>1	<1	>1	<1	>1	<1	>1	<1	>1	<1	>1	<1	>1	<1	>1	<1	>1
Management	93	96	95	95	95	98	86	87	97	99	92	100	96	97	92	97	94	91	94	98	82	83	90	92
Professional/Technical	33	28	54	52	57	62	45	43	86	89	62	75	66	60	73	73	47	73	46	45	43	44	60	58
Clerical	14	12	42	37	19	14	28	29	52	46	43	44	54	44	31	28	18	18	46	41	17	17	36	31
Manual	6	7	27	23	11	13	21	20	43	40	43	41	53	42	27	27	16	18	37	37	14	15	30	26

Table 6.5b: Percentage organisations with the following employee categories formally briefed about the financial performance of their organisation.(+)

Country	D(W)	DK	E	F	FIN	IRL	N	NL	P	S	T	UK
Management	90	95	88	90	94	94	95	95	83	97	72	90
Professional/Technical	71	77	44	66	91	65	74	73	48	65	29	70
Clerical	55	72	16	55	85	41	67	44	22	75	12	53
Manual	44	54	9	42	83	36	66	40	18	68	8	49

Private and public sector

	D(W)		DK		E *		F		FIN		IRL		N		NL *		P *		S		T *		UK	
	Pu	Pr	Pu	Pr	Pu	Pr	Pu	Pr	Pu	Pr	Pu	Pr	Pu	Pr	Pu	Pr	Pu	Pr	Pu	Pr	Pu	Pr	Pu	Pr
Management	83	91	95	94	69	90	79	93	92	95	93	94	93	96	50	94	69	88	98	97	75	71	85	92
Professional/Technical	64	73	74	78	50	44	45	71	90	94	53	69	62	82	0	74	23	53	51	77	44	28	54	76
Clerical	41	58	71	73	13	16	34	58	82	90	28	44	46	82	50	45	8	26	63	85	13	13	25	64
Manual	18	48	55	54	13	8	27	45	84	88	23	39	44	82	50	41	0	23	56	77	13	8	23	59

Less than 1,000 or greater than or equal to 1,000 employees

	D(W)		DK		E		F		FIN		IRL		N		NL		P		S		T		UK	
	<1	>1	<1	>1	<1	>1	<1	>1	<1	>1	<1	>1	<1	>1	<1	>1	<1	>1	<1	>1	<1	>1	<1	>1
Management	90	91	95	95	88	89	91	89	92	95	95	88	94	99	93	96	83	82	98	98	70	76	89	90
Professional/Technical	68	76	76	78	40	52	67	65	90	91	63	72	74	74	71	81	41	73	68	62	25	35	69	71
Clerical	51	62	72	73	15	19	53	57	84	83	39	47	69	62	44	43	20	27	79	71	13	11	55	52
Manual	40	49	53	58	7	13	41	42	80	86	33	41	67	63	41	35	16	27	70	65	8	9	50	48

Table 6.6: Methods used for employees to communicate their views to management: percentage organisations.(+)

Country	D(W)	DK	E	F	FIN	IRL	N	NL	P	S	T	UK
Immediate supervisor	90	94	96	92	91	96	93	91	94	94	98	96
Trade unions/works council	78	86	79	86	89	73	95	78	29	89	63	69
Regular workforce meetings	63	74	25	52	88	49	44	37	40	22	18	52
Quality circles	19	10	17	20	18	11	8	15	11	9	13	18
Suggestion schemes	47	21	14	10	45	22	25	35	14	47	16	27
Attitude survey	20	19	19	21	50	14	27	6	13	43	4	30
No formal methods	40	10	53	22	4	10	9	32	34	11	2	8

Private and public sector

	D(W)		DK		E *		F		FIN		IRL		N		NL *		P *		S		T *		UK	
	Pu	Pr	Pu	Pr	Pu	Pr	Pu	Pr	Pu	Pr	Pu	Pr	Pu	Pr	Pu	Pr	Pu	Pr	Pu	Pr	Pu	Pr	Pu	Pr
Immediate supervisor	92	90	92	95	88	97	91	92	89	92	98	94	92	92	50	91	77	96	95	93	100	97	94	97
Trade unions/works council	75	79	96	79	94	78	92	84	97	86	93	65	96	95	50	78	23	32	88	89	69	60	89	63
Regular workforce meetings	49	66	80	69	38	25	42	53	87	88	33	54	40	46	50	37	39	41	15	27	13	18	47	55
Quality circles	9	21	8	13	31	16	14	22	11	22	3	12	5	12	0	16	8	14	6	11	0	16	17	19
Suggestion schemes	54	46	13	26	6	14	10	10	42	53	20	20	18	32	100	34	15	15	41	50	19	24	24	28
Attitude survey	23	19	12	23	19	19	23	21	40	52	10	17	16	38	0	7	0	16	40	45	5	28	7	31
No formal methods	38	40	12	9	56	9	27	21	5	40	10	11	5	15	0	33	39	36	11	11	3	7	7	8

Less than 1,000 or greater than or equal to 1,000 employees

	D(W)		DK		E		F		FIN		IRL		N		NL		P		S		T		UK	
	<1	>1	<1	>1	<1	>1	<1	>1	<1	>1	<1	>1	<1	>1	<1	>1	<1	>1	<1	>1	<1	>1	<1	>1
Immediate supervisor	90	91	93	96	94	100	92	91	92	94	95	97	93	92	90	92	94	91	93	95	99	96	96	96
Trade unions/works council	77	79	83	92	78	82	85	87	91	89	71	81	95	96	80	65	21	55	89	88	58	70	64	74
Regular workforce meetings	58	69	73	75	24	29	51	52	88	89	48	53	43	49	36	39	39	41	25	21	20	15	51	53
Quality circles	15	25	12	7	13	22	16	24	19	18	11	9	8	9	11	35	13	5	5	13	13	13	13	22
Suggestion schemes	40	57	24	16	12	16	9	12	46	46	17	38	24	27	31	50	10	27	44	50	17	15	25	29
Attitude survey	17	25	21	16	15	28	16	29	47	56	15	13	26	35	4	15	10	23	31	47	1	9	8	34
No formal methods	41	37	8	14	53	51	24	18	5	3	10	9	9	6	34	23	32	9	15	9	4	1	4	7

Table 6.7: Responsibility for formulating policy on staff communication: percentage organisations.

Country	D(W)	DK	E	F	FIN	IRL	N	NL	P	S	T	UK
HR/Personnel Dept	43	40	68	60	46	69	45	24	28	36	48	65
Public relations Dept	11	10	2	9	9	1	6	2	11	37	2	6
Marketing department	2	1	2	1	2	2	2	1	4	3	1	2
Line management	37	35	14	9	29	19	33	60	41	20	30	16
Other	6	11	10	16	8	5	10	11	12	5	9	8

Private and public sector

	D(W)		DK		E *		F		FIN		IRL		N *		NL *		P *		S *		T *		UK	
	Pu	Pr	Pu	Pr	Pu	Pr	Pu	Pr	Pu	Pr	Pu	Pr	Pu	Pr	Pu	Pr	Pu	Pr	Pu	Pr	Pu	Pr	Pu	Pr
HR/Personnel Dept	50	42	41	41	50	69	50	63	50	44	65	70	44	46	0	24	23	29	23	46	38	50	61	68
Public relations Dept	12	11	9	12	13	1	14	7	7	8	0	1	5	8	0	2	15	11	39	36	2	6	8	5
Marketing department	2	2	1	1	0	2	1	1	0	4	5	1	0	4	0	1	0	4	3	2	0	1	2	2
Line management	28	38	41	31	19	14	9	24	26	29	18	19	34	31	0	60	54	38	31	31	31	29	16	15
Other	8	6	7	12	6	10	10	24	14	7	5	6	13	7	100	10	8	12	4	5	13	8	9	8

Less than 1,000 or greater than or equal to 1,000 employees

	D(W)		DK		E		F		FIN		IRL		N		NL		P		S		T		UK	
	<1	≥1	<1	≥1	<1	≥1	<1	≥1	<1	≥1	<1	≥1	<1	≥1	<1	≥1	<1	≥1	<1	≥1	<1	≥1	<1	≥1
HR/Personnel Dept	39	48	42	39	68	67	56	63	46	48	70	66	46	41	26	19	27	32	41	29	55	37	65	66
Public relations Dept	7	18	9	14	0	5	6	14	6	11	0	3	5	10	2	4	7	23	33	41	1	4	3	8
Marketing department	2	1	1	2	2	2	2	1	4	0	3	0	2	3	1	0	4	5	5	4	0	2	1	2
Line management	42	28	35	34	18	19	9	10	30	21	17	25	32	33	56	69	45	27	15	24	25	39	18	14
Other	8	4	12	8	10	11	13	20	6	15	6	3	10	10	12	8	11	14	14	5	4	10	7	10

SECTION VII: FLEXIBLE WORKING PATTERNS

Table 7.1a: Percentage organisations reporting a change in the use of weekend work

Country	D(W)	DK	E	F	FIN	IRL	N	NL	P	S	T	UK
Increased	19	14	11	16	13	15	19	13	19	11	9	17
Same	43	57	42	40	46	51	63	39	52	59	48	56
Decreased	18	6	10	4	15	15	7	8	19	12	32	16
Not used	17	18	29	32	24	15	7	35	8	15	6	6
Don't know	2	3	0	0	2	6	1	0	0	1	0	1

Private and public sector

	D(W)		DK		E		F		FIN		IRL		N		NL		P		S		T		UK	
	Pu	Pr	Pu	Pr	Pu	Pr	Pu	Pr	Pu	Pr	Pu	Pr	Pu	Pr	Pu	Pr	Pu	Pr	Pu	Pr	Pu	Pr	Pu	Pr
Increased	7	20	8	19	6	11	10	17	11	15	5	18	9	25	0	14	23	19	4	16	6	9	11	19
Same	44	44	53	65	69	40	60	35	47	46	60	48	71	56	100	37	77	47	63	57	50	50	71	51
Decreased	12	19	3	7	0	11	4	5	15	15	8	15	8	6	0	8	0	22	15	10	25	32	6	20
Not used	30	14	16	18	13	31	19	35	26	22	20	15	6	10	0	35	0	10	14	16	6	6	5	6
Don't know	5	1	5	2	2	0	0	0	2	2	0	0	3	1	0	1	0	0	1	1	0	0	3	1

Less than 1,000 or greater than or equal to 1,000 employees

	D(W)		DK		E		F		FIN		IRL		N		NL		P		S		T		UK	
	<1	>1	<1	>1	<1	>1	<1	>1	<1	>1	<1	>1	<1	>1	<1	>1	<1	>1	<1	>1	<1	>1	<1	>1
Increased	19	18	13	16	10	13	16	16	15	11	13	22	18	21	15	8	18	23	13	8	10	7	18	16
Same	38	50	54	63	41	44	34	49	41	55	49	53	62	64	35	50	55	41	55	64	48	48	49	62
Decreased	20	15	6	5	10	11	5	4	16	10	14	16	8	5	9	4	17	27	10	13	31	33	21	12
Not used	19	15	21	11	33	25	36	25	28	20	19	3	8	3	37	27	9	5	20	11	4	9	7	5
Don't know	2	2	2	5	0	0	0	0	4	4	0	0	1	3	0	4	0	0	1	2	0	0	1	2

Table 7.1b: Percentage organisations reporting a change in the use of shift work

Country	D(W)	DK	E	F	FIN	IRL	N	NL	P	S	T	UK
Increased	29	12	19	26	11	15	14	24	19	8	11	17
Same	46	54	62	53	59	54	62	46	50	54	64	58
Decreased	6	6	6	3	10	8	5	5	20	7	11	10
Not used	14	23	8	12	18	16	12	24	7	26	8	10
Don't know	1	2	0	0	1	0	1	0	1	1	1	1

Private and public sector

	D(W)		DK		E		F		FIN		IRL		N		NL		P		S		T		UK	
	Pu	Pr	Pu	Pr	Pu	Pr	Pu	Pr	Pu	Pr	Pu	Pr	Pu	Pr	Pu	Pr	Pu	Pr	Pu	Pr	Pu	Pr	Pu	Pr
					*										*		*				*			
Increased	7	33	5	17	13	20	15	29	8	15	0	21	6	22	0	23	8	21	4	12	0	11	8	21
Same	53	46	61	49	63	61	68	50	77	54	60	53	66	57	100	46	23	48	51	57	75	64	70	53
Decreased	4	7	2	8	6	6	3	3	7	13	5	8	4	4	0	5	54	22	5	10	6	12	6	10
Not used	22	12	24	21	13	8	8	12	6	15	30	11	10	15	0	24	15	7	7	31	0	0	8	10
Don't know	5	1	4	2	0	0	0	0	0	1	0	0	0	4	0	0	0	0	0	1	0	1	3	1

Less than 1,000 or greater than or equal to 1,000 employees

	D(W)		DK		E		F		FIN		IRL		N		NL		P		S		T		UK	
	<1	>1	<1	>1	<1	>1	<1	>1	<1	>1	<1	>1	<1	>1	<1	>1	<1	>1	<1	>1	<1	>1	<1	>1
Increased	30	28	11	13	18	21	26	26	14	8	16	13	13	15	26	15	21	14	12	6	10	11	18	16
Same	39	58	55	60	61	62	50	57	55	68	53	59	61	64	46	46	47	59	45	62	61	70	51	63
Decreased	7	5	5	7	8	3	3	9	9	11	7	13	5	5	6	0	18	27	8	7	10	13	11	9
Not used	19	7	26	15	8	7	14	8	19	13	18	9	13	9	22	31	9	0	31	21	10	4	15	6
Don't know	2	1	2	3	0	0	0	0	1	1	0	0	2	1	0	0	1	1	1	1	1	0	1	2

Table 7.1c: Percentage organisations reporting a change in the use of overtime

Country

Country	D(W)	DK	E	F	FIN	IRL	N	NL	P	S	T	UK
Increased	43	24	15	23	12	23	36	30	30	24	12	14
Same	36	46	32	44	39	34	39	52	34	48	29	38
Decreased	20	26	42	21	47	34	21	17	30	23	55	41
Not used	0	1	8	7	1	3	0	0	3	1	1	2
Don't know	0	1	0	1	1	0	1	0	1	3	1	1

Private and public sector

	D(W)		DK*		E		F		FIN		IRL		N		NL*		P*		S*		T*		UK	
	Pu	Pr	Pu	Pr	Pu	Pr	Pu	Pr	Pu	Pr	Pu	Pr	Pu	Pr	Pu	Pr	Pu	Pr	Pu	Pr	Pu	Pr	Pu	Pr
Increased	51	42	21	27	25	14	19	25	11	8	20	26	32	39	0	29	46	29	28	21	13	12	13	14
Same	38	35	40	51	31	33	48	44	42	36	38	35	44	36	50	51	46	33	45	50	6	33	41	37
Decreased	7	22	21	32	31	42	21	19	44	54	30	34	18	23	50	19	8	32	19	26	69	52	37	45
Not used	1	0	0	2	6	8	8	6	0	1	8	1	1	0	0	0	0	4	4	1	0	1	1	2
Don't know	2	0	2	2	1	0	0	0	3	1	0	0	0	2	0	0	0	1	5	2	0	1	3	1

Less than 1,000 or greater than or equal to 1,000 employees

	D(W)		DK		E		F		FIN		IRL		N		NL		P		S		T		UK	
	<1	>1	<1	>1	<1	>1	<1	>1	<1	>1	<1	>1	<1	>1	<1	>1	<1	>1	<1	>1	<1	>1	<1	>1
Increased	42	43	25	23	13	17	24	21	15	6	23	22	35	40	30	27	28	36	28	21	13	11	16	12
Same	35	37	49	41	31	34	43	46	33	49	36	28	38	41	50	58	38	23	45	50	27	30	38	39
Decreased	21	18	23	32	40	46	18	25	50	41	31	47	24	14	19	15	36	36	25	21	55	54	40	42
Not used	0	0	1	0	12	2	2	10	1	0	4	0	1	0	0	0	0	5	1	6	1	0	2	2
Don't know	0	1	1	3	0	0	0	1	0	4	0	0	0	0	0	0	1	0	1	1	0	0	1	2

Table 7.1d: Percentage organisations reporting a change in the use of annual hours contracts

Country	D(W)	DK	E	F	FIN	IRL	N	NL	P	S	T	UK
Increased	9	ni	19	5	1	4	9	29	22	2	1	11
Same	11	ni	25	18	40	17	31	42	20	23	59	17
Decreased	1	ni	6	1	21	9	9	6	23	4	2	3
Not used	63	ni	39	61	28	50	32	18	27	54	21	62
Don't know	9	ni	0	1	3	1	9	1	0	7	1	1

Private and public sector

	D(W)		DK		E*		F		FIN		IRL		N*		NL*		P*		S		T*		UK	
	Pu	Pr	Pu	Pr	Pu	Pr	Pu	Pr	Pu	Pr	Pu	Pr	Pu	Pr	Pu	Pr	Pu	Pr	Pu	Pr	Pu	Pr	Pu	Pr
Increased	9	9	ni	ni	25	18	6	5	2	2	10	2	8	12	50	29	39	16	2	1	6	0	19	8
Same	9	11	ni	ni	25	25	24	17	40	40	23	15	30	31	50	40	23	22	19	24	44	60	15	18
Decreased	1	1	ni	ni	0	7	1	1	21	21	5	11	9	11	0	6	23	19	3	5	0	3	2	3
Not used	64	64	ni	ni	38	38	55	63	29	27	48	54	29	34	0	20	0	34	56	55	19	23	55	65
Don't know	6	9	ni	ni	0	0	0	2	3	4	0	2	11	6	0	1	0	0	8	7	0	1	1	1

Less than 1,000 or greater than or equal to 1,000 employees

	D(W)		DK		E		F		FIN		IRL		N		NL		P		S		T		UK	
	<1	>1	<1	>1	<1	>1	<1	>1	<1	>1	<1	>1	<1	>1	<1	>1	<1	>1	<1	>1	<1	>1	<1	>1
Increased	9	11	ni	ni	17	21	5	5	1	3	4	6	10	5	31	19	21	23	2	1	0	2	8	13
Same	10	12	ni	ni	24	27	15	23	36	45	15	25	27	42	41	42	18	21	19	25	56	63	15	19
Decreased	1	1	ni	ni	5	9	1	0	19	21	10	6	9	9	4	12	27	21	6	2	4	0	3	2
Not used	63	63	ni	ni	43	30	63	58	32	24	53	41	34	26	21	12	23	28	57	54	21	22	66	58
Don't know	9	9	ni	ni	0	0	0	1	2	3	2	0	9	8	8	0	0	0	7	8	8	1	0	2

ni question not included in country

Table 7.1e: Percentage organisations reporting a change in the use of part-time work

Country

	D(W)	DK	E	F	FIN	IRL	N	NL	P	S	T	UK
Increased	49	11	15	27	22	31	28	49	5	14	0	39
Same	40	64	26	48	42	27	54	39	26	57	21	40
Decreased	6	17	5	5	6	4	10	2	7	24	2	8
Not used	2	5	43	12	25	26	2	9	50	0	45	8
Don't know	0	2	0	0	2	0	2	1	0	2	1	1

Private and public sector

	D(W)		DK		E *		F		FIN		IRL		N		NL *		P *		S *		T *		UK	
	Pu	Pr	Pu	Pr	Pu	Pr	Pu	Pr	Pu	Pr	Pu	Pr	Pu	Pr	Pu	Pr	Pu	Pr	Pu	Pr	Pu	Pr	Pu	Pr
Increased	85	42	13	9	13	14	36	23	11	24	40	26	41	21	0	49	0	6	7	20	0	0	62	30
Same	12	46	61	64	25	25	50	49	48	36	33	27	45	61	100	37	23	25	53	59	25	20	31	44
Decreased	0	7	19	16	0	5	6	5	8	7	3	6	8	12	0	2	0	7	35	17	2	0	2	10
Not used	1	3	1	8	50	44	5	15	27	28	15	34	0	4	0	9	54	51	1	1	31	47	1	11
Don't know	0	0	4	1	0	0	0	0	3	2	0	0	4	0	0	1	0	0	1	2	0	1	1	1

Less than 1,000 or greater than or equal to 1,000 employees

	D(W)		DK		E		F		FIN		IRL		N		NL		P		S		T		UK	
	<1	>1	<1	>1	<1	>1	<1	>1	<1	>1	<1	>1	<1	>1	<1	>1	<1	>1	<1	>1	<1	>1	<1	>1
Increased	46	54	11	11	15	15	27	26	24	19	27	45	29	27	44	65	6	5	13	14	0	0	30	47
Same	41	38	63	64	25	28	45	53	36	53	25	31	54	56	39	31	24	32	61	52	20	24	44	37
Decreased	7	4	17	18	5	4	5	5	5	9	6	0	11	8	3	0	4	14	21	28	1	2	9	7
Not used	2	2	6	3	45	38	5	15	30	15	32	6	2	3	11	4	55	32	1	0	46	45	13	4
Don't know	0	0	1	4	0	0	0	0	0	5	0	0	2	3	1	0	0	0	1	3	1	1	1	2

Table 7.1f: Percentage organisations reporting a change in the use of temporary/casual work

Country	D(W)	DK	E	F	FIN	IRL	N	NL	P	S	T	UK
Increased	24	13	29	28	18	38	30	40	19	32	10	39
Same	25	42	33	35	27	36	38	42	25	40	9	34
Decreased	13	34	11	21	46	9	20	9	12	20	7	19
Not used	31	6	19	10	7	7	6	6	36	4	39	5
Don't know	3	1	0	0	0	1	3	0	1	1	2	1

Private and public sector

	D(W)		DK		E *		F		FIN		IRL		N *		NL *		P *		S		T *		UK	
	Pu	Pr	Pu	Pr	Pu	Pr	Pu	Pr	Pu	Pr	Pu	Pr	Pu	Pr	Pu	Pr	Pu	Pr	Pu	Pr	Pu	Pr	Pu	Pr
Increased	12	27	7	17	31	29	20	31	19	20	40	34	35	22	100	39	19	8	29	33	6	11	55	33
Same	11	28	47	40	31	32	40	33	24	25	40	38	39	40	0	42	23	31	44	39	6	10	28	36
Decreased	3	15	38	30	13	11	12	24	53	43	5	10	17	25	0	9	12	8	21	19	6	6	11	22
Not used	54	26	2	9	13	20	22	7	3	10	8	7	3	9	7	0	38	31	1	1	31	39	1	6
Don't know	8	2	1	1	0	0	0	0	0	1	1	0	3	2	0	0	1	0	1	1	0	2	1	1

Less than 1,000 or greater than or equal to 1,000 employees

	D(W)		DK		E		F		FIN		IRL		N		NL		P		S		T		UK	
	<1	>1	<1	>1	<1	>1	<1	>1	<1	>1	<1	>1	<1	>1	<1	>1	<1	>1	<1	>1	<1	>1	<1	>1
Increased	24	25	14	12	27	32	32	32	18	20	37	41	30	32	40	39	18	23	37	26	5	17	36	41
Same	21	30	46	32	28	39	31	40	28	23	34	44	38	37	41	42	27	18	36	45	8	11	32	35
Decreased	13	13	27	47	14	5	20	22	41	55	10	3	21	18	8	12	10	18	18	21	7	7	22	16
Not used	33	28	8	4	22	14	11	8	3	0	8	0	6	5	4	0	37	32	5	3	43	33	7	3
Don't know	3	2	1	1	0	0	0	0	1	0	1	0	2	4	0	0	0	5	1	2	3	0	0	2

Table 7.1g: Percentage organisations reporting a change in the use of fixed term contracts

Country	D(W)	DK	E	F	FIN	IRL	N	NL	P	S	T	UK
Increased	47	24	29	32	26	38	37	20	29	20	13	29
Same	33	36	44	37	26	29	37	56	37	31	24	26
Decreased	12	3	8	19	44	4	13	20	27	4	7	6
Not used	5	33	11	5	3	20	6	0	7	39	23	34
Don't know	1	2	0	0	1	1	2	0	0	5	1	1

Private and public sector

	D(W)		DK		E*		F		FIN		IRL		N		NL*		P*		S		T*		UK	
	Pu	Pr	Pu	Pr	Pu	Pr	Pu	Pr	Pu	Pr	Pu	Pr	Pu	Pr	Pu	Pr	Pu	Pr	Pu	Pr	Pu	Pr	Pu	Pr
Increased	49	47	33	19	25	30	35	32	32	22	48	30	39	31	50	20	23	30	21	19	6	15	56	18
Same	32	32	34	37	31	44	38	37	16	29	35	29	36	39	50	55	54	36	32	30	19	24	26	26
Decreased	11	13	1	3	6	8	9	22	50	42	3	3	10	16	0	20	23	26	2	4	6	8	3	7
Not used	4	5	28	36	25	11	10	0	2	4	13	24	6	8	0	0	0	7	35	38	13	25	10	43
Don't know	1	0	1	3	0	0	0	0	0	2	0	1	3	2	0	0	0	0	4	5	0	1	1	1

Less than 1,000 or greater than or equal to 1,000 employees

	D(W)		DK		E		F		FIN		IRL		N		NL		P		S		T		UK	
	<1	>1	<1	>1	<1	>1	<1	>1	<1	>1	<1	>1	<1	>1	<1	>1	<1	>1	<1	>1	<1	>1	<1	>1
Increased	47	47	20	32	27	34	33	31	26	26	35	44	37	36	21	15	32	18	18	22	12	15	24	32
Same	30	37	36	35	45	40	36	39	27	21	29	31	36	39	52	69	38	32	29	31	25	24	21	29
Decreased	13	11	2	4	11	3	20	18	42	49	5	3	14	12	23	8	21	46	6	1	7	9	6	5
Not used	7	2	37	24	10	14	4	7	5	1	22	9	6	5	0	4	7	5	37	35	25	20	41	28
Don't know	0	1	2	2	0	0	0	0	0	3	1	0	2	3	0	0	0	0	4	5	1	0	0	1

Table 7.1h: Percentage organisations reporting a change in the use of homebased work

Country	D(W)	DK	E	F	FIN	IRL	N	NL	P	S	T	UK
Increased	3	5	0	1	10	1	6	2	1	8	2	9
Same	10	22	6	9	13	4	20	9	3	17	2	12
Decreased	6	2	0	1	0	0	3	1	0	1	2	7
Not used	67	63	79	74	68	70	55	0	83	67	57	69
Don't know	7	3	0	1	2	1	7	0	0	3	1	1

Private and public sector

	D(W)		DK		E *		F		FIN		IRL		N *		NL *		P *		S *		T *		UK	
	Pu	Pr	Pu	Pr	Pu	Pr	Pu	Pr	Pu	Pr	Pu	Pr	Pu	Pr	Pu	Pr	Pu	Pr	Pu	Pr	Pu	Pr	Pu	Pr
Increased	3	4	5	5	0	0	0	2	8	11	0	2	4	5	0	2	0	0	11	7	0	3	13	7
Same	7	11	26	21	6	0	13	8	13	15	3	6	20	22	50	8	0	4	19	14	6	2	10	12
Decreased	1	6	1	3	0	0	0	1	0	0	0	0	0	3	3	1	1	0	0	1	1	2	0	2
Not used	71	66	67	57	88	77	75	74	73	67	73	72	58	57	50	81	69	84	59	73	38	59	61	72
Don't know	5	6	5	3	0	0	0	1	0	2	3	0	8	7	0	0	0	0	3	4	0	1	2	1

Less than 1,000 or greater than or equal to 1,000 employees

	D(W)		DK		E		F		FIN		IRL		N		NL		P		S		T		UK	
	<1	>1	<1	>1	<1	>1	<1	>1	<1	>1	<1	>1	<1	>1	<1	>1	<1	>1	<1	>1	<1	>1	<1	>1
Increased	4	3	6	3	0	0	0	2	8	13	1	3	7	5	2	4	1	0	9	9	1	4	5	11
Same	9	12	24	20	7	3	6	14	11	20	5	3	19	23	9	8	3	5	14	19	0	7	11	13
Decreased	7	5	1	4	1	0	1	1	0	1	1	0	3	3	1	0	0	0	1	1	3	0	2	2
Not used	67	68	62	66	78	78	75	72	72	60	73	59	56	51	83	69	82	86	69	62	60	52	72	67
Don't know	6	7	3	4	0	0	0	1	0	4	0	3	3	6	0	2	0	0	2	4	0	2	0	2

Table 7.1i: Percentage organisations reporting a change in the use of government training schemes

Country

	D(W)	DK	E	F	FIN	IRL	N	NL	P	S	T	UK
Increased	6	32	16	14	22	13	20	10	33	14	4	11
Same	12	25	18	17	21	29	32	18	16	47	10	34
Decreased	6	4	3	3	4	0	8	1	9	14	2	25
Not used	63	34	48	53	47	36	29	61	31	18	46	22
Don't know	5	2	1	0	2	2	3	2	1	3	1	1

Private and public sector

	D(W)		DK		E *		F		FIN *		IRL		N		NL *		P *		S		T *		UK	
	Pu	Pr	Pu	Pr	Pu	Pr	Pu	Pr	Pu	Pr	Pu	Pr	Pu	Pr	Pu	Pr	Pu	Pr	Pu	Pr	Pu	Pr	Pu	Pr
Increased	17	4	60	13	6	17	30	9	34	8	20	9	26	17	0	11	31	36	11	19	0	5	15	10
Same	12	13	26	25	19	19	26	15	16	18	35	27	29	28	50	17	31	14	41	53	6	11	34	35
Decreased	23	4	4	4	6	3	2	2	13	2	0	0	6	12	0	1	0	10	11	20	6	1	24	27
Not used	39	65	5	53	56	46	33	60	36	63	25	43	25	36	50	61	15	33	29	5	25	48	19	23
Don't know	4	5	1	2	2	0	0	0	2	3	3	2	6	0	0	2	2	0	5	1	0	1	3	1

Less than 1,000 or greater than or equal to 1,000 employees

	D(W)		DK		E		F		FIN		IRL		N		NL		P		S		T		UK	
	<1	>1	<1	>1	<1	>1	<1	>1	<1	>1	<1	>1	<1	>1	<1	>1	<1	>1	<1	>1	<1	>1	<1	>1
Increased	5	7	27	42	16	15	13	15	19	23	15	6	19	22	11	12	32	36	15	13	3	7	11	12
Same	11	13	26	23	17	21	15	20	22	18	30	28	33	30	18	19	14	23	44	48	8	13	35	34
Decreased	5	9	4	4	3	3	2	3	2	9	0	0	8	6	1	0	7	14	12	17	1	2	23	26
Not used	64	60	39	25	51	43	56	51	49	46	35	37	30	27	65	46	35	18	23	13	47	46	25	20
Don't know	5	5	1	2	2	0	1	0	1	5	3	0	3	1	1	8	1	0	3	4	0	2	0	2

Table 7.1j: Percentage organisations reporting a change in the use of subcontracting

Country	D(W)	DK	E	F	FIN	IRL	N	NL	P	S	T	UK
Increased	41	22	35	31	21	36	14	15	24	9	30	31
Same	26	34	25	32	35	30	35	22	17	27	10	31
Decreased	4	6	6	8	29	4	16	8	7	5	33	10
Not used	21	26	23	17	11	20	21	44	38	44	29	20
Don't know	3	5	0	1	2	1	5	2	1	7	0	2

Private and public sector

	D(W)		DK		E *		F		FIN		IRL		N		NL *		P *		S *		T *		UK	
	Pu	Pr	Pu	Pr	Pu	Pr	Pu	Pr	Pu	Pr	Pu	Pr	Pu	Pr	Pu	Pr	Pu	Pr	Pu	Pr	Pu	Pr	Pu	Pr
Increased	31	44	19	25	25	36	23	34	18	22	38	35	8	18	0	15	15	25	6	11	6	33	31	31
Same	12	28	34	35	44	24	24	33	29	35	28	33	32	31	50	22	15	16	21	33	6	10	34	30
Decreased	2	5	3	7	0	6	6	8	44	26	3	3	13	20	0	7	0	7	1	8	0	4	2	14
Not used	38	16	27	25	19	24	33	14	3	15	23	20	27	21	50	44	39	38	56	34	31	28	22	18
Don't know	7	3	7	4	4	0	0	1	3	2	3	0	7	4	0	2	2	1	5	8	0	0	0	5

Less than 1,000 or greater than or equal to 1,000 employees

	D(W)		DK		E		F		FIN		IRL		N		NL		P		S		T		UK	
	<1	>1	<1	>1	<1	>1	<1	>1	<1	>1	<1	>1	<1	>1	<1	>1	<1	>1	<1	>1	<1	>1	<1	>1
Increased	40	44	22	23	31	43	31	33	19	24	32	50	15	12	15	15	24	23	7	11	29	33	27	34
Same	23	30	35	32	27	22	30	36	39	26	32	22	34	39	22	23	13	32	27	27	9	11	31	31
Decreased	4	4	6	5	5	9	7	10	28	34	5	0	16	15	8	8	4	14	6	4	3	4	12	8
Not used	23	16	27	23	28	14	21	10	10	12	23	9	23	15	47	35	42	23	46	42	30	26	21	18
Don't know	3	4	4	8	1	0	0	0	0	5	1	0	5	5	2	0	1	0	6	8	0	0	1	3

Table 7.2a: The approximate proportion of workforce on part-time contracts: percentage organisations.

Country	D(W)	DK	E	F	FIN	IRL	N	NL	P	S	T	UK
Less than 1%	11	15	46	34	52	41	11	17	55	5	15	29
One to 10%	62	44	17	49	34	28	47	59	10	42	7	40
Eleven to 20%	16	19	4	8	1	7	16	9	0	23	1	9
More than 20%	7	18	2	4	5	5	21	11	0	28	3	17
Don't know	1	1	5	1	2	1	3	2	1	2	7	2

Private and public sector

	D(W)		DK		E *		F		FIN		IRL		N		NL *		P *		S		T *		UK	
	Pu	Pr	Pu	Pr	Pu	Pr	Pu	Pr	Pu	Pr	Pu	Pr	Pu	Pr	Pu	Pr	Pu	Pr	Pu	Pr	Pu	Pr	Pu	Pr
Less than 1%	0	13	1	25	63	46	15	39	61	50	30	44	3	17	0	16	39	62	4	6	6	16	4	38
One to 10%	40	68	23	57	0	17	58	45	27	35	40	24	26	63	0	59	8	7	28	52	0	8	34	41
Eleven to 20%	42	10	33	9	6	4	20	5	0	2	13	3	21	9	50	9	0	0	23	22	0	1	19	5
More than 20%	16	5	38	5	0	1	4	4	2	6	3	8	43	8	50	11	0	0	44	16	6	3	37	11
Don't know	1	1	2	1	0	6	2	1	3	1	0	2	8	0	0	2	0	1	1	4	13	7	3	2

Less than 1,000 or greater than or equal to 1,000 employees

	D(W)		DK		E		F		FIN		IRL		N		NL		P		S		T		UK	
	<1	>1	<1	>1	<1	>1	<1	>1	<1	>1	<1	>1	<1	>1	<1	>1	<1	>1	<1	>1	<1	>1	<1	>1
Less than 1%	11	10	17	12	45	49	34	34	54	50	45	25	11	10	17	15	54	59	6	4	14	15	36	22
One to 10%	62	63	48	35	19	12	48	50	32	39	26	31	48	44	62	46	9	14	54	30	7	7	44	36
Eleven to 20%	16	15	18	20	4	4	8	7	7	6	19	6	14	19	8	15	0	0	21	25	0	2	9	9
More than 20%	6	7	12	29	1	2	3	3	6	3	3	16	21	22	9	19	0	0	18	37	4	4	6	27
Don't know	0	3	1	2	5	5	2	1	2	0	0	0	2	4	2	0	1	0	1	3	9	4	1	3

Table 7.2b: The approximate proportion of workforce on temporary/casual contracts: percentage organisations.

Country	D(W)	DK	E	F	FIN	IRL	N	NL	P	S	T	UK
Less than 1%	48	48	24	34	45	22	37	22	40	32	17	37
One to 10%	23	44	33	47	41	50	44	55	23	49	12	48
Eleven to 20%	1	2	16	7	5	10	4	15	1	8	1	5
More than 20%	1	2	8	2	1	4	2	3	0	5	2	2
Don't know	11	5	3	2	2	1	5	2	2	3	7	3

Private and public sector

	D(W)		DK		E *		F		FIN		IRL		N		NL *		P *		S		T *		UK	
	Pu	Pr	Pu	Pr	Pu	Pr	Pu	Pr	Pu	Pr	Pu	Pr	Pu	Pr	Pu	Pr	Pu	Pr	Pu	Pr	Pu	Pr	Pu	Pr
Less than 1%	39	50	29	60	25	22	41	32	53	49	13	27	25	47	0	23	23	45	23	41	0	20	26	42
One to 10%	8	27	63	32	31	34	39	50	32	40	63	45	51	37	100	54	31	19	52	46	0	14	58	44
Eleven to 20%	0	2	2	2	31	15	3	8	5	2	10	9	7	3	0	15	0	0	0	15	0	3	1	5
More than 20%	0	1	0	0	6	7	2	3	2	1	1	0	3	2	0	3	0	0	0	6	6	2	2	1
Don't know	18	9	3	1	0	3	4	2	2	3	3	0	1	7	3	0	2	0	3	3	3	8	6	2

Less than 1,000 or greater than or equal to 1,000 employees

	D(W)		DK		E		F		FIN		IRL		N		NL		P		S		T		UK	
	<1	>1	<1	>1	<1	>1	<1	>1	<1	>1	<1	>1	<1	>1	<1	>1	<1	>1	<1	>1	<1	>1	<1	>1
Less than 1%	45	53	52	40	21	29	34	35	50	44	24	13	40	28	22	23	39	41	36	28	13	24	42	33
One to 10%	24	21	39	54	33	34	48	45	37	44	48	59	42	49	55	54	21	27	50	47	13	11	45	50
Eleven to 20%	1	2	2	2	18	13	6	8	4	11	6	3	3	6	16	12	1	0	6	11	0	0	2	5
More than 20%	1	0	0	0	8	5	3	2	1	0	4	3	3	3	3	4	0	0	4	6	1	4	2	2
Don't know	10	12	1	3	2	3	2	2	3	1	0	3	4	8	2	0	1	5	2	4	9	4	1	5

Table 7.2c: The approximate proportion of workforce on fixed term contracts: percentage organisations.

Country	D(W)	DK	E	F	FIN	IRL	N	NL	P	S	T	UK
Less than 1%	27	66	22	27	16	46	31	0	17	67	11	54
One to 10%	58	15	29	56	68	20	49	2	38	11	11	21
Eleven to 20%	6	2	15	10	9	4	6	1	17	1	5	2
More than 20%	1	5	11	2	5	9	3	91	19	0	32	3
Don't know	3	3	3	2	1	1	3	1	0	7	5	4

Private and public sector

	D(W)		DK		E *		F		FIN		IRL		N		NL *		P *		S		T *		UK	
	Pu	Pr	Pu	Pr	Pu	Pr	Pu	Pr	Pu	Pr	Pu	Pr	Pu	Pr	Pu	Pr	Pu	Pr	Pu	Pr	Pu	Pr	Pu	Pr
Less than 1%	24	27	75	58	38	21	34	26	23	16	40	47	24	37	0	0	23	18	67	69	6	11	48	47
One to 10%	59	58	11	18	25	29	52	56	57	74	25	19	48	51	50	1	31	38	6	14	0	13	35	23
Eleven to 20%	6	6	0	4	0	16	5	11	10	5	8	2	9	4	0	1	15	16	0	1	19	3	4	3
More than 20%	0	1	5	6	6	12	0	0	8	2	13	6	4	2	50	91	23	21	0	0	38	32	3	4
Don't know	4	3	1	4	0	3	3	3	0	1	0	2	6	0	0	1	0	0	9	5	6	5	4	1

Less than 1,000 or greater than or equal to 1,000 employees

	D(W)		DK		E		F		FIN		IRL		N		NL		P		S		T		UK	
	<1	>1	<1	>1	<1	>1	<1	>1	<1	>1	<1	>1	<1	>1	<1	>1	<1	>1	<1	>1	<1	>1	<1	>1
Less than 1%	29	24	61	75	33	20	27	27	21	10	47	38	34	23	0	0	11	36	64	69	9	15	56	53
One to 10%	56	61	17	12	25	36	56	55	65	70	19	25	48	50	2	0	41	27	13	8	9	13	18	22
Eleven to 20%	6	6	2	2	19	7	10	9	8	11	5	0	5	10	1	0	18	14	1	1	4	7	2	2
More than 20%	2	1	5	6	13	9	2	2	4	5	9	9	3	4	91	89	21	14	1	0	36	24	2	3
Don't know	1	5	3	3	3	2	2	2	0	1	0	6	3	4	0	1	0	0	6	8	2	1	1	6

Table 7.2d: The approximate proportion of workforce on homebased work: percentage organisations.

Country	D(W)	DK	E	F	FIN	IRL	N	NL	P	S	T	UK
Less than 1%	39	68	34	61	71	45	65	58	36	68	11	61
One to 10%	7	7	0	2	4	0	4	1	2	3	2	4
Eleven to 20%	1	1	0	0	0	0	0	1	0	1	1	0
More than 20%	0	1	0	0	0	0	0	1	0	0	0	0
Don't know	23	6	9	3	7	3	11	6	5	7	7	4

Private and public sector

	D(W)		DK		E		F		FIN		IRL		N		NL		P		S		T		UK	
	Pu	Pr	Pu	Pr	Pu	Pr	Pu	Pr	Pu	Pr	Pu	Pr	Pu	Pr	Pu	Pr	Pu	Pr	Pu	Pr	Pu	Pr	Pu	Pr
					*						*		*		*		*				*			
Less than 1%	29	41	64	69	44	33	60	62	73	72	43	46	55	77	50	57	23	41	56	79	0	13	62	62
One to 10%	4	8	10	5	0	0	3	4	0	5	0	0	4	3	0	1	0	3	7	1	0	3	3	4
Eleven to 20%	0	1	2	1	0	0	0	0	0	0	0	0	0	0	0	0	0	0	0	1	0	1	0	0
More than 20%	0	0	0	1	0	0	0	0	0	0	0	0	0	0	0	1	0	0	0	1	0	0	0	0
Don't know	20	23	7	5	0	9	0	10	7	7	3	3	15	6	0	6	8	4	8	5	6	8	6	4

Less than 1,000 or greater than or equal to 1,000 employees

	D(W)		DK		E		F		FIN		IRL		N		NL		P		S		T		UK	
	≤1	>1	≤1	>1	≤1	>1	≤1	>1	≤1	>1	≤1	>1	≤1	>1	≤1	>1	≤1	>1	≤1	>1	≤1	>1	≤1	>1
Less than 1%	36	43	63	78	36	30	61	62	68	76	46	38	66	63	58	54	35	36	72	64	9	15	59	64
One to 10%	8	5	6	7	1	0	0	2	4	1	0	0	5	3	1	0	0	3	0	1	3	2	3	3
Eleven to 20%	1	0	2	0	0	0	0	0	0	0	0	0	0	0	0	0	0	0	0	0	0	2	0	0
More than 20%	0	0	1	1	0	0	0	0	0	0	0	0	0	0	1	1	0	0	0	0	0	0	1	0
Don't know	22	25	5	8	8	10	7	3	3	7	2	6	9	14	6	4	6	5	8	8	10	2	2	6

Table 7.2e: The approximate proportion of workforce on government training schemes: percentage organisations.

Country	D(W)	DK	E	F	FIN	IRL	N	NL	P	S	T	UK
Less than 1%	ni	56	31	58	59	50	57	50	38	59	13	61
One to 10%	ni	27	13	14	18	11	19	7	20	27	6	19
Eleven to 20%	ni	2	2	1	2	0	1	0	2	<1	1	<1
More than 20%	ni	1	0	0	2	0	1	0	2	1	0	0
Don't know	ni	3	7	3	6	2	6	9	1	3	9	3

Private and public sector

	D(W)		DK		E		F		FIN		IRL		N		NL		P		S		T		UK	
	Pu	Pr	Pu	Pr	Pu	Pr	Pu	Pr	Pu	Pr	Pu	Pr	Pu	Pr	Pu	Pr	Pu	Pr	Pu	Pr	Pu	Pr	Pu	Pr
Less than 1%	ni	ni	34	71	38	30	43	61	60	66	55	47	59	59	50	50	31	40	49	67	0	15	63	60
One to 10%	ni	ni	54	10	14	36	36	9	26	7	18	9	13	23	0	7	15	23	42	17	0	7	17	20
Eleven to 20%	ni	ni	5	0	6	2	3	0	2	2	0	0	2	2	0	0	8	1	0	1	0	1	1	0
More than 20%	ni	ni	1	1	0	0	0	0	0	0	0	0	1	1	0	0	3	0	0	1	0	0	0	0
Don't know	ni	ni	1	3	6	7	3	3	3	9	0	3	6	5	0	11	0	0	1	4	6	10	4	3

Less than 1,000 or greater than or equal to 1,000 employees

	D(W)		DK		E		F		FIN		IRL		N		NL		P		S		T		UK	
	<1	>1	<1	>1	<1	>1	<1	>1	<1	>1	<1	>1	<1	>1	<1	>1	<1	>1	<1	>1	<1	>1	<1	>1
Less than 1%	ni	ni	57	54	33	26	60	55	61	56	53	41	56	59	54	35	38	36	58	60	12	15	59	63
One to 10%	ni	ni	24	34	11	15	13	16	17	18	12	9	22	12	6	12	20	23	28	26	5	7	20	18
Eleven to 20%	ni	ni	1	3	2	2	0	1	2	4	0	0	2	1	0	0	0	9	0	1	0	2	0	0
More than 20%	ni	ni	1	1	0	1	0	0	0	1	0	0	0	0	0	0	3	0	0	1	0	0	0	0
Don't know	ni	ni	3	3	8	5	3	3	3	11	1	6	5	9	8	19	1	0	3	3	10	7	1	5

ni question not included in country

Table 7.3a: Major change in the specification of managerial jobs over the last three years: percentage organisations.

Country	D(W)	DK	E	F	FIN	IRL	N	NL	P	S	T	UK
Jobs made more specific	28	ni	34	55	52	21	52	32	27	10	35	25
No major change	14	ni	44	32	21	37	18	32	28	28	38	31
Jobs made wider/more flexible	61	ni	19	16	37	42	38	28	32	59	25	45

Private and public sector

	D(W)		DK		E		F		FIN		IRL		N		NL		P		S		T		UK	
	Pu	Pr	Pu	Pr	Pu	Pr	Pu	Pr	Pu	Pr	Pu	Pr	Pu	Pr	Pu	Pr	Pu	Pr	Pu	Pr	Pu	Pr	Pu	Pr
Jobs made more specific	22	29	ni	ni	19	34	64	52	50	54	18	21	49	55	0	32	23	29	8	11	25	38	31	23
No major change	18	13	ni	ni	44	45	28	34	18	26	63	26	17	15	50	33	39	23	21	34	56	34	33	26
Jobs made wider/more flexible	57	61	ni	ni	13	19	17	12	30	44	20	53	37	42	50	28	23	34	69	52	19	27	43	46

Less than 1,000 or greater than or equal to 1,000 employees

	D(W)		DK		E		F		FIN		IRL		N		NL		P		S		T		UK	
	<1	>1	<1	>1	<1	>1	<1	>1	<1	>1	<1	>1	<1	>1	<1	>1	<1	>1	<1	>1	<1	>1	<1	>1
Jobs made more specific	30	25	ni	ni	28	44	53	59	51	58	21	22	51	54	33	27	30	18	9	11	35	35	25	25
No major change	13	14	ni	ni	49	34	32	30	27	11	36	41	17	21	35	19	31	18	29	29	38	39	33	30
Jobs made wider/more flexible	60	62	ni	ni	16	26	17	15	35	40	43	38	39	36	24	42	24	59	60	60	22	30	45	46

ni question not included in country

Table 7.3b: Major change in the specification of professional/technical jobs over the last three years: percentage organisations

Country	D(W)	DK	E	F	FIN	IRL	N	NL	P	S	T	UK
Jobs made more specific	32	ni	37	44	50	13	36	36	31	7	38	19
No major change	16	ni	36	36	20	45	29	29	33	48	37	40
Jobs made wider/more flexible	55	ni	29	20	49	34	33	31	25	30	21	37

Private and public sector

	D(W)		DK		E		F		FIN		IRL		N		NL		P		S		T		UK	
	Pu	Pr	Pu	Pr	Pu	Pr	Pu	Pr	Pu	Pr	Pu	Pr	Pu	Pr	Pu	Pr	Pu	Pr	Pu	Pr	Pu	Pr	Pu	Pr
Jobs made more specific	30	33	ni	ni	44	36	51	42	48	53	13	14	25	48	0	36	23	34	4	9	25	42	20	20
No major change	16	16	ni	ni	31	37	31	38	16	23	65	36	27	27	50	29	46	30	42	54	50	34	44	38
Jobs made wider/more flexible	56	54	ni	ni	19	29	21	21	58	40	13	45	33	34	50	31	15	25	35	26	19	22	33	39

Less than 1,000 or greater than or equal to 1,000 employees

	D(W)		DK		E		F		FIN		IRL		N		NL		P		S		T		UK	
	<1	>1	<1	>1	<1	>1	<1	>1	<1	>1	<1	>1	<1	>1	<1	>1	<1	>1	<1	>1	<1	>1	<1	>1
Jobs made more specific	33	32	ni	ni	33	45	42	49	46	58	13	16	39	30	40	19	32	27	9	5	35	44	20	20
No major change	16	16	ni	ni	39	31	38	32	26	11	44	50	29	30	31	19	35	27	48	48	34	34	39	40
Jobs made wider/more flexible	53	58	ni	ni	27	30	20	19	46	50	34	31	32	36	27	46	18	46	28	31	20	24	38	37

	D(W)	DK	E	F	FIN	IRL	N	NL	P	S	T	UK
Jobs made more specific	20	ni	23	33	42	7	29	25	15	4	33	12
No major change	33	ni	51	44	23	49	29	38	46	46	46	43
Jobs made wider/more flexible	36	ni	19	19	51	39	41	29	22	47	15	41

Private and public sector *

	D(W)		DK		E		F		FIN		IRL		N		NL		P		S		T		UK	
	Pu	Pr	Pu	Pr	Pu	Pr	Pu	Pr	Pu	Pr	Pu	Pr	Pu	Pr	Pu	Pr	Pu	Pr	Pu	Pr	Pu	Pr	Pu	Pr
Jobs made more specific	23	20	ni	ni	38	22	39	31	39	45	5	7	19	41	0	24	8	18	2	5	25	36	11	12
No major change	24	33	ni	ni	38	51	41	45	21	25	55	46	23	28	50	37	39	47	33	57	50	44	47	41
Jobs made wider/more flexible	39	36	ni	ni	13	20	14	21	60	44	33	43	47	41	50	29	31	21	61	35	37	15	37	43

Less than 1,000 or greater than or equal to 1,000 employees

	D(W)		DK		E		F		FIN		IRL		N		NL		P		S		T		UK	
	<1	>1	<1	>1	<1	>1	<1	>1	<1	>1	<1	>1	<1	>1	<1	>1	<1	>1	<1	>1	<1	>1	<1	>1
Jobs made more specific	20	19	ni	ni	20	28	32	34	39	44	8	3	32	23	28	12	17	9	4	3	35	30	13	10
No major change	33	33	ni	ni	53	48	43	45	25	21	47	53	28	30	39	31	52	27	50	42	38	59	41	45
Jobs made wider/more flexible	34	40	ni	ni	19	19	20	18	52	50	40	34	42	41	25	46	13	50	43	50	12	20	43	39

ni question not included in country

Table 7.3d: Major change in the specification of manual jobs over the last three years: percentage organisations.

Country

	D(W)	DK	E	F	FIN	IRL	N	NL	P	S	T	UK
Jobs made more specific	8	ni	15	24	23	9	20	21	15	2	22	9
No major change	42	ni	48	36	33	42	34	41	50	38	48	39
Jobs made wider/more flexible	14	ni	18	22	44	29	30	31	22	48	13	38

Private and public sector *

	D(W)		DK		E		F		FIN		IRL		N		NL		P		S		T		UK	
	Pu	Pr	Pu	Pr	Pu	Pr	Pu	Pr	Pu	Pr	Pu	Pr	Pu	Pr	Pu	Pr	Pu	Pr	Pu	Pr	Pu	Pr	Pu	Pr
Jobs made more specific	2	9	ni	ni	31	14	29	23	29	23	8	8	10	29	0	20	15	16	0	4	19	23	10	8
No major change	36	43	ni	ni	50	47	39	36	27	37	60	47	30	34	50	41	39	49	39	39	50	47	45	38
Jobs made wider/more flexible	10	15	ni	ni	0	19	21	23	35	55	15	34	31	33	50	31	15	25	51	47	13	14	31	41

Less than 1,000 or greater than or equal to 1,000 employees

	D(W)		DK		E		F		FIN		IRL		N		NL		P		S		T		UK	
	<1	>1	<1	>1	<1	>1	<1	>1	<1	>1	<1	>1	<1	>1	<1	>1	<1	>1	<1	>1	<1	>1	<1	>1
Jobs made more specific	8	9	ni	ni	11	22	23	26	21	28	9	6	21	17	23	12	14	18	3	2	17	30	9	8
No major change	40	46	ni	ni	50	46	36	35	34	34	50	50	35	32	44	27	55	32	41	37	44	54	36	42
Jobs made wider/more flexible	13	15	ni	ni	20	15	22	22	43	44	28	31	30	31	25	54	17	36	45	51	16	9	40	36

ni question not included in country

SECTION VIII: THE EUROPEAN COMMUNITY

Table 8.1a: Percentage of organisations who have developed a business strategy in response to the Single European Market

Country	D(W)	DK	E	F	FIN	IRL	N	NL	P	S	T	UK
Yes, written	13	18	13	13	17	15	15	15	18	14	9	20
Yes, unwritten	31	16	29	20	17	22	8	25	33	17	22	20
No	54	63	52	61	63	59	74	58	41	68	58	56

Private and public sector

	D(W) Pu	D(W) Pr	DK Pu	DK Pr	E Pu	E Pr	F Pu	F Pr	FIN Pu	FIN Pr	IRL Pu	IRL Pr	N Pu	N Pr	NL Pu	NL Pr	P Pu	P Pr	S Pu	S Pr	T Pu	T Pr	UK Pu	UK Pr
Yes, written	6	14	3	28	6	14	14	14	19	18	13	18	8	21	50	15	8	22	9	19	6	10	8	23
Yes, unwritten	13	34	9	20	13	31	13	21	13	19	15	25	3	10	0	25	0	40	16	17	13	25	9	25
No	81	50	83	50	81	48	67	61	66	63	65	55	87	66	50	59	77	33	74	63	69	55	79	49

Less than 1,000 or greater than or equal to 1,000 employees

	D(W) <1	D(W) >1	DK <1	DK >1	E <1	E >1	F <1	F >1	FIN <1	FIN >1	IRL <1	IRL >1	N <1	N >1	NL <1	NL >1	P <1	P >1	S <1	S >1	T <1	T >1	UK <1	UK >1
Yes, written	10	16	19	15	10	18	10	18	15	21	16	13	15	14	14	19	16	27	12	15	8	11	16	23
Yes, unwritten	27	38	15	17	25	35	19	21	13	21	22	22	8	8	26	23	34	32	13	21	25	17	22	18
No	61	44	63	65	57	42	66	55	70	54	59	53	75	73	60	54	45	27	74	63	62	50	60	54

Table 8.1b: Percentage of organisations who have developed a human resource strategy in response to the Single European Market

Country	D(W)	DK	E	F	FIN	IRL	N	NL	P	S	T	UK
Yes, written	3	4	8	7	5	4	4	6	4	2	7	7
Yes, unwritten	11	9	19	13	12	16	6	9	28	10	16	15
No	78	82	68	72	81	70	85	79	58	87	60	72

Private and public sector

	D(W) Pu	D(W) Pr	DK Pu	DK Pr	E Pu	E Pr	F Pu	F Pr	FIN Pu	FIN Pr	IRL Pu	IRL Pr	N Pu	N Pr	NL Pu	NL Pr	P Pu	P Pr	S Pu	S Pr	T Pu	T Pr	UK Pu	UK Pr
Yes, written	1	3	0	7	6	8	5	8	5	6	5	5	1	6	0	7	0	6	1	3	0	8	4	9
Yes, unwritten	4	12	5	12	6	20	8	14	7	14	15	14	4	8	9	10	15	30	9	10	13	18	9	17
No	74	79	91	77	88	65	77	72	86	79	70	72	91	81	50	79	77	55	88	86	56	60	83	70

Less than 1,000 or greater than or equal to 1,000 employees

	D(W) <1	D(W) >1	DK <1	DK >1	E <1	E >1	F <1	F >1	FIN <1	FIN >1	IRL <1	IRL >1	N <1	N >1	NL <1	NL >1	P <1	P >1	S <1	S >1	T <1	T >1	UK <1	UK >1
Yes, written	2	4	4	4	4	14	6	10	4	8	6	0	5	3	5	12	6	0	2	2	4	11	6	8
Yes, unwritten	7	18	8	12	15	27	13	13	10	13	15	19	6	5	10	4	24	41	6	14	20	11	14	16
No	84	68	83	81	74	56	76	66	84	77	69	72	85	87	80	73	62	46	90	84	62	57	76	70

Table 8.2: How organisations keep abreast of EC initiatives and developments.(+)

Country	D(W)	DK	E	F	FIN	IRL	N	NL	P	S	T	UK
Through a specialist/team within organisation	7	37	14	20	23	24	20	15	14	31	2	26
Through a specialist based in Brussels	3	9	5	8	6	10	3	7	5	10	2	7
By participating in local employers/trade events	70	34	22	22	59	51	41	43	53	55	39	41
Through IPM briefings/local Assoc.	29	47	57	33	30	46	6	25	18	46	20	50
By following general media	78	63	73	58	83	73	63	72	71	81	64	73

Private and public sector

(markers: * above E, NL, P, T)

	D(W)		DK		E		F		FIN		IRL		N		NL		P		S		T		UK	
	Pu	Pr	Pu	Pr	Pu	Pr	Pu	Pr	Pu	Pr	Pu	Pr	Pu	Pr	Pu	Pr	Pu	Pr	Pu	Pr	Pu	Pr	Pu	Pr
Through a specialist/team within organisation	27	62	43	56	11	89	17	74	33	47	44	50	22	58	0	15	15	78	46	51	0	3	28	61
Through a specialist based in Brussels	8	92	8	59	15	85	22	69	17	50	36	50	40	40	0	7	20	80	31	69	0	3	21	67
By participating in local employers/trade events	10	81	19	78	8	90	8	87	24	75	19	73	22	55	0	42	2	92	42	54	13	45	17	76
Through IPM briefings/local Assoc.	8	84	35	63	5	93	8	85	22	73	22	69	25	50	0	27	6	82	42	55	0	24	28	64
By following general media	12	80	38	59	5	93	16	77	28	62	25	67	34	45	0	73	9	85	42	54	50	67	23	68

Less than 1,000 or greater than or equal to 1,000 employees

	D(W)		DK		E		F		FIN		IRL		N		NL		P		S		T		UK	
	<1	>1	<1	>1	<1	>1	<1	>1	<1	>1	<1	>1	<1	>1	<1	>1	<1	>1	<1	>1	<1	>1	<1	>1
Through a specialist/team within organisation	4	12	32	46	9	23	15	28	17	33	23	28	16	30	12	27	9	32	24	38	1	4	18	32
Through a specialist based in Brussels	2	5	8	11	3	9	7	10	5	5	12	3	3	5	5	15	7	0	9	12	1	4	3	10
By participating in local employers/trade events	68	73	35	32	21	26	24	19	57	65	52	53	44	45	45	31	49	64	45	65	43	33	41	41
Through IPM briefings/local Assoc.	26	33	46	49	54	62	33	34	28	38	45	47	5	8	25	31	17	23	46	48	17	26	48	52
By following general media	78	77	65	60	74	71	60	55	82	85	74	66	65	55	73	69	75	59	83	79	68	59	75	71

Table 8.3a: Percentage organisations indicating full implementation of the EC Social Charter would require change in their policies on the use of working hours/shifts.

Country	D(W)	DK	E	F	FIN	IRL	N	NL	P	S	T	UK
Major change	4	5	23	5	1	22	11	1	9	1	4	27
Minor change	13	15	34	20	15	31	11	26	36	19	32	34
No change	44	42	25	42	37	34	41	47	39	27	25	25
Don't know	33	34	9	24	45	11	43	25	11	52	21	12

Private and public sector *

	D(W)		DK		E		F		FIN		IRL		N		NL		P		S		T		UK	
	Pu	Pr	Pu	Pr	Pu	Pr	Pu	Pr	Pu	Pr	Pu	Pr	Pu	Pr	Pu	Pr	Pu	Pr	Pu	Pr	Pu	Pr	Pu	Pr
Major change	3	4	4	6	25	23	2	5	0	2	25	21	1	0	0	1	8	8	1	1	0	5	21	29
Minor change	10	14	11	18	19	35	14	22	18	16	20	34	6	17	50	26	8	41	16	21	13	34	37	35
No change	46	43	40	44	38	25	37	41	36	40	35	35	36	43	50	46	51	36	24	30	25	25	25	24
Don't know	37	33	28	41	13	9	30	23	45	40	18	8	51	39	0	26	15	11	58	46	25	22	14	11

Less than 1,000 or greater than or equal to 1,000 employees

	D(W)		DK		E		F		FIN		IRL		N		NL		P		S		T		UK	
	<1	>1	<1	>1	<1	>1	<1	>1	<1	>1	<1	>1	<1	>1	<1	>1	<1	>1	<1	>1	<1	>1	<1	>1
Major change	3	5	3	10	21	27	5	4	1	3	19	31	1	1	1	0	7	14	1	1	3	7	25	28
Minor change	11	17	14	17	32	38	20	21	14	16	31	31	10	13	23	42	38	27	17	20	38	22	31	37
No change	45	43	42	41	27	22	43	40	39	38	38	38	40	45	51	27	39	36	28	26	23	28	30	21
Don't know	37	26	37	28	13	4	24	23	45	44	11	9	45	36	25	27	10	14	52	53	25	15	13	11

Table 8.3b: Percentage organisations indicating full implementation of the EC Social Charter would require change in their policies on the use of part-time, temporary, fixed term contracts.

Country	D(W)	DK	E	F	FIN	IRL	N	NL	P	S	T	UK
Major change	3	2	25	4	2	4	1	5	5	2	6	12
Minor change	18	14	38	16	14	24	6	21	32	13	12	33
No change	38	43	22	44	38	49	42	47	41	30	23	35
Don't know	34	37	9	25	45	17	46	24	11	54	28	16

Private and public sector *

	D(W)		DK		E		F		FIN		IRL		N		NL		P		S		T		UK	
	Pu	Pr	Pu	Pr	Pu	Pr	Pu	Pr	Pu	Pr	Pu	Pr	Pu	Pr	Pu	Pr	Pu	Pr	Pu	Pr	Pu	Pr	Pu	Pr
Major change	4	3	1	2	6	27	2	4	2	2	5	2	0	2	0	6	8	6	2	2	6	6	14	12
Minor change	12	20	13	15	38	37	14	17	18	15	20	25	2	9	50	20	31	33	15	11	6	14	35	33
No change	43	36	39	45	38	20	34	45	34	43	48	51	37	48	46	50	31	41	23	37	25	25	30	37
Don't know	36	34	43	37	6	9	32	24	45	40	15	19	55	41	0	24	8	12	57	49	31	27	17	14

Less than 1,000 or greater than or equal to 1,000 employees

	D(W)		DK		E		F		FIN		IRL		N		NL		P		S		T		UK	
	<1	>1	<1	>1	<1	>1	<1	>1	<1	>1	<1	>1	<1	>1	<1	>1	<1	>1	<1	>1	<1	>1	<1	>1
Major change	2	4	1	3	22	31	3	5	2	1	5	0	1	3	6	4	4	9	1	3	7	4	9	15
Minor change	18	19	13	14	40	35	16	15	14	16	20	38	8	6	17	39	32	32	10	15	13	11	30	37
No change	36	41	41	41	19	25	46	41	39	38	38	52	43	41	51	31	41	41	31	30	23	22	42	28

Table 8.3c: Percentage organisations indicating full implementation of the EC Social Charter would require change in their policies on health and safety.

Country	D(W)	DK	E	F	FIN	IRL	N	NL	P	S	T	UK
Major change	1	3	51	7	0	15	1	10	29	0	12	13
Minor change	10	19	31	28	9	41	14	36	42	25	30	48
No change	47	38	8	32	45	30	37	28	12	24	19	25
Don't know	34	36	5	22	44	11	44	24	10	49	16	11

Private and public sector *

	D(W)		DK		E		F		FIN		IRL		N		NL		P		S		T		UK	
	Pu	Pr	Pu	Pr	Pu	Pr	Pu	Pr	Pu	Pr	Pu	Pr	Pu	Pr	Pu	Pr	Pu	Pr	Pu	Pr	Pu	Pr	Pu	Pr
Major change	3	1	3	4	44	52	5	8	0	1	25	10	2	0	0	11	39	29	0	1	6	12	18	12
Minor change	8	10	17	20	38	30	21	29	10	11	25	45	7	22	50	35	23	43	24	26	25	32	49	49
No change	47	47	30	43	6	8	25	33	42	51	28	33	30	42	50	28	15	12	21	27	6	20	17	27
Don't know	35	34	45	30	6	4	32	21	45	37	15	10	54	35	0	25	0	12	51	45	31	15	12	10

Less than 1,000 or greater than or equal to 1,000 employees *

	D(W)		DK		E		F		FIN		IRL		N		NL		P		S		T		UK	
	<1	>1	<1	>1	<1	>1	<1	>1	<1	>1	<1	>1	<1	>1	<1	>1	<1	>1	<1	>1	<1	>1	<1	>1
Major change	1	2	4	3	49	53	6	9	1	0	14	19	0	3	10	12	31	23	0	1	13	11	13	14
Minor change	9	12	15	25	30	33	29	26	9	11	39	47	11	19	34	42	39	50	28	23	29	33	48	48
No change	45	50	39	36	8	7	34	30	46	46	32	22	39	32	31	15	13	9	24	23	22	13	27	23
Don't know	38	27	37	32	6	1	22	23	43	41	11	9	46	40	24	27	11	5	47	51	20	11	11	11

Table 8.3d: Percentage organisations indicating full implementation of the EC Social Charter would require change in their policies on equal treatment of men and women.

Country	D(W)	DK	E	F	FIN	IRL	N	NL	P	S	T	UK
Major change	3	2	22	4	0	2	0	8	1	2	4	7
Minor change	11	10	36	16	7	10	6	39	11	18	7	28
No change	49	53	29	50	52	73	47	34	72	30	51	53
Don't know	29	31	5	21	39	10	42	18	8	49	14	9

Private and public sector *

	D(W)		DK		E		F		FIN		IRL		N		NL		P		S		T		UK	
	Pu	Pr	Pu	Pr	Pu	Pr	Pu	Pr	Pu	Pr	Pu	Pr	Pu	Pr	Pu	Pr	Pu	Pr	Pu	Pr	Pu	Pr	Pu	Pr
Major change	3	3	2	2	25	22	2	4	0	1	3	2	1	0	0	8	1	1	3	1	0	4	8	7
Minor change	9	12	12	10	31	36	10	18	5	7	13	9	3	10	50	37	8	11	19	17	0	8	31	28
No change	52	49	41	61	31	30	47	49	55	58	60	76	36	55	50	33	77	71	27	34	31	55	47	55
Don't know	31	29	41	23	6	4	24	21	39	33	15	9	53	34	0	20	10	10	49	47	25	13	11	8

Less than 1,000 or greater than or equal to 1,000 employees *

	D(W)		DK		E		F		FIN		IRL		N		NL		P		S		T		UK	
	<1	>1	<1	>1	<1	>1	<1	>1	<1	>1	<1	>1	<1	>1	<1	>1	<1	>1	<1	>1	<1	>1	<1	>1
Major change	2	5	3	1	22	25	3	4	1	0	2	6	0	1	8	8	1	0	1	3	4	4	7	7
Minor change	10	14	9	13	36	34	15	19	4	10	11	6	5	8	38	39	10	14	18	18	8	7	23	32
No change	48	52	51	57	28	31	53	44	57	50	70	78	47	47	34	31	70	77	31	29	55	46	57	50
Don't know	33	21	33	26	6	1	20	21	37	40	11	6	44	37	19	19	10	0	49	49	17	9	11	7

Table 8.3e: Percentage organiations indicating full implementation of the EC Social Charter would require change in their policies for procedures for consultation and participation of employees.

Country

	D(W)	DK	E	F	FIN	IRL	N	NL	P	S	T	UK
Major change	4	2	33	8	1	20	0	6	18	1	17	28
Minor change	9	18	36	23	13	28	9	37	22	17	24	32
No change	46	41	15	31	42	33	43	32	32	30	20	23
Don't know	34	35	9	27	43	17	44	24	18	50	19	13

Private and public sector

	D(W)		DK		E	F		FIN		IRL		N		NL		P		S		T		UK	
	Pu	Pr	Pu	Pr	*	Pu	Pr	Pu	Pr	Pu	Pr	Pu	Pr	Pu	Pr	Pu	Pr	Pu	Pr	Pu	Pr	Pu	Pr
Major change	5	3	2	2	*	5	9	0	2	15	23	0	0	0	0	23	18	1	1	6	18	19	33
Minor change	3	9	9	24	*	15	24	10	15	18	30	6	12	50	36	8	25	21	16	13	27	35	33
No change	49	46	42	41	*	27	32	44	45	43	28	30	50	50	31	46	32	24	36	6	21	27	20
Don't know	39	33	43	29	*	33	26	45	38	20	17	57	36	0	26	8	19	52	45	31	18	17	11

Less than 1,000 or greater than or equal to 1,000 employees

	D(W)		DK		E		F		FIN		IRL		N		NL		P		S		T		UK	
	<1	>1	<1	>1	<1	>1	<1	>1	<1	>1	<1	>1	<1	>1	<1	>1	<1	>1	<1	>1	<1	>1	<1	>1
Major change	3	4	2	1	28	42	8	9	1	1	19	19	1	0	5	8	21	9	0	2	16	20	24	32
Minor change	8	10	15	23	38	32	22	24	12	13	29	22	74	14	39	27	23	18	17	18	23	24	33	32
No change	43	51	41	42	15	16	33	28	44	41	31	41	43	41	31	31	25	55	32	28	26	9	25	22
Don't know	38	26	37	30	2	11	27	27	41	45	18	19	46	39	24	31	23	5	50	50	21	15	16	11

Table 9.1: Industry sector breakdown

Country	D(W)	DK	E	F	FIN	IRL	N	NL	P	S	T	UK
Agriculture	0	2	0	2	0	1	3	4	3	3	3	1
Energy and water	5	3	5	3	7	2	7	7	2	3	2	3
Chemical products	8	4	0	6	4	5	4	6	8	2	19	4
Metal manufacturing	32	15	18	30	13	15	10	14	11	15	24	16
Other manufacturing	15	8	20	11	23	28	9	20	28	13	35	18
Building/civil eng.	3	5	2	3	5	2	4	6	3	4	3	4
Retail & distribution	5	9	6	6	8	7	5	10	4	7	1	11
Transport/communication	2	4	5	3	7	3	5	10	4	6	1	4
Banking & finance	12	7	19	10	9	5	5	13	14	8	9	10
Personal services	0	2	1	0	0	1	0	1	0	1	0	1
Health services	1	9	3	7	4	10	5	1	0	8	1	10
Other services	3	2	0	0	1	1	2	2	1	1	0	2
Education	0	3	0	0	2	7	1	0	0	3	0	3
Local government	5	20	1	8	4	6	25	0	9	10	0	10
Central government	0	4	0	1	9	4	4	0	1	9	0	2
Other	6	5	7	11	4	3	9	6	12	10	3	2

Table 9.2a: Total size of organisations

Country	D(W)	DK	E	F	FIN	IRL	N	NL	P	S	T	UK
200 – 499	34	42	36	27	28	52	45	59	47	28	33	20
500 – 999	28	24	27	32	26	25	28	21	29	23	29	25
1000 – 4999	31	26	28	31	15	15	25	17	20	36	35	37
5000 and above	9	7	9	11	17	7	3	2	4	14	3	18

Private and public sector

	D(W)		DK		E		F		FIN		IRL		N		NL		P		S		T		UK	
	Pu	Pr	Pu	Pr	Pu	Pr	Pu	Pr	Pu	Pr	Pu	Pr	Pu	Pr	Pu	Pr	Pu	Pr	Pu	Pr	Pu	Pr	Pu	Pr
Sig.					*										*		*		*		*			
200 – 499	28	35	25	52	31	38	21	30	23	41	38	58	38	51	0	58	46	49	22	32	19	36	9	25
500 – 999	24	28	28	23	31	27	28	33	27	29	27	26	31	26	50	21	23	30	23	30	25	28	22	25
1000 – 4999	33	29	33	23	31	27	32	27	29	26	25	10	27	21	50	18	23	16	44	30	50	32	45	34
5000 and above	15	8	15	3	6	9	20	8	21	4	10	6	4	3	0	2	8	2	17	12	6	3	25	16

Table 9.2b: Number of part-time employees in organisations

Country	D(W)	DK	E	F	FIN	IRL	N	NL	P	S	T	UK
0	8	14	53	27	0	35	13	9	58	15	76	20
1 – 10	17	20	24	23	27	22	14	27	33	7	11	20
11 – 50	38	26	11	28	21	16	30	34	5	27	5	22
51 – 200	25	21	9	16	0	17	23	19	2	20	5	14
201 and above	13	20	3	7	15	11	20	12	1	32	3	24

Private and public sector

	D(W)		DK		E		F		FIN		IRL		N		NL		P		S		T		UK	
	Pu	Pr	Pu	Pr	Pu	Pr	Pu	Pr	Pu	Pr	Pu	Pr	Pu	Pr	Pu	Pr	Pu	Pr	Pu	Pr	Pu	Pr	Pu	Pr
Sig.					*										*		*		*		*			
0	6	8	15	13	44	54	29	27	40	37	15	44	13	12	0	10	69	57	18	14	94	74	15	21
1 – 10	2	20	3	31	31	24	8	28	23	29	10	24	4	22	0	26	23	36	6	6	6	11	3	26
11 – 50	18	42	13	34	12	11	22	29	23	19	30	11	22	38	0	34	8	3	12	38	0	6	12	26
51 – 200	42	21	29	15	6	6	29	12	8	9	20	15	25	20	50	19	0	3	16	23	0	5	20	11
201 and above	32	10	39	7	6	3	13	4	6	6	25	7	36	7	50	11	0	1	48	19	0	4	50	15

Less than 1,000 or greater than or equal to 1,000 employees

	D(W)		DK		E		F		FIN		IRL		N		NL		P		S		T		UK	
	<I	>I	<I	>I	<I	>I	<I	>I	<I	>I	<I	>I	<I	>I	<I	>I	<I	>I	<I	>I	<I	>I	<I	>I
0	6	10	12	19	48	63	21	36	35	33	39	22	11	18	7	19	63	41	10	21	74	78	17	23
1 – 10	25	4	27	4	30	14	33	9	36	12	25	9	18	4	33	0	0	34	11	2	17	2	36	6
11 – 50	48	21	33	11	13	8	31	26	19	0	20	0	35	17	38	15	3	14	45	8	1	11	29	17
51 – 200	19	35	15	23	8	9	13	19	7	16	13	28	24	19	17	27	0	9	26	13	5	5	13	14
201 and above	2	29	4	51	1	6	2	13	2	13	3	41	12	42	5	39	0	5	7	57	3	4	5	40

Table 9.4a: Number of employees in country if organisation is part of a larger group. (Valid %)

Country	D(W)	DK	E	F	FIN	IRL	N	NL	P	S	T	UK
1 – 999	26	50	31	19	0	42	26	51	59	9	29	20
1000 – 1999	18	18	18	12	0	13	21	14	27	6	11	11
2000 – 4999	19	17	19	15	0	25	13	14	12	12	18	23
5000 – 14999	19	9	18	20	0	8	27	10	3	11	21	18
15000 – 49999	9	6	8	22	0	8	9	6	0	12	18	14
50000 and above	9	0	6	13	0	4	4	6	0	3	3	15
n=	371	125	95	396	110	25	106	73	34	166	38	485

Table 9.4b: Total number of employees world-wide. (Valid %)

Country	D(W)	DK	E	F	FIN	IRL	N	NL	P	S	T	UK
1 – 4999	35	45	17	15	8	30	37	47	25	12	25	21
5000 – 14999	21	11	13	17	15	25	20	16	17	10	6	19
15000 – 49999	21	21	38	31	10	17	16	26	29	6	38	28
50000 – 99999	11	4	17	17	0	11	7	5	4	3	13	18
100000 and above	12	19	17	20	3	19	21	7	25	4	19	14

Table 9.5: Organisations reporting an increase or decrease in employees in excess of 5% in the last three years

Country	D(W)	DK	E	F	FIN	IRL	N	NL	P	S	T	UK
Increased	52	23	43	31	11	46	38	54	31	23	26	26
No change	26	30	24	26	22	19	27	27	26	22	14	26
Decreased	20	46	32	42	66	34	34	19	41	54	58	47

Private and public sector

	D(W)		DK		E		F		FIN		IRL		N		NL		P		S		T		UK	
	Pu	Pr	Pu	Pr	Pu	Pr	Pu	Pr	Pu	Pr	Pu	Pr	Pu	Pr	Pu	Pr	Pu	Pr	Pu	Pr	Pu	Pr	Pu	Pr
					*										*		*		*		*			
Increased	51	52	5	35	56	43	14	34	11	10	28	56	50	28	100	53	31	30	19	27	6	27	22	27
No change	36	24	42	22	19	24	47	22	28	20	35	11	35	24	0	27	46	23	34	12	19	14	47	18
Decreased	13	22	50	42	25	33	38	43	61	69	33	33	15	48	0	20	15	45	46	61	75	57	29	55

Less than 1,000 or greater than or equal to 1,000 employees

	D(W)		DK		E		F		FIN		IRL		N		NL		P		S		T		UK	
	<1	>1	<1	>1	<1	>1	<1	>1	<1	>1	<1	>1	<1	>1	<1	>1	<1	>1	<1	>1	<1	>1	<1	>1
Increased	50	56	26	19	40	48	32	30	9	16	49	38	37	41	55	50	35	18	21	25	31	17	24	28
No change	29	22	27	34	27	20	29	23	21	26	16	28	28	27	26	31	25	27	20	24	10	17	21	29
Decreased	20	21	47	44	33	32	39	47	70	58	34	34	36	31	20	15	37	55	59	50	57	59	54	41

Table 9.6: How the workforce was downsized if the decrease was more than 5%.(+)

Country	D(W)	DK	E	F	FIN	IRL	N	NL	P	S	T	UK
Voluntary redundancies	13	58	71	70	48	85	46	88	82	55	61	73
Compulsory redundancies	9	86	25	64	51	23	44	54	5	44	59	76
Early retirement	15	49	81	70	65	55	67	83	42	59	27	74
Natural wastage	18	81	56	71	96	68	97	100	84	80	63	87
n=	79	151	85	273	149	47	96	24	38	175	71	583

Private and public sector

Private and public sector	D(W)		DK		E*		F		FIN		IRL		N		NL*		P*		S		T*		UK	
	Pu	Pr	Pu	Pr	Pu	Pr	Pu	Pr	Pu	Pr	Pu	Pr	Pu	Pr	Pu	Pr	Pu	Pr	Pu	Pr	Pu	Pr	Pu	Pr
Voluntary redundancies	31	65	77	43	100	71	76	69	23	49	64	93	31	48	0	88	50	82	61	45	50	62	22	74
Compulsory redundancies	38	48	83	90	25	23	21	73	11	64	0	34	31	41	0	54	0	6	31	55	8	69	15	83
Early retirement	23	79	57	44	75	81	60	73	11	64	57	55	25	76	0	83	39	0	63	62	25	80	24	73
Natural wastage	77	92	88	75	75	54	81	68	25	69	64	69	100	98	0	100	100	100	88	80	75	80	26	88
n=	13	156	65	81	4	79	42	211	80	100	14	29	16	58	0	24	2	33	64	102	12	58	316	440

Less than 1,000 or greater than or equal to 1,000 employees

	D(W)		DK		E		F		FIN		IRL		N		NL		P		S		T		UK	
	<1	>1	<1	>1	<1	>1	<1	>1	<1	>1	<1	>1	<1	>1	<1	>1	<1	>1	<1	>1	<1	>1	<1	>1
Voluntary redundancies	57	73	47	80	69	73	57	85	47	72	86	82	36	75	90	75	77	92	48	63	48	81	66	82
Compulsory redundancies	55	34	85	88	20	33	63	65	45	83	25	18	38	63	45	100	4	8	46	42	57	63	80	71
Early retirement	67	86	43	61	76	90	63	79	45	83	47	82	58	92	80	100	42	42	50	71	23	33	65	84
Natural wastage	92	88	78	88	45	77	68	76	65	94	64	82	93	100	100	100	92	75	77	84	52	81	83	91
n=	106	73	102	49	55	30	148	125	95	36	36	11	72	24	20	4	26	12	96	79	44	27	301	282

Table 9.9: How percentage organisations demand for main product or service altered over previous three years apart from normal seasonal variations.

Country

	D(W)	DK	E	F	FIN	IRL	N	NL	P	S	T	UK
Increased	70	52	59	46	29	66	54	67	55	39	46	45
No change	17	26	19	26	28	18	20	21	25	32	36	22
Decreased	10	18	20	22	41	13	19	10	14	27	15	31

Private and public sector

	D(W)		DK		E *		F		FIN *		IRL		N *		NL *		P *		S		T *		UK	
	Pu	Pr	Pu	Pr	Pu	Pr	Pu	Pr	Pu	Pr	Pu	Pr	Pu	Pr	Pu	Pr	Pu	Pr	Pu	Pr	Pu	Pr	Pu	Pr
Increased	62	70	56	48	50	61	45	47	31	24	68	66	69	50	0	68	46	60	44	35	31	47	61	39
No change	13	17	32	23	38	16	32	25	36	22	20	18	19	24	0	22	15	23	37	28	19	39	30	19
Decreased	2	11	5	27	6	21	12	24	32	51	7	15	3	25	50	9	8	15	15	37	38	11	5	41

Less than 1,000 or greater than or equal to 1,000 employees

	D(W)		DK		E		F		FIN		IRL		N		NL		P		S		T		UK	
	<1	>1	<1	>1	<1	>1	<1	>1	<1	>1	<1	>1	<1	>1	<1	>1	<1	>1	<1	>1	<1	>1	<1	>1
Increased	68	72	51	52	57	63	47	44	24	35	66	69	52	59	68	65	55	55	31	47	48	41	38	51
No change	19	15	27	27	19	18	27	24	29	25	18	19	20	21	20	27	30	9	34	29	38	33	23	21
Decreased	10	9	20	14	22	17	20	23	46	35	15	6	21	11	12	4	11	23	31	23	12	20	37	26

Table 9.10: Description of market(s) for products or services: percentage organisations.

Country

	D(W)	DK	E	F	FIN	IRL	N	NL	P	S	T	UK
Local	6	25	3	13	7	9	29	2	8	21	3	18
Regional	12	10	13	12	23	8	11	17	4	17	14	8
National	15	24	29	23	33	23	22	24	26	31	34	24
European	18	11	19	15	9	15	10	24	20	14	14	8
World–wide	44	28	36	35	24	43	24	33	40	14	35	39

Private and public sector

	D(W)		DK		E *		F		FIN *		IRL		N *		NL *		P *		S		T *		UK	
	Pu	Pr	Pu	Pr	Pu	Pr	Pu	Pr	Pu	Pr	Pu	Pr	Pu	Pr	Pu	Pr	Pu	Pr	Pu	Pr	Pu	Pr	Pu	Pr
Local	21	3	57	4	23	2	51	4	13	3	22	5	59	5	0	2	54	0	37	8	0	2	57	5
Regional	22	10	18	4	19	12	7	11	26	21	25	0	9	15	50	17	8	3	24	12	19	14	13	6
National	4	17	14	30	13	31	8	27	21	35	28	21	14	30	0	24	15	29	31	32	63	29	14	28
European	4	20	2	17	6	20	5	17	10	13	10	17	2	17	0	24	0	22	3	24	0	16	2	11
World–wide	5	50	5	44	31	35	20	40	31	23	10	57	8	32	0	33	8	47	3	23	19	39	13	50

Less than 1,000 or greater than or equal to 1,000 employees

	D(W)		DK		E		F		FIN		IRL		N		NL		P		S		T		UK	
	<1	>1	<1	>1	<1	>1	<1	>1	<1	>1	<1	>1	<1	>1	<1	>1	<1	>1	<1	>1	<1	>1	<1	>1
Local	8	4	20	36	4	2	13	13	4	7	8	12	28	31	2	0	10	0	14	29	4	2	14	22
Regional	14	9	9	12	12	13	13	13	26	20	7	13	13	4	17	19	4	5	20	15	16	11	7	10
National	17	13	27	16	31	28	8	23	36	29	22	28	23	19	24	23	25	27	31	31	34	35	23	25
European	19	15	14	6	18	21	16	13	11	9	16	9	10	12	27	8	20	23	17	11	17	9	11	6
World–wide	39	50	31	24	35	35	32	38	20	28	46	31	22	29	30	46	39	41	14	13	30	44	45	35

Table 9.11: Percentage organisations involved in a major change of ownership in the last three years

Country	D(W)	DK	E	F	FIN	IRL	N	NL	P	S	T	UK
Yes	21	22	36	38	44	34	29	36	22	35	15	32
No	73	75	62	57	55	61	63	64	71	61	82	65

Private and public sector

	D(W)		DK		E *		F		FIN		IRL		N		NL *		P *		S		T *		UK	
	Pu	Pr	Pu	Pr	Pu	Pr	Pu	Pr	Pu	Pr	Pu	Pr	Pu	Pr	Pu	Pr	Pu	Pr	Pu	Pr	Pu	Pr	Pu	Pr
Yes	4	24	7	31	25	37	16	43	27	57	20	38	5	50	0	37	0	26	16	51	13	15	13	41
No	52	75	85	67	69	61	68	55	69	43	70	61	81	46	100	63	54	73	78	49	87	82	82	59

Less than 1,000 or greater than or equal to 1,000 employees

	D(W)		DK		E		F		FIN		IRL		N		NL		P		S		T		UK	
	<1	>1	<1	>1	<1	>1	<1	>1	<1	>1	<1	>1	<1	>1	<1	>1	<1	>1	<1	>1	<1	>1	<1	>1
Yes	19	23	21	23	30	48	35	42	42	44	34	31	27	32	40	23	20	27	37	32	14	15	<1	33
No	77	67	77	71	68	50	60	52	57	53	63	56	62	64	60	77	73	64	56	65	82	83	66	64

Table 9.12 Type of organisation

Country	D(W)	DK	E	F	FIN	IRL	N	NL	P	S	T	UK
Public limited company (PLC)	19	16	80	68	51	36	22	85	66	46	2	39
Trust/friendly society/cooperative	1	8	6	4	4	0	8	7	1	6	0	2
Other private sector organisation	60	35	5	3	5	28	14	4	12	1	81	23
State owned industry (trading)	3	4	3	5	16	5	2	0	0	7	11	1
Other state owned corporation	0	2	1	4	2	3	4	1	3	4	2	1
Public administration (local/central government, health, education)	4	34	3	9	10	21	32	1	17	32	0	23
Other	10	3	3	6	11	7	15	1	1	2	4	8

Table 9.13: Nature of organisation

Country	D(W)	DK	E	F	FIN	IRL	N	NL	P	S	T	UK
Corporate headquarters of an international group	15	15	16	8	5	9	4	10	1	9	3	10
Corporate headquarters of a national group	9	10	17	9	5	7	10	6	13	15	9	9
Subsidiary/division of a larger group	25	17	19	20	32	38	29	49	28	36	29	39
Independent single site organisation	15	9	26	13	6	5	14	9	11	6	24	4
Independent company with more than one site	26	16	13	36	24	9	5	19	33	13	31	13
Headquarters national local gov. service	1	20	4	9	22	14	18	0	3	11	0	11
Health authority	2	9	1	0	4	5	3	0	0	4	0	8
Other	0	3	2	4	2	9	7	6	9	4	2	5

Table 9.14: Country of corporate headquarters if organisation is part of a larger group

Country	D(W)	DK	E	F	FIN	IRL	N	NL	P	S	T	UK
Denmark	0	82	0	1	0	0	2	0	1	0	0	0
France	1	1	5	73	0	4	2	2	4	0	2	2
Germany	71	2	4	5	0	1	0	5	3	1	2	2
Italy	1	0	2	1	0	0	0	0	0	0	1	1
The Netherlands	1	0	2	2	0	2	1	63	2	0	0	1
Republic of Ireland	0	0	0	0	0	56	0	0	0	0	0	1
Spain	0	0	70	0	0	0	0	0	2	0	0	0
UK	2	3	3	2	1	5	1	4	4	1	4	73
Other EC Europe	0	0	0	1	0	0	0	0	0	0	0	0
Norway	0	1	0	0	0	0	78	0	0	1	0	0
Sweden	1	3	2	1	1	1	2	2	0	74	0	0
Switzerland	3	1	3	3	1	0	1	4	2	2	1	1
Other Non-EC Europe	0	0	1	0	0	0	0	0	0	0	0	0
USA	7	3	6	9	1	24	3	11	8	1	3	11
Japan	1	1	1	1	0	2	0	0	0	1	0	1
Portugal	0	0	0	0	0	0	0	0	65	0	0	0
Turkey	0	0	0	0	0	0	0	0	0	0	87	0
Finland	0	0	0	0	91	0	0	0	0	0	0	0
Other	0	1	3	1	0	5	10	1	0	0	1	2

*(West Germany)

Index